D0699818

083

DATE DUE

JA 4'85 JA 20'85			
JE 5 87 JE 30'01			
JL 8'88			
JE 3'98			
JE 21'88			
NO 18'88			
NO 27'85			
JE 19'90			
JA 8'92			
JE 10'04			

THE CORRESPONDENCE OF

W. E. B. DU BOIS

VOLUME III   SELECTIONS, 1944–1963

W. E. B. Du Bois, 1954

W. E. B. Du Bois

THE CORRESPONDENCE OF

W. E. B. DU BOIS

VOLUME III   SELECTIONS, 1944–1963

EDITED BY HERBERT APTHEKER

UNIVERSITY OF MASSACHUSETTS PRESS   1978

Library of Congress Cataloging in Publication Data
Du Bois, William Edward Burghardt, 1868-1963.
The correspondence of W. E. B. Du Bois.
Includes bibliographical references.
CONTENTS: v. 1. Selections, 1877-1934.—v. 2.
Selections, 1934-1944.—v. 3. Selections, 1944-1963.
1. Du Bois, William Edward Burghardt, 1868-1963.
2. Afro-Americans—Correspondence. 3. Intellectuals—
United States—Correspondence. I. Aptheker, Herbert,
1915- ed,
E185.97.D73A4 1973 301.24'2'0924 [B] 72-90496

Grateful acknowledgment is extended to the following for permission to print their letters: Bettina Aptheker, Robert C. Bennett, Thaddeus L. Bialek, Joseph Boromé, Fenner Brockway, Opal Brooten, Kathleen R. Bruyn, Emmett Carter, James S. Coleman, John W. Copeland, Merle Curti, Thomas L. Dabney, Arthur Huff Fauset, Eleanor Flexner, L. H. Foster, Eric F. Goldman, Carlton B. Goodlett, Dewey W. Grantham, Jr., William Jaffé, Virginia Lacy Jones, Corliss Lamont, Alfred Baker Lewis, Rayford W. Logan, Lee Lorch, Curtis D. MacDougall, Ernst Moritz Manasse, Benjamin E. Mays, Maribel Meisel, Eve Merriam, Henry Lee Moon, Gunnar Myrdal, F. D. Patterson, Linus Pauling, Dean G. Pruitt, Thomas Sancton, Elliott P. Skinner, Louis M. Starr, Sterling Stuckey, Charles H. Thompson, Nathaniel P. Tillman, Jr., Charles H. Wesley, Roy Wilkins.

Grateful acknowledgment for permission to publish is also extended to: Mrs. Hamilton Fish Armstrong for the letter of Hamilton Fish Armstrong; Julia E. Bender for the letter of W. A. Bender; Alumni Affairs, Fisk University, for the letter of L. Howard Bennett; Gladys Brooks for the letter of Van Wyck Brooks; Dorothy Burnham for the letter of Louis E. Burnham; Myra C. Callis for the letter of Henry Arthur Callis; National Archives and Records Service, Washington, D.C., for the letter of Matthew J. Connelly; The Office of the Mayor of Chicago for the letter of Richard J. Daley; Edmonia W. Davidson for the letter of Eugene Davidson; Emily Davis and Nina Goodman for the letters of Benjamin J. Davis, Jr.; Jonathan Dodd for the letters of Edward H. Dodd, Jr., and Mary McPartland; Department of Justice, Washington, D.C., for the letters of William E. Foley; History Commission, Communist Party, U.S.A., for the letters of James W. Ford; Marie Brown Frazier for the letter of E. Franklin Frazier; Solomon C. Fuller, Jr., for the letters of Meta Warrick Fuller; Department of State for the letter of Benjamin Gerig; Consumer Protection Office for the letter of Abe McGregor Goff; American Federation of Labor and Congress of Industrial Organizations for the letter of William Green; Robert Nemiroff for the letters of Lorraine Hansberry; Jane Hays Butler for the letter of Arthur Garfield Hays; Dorothy S. Himstead for the letter of Ralph E. Himstead; Roger Holmes for the letter of John Haynes Holmes; Everitte E. Hurston, Sr., for the letter of Zora Neale Hurston; Office of the President, Howard University, for the letter of Mordecai W. Johnson; Pierre Joliot and Hélène Langevin-Joliot for the letter of Frédéric Joliot-Curie; The Rockwell Kent Legacies for the letter of Rockwell Kent; Passport Office, Department of State, Washington, D.C., for the letters of Frances G. Knight and Ruth B. Shipley; The Estate of Winifred Mary Laski for the letters of Harold Laski; Robert Threatt for the letter of John H. Lewis; Ruth M. Lewis for the letter of Oscar Lewis; Franklin H. Littell for the letter of C. F. Littell; W. G. Mathews for the letter of Basil Mathews; Margaret M. Mills for the letter of Douglas S. Moore; Louis M. Starr for the letter of Allan Nevins; National Association for the Advancement of Colored People for the letter of Dorothy Parker; The Estate of Joseph M. Proskauer for the letter of Joseph M. Proskauer; Paul Robeson, Jr., for the letters of Paul Robeson; Mrs. James H. Hollis, Jr., for the letter of George P. Shannon; Alan H. Shapley for the letter of Harlow Shapley; The Society of Authors on behalf of the Bernard Shaw Estate for the letter of George Bernard Shaw; H. H. Zand for the letter of Arthur B. Spingarn; Anson Phelps Stokes, Jr., for the letters of Anson Phelps Stokes; Pala Stout for the letter of Rex Stout; Czechoslovak Theatrical and Literary Agency for the letter of Vojtech Strnad; Mary Tobias Messner for the letters of Channing H. Tobias; The Estate of Carl Van Vechten for the letter of Carl Van Vechten; Henry H. Villard for the letters of Oswald Garrison Villard; George Philip Wells for the letter of Marjorie Wells; Jane C. Wright for the letters of Louis T. Wright; Fisk University Library Special Collections for the letter of S. J. Wright.

CONTENTS

Contents [ix]

1950

Contents [xix]

ILLUSTRATIONS

INTRODUCTION

The final two decades (1944–1963) in the fabulous life of W. E. B. Du Bois were years of extraordinary activity. From 1944 to 1947 he was back with the National Association for the Advancement of Colored People. Thereafter, until its demise in 1955, Du Bois, with Paul Robeson and Alphaeus Hunton, made a unique contribution through the Council on African Affairs to the struggle against colonialism and imperialism. Simultaneously, as leader of the Peace Information Center in the early 1950s, Du Bois became a figure of international significance in the effort to prevent World War III and to turn back the armaments race and, especially, to ban atomic weaponry.

The years with the NAACP were personally very difficult—especially because of his developing radicalism and consequent clashes with key members of its Board, notably Walter White. But they were fruitful years which saw Du Bois in the midst of the founding of the United Nations, leading the renewed Pan-African movement and producing historic petitions to the UN on behalf of African and Afro-American peoples.

Du Bois's outspoken attacks upon colonialism and racism, and his support of all efforts for national liberation and disarmament brought him to the very edge of prison—at a time when he was past eighty years of age. His arrest, indictment, trial and acquittal (1950–1951) on the charge of being an "un-registered foreign agent" were part of the Cold War wave of reaction known as McCarthyism; Du Bois was one of the most principled and effective op-ponents of that monstrosity in the United States.

With his almost unbelievable energy, while engaged in these efforts, the final twenty years of his life witnessed the continuation of his habit of travel—not only throughout the United States, but also to the West Indies, Western and Eastern Europe, the People's Republic of China and West Africa. Articles for magazines and newspapers poured out of him, and in his final years Du Bois produced several significant books: *Color and Democracy: Colonies and Peace* (1945); *The World and Africa* (1947); *In Battle for Peace* (1952); the trilogy, *The Black Flame* (1957–1961); and *ABC of Color* (1963). He also saw through the press a somewhat revised fiftieth-anniversary edition of his classic, *The Souls of Black Folk*, first published in 1903.

Du Bois's correspondence in these years illuminates all these efforts and movements. It throws light, also, on third-party movements after the Second World War, particularly that led by Henry Wallace; the revived effort to produce an *Encyclopedia Africana*—which was a basic cause of his move to Ghana; and of his movement to the Left, culminating in his decision in 1961 to join the Communist Party, U.S.A.

Particularly illuminating are Du Bois's exchanges with Albert Schweitzer,

E. Sylvia Pankhurst, Henry Wallace, Paul Robeson, Kwame Nkrumah, George Padmore, Amy A. Garvey and Amy Jacques Garvey, Benjamin J. Davis, Jr., and Walter White.

While in this volume, as in the earlier two, the editor has concentrated upon correspondence illuminating Du Bois's public life, the letters published herein involving his first wife and their daughter and granddaughter, and to Shirley Graham and to me, do convey a sense of his own personal feelings, moods and qualities.

Editorial principles shaping the first two volumes of this collection mark the third. The effort has been made again to include correspondence illuminating the public life of Du Bois and to do so while avoiding repetition in the interests of space. Letters when published are printed precisely as written and in full with two exceptions: where obvious typographical errors were made these are silently corrected; where a slip was made this has been corrected but the correction is noted. An example occurs in one of Du Bois's letters to E. Sylvia Pankhurst (p. 380) where he uses the word, "Negro," and clearly means, "African."

In this volume, as in those preceding, it was rare for permission to publish letters to be refused. This happened in one instance, and in an additional case, involving a professor in a midwestern state, two letters from the editor failed to bring any response.

From time to time, within the text itself, acknowledgment is made of assistance. Here, however, I wish to thank specifically the following people: Adele Ausink, of Cottey College, Nevada, Missouri; Lloyd L. Brown; John W. Copeland; Elaine Druesedow, reference librarian, Oberlin College Library; Stanley Faulkner, Esq.; Eleanor Flexner; the late Harry Freeman; Carlton B. Goodlett, M.D.; Bernetta L. Hux, secretary, African American Studies Program, University of Maryland (Baltimore); Virginia Lacy Jones, dean, School of Library Service, Atlanta University; Corliss Lamont; Arthur S. Link; Rayford W. Logan; Carl Marzani; Robert F. Munn, director of libraries, West Virginia University; George B. Murphy, Jr.; Erwin A. Salk; Abbott Simon, Esq.; Elliott P. Skinner; Louis M. Starr; Sterling Stuckey; and Charles H. Wesley.

The entire manuscript of this volume, as of the earlier two, was read by Professor Sidney Kaplan of the University of Massachusetts and by Mr. Ernest Kaiser of the Schomburg Library in New York City. As was true earlier, in this case also, both found errors, offered helpful suggestions and generally improved the work.

Staying with this project from the beginning was Leone Stein, director of the University of Massachusetts Press. The project has had more than its share of difficulties but the enthusiastic support of Mrs. Stein never wavered and was indispensable to the completion of the effort. Malcolm Call, formerly editor of the Press and now editor of the University of North Carolina Press, labored on this project from the beginning and assisted it even after his move south; his help also was most important. Others at the Press, especially Janis Bolster and Carol Schoen, labored beyond the call of duty to bring this third volume to fruition. The index was prepared by Jody Simpson.

That the late Shirley Graham Du Bois did not live to see the completion of this project in the publication of the work of Du Bois is terribly painful. From the beginning of this effort, now over thirty years ago, she supported it in her characteristically vibrant and effective way.

The criticism and participation of Fay P. Aptheker in this—as in everything else done by the editor—has been vital and sustaining.

All inadequacies and errors that remain are the responsibility of the editor alone.

The year of the appearance of this third volume is the 110th anniversary of the birth of W. E. B. Du Bois. His mark upon the twentieth century is indelible. I think that his insights, hopes and staunchness will serve humanity for centuries to follow.

Herbert Aptheker

THE CORRESPONDENCE OF

W. E. B. DU BOIS

VOLUME III SELECTIONS, 1944–1963

1944

By February 1944, Du Bois was manifesting growing interest in the post-war world and especially the place of Africa and peoples of African descent in that world. Correspondence reflecting this concern—with Paul Robeson, Harold A. Moody, and Mrs. Amy Jacques Garvey—has been published in the second volume of this work (pp. 375-83).

After his forced resignation from Atlanta University and the termination of his services there as of 30 June 1944, Du Bois accepted a position as Director of Special Research for the NAACP. Summing up his duties as agreed upon in a meeting with the officers of that organization, Du Bois had written to Walter White on 5 July 1944 that his "main work" would be the collection and publication of data "concerning the people of Africa and their descendants, and concerning other colored races," and also "the preparation of material to be presented" at the post-war peace conferences (see volume two of the present work, p. 413). In line with this understanding, a group of identical letters, dictated by Du Bois before he left on a visit to Haiti in early September 1944,* were mailed under his signature to African leaders in the Gold Coast, Gambia, Sierra Leone, and Nigeria.

New York City, September 12, 1944

My dear Dr. Danquah:[1]

Persons of Negro descent resident in the United States of America are deeply interested in the postwar condition of Negroes in Africa, the West Indies and other parts of the world. For this reason the National Association for the Advancement of Colored People has established a Department of Special Research, of which they have made me Director.

My first effort is to correspond with groups of Negroes in order to ascertain:

1. What plans they have for action after the War to secure greater powers

---

* Du Bois spent most of September in Haiti at the invitation of its government. See pp. 417-18 of volume two of this *Correspondence* for details.

1. Dr. J. B. Danquah (1895–1965) at this time was general secretary of the Gold Coast Youth Conference in Accra—now Ghana. Danquah was educated at the University of London and practiced law in England from 1927 to 1930. In the 1930s and 1940s he was among the foremost leaders of West African intellectual and political development. In the 1950s he became a leader of a moderate group opposed to Nkrumah; he ran against the latter in 1960 for the presidency and was overwhelmingly defeated. In 1964 Danquah was imprisoned. He died in detention in February 1965.

of self-government, better conditions of work and wage, wider and more effective education and a chance to share in modern democracy and civilization.

2. What organizations they have or plan for to achieve these ends.

3. Whether they are willing to cooperate with other groups of Negroes and Colored people seeking similar ends for such joint consultation and cooperation as seems desirable.

Already correspondence with the President of the London Missionary Society, the Secretary of the West African Student Union, the Garvey organization of Jamaica, and others has brought offers of cooperation and suggestions for a Pan-African Congress in London after the close of the War.[2]

Your name has been sent to me as one in position to furnish me information and names of other persons with whom I may correspond, and I would appreciate an early answer and any suggestions as to cooperation and action.

I am, Sir,

Your obedient servant,
W. E. B. Du Bois

Du Bois did not neglect the West Indies in his plans to help develop a united front of colonial peoples. Illustrative is a letter written to Norman W. Manley (1893-1969), at this time Jamaica's most distinguished lawyer and destined to be in the 1950s Jamaica's chief minister. No response was forthcoming—or, at any rate, none seems to have survived.

New York City, October 10, 1944

Norman Manley, Esq.

My dear Sir:

Your name has been suggested by a number of persons who are interested in the development of your island. I was one of the founders of the National Association for the Advancement of Colored People but left this work about ten years ago and have been engaged in teaching in Atlanta University. September first I returned to the Association to take up especially the situation of colonies in the postwar world.

I am convinced that the majority of the people of the world live in colonies or quasi-colonies and that any plan for peace and democracy has got to include their welfare and their development.

2. The Fifth Pan-African Congress, chaired by Du Bois, actually convened in Manchester, England, in October 1945. There had been held in London on 21-23 July 1944 a Conference of the League of Coloured Peoples; this conference adopted a suggested "charter," which it urged the governments of the United Nations also to adopt. It began by demanding the elimination of all forms of discrimination based upon color or sex and the swiftest possible implementation of the independence of colonial peoples. A mimeographed copy of this proposed charter was found in the Du Bois papers.

I am, therefore, writing to leaders in the various colonies in the world starting with those inhabited by people of African descent and am asking them if they would be willing to write me at length concerning the present conditions in their colonies and plans for the future: plans originating with the government and with groups of forward-looking people.

I hope that you will be willing to give me some information and send me any literature that you think of. In this way the colored people of the United States and those of Jamaica may seek for acquaintanceship and understanding and such cooperation as is advisable for the uplift of the people in our respective countries.

I shall be very glad to hear from you at your convenience.

Very sincerely yours,
W. E. B. Du Bois

The first wife of Marcus Garvey was a Jamaican woman named Amy Ashwood. They met in their native Jamaica, but from 1916 to 1918 she lived in Panama. When she came to the United States in 1918, she resumed a relationship with Garvey; they married late in 1919. The marriage was terminated by divorce—with great acrimony and mutual charges of ill conduct—early in 1920. Amy Ashwood-Garvey lived thereafter in the United States, mostly in New York City, and maintained an interest in anti-colonial movements. When Du Bois wrote to her in 1945 concerning proposals for an anti-colonial conference to be held in New York City, she replied promptly.

New York City, February 1, 1945

My dear Dr. Du Bois:

I want to thank you for your important communication of January 24th in connection with your proposal for a conference on the colonial question.[1]

I think that your plan is worthy of immediate consideration, and pledge my efforts to insure the success of the conference. However, I take the view that the technical organization of the conference will require some study preliminary to its convening.

I suggest the following names:

Mr. H. P. Osborne of the West Indies National Council
    360 W. 125th Street, N.Y.C.

1. With Du Bois's inspiration, the NAACP sponsored a Conference on Colonialism held in Harlem on 6 April 1945. Cooperating were the Council on African Affairs and the West Indies National Council; several Africans, including Kwame Nkrumah, participated. For further details and the text of the resolution adopted by this conference see *A Documentary History of the Negro People in the United States, 1933–1945*, ed. Herbert Aptheker (Secaucus, N.J.: Citadel Press, 1974), 3: 558–60 (hereinafter cited as *Documentary History*).

The Council on African Affairs
   23 West 26th Street, N.Y.C.
Mr. W. Adolph Roberts of the Jamaica Progressive League
   2286 Seventh Avenue, N.Y.C.
Mr. Cecil Holmes, Sec., United Mutual Life Insurance Co.
   360 West 125th Street, N.Y.C.
Mr. George Weston
   100 St. Nicholas Ave., N.Y.C.
Mr. George Harris, Pres., Ethiopian World Federation
   Lenox Avenue, N.Y.C.
Dr. Charles A. Petioni, Chairman, West Indies National Council
   114 West 131st Street, N.Y.C.
Mr. Herbert Seale, c/o Advertising Dep't., People's Voice
   210 West 125th Street, N.Y.C.
Atty. Joseph C. Morris
   209 West 125th Street, N.Y.C.
Rev. Ethelred Brown, Secretary; Jamaica Progressive League
   2286 Seventh Avenue, N.Y.C.
With assurance of my highest consideration

Very sincerely yours,
Amy Ashwood-Garvey

From 1 July to 22 July 1944, forty-four nations attended a United Nations Monetary and Financial Conference in Bretton Woods, New Hampshire. Plans were developed for post-war economic recovery and trade, and the International Monetary Fund and the International Bank for Reconstruction and Development were established. At the end of February 1945, a briefing on the Bretton Woods conference was held in Washington, with the secretary of the treasury and other officials speaking. Du Bois attended and, as a result, sent a note to Roy Wilkins, acting-secretary of the NAACP during Walter White's travels abroad.

New York City, March 2, 1945

Memorandum to Mr. Wilkins:

I attended the conference on the Bretton Woods proposals held in Washington, February 28. There were present representatives from 106 organizations as per the enclosed memorandum [not included here]. Luncheon was served at the Willard Hotel.

In the afternoon I took the occasion to propound the following question: 'There is in the Bretton Woods proposals so far as I can gather no reference to colonies or colonial conditions. Yet colonies are economic rather than solely political problems. Seven hundred and fifty millions of people, a third of mankind, live in colonies. Cheap colonial labor and materials are basic to post-war industry and finance. Was this matter mentioned in any form at Bretton Woods?'

The answer was no; that there were other important matters also that had not been considered as for instance cartels. Someone suggested that in determining the fitness of countries for loans certain control over their action toward dependent peoples might be exercised.[1]

W. E. B. Du Bois

Rex T. Stout (1886–1975) is best known as the prolific mystery writer Nero Wolfe. He was president of the Authors' Guild from 1943 to 1945 and chairman of the Writers' War Board from 1941 to 1946. In the latter capacity he endeavored to muster public support for positive action from Congress in connection with proposals coming from the Bretton Woods conference. In this connection he wrote to Irene Diggs, Du Bois's secretary.

New York City, March 28, 1945

Dear Miss Diggs:

May we ask you three questions, not counting this one?

1. Are you working for the ratification of the Bretton Woods agreement without amendment by our Congress?

2. If so, do you need any kind of information or material which you do not have?

3. If not, may we send you material we hope and believe will arouse your active support of Bretton Woods?

Various organizations are conducting educational campaigns on Bretton Woods. That is of course essential. But since the decision will be made on Capitol Hill and will be made soon, we believe the immediate need is for an avalanche of requests for the approval of Bretton Woods on the desks of all Senators and Representatives. Perhaps you are already working on that. Would you care for more detailed suggestions from us?

Sincerely,
Rex Stout

New York City, March 30, 1945

Mr. Rex Stout
My dear Sir:

Replying to your letter of March 28 sent to the National Association for the Advancement of Colored People, may I say that our attitude toward the Bret-

---

1. Du Bois devoted his 17 March 1945 column in the *Chicago Defender* to the Bretton Woods Conference.

ton Woods proposals is this: we recognize the necessity for economic reconstruction after the war and we believe that so far as technical banking is concerned the Bretton Woods proposals are good. But we deplore the fact that the well-being of groups like the seven hundred and fifty million colonial peoples is entirely ignored in these proposals and it is assumed that the social and ethical questions connected with their labor, wages and social conditions have nothing to do with economic proposals.

This is simply a continuation of the insistence of nineteenth century economists that economic science has nothing to do with social uplift.

Very sincerely yours,
W. E. B. Du Bois

From 25 April through 26 June 1945, the founding meeting of the United Nations Organization was held in San Francisco. Du Bois was vitally concerned with this historic event. In the same period, African and African-derived peoples throughout the world were expressing concern about and preparing plans for the kinds of societies in which they were to live when World War II finally ended. Here again Du Bois, with his personal preeminence, his pioneering role in Pan-Africanism, and his position with the NAACP, was fully involved.

In the pages that follow, both decisive phases in his life are reflected through the sampling of scores of letters sent and received. The first letters deal with the formation of the United Nations; thereafter, letters follow the events related to the Fifth Pan-African Congress held in England in October 1945.

The first of the letters concerning the United Nations was addressed to the secretary of state, then Edward R. Stettinius, Jr.

New York City, March 10, 1945

The Secretary of State
Dear Sir:

The National Association for the Advancement of Colored People wishes to ask if on the agenda of the approaching conference in San Francisco the question of colonies and their future status and treatment will be considered? We have in mind not only colonies which formerly have belonged to enemy nations or international territory taken from them after this war but in particular colonies of empires and free states which are not self-governing.

Morever, the Association would like to ask if there will be present any commissions or spokesmen from the colonial peoples themselves who can directly or indirectly speak for their aspirations and progress?

Finally, the Association would like to ask if any provision will be made for the representation of American Negroes at the San Francisco meeting in order that they may advocate and advise measures for their own social progress and also be given opportunity to speak for other peoples of African descent whom they in a very real sense represent?

We would be deeply obliged if we could have in the near future an answer to these questions.

I am, Sir,

Very sincerely yours,
W. E. B. Du Bois

Two days after this letter was sent to the secretary of state, the board of directors of the NAACP issued a statement drafted by Du Bois, entitled, "Colonialism, Peace, and the United Nations."* The essence of this six-hundred-word declaration was a call for the outlawry of racism and the implementation of repeated promises to terminate colonialism. Both were necessary to ensure real peace in the post-war world.

Meanwhile, Du Bois heard not a word in response to his letter of 10 March. Therefore, on 21 March, he wrote to Benjamin Gerig, chief of the State Department's Division of Dependent Area Affairs, enclosing a copy of the 10 March letter and of the 12 March declaration.† This letter did bring a reply.

Washington, D. C., April 2, 1945

My dear Dr. Du Bois:

I wish to thank you for your letter of March 21, enclosing a copy of the letter which you had written to the Secretary of State, and the resolutions recently adopted by the Association.

In response to your specific inquiries I am happy to give you the following information:

1. The Division of Dependent Area Affairs has responsibility for the formulation and coordination of policy and action with respect to the activities of the projected international organization affecting dependent areas generally, and maintains liaison with international agencies and organizations and with other Government Departments and agencies on these matters.

2. This Division, in collaboration with other interested divisions and officers in the Department, does, of course, undertake the formulation of recommended policies and positions with respect to international arrangements affecting dependent areas.

3. As you know, the United Nations Conference is exclusively a conference

---

* The full text of the 12 March declaration will be found in Aptheker, *Documentary History*, 3:557-58.

† Benjamin Gerig was born in Ohio in 1894 and educated at the University of Illinois and the University of Geneva. He taught at the University of Illinois, Simmons College, and Haverford College and in the 1930s held posts with the League of Nations. He was the author of *The Open Door and the Mandates System* (1930).

of governmental delegations and there can be no opportunity for official participation in the deliberations of the Conference itself by unofficial representatives. The Department, however, in recognition of the keen interest manifested by national organizations in the proposed international organization, has invited a limited number of these organizations, constituting a fair cross section of citizen groups, to designate representatives to serve as consultants to the American Delegation at the Conference. In pursuance of this policy the Department has invited the National Association for the Advancement of Colored People to appoint one representative to be available for consultation with the American Delegation, and I am happy to learn that you and Mr. Walter White are to come to San Francisco in this capacity.[1]

Sincerely yours,
Benjamin Gerig

When the leaders of the NAACP *were given the right to hold consultative status to the United States delegation in San Francisco, it occurred to Du Bois that it would be well if leaders of other relevant organizations were given the opportunity to put before the* NAACP *group proposals which might then influence what was suggested to the national delegation. As a result of Du Bois's recommendation, such meetings were held with officers of the Council on African Affairs, several sororities, fraternities, and churches, and West Indian organizations with offices in the United States.*

April 12, 1945

Memorandum to Mr. White:

What do you think of this suggestion? That the NAACP write to the great Negro church organizations, fraternities and other national Negro groups saying something like this: The NAACP has been designated as one of the bodies which has a right to appoint consultants for the American delegation to the San Francisco conference. We realize that in carrying out this duty we represent not simply this organization but the whole body of American Negroes. We are anxious, therefore, to do anything in our power to assist the work and make known the decisions of such groups. If, therefore, you have passed any resolutions or come to any conclusions concerning what ought to be done at San Francisco, if you will send us a copy of this action we will be glad to make representation to whatever authorities we have access. We would, of course, take no action and give no publicity unless duly authorized. Will you kindly communicate with us and let us know just how we can be of service?

W. E. B. Du Bois

1. The NAACP appointed Walter White as its consultant and Du Bois and Mary McLeod Bethune as advisors to the consultant.

Du Bois drew up important proposals on the trusteeship concepts of the United Nations; during the San Francisco conference these were sent as a memorandum from White, Du Bois, and Bethune, at the Sir Francis Drake Hotel, to the suite of the secretary of state at the Fairmont Hotel.

May 7, 1945

To the Honorable Edward R. Stettinius, Jr.

The undersigned consultants respectfully place before the American delegation the following comments on the trusteeship proposal made by it. We are pleased that the United States has made a proposal on this most basic problem in which is involved the whole question of peace. We recognize the difficulty of reconciling security needs with humanitarian considerations but we urge that the American delegation seriously consider and vigorously support the changes set forth herewith to make its trusteeship proposal even more effective. Several other consultants have indicated their desire to join in submission of these suggestions. Their names will be transmitted to you as soon as they have had opportunity to read the full text.

*   *   *

It has been agreed by four of the Great Powers that one of the purposes of the international organization is "promotion and encouragement of respect for human rights and fundamental freedom for all without distinction as to race, language, religion or sex" but the agreement also provides that in case discrimination does occur the organization has no right to intervene within the "domestic jurisdiction" of the state concerned. This means that the international organization cannot interfere in colonial affairs, and it may also make impossible any attempt to safeguard the rights of any groups in any nation; for instance, it could not combat the race and religious persecution of another Hitler.

This declaration in Chapter I, Paragraph 3, is encouraging as far as it places the international organization on the side of justice and nondiscrimination but it is especially dangerous in leaving out the mass of people living in colonies, against whom discrimination is customary and unjustifiable. We believe that a declaration should lay down the principle and implement it so as to provide for the transition of all colonial peoples from colonial status to such autonomy as they desire. The eventual disappearance of the colonial system is the best insurance of peace. This domestic principle, the international organization has not recognized.

With regard to trusteeship, the American proposal is permissive only and ought to be mandatory.

The American proposal is that only such territory or parts of territories where strategic considerations are of paramount importance should be designated as strategic; other parts and populations should be under a trusteeship system. The British proposal on the other hand would not recognize the feasibility of separating strategic areas from other trustee areas, and would permit the operation of strategic controls in the interest of security in any territory or part thereof. This, as it seems to us, is a possible encroachment of military considerations upon considerations of humanity.

With regard to mandates distributed after the first World War, and to territories taken by the United Nations after this war, there is proposed a trusteeship administered by the nations who held the mandates and by other interested nations, but there is no provision for Native representation. This failure to include Natives in the governing council does not carry out the stated objectives of the proposal to train the Natives for "progressive development toward self-government." Neither is there provision for Native representation in territories voluntarily put under the trusteeship.

It is unthinkable that the mandated colonies distributed after the first World War should be returned to the position of colonies owned by other countries or that the terms upon which they were mandated should not be subject to revision.

All this refers to a colonial population of not more than 25 millions. This leaves at least 725 millions of colonial inhabitants concerning whom nothing is said except that some of these territories may voluntarily be placed under the trusteeship by the countries controlling them.

Walter White, Consultant
W. E. B. Du Bois, Associate Consultant
Mary McLeod Bethune, Associate
Consultant, National Association for the
Advancement of Colored People

Toward the close of the conference, Du Bois sent a personally signed communication to each of the members of the United States delegation.

San Francisco, Calif., May 16, 1945

To The American Delegation:

The attempt to write an International Bill of Rights into the San Francisco Conference without any specific mention of the people living in colonies seems to me a most unfortunate procedure. If it were clearly understood that freedom of speech, freedom from want and freedom from fear, which the nations are asked to guarantee, would without question be extended to the 750 million people who live in colonial areas, this would be a great and fateful step. But the very fact that these people, forming the most depressed peoples in the world, with 90% illiteracy, extreme poverty and a prey to disaster, who hitherto for the most part have been considered as sources of profit and not included in the democratic development of the world; and whose exploitation for three centuries has been a prime cause of war, turmoil and suffering—the omission of specific reference to these peoples is almost advertisement of their tacit exclusion as not citizens of free states, and that their welfare and freedom would be considered only at the will of the countries owning them and not at the demand of enlightened world public opinion.

To insist, therefore, upon this flagrant omission would, Sir, as it seems to me, be missing the greatest opportunity of our age. For the first time in modern history it is possible for three great nations which do not depend upon the exploitation of colonies for their development to unite and open a new path of progress.[1] We all know that the opposition of Great Britain to any international action on the colonial problem has made the United States refrain from this step and make no allusion to the festering problems of India, of the Netherlands Indies and of West and South Africa.

But is this wise, not only for our own sakes but for the future of the people of Britain, many of whom have denounced the colonial system? We have allowed ourselves in this conference to be estranged from Russia by the plight of a dozen reactionary and Jew-baiting Polish landlords, and have made no comment and taken no action on the great words spoken by Molotov: 'We must first of all see to it that dependent countries are enabled as soon as possible to take the path of national independence.'

May I beg of you in the name of 13 million Americans who are blood brothers of many millions of these colonists

First, to make a preliminary statement on the essential equality of all races, the same statement which the United States and Great Britain once refused to grant Japan, and identical with the suppressed proposal of the Chinese delegation at Dumbarton Oaks;[2] and that

Secondly, the United States delegation propose this article for the Charter of the United Nations: 'The colonial system of government, however deeply rooted in history and custom, is today undemocratic, socially dangerous and a main cause of wars. The United Nations, recognizing democracy as the only just way of life for all peoples, make it a first statute of international law that at the earliest practical moment no nation or group shall be deprived of effective voice in its own government and enjoyment of the four freedoms.' An international colonial commission on which peoples shall have

---

1. By the "three great nations" Du Bois meant the United States, China, and the Soviet Union.

2. Du Bois referred to Chinese anti-racist efforts at the Dumbarton Oaks Conference in an essay in the *Pittsburgh Courier*, 28 October 1944, p. 4. There are references to this Chinese attempt and to Japan's 1920s anti-racist proposals in his *Color and Democracy: Colonies and Peace* (New York: Harcourt, Brace and Co., 1945).

representation will have power to investigate the facts and implement this
declaration under the Security Council.

Respectfully yours,
W. E. B. Du Bois
Consultant of the American Delegation
representing the National Association for
the Advancement of Colored People

*To this statement Du Bois received one response which came from the ranking
Republican member of the United States delegation, Arthur H. Vandenberg
(1884–1951), a senator from Michigan from 1928 until his death, who was especially influential during the 1940s.*

San Francisco, California, May 19, 1945
My dear Mr. Du Bois:

This will acknowledge your fine letter of May 16th.

I shall hope—before the Conference ends—to have a chance to talk with you
personally about the matters to which you refer. Certainly I totally share your
general point of view. Even though we cannot achieve the total goal which you
define, I am very sure that we *are* going to make great progress in this direction
in the text of the new Charter. We must face the fact—in this connection—that
we have to get an agreement with forty-five other nations in connection with
whatever we do and this prohibits the full freedom of action which we enjoy.

I am indebted to you for your fine statement.

You will forgive the necessary haste of this acknowledgment.

Cordially and faithfully,
A. H. Vandenberg

Lawrence E. Spivak, then the editor of the American Mercury, *noticed press
announcements of the May 1945 appearance of Du Bois's* Color and Democracy: Colonies and Peace.* *He wrote Du Bois on 17 May, asking if there was
something else Du Bois wanted to say and suggesting that he let the* Mercury
*know. The response from Du Bois is substantial; nothing came of the sugges-
tions, though Spivak did express some interest in an essay on Pan-Africanism.*

* Lawrence E. Spivak was born in New York City in 1900 and educated at Harvard.
He was associated with the *American Mercury* from 1934 to 1954. In the late 1940s and
through the 1950s his radio and television program, "Meet the Press," gained unusual
national interest.

New York City, May 22, 1945

My dear Mr. Spivak:

There is always much to be said about the 200 million Negroes in the world and I especially think that just now a restatement of their problems and re-orientation of their relationship to the modern world is due. Much depends on how far my ideas correspond with those of the *American Mercury*.

I suggest that from two or four articles might be built out of the following subjects under the general title, "The Darker World after San Francisco":

1. *The Plight of Colonies at San Francisco*   Nothing was done at San Francisco to face or settle the colonial problem. Rather, colonial imperialism was strengthened.

2. *San Francisco and Human Rights*   The conclusions at San Francisco were to mention human rights and close the door to every practical possibility of realizing them.

3. *The Pattern at San Francisco*   This leads straight toward race war between the Nordics and Asia with Russia ranged with Asia.

4. *The Negro in the American Army*   Either race separation will disappear in the American armed forces or the pattern will be torn to pieces in the next war.

5. *The Caribbean*   Race developments in the Caribbean of importance to the world in economics and culture are pending.

6. *Ethiopia, Haiti and Liberia*   The facts about Negro governments are that their success in view of the opposition has been surprising, and their future critical for the world.

7. *France and Eboue*   Post-war France is going to develop faster in Northern Africa than anywhere else.

8. *Pan Africa*   The movement to unite peoples of African descent in Africa and America is today rising and facing the attempt of Smuts and Kenya to dominate Africa with a handful of whites.

9. *Georgia*   The development of race conflicts in Georgia for the last 25 years, and the present status.

If any of these subjects interest you I would be glad to develop them further for your information.

Very sincerely yours,
W. E. B. Du Bois

On his way back from San Francisco, Du Bois sent a frank and brief summary of his estimate of the United Nations experience to his old friend, Arthur B. Spingarn, then the president of the NAACP.*

* Arthur B. Spingarn (1878-1971) was born in New York City and educated at Columbia University. He practiced law in New York City, and was the attorney in the 1911 incorporation of the NAACP. He served as NAACP president from 1940 to 1966.

Denver, Colo., May 30, 1945

Dear Mr. Spingarn:

I am on my way back from San Francisco, and have stopped here for a speech for some inter-racial organizations.

The San Francisco conference was most interesting as an experience and spectacle; its net result was to leave the door open for a real internation and at the same time to oppose no obstacle to increased colonialism and another world struggle between Asia and Russia on the one hand and America and Eastern Europe on the other. A mighty development of world opinion towards human rights will determine the outcome. Not a whisper against colonialism could be heard except from Molotov.

As consultants, we could do little, although we exercised some little influence. They would not take a stand for any race equality or for colonies, but did back a contradictory statement on human rights. Walter was listed as consultant and I as associate. This was justifiable since he was head of the organization; at the same time it handicapped me as several of the important consultations were for consultants; I think they put over certain decisions on Walter by reason of his unfamiliarity with the broader implications. In the end however I doubt if this made much difference. Mrs. Bethune was rather a nuisance, but a harmless one.

We did get before the world a pretty clear statement of the colonial problem and its connection with minority problems. San Francisco was a beginning, not an accomplishment.[1]

We were treated royally by the city, and Walter's flair for personal acquaintanceships of every sort was marvellous. He was very thoughtful in giving me every opportunity to meet people I never would have seen otherwise.

I have kept in excellent health and am quite rested and fit. I'm speaking in Chicago and then rushing through New York to make three commencement speeches in the south. I'll get back to my desk about the middle of June. Hope you and Mrs. Spingarn have kept in health. My best regards to both.

Very sincerely,
W. E. B. Du Bois

From 9 July to 13 July 1945, the Committeee on Foreign Relations of the United States Senate held hearings on the charter of the United Nations. In this connection Du Bois wrote to the committee's chairman, Senator Tom Connally (D., Tex.).

1. Du Bois published two articles on the San Francisco meeting in the *New York Post*, 9 May 1945, p. 8, and 15 May 1945, p. 14. The *Rocky Mountain News* of Denver, Colorado, published the text of an interview with Du Bois on the meaning of San Francisco on 28 May 1945.

New York City, July 2, 1945

[Senator Tom Connally]
Sir:

I am writing to ask the privilege of appearing for 15 minutes before the committee which will hold hearings on the United Nations Charter. I am aware that this is asking a great deal, that the hearings will, of necessity, be short and selected, but I think someone should speak concerning certain reservations with regard to colonies. I have long been a student of the colonial question. I was Consultant to the American Delegation at San Francisco, and as you are probably aware, sent the members various memoranda. On May 25th I published a book on the subject.

I want to ask that the Senate in ratifying the Charter shall make reservations so that all of the mandated territory taken over after the First World War shall ultimately be put under trusteeship and that no such territory shall be integrated into the colonial system of any imperial power without consent of the Board of Trusteeship on which the colonial people themselves shall be represented.

I wish also to strengthen the declaration concerning all colonial peoples who do not today have effective voice in their own government so as to provide them some form of representation in the organization of the United Nations.

I can include this statement in a short written memorandum but it will, of course, be much more effective if I could make this statement in person before your committee.[1] You will find my biography in *Who's Who in America*.

I am, Sir,

Very respectfully yours,
W. E. B. Du Bois

Du Bois contributed with regularity to the influential quarterly Foreign Affairs; *essays by him appeared in 1925, 1933, 1935, 1938, and 1943. During this period Hamilton Fish Armstrong was associated with the magazine, as managing editor from 1922 to 1928 and then as editor until 1972, a year before his death.* But

1. On 7 July 1945, Du Bois received a wire from the clerk of the committee inviting him to testify on 11 July. His testimony is printed in u.s., Congress, Senate, Committee on Foreign Relations, hearings on *The Charter of the United Nations*, 79th Cong., 1st sess., 11 July 1945, pp. 391-93. For a summary see Herbert Aptheker, *An Annotated Bibliography of the Published Writings of W. E. B. Du Bois* (Millwood, New York: Kraus-Thomson, 1973), p. 504. There is a full report of Du Bois's appearance before this Senate committee in the *Chicago Defender*, 21 July 1945.

* Hamilton Fish Armstrong (1893–1973) was born in New York City and educated at Princeton University. In addition to his work with *Foreign Affairs*, he served the State Department in various advisory capacities and was an adviser to the United States delegation at the founding of the United Nations in San Francisco. He was the author of over fifteen books and co-author, with Allen W. Dulles, of *Can We Be Neutral?* (1936).

with the end of World War ii, *Du Bois's work was no longer published in this periodical.*

New York City, July 9, 1945

My dear Mr. Armstrong:

I was at San Francisco for five weeks as one of the Consultants to the American Delegation, representing the National Association for the Advancement of Colored People. I know that you were there at the same time but I did not have the pleasure of seeing you.

I am, of course, very much dissatisfied at what the Conference did concerning colonies, and I want to express that somewhere. You perhaps know of my book, *Color and Democracy*. To this eventually I want to add a chapter on San Francisco and I should like to write for *Foreign Affairs* a preliminary statement of that proposed chapter. Possibly you have already covered this matter sufficiently, but if you have not, won't you please let me know?

The gist of what I want to say is that while the San Francisco Conference took steps to prevent further wars in certain emergencies they did not go nearly far enough in facing realistically the greatest potential cause of war, the colonial system. All that they said about trusteeships applied to a few millions of people and to them only if it was decided later to put them under trusteeship; the great mass of over 700 million people in colonies were touched only by the general and rather vague declaration concerning the attitude which imperial states should take toward their colonies. This was implemented in no way.

I should be glad to hear from you and to know if you would be interested in such an article. As you will see by my letterhead, I am now in New York and connected with the National Association for the Advancement of Colored People.

Very sincerely yours,
W. E. B. Du Bois

New York City, July 12, 1945

Dear Dr. Du Bois:

Thank you for your letter of July 9 in which you were kind enough to suggest the possibility of preparing an article for *Foreign Affairs* dealing with the trusteeship aspects of the Charter. I am sorry to say that our schedule is already more than full and that I, therefore, am not able to encourage you to prepare anything for us at this moment.

With much regret, and hoping that at some future time we may be able to number you again among our contributors, believe me.

Yours sincerely,
Hamilton Fish Armstrong

In the midst of his preoccupation with international affairs, Du Bois maintained a considerable correspondence treating of his many other interests. This exchange with Ada P. McCormick illuminates not only many aspects of Du Bois's thinking in general but also his opinions concerning the requirements for a successful magazine.

Tucson, Arizona, August 30, 1944

Dear Dr. Du Bois:

Every time I open a copy of *Phylon* I am overcome with how able, scholarly and interesting it is and I've been wondering for quite a while whether you would be willing to have some sort of editorial connection with *Letter*.[1]

Letter of course is a very informal and uneducated sort of thing compared to your standards, but it seemed to me if you were willing you could help me right where you are by making suggestions on the set up of the magazine.

The purpose of the magazine is perfectly simple and direct. It is to work for world federation of nations and for understanding, friendliness and equality between different races. This would take in Negroes, Hindus, Chinese, Mexicans and Japanese. I am also interested in human beings as individuals but alone that would not be reason enough for getting out a magazine. A magazine is only a means to an end. Other propaganda methods might be far more effective.

I am sending you a list of the departments (many would only be a paragraph) I think of in the magazine and am enclosing a check for $100 for consultant fee.

Would you have time and freedom to sit down and do a $100 worth of consulting on this effort?

Would you ever be likely to be spending a winter in Tucson? This letter is very vague on a specific job but the future of the magazine itself is vague.

Please write me suggestions as to how you would run *Letter* if you were I and how one can successfully use editorial help from different towns. I hesitate to uproot people on a magazine so uncertain as this.

I wouldn't attempt to get out anything like *Phylon* because I haven't the scholarship or the brains. Also I want something that simple, average people will read. A nonsense gay touch—

I have considerable qualms naturally enough on whether *Letter* is worth publishing—good enough to have any effect. So don't hesitate to speak your mind.

Who printed *Phylon*—the actual mechanical printers? Fine job!

1. The first number of *Letter* was dated January 1943, with twelve thousand copies printed. Ida M. Tarbell was listed as a consultant. Though announced as a monthly, it appeared irregularly; apparently its last issue was volume 5, number 9, dated September 1947. Among those who wrote for it were Edgar Snow, Dorothy Thompson, Lillian Smith, Shirley Graham, and John Henrik Clarke. An effort to obtain additional biographical material on Ada P. McCormick has not been successful.

If I get some professional contributing editors would you be interested in being one? The sort of thing the *Pittsburgh Courier* does might not be bad in a magazine. Say four brilliant people if we could land them running short departments.*

I am so green at this. We are sending you the four copies issued, the next drags at the printers. Do tear them apart and rebuild—up to fee enclosed.

Sincerely,

Ada P. McCormick

*[McCormick's note] Or one editor running 4 departments. Could get varying guest editors for departments in different issues. Negroes—Latin America—Chinese—Anglo-Americans. Does that sound better or not?

p. s. I want to do a work-up of you and *Phylon* some time—i.e., the history of *Phylon* as created by you—so any notes on that would be of interest!

New York City, October 4, 1944

My dear Miss McCormick:

Your letter of August 30 was delayed in answering because of my absence in Haiti—that amazing island, whose beauty surpasses anything I have ever seen. I have just returned to a new job and have as yet neither permanent office nor my books and papers, nor my secretary (she's finishing work for her Ph.D. at the University of Havana, but returns in October loaded with Spanish.)

My month-late answer therefore must be tentative and subject to revision on further thought.

I should be glad to collaborate on the *Letter*, if it can be arranged. As I have written you, I have left Atlanta University and returned to New York where I am Director of Special Research for the National Association for the Advancement of Colored People. The scope of my work is not yet settled but I enclose a preliminary forecast.

In leaving Atlanta, I had to relinquish, to my regret, all connection with *Phylon*. *Phylon* is the fourth magazine which I have founded and edited:[1] first the *Moon*, a weekly, in Memphis, Tenn. Then the *Horizon*, in Washington, D. C. Then the *Crisis*, in New York, monthly, which ran for twenty-three years in New York, and once reached a circulation of 100,000. Then *Phylon*. The name was my suggestion. For the format I sought expert advice—Elmer Adler, who planned the format of the New York *Times*, and now lives in Princeton.[2] I'd like to write the history of this magazine sometime for the *Letter*.

1. Du Bois inadvertently omitted *Brownies' Book*, a monthly magazine for children, which he founded and edited during its existence from January 1920 to December 1921.
2. Elmer Adler (1884-1962) was at this time a consultant for the library and press of Princeton University. Volume two of this work includes an exchange between him and Du Bois, pp. 388-89.

Now for advice and suggestion: (1) Your magazine must appear regularly and on time. No body of subscribers will endure irregular appearance and omitted and doubled numbers. A monthly is best for general readers such as you may attract and 60 pages is sufficient. If quarterly, then you must have 100 pages at least.

(2) Regularity can be assured only by having a business manager on the spot for mailing and sales promotion. Small use in publishing unless the magazine reaches readers and on time. Subscriptions must be carefully recorded and kept up.

(3) Your ideas on contents are good, but all depends on carrying out. Life-Time-Fortune have shown us the value of a group of carefully selected, well-paid editors, doing special research in various lines. I suggest for *Letter*, a board of five editors: you, yourself, as managing editor, for make-up and general direction; four other editors scattered in various parts of the world, with special assignments which might vary from time to time. They should be good writers, clear thinkers, and get their stuff in on time. They would have to be paid enough to ensure a living when combined with other work which would leave time for this job. Their personality should be the major consideration, and the subjects adjusted to their gifts.

(4) This involves the question of expense. The expense of your magazine should be carefully calculated and budgeted. You should live within your budget, allowing for income only what the magazine actually brings in. Within that frame, you should try to give something people would not only want to read, but insist on reading.

(5) Subjects treated, in order of importance, seem to me:

(a) Income   The question of wage, salary, profits, etc. This is the primary and fundamental question of this age as indeed of all ages. It must be faced and solutions sought.

(b) Race   The problems which lurk under the concept of race, no matter how we define the word, and which are most influential in human affairs today.

(c) Sex   The problem not only of the place and function of woman, but the problems of marriage, family, children, etc.

(d) Education   The training of human beings, young and old, into an intelligent working knowledge of the world in which they live.

(e) Religion   The problem of dogma as a fact and of faith as a method.

(f) Law and Government   The problems of democracy, crime and social control.

These primary subjects must receive continuous attention; the method of attack should include the human approach—how these broader matters affect prisoners, landlords and tenants, relatives, merchants and mechanics, laborers; people in China, India, Latin America; children, girls in love, etc.

These are my initial comments. Read them over; by that time, I shall probably have other ideas, and have changed these in some respects.

Very sincerely yours,
W. E. B. Du Bois

Raymond Leslie Buell (1896–1946) was a distinguished authority on international affairs. He taught at leading universities and served as research director of the Foreign Policy Association in New York City from 1927 to 1933. His best-known work was the two-volume study The Native Problem in Africa *(1928). In his later years he served as an international affairs editor for* Time *magazine, and in that capacity he wrote to Du Bois, addressing his letter to Atlanta.**

New York City, October 5, 1944

Dear Professor Du Bois:

I am making another study of Liberia, its progress, if any, since the dark days of 1932, and the prospects for the future. I am anxious to get your views on this question, and any suggestions of people I should contact. Do you think the Liberian Republic should continue in the future as in the past; do you see any evidence that the American-Liberians are giving way to the native-born aborigines? I shall be grateful for any ideas you can send me on this subject.

Sincerely yours,
Raymond L. Buell

New York City, October 11, 1944

My dear Mr. Buell:

I have your letter of October 5, sent to Atlanta. I have been retired from my work at Atlanta University and have rejoined the NAACP with offices in New York for special study of the problems of Colonial peoples after the war. This, of course, increases my direct interest in Liberia since Liberia is a quasi-colony of the United States.

I have made no special study of Liberia since the Liberian appeal to the League of Nations which I treated in an article in *Foreign Affairs*.[1] I have, however, gotten information from time to time from the American Minister, Lester Walton, who is a friend of long standing. I believe that Mr. Walton is on his way to the United States and I should certainly advise conferring with him. I think that the Liberian Republic should continue as an independent country acquiring as time goes on an increasing amount of economic independence, to support its political interests.

* A 1929 exchange between Buell and Du Bois appears in volume one of this work, pp. 403-4.

1. "Liberia, the League and the United States," *Foreign Affairs* 9 (July 1933): 682-95.

There are no American-Liberians in the biological sense. The Liberians are all of them today overwhelmingly mixed with native African blood. There remains, however, a strong cultural separation of the ruling class of Liberians from those still under tribal government or influence. The future problem is the blending of these two ideas.

I shall be glad to talk with you about Liberia at any time you may wish.

Very sincerely yours,
W. E. B. Du Bois

It was not unusual for Du Bois to receive requests for his photograph from schools or organizations conducted by Black people, but such requests from white institutions were rare. One came from a youngster in a Brookfield public school, District 95, Cook County, Illinois; it is printed as written. It was followed by a letter from the child's teacher.

Brookfield, Illinois, October 18, 1944

Dear Dr. Du Bois:

We began studying about Negros in school last year. We became so interested that we organized a club so that we might learn about them during our lunch hour. We feel badly about the way some people treat Negroes. It is wrong and we want to do everything we can to make other people realize it.

Last year we wrote letters to Negro children and invited them to visit our school. Their teacher and our teacher are friends. One of them is Mrs. Madeline R. Morgan, who wrote stories for the Chicago school children, which we have enjoyed reading too. Mrs. Morgan visit our school and talked to us in an assembly. We visited a Negro library in Chicago and read read stories of Negros.

This year we are in the sixth grade and being older, we want to do something Bigger. We want to make a collection of pictures and stories of famous Negros which we can share with people of our town and children in other schools all through our state.

We have read stories about you in Mrs. Morgans book. You are doing a wonderful part by your [one word illegible] in starting the magazine *The Crisis* and by teaching so long, since from 1896 to now is a great deal of time. We thought perhaps you would help us by sending us your picture for our exhibit on Negro achievement.

Thank you so much we will try to show are gratefulness by helping make others feel that discrimination is wrong.

Yours very truly
Marilyn Breenson—Junior Social Studies
Council

Brookfield, Illinois, November 2, 1944

Dear Sir:

I believe Marilyn has explained what we hope to do and I hope it is not too
great an imposition. There is so much to be done and so much that can be done
in the training of our school children. Miss Jensen of the N.A.A.C.P. assured
us that, if possible, you would assist us in securing pictures for our exhibit by
sending us yours.

Very sincerely yours,
Grace Markwell

New York City, November 4, 1944

My dear Miss Breenson:

I am sending herewith a picture of myself which I hope will help your
collection.

Very sincerely yours,
W. E. B. Du Bois

*One of the means that Du Bois employed to make his views known was the
newspaper column. He contributed in 1927 and in 1931 to the* Amsterdam
News. *From 1936 until early 1938 he contributed to* The Pittsburgh Courier
and from October 1939 until 14 October 1944 to the Amsterdam News *once
more. In a letter to that paper's managing editor, Julius J. Adams, written
29 March 1943, Du Bois complained of the garbling of one of his columns; why
he discontinued his association with the* Amsterdam News *is explained in the
letters that follow.*

C. B. Powell was the editor and publisher of the newspaper.

New York City, October 20, 1944

My dear Mr. Powell:

I have received the check from the *Amsterdam News* this morning for the
first half of October. As I furnished you material for columns up until the
fifteenth, I shall keep this check but I think you may consider this payment
as ending the contract between us as I shall send you no more material.

I want to thank you for the courtesy and consideration given me in the past
and I am sorry that our relationships cannot continue longer but, as I think you
understand, I cannot allow my material to be changed and distorted at the will
of any publisher. I realize, on the other hand, that you have a right to publish
or refuse to publish anything you please. By the same token I have the right to
refuse to furnish matter which is changed without my consent.

Very sincerely yours,
W. E. B. Du Bois

New York City, October 26, 1944

Dear Dr. Du Bois:

We are in receipt of your letter of the 20th.

Unfortunately Dr. Powell is still away from his Editorial desk, however you may be assured that your letters will be referred to him immediately upon his return.

Very truly yours,
M. J. Lloyd, Secretary
C. B. Powell, Editor

Brooklyn, New York, November 8, 1944

My dear Dr. Du Bois:

The Youth Council of the Brooklyn Branch NAACP is engaged in a campaign against the yellow journalism of the *Amsterdam News,* and we would like your cooperation if possible.

As Negro youth, we feel that this type of journalism is doing our race irreparable harm and we are determined to do something about it. We have written a letter to Editor C. B. Powell, asking for a conference for the discussion of our criticisms, but to date we have not been granted same.

Included in our points for discussion was the fact that the paper was biased politically—so much so that many articles by feature writers were omitted, presumably because of the political beliefs of the writer. We can understand a paper supporting this or that political party in its editorial column, but the *Amsterdam News* did much more than just that.

I wonder if you would be good enough to favor us with a statement regarding your resignation from the staff of the Amsterdam? When we finally succeed in holding a conference with Dr. Powell we want to have specific information to back up each and every one of our arguments.

Very sincerely yours,
Walter McKay, Chairman
Education Committee

New York City, November 9, 1944

My dear Mr. McKay:

I discontinued my contributions to the Amsterdam News because without consultation or notice the editor changed my column twice so as to prevent me from expressing my political views on the presidential campaign.

Very sincerely yours,
W. E. B. Du Bois

Joseph M. Proskauer (1877–1971), born in Mobile, Alabama, was educated at Columbia University and admitted to the New York bar in 1899. He practiced law there until 1923, when he became a justice of the New York Supreme Court. After his judgeship ended in 1930, he resumed the private practice of law. In his capacity as president of the American Jewish Committee, he sent Du Bois a letter late in October 1944, addressing it to Atlanta University.

New York City, October 24, 1944

Dear Dr. Du Bois:

Believing that the sanctity of the individual is a principal basic to future world order and peace, the American Jewish Committee plans to issue a Declaration of Human Rights, two copies of which are enclosed.[1] We feel sure that the sentiments expressed are not only those of the Committee, but those held by thousands of distinguished and thoughtful Americans of all faiths. We, therefore, urge that you join with us in signing this Declaration.

On the eve of Liberation, we feel a particular urgency for all men of peace and good will to emphasize and reaffirm the godly concept of the dignity of the individual man.

We trust that you will join with us in presenting the Declaration of Human Rights to the American public. To this end, will you please sign and return one copy in the enclosed self-addressed envelope; the other copy we believe you will want to keep for your own records.

Sincerely yours,

Joseph M. Proskauer

New York City, November 14, 1944

Mr. Joseph M. Proskauer

My dear Sir:

I have received your declaration of human rights and want to say frankly that I am greatly disappointed. You say under paragraph two of your creed: "No plea of sovereignty shall ever again be allowed to permit any nation to deprive those within its borders of these fundamental rights on the claim that these are matters of internal concern." How about depriving people outside the borders of a country of their rights?

Under paragraph five you appeal for sympathy for persons driven from the land of their birth; but how about American Negroes, Africans and Indians who have not been driven from the land of their birth but nevertheless are deprived of their rights? Under paragraph six you want redress for those who wander the earth but how about those who do not wander and are not allowed to travel and nevertheless are deprived of their fundamental human rights?

1. References to the declaration will be found in the *New York Times*, 5 February 1945, p. 28, and 22 March 1945, p. 15.

In other words, this is a very easily understood declaration of Jewish rights but it has apparently no thought of the rights of Negroes, Indians and South Sea Islanders. Why then call it the Declaration of Human Rights?

Very sincerely yours,
W. E. B. Du Bois

The immediate genesis of Du Bois's Color and Democracy: Colonies and Peace *was a letter Du Bois sent to Harcourt, Brace—the publishers of his* Darkwater *(1920),* Dark Princess *(1928), and* Black Reconstruction *(1935)—late in November 1944, shortly after he had gotten himself settled in his new post with the* NAACP. *The response was positive, and the book itself was published on 25 May 1945.**

New York City, November 20, 1944

Gentlemen:

I propose to write a book on the subject "Color and Democracy: Color and Peace." I have come to this idea because of the demand for lectures and broadcasts on this subject and because of my new position as Director of Special Research for the NAACP this has been made my field of work and study.

I am enclosing a short synopsis for a book of seven chapters to fill about one hundred and fifty pages of a small octavo. This is but a bare outline. I want to add to it some factual and illustrative material and more specifically I want to put it into very careful finished English which will make it agreeable reading for the average American.

I am quite sure that a book of this sort sold at a small price can find considerable circulation among the large and widespread membership of the National Association for the Advancement of Colored People as well as among others.

I am writing to ask if you would consider undertaking the publication of this work?

Very sincerely yours,
W. E. B. Du Bois

Barely two weeks after hearing positively from Harcourt, Brace, Du Bois— with his incredible energy and drive—was writing a letter to Henry Holt and Company, the publishers of his Negro *(1915) and* Black Folk Then and Now *(1939), proposing a book on Africa. In this case, however, while the response was prompt it was not encouraging, and the book proposed never was written.*

* For details on this book, additional correspondence about it, and its critical reception, see the editor's introduction to the Kraus-Thompson edition of the volume (Millwood, New York, 1976).

New York City, December 14, 1944

Henry Holt and Co.

Gentlemen:

I have in mind a book on Africa, "Africa and Two World Wars." I plan short statements concerning the impact of the first World War on Africa and events between the wars. The main part of the book I want to devote to an examination of what effect the war is having on Africa, both independent states and the colonies; what the colonial powers are proposing to do after the war; and what the colonies and other states are demanding.

I think a short book of one hundred fifty or two hundred pages on this subject would find readers. If you are interested, I would be glad to outline this book more definitely by chapters in January and I think I can have the completed manuscript in your hands by April.

Very sincerely yours,

W. E. B. Du Bois

A response from Du Bois characteristically illuminating his view of religion occurs in correspondence initiated by a priest connected with St. Peter Claver's Church in Tyler, Texas; one regrets that in the priest's letter he does not give the substance of "the remark of my housekeeper."

Tyler, Texas, December 10, 1944

Dear Doctor Du Bois,

I have read with pleasure your article in the book *What the Negro Wants.*[1] It is quite an autobiography of your life. Incidents of loss of hope and courage waning are recalled and bring to my mind the remark of my housekeeper when I spoke words of praise for your name.

But to the point—on page 68 you say, "To the third category of social activity, concerned with social uplift, one would say at first that not only should everyone be admitted but all even urged to join."

I write this letter to urge you not only to consider the Catholic Church but to urge you to join her. Maybe I am wrong and you are already a Catholic but nevertheless I seem to see in your writing that you expect a great deal from the church by your phrase "If a church is a social clique." The Catholic Church in the United States has not given to the Negro all that she can and should do, but I believe that for yourself she will be able to give you greater strength and courage to carry on your life work. She will help you when men fail you.

The first native of North or South America raised to the Episcopacy was a Negro—Victoria Bishop of Panama—I pray that we have more like him now.

1. "My Evolving Program for Negro Freedom," in *What the Negro Wants,* ed. Rayford W. Logan (Chapel Hill: University of North Carolina Press, 1944), pp. 31-70. The second quotation, unidentified in the letter, is from p. 69 of Du Bois's essay.

Toussaint, a Catholic, kept his hope and courage unto the end under bitter punishment of body and mind. If Jesus Christ—the God-Man—has not converted the world as yet, how expect a man to do it.

"So far as human friendship and intermingling are based on broad and catholic reasoning and ignore petty and inconsequential prejudices, the happier will be the individual and the richer the general social life." This the Catholic Church offers you. This is what the Catholic Church without state interference but aid has done for Brazil and other places.

Do write me, and [if] I can be of any service to you in whatsoever manner —do not hesitate to call on me.

Sincerely yours in Christ,
John R. Timpany S. S. J.[2]

New York City, January 17, 1945
Reverend John R. Timpany, S. S. J.
My dear Sir:

Answering your letter of December 10, I may say that I have great sympathy with the Catholic Church and know something of its history. My granddaughter is at present in the eighth grade of the elementary school conducted by the Sisters of St. Francis Academy in Baltimore. On the other hand, I cannot assent to any creed which demands that I accept on faith the elaborate doctrine and dogma of the Catholic Church. As a scientist I am perfectly aware that there are some things in this world we must accept on faith so long as we rigorously test them by the data of experience. Beyond that I cannot go.

I regret to say that the human friendship and intellectual fellowship offered by the Catholic Church now and in the past is not as perfect as I wish it could be. There are separate white and Negro congregations in the South. The Catholics refuse to receive colored students in a large number of their schools and their training of Negro Catholic priests in America has been ridiculously below the demand.

Very sincerely yours,
W. E. B. Du Bois

2. Father Timpany describes missionary work among Black children in "Texas Comes Through," in the *Colored Harvest* (published by St. Joseph's Society in Baltimore) for June-July 1934 (22:11.) At that time he served at a church in Beaumont. In the *Colored Harvest* 31 (October-November 1944): 15, his appointment as the rector of the church in Tyler, Texas, was announced.

James W. Ford (1896-1957), born in Alabama, was a founder of the American Negro Labor Congress in 1925. He joined the Communist Party the next year and during the 1930s and 1940s in particular was an outstanding leader of that party; he was the Communist vice-presidential candidate in 1932, 1936, and 1940. Beginning in the 1920s, Ford and Du Bois occasionally exchanged letters. Illustrative is an exchange from early 1945.

New York City, January 8, 1945

Dear Dr. Du Bois:

Some time ago I wrote to your office requesting a copy of a speech which you delivered over Station WEVD on the Colonial question. I did not receive the address. But I have since read an article of yours on the subject which I take to be the substance of your radio broadcast.[1]

I am therefore writing this to you because I had hoped to make some comment on some of your views on the Colonial question with which I do not agree. Nevertheless, I want you to know that I disagree entirely with the manner and content of the criticism expressed in the *Daily Worker* article by Max Gordon, who incidentally expressed his own individual opinion.[2]

Sincerely yours,
James W. Ford

New York City, January 17, 1945

My dear Mr. Ford:

I am sending you another copy of my broadcast. I am sorry that the first did not reach you. I may say that so far as the publication in the *New Leader* is concerned, I simply sent them, at their request, the broadcast and gave them the permission to republish it if they wished.

Very sincerely yours,
W. E. B. Du Bois

1. The article was "Imperialism, United Nations and Colonial People," *New Leader* 27 (December 30, 1944): 5. This essay—which was indeed the text of a radio speech by Du Bois—warned that colonialism had been an important cause of both world wars and that, unless excised, it would encourage still further wars.

2. Max Gordon, a staff writer for the *Daily Worker*, in its issue of 5 January 1945 (p. 7), criticized Du Bois's *New Leader* piece as ultra-leftist.

*On 16 January 1945, Du Bois returned to Harcourt, Brace the corrected copy
of his manuscript of* Color and Democracy; Colonies and Peace. *The very next
day he sent a proposal for another book to Viking Press.*

New York City, January 17, 1945

[Viking Press]
Gentlemen:

I have in mind a book along the following lines: title to be "The Africas"
emphasizing the fact that Africa is not one country, one group or one race but
a conglomerate of peoples with various degrees of importance and possibilities
who are going to play roles in the post-war world.

The book will be a study of the condition of the various African nations,
colonies and groups at the time of the first World War, since that war, during
the present war, with a forecast of what is going to happen in Africa after the
war.

I want to emphasize the fact that merely because news from Africa is not
broadcast, this does not mean that important developments are not taking place.
The people of Africa are normal human beings with all possibilities for development. Their country is extraordinary for its climate and possibilities and the
geography of Africa places it today in the midst of world events.

I think that a small book of one hundred and fifty or two hundred pages on
this subject might attract readers. I should be glad to know what you think of
the proposition.

Very sincerely yours,
W. E. B. Du Bois

New York City, January 23, 1945

Dear Dr. Du Bois:

Your suggestion of a book to be entitled "The Africas" appeals to our interest
and your brief remarks about the subject matter lead us to believe that you have
a significant contribution to make. Could you give us a little more to go on,
say in the form of an elaborate statement, or table of contents with annotations,
or perhaps an elaboration in an interview which could be arranged to suit your
convenience?

You may remember that in another day we used to meet occasionally. I
should be glad to renew the acquaintance and I will await word as to your
pleasure.

Sincerely yours,
B. W. Huebsch[1]
[President, The Viking Press, Inc.]

1. B. W. Huebsch (1876–1964) studied at Cooper Union in New York City and for
a period was music critic on the *New York Sun.* From 1920 to 1924 he published the

It was typical of Du Bois that he took the time to write the following letter to Karl Earl Mundt (1900–1975), from 1939 to 1948 a member of the House from South Dakota and then (1948-73) a United States senator. Karl Mundt's main congressional work was investigating "subversives," along with his colleagues, Richard Nixon and Joseph McCarthy. There seems to have been no reply to Du Bois's letter.

New York City, January 22, 1945

Mr. Karl E. Mundt
My dear Sir:

I understand you have been asking various persons concerning their ideas of un-American activities. May I suggest the following:

1. the widespread conspiracy especially in the South to keep persons from registering as voters.

2. the widespread effort and organization to keep registered voters in the South from casting their ballot.

3. the present activities of the Ku Klux Klan and other organizations.

4. the effort through secret societies and social organizations to coordinate efforts to make laws and ordinances curtailing and limiting the freedom and citizenship of Negroes.

5. widespread efforts to increase and advertise anti-Semites.

6. similar effort to prevent the organization and unionization of labor in the South and to induce labor unions as exist to exclude Negroes.

7. the systematic suppression of news concerning Negroes in the South and especially favorable news.

8. the opposition to Negro education particularly in the public elementary and high schools.

I think the above matters call for earnest and careful investigation and I am sure Mr. [John] Rankin, a member of your Committee, can furnish a great deal of information on practically all these points.

I am, Sir,

Very sincerely yours,
W. E. B. Du Bois

A letter which reflected (and still reflects) the feelings of many white people

----

weekly *Freeman;* in 1925 he joined Viking. He was a translator of Stefan Zweig and for many years treasurer of the American Civil Liberties Union. It was probably in his editorial work and his efforts with the ACLU that he and Du Bois "used to meet occasionally." In February 1945, Viking and Du Bois signed a contract; the resulting book was *The World and Africa*, published in January 1947. For details and additional correspondence, see this editor's introduction to the Kraus-Thomson edition of that book (Millwood, New York, 1976).

in the United States produced a reply manifesting Du Bois's compassion and earnestness.

Pass Christian, Miss., March 2, 1945

Dear Dr. W. E. B. Du Bois:

I don't know quite how to write what I have in mind without it degenerating into something typical of a Christian Scientist testimonial.

I want to be able to *do* something for and preferably in your organization, yet my technical qualifications, outside a genuine interest and will to act, are practically non-existent.

I happen to have been born of white parents and am the wife of a soldier stationed temporarily in nearby New Orleans and am also the mother of two.

The community here, the white part of it, is as a whole bitterly prejudiced. This is Pass Christian where they speak of Lincoln, if they speak of him at all, as having been fortunate to have died so soon.

Just what can a person like me *do*, Dr. Du Bois, to further the much needed understanding between black and white?

In all sincerity,
Johanna Griggs
[Mrs. C. L. Griggs]

P.S. Am mailing duplicate letter to Donald Jones, who has written an article for December *Common Sense!*[1]

New York City, March 13, 1945

My dear Mrs. Griggs:

There is no categorical or exact answer to your letter of March second. What one can do in great causes and in particular places depends on so many variables that the perfect answer is only possible for the person involved at the particular time and in the particular place. Generalities are only meaningless but I may say this: what is conspicuously lacking in race relations is courage in particular persons who have the right ideas to express themselves clearly when occasions occur. I do not mean speeches or harangues but I do mean that there come specific times when it is the duty of a person to say clearly: I believe in race equality; I do not subscribe to the color line; I think the conduct just mentioned was wrong and contemptible.

I am afraid this letter will not help you very much.

Very sincerely yours,
W. E. B. Du Bois

1. Donald Jones, "If I Were a White Man," *Common Sense* 13 (December 1944): 429–31. Jones had been director of publicity for Dillard University in New Orleans; at the time this article was published he was assistant field secretary of the NAACP. His article offered several suggestions for specific actions by white people to help overcome racism.

In 1939 the American Association of University Professors held its annual meeting in a hotel in New Orleans which would not serve Black people; in April 1944, local groups of the AAUP held a dinner meeting at a hotel in Washington, D.C., which refused to serve Black people, and the AAUP leadership therefore did not invite its Black members to that dinner. As a result, Du Bois resigned from the AAUP through a letter to its general secretary, Dr. Ralph E. Himstead,* with copies to each of the remaining thirty-nine officers and members of the AAUP council. In addition to the reply from Himstead, Du Bois received replies from four of the other thirty-nine professors.

New York City, March 13, 1945
[Dr. Ralph E. Himstead]
My dear Sir:

I have hesitated about renewing my membership in your Association but finally after talking with Dr. Rayford W. Logan of Howard University, I have decided that I will not.[1] I think that the persistent policy which you follow in spite of our protest of holding your meetings, national and local, in places where your Negro members are not allowed to attend is not only unfair but contemptible. I do not wish, therefore, any further connection with an organization that persists in such conduct.

Very sincerely yours,
W. E. B. Du Bois

Washington, D.C., April 19, 1945
Dear Dr. Du Bois:

I have your letter of March 13 in which you submit your resignation as a member of the American Association of University Professors. Your resignation is accepted with deep regret.

In stating the reason for your resignation, you write as follows:

"I have hesitated about renewing my membership in your Association but finally after talking with Dr. Rayford W. Logan of Howard University, I have decided that I will not. I think that the persistent policy which you follow in spite of our protest of holding your meetings, national and local, in

---

* Ralph Ebner Himstead (1893–1955) was born in Illinois and educated at the University of Illinois, Northwestern, and Harvard, receiving from the latter an LL.D. in 1929. He was a professor of law at the University of Syracuse from 1924 to 1936; thereafter, until his death, he served with the AAUP.

1. In a letter to the editor dated Washington, D.C., 28 May 1976, Logan stated that he did not recall a conversation with Du Bois about the AAUP at Atlanta. He did remember the 1939 incident at New Orleans and he enclosed a copy of a 26 December 1939 letter from Professor Mercer Cook, chapter president of the AAUP at Howard University, to Himstead, protesting the jim-crow arrangements at New Orleans and urging that future AAUP affairs not be marred by such insulting and backward practices.

places where your Negro members are not allowed to attend is not only unfair but contemptible. I do not wish, therefore, any further connection with an organization that persists in such conduct."

I should like to comment on your statement quoted above. Although the American Association of University Professors has always experienced difficulty in finding places for its Annual Meeting free of discrimination against Negroes, its policy has been and is to find such places. In the pursuit of this policy, the Association has for the most part been successful. During my nine years as General Secretary of the Association, only one of the Association's Annual Meetings was scheduled at a hotel whose management discriminated against Negroes. I refer to the 1939 Annual Meeting, which was held in New Orleans, Louisiana, at the Hotel Jung. All the other Annual Meetings of this Association during my Secretaryship have been held free of discrimination against Negroes.

The American Association of University Professors usually holds its Annual Meeting in connection with the Annual Meeting of one or more of the special discipline organizations. The decision to hold the 1939 meeting with the meeting of the Modern Language Association was made before the Modern Language Association had made a final selection of the city for the meeting. With reference to the city in which that meeting was held, therefore, the American Association of University Professors had no choice nor did it have any choice as regards hotel accommodations. The Modern Language Association is a large organization with many sections and in the very nature of the case that Association had first choice of hotel accommodations. The only hotel in which the American Association of University Professors could get accommodations was the Hotel Jung, whose management discriminates against Negroes. Our Negro members were permitted to attend the business sessions of the meeting, but were not permitted to attend the annual dinner. With reference to the scheduling of this meeting at the Hotel Jung I received a few protests from our Negro members to which I replied presenting the facts as indicated above. The Association has received no similar protests with reference to any other meeting during my term of office as General Secretary. It is difficult for me, therefore, to understand your reference to "the persistent policy which you follow in spite of our protest."

In your letter of March 13 you also refer to local meetings of the Association. Except for a few regulations in the Constitution and By-Laws of the Association concerning procedures, chapters of this Association are autonomous. To my knowledge, no chapter of this Association in holding a meeting open to members of the Association at other institutions has ever excluded a Negro member. On the other hand, I have firsthand knowledge of several regional meetings sponsored by chapters to which members of chapters of Negro institutions were invited and in which they participated. There is no policy of this

Association, "persistent" or otherwise, to discriminate against Negro members either locally or nationally in the manner you indicate in your letter of March 13.

Occasionally chapters of the Association in arranging for regional meetings experience difficulty in finding places for such meetings free of discrimination against Negroes. I have in mind one such instance. On April 14, 1944, there was held in Washington, D.C. a dinner meeting of the Association sponsored by local groups in the Washington area. The Committee on Arrangements for this meeting had difficulty in finding a place on the date set for the meeting that would serve a dinner for a group of the size that was expected to attend. There were only two such places available, both hotels, and the management of both these hotels discriminates against Negroes. On March 31, 1944 I wrote to Professor [Rayford] W. Logan, President of the Association's chapter at Howard University, with reference to this situation. In my letter to Professor Logan, I said:

"With deep regret I write that the regulations of both these hotels are such as to bar the attendance of our colored members. In order that there may be no misunderstanding concerning this situation and to avoid embarrassment we are not sending to our members at Howard University the special postal card announcement of the dinner.

"I am confident you understand that the national officers of the Association regret the fact of the discrimination referred to above but this discrimination is a fact which apparently only the slow process of education can change and concerning which in this instance there is no other course we can follow than to comply. As you know, when the City of Washington was less crowded, we held Association meetings at places whose regulations were not discriminatory. This policy the Association has followed whenever possible, and it should be possible in Washington as soon as conditions become more normal.

"If you think it would be advisable, I should appreciate it if you would bring this letter to the attention of the chapter at Howard University."

To this letter Professor Logan did not reply.

During my nine years as General Secretary of the American Association of University Professors, chapters in the Washington area have held a number of regional meetings. The dinner meeting on April 14, 1944 was the only one held at a place whose management discriminates against Negroes.

In the light of the record of the American Association of University Professors and of my own record as General Secretary of the Association with reference to the scheduling of meetings at places that do not discriminate against Negroes, the charge you make in your letter of March 13 is, I submit, unfair and regrettable.

The American Association of University Professors has chapters at 321 institutions. Nine of these chapters are at Negro institutions: Atlanta University, Hampton Institute, Howard University, Lincoln University (Missouri), North Carolina College for Negroes, Stowe Teachers College, Virginia State College for Negroes, West Virginia State College, and Xavier University. In addition to its Negro members at these nine institutions, the Association has Negro members from the faculties of six other institutions where chapters have not been organized. To the faculties of Negro institutions, the Association has given much service. Proportionately, more requests for professional service, particularly requests for intervention in situations involving issues of academic freedom and tenure, have come to the Association from members of Negro universities than from other institutions, and the services requested have been given to the full extent of the Association's ability. The American Association of University Professors is deeply interested in the education and the advancement of Negroes, as am I personally. That fact constitutes another reason why the charge you make in your letter of March 13 is regrettable. It is difficult for me to understand why you did not ascertain the facts before making so serious a charge.

Several members of the Council of this Association inform me that they have received a copy of your letter to me of March 13. Did you send copies of this letter to all members of the Association's Council? Please advise me on this point and also send me the names of all other persons to whom you sent copies of this letter. I shall wish to send to the persons who received copies of your letter of March 13 copies of this my reply.

Enclosed with this letter is a statement of your indebtedness to the American Association of University Professors for membership dues for the portion of the current year you were a member; i.e., up until the time of receipt of your resignation. If, in the light of the facts stated in this letter, you should decide to resume membership in the Association, and I hope that you will so decide, please disregard the statement enclosed and make the regular payment of annual dues some time during the current year.

I was interested to learn of your retirement from the faculty of Atlanta University and of your present position on the staff of the National Association for the Advancement of Colored People. I hope that you are finding your present work congenial and that in it you will find an even greater opportunity for significant service to society than as a member of a faculty of a university.

With best wishes for you in your new work, I am

Very sincerely yours,
Ralph E. Himstead

Among the council members who did reply to Du Bois was Clair Francis Littell (1887-1966), born in Pennsylvania and educated at Syracuse and Columbia

*universities. From 1924 through 1954, Littell was on the faculty at Cornell
College in Mount Vernon, Iowa; he was a member of the* AAUP *council from
1944 to 1947.*

Mount Vernon, Iowa, April 6, 1945

Dear Dr. Du Bois:

I assure you that I am heartily in sympathy with your remonstrance against
racial discrimination, if there is such, in the American Association of University
Professors. I was not aware of any tendency in that direction, although it is
highly probable that there are many of our members, particularly from the
South, who are still slaves to the notion of segregation, etc.

I was on an errand not a month ago, to one of our best colored schools in
the Middle West, to give them advice as to how best to handle some problems
that had arisen in their faculty with regard to promotions in rank, and also to
encourage their fine chapter of the AAUP that has recently been started. I found
there what seemed to me as a visitor, a satisfaction in having their own institution, state supported and independent, and a desire NOT to be incorporated into
the regular State University. I realize that much of this local sentiment was due
to the desire to avoid as much as possible of the inevitable discrimination that
would exist on the campus of the university.

It is undoubtedly true that a great many broad-minded and sincere Americans are doing all in their power to forward the cause of true Americanism
and Christianity through evolutionary methods. I personally feel that great
progress has been made in many ways since I first became interested in such
questions, many years ago.

Whenever occasion arises in the National Council to deal with the problem
that you raise, I shall certainly do all in my power to have the wrong righted.

Yours sincerely,
C. F. Littell

*Another respondent was William Jaffé, born in New York City in 1898 and
educated at the City College of New York, Columbia and the University of
Paris. Jaffé was a professor of economics at the University of Chicago from
1928 to 1966 and now is professor emeritus there. Most recently he has taught
economics at York University in Ontario, Canada.*

Evanston, Illinois, April 9, 1945

Dear Dr. Du Bois:

I want to thank you for sending me a copy of your letter of March 13, 1945
addressed to Dr. Ralph E. Himstead, Executive Secretary of the A.A.U.P.

As a member of the Council of the Association I feel a sense of responsibility
for the state of affairs which led you to refuse to renew your membership for

this year. May I trouble you to send me an account of the specific facts and circumstances of which you complain? I wish to come well armed to the next Council Meeting to be held at the Stevens Hotel on May 18.

Even before your letter reached me I had been planning to ask the disturbing question why the Association has been so ominously quiet about the prevalence of racial, religious and national discrimination in the administration of institutions of higher learning. This is a matter of professional interest which it is the business of the A.A.U.P. to consider.

I need not add that I take a serious view of the evil of race and other abominable prejudices not only on grounds of human justice but also on personal grounds. The frequent sign "gentiles only" is aimed at me and the likes of me.

Sincerely yours,
William Jaffé

A third reply came from Dr. Francis E. Ray (1887-1966), then a professor of chemistry at the University of Cincinnati. Ray had previously been on the faculties of the University of Illinois and Grinnell College; from 1949 to his death he was a professor at the University of Florida. His main specialization was the study of cancer.

Cincinnati, Ohio, April 9, 1945

My dear Mr. Du Bois:

Thank you for sending me a copy of your letter of March 13 to Dr. Himstead.

I am sure that there is no policy to exclude our negro or any other group. There may be some carelessness in making it perfectly clear to the hotels that we insist that there be no discrimination.

The American Chemical Society has a no-discrimination clause in their contracts with hotels and halls to which notice is always directed. I shall certainly urge that such be done in future A.A.U.P. meetings.

I would urge you to reconsider your decision to resign from the A.A.U.P. It is only by your presence that you can contribute to the improvement of conditions. We need your vigilance and support.

Yours sincerely,
Francis E. Ray

The final response came from George Pope Shannon (1892-1964). Shannon was born in Tennessee and educated at Vanderbilt and Stanford universities. He taught at Stanford and the University of New Mexico in the 1920s and 1930s, and from 1935 through 1947 was professor of English at the University of Alabama. In the late 1950s, Shannon edited the Bulletin *of the* AAUP.

University, Alabama, April 20, 1945

My dear Mr. Du Bois:

Your letter of March 13 to Dr. Himstead, a copy of which you sent me, has puzzled me, for three reasons: First, I am not aware that our Association has a policy of excluding Negroes from meetings; second, I have assumed, perhaps mistakenly, that the large Northern hotels freely admit Negroes; and third, it has been several years since our Association has held a national meeting open to the general membership.

May I say with reference to the third point above that, according to my recollection, there has not been a general meeting since December, 1941. There have been Council meetings, but since you are not a member of the Council, I do not see how you could have been adversely affected.

So far as I am personally concerned, I feel no disposition to exclude Negroes from any AAUP meeting, whether business or social, and I am inclined to believe that most members feel as I do. Whether they do or do not so feel, the issue cannot become acute during the war, since no meetings are being held. Meanwhile, the problems of higher education *are* acute. Why, then, should one resign from an organization whose efforts are presently needed, over an issue which at present cannot exist in a practical sense?

If your resignation was intended as a gesture, it seems to me so ill-timed as to lose all effect. If it was a sincere reaction to a present issue, I hope that my analysis above may help you to see it in a different light. In short, since the welfare of Negroes cannot be practically advanced by your resignation, and since higher education needs the continued support of all sincere friends, I hope that you will reconsider your action.

Very truly yours,
G. P. Shannon

Early in 1945, Saul Carson (1895-1971) wrote to Du Bois asking his ideas for a radio program Carson was then producing. The Carson letter seems not to have survived, but the reply is substantial. A well-known journalist in his day, Carson had been a founder of the Philadelphia Newspaper Guild. From 1953 until his retirement in 1969, he was United Nations correspondent for the Jewish Telegraph Agency.

New York City, April 10, 1945

Mr. Saul Carson
My dear Sir:

With regard to a radio program for "New World A-Coming" may I suggest the following policy as far as white and colored nations are concerned: You ought to stress the fact that differences of skin color and of hair and physique between the great groups of human beings are not of primary importance and do not of themselves call for action. On the other hand, differences of education, of health and particularly of work, wage and income and of political autonomy are of tremendous importance.

It happens today that most of the people of darker skin throughout the world occupy colonial or semi-colonial status; and because of their political subordination to imperial countries they suffer from extreme poverty, great illiteracy and disease. This binds the colored peoples together in common action today and will increasingly unite them in the future; but this union is not because of color and not for oppressing peoples of other colors, but for the primary necessity of getting the rights to a decent standard of living, to education and to health.

If these reforms are accomplished, the world has nothing to fear from race conflict, or from world war between yellow and white people or between white and black.

On the other hand, all people in the modern world have everything to fear from poverty, ignorance, disease and slavery.

I trust the above statement will be what you asked for.

Very sincerely yours,
W. E. B. Du Bois

In response to a request from the Chicago Defender *for a statement on the defeat of Germany, Du Bois sent a telegram to the editor, Metz T. P. Lochard.*

New York City, May 4, 1945
Germans have followed 12 years ideas of race superiority, the right of might and the use of lies. We have conquered Germany but not their ideas. We still believe in white supremacy, keeping Negroes in their places and lying about democracy, when we mean imperial control of 750 millions of human beings in colonies.

W. E. B. Du Bois

An exchange with a biographer of Booker T. Washington is of interest. Basil Mathews (1879-1951) was born in England and educated in Oxford; he taught at Boston University and Andover-Newton Theological Institution and in his last years at the University of British Columbia. Booker T. Washington *(1948) was one of forty books by Mathews; most treated religious subjects.*

Vancouver, Canada, June 8, 1945
Dear Dr. Du Bois:
As I have been trying to shape an appraisal of the strengths and defects of Booker T. Washington's program and policy my mind has gone back to a talk

that I was privileged to have with you some years ago when I was staying at Atlanta University and Spelman College. And I have been re-reading your *The Souls of Black Folk*, which—with your *Darkwater*—has given me so much stimulus and guidance (as well as sheer enjoyment of your enviable command of the nuances of our English prose).

Should I be imposing too much on you if I asked whether, during the forty years of experience and reflection since you wrote the chapter "Of Mr. Washington and Others," your appraisal has modified to any degree; and, if so, whether you would care to indicate in what direction?

I know how busy you are and hesitate to impose on your time and energy. But I know no one whose mature judgement I should value as highly as yours; and I do want, in lecturing and writing, to arrive at the most just estimate possible.

If you should happen to see President Clement or Miss Read would you be so good as to convey my kind greetings and good wishes.

Ever sincerely yours,
Basil Mathews

New York City, July 11, 1945

My dear Mr. Mathews:

Answering your letter of June 8th may I say that I do not think my opinion of Mr. Washington has changed essentially but there is a more recent interpretation of my attitude in the book, *What the Negro Wants*. The editor is Dr. Rayford Logan and the publisher is the University of North Carolina, Chapel Hill, North Carolina. I have a chapter in that on my evolving program of Negro education; also in my autobiography, *Dusk of Dawn* (Harcourt, Brace [1940],) the matter of Mr. Washington's policy is treated.

I am very glad indeed to hear from you.

Very sincerely yours,
W. E. B. Du Bois

Zora Neale Hurston (1903-60), one of the best-known writers of the 1930s and 1940s, was born in Florida and educated at Morgan College in Baltimore, Howard University, and Barnard College. For a time she was a secretary to the novelist Fannie Hurst, and she also served as a research assistant for Franz Boas. Among her most widely known books were Mules and Men *(1935),* Their Eyes Were Watching God *(1937) and* Tell My Horse *(1938). Her autobiography,* Dust Tracks on a Road, *was published in 1942. There are recent reprints of some of her works. Her letter to Du Bois, with its somewhat peculiar proposal, is rather characteristic of her work in general. It was addressed to Du Bois at Atlanta University, though its last sentence referred to the anti-colonial stand which Du Bois had taken as one of the* NAACP *consultants to the United States delegation at the founding meeting of the United Nations in San Francisco.*

Daytona Beach, Fla., June 11, 1945

My dear Dr. Du Bois:

As Dean of American Negro Artists, I think that it is about time that you take steps towards an important project which you have neglected up to this time.

Why do you not propose a cemetery for the illustrious Negro dead? Something like Pere la Chaise in Paris. If you like the idea, may I make a few suggestions to you?

1. That you secure about one hundred acres for the site in Florida. I am not saying this because this is my birth-state, but because it lends itself to decoration easier than any other part of Florida for that world famous Bok Tower.[1] I hope that you have seen it, for it is a thing of wondrous beauty. And the thing I want you to note is that two-thirds of the beauty is not in the Tower itself, but in the surroundings. You see, Dr. Du Bois, the very woods of Florida afford trees and shrubs free that would cost a fortune north of here, even provided that they could be made to grow. Magnolias, bay, oaks, palms, pines, all free for the taking. Beautiful shrubs while not wild, so plentiful that you could get thousands of cuttings of hibiscus, crotons, oleanders and the like for the mere asking. And don't forget the beautiful, disease and insect repelling camphor tree which grows here so free and quickly. By the time that each well known Negro contributed a tree or two, you would have a place of ravishing beauty. Ceremonies of tree-setting of course. You would, like Bok, select a site in the lake country of Florida, where thousands of acres are available and as cheap as five to ten dollars an acre on lakes.

2. That there be no regular chapel, unless a tremendous amount of money be secured. Let there be a hall of meeting, and let the Negro sculptors and painters decorate it with scenes from our own literature and life. Mythology and all. Funerals can be held from there as well.

Addition to first suggestion: In Florida, the vegetation would be green the year round, so that visitors during the winter months would not see a desolate looking place. For you must know the place would attract visitors [from] all over the world.

1. The reference to the Bok Tower indicates one of the conceptions of Edward William Bok (1863–1930), who was born in the Netherlands and came to the United States as a child. Bok became a very well-known journalist and a pioneer in what is today known as public relations. He was chief editor of the *Ladies' Home Journal* from 1889 to 1910. *The Americanization of Edward Bok* (1920), an autobiography, had a wide sale in its day. Bok conceived of the idea of a sanctuary and a carillon tower to be built in Florida and provided the funds for the project, which was executed by the famous landscape architect Frederick Law Olmsted and the Philadelphia architect Milton B. Medary. The sanctuary and tower were dedicated by President Calvin Coolidge in 1929. Bok told the story of the tower in the *Ladies' Home Journal* 46 (May 1929):12,205.

3. As far as possible, remove the bones of our dead celebrities to this spot.

4. Let no Negro celebrities, no matter what financial condition they might be in at death, lie in inconspicuous forgetfulness. We must assume the responsibility of their graves being known and honored. You must see what a rallying spot that would be for all that we want to accomplish and do. There one ought also to see the tomb of Nat Turner. Naturally, his bones have long since gone to dust, but that should not prevent his tomb being among us. Fred Douglass and all the rest.

You will naturally ask me why I do not approach Mary McCleod Bethune, since she is right here in town with me. But my objection is that she has never uttered nor written a quotable line, never created any art form, nor even originated an educational idea. She has not even improved on any that have been originated. So I think that she should come into the thing later on. In fact, having made the suggestion to you, I shall do nothing more if you like the idea and take it up. I mean, nothing that is not asked of me. I am no organizer, and I know it. That is why I have never accepted any political appointment, though three have been offered to me since the War began. I like to sit and meditate and go my own way without strings, so that I can say what I want to. That is precious little at present, because the publishers seem frightened, and cut every thing out that seems strong. I have come to the conclusion that for the most part, there is an agreement among them to clamp on the lid. But I promise you, that if you like the idea and go ahead, I will fall in behind you and do all that I can.

I feel strongly that the thing should be done. I think that the lack of such a tangible thing allows our people to forget, and their spirits evaporate. But I shall not mention the matter to any one else until you accept or refuse. If you accept, there is no need for me to say anything more, as that will be your province. If you refuse, then maybe Walter White and the N.A.A.C.P. might take it up.

Oh yes, the reason that I suggested so much as 100 acres was because it would prevent white encroachment, and besides, it would afford space for an artist colony if ever the need arose. You can call on me for the first contribution. If you came down to look over sites, I could save you a lot of trouble by driving you around to look, since I know the State pretty well. I think that I know where to get some mahogany from Central America for the inside woodwork of the building.

Your own mind can furnish you plenty of details, so there is nothing more for me to say except congratulations on your stand at San Francisco, and many good wishes for the future.

Sincerely,
Zora Neale Hurston

New York City, July 11, 1945

My dear Miss Hurston:

I have been out of the city for some time and this is in answer to your note of June 11th.

The idea of the cemetery for illustrious Negroes has its attractions but I am afraid that the practical difficulties are too great, and I regret to say I have not the enthusiasm for Florida that you have, naturally. I do know of its magnificent weather and vegetation, but in other matters more spiritual it is not so rich.

My work with the NAACP is limited in scope and I should hardly feel like suggesting this, but why not go ahead and suggest the matter not only to Mr. White, but to others? You might be able to carry it through.

It is nice to hear from you again after all these years.

Very sincerely yours,
W. E. B. Du Bois

Joseph A. Boromé was born in New York City in 1919 and educated there at City College and Columbia University. He was a Rosenwald Fellow from 1946 to 1948 and a librarian at Columbia from 1947 to 1950; in the latter year he joined the history department at City College of New York. He has produced significant studies in United States and Latin American history. His massive doctoral dissertation, "The Life and Letters of Justin Winsor," was completed at Columbia in 1950; it was in connection with the dissertation that he wrote Du Bois. In addition to the letter of 10 July 1945, published below, Boromé wrote a follow-up request to Irene Diggs, Du Bois's secretary, on 10 September.

Long Island City, New York, July 10,
1945

Dear Dr. Du Bois:

I am at present engaged in writing a biography of Justin Winsor, Librarian of Harvard from 1877 to 1897. I noted that you read part of your dissertation on the African slave trade at an annual meeting of the American Historical Association, in 1891 I believe. Because I thought you might have some personal impressions or reminiscences of Dr. Winsor, either at Harvard or at the American Historical Association's meetings, I now write this letter.

I am seeking any aid, or suggestions or any personal material or impressions of Dr. Winsor. If you are able to help me in any of these items, or if you would care to take the time to send me your memories of the Harvard Library at the time you were using it—how it operated to the students' advantage or disadvantage; whether Winsor helped the struggling student, or indeed whether the students ever saw him—I shall indeed be most grateful. Needless to say I shall not, under any conditions, publish any letter you might care to send me without your expressed approval. Any material you might send will be safely kept in my study in the Columbia University Library.

Thank you for your kind consideration in this matter.

Sincerely yours,
Joseph Boromé

New York City, October 5, 1945

My dear Mr. Boromé:

I am sorry not to have been able to get in touch with you with regard to your letters of July 10 and September 10th.

I am afraid that there is not much I can say to help you concerning Justin Winsor. I entered Harvard as a Junior in the Fall of 1888 and stayed two years in college and two years in the graduate school, leaving in the Spring of 1892. Winsor, at that time, was an authority and almost a legend and I had no personal contact with him as most of my work was done under [Albert Bushnell] Hart in the Department of American History. I never met him personally although I saw him a few times. I do not think I ever heard him lecture. His historical method and general guidance of the library was felt throughout my work. I worked a good deal in the library and I think that some of my requests for guidance and access to material went up to Winsor but I have no recollection of any direct response.

I am sorry not to be able to help you more.

Very sincerely yours,
W. E. B. Du Bois

Ernst Moritz Manasse was born in Germany in 1908 and educated at the University of Heidelberg; he taught in the 1930s in Italy and England and from 1939 to 1973 was on the faculty at North Carolina Central University in Durham, where he is now professor emeritus. He has written in philosophy and German literature.

Durham, N. C., July 18, 1945

Dear Professor Du Bois:

Several months ago, I asked you whether you are in possession of any material which would be of interest for the establishment of Max Weber's views on the American race problem. You kindly answered me at that time you could not get to your files due to the transfer of your household from Atlanta to New York.

In the meantime I have almost finished a paper which I hope to publish under the title "Max Weber on Race."[1] I would however not finish my manuscript

1. The footnote observed that Du Bois had contributed to a 1906 number of the

without having asked you once more whether you could check my material by personal records. I take the liberty to enclose the wording of a footnote of my manuscript. In case you could either confirm or correct the statements made therein, I would be very thankful. My doubt as to whether you had met Weber already in 1892 is due to the fact that at the time Weber was a very young instructor of commercial law. I have however not been able to look up a catalogue of the University of Berlin of that year.

I certainly would greatly appreciate any information you would be willing to pass on to me.

I am, dear Professor Du Bois,

Sincerely yours,
Ernst Moritz Manasse

New York City, August 1, 1945

Dear Mr. Manasse:

I am not yet in such position with my books and files so as to be able to use them. We are planning to move into a new building in September and I hope then to be able to get at things.

I remember the article in the *Archiv* and I am sure it was written at the personal solicitation of Max Weber. I think he visited me in Atlanta. In Berlin, while I was in his class I did not have, as I remember, any personal contact.

Very sincerely yours,
W. E. B. Du Bois

Alfred Baker Lewis was born in Philadelphia in 1897, studied at the University of Pennsylvania, and practiced law from 1919 to 1924. Thereafter he was active with the Socialist party, managing its Rand School in New York City and acting as secretary of the party in Massachusetts. In 1943 he became an officer in the Union Casualty Company and more recently was president of the Mt. Vernon (New York) Life Insurance Company. He has been associated with the League for Industrial Democracy and, since 1924, with the NAACP.

New York City, July 18, 1945

Dear Dr. Du Bois:

I have read with a great deal of interest and enjoyment your "Color and Democracy," and particularly appreciate your "class struggle" analysis of the

---

Archiv für Socialwissenschaft and that his *Dusk of Dawn* mentioned contact with Max Weber when Du Bois was a student at the University of Berlin. Manasse's essay was published in *Social Research* 14 (1947):191-222. Weber visited Du Bois at Atlanta University in 1904, and Du Bois's 1906 article resulted from that visit. A 1905 letter from Weber to Du Bois is relevant; see volume one of this work, pp. 106-7.

political democracy plus private capitalism which constitutes the social order of the countries, except Russia, having an advanced industrial civilization.

I would like to suggest that you somewhat under-estimate the extent to which the interests of labor groups in the industrially advanced and imperialistic nations are opposed to imperialism.

I worked for some years in Massachusetts and was impressed by the extent to which the textile industry (and other industries to a slighter extent) was moving South—because labor there was cheap. Within Massachusetts the women's shoe manufacturing industry was moving from the larger towns where the unions were well organized into smaller towns where the union was non-existent. New England towns were getting run-away shops from New York's high wage clothing industry. In all cases the reasons for the movement of industry was to get cheaper labor.

The organized workers knew very well that the relocation of industry in cheap labor areas was a threat to their standard of living, and they did all they could possibly do to organize the workers in the low wage areas and get higher wages for them. The economic motive of seeking cheap labor of course does not cease to operate at the Rio Grande River nor at the borders of any other industrially advanced country. Large investors seek foreign investment in so-called backward lands, i.e., lands where the standard of living is low, for one important reason, because labor there is cheap. By the same token the labor forces in the industrially advanced nations have a direct interest in raising the living standards and wages of the exploited lands. For cheap labor is a threat to their standards of living, and they would prefer, other things equal, to have capital invested at home and giving more employment there rather than having capital invested abroad to take advantage of low wages.

Of course imperialism would be no more objectionable than the ordinary processes of capitalism if it merely involved industrialization of those areas of the world to which modern machinery production has not yet spread. Capitalism is a definite advance over pre-capitalist modes of production. The especially objectionable feature of imperialism is the attempt of foreign investors acting through their governments to establish political as well as economic control over the backward areas to prevent the workers there from unionizing or from gaining the protection of labor legislation or of social security laws and the advantages of social services financed in part by adequate taxation of the profits of foreign investors. It is just such imperialist policies to which the interests of organized labor in the industrially advanced nations are opposed so far as those interests are rightly understood.

To be sure there are all sorts of qualifications on this. But I think it is fair to say that the chief qualifications are two. One is just plain lack of knowledge of the facts regarding imperialism. The members of organized labor have been until very recently not deeply interested in foreign policy, and they are still mostly ignorant, like other sections of the population, of the available facts regarding imperialism.

The other qualification is that imperialist policies have been "sold" to the workers in the industrially advanced nations as a necessity for national security. In the absence of any system of international collective security, impressive arguments can be marshalled to support that position. On the whole the labor forces have been more consistent supporters of collective security than have other economic interest groups (although the Communists deserted the collective security program while the Hitler-Stalin Pact was in effect, following the foreign policy of Russia). To the limited extent that the new United Nations Charter provides a system of collective security we may expect and should demand from the labor forces a more forthright and consistent anti-imperialist stand.

Finally I suggest that we should be careful to subject anti-imperialist movements to the test of opposition to economic exploitation. Off hand, I should say that the Moslem League in India, though opposed to British rule, was not opposed to exploitation; and Argentina's present government, although at the beginning it claimed to be opposed to Yankee imperialism, is certainly not pro-democratic or opposed to exploitation.

Very truly yours,
Alfred Baker Lewis

New York City, July 31, 1945

Dear Mr. Lewis:

Thank you for your letter of July 18th.

I am glad you liked my book, and I agree with you wholeheartedly concerning the attitude of labor toward imperialism. In the United States, of course, the best organizations of labor have traditionally been a part of the capitalist system and willing to exploit anybody anywhere if they could for a share in the profits. The railway unions are an example of this. As you say, even in the Labor party of England imperialism has been sold to them as part of the glory of their country and they have not understood clearly what exploitation in Africa and Asia means.

Also, it is true in India that the Moslem League backed the great landlords, and even some elements in the National Congress are exploiters of cheap labor, pure and simple.

Perhaps I did not stress this enough in my book but I think you will find it implied.

Very sincerely yours,
W. E. B. Du Bois

The perennial questions about the actual meaning of segregation in the United States and what to do about its existence recur in the following letters. Du Bois's response was to cause later difficulties between him and the board of the NAACP, *as subsequent correspondence in this volume will show (see pp. 99– 102 below).*

Dayton, Ohio, Aug. 6, 1945

Dear Dr. Du Bois:

I send this letter at the request of a group of Dayton citizens who are much perturbed over the school situation in our city. I had hoped to have been able to see you and talk the matter over with you personally while I was in New York in June but was unable to reach you either time I called at the office. Letters are quite inadequate to explain the setup, but I shall endeavor to give you somewhat of a picture of the situation.

As you perhaps know, we have in Dayton one segregated Negro high school, the Paul Laurence Dunbar. Its principal is Mr. Frederic C. MacFarlane, who has been at its head for over ten years. Despite the fact that Negroes are themselves partly to blame for its erection, there are those who now see their error and are anxious to atone for their sin. This is true because they have come to see that the local Board of Education is determined to continue its policy of seg-regating Negro children by a subtle system of zoning. So now, instead of one Negro school, we have three elementary ones—the last one, Wogaman, where an all white faculty has been replaced by an all Negro faculty and where the white children living in this school district have been transferred out into another one leaving most of the school population Negro.

Resentment is high against this incident and Dunbar high school has become the sore spot in the city. Mr. MacFarlane has been under attack for some years, because he has openly approved segregation and supports the Board in its policy. He has a few followers—but very few, as the majority of the Negro citizens have severely condemned him and have asked the Board for his re-moval. The Board so far has refused to do so, because he preaches the gospel of segregation, which fits into their scheme.

Mr. MacFarlane has advocated to white audiences the establishment of a "49th" state to be Federally supported for Negroes. He has indoctrinated the students attending Dunbar with his philosophy of racism and continually quotes you as favoring segregation as the only solution to the race problem in America.

I am enclosing first, a copy of charges made against him by the Citizens' Committee, a copy of his "Farewell to the Graduates" and some newspaper clippings taken from the Daily press, in which he writes under an assumed name of "Charles S. Motley."

We are much disturbed over the influence that he is exerting on the students. They are developing a hatred for whites which reacts against any effort at obtaining a democratic educational system. We are most anxious that you disclaim through the press any approval of segregation, as the solution to the problem of the Negro minority. There are many people who do not read and young minds are easily influenced by Mr. MacFarlane's quotations from your writings as favoring segregation.

We would be much relieved if you could make statements in the Ohio edition of the *Pittsburgh Courier*, Ohio *State News* and in both of our daily papers, the *Herald* and the *News*, to refute this dangerous propaganda.

I know that you are quite busy, but such a statement coming from you would clarify this issue to no mean degree. My friend Mrs. Hathcock has insisted that I reach you about this matter. I also talked with our friend, Father J. N. S. Belboder, shortly before his passing and he too was quite anxious to have you come to Dayton and publicly refute these theories.

Anything you can do we will appreciate as we are determined to put an end to discrimination in the Dayton schools.

> Respectfully yours,
> Marian Smith Williams[1]

New York City, August 31, 1945

Mrs. Marian S. Williams
My dear Madam:

I have your letter of August sixth and have been trying to get time to answer it not simply as a letter but perhaps to write about it in my column in the *Defender*.[1]

I do not believe in jim crow schools. They are undemocratic and discriminatory. At the same time, as I have said from time to time, the majority of Negroes in the United States depend today upon separate schools for their education and despite everything we can do and should do that situation will continue longer than any of us now living survive. We must, therefore, make the best of a bad situation and take every advantage of that situation.

The separate schools provide employment for colored teachers and in many cases as in the schools of Washington, D. C. they are in themselves very excellent schools. Usually, of course, a separate school is a poorer school run with fewer funds with less trained supervision and with a poorly trained staff. Under these circumstances there is no single answer which will apply to all situations.

---

1. In the *Crisis* 53 (February 1946):55, there appears an account of a two-day meeting held in Columbus, Ohio, with representatives of that state's NAACP chapters and Thurgood Marshall, special counsel of the NAACP, to map plans to combat school and housing segregation. This meeting was presided over by Marian Smith Williams, described as president of the Dayton NAACP branch and chairperson of the education committee of the Ohio State Conference.

1. Du Bois devoted two of his *Chicago Defender* columns to this question—6 October and 13 October 1945. For a summary of their contents, see Aptheker, *Annotated Bibliography*, p. 448.

There are cases where the establishment of a separate school would be nothing less than a crime permitted by carelessness. There are other cases when the establishment of a separate school is not only advisable but a bounden duty if colored children are going to get education.

What the exact situation is in Dayton, I, of course, do not know.

Very sincerely yours,
W. E. B. Du Bois

Channing H. Tobias (1882–1961) was born in Augusta, Georgia, and graduated from Paine College in that city in 1902; three years later he earned a bachelor of divinity degree from Drew University. He served as a professor at Paine College until 1911 and then began work with the YMCA which continued until 1946. He participated in the 1921 meeting of the Pan-African Congress. In 1948 he received the Spingarn Medal from the NAACP.

His selection in 1946 as director of the Phelps-Stokes Fund represented the first appointment of a Black person to the leadership of a nationally known foundation. Du Bois wrote to him in this connection.

New York City, November 29, 1945

My dear Dr. Tobias:

I have just heard of your election as Director of the Phelps-Stokes Fund. May I congratulate you heartily. It is a sign of the progress which the American Negro is making to think that Thomas Jesse Jones has been succeeded by Channing H. Tobias.[1] Glory to God in the highest!

Very sincerely yours,
W. E. B. Du Bois

New York City, November 30, 1945

Dear Dr. Du Bois:

No congratulatory expression that I have received means more to me than yours. In the first place, I happen to know that Dr. Stokes wrote you some time ago, asking your opinion of certain persons whose names he submitted to you for comment, and that you spoke very highly of me in your reply. In the

1. Thomas Jesse Jones was a white man from Alabama who specialized in advising various national foundations—especially the Phelps-Stokes Fund, of which he was director for many years—on proper policies to pursue in connection with the so-called Negro Question. He was chief author of a two-volume study, *Education in Africa*, issued by the fund in 1922 and 1925 and scathingly reviewed by Du Bois in the *Crisis* 32 (June 1926): 86–89. Earlier Du Bois had critically reviewed another two-volume study by Jones, *Negro Education*, published in 1917 by the United States Bureau of Education; see the *Crisis* 15 (February 1918):173–78. Du Bois wrote an overall evaluation of Jones that appeared in the *Crisis* 22 (October 1921):252–56.

second place, you are so well acquainted with the Fund and the field that it serves that your expression of confidence has a depth of meaning that would not be true of anyone who did not have this intimate knowledge. Rest assured that I fully appreciate the significance of your reference to the present occupant of the office.

I kept up fairly well with your reports from London, and shall be looking forward to an early opportunity of talking with you about the Pan African Congress and your observations in general while you were in Europe. From what I have read, I am sure that it was worth all the time that was spent in trying to convince some of our friends that the trip was worthwhile.

With every good wish, and again thanking you, I am

Sincerely yours,

Channing H. Tobias

Albert Schweitzer (1875–1965), the world-famous medical missionary, theologian, musicologist, and philosopher, whose honors included the Goethe Memorial Prize (1928) and the Nobel Peace Prize (1952), sent Du Bois a long letter from his hospital in what was then French Equatorial Africa and is now Gabon. The letter was addressed to Du Bois in Atlanta; this address and the mailing time from Africa no doubt explain the delay in Du Bois's reply.

Lambaréné, French Equatorial Africa

December 5, 1945

Dear Professor Du Bois:

I wish to express my appreciation to you for your kindness in responding to the request of Dr. Robach and for your contribution to the book in which he proposed to analyze my thinking and work.[1]

You have made an intensely interesting contribution not only for others but

1. Schweitzer refers to an essay by Du Bois, "The Black Man and Albert Schweitzer," appearing in *The Albert Schweitzer Jubilee Book*, ed. A. A. Roback, (Cambridge, Mass.: Sci-Art Publishers, n.d.), pp. 121–27. The essay gave a succinct account of Schweitzer's career and observed that Black people's attitude toward missionaries "is tinged with bitterness"—for understandable reasons—but that men like Mungo Park and David Livingstone are "revered" among them. But, Du Bois went on, Schweitzer "had no broad grasp of what modern exploitation means ... if he had, he probably would have tried to heal the souls of white Europe rather than the bodies of black Africa." In a later book, also edited by A. A. Roback, Du Bois's essay "Whites in Africa after Negro Autonomy" remarked that it would be well if people like Schweitzer would "train Negroes as assistants and helpers ... who can in time carry on and spread his work and see that it is supported by the new African states and does not continue to be dependent on European charity"; such training, Du Bois thought, would be "fundamental" and not "paternalistic." In *Albert Schweitzer's Realm: A Symposium* (Cambridge, Mass.: Sci-Art Publishers, 1962), pp. 243–55.

particularly for myself, in showing how my treatment of Lambaréné presented itself—judged in the great and historic problem as a whole of the relationship of blacks and whites.

As far as I am concerned, I realized right along that my work should deal
only with one of the questions of the great problem. I purposely limited myself
to this plan because I believe that it is more suitable to my nature (and in
keeping with my talents) to follow a certain pattern than to seek to orient
myself to a whole picture of a vast problem.

Here, on the spot, for many years, I have had the opportunity to study the
problem of the relationship between the whites and blacks in all its details
within a given situation or precise setting. The particular case here is that this
country was the theatre of continuous war between the tribes, and that European occupation put an end to this deplorable situation or state of affairs.

Some old residents told me that this sort of "pax Romana" (the significance
of this expression is that the Europeans conducted themselves like masters) was
felt by all as a great benefit. It was beneficial also for the population here no
longer to be subjugated to the will of the cruel chiefs and to fetichisms exer-
cising a terrible power over the people.

At this place from which I am writing to you, there lived a king of the race
"Galos" who every night caused a woman to be put to death in order to determine the most cruel form of death and thus provide himself with the maximum feeling of satisfaction.

The problem of the blacks working for the whites is exceedingly complex
when seen at close range. It is very difficult for one to form a clear or definite
opinion. Here I know many whites who are very good to the natives and who
have it at heart to be fair with them and who concern themselves with their
well being.

How happy I should be were it possible for us to discuss together all these
problems, to which I would contribute my knowledge of details for a known
or definite location and you the knowledge of the problem as a whole.

At this moment, when in our colony the natives are, more and more, being
liberated from the tutelage of the whites, the problem becomes passionately
absorbing. What will result from this rapid emancipation? What authority will
replace that which increasingly is disappearing? The first result will be that the
populations will again become more dependent upon native chiefs and native
groups who will take the power in their hands. What will be the final result of
this evolution? What will it contribute to the moral development of the natives
and to the development of an organization leading to progress?

It is a chapter of history that we are experiencing here in these large and
small events. And we do not see the orientation which the evolution will take.
We are seized or caught in the train of circumstances. So, I will allow myself
to tell you of the situation just as I see it here. I should like to have a little
more leisure and a keener vision so that I might make for my own use a true

analysis of the evolution of ideas and march of events. But I am entirely taken up by my work at the hospital. My strength and that of my co-workers does not suffice for the task.

Pardon me, I pray you, for not having written to you in English. It is so much easier to write in French.[2]

Thank you again for your great kindness. With my best wishes I am

Sincerely yours,
Albert Schweitzer.

New York City, July 31, 1946

My dear Mr. Schweitzer:

I have here your kind letter of December 5, 1945 and I thank you for your words of appreciation. On the other hand, I presume that you will not mind if I add a word to my thesis: I trust you will not receive without careful examination the legend that it was white Europe which brought peace and leadership to West Africa and that without the influence of the whites, Africa would retrograde into barbarism. You should certainly read, if you have not already, the works of Maurice Delafosse, formerly the governor of the French colonies and professor at the Colonial School and the School of Oriental Languages in France. Monsieur Delafosse published in 1921 *Les Noirs de l'Afrique* and in 1925 *Civilizations negro Africaines.*[1]

These and many other works which I could name prove that civilization in West Africa was not the gift of white folk but on the other hand around the Gulf of Guinea there was an ancient culture dating back a thousand years or more, which was one of the most interesting primitive cultures of the world. It was the American slave-trade carried on by Europeans that degraded and spoiled this civilization.

Later white men rationalized their crime by claiming the highest motives first in their man-stealing, then in their missionary work and finally in their system of colonial government. The fact of the matter is that West Africa, just as the rest of Africa, has been organized for the profit of white Europe and America. Until this basic idea of making money out of the stolen toil and material of black folk ceases to be the leading idea, Africa will never recover from her degradation.

The withdrawal of whites from Africa like any sudden social change would bring difficulties and even momentary disaster, but in the long run it would

2. Du Bois's French was not as good as his German. His earlier French letters were translated by Jessie Fauset; this translation, made by Du Bois's friend Mrs. M. V. Boutté has been slightly revised by the editor.

1. These two books were issued in English in one volume, as *The Negroes of Africa* (Washington, D.C.: Associated Publishers, 1931). The book is noted briefly and favorably by Du Bois in the *Crisis* 38 (September 1931): 304.

restore the dignity and initiative of the black race and give them that independence and self-rule which made Belgium and France and all free countries.

The great difficulty is that most white men do not believe in the humanity
and ability of the black race; they have not seen independent Negro countries
with initiative; they do not believe them possible. I think however, if you
should visit the United States[2] and see the condition of fifteen million descendants of African slaves, you would begin to realize what the possibilities of black
folk are. The American Negroes are not in the position we want to be and
will be, but we have made such progress that no one doubts our ultimate
accomplishment. In one of the greatest, most powerful and most ruthless countries of the earth, we have fought our way forward until today we own property; we share political power; we make art and literature; we sit in Congress
and in the legislatures and on the bench. In other words we are Americans,
not completely but progressively and inevitably.

What we have done, Africa did in earlier ages and can do again if the dead
hand of Europe is taken from her throat. Fetichism and tyranny have ruled in
Africa and will; but no more and not as disastrously as they have ruled in
Europe and Asia. Africa has no monopoly on cruelty, and more Negroes have
died under European rule than ever died under Negro rule.

I hope you will forgive me for this plain speaking but it is my deep belief. I
wish you every success with your work. I am sir,

Very sincerely yours,
W. E. B. Du Bois

*If Du Bois felt it necessary to offer a person like Albert Schweitzer some ele-
mentary references in African history, it is not surprising that a Black woman
in San Francisco would write the following letter late in 1945. Mrs. Williams's
letter is printed verbatim.*

San Francisco, Calif., December 14, 1945

Dear Mr. Du Bois:

Kind sir, I just finished reading your book "Darkwater". I thought it very
true, worded genuinely, wonderfully, and explicit, except the last Chapter
"The Comet". Was this a parable of what would be the relations, were such a
catastrophe to happen. I am sorry and ashamed to be such a bumpkins, but
since I enjoyed it so much, and always read your column in the Defender, I said
it would be better to understand clearly, which I did not. I am a married
woman of twenty-five with eleventh-grade education, but was never taught

---

2. Schweitzer did visit the United States in 1949 in connection with a Goethe Festival held in Aspen, Colorado.

very much Negro history in school. I have a library card and decided to avail myself to some of this literature and naturally thought of you as the first author.

Sincerely yours,
Ruth K. Williams (Mrs.)

p.s. Also I obtained the book "America's Greatest Problem: The Negro", as a balance to my idea of a black man's thoughts to a fair-minded white's and was horrified and shocked. Could you please tell me if all this Mr. R. W. Shyfeldt, M.D. possess truth.[1] To my mind a person would have to possess intense hate not to find one good thing about a person or race. There are pictures here that we evolved from apes. Of course, I've read before we're supposed to be more odorous than any other race. Also are [our] heads are inferiorially shaped long, our brain fogs at maturity, and that Negroes sexual organs are larger and therefore more demandatory and ruthless than Caucasians. There is a comparison on page 103 of a Negro sexually to a bull elk toward a menstrual girl. Do we really have straining periods of "sex madness". I have never been aware of such feelings? Is there truly in Africa near Sierra Leone, a secret black order Human Leopards, who eat and sacrifice barbarically other blacks or what have you?

You are a learned and well read and taught man in all fields; it can't be true that Negroes main ambition, objective, and greatest desire is the violation of white women, beastially. Does "States Rights", mean foremost the right to lynch a person, nominally Negro undisturbed. Are we the main carriers of malaria and tuberculosis, as well as syphillis. All this I read, but I shall not believe it until one of my race of culture says o.k. I wish you'd accept this letter as very personal from me to you, as I am much perturbed. Again I write

Sincerely yours,
Ruth K. Williams

New York City, September 10, 1946

My dear Madam:

Your letter of December 14, 1945 has just come to my attention. I am sorry that it was misplaced so long. With regard to the story of the Comet in *Darkwater*, it is simply a story showing how some unusual catastrophe may change the attitude of persons toward each other. The book by Shufeldt is of no im-

---

1. The reference is to Robert W. Shufeldt, *America's Greatest Problem: The Negro* (Philadelphia: F. A. Davis, 1915). Earlier Shufeldt had published a substantially similar work, *The Negro: A Menace to American Civilization* (Boston: R. E. Badger, 1907). These books were representative of the poison produced during the era well called by Professor Rayford Logan *the nadir*.

portance whatsoever and has long been outdated. You should read Ruth
Benedict on *Race*.[1]

Very sincerely yours,
W. E. B. Du Bois

*In addition to the founding of the United Nations, another matter of central
concern to Du Bois in 1945, both personally and officially, was the development
of the Pan-African movement and, specifically, the holding of the Fifth Pan-
African Congress. Ensuing letters concern this area of Du Bois's work.*

*Of great consequence to the holding of the Fifth Pan-African Congress in
October 1945 was the work of George Padmore.* While Du Bois and Padmore
knew each other before, during the work that led to this congress they became
friends, though significant disagreements marked their relationship. In the
17 March 1945* Chicago Defender—*to which Du Bois was then contributing a
weekly column—Padmore published a call from his London home for a Pan-
African Congress to be held when the fighting in Europe had terminated.*

New York City, March 22, 1945

My dear Mr. Padmore:

I notice in the *Defender* a statement concerning a proposed Pan African
Congress. You know, of course, that I am interested in such a meeting and have
been connected with attempts along this line since 1918. I have written to Mr.
Harold Moody and to the Secretary of the wasu [West African Students'
Union] concerning a congress after this war.

Your statement calls for a definite meeting six months after the war in Paris.
May I bring to your attention the fact that it is by no means certain that six
months after the end of the war in Europe it would be possible to secure passage
for any significant number of colonials.

Secondly, a Pan African Congress ought to be held in Africa. We have held
them in the past in London, Paris, Brussels, Lisbon and New York. We should
meet this time in Africa. This seems to me of the greatest importance.

Thirdly, the meeting should not be set for a definite date as yet. We might
say six months after the close of the European war or six months after the close

---

1. Ruth Benedict, *Race: Science and Politics* (New York: Modern Age Books, 1940).
* George Padmore, the pseudonym of Malcolm Ivan Nurse, was born in Trinidad
in 1902 and died in Ghana in 1959. For some years he was active in the Communist
movement, but he was expelled in 1934. He was deeply anti-Communist thereafter but
tended to retain regard for the Soviet Union, especially during and after World War
II. In his final years he held influential positions in Ghana, particularly as adviser to
Nkrumah on foreign policy. See James R. Hooker, *Black Revolutionary: George Padmore's Path from Communism to Pan-Africanism* (New York: Praeger Publishers,
1967, 1970)—a book marred by a rather condescending tone toward Du Bois.

of the World War. I hardly think we could be more definite than this and be able to carry the matter through.

Finally, you give the text of a manifesto. Could you send me the names of the organizations which are participating in this statement? It is, of course, in the main what we should all agree with but I think we should be careful not to bind colonial peoples in support of a statement which they have not had ample opportunity to consider beforehand. In other words, the definitive statement should come after the congress and not before.

I should be very glad to hear from you at your convenience and to know what organizations are participating and just what has actually been done up to this point. The National Association for the Advancement of Colored People has at present nearly five hundred thousand paid members and it has definitely adopted a Pan African Congress as a part of its program after the war and designated me officially to help in carrying out this project. I would like, therefore, your advice and the names of persons and organizations who have similar ideas.

Very sincerely yours,
W. E. B. Du Bois

As assistant to the director of the Political Action Committee of the CIO, *Henry Lee Moon* was present at the organizing meeting of the World Federation of Trade Unions held in London early in 1945. Upon his return he sent what he called a memorandum to Du Bois.*

New York City, April 9, 1945

TO: Dr. W. E. B. Du Bois

Colored people in Britain express a great deal of interest in proposals for a Pan-African Congress. All of them look to you for leadership in calling and guiding such a Congress. I talked with resident colored persons in London, Manchester, Liverpool and Cardiff, as well as with colonial delegates to the World Trade Union Conference, all of whom indicated that they would like to see such a congress called.

At the meeting held in Manchester on February 24, representatives of the International African Service Bureau, Negro Welfare Association and the

* Henry Lee Moon was born in South Carolina in 1901; he was educated at Howard University and Ohio State University and took postgraduate work at the Brookwood Labor College and at American University in Washington. He worked on several newspapers and then served as an adviser for the United States Housing Authority from 1938 to 1944. From 1944 to 1948 he held the above-mentioned position with the CIO; thereafter he served as director of public relations for the NAACP and in 1966 became editor of the *Crisis* as well. He retired from these positions in June 1974. He is the author of *Balance of Power: The Negro Vote* (1948) and the editor of *The Emerging Thought of W. E. B. Du Bois* (1972), a collection of essays and editorials from the *Crisis*.

Negro Association of Manchester joined with labor delegates in formulating a proposal to have the conference called in September at Paris immediately following the World Labor Congress scheduled for that time. The labor delegates expected to return for this Congress and felt that they could represent their organizations both at the Labor meeting and at the Pan-African Congress. It was therefore proposed that in each country Negro leadership should set up a national committee to obtain the broadest possible representation at the Congress. It was urged that invitations to participate in the Congress should be sent to labor organizations, churches, civic and political groups and such other organizations as were interested in the progress and development of colored people.

A provisional committee was set up to coordinate activities leading to a Pan-African Congress. This committee was composed of James Taylor, from the Gold Coast; Jomo Kenyatta, from Kenya; Dr. Peter McD. Milliard, from British Guiana; Ato Makonnen of Ethiopia and I. A. T. Wallace [Johnson] of Sierra Leone. All of these save Wallace Johnson are resident in Manchester. George Padmore is acting as secretary to this committee.

In London I also talked with Dr. Harold A. Moody. Dr. Moody believes that such a congress should be held, but doubts the wisdom of relating it in any way to the labor movement. The problem, he maintains, is humanitarian and not political or economic. Accordingly he believes that there should be no correlation between the Pan-African Congress and any other organization or movement.

In Cardiff I talked with representatives of the United Committee of Colored and Colonial People's Organization. This group is primarily a working class group composed of African and West Indian seamen and factory workers. The members of this committee likewise expressed an interest in the convening of a Pan-African Congress. The chairman of this committee is A. E. Mossell.

Following are the names and addresses of some of the persons with whom I talked and who expressed interest in the Congress:

George Padmore, Press Room, Ministry of Information, London

Dr. Harold A. Moody, President, League of Colored Peoples, 164 Queens Rd., S. E. 15, Peckham, London

James Taylor, President, Negro Welfare Association, 26 Ducie St., Con M. Manchester.

Jomo Kenyatta, General Secty. Kukua African Association

Ato T. R. Makonnen, Int'l. African Service Bureau, Cosmopolitan Restaurant, Manchester

Dr. Peter McD. Milliard, President, Negro Association of Manchester, 76 Gt. Clowes St., Lower Broughton, Manchester.

Hussein Sheir, 10 Sophia St., Cardiff

I. A. T. Wallace Johnson, All-Seamen's Union, Freetown, Sierre Leone, Africa

Kenneth Hill, Vice President Jamaica Trade Union Council, 7 Eastwood Avenue, Halfway Tree, Kingston, Jamaica
   Hubert H. Critchlow, British Guiana Trade Union Council
   Learie Constantine, Colonial Welfare Officers, British Ministry of Labor, Liverpool
   Dr. C. B. Clarke, 112 Newington Causeway, S. E. 1, London
   A. E. Mossell, Chairman, United Committee of Colored and Colonial People's Organizations, 9 Loudoun Sq., Cardiff
   A. Shepherd, Colonial Defense Association, Cardiff, 8A Maria St., Cardiff
   Others with whom I talked, who may be interested in the Congress, include K. A. Korsah, of the Gold Coast, who may be reached at the Colonial Office in Downing Street, where he is temporarily working with the cocoa control plan, and Dr. Arthur Lewis of Jamaica, who is now a lecturer at the London School of Economics, located during the war at Peter House College, Cambridge University, Cambridge, England.

[Henry Lee Moon]

*The memorandum from Moon no doubt was one of the sources for a letter Du Bois sent to Jean de la Roche, chief of the French Press and Information Service in New York City.**

New York City, April 11, 1945

My dear Mr. de la Roche:
   I want in confidence to take up a matter with you in which I am deeply interested. Mr. [Wilfred] Benson of the International Labor Office called on me the other day and told me that they would have a meeting in Paris in September at the invitation of the French Government. Also I learned from London that a conference of the new world labor movement will take place in Paris in September.
   I am anxious to have a meeting of the Pan African Congress in Paris that same month. You perhaps have heard of the Pan African Congress. The first congress was convened in Paris directly after the armistice following the first World War early in 1919. The French Government was officially represented. Blaise Diagne and M. Candace presided at various meetings and we met by special permission of Premier Clemenceau. In 1921, a second session of the Pan African Congress was held. It was larger and more representative; we had sessions in London, Paris and Brussels. Some two hundred delegates attended

---

  * In addition to his government position, de la Roche published books and papers on French colonial questions, including *Indo-China and French Colonial Policy*, submitted to the Ninth Conference of the Institute of Pacific Relations, January 1945, and the study *Le Gouverneur Général Félix Eboué*, 1884-1944 (Paris, 1957).

representing the majority of the Negro groups in Africa and in America. Later a third congress was held in London and Lisbon in 1923 and a small one in New York in 1925. Then the depression precluded further meetings.

It seems now that after the conclusion of the second World War that it is time for a Fifth Pan African Congress to be held. It would be attended by delegates from the various colonies in Africa and the various countries and colonies in America; its object would be to consider the present situation and the future of the Negro race and its descendents. My idea is that following the liberal program of M. de Gaulle and the late Governor Eboué, France would represent the most encouraging prospect of a solution for the problem of colonies and the development of black folk in the modern world.

It would be, therefore, of tremendous encouragement if we could receive from the French Government an intimation that such a meeting would be welcome in Paris in September or even something further in the guise of an official invitation to the National Association for the Advancement of Colored People to call such a conference there and then.

Will you think this matter over and let me confer with you concerning it?[1]

Very sincerely yours,
W. E. B. Du Bois

On the same day he wrote to de la Roche Du Bois wrote to Padmore and to Dr. Harold A. Moody, the president of the League of Coloured Peoples, concerning the proposed Pan-African Congress.

New York City, April 11, 1945
My dear Mr. Padmore:

I am writing you hurriedly again before you have had a chance to read my last letter. Since writing you I have had direct communication with the meeting of colored labor leaders at Manchester and I think I understand their wishes and point of view, with which I am in complete sympathy. I have, therefore, approached the Board of Directors of the National Association for the Advancement of Colored People with the proposal that this organization call a Pan African Congress in Paris. Also I have changed my mind as to the time.

The head of the International Labor Office in Montreal has called on me and tells me that they are going to meet in Paris in September and the world labor conference will take place at that time. If, therefore, it is possible for them to meet at that time and place, it ought to be possible for us.

1. Later correspondence shows that the French government did approve the holding of the proposed congress in Paris in September; meanwhile, however, as subsequent letters will show, it was decided to hold the meeting in England rather than France and to assemble in October rather than September.

The National Association for the Advancement of Colored People will assume a considerable part of the expense of the meeting; the exact amount will be determined in the next few days by a committee appointed yesterday.

I shall be glad to hear from you on this subject at your convenience.

Very sincerely yours,

W. E. B. Du Bois

New York City, April 11, 1945

My dear Mr. Moody:

I am rushing another letter to you despite the fact that you have hardly had time to answer my last letter. Since writing I have been in receipt of direct communication from the colored labor leaders who met in Manchester in February. I have also talked with the executive head of the International Labor Office with headquarters in Montreal.

I took up yesterday with the Board of Directors of the National Association for the Advancement of Colored People the matter of the Pan African Congress. From all these sources I am persuaded that we ought to call a Pan African Congress in Paris in September. The world labor organization is going to meet there in September and the International Labor Office. The Pan African Congress should, of course, have no organic connection with these organizations but if we met at or near the same time we would have a chance to have direct representation from Africa and the Caribbean which would be impossible under other circumstances.

Moreover, I think you will be convinced on reflection that the intellectual leaders of the Negro throughout the world must in the future make close alliance and work in cooperation with the leaders of labor. If Europe has consented more and more to cooperate with organized labor, Africa cannot neglect this necessary extension of democracy. Our problems of race are not simply philanthropic; they are primarily economic and political: the problem of earning a living among the poorest people in the world, the problem of education, of health and of political autonomy, either within or without the empires. Here in the United States we have achieved cooperation between the intelligentsia and labor. For a long time the university men fought against this and the labor leaders, on the other hand, distrusted higher education. We see now that only in union can progress be made.

I trust, therefore, your organization, the League of Coloured Peoples, and the London Missionary Society will be willing to join with the National Association for the Advancement of Colored People in a call for a Fifth Pan African Congress to be held in Paris in September.

The National Association for the Advancement of Colored People is prepared to assume a considerable proportion of the expense and a committee on that subject will come to definite conclusions within a few days.

Another reason which compels me to hurry and make definite the call for this meeting is the threat of Jan Smuts to call a Pan African Congress which virtually would be confined to the whites of South Africa, Tanganyika and Kenya.[1] I want to forestall any use of this name in a movement which would disfranchise the great mass of Africans and their descendents.

Will you let me hear from you at your earliest convenience and give me frankly your reaction to points made in this letter?

Very sincerely yours,
W. E. B. Du Bois

Padmore's response was prompt and substantial.

London, England, April 12, 1945

Dear Dr. Du Bois:

I have just received your letter of the 22nd of March and am availing myself of the good offices of a friend who is returning to the States to send you this reply.

I am delighted to hear that progress is being made in connection with the Pan African Conference at your end. But first a few words of clarification. Putting on one side the use of terms (Pan African was only employed because it epitomises the conception behind the idea endorsed by Colonial Organizations in this country), there is no attempt to monopolise or by-pass the work of others engaged on a similar undertaking. We are well acquainted with the historical origin of the Pan-African Movement, especially me, as I am a nephew of the late Sylvester-Williams, a West Indian barrister who initiated the project with which you, Bishop Walters and others have been associated.[1]

During the visit in this country of Mr. Walter White, we explored the possibility of reviving the idea of convening such a conference at the most con-

1. Jan Christiaan Smuts (1870–1950) was prime minister of South Africa; the contemporary press seems not to have mentioned any such threat from him.

1. The reference is to Henry Sylvester-Williams, main convener of the first Pan-African Conference, held in London in 1900. Bishop Alexander Walters of the African Methodist Zion Church presided; Du Bois was secretary and wrote the "Appeal to the World." Owen Charles Mathurin's *Henry Sylvester Williams and the Origins of the Pan-African Movement, 1869–1911* (1976) is the first really full-length biography of Williams, a Black teacher from Trinidad who immigrated to the United States and Canada and studied law in England in the late 1890s. James R. Hooker, Padmore's biographer (see above, p. 56, n. 1), published *Henry Sylvester Williams: Imperial Pan-Africanist* (London: Rex Collings) in 1975.

Padmore states that he was the nephew of Sylvester-Williams; Du Bois repeated this statement later and Hooker wrote concerning Du Bois's remark: "To my knowledge Padmore was not related to the lawyer, though it would have been satisfying to detect a kinship. Perhaps the elderly Du Bois saw himself as the link between these men and their conference, a pardonable fancy." Hooker's error may be pardonable, but his condescension toward the "elderly" Du Bois verges on the unpardonable.

venient time. Towards this end I was able to arrange a gathering with the West African Students Union, at which Mr. White told them about the activities of the NAACP and other groups in America in connection with the whole question of race and world politics. I was therefore delighted to hear that you had returned to the NAACP to take charge of their Special Research Department.

Now the Manifesto issued out of certain concrete proposals which were put forward on the occasion of the visit of the Colonial delegates to the World Trade Union Conference in London.[2] A number of Colonial organizations in Manchester organized a coordinating committee for the purpose of entertaining these overseas delegates; and they secured the endorsement of the mass organizations which these Colonial delegates represented to the coordinating committee constituting itself as a sort of convening body to issue a call to the Colonial peoples and other Coloured communities for a world conference. The question of the proposed date arose in relation to the fact that in September next a large group of Colonial representatives is expected to arrive in Europe in connection with the formal launching of the new Trade Union International. It was therefore thought that if we could avail ourselves of their presence, the Pan African Conference could be held, or, if it was considered inopportune, that at least a preliminary conference could take place, to set a date for a world conference, when the convenience of travel and other factors permitted. Everything was tentative; there were no definite commitments. Now that I have had the good fortune of establishing direct contact with you, I shall assume the responsibility of placing your letter before the coordinating committee. I know that they will endorse your suggestions. As soon as we have been able to meet together and discuss things, you will receive an official communication.

With regard to the text of the Manifesto which appeared in the *Defender*, this was prepared by one of our colleagues, Mr. Desmond Buckle of the Gold Coast, then discussed, amended and endorsed by the organizations constitut-

2. This manifesto was the one quoted at length in Padmore's article in the *Chicago Defender*, 17 March 1945. The printed manifesto, enclosed by Padmore in his letter, is a four-page leaflet headed "Manifesto on Africa in the Post-War World for Presentation to the United Nations Conference, San Francisco, April 1945." It was "promulgated and supported" by the League of Coloured Peoples, in cooperation with the West African Students' Union (London), the International African Service Bureau (London), the Negro Association (Manchester), the Negro Welfare Center (Liverpool and Manchester), and the Coloured Men's Institute (East London); it was "endorsed" by the following colonial trade-union leaders "on behalf of their unions": J. S. Annan, Gold Coast Trade Unions; T. A. Bankole, president, Nigerian Trade Union Conference; H. N. Critchlow, British Guiana Trade Unions; J. A. Garba-Jahumpa, secretary, Gambia Trade Union Conference. The manifesto proposed measures looking toward the termination of colonialism in Africa and urged that this goal be accepted by the United Nations as a necessary part of the commitment to a peaceful future world.

ing the coordinating committee, as well as the League of Coloured People, which had been invited to participate in promulgating the Manifesto. I note that you are in direct touch with Dr. Moody and WASU. I am not sure of the attitude of the League in regard to cooperating with the existing coordinating committee of the proposed conference, but I can guarantee the support of the other groups. I mention this because our major criticism of the League is their single-handed attitude, but I think that pressure of public opinion may force them into line. This, however, will present no great difficulty in our trans-Atlantic collaboration.

There is one other observation I would like to make, and that is about the venue. We agree in principle that Africa is the best place to hold a Coloured Conference, but whether or not the Colonial Governments would allow us the possibility of calling a meeting of Negro peoples in their territories is a matter open to debate. I am very certain that if we could hold our conference in Sierra Leone or Nigeria, for instance, we should have the masses of the people behind us, and there is not the least shadow of our doubt about the success of such a Conference, and we shall certainly explore the possibilities. But failing this, it seems to me that, considering the closer ties which the war has brought between Liberia and the United States, and since America is not a Colonial Power in Africa, it might be possible for the NAACP and other participating organizations to secure facilities for us to meet in Monrovia. And that again is a matter we shall have to investigate.

The organizations which participated in the promulgation of the manifesto are:

International African Service Bureau, 58 Oxford Road, Manchester
Negro Association, c/o Dr. Milliard, 191 Slade Lane Levenshulme, Manchester
Negro Welfare Association, Mr. J. Cowan, Secretary, c/o 66 Oxford Road, Manchester

If we want to make this thing a success, the concrete procedure would be for your group in America to recognize the principle of democratic decentralization. Since you have greater facilities at your disposal, you should set up in New York a Committee which will take care of organizing the American delegation as well as the West Indian one. As to the West Indies, we can send you all the contacts we have with the mass organizations, and this would make things easier than from here. We can give you all the data, and you should prepare the necessary draft resolutions, which should cover:

a) a general resolution
b) specific resolutions relating to specific areas such as the Caribbean, Latin America.

We will try to broaden the existing Coordinating Committee by co-opting all other organizations which are now outside of it, and to transform it into the Pan African Convening Committee in Great Britain. Our task will be to contact all organizations in Africa, which I think we should consider our sphere, and to circularize them direct with the draft documents, which you will be preparing, to get their amendments and observations. When this preparatory work has been done, the two Co-ordinating Committees in London and New York will decide upon the best time and place to have this conference, and will inform their respective contacts—you in the New World and we in Africa—as to the concrete steps to be taken for us all to get together.

I am enclosing a copy of the Manifesto which, although printed upon the League of Coloured People's letterhead, is a collective document, not of any one organization, but of all the participating groups. I only mention this, because if we are going to make the thing a success, we must not have a false impression. We hope to have a meeting of the delegates of the participating organization, and the general feeling is that Dr. Moody, who took it upon himself arbitrarily to do this sort of thing, will be slated. I shall do my best to prevent the splitting of this cooperation, because in the light of your letter, we now have a wider conception in relation to the conference, and this can only be made possible from our end by team-work. But there is unfortunately too much egotism, and this hampers cooperation.

You see, there are no mass organisations in Britain, because we have no mass communities, but we all have, in varying degrees, contact and influence with the mass organisations in the British Colonies, and unless we pool our forces we do not get anywhere. I want to emphasize this, because you may have the impression that any one of the groups represents large followings. And the League has an outlook which concerns itself chiefly with the student community here, and therefore has a floating membership, while the other organizations are primarily concerned with the workers and peasants, who must be the driving force behind any movement which we middle class intellectuals may establish. Today, the African masses, the common people, are awake and are not blindly looking to doctors and lawyers to tell them what to do. This was particularly sharply reflected in the composition of the trade union delegates which came here. They came from the masses and have their roots deep in the masses.

I have written at some length as I wanted to make the position as clear as possible, and I look forward with very great interest to your subsequent observations.

Assuring you of my sincere desire to cooperate in every way, and of my complete interest in the work which you are doing.

Very sincerely yours,
George Padmore

At about the same time, Du Bois received an undated reply to his letter of April 11 from Moody in London.

London, England [undated]

My dear Dr. Du Bois,

I have now received your further letter dated April 11 with reference to the calling of a Pan African Congress. I note that you have further considered the matter with your Board of Directors and have decided to call one in Paris in September next. From all that I can gather, on this side, I do think that it will be quite impossible to run a representative Conference in Paris then. Transport will not be much easier than it is at the present moment and conditions in Paris are not likely to be such as will enable the City to cater to two large Conferences at the same time, and except the British and French Governments considered that such a Conference as ours could be held at the same time as the T.U.C. Conference, I feel certain that they would not make matters easier for us.

Why not adhere to your original idea and plan for a big Conference in Africa as soon as world conditions make this a possibility and regard a Conference in Paris in September next as something in the shape of a preliminary exploratory meeting to plan and prepare for the larger affair, to set afloat investigations which will render the later conference a much more effective gathering? Why not let it be "Dumbarton Oaks" in preparation for our "San Francisco"? Please think about this. I am in full agreement with all you say about working with Labour Groups, but I do not want us to tie ourselves to any one group either politically or in any other way. We have to stand on our own legs, decide our own future and carve out a policy for our people, which will command the attention of the world because of its sanity, reasonableness and practicability; and I would suggest to you that we will not be able to do this as early as September. We want to see what the United Nations are purposing to do in relation to us. They have our Manifesto, which you have seen by this [time]. What are they going to do about it? We want to know what will be the reaction of our people the world over to the results of San Francisco. We want to stir them up to realise that now is our time when we must make the world feel that we are no longer asleep, but that we mean to think together, work together and act together for the benefit of all our people. Our people are still far away for this goal. In Paris in September next we could work up steam towards this great objective and the place for staging this is surely Africa.

I hope you will agree with me in these conclusions. Let me say, finally, that the London Missionary is constitutionally unable to associate themselves with us in the calling of this Conference, which should, in my opinion, be called entirely by our own people. Other American and European groups may and I hope will associate themselves with us in the shape of sending delegates to the Conference, but the responsibility of giving shape to the Conference must rest with our own groups. I hope you and your Committee will agree with me in this decision.

With respect to preventing Smuts using the term Pan-African, we could forestall him by associating the name with the Conference in Paris and making clear that it is wholly a preliminary Conference in preparation for the larger meeting to be held at a suitable time in Africa.

There are many other reasons which make me feel that this is the correct thing to do, but I cannot now stay to relate them herein.

With my very best wishes,

Yours very sincerely,
Harold A. Moody

New York City, July 9, 1945

My dear Mr. Padmore:

You will pardon my delay in answering your kind letter of April 12th. The following week I was called out of town to serve as Consultant to the American Delegation at the San Francisco Conference. I stayed for five weeks and then had a number of lecture engagements. Indeed, I have just gotten back permanently to my desk.

We are still working on the Pan-African Congress. We have received notice that the Colonial Minister of France will be willing and pleased to have such a Congress meet in Paris. But on the other hand, there are going to be difficulties about transportation from the United States, more especially as to the return trip because of the great number of soldiers who will be returning during the rest of the year. Whether or not we can get visas from the State Department I am not yet sure, but am working on the matter. I expect to be able to write you very soon again.

If we cannot arrange to have the proposed meeting in September we shall try again for the spring. Of course, the great advantage of meeting in September will be, as you emphasize, the presence of the colonial delegates to the World Trade Union Conference.

I am not quite sure as to how far we should go in drafting resolutions before the conference. There are already a number of such resolutions in existence, and these should become a part of the matter which we will study but I think we should go slowly as to further resolutions until the Congress actually meets.

I do not like the idea of dividing up the calling of the Congress into the hands of a number of convening committees. I think that would be cumbersome and quite unnecessary at present. We have certain direct contacts with Africa and would want to feel free to extend invitations. You and your committees undoubtedly have various contacts with America, especially with the West Indies. My experience teaches me it is a good deal better in a meeting of this sort to have as little preliminary machinery as possible and let the meeting find itself and organize its own machinery after the convocation. Eventually,

of course, we want to have the Pan-African Congress a meeting of duly ac-
credited delegates from groups, organizations and states; but this plan will develop slowly and will call for a great deal of care and thought.

The Congress which we propose calling in September will have to be exploratory and tentative, a matter of getting acquainted and comparing ideas. I think
we should be very catholic and cooperative and avoid trying to push people
too far or to get any particular set of ideas adopted too quickly. It would be
very easy in a case like this for us to get split up before we began. Mr. Moody
and his organization is conservative, especially when it comes to trade unions
and communism. I imagine the wasu has the same kind of tendencies. American
Negroes on the other hand are much more radical and broadminded than they
were a generation ago and wish to go far in cooperating with the labor movement. All of this requires time and care to bring out the best unity and the
widest results. I shall write further on this matter and on the exact steps.

With regard to the historical origin of the Pan-African movement, the late
Sylvester-Williams initiated the Pan-African "Conference" in 1900. The matter
then lapsed for 19 years until I, with the assistance of the NAACP, called a Pan-
African "Congress" (note the change in name) in Paris that year. The second
Pan-African Congress was held in 1921, the third in 1923, the fourth in 1927.
This, then would be the fifth in the series. Your uncle should have the credit of
initiating the idea and the name, although I think it would be a good plan to
keep now to the series of "Congresses."

As I have said I shall write you very soon as our plans develop here.

Very sincerely yours,
W. E. B. Du Bois

*At Du Bois's suggestion, the NAACP established a committee on the Pan-African
Congress, consisting of Du Bois; Walter White (as secretary); Professor
Rayford W. Logan, then at Howard University; Dr. Ralph J. Bunche, then
with the Bureau of Dependent Peoples of the United States Department of
State; Judge William H. Hastie of Washington; the writer Russell W. Daven-
port; Elmer A. Carter, then a member of the New York State Commission
against Discrimination; Channing H. Tobias; Arthur B. Spingarn; and the
surgeon Dr. Louis T. Wright.*

July 10, 1945
Memorandum to Committee on Pan-African Congress
From: Dr. Du Bois

1. It is proposed that the NAACP should call a Pan-African Congress but the
Congress, when it convenes, will be an independent body and adopt such program and take such action as seems best. The NAACP, as the organization originally sponsoring this series of Congresses, would offer to meet certain of the

expenses of the Congress: for example, to pay for an office in Paris during the session of the Congress and to pay for a place of meeting. Also, to contribute toward secretarial expenses and the expense of translation. It might also offer to meet the expense of printing the final report and to assist with publicity. All funds contributed by the NAACP would be under the control of the delegates which it sends.

2. It would be probable that the Congress itself would supplement its expense funds from contributions from other organizations. This might help in the secretarial and translating expenses. Organizations in the United States, West Indies, and other countries might contribute to such expenses. Such contributions would be entirely under the control of the Congress when organized.

3. It would be of the greatest advantage if the NAACP should designate and offer to pay, at least in part, a trained student of French and English who could do the translation. Dr. Rayford Logan did this in 1921 and 1923. If he should be present in Paris, at his own expense, we might offer to pay him something for services as translator.

4. The program of the conference is, of course, a matter for the conference to decide. However, it would be quite in order for the NAACP to suggest as a tentative program something like the following (I think that persons could be secured to speak on all of these subjects):

a. Colonial Conditions

1. British Africa
   (a) Union of South Africa
   (b) Kenya
   (c) Nigeria
   (d) Gold Coast
   (e) Tanganyika
   (f) Sierra Leone and Gambia
   (g) Uganda
   (h) British Somaliland
3. Belgian Congo

2. French Africa
   (a) French West Africa
   (b) French Equatorial Africa
   (c) Morocco
   (d) Algeria
   (e) Tunis
   (f) Madagascar

4. Portuguese Africa
   (a) Angola
   (b) Mozambique

5. Spanish Africa
6. Italian Africa
   (a) Libya
   (b) Somaliland
   (c) Eritrea

7. Autonomous or Semi-Autonomous States
   (a) Liberia
   (b) Ethiopia
   (c) Egypt
   (d) Anglo-Egyptian Sudan

8. Descendants of Africans overseas
   (a) United States of America
   (b) Caribbean Area

5. From the above territories there should be collected:
a. Recent published statements concerning conditions
b. Recent demands of organized bodies
c. Oral statements and communications
6. Colonial Powers
Great Britain, France, Belgium, Italy, Spain and Portugal should be invited
to send representatives, or to present written statements of colonial policies and
conditions. The charter of the United Nations should be examined as to its
provisions for, and effect upon, colonies. Statements concerning colonies and
colonial policies should be made by
a. Representatives of organized labor
b. Representatives of the ILO
c. Churches and missionary bodies
d. Scientific bodies
7. Special efforts should be made to get statements on the following matters:
a. Education
b. Work and Wages
c. Health and Housing
d. The family
e. Tribes and Clans
f. Government
8. Visitors from organizations, states and other colonies would be welcome.
9. A survey of all these conditions should be projected for report in 1947 at a
6th Pan African Congress. Such a report should make careful estimate of the
Hailey survey on Africa and the various accompanying reports.[1] Effort should
be made to secure a more accurate set of maps of Africa in accordance with
present conditions.
10. Five sessions covering three days might be proposed:
First Day—Morning and Night (Afternoon for Committees)
Second Day—Morning and Night (Afternoon for Committees)
Third Day—Morning for Resolutions and Adjournment
11. Finally, a permanent organization should be formed with membership
based on delegates from participating states and groups with votes according to
populations and interests involved.
The expenses of this Congress to the NAACP may be estimated as follows:

Two delegates—Passage and Return	$1,000
Living Expenses	1,000
Expenses of Congress:	
Promotion to Sept. 15	100

1. The reference is to William M. Hailey, *An African Survey: A Study of Problems Arising in Africa South of the Sahara* (London: Oxford University Press, 1938).
In 1957 the same publisher issued a version of this work revised as of 1956.

Office and Hall	200
Clerical Expense and	
Translation	350
Publication of Report	350
	$3,000

*Among the groups and individuals with which Du Bois corresponded in April
1945 in reference to plans for a Pan-African Congress was the West African
Students' Union, wasu. Founded in London in 1924, wasu by this time had a
membership of several hundred in England and in Africa; the group ran a
hostel, published a journal, and served as an important center for the dissemi-
nation of information about West Africa and for the building of national pride
and awareness of African peoples.*

*A reply from wasu finally reached Du Bois some four months after he had
written to its general secretary.*

The West African Students' Union
London, England, July 24, 1945

Re: Pan-African Congress
My dear Dr. Du Bois:

I am directed to acknowledge the receipt of your letters dated the 3rd and
the 11th of April, 1945, respectively, and to inform you that the Executive
Committee of the West African Students' Union have given careful consideration to the several points which you raised.

2. We have been unable to forward our observations to you at an earlier
date, since the proposition you have made regarding a Pan-African Congress
is an important matter and demands the most serious comprehensive deliberation that we can give to any question affecting the future of Africa and the
welfare of peoples of African descent throughout the world. The views we
express represent the approach of West African students here in Great Britain
and Ireland to the proposition that you have put before us. We have no doubt
that your good friend, Mr. Lapido Solanke, our Secretary-General and War-
den, who is out at present on a short mission to West Africa on behalf of our
Union, shares our views. However, in an important matter like this, we consider that full consultation with responsible political leaders and organizations,
as well as with the intelligentsia, in the respective African States is essential if
the proper objectives of the proposed Congress are to be achieved. We believe
that the suggestion will be welcomed by all sections of progressive and enlightened opinion in our common Mother-Continent and have no doubt that your
Association is already in direct touch with African opinion at home. Therefore,
in the circumstance, since as students we have no pretensions to such African
representation as we consider necessary in this important matter of far-reaching

consequences, at present we can only say that our Union would be willing to participate in the Congress when once we have been able to ascertain the views of responsible men of affairs in Africa on this useful proposition.

3. The idea of a Congress of African nationals and all peoples of African descent throughout the world is both useful and timely. Perhaps it is even long over due. But we observe that four of such Pan-African Congresses had been held in the past, all within recent memory, and that the one at present under discussion will be the fifth. It is unfortunate that all these important conferences should have been held outside of Africa but in European capitals. This point is significant and should deserve our careful attention.

4. We notice also that you would want our Pan-African Congress to be held in ample time to forestall the Pan-African Conference which General Smuts is planning to convene in the near future. As you indicated, he will certainly invite the small but influential European minorities in East Africa to represent the governments of their respective States. The Africans will be left in the pan as usual. The aim of the Smuts Conference will be to achieve a greater measure of political solidarity and a more effective cooperation in other spheres between the States concerned. This appears to us to be an important reason why it is all the more necessary that this time our fifth Congress should not be held in Europe, as you have already suggested. Perhaps one of the countries in Africa would be the best place where we should meet. Our Executive Committee are certainly not in favour of this or any future Pan-African Congress being held anywhere in Europe. We do rather suggest the Republic of Liberia as perhaps an ideal choice. All considerations seem to make that country the most favourable place for our Fifth Pan-African Congress. And, especially, at a time like this when Liberia is planning to celebrate the centenary of the founding of the Republic two years hence, the holding of our Congress there seems most desirable. We have good reason to believe that the Government of Liberia would welcome this idea and would give us the encouragement and diplomatic assistance that might be necessary to ensure success. Moreover, it will be possible to have a wider and more effective representation of different sections of progressive African opinion when the Congress is held in Liberia than would be possible in France or anywhere else in Europe. It is also likely that we might not succeed in frustrating the ends of General Smuts' proposed African Conference if we held our Congress in Europe.

5. It appears from our suggestion that there is urgent need for reconsidering the principles on which any future Pan-African Congresses are to be held. We favour the view that, in the present as well as in the future, independent States in Africa and in the Caribbean area be approached with a view to asking the governments of these States to lend a larger measure of support as conveners. Representatives of African States and territories in the West Indies that have not yet attained their national independence and international recognition, as well as representatives of the major national organizations of our

Negro brethren in the United States and Canada, will be invited by the "League of Independent Black Nations" to share in the burden of planning and to participate fully and actively in the deliberations of the Conference, with due regard to their present status in international affairs. The application of this principle would mean that the governments of the Republic of Liberia, the Republic of Haiti, and the Kingdom of Ethiopia will have to be called upon to assist in the present instance.

6. This, in our opinion, seems to be the most realistic approach to the matter under discussion that we are able to suggest. The problems of black peoples throughout the world are in the main a question of politics. And our experience in the four previous Pan-African Congresses, guided by the trend of current international affairs, leads us to believe that closer collaboration with the independent black Nations, as well as with the representatives of the countries and peoples not yet free, is necessary in all our long-distance planning in the future.

7. It is clear from our observations that our Executive Committee would favour postponement of the proposed date of the Congress from September this year to a date nearer to the national centenary celebrations in Liberia in 1947, assuming that the Congress would meet in that country instead of France. We could well imagine the great amount of ground work and other diplomatic arrangement that our proposals would entail. But we have no doubt that your Association is placed in an advantageous position to undertake the task.

8. Besides information and particulars that you may have already on your files, we have pleasure in forwarding the addresses of the following political, labour, and other national progressive organizations in West Africa which might be interested in a Pan-Africa Congress along the lines you have proposed:

I. *Nigeria:*

The Secretary-General,
The Nigerian Youth Movement,
Lagos, Nigeria, West Africa.

The Secretary-General,
The Trade Union Congress
of Nigeria,
Lagos, Nigeria, West Africa.

Mr. Nnamdi Azikiwe,
Secretary-General,
The National Council of Nigeria,
Lagos, Nigeria, West Africa.

His Highness,
The Alake of Abeokuta,
Abeokuta, Nigeria, West Africa.

The Secretary-General
The Nigerian Teachers' Union
Lagos, Nigeria, West Africa.

II. *Gold Coast:*

Dr. J. B. Danquah,
Secretary-General,
The Gold Coast Youth Conference,
Accra, Gold Coast, West Africa.

The Secretary,
The Joint Provincial Council
of Chiefs
Dodowa, Gold Coast, West Africa.

Mr. Joseph Annan,
Secretary-General,
Trades Union Congress,
Sekondi, Gold Coast, W. Africa

The Secretary,
Ashanti Confederacy Council,
Kumasi, Ashanti, Gold Coast,
West Africa.

The Secretary-General,
Gold Coast Teacher's Union
Accra, Gold Coast, W. Africa.

III. *Sierra Leone:*

Mr. Wallace Johnson,
Secretary-General,
Sierra Leone Youth League,
Freetown, Sierra Leone, W.A.

The Secretary-General,
Trades Union Congress,
Freetown, Sierra Leone, W.A.

IV. *Gambia*

The Secretary-General, Trades Union Congress, Bathurst, Gambia.

9. We should be pleased to hear from you again on this matter and our Union would do their best to cooperate with your Association in any measure for which we are capable.

I am

Very truly yours,
[Signature illegible]
Acting Secretary-General

New York City, September 14, 1945

The Acting Secretary General
West African Students Union
Gentlemen:

I have your kind letter of July 24, 1945. In reply, I beg to say that the National Association for the Advancement of Colored People has asked me to attend the projected Pan African Congress which is called to meet October 15th to 21st in London.

The Association, however, definitely agrees with you in regarding this meeting as preliminary to a real Pan African Congress of delegates to take place in 1946 or 1947 and my credentials authorize my affiliation with the movement only on condition that such a Congress is called and arranged for. In that case, this organization will be glad to be affiliated and prepared to give some financial support.

You probably know that the National Association for the Advancement of Colored People has some 400,000 paid members and is the largest organization of its kind working among the 13 or 14 million Americans of Negro descent. We have been a little hesitant in cooperating with the present movement, because, as you know, the committee has gone ahead without very much consultation with us and consequently, we do not feel that we are among the sponsoring bodies. At the same time, difficulties of time and space were great and we realize that it was not possible to have as much consultation and arrangement as would have been desirable. The main object is, of course, to unite persons of African descent for the freedom and autonomy of the Peoples of Africa and if this meeting proves to be a step in that direction, we are only too eager to take part.

I may find some difficulties in getting transportation to England and in getting a British visa. I am writing Mr. [Arthur] Creech-Jones and Mr. [Harold J.] Laski with both of whom I am acquainted to ask their good office.[1] Anything that your organization can do to help will be appreciated. Also, I shall want good hotel accommodations, comfortable even if costly. I shall be glad to have your recommendation.

Very sincerely yours,
W. E. B. Du Bois

Late in July 1945 Du Bois concluded that it would probably not be possible for him to be present at a September meeting of a Pan-African Congress. He wrote of this matter to Padmore. Before his letter reached its destination, however, Padmore sent Du Bois a long letter describing developments as of mid-August and replying to an earlier letter from Du Bois. The August letter from Padmore had a running head reading, "Pan-African Congress," and indicated that the congress was being sponsored by the Pan-African Federation, the League of Coloured Peoples, and the West African Students' Union.

New York City, July 20, 1945

My dear Mr. Padmore:

I am writing to let you know that the chances are that I will not be able to come to Paris for the proposed September meeting. The NAACP has voted in favor of helping to promote a Pan-African Congress and appropriated the money, but unfortunately the situation in the United States as to transportation is such that arrangements will be difficult, if not impossible. We could get over to Paris with perhaps a half dozen delegates but American soldiers are streaming back from Europe now in such numbers that I do not think we are

1. Du Bois had met both Creech-Jones and Laski during his visits to Europe soon after the First World War in connection with the Pan-African movement; financing for the congress meeting then had come, in part, from both the NAACP and the Labour party, of which Creech-Jones and Laski were leaders. Arthur Creech-Jones (1891–1964) was secretary from 1940 to 1945 to Ernest Bevin, minister of labour; in 1945–46 he was undersecretary of state in the colonial office. Harold J. Laski (1893-1950) was an internationally renowned writer, lecturer, and teacher in political theory and governmental practice. Du Bois referred several times in his writings to the work of Laski; see the index to Aptheker, *Annotated Bibliography*.

going to be able to obtain any assurance of transportation from France to America during the year 1945. If it is possible, I will, of course, hasten to let you know. But as I see it now it looks impossible.

In the meantime I hope you will be present at the Paris meeting of the Trade Union delegates and that you will assemble them in a conference on Africa. I think it would better be called a consultative conference rather than a congress. You might, therefore, make preparations for a real and fairly complete Pan-African Congress in the future. As Acting Permanent Secretary of the last four Congresses I had delegated to me the power to assemble the Fifth Congress. Whatever that power amounts to I very gladly turn over to any meeting in Paris so that they will feel free to take any action that they may wish and I want to assure you and them that I shall be willing to cooperate in the future in any way in accordance with my ability.

I shall follow this letter by another just as soon as the decision of the NAACP is final, but I thought this warning letter ought to go immediately.

I am sending a letter identical with this to Mr. Moody.

Very sincerely yours,
W. E. B. Du Bois

London, England, August 17, 1945

Dear Dr. Du Bois:

Even before your letter of the 9th July arrived we read of your presence at San Francisco. Consequently we can well understand the delay in acknowledging our letter of April 12th. A few days before your July 9th letter arrived we addressed to you a communication dated July 16th in which we summarised in concrete fashion the plans and progress made up to that date. On August 11th and 12th there was convened at Manchester, the headquarters of the Pan-African Federation, a delegate conference representing all of the organisations which have been invited to participate in the forthcoming Conference. At that ad hoc meeting a review of the preparatory work was made. From the reports it was revealed that the position was as follows.

A number of replies had been received from Labour, Trade Union, Co-operative, and other progressive organisations in the West Indies, West Africa, South and East Africa, in acknowledgment of the formal invitation to attend the Conference. Most of these bodies not only approved and endorsed the agenda, making minor modifications and suggestions here and there, but pledged themselves to send delegates. In cases where either the time is too short or the difficulties of transport at the present time too great to be overcome at such short notice, the organisations will give mandates to the natives of the territories concerned who are travelling to Paris to attend the World Trade Union Conference. Where territories will not be sending delegates to the Trade Union Conference, organisations will mandate individuals already in Great Britain to represent them.

In this way we are assured of the widest representation, either through people travelling directly from the Colonial areas to Britain, or individuals from those territories who are already in the British Isles. Apart from these overseas delegates, more than 14 organisations of the Africans and peoples of African descent in Great Britain and Ireland will participate in the Conference.

A few words about procedure. Our provisional committee appreciates the view you have expressed that no attempt should be made to impose any fixed ideological pattern upon the Conference, but we have every reason to believe that there will be unanimous agreement upon the fundamental aims and objects which the Conference desires to arrive at. I do not know what is the situation in America among coloured organisations regarding the future political outlook of Afro-Americans in relation to the American scene, but I can assure you that there is complete unity of purpose and outlook among the Colonial peoples of the British Empire. This, as you realise, is easily understandable. They are all inhabitants of territories to which they constitute the overwhelming majority of the population. Living under alien rule, their first manifestation of political consciousness naturally assumes the form of national liberation, self-determination, self-government—call it what you may. They want to be able to rule their own countries, free from the fetters of alien domination. On this all are agreed, from even the most conservative to the most radical elements. There might be differences as to the rate at which improvement is made towards the goal and regarding the political form which the objective should take.

For example, Left-wing elements among Colonials emphasise self-determination to the point of secession from the British Empire, while the more conservative elements, although endorsing our claim for self-determination, clarify it in terms of Dominion status within the British Empire. But again I repeat there is no cleavage as regards the desired objective. Consequently there is complete unity of purpose among all of our participants in the Conference.

In our ranks the question of Communism or anti-Communism, Stalinism, or Trotskyism, and all the other ideological tendencies which may obtain in the American Negro scene, do not exist here, for the simple reason that the American Negro is part and parcel of the American body politic and he finds it difficult to isolate himself from the political currents which may prevail in American society. The British Negro lives away from the British Isles, and those individuals who are here constitute an alien minority, although they are subjects of the same Crown. As a result, when the Negro comes to this country he does not ally himself with the existing political organisations and become a vehicle within his own racial group for the ideologies prevailing among the British political parties. Rather he tends to get together with other Colonial organisations to advocate and propagate his own political aspirations which, as I have suggested above, concentrate on the question of self-determination for the country whence he comes. This does not mean that there are no individual Negroes who subscribe to political philosophies, whether they be Socialism,

Communism, Anarchism, etc. But these are more in the nature of personal idiosyncrasies than practical politics.

In brief, even those who call themselves Communist are nationalist. That is to say, they realise that their countries must first be nationally free before they can begin to practice their Communism. I mention this, because living as you do on the other side of the Atlantic, it is very easy for you to interpret political trends among British Colonials in terms of the American scene. If you will permit me a personal allusion: As an individual I have very strong political views on the Left, views which a man like Dr. Moody does not subscribe to. While it would be unfair to say that Dr. Moody is hostile to Socialism, he does not advocate the Marxian philosophy as I do. But regardless of our personal views, there is no cleavage as regards the immediate steps which confront our people, which, as I said, are self-government for the West Indies, self-government for Africa, etc. You would be surprised to know how easy it was to bring into existence the Pan-African Federation, which is a federated body comprising more than 14 constituent organisations composed of workers, students, intellectuals, Africans, West Indians, and other peoples of African descent. When it comes to the struggle against Imperialism, British or otherwise, these people feel as one. They do have their little petty squabbles, but they are never of a fundamental character.

Having made this clarification, I would like to say a few words about the machinery of the Conference. Our Committee here agrees with you that we should have few pre-arranged plans but allow the Conference to evolve. However, there must be a minimum amount of machinery, otherwise we shall have anarchism, and that is one philosophy from which I think the average Negro has an instinctive aversion. We are well acquainted with the modus operandi of running Conferences. The truth is that we have too many conferences. Conferences of one kind or another are a typical British institution, and this is a malady which we as British subjects have not been able to escape. But the Committee which is now functioning is a provisional committee. Its specific task is to establish contact with organisations in this country and overseas and to issue invitations. It has further set itself the task of preparing the technical facilities for the Conference, budgeting, entertainment, securing meeting hall, etc. Such machinery is inevitable, as without it the Conference could not bring itself into existence. When the delegates arrive we propose that the provisional committee shall turn itself into a Standing Orders Committee, to register credentials, elect reporters for the various subjects on the agenda, and such matters. When the Conference officially opens, the whole machinery will be in the hands of the delegates, who can then do what they like. That is surely the minimum machinery which we contemplate.

Concerning resolutions: We do not intend to have any resolutions cut and dried for the delegates to approve or reject. All that we are proposing is that we should have reports upon the various parts of the world which are to come under review. Out of these reports we take it that sub-committees will be set up to draft their resolutions, which will embody the salient problems emerging from the different reports and discussion. For example, we are expecting American delegations to give us a report on the problems of the American Negro today and the perspective before him. Discussion will follow these reports, and a resolution will be adopted by the Conference as a final document. In this connection it is suggested that it would be very helpful if our American friends, who are better acquainted with the Negro problem in their country, would undertake the preparation of reports on these problems and be responsible for drafting such documents. We hope to get some of the delegates from other parts of the black world to do likewise.

Our suggestion to get committees together in each of the territories was merely to facilitate the gathering together of delegates, particularly in view of the shortness of time, and they are only regional committees. There are so many Negro organisations in America—political, religious, labour, cultural, etc.—and our proposal was that if you could issue invitations to those groups to set up their own American Committee it would help matters, because they would then either send individual delegates or have a delegation to represent them collectively.

In the case of the Colonial organisations the situation is entirely different. They are in scattered territories, very often having no contact with one another. Hence it was more expedient for the provisional committee to invite the organisations in these different territories, since we could act centrally. Over eighty invitations went out to such organisations and replies are coming in, our Committee centralising the plan. In your situation all of the coloured organisations are in one country, and all that we are suggesting is that you in New York, like us in Britain, should act as the co-ordinating link for the American scene, while we do likewise for the British, French and other imperial areas. You mention that you have some contacts in Africa, but we doubt whether your contacts are any different from ours. In truth, there is no organisation in the British Colonial Empire with which we are not in contact. Our problem is not lack of contact, but how it will be possible for these people to travel at such short notice to Britain. If they could all send delegations to Britain we would have to hire the Albert Hall.

After reviewing the situation we do feel like you that our Conference should be merely a preliminary one to a greater, more representative Congress to be held some time next year, especially as a new Government has come into being in Britain since we started planning the forthcoming Conference.

The Pan-African Federation has recently addressed an Open Letter to Mr. [Clement] Attlee, the Labour Prime Minister, and we are hoping to have long discussions with the new Labour Secretary of State for the Colonies, Mr. George Hall, and it is hoped that out of these talks we shall be able to get the support of the British Labour and Trade Union movements in facilitating the

bigger Conference which we have in mind for 1946, when more normal ship-
ping and travelling facilities will exist. The situation here in this respect is at
the moment so topsy-turvey that it is even impossible to get travelling facilities
from London to Paris, which is, as it were, just a stone's throw away. Apart
from that, every one who comes back from Paris warns us to keep away from
there, for Europe is facing famine, and what with the shortage of coal, holding
a conference in Paris in September would just be inviting trouble.

It is not surprising that the French Colonial Minister expressed such willingness for us to meet in his capital. In this connection, if the French Colonial Minister really knew that we are uncompromisingly opposed to all forms of Imperialism, that we would like to break up the French Empire as much as we
would like to liquidate the British Empire, it is doubtful whether he would be
so pleased to have us denounce French Colonial rule from the very metropolis
of his Empire. For while we hold no brief for British Imperialism, the latter
is a humanly run institution by comparison with the French. In spite of the
popular impression which exists among Western Negroes that France has a
liberal policy towards her Colonials, because of the absence of the Colour Bar
in Paris prior to the war, in Africa the French policy is so repressive that
whereas we have legal political and trade-union movements in the British Colonies, in the adjoining French Colonies there is no such thing. The facts in the
recent articles of Rene Maran in the *Chicago Defender*, while they may come
as a shock to Afro-Americans, are common knowledge to us.[1] And with the
present Labour Government in power in this country we have more possibility
to manoeuvre than the French Colonials have under the semi-dictatorial regime
which exists in France. After all, all the Negroes here voted for the Labour
Party and supported them. They are members of the Labour Party and surely
have a constitutional voice in shaping policy. All the Negroes in Britain are
members of the Trade-Union Movement. Our French African comrades are
not in that position, and unless France makes a bloodless revolution like the
one which occurred here a few weeks ago, we see no prospects for French black
Colonials.

Since it is now officially announced that the World Trade Union Conference
will begin on September 25th and close on October 9th, we are planning to
convene the Pan-African Congress on October 15th. It should last a week.
This will enable the Colonial delegates to get from France to England between

1. In the *Chicago Defender*, 30 June and 7 July 1945, appeared a two-part article
by Rene Maran describing a massacre of French colonial troops in Dakar in 1944,
mentioning something of the realities of colonialism in Indo-China, and affirming the
appearance inside France itself of racist discriminatory practices. Maran (1887–1960),
born in France of Black West Indian parents gained fame as the first Black author to
receive the Prix Goncourt—this for his novel *Batouala* (French ed. 1921; second
English reprint, 1973).

the 9th and 15th October. It will also enable us to hold some informal meetings and finish off our plans.

We heard from Mr. George Weaver of the c.i.o. Committee for the Abolition of Racial Discrimination in Washington. They would like to participate in the Conference and will no doubt give a mandate to the coloured members who are likely to be included in the delegation to the World Trade Union Conference.

Mrs. Garvey writes us that she had issued instructions to the Garvey Association in America to support the Conference. It might not be practicable for them to send delegates, but I am suggesting to the New York headquarters at 100-2, West 116th Street that they should get into touch with you and to indicate what they would like to do.

Regarding the c.i.o. again, if you contact Mr. Henry L. Moon, he would be able to inform you whether the c.i.o. will be sending any Negroes in their delegation this time.

One more thing. There seems to have been some confusion caused through the use of the term "Pan-African Congress." Whether it is Congress or Conference, our Committee does not mind in the least. If you would like it to be called Congress, all well and good; if not, then Conference is all the same. Like typical Britishers, the people here have a great capacity for compromise and are not much carried away by nomenclature. It doesn't matter much to them whether it is conference or congress. The truth is they wanted to call theirs the African Peoples Conference, but somehow or other, the secretary, in preparing the letterheading, used the term Pan-African Congress. But this is a very minor matter and can easily be straightened out. It's the purpose that really counts.

Yours very sincerely,
George Padmore

At the end of August, Du Bois sent Walter White a report on the status of the projected congress and suggested that practical steps be taken. The Pan-African Committee of the NAACP did vote in support of the congress and in support of sending Du Bois to that congress as its representative.

New York City, August 31, 1945

Memorandum to the Secretary of the
Pan-African Committee:

According to my latest reports from Europe the present situation is as follows: the convening committee has officially announced that since the World Trade Union Conference will meet in Paris, September twenty-fifth to October ninth, the Pan African Congress will meet in London for one week beginning October fifteenth. All idea of a Paris meeting has been given up because of

difficulties of transport between London and Paris. Also the West African
Student Union, an important organization sponsoring the congress, would prefer to have the meeting postponed and held in Africa in 1947 but nevertheless
is apparently concurring in the present meeting.

It seems to me since correspondence is coming to me from Europe and the
West Indies I ought to send out some kind of publicity. I suggest, therefore, one
or two things: that in my capacity as organizer of four Pan African Congresses
I should inform the Negro press of the present plans of the London convening
committee and in their name should invite any persons or organizations to let
me know of their wish or plans to attend. Two, if the Committee wishes the
publicity could go out in the name of the NAACP stating the facts and naming
the NAACP as one of the sponsoring organizations.[1]

I think a decision on this point ought to be made not later than the first week
of September.

W. E. B. Du Bois

*The board of the NAACP having acted positively, Du Bois turned at once to
writing a letter to Padmore conveying matters he considered most urgent.*

New York City, September 12, 1945

Dear Mr. Padmore:

After long deliberation, the Board of Directors of the National Association
for the Advancement of Colored People voted to be represented at the Pan-
African Congress to be held in London October 15–21, 1945. They have asked
me to attend the meeting as their delegate. As the meeting has already been
planned and called without our official participation, I come officially simply
as an observer; but I am authorized to say that if a permanent organization
results, and a representative congress is called for 1946 or 1947, this organization will take part and will aid with an appropriation toward expenses. Final
decision on these points will be made by the directors after my report to them
on the present meeting. As you doubtless know, the NAACP has at present a paid
membership of 400,000 persons and is the largest organization of its kind, representing 13,000,000 Americans of Negro descent.

The chief difficulty now facing me is obtaining facilities of travel to London
and return, and also obtaining a British visa. I am writing to our Department
of State today and also to Harold Laski and Mr. Creech-Jones, both of whom
I know, to help get me a visa. If the Labor government is favorable to the
Congress they can do much to help foreigners get visas. On the other hand if
they take no action, you may find it very difficult to get your delegates

---

1. In his column in the *Chicago Defender* for 29 September 1945, Du Bois reported
that the NAACP had voted to send him as a delegate to the Fifth Pan-African Congress.

together. Also the matter of hotel accommodation is of importance, and I will be glad of advice and help.

There are many matters that ought to be thoroughly thrashed out before the meeting which time and distance precluded. Perhaps only one aspect ought to be emphasized as a sine qua non of success: avoid the appearance of making this predominantly a "British" meeting; we must not neglect the interests and opinions of French, Belgian, Portuguese and Spanish Africans as well as Africans of West Indian and American descent. Many of these last will be slimly represented and some not at all; but all will count in complete Pan-Africa. Union of effort among us will count as never before.

Sincerely,
W. E. B. Du Bois

Because of the precarious conditions of travel in the immediate post-war world, Du Bois sent several letters to various officials in an effort to arrange for his travel to England. One went to the under-secretary of state, then Dean Acheson, who had just been promoted from a position as assistant secretary of state at the end of August 1945. A few years later, Acheson, as secretary of state, would take the lead in condemning the peace efforts which would result in Du Bois's arrest, trial, and ultimate acquittal.

New York City, September 12, 1945

The Under-Secretary of State,
Sir:

There is to be held in London, October 15 to 21, 1945 a Pan-African Congress. This will be the fifth congress held since the first which organized in 1919, at the time of the Congress of Versailles. Three other congresses have been held since in London, Paris, Lisbon and New York, in 1921, 1923, and 1927. These were all called by the National Association for the Advancement of Colored People, of which I am an official and one of the incorporators. Among those speaking and cooperating at these congresses have been Paul Otlet, "Father of the League of Nations," the late Lord [Sidney] Olivier, Harold Laski, H. G. Wells, President [C. D.] King of Liberia, and from fifty to one hundred and fifty delegates from Africa, Europe, the West Indies and the United States.

The present movement originated among the African delegates to the trades union congress held in London last winter. My cooperation was asked because of my connection with previous congresses and because I was associate consultant at San Francisco, and am particularly interested in colonies.

The NAACP, at the last meeting of the directors, has asked me to attend the London meeting. This will involve travel by air or water, and I am writing to ask you or the appropriate official how I may obtain permission or facilities for this trip. I would be glad to come to Washington for consultation, or to furnish any further data which you may wish. My biography is in *Who's Who in America.*

I am, Sir, very respectfully yours,

W. E. B. Du Bois

The Du Bois papers do not show a reply from Acheson. The same day Du Bois wrote to him, he also wrote to President Truman. This letter brought a reply from a secretary and resulted in an interview between Du Bois and Acheson.

New York City, September 12, 1945

The President of the United States
Sir:

I am writing to ask if it would be possible for me to talk with you a few minutes next week concerning the Pan-African Congress which is to meet in London, October 15 to 21, 1945. The First Pan-African Congress met in Paris in February, 1919, at my suggestion, and with the consent of Prime Minister Clemenceau. Subsequent congresses met in Paris, Brussels, London and New York, in 1921, 1923 and 1927, with me in each case acting as secretary. Among those speaking and co-operating have been Paul Otlet, "Father of the League of Nations," the late Lord Olivier, Harold Laski, H. G. Wells, President King of Liberia and a total of fifty to one hundred and fifty delegates at the various meetings, from Africa, Europe, the West Indies and the United States.

The present movement toward a Fifth Pan-African Congress arose among the African delegates to the trade union conference held in London last winter. They appealed for co-operation to the National Association for the Advancement of Colored People, which had initiated and sponsored the previous congresses. It was finally decided by the London committee to call a Congress directly after the Paris meeting of the international trade union organization. The French minister of colonies invited the group to meet in Paris, but London seemed more suitable. The NAACP, of which I am an official and one of the original incorporators, have voted to send me as a delegate to this Congress.

I know how busy you are at this time, but I venture to ask a few minutes to discuss this matter with you.

I am, Sir, respectfully yours,

W. E. B. Du Bois

The White House
Washington, D. C., Sept. 19, 1945

Dear Mr. Du Bois:

The President is very much interested in the problems which will be discussed at the forthcoming Pan-African Congress, but his schedule, as you can well imagine, is very full right now. I would suggest that you take the matter up with the Honorable Dean Acheson, Acting Secretary of State, who will be glad to see you next week.

I am forwarding your letter to him and suggest that you call him for an appointment. Then, if the President's schedule lightens, we will try to arrange an interview later.

Sincerely yours,
Matthew J. Connelly[1]
Secretary to the President

*The most liberal of the daily newspapers in New York City in the 1940s was PM. Du Bois thought it possible, therefore, that the PM staff might be interested in publishing dispatches on the forthcoming Pan-African Congress. He wrote to the managing editor, John P. Lewis, with this suggestion.**

New York City, September 17, 1945
[John P. Lewis]
My dear sir:
A Pan African Congress has been called to meet in London, October 15th to 21st. The convening committee was organized by American Negro delegates to the Trade Unions Conference which met in London last winter. The original plan was to have the meeting in Paris after the projected Trade Unions Conference. Difficulties of travel and probably other considerations led the committee finally to call the conference in London.

The idea of "Pan Africa" was initiated after the first World War when I got together a small Pan African Congress in Paris during the Peace Conference at Versailles. Later, larger conferences were held in Europe in 1921 and 1923 and one in New York in 1927. At all these conferences, a majority of the delegates were persons of African descent living outside Africa in Europe, America and the West Indies; but there were always a number of Africans. If the present Congress is successful, there will probably be a larger number of Africans than ever before and the motive power will be from Africa itself, although colored folk in England and the West Indies will play a considerable part.

1. Matthew J. Connelly (1907-76) was educated at Fordham University. He was an investigator for a Senate committee headed by Truman during the war, and when Truman became president was named his appointments secretary. He held this position throughout Truman's presidency, but in 1955 Connelly was tried for corruption while in office; he was convicted and sentenced to two years in prison in 1957.

* John P. Lewis was born in Denver, Colorado, in 1903 and worked on newspapers in that city from 1920 to 1931. He then worked for the *Buffalo* (New York) *Times* until joining *PM* in 1940. He was managing editor and then editor of *PM* until he moved in 1948 to do newspaper work in New Hampshire; he died there in 1961.

I am not at all sure that, even with the present Labor Government, England is going to allow an effective Pan African Congress and if such a Congress should assemble in London I am afraid that notice and comment upon it may be quietly suppressed.

In the previous Congresses, the National Association for the Advancement of Colored People has been the moving spirit through my agency. The Association is not the main instigator of this Congress but it has asked me to attend it and if there are favorable results to try to organize a more inclusive and representative Congress for 1946 or 1947. I shall probably have difficulty in getting passage to London and especially in returning and I may have difficulty about visas although I have written to Harold Laski and Creech-Jones, whom I know.

I am venturing to write you to ask if, in case I go, you would like to have one or more articles about the Congress, provided of course it turns out to be a real worthwhile meeting. Previous Congresses have represented professional men and the intelligentsia; this Congress promises to represent also organized African labor. If it is successful, it may be an epoch making meeting and movement; on the other hand, it may be just a flop.

I should be very glad to hear from you and to have your ideas on the matter.[1]

Very sincerely yours,
W. E. B. Du Bois

A long letter from George Padmore, received shortly before Du Bois left for England, supplies significant information.

London, England, September 18, 1945

Dear Dr. Du Bois:

No doubt this will be the last opportunity I shall have to write you before the Congress convenes. As I have informed you, the date has been officially fixed for the 15th October, 1945, but even that is still contingent upon the conclusion of the World Trade Union Conference in Paris. That conference begins on September 25th, and is supposed to end on the 9th October. But there might be some delay, which would mean we should have to push our conference back a little. But we hope that everything will go to schedule.

Several delegates to the Pan-African Congress have already arrived in this country and others are on their way. This past weekend the Executive Committee of the Pan-African Federation, which comprises all of the organizations

1. Lewis invited Du Bois—probably by telephone, since no written communication seems to exist—to wire *PM* accounts of the congress. Du Bois sent four wires; according to a later letter from Du Bois to Henry Luce (17 December 1945), the newspaper published one account, but it has not been identified.

of Africans and peoples of African descent in the British Isles, with the exception of the League of Coloured People, met in London to complete final plans
for the forthcoming Congress. Your letter of September 12th was put on the
agenda and its contents discussed. I am therefore able to report to you the sentiments of our Executive.

1) We are glad to hear that you are making every effort to attend and sincerely hope that you will be able to undertake the trip.

2) We get the impression from your letter that you were having some difficulty in securing visas. This is rather surprising, as we thought the only
difficulty in your way was to get passage facilities. We hope that the intervention of Prof. Laski and Mr. Creech-Jones will be of aid in obtaining a
British visa. Had we known of this obstacle in your way sooner, we could have
set our machinery in motion to assist you. However, we must hope for the best.

3) While the Colonial peoples expect a more sympathetic attitude towards
their problems and aspirations from Labour than from the Tories, they have
no illusions about either party, for on matters affecting imperial policy there
is only a difference of degree rather than of kind. Therefore, in launching our
Congress we were not concerned with whether the Labour Government wel-
comes it or not. We do hope they welcome it, but this is immaterial. We shall
make our deliberations, pass our resolutions, and make our representations to
them to implement their pre-election promises. If they don't fulfill those promises, we shall expose them even more ruthlessly than the Tories, for the Tories
never promised us anything but blood, tears, toil and sweat.

4) Hotel accommodation here is on the difficult side, but we shall always be
able to fix you up, if you will let me know a few days in advance of your arrival here. We have one or two middle-class supporters, who will be delighted
to welcome you in their homes.

5) As you will see from our agenda, our whole approach is an international
one, an inclusive one. But we are realistic enough to know that a Congress
taking place immediately following a war in which the whole machinery of international communication was broken down, would find it difficult to get
delegates from all parts of the Colonial world and the Americas. Nevertheless,
the response to our invitation has been much greater than our most optimistic
anticipations. There will be two kinds of delegates:

   a) Those travelling directly from the West Indian Colonies, South America,
      and various parts of Africa, to attend the Congress;
   b) Those mandated by organisations unable to send delegates directly be-
      cause of passport and transport obstacles.

We are, however, expecting to have representation from every territory in
British West, South and East Africa, and also some French Negroes. We have
not forgotten the French, Belgian, Portuguese and Spanish parts of Africa. The
thinking of the young Africans who form the vanguard of the new Pan-
Africanism is in terms of Africa as a whole. Their ideological outlook trans-

cends the arbitrary frontiers which European imperialists have set up in Africa. But our problem is a technical one, for while we have contacts in all parts of the Continent, and that with organisations and not merely individuals, our difficulty is to get them out.

There is one point which my Executive has asked me to put clearly before you. If we were satisfied to have at our Congress merely people who come from various parts of Africa, then it would be 100% represented, for there are to be found in Britain natives from every part of the world. All we should have had to do would have been to bring them together at a meeting and call it a Pan-African Congress. But this is not our purpose. All our delegates must have mandates from organisations, and they will therefore speak not for themselves but for masses of people, representative, not of the middle class strata and professionals in the Colonies, but of the workers' organisations, the co-operative societies, peasant associations, labour parties and national liberation organisations. This was the emphasis with which the Congress was conceived and brought into being.

In reviewing the work of our Congress, my Committee this weekend came to the conclusion that the weakest representation we shall have is from the United States. In this respect we are largely to blame. We had assumed that the relationship between the various progressive organisations in America, as for example, the NAACP, Urban League, the March on Washington Movement, the [National] Negro Congress, the West Indian National Council, and the various trades unions associated with the C.I.O., would have been able to get together, as we have done here, and get up a provisional committee. And we had thought that out of this united front a delegation would have been selected from America to represent these various sections of Negro opinion. But it seems that this was not possible. Unfortunately though, we did not address our invitations directly to those different organisations, and it does not seem possible to do so at this late date. We very much regret this because we did not want to give the impression that we did not want to treat with any organisation other than the NAACP.

It is therefore all the more disappointing to us to hear that your organisation is unable to give you a plenipotentiary mandate. However, we shall be most happy to welcome you in whatever capacity you come, realising as we do the valuable contribution which you have made to the progress and emancipation of our people in the United States.

Yours sincerely,
George Padmore

P.S. Your telegram was received just before dispatching this letter. We shall arrange accommodation for you with Dr. Belfield Clarke. I might be away from London at the time of your arrival, so please cable Dr. Clarke at 112 Newington Causeway, S.E.1 saying when you are arriving. Try and supply the name of *railway station, date and time* of arrival. He will meet you.

Just before his departure, Du Bois summarized for Walter White and other members of the Pan-African Committee of the NAACP what steps he had taken in preparation for the congress.

September 25, 1945

TO: Secretary and the Members of the Pan African Committee

FROM: W. E. B. Du Bois

In accordance with the vote of the Board of Directors at the September meeting, I have taken the following action:

1. Cabled to London asking the latest developments concerning the proposed Congress and all printed matter which has been published. In reply to this, I have had a cablegram confirming the meeting, October 15 to 21, and saying that data and printed matter were being forwarded.

2. I applied for a renewal of my passport which has expired and explained to the Passport Division the reasons for my desiring a trip to London.

3. I have also written explaining the Pan African Congress to the President of the United States, the Under-Secretary of State and the War Department.

4. I wrote explaining the attitude of the N.A.A.C.P. toward the Congress to Dr. Moody of the League of Colored People, London, and to the West African Students Union.

5. I have written to persons whom I know in London concerning the Congress and my obtaining visas to attend. Among these are: Mr. Creech-Jones, Under-Secretary for Colonies, Mr. Harold Laski, Chairman of the Labor Party, and Mr. E .W. Smith, Editor of *Africa*.[1]

6. I have written to the British Embassy in Washington asking if they would be willing to give me a visa if I obtained permission from the State Department to make the journey.

7. I have written to Senator [Robert F.] Wagner and Congressman [Adam C.] Powell asking their good offices.

8. I have written to Mr. [George L. P.] Weaver and Mr. [Henry L.] Moon of the C.I.O. in Washington asking their cooperation.

9. I have written the U.S. Steamship Lines concerning possible passage.[2]

If there are any other steps which I should take or contacts which I should

---

1. Edwin Williams Smith (1876–1957), born in South Africa, was a missionary, anthropologist, and author. His two best-known books were *The Golden Stool* (1926) and *Aggrey of Africa* (1929). In the 1920s and 1930s he was associated with the Phelps-Stokes Fund and was a visiting professor at Fisk. He was editor of *Africa*, the journal of the International African Institute in London, from 1945 through 1947.

2. Actually, Du Bois flew to England—then a rather unusual adventure. He described the flight in his *Chicago Defender* column of 17 November 1945, remarking, "One of these days we will breakfast in New York, lunch on the moon, and after dinner, shake hands with God." Only the last of these prophecies now seems unlikely.

make in this matter, I would be very glad to have advice from the Secretary
or any other member of the committee.³

W. E. B. Du Bois

*As noted, Du Bois had written to Harold J. Laski about his intended visit to
England. Laski responded with a very cordial note late in September and then,
after Du Bois's arrival, asked him to visit.*

London, England, September 25, 1945

Dear Dr. Du Bois,

Of course I remember you. And I have gladly sought to redeem some small
part of the debt I owe to your books by writing urgently to Mr. Bevin on
your behalf. I hope greatly that you will come, and that I shall have the pleasure
of seeing you again.

Yours sincerely,
Harold J. Laski

London, England, November 6, 1945

Dear Dr. Du Bois,

Will you come and see me here on Friday morning about 11?¹ It will be a
great pleasure to have a talk with you after so many years.

Yours sincerely,
Harold J. Laski

*As late as 5 October, Du Bois still was not certain that he would be able to get
to England for the congress; on that date he wrote Padmore.*

New York City, October 5, 1945

My dear Mr. Padmore:

Matters are slowly shaping up so that it looks as though I may be able to
attend the Pan African Congress. I appealed to the President of the United
States and got an interview with the Acting Secretary of State. He is taking

3. The only written response in the Du Bois papers to this memorandum is an 8
October 1945 letter from Washington, D.C., from William H. Hastie (1904–1976),
then dean of the School of Law at Howard, later governor of the Virgin Islands, and
from 1949 through 1971 a judge of the Third United States Circuit Court of Appeals,
the first Black on the court. In this brief note, Hastie told Du Bois that Norman W.
Manley of Jamaica was visiting in New York City and suggested they get together
before Du Bois left. Whether they did so is not known.

1. By "here" Laski meant his office at the London School of Economics. Du Bois
devoted a column to his visit with Laski—*Chicago Defender*, 15 December 1945.

the matter of priorities under consideration. I hope to hear from him in a day or two. I have received my passport but British consent to a visa has not yet been obtained. The consul office here has cabled to London but has as yet received no reply. Then too, if I come, I shall have to fly and that will greatly increase the expense. I do not yet know whether the National Association for the Advancement of Colored People will consent to this increased expense but I think it will.

If I do come, I appreciate the stopping place which you have secured for me at Dr. Clarke's, 112 Newington Causeway, S.E.1. I will cable him as soon as I know my plans. In the meantime, will you please see if he can arrange a comfortable room for me which I can occupy alone and also will you try to secure for me the services of a typist and a small office or desk space where I can work. I shall of course expect to pay for all these accommodations. I shall bring my own portable typewriting machine.

If I do not succeed in getting to London, I shall try to rush to you, in time for the Congress, certain proposals and considerations which I should like laid before it.

I thank you for your cooperation.

Very sincerely yours,
W. E. B. Du Bois

Du Bois arrived in London 12 October 1945. Because of war damage and numerous conferences being held in London, more adequate facilities for the Pan-African Congress were found in Manchester, and registration of delegates took place at the Congress Hall there on 13 October. The conference itself opened on Monday, 15 October, with a welcoming address by the city's lord mayor. Of the seven people selected to chair sessions, Du Bois was one (and Mrs. Garvey another); Du Bois and Mrs. Garvey were two of the five members of the resolutions committee.* Du Bois also was named permanent chairman. On 16 and 17 October the sessions concerned Africa; on 18 and 19 October the West Indies and North and South America. The twentieth was devoted to summing up, decisions, and a banquet, while on Sunday, 21 October, there was a well-attended public meeting.

On 19 October, Du Bois sent a preliminary report to Arthur Spingarn, president of the NAACP.

---

* Of notable interest is the single resolution that did not deal with Africa. It read: "That the Pan-African Congress comprising of peoples of Africa and African descent now in session in the city of Manchester, extends its fraternal greetings to the struggling peoples of Java and Indo-China in their fight against Dutch and French imperialism, and pledges its solidarity in their struggle for freedom. Hands off Java! Hands off Indo-China!"

Manchester, England, October 19, 1945

Dear Mr. Spingarn:

I had a most interesting flight to England; breakfast in New York, supper in Newfoundland, breakfast again in Ireland and dinner in London. The Congress which is meeting in Manchester, where it found better accommodation, is really an excellent body. It has a much stronger African representation than any of the previous Congresses and the men of Africa on the whole are of high character, and have given us a lot of facts, together, of course, with considerable emotion.

I am very glad I came; I think much good will come out of the Meeting.[1] Just when I can get back and how, I am not sure. I am afraid it is going to be hard to find a ship, but I am already trying.

My best regards to you and Mrs. Spingarn.

Very sincerely yours,
W. E. B. Du Bois

Among the people whom Du Bois had met on earlier visits to Britain was the world-famous author H. G. Wells (1866–1946). Indeed, Wells, as well as Harold Laski, had spoken at the 1923 Pan-African Congress in London, which Du Bois had chaired. Soon after the Manchester meeting adjourned, Du Bois wrote to Wells a letter that seems not to have survived; the result was a reply from Marjorie Wells—the wife of H. G. Wells's eldest son, G. P. Wells—who served as the writer's secretary.

London, England, November 5, 1945

Dear Mr. Du Bois,

Mr. H. G. Wells asks me to thank you for your letter. He would very much like to see you, but he has not been in good health for some time, and tires very easily, so that the visit would have to be a short one. Perhaps you would telephone after 10 a.m. to suggest a time that would suit you. About 4 or 4:30 in the afternoon is his usual time for visitors, but he asks me to find out what time would be most convenient for you.[1]

Yours sincerely,
Marjorie Wells

1. Du Bois devoted his 24 November 1945 column in the *Chicago Defender* to a description of the work of the congress, discussing especially what related to the West Indies and to the participation of Mrs. Garvey. In his posthumously published *Autobiography* (ed. H. Aptheker [New York: International Publishers, 1968]), Du Bois does no more than simply mention this Manchester congress (p. 330). A fairly full report is given in J. Ayodele Langley, *Pan-Africanism and Nationalism in West Africa* (London: Oxford University Press, 1973), pp. 347–57. See also Hooker, *Black Revolutionary*, pp. 80–98.

1. Du Bois described this visit with Wells in the *Chicago Defender*, 1 December

An exchange with George Bernard Shaw (1856–1950) is less pleasant, but is quite Shavian.

London, England, November 9, 1945

Mr. George Bernard Shaw,
Sir:

I am an American Negro, and have had some little correspondence with you in the past[1]. Once Mrs. Havelock Ellis was about to take me to call on you, but you were out of town. I am venturing to ask if while I am in London awaiting a chance to return home, I could have a few words with you?

Very sincerely yours,
W. E. B. Du Bois

To this letter, Shaw replied, on a card, in ink:*

Ayot Saint Lawrence
14.11.45

I am sorry; but the whole American army wants to visit me or has actually crashed my gate and done so.

I can entertain no more visitors, plain or colored, for another year at least

GBS

The day after his return from England, Du Bois sent a memorandum to Walter White.

New York City, November 27, 1945

Memorandum to Mr. White:

I landed at LaGuardia Field, Monday, November 26, at 12:27. I shall send you my expense account within a few days.

On the plane coming over I met John Marshall of the Rockefeller Foundation. He suggested to me confidentially that perhaps the NAACP would like to take up the matter of the illegitimate children of American Negro soldiers in England. It has been estimated that there are at least one thousand of them. There is no provision in the English social service machinery adequately to

---

1945. The conversation was brief; Du Bois served tea for both of them. "The end of man is always sad," he wrote. "But the shadow which hovers about a great genius is ultimate tragedy." In his column of 28 September 1946, Du Bois paid glowing tribute to Wells, who had just died.

1. No other correspondence either to or from Shaw has been found.

* © The Trustees of the British Museum, The Governors and Guardians of the National Gallery of Ireland and Royal Academy of Dramatic Art.

take care of these children although there is goodwill and concern. Mr. Marshall suggests that American Negroes might adopt these children and provide for them. I told him I would lay the matter before you. He says that Victor Weybright, who was formerly on the *Survey Graphic* and now connected with Penguin Books, can give you a great deal of information.[1]

I shall be glad to confer with you concerning this or any other matters at such time as you may wish.

W. E. B. Du Bois

Du Bois was a principled optimist and believed in giving all people a chance to do something worthwhile. Therefore, on his return from England, he suggested to Henry R. Luce, of Time, Life, Fortune, *and so on, that developments in Africa and among Africans might be worth some space in his publications.* Whether or not Luce granted the meeting requested is not known; certainly his publications never carried a word from Du Bois.*

New York City, December 17, 1945

Personal

Mr. Henry Luce

My dear Sir:

I have just returned from a Pan African Congress held in Manchester, England with representatives especially of the labor classes from West Africa and the West Indies. I was tremendously impressed by the new meaning of Africa to the modern world which I think most people and thinking people of today are missing. Africa is still not news. The editors of PM invited me to wire them statements on the Congress and I sent four telegrams from which they made one short article.

But the main story, that of the new development of cocoa on the West Coast and the extraordinary paradox which it presents to the new English Labor Government, that they did not touch. If the world today is art and luxury, electricity and food, among other things, Africa is contributing through its gold and diamonds, its copper and chocolate an extraordinary part. In return

1. John Marshall was born in Maine in 1903 and educated at Harvard; he taught there briefly in the late 1920s and in 1933 began his association with the Rockefeller Foundation. Victor Weybright was born in 1903 in Maryland and educated at the universities of Pennsylvania and Chicago. During the Second World War he was a special assistant to the United States ambassador in London; earlier he had been associated with Survey Associates. In the 1960s he founded the publishing firm of Weybright and Talley. For the illegitimate children, see the brief account by St. Clair Drake, "A Report on the Brown Britishers," *Crisis* 56 (June 1949):174.

* Henry R. Luce (1898–1967) was educated at Yale and Oxford; in 1923 he founded *Time* magazine with Briton Hadden and went on thereafter to edit and publish *Fortune, Life, Architectural Forum*, and other periodicals.

it is not only not getting a fair share of the results, but the fact that this is true is bedeviling and will continue to frustrate the restoration and advance of civilization.

I should like to talk with you about this and see if I can secure your interest. Would you be willing to grant me a little of your time?

Very sincerely yours,

W. E. B. Du Bois

A final significant component of Du Bois's life in 1945 was his strained relationship with Walter White, the executive secretary of the NAACP. *Of the many people with whom Du Bois worked in his long life, the person for whom he seems to have had least regard was Walter White. Difficulties and even clashes developed quite early after Du Bois's return to the* NAACP; *illustrative are the letters and memoranda published below. The first memorandum is one sent to White's assistant, Roy Wilkins.*

January 31, 1945

Memorandum to Mr. Wilkins:

I do not wish mail or telegrams addressed to me opened by any one except Miss [Irene] Diggs. If telephone calls of any sort come for me they will be referred to me or Miss Diggs. In the absence of both of us, the reply will be that we are not in the office and it is not known exactly when we will return.

W. E. B. Du Bois

April 10, 1945

Memorandum to Mr. White:

Something must be done immediately about office space for my work. Mr. White's sudden return leaves all my books in his office together with my dictaphone installation, my encyclopaedia, papers, clippings and part of my files. The small office in which Miss Diggs and I have been working must accommodate the clerk who has been helping with the Colonial Conference and must help with preparations for the Pan African Congress. A visitor coming in would scarcely have space to sit down. It is inconceivable for me to carry on my work under such handicaps until September.[1] May I, therefore, ask for immediate action?

W. E. B. Du Bois

cc to Messrs. [Arthur B.] Spingarn, [Roy] Wilkins, Dr. [Louis T.] Wright and Judge [Charles E.] Toney

1. In the fall of 1945 the NAACP was to move into its own headquarters at the Willkie Building at 20 West Fortieth Street, New York City.

June 14, 1945

Memorandum to Dr. Du Bois from Mr. White

Pending meeting of the committee appointed by the Board at the April meeting to consider the matter of a Pan-African Congress and action by the Board on whatever report that committee makes, I think it both premature and unfortunate that announcement has been made by you that a Pan-African Congress will be held in Paris in September. All that the Board has done to date is "go on record as favoring the idea of a Pan-African Congress to be held in Paris in September under the sponsorship of the N.A.A.C.P." (April minutes of the Board), subject to the investigations of a committee which was appointed to look into "costs and possible dates, which committee is to report back to the Board."

At the May meeting of the Board, on the basis of your report, the Board further voted that "the report and the estimated cost of the proposed Pan-African Congress be referred to the special committee on the Pan-African Congress, awaiting the return of Dr. Du Bois who is a member of that committee."

It would be unfortunate to announce the definite date and place of a Pan-African Congress until such matters as costs, transportation, accommodations, program objectives and other such pertinent points are determined, especially since there will be both added work and disappointments in explaining if for any reason the Congress cannot be held at the time and place announced.

May I further suggest that future statements regarding the Congress be made through either the committee or the regular Association channels as only by such cooperative clearance can confusion or misunderstanding be avoided.

As you know, from my memorandum to you of June 12th, efforts are now being made to hold a meeting of the Pan-African Congress Committee, which meeting could not be held because of your absence in San Francisco and in filling speaking engagements, at the earliest possible date. In this connection please let me discuss with you date, etc., as soon as you return to the office.

Walter White

June 27, 1945

Memorandum to Dr. Du Bois from Mr. White
(Copy to Messrs. Spingarn and Wright)

Your memorandum of June 26 raises a question of procedure that I think it would be best for all concerned to clarify now.

It is perfectly proper for you or any other executive to confer with Mr. Spingarn, as President, and Dr. Wright, as Chairman of the Board, on any matter you choose.

But the responsibility of administration of the office has been placed by the Board upon its executive officers, namely, the Executive Secretary, and in his absence, the Assistant Secretary. In case of the absence of both the Secretary and the Assistant Secretary, Mr. [Thurgood] Marshall, the Special Counsel, is in charge. Since he has said nothing to me about it, I assume Mr. Wilkins had no knowledge of your renting an office at 55 West 42nd Street. I knew nothing about it until I received your memorandum this morning.

All of us are well aware of the difficulties of limitation of space under which you have labored. But those same difficulties have applied, in some instances to an even greater degree, as in the Legal Department, to other members of the staff. We have been informed that we shall probably be able to move into new offices sometime in August. I am, therefore, unable to approve your action in renting an office, particularly without having consulted with any of the administrative officers, and shall not favor reimbursement of any expenditures, which I presume will include any cost of moving which may have been incurred.

As for the date of the Pan-African Committee meeting, you have been informed in various memoranda of the efforts which I have made to arrange for a full meeting of the committee. I am communicating with the out-of-town members of the committee to see if it will be possible for them to be present for a meeting on July 2nd. If they and the members who reside in New York are able to attend a meeting on that date, it will be set for July 2nd.

Let me sum up what is said in this and in one or two previous memoranda by pointing out that over a period of years we have succeeded in building up a spirit and procedure of cooperation among the various departments of the Association's work. Unless there is mutual cooperation and responsibility by all departments, there will be lost one of the Association's most valued assets. If one department is permitted to operate independently of others, there will inevitably develop in time an unwillingness on the part of other departments to function as integral parts of the total organization. I am certain that you would not approve of this, and I hope that I may have your cooperation.

July 5, 1945

To The Board of Directors:

When I joined the N.A.A.C.P. in September, 1944, I was promised by the committee which engaged me that I would have two offices which I said were necessary for my work. The secretary undertook to secure me this office space, but to date has not succeeded. While he was absent in the Pacific I used his office and installed my books. When he returned, I was deprived of his office and had no access to my books. I asked relief repeatedly, and the Board voted $50 a month rental when an office was secured, but the secretary was still not able to find space and did not answer my memorandum dated April 10th on the matter nor acknowledge it.

After returning from San Francisco, I started looking for an office and secured one for $100 per month. I notified the secretary, offering to pay the $50 extra myself if the Board did not approve. The Secretary complained that my selecting an office was an infringement on his prerogative and that he would not consent. I replied that he had himself been seeking an office for me and that the fact that I had found one was no invasion of his rights except as to the amount of rent.

I moved to the new office July 6th. I must have such an office if I am to fulfill my contract already signed with the Viking Press to write a book on African colonies[1]. The writing was postponed for my duties at San Francisco. I must for this work have my books and space. Under somewhat similar circumstances the secretary himself worked in a separate office last summer to write his book. It is a technical objection that I did personally what the Board had requested the secretary to do, and what the secretary had repeatedly promised to do. I have no desire to invade the authority of any official or to disrupt the harmony of this organization in any degree. The actual money involved is unimportant. It is important for me to have a chance to work for the best interests of the Association and of the Negro race, and I ask the Board to help me do this.

W.E.B. Du Bois

July 5, 1945

Memorandum To Dr. Du Bois From Mr. White:

I have neither time, energy nor inclination to give to exchange of memoranda, but I want in fairness to you to know in advance what I shall say to the Board with respect to certain items in your memorandum of July 5th. You state that "under somewhat similar circumstances the Secretary himself worked in a separate office to write his book." The expenses of the office I used were paid in toto by myself, no penny of it being charged to the NAACP. In addition, this was on my own time, being three weeks of the month's vacation due me and, incidentally, my first vacation in seven years. I see no parallel whatever between the two circumstances, particularly as I was using my own and not the Association's time in which to write *A Rising Wind*.

You refer repeatedly to "prerogative." The issue is not one of any executive's prerogative, but one of administrative procedure.

July 17, 1946

My dear Dr. Du Bois:

I transmit to you herewith the following action taken by the Board of Directors at its meeting in Cincinnati on July 7:

Voted: That in contracting for office space for the office of the Director of Special Research without the knowledge or consent of the Secretary, or in his absence, the Assistant Secretary, the Director of Special Research exceeded his authority. When thereafter the Secretary was notified and did not approve the

1. This book was *The World and Africa: An Inquiry into the Part Which Africa Has Played in World History* (New York: Viking, 1947). Its preface is dated May 1946.

removal, the Director of Special Research further exceeded his authority by proceeding with his plans and moving from the offices of the Association to new quarters. In these circumstances the Board of Directors disallows the expenditure of any funds for rental of or removal to the space now occupied by the Director of Special Research.

Voted: That Dr. Du Bois be required to submit to the Budget Director a factual justification of his request for a clerical assistant in addition to a research assistant; and that decision be made by the Secretary and the Budget Director.

Voted: That the Committee on the Pan African Congress determine, with power to act, whether a Pan African Congress should be held; that among the items considered be Program, Follow-up, Costs.

Voted: That before the proposal (of pamphlet publications) be considered, Dr. Du Bois be requested to comply with the request of the Committee that he submit to the Committee a memorandum outlining the series of pamphlets referred to in connection with his submission of the pamphlet, "Africans' Claims," together with his suggestions as to methods of printing, distribution, advertising, selling, etc.

Ever sincerely,
Walter White
Secretary

New York City, December 21, 1945

Dear Dr. Du Bois:

As we begin a new year it is necessary that we reach an understanding and definite agreement regarding the relation of the Department of Special Research to other departments of the NAACP.

During the year 1945 certain actions by yourself seriously interfered with the smooth operation of the NAACP as a whole. Specifically, among others, are the following:

(1) The correspondence you had with an individual in Dayton, Ohio, which you later used in columns in the *Chicago Defender*, stating that while you were opposed to segregation, Negroes must recognize the gains they may obtain from segregated schools. When our Dayton branch appeared before the Board of Education to protest the extension of segregated schools in that city, they were confronted with your statement and the Superintendent of Schools dismissed their complaint saying that you, as a national executive of the NAACP, had taken the position in favor of segregated schools. I was informed in Dayton recently that this had cost the branch to lose a number of memberships from persons who resented any NAACP national officer defending segregation.

(2) Your action in moving from 69 Fifth Avenue to 55 West 42nd Street without either consultation with or approval by any responsible executive and

your attitude in your memorandum to the Board in which you stated that "with or without the Secretary's consent" you were going to move.

(3)   Your appearance before a Senate Committee in connection with the San Francisco Charter without notifying the Association or ascertaining what plans it had which cut across Association plans and also got us into difficulty with the press because they were not given notice of your appearance.

It is imperative to the successful smooth operation of the Association that all departments function as integral parts of the Association as a whole. I would like to have assurance from you that this can be accomplished. One of the difficulties, in my opinion, has arisen from the request you made of Mr. Wilkins as Acting Secretary when I was overseas that the mail of the Department of Special Research be not opened and that it be treated in an entirely different fashion from mail addressed to other executives. In the light of the Dayton situation it will be necessary that all mail be handled precisely the same for all executives with your secretary making a digest of mail to be supplied to other executives so that each of us knows what is going on in other departments.

Will you be good enough to let me have your reaction to these requests.

> Ever sincerely,
> Walter White

December 26, 1945

Memorandum to Dr. Du Bois from Mr. White
(Copy to Mr. Wilkins, Budget Director)

When I approved your memorandum of November 29th requesting permission to select two desks for yourself and Miss Diggs, and chairs, waste-paper baskets and a tree for coats I did so on the assumption that you would purchase desks and other equipment in keeping with that used by other executives. It is therefore with surprise that I see the bills from Berry, Dickie and Stettler totaling $671.15, including

1 walnut desk	$260.00
1 red leather revolving armchair	68.00
1 red leather desk lamp, with bulb	30.00
2 walnut armchairs	50.00
2 brown leather armchairs	87.00
1 walnut revolving armchair, brown leather	68.68
1 red leather ashtray	3.50

The desks used by other executives cost $60.00 each. The desk in my office which was bought while I was out of the country, cost only $125.00—less than half the one which you have just purchased. The walnut hat-tree purchased for me cost only $9.75 as against $24.00 for the one you bought.

I cannot approve the purchase of such expensive furniture.

I understand that you have additional furniture on order for Miss Diggs. That must be of the same quality as the rest of the general office.

We are informed by Messrs. Berry, Dickie and Stettler that you have on order over two hundred dollars worth of steel shelving. I did not authorize this. You requested "the services of a carpenter and cabinet maker to arrange and add to the bookcases." Mr. Wilkins informs me that he told Miss Diggs to inquire of the Blank Company about the cost of steel shelving. It is Mr. Wilkins' impression that Blank's prices are lower than those of Berry, Dickie and Stettler. Was inquiry made by Miss Diggs or yourself before the order was placed?

Du Bois had gone to his Baltimore home for the Christmas holidays, so that just when he saw White's furniture memorandum is not certain. But on December 27, 1945 he sent a night letter to Arthur B. Spingarn in New York City.

[Baltimore], December 27, 1945

[To Arthur B. Spingarn]
Night Letter
Desire a place on program of Annual Meeting to defend myself against the attacks of Walter White. Am forwarding correspondence. Wire me date of meeting and kindly arrange conference between me, you and Dr. Wright before meeting. Plan to leave here January second but will leave sooner if necessary.

W.E.B. Du Bois

To the foregoing, Spingarn replied late in the afternoon of 28 December 1945 with a telegram to Du Bois in Baltimore.

[New York City], December 28, 1945

Telegram received. Annual meeting January seventh. In my opinion matter has no place at annual meeting but should be taken up at meeting of board of directors. Will discuss this further with you upon your return.[1]

Arthur B. Spingarn

1. These differences and clashes persisted throughout 1946 and 1947, when Du Bois's second employment by the NAACP terminated. Profound political and ideological disagreements were fundamental in this matter, as later correspondence will help demonstrate. Du Bois's chapter "I Return to the NAACP" in his posthumously published *Autobiography* (pp. 326–39) is especially illuminating on the sources and nature of the differences.

1946

Again for 1946, as for 1945, Du Bois's public life may be divided into his problems and quarrels with Walter White, his activities in the sphere of international affairs, and other interests relating largely to internal United States matters.

The confrontation with White, which reached a critical stage late in 1945, continued into the following year.

New York City, January 3, 1946

My dear Mr. White:

Answering your letter of December twenty-first, may I say

1. Persons in the Department of Education of Dayton quoted not from a letter of mine but from my statement on segregation as made in my autobiography published in 1940. A member of the Dayton Branch wrote to ask me if I was correctly quoted. I replied with a statement of my general attitude but was careful to add that I was passing no judgment on the current controversy.

2. The Committee on Foreign Affairs of the United States Senate invited me to testify on the proposed UNO Charter. They did not mention the NAACP, and in my first sentence I stated that my testimony represented my personal opinion and not that of any organization. Mr. White was also asked to testify and my appearance in no way hindered him from so doing.

3. I rejoined the NAACP at the request of the president of the Association, the Chairman of the Executive Committee and the Secretary. I had not before then dreamed of returning nor been asked to do so. I had at the time three other offers of employment. I preferred the NAACP, but I hesitated in accepting until I had thorough understanding with the officials above and with a special committee. By personal conference and correspondence we came to apparent agreement and that agreement I finally put in writing and sent to the officials and the committee as embodying my understanding of the conditions upon which I was to rejoin the organization.

One of the requests that I made of the committee was that I should have for my work two offices: one for myself and my books and one for my assistant and other clerical help. I asked this because I have a library of two thousand five hundred volumes collected over long years and at considerable cost, which in its line is unequalled and which is absolutely necessary to my work. I have also an accumulation of letters, papers and pamphlets covering fifty years of active life.

When I reported for work in September, 1944, I was assigned a single office eight feet wide, separated by thin board partitions from two of the busiest and noisiest offices in the building. The Secretary explained that this assignment was temporary, and that he was searching for suitable accommodations, outside the building if unobtainable within. I waited three months. Finally, I was assigned the Secretary's office in addition to my own, while he was absent in the Pacific. I had temporary bookcases built, unpacked about half of my books and settled down to work.

In May the Secretary returned permanently to occupy his office. I was worse off than before. My books and part of my files were in the Secretary's office, to which I had no right of access. I made written and urgent appeal to the Secretary and received no reply.

Thereupon, I secured an office outside the building to be used in conjunction with my own. I notified the Secretary of my action, offering to pay part of the rent if he considered one hundred dollars a month too high. The Secretary replied refusing to consent to my removal under any condition and offering no other relief or solution. I considered this a direct repudiation of the understanding upon which I had entered the service of the Association. I therefore moved a part of my books and files to the new office, leaving the rest in the old. I then appealed to the Board of Directors asking to be heard personally in my defense.

The Board met in Cincinnati and without permitting me to appear before them declared that in moving I had "exceeded my authority," and that the Association would not pay the rent of the new office. I considered the decision unjust, but I paid out of my own funds four hundred dollars for four months rent and seventy-six dollars for moving expenses. I visited the old office daily for mail and consultation until, after two months, the Secretary turned that office over to his new assistant. My books and files remained piled at one end.

When the new building was occupied I again asked for adequate office space. The Secretary declared that he could furnish only one of the smaller offices. I submitted again, moved into the office and have been trying since to adjust myself to its limitations.

The Secretary now asks me in view of my actions what attitude I propose to take toward his decisions in the future. I wish to make my answer clear: I will in the future comply as I have complied in the past with any request or decision of the Secretary which I consider in reasonable accord with the understanding on which I consented to rejoin the staff of the NAACP. If, on the other hand, the action of the Secretary seems to me in clear contravention of this understanding I shall appeal from his decision to the Board of Directors.

I can best illustrate my meaning by referring to the new demand of the Secretary to open and censor my mail. I will not permit anyone but myself to open my personal mail. No suggestion of such demand was made when I was consulted as to the conditions of my return. Had it been made I should have refused to assent. My mail is not personal in the narrow sense but it has grown up from fifty years of life and covers my whole career of activity, research and writing. I shall be glad to turn over to the Secretary my correspondence that concerns him or the work of the Association. But I will not allow him or anyone else to open mail addressed personally to me.

In view of this serious difference of opinion, I agree with the Secretary that it is time for a careful reconsideration of my position in the organization. During my incumbency of this office I have strained every nerve to serve the Association to the best of my ability: I have refrained from interfering in any way with the policy of the organization; whenever I have written or spoken I have made it clear that I was expressing my own opinions; I have lectured on subjects which lay within the scope of my department and my recognized fields of knowledge.

In the last year and a half, I have delivered over forty lectures in fourteen states and two foreign lands; I have published one book and contributed chapters to four others; I have taken part in six international conferences and in three of these active part, including the Colonial Conference in New York and the Pan African Congress in England, over both of which I presided. I have written in this time over one hundred articles and reviews and answered correspondence from every continent and nearly every state in the union.

I have recognized from the start that in the case of one who for so long a time has expressed frankly and aggressively opinions on controversial subjects, there would inevitably arise the problem as to how far I could talk and write without compromising the NAACP. I have sought earnestly to avoid any such misunderstanding and yet to preserve, as in justice to myself I must, my freedom of expression. I am gratified that only in one case, that of Dayton, have I been accused of misrepresenting the Association. And in that case, as I have shown, the accusation was untrue. I want to emphasize the fact that in sixteen months of employment in New York, I have not been furnished office accommodations which give me even a fair chance of functioning properly in my work.

Unless I have failed to carry on my work in accord with my promises, or unless the agreements made with me were invalid and misunderstood by those who engaged me, it is obviously unjust to change them without consultation and new understanding. I am sending copies of this correspondence to the President of the Association and the Chairman of the Board and demanding a hearing before the Board of Directors.

Very sincerely,
W.E.B. Du Bois

January 4, 1946

Memorandum to Mr. White:

1. On November thirtieth you approved my memorandum concerning new furniture for my office and re-building and extension of my temporary wooden

bookcases. You suggested a reliable firm with whom I might deal. You left it apparently to my discretion as to how much I should spend.

2.   Office furniture today is scarce and most of the ordinary models are not on the market. The desk model which I wished is larger than the ordinary small desk because the desks in this small office must serve both as desks and tables. I chose medium priced desks among those available. The same is true of the other furniture.

3.   After consulting with the firm whom you recommended and with Mr. Wilkins, I concluded that in the long run, and taking into account possibilities of removal, steel bookcases were nearly as cheap as building and re-building these wooden cases. I asked bids from your firm and also from the firm recommended by Mr. Wilkins. The latter firm to whom I wrote December eleventh has not yet replied. I, therefore, ordered the shelving from the firm whom you recommended. I am told that there could not be much difference between the bids of the two firms as the shelving comes practically from the same sources.

4.   I do not think my expenditure for office equipment is extravagant according to present conditions, but if this expenditure is larger than you wish to allow and since what I have ordered is practically a matter of contract which we are bound to carry out, I suggest that the NAACP pay such part of this expenditure as you consider reasonable, and I will undertake to pay the balance.

W.E.B. Du Bois

A brief note from White indicates that the board decided in Du Bois's favor at this time.

New York City, March 1, 1946

Dear Dr. Du Bois:

I am herewith informing you of your appointment for the calendar year beginning January 1st as Director of Special Research. I regret my absence from the city has delayed this formal notification.

Ever sincerely,
Walter White
Secretary

Further correspondence between White and Du Bois in October 1946 reflects the stiffness in the relationship that continued to exist. Letters presented elsewhere in this volume in connection with Du Bois's major interests in 1946, indicate ongoing tension.

October 23, 1946

Memorandum to Dr. Du Bois from Mr. White:

Do you know how George Streator of the New York *Times* gained possession of a copy of your memorandum of October 10th [published hereafter pp. 120–24] in response to my request to members of the staff to suggest subjects for discussion at the week-end conference?

My reason for asking this is because Mr. Streator called Mr. Wilkins and said that he had a copy and wanted a statement from us as the basis for a news story he was planning to write in the *Times*. Fortunately, Mr. Wilkins was able to convince Mr. Streator that this was strictly an inter-office memorandum and that the conference was one of staff members solely to discuss ways and means of improving our machinery and that it was not a matter which should have gone outside of this office.

October 25, 1946
Memorandum to Dr. Du Bois from Mr. White:

Will you be good enough to advise me if you know how George S. Schuyler obtained a copy of your memorandum in reply to mine to all staff members asking for suggestions of subjects to be discussed at the weekend staff conference?

October 28, 1946
Memorandum to Mr. White:

Answering your memoranda of October 23 and October 25th, may I say that my statement to the staff was sent only to the staff members. However, if Mr. Streator or Mr. Schuyler had asked me for a copy, I should have been glad to furnish it. I did not regard it as confidential in any sense.

W. E. B Du Bois

In March 1945 the Phelps-Stokes Fund published Encyclopedia of the Negro: Preparatory Volume with Reference Lists and Reports, *by Du Bois and Guy B. Johnson (then of the University of North Carolina), with the assistance of Irene Diggs, Agnes Donohugh, Guion Johnson, Rayford Logan, and L. D. Reddick, and with an introduction by Anson Phelps Stokes. A revised and slightly enlarged edition of this book was published in 1946. It is to the first edition that a letter from Eric F. Goldman, then an assistant professor of history at Princeton, refers.*

* Eric Frederick Goldman was born in 1915 in Washington, D.C. He was educated at Johns Hopkins University, taught there briefly, worked at *Times* magazine, and from 1943 to the present has been teaching at Princeton. From 1963 to 1966 he served as a special consultant to President Lyndon B. Johnson. He edited *Historiography and Urbanization* (1941); among his best-known books are *Rendezvous with Destiny* (1952), *The Crucial Decade* (1956), *The Tragedy of Lyndon Johnson: A Historian's Personal Interpretation* (1969), and *John Bach McMaster: American Historian* (1943, 1971).

Princeton, New Jersey, January 14, 1946

Dear Dr. Du Bois:

I have just finished going over the printed prospectus of the *Encyclopedia of the Negro* and I am so delighted at seeing so thorough and useful a work under way that I venture to make a suggestion which I hope will be helpful. I notice under the proposed list of major subjects that there is no entry on "Historiography" or "History." Some Negro historians seem to be treated in separate articles but I gather that the plan does not call for one sweeping article which shall treat the rise of Negro history.

Perhaps it is because my own research interests have been primarily historiographical, but I do feel that Negro historiography is one of the most neglected of all fields. The *Jernegan Essays in American Historiography*, a more or less standard book, treats no Negro. Michael Kraus' *A History of American History* has only one paragraph.[1] All this seems to me an appalling neglect when the story is so significant a one, both for the intellectual history of the Negro and for the intellectual history of the United States. I wonder if it would fit into your plans to include such an article.

With best wishes for the success of the project,

Sincerely yours,

Eric F. Goldman

New York City, January 18, 1946

My dear Mr. Goldman:

Thank you for your letter of January fourteenth. The prefatory volume of the *Encyclopedia of the Negro* falls far short of being the scientific contribution we had in mind. Today we have just sent a revised edition to the printers which may be a little more satisfactory.

The history and historiography of the Negro was omitted from the first edition because so little has been done on the matter. By general consent Negro history has either been attributed to other people or lost sight of entirely.

I thank you very much for your word of appreciation.

Very sincerely yours,

W. E. B. Du Bois

At the 1946 annual meeting of the NAACP, *the board of directors did not suggest the reappointment of Oswald Garrison Villard to his position as one of its vice presidents. Villard (1872–1949) had been, of course, one of the founders of the* NAACP *and its staunch supporter ever since 1910. Du Bois's relationship*

---

1. William T. Hutchinson, ed., *The Marcus W. Jernegan Essays in American Historiography* (Chicago: Universityof Chicago Press, 1937, 1972); Michael Kraus, *A History of American History* (New York: Farrar and Rinehart, 1937).

with him—not always pleasant—went back to 1905; evidences of this connection can be found in the first two volumes of Du Bois's correspondence.

It is likely that Villard was dropped as a reaction to his consistent pacifism, which he maintained even during the Second World War. It is possible, also, that an article he published in the Negro Digest *in January 1946, entitled, "The Strategy of Good Manners," did not endear him to other board members; in this essay Villard suggested that bad manners, allegedly common among Black people, made it difficult for white people to support effectively the just demands of Afro-Americans for equal rights.*

The board's action incensed Du Bois.

New York City, February 13, 1946

My dear Mr. Villard:

I want to tell you how ashamed I am of the action of the NAACP in removing your name from the list of vice-presidents. This will not hurt you but it certainly hurts the Association. I did not attend the meeting in which this action was taken and just learned of it yesterday.

Very sincerely yours,
W. E. B. Du Bois

New York City, February 16, 1946

Dear Du Bois,

Many thanks for your note and the sentiment it contains. It gave me the first news that I had been dropped, as a letter from Miss Ovington, received in the same mail, assumed I had heard and left me without any idea of what she was writing about. You remember the old German saying "Undank ist der Welt Zorn"?[1] This move would seem to mean that a colored group has caught up with the whites in practicing intolerance!

Of course it is based upon a misunderstanding and I shall probably ask my right as a member of the NAACP to appear before the Board and explain the situation. It made a mistake in not asking me to appear before passing judgment—there it injured itself.

I assure you this action leaves no sting. I am about at the end of my active life and my deafness makes me useless as a board member—indeed I have been of little help for years past. A far, far greater loss to the Board is the death of William Allan Neilson.[2] He was a prince of men and an extremely wise counsellor. His loss concerns me greatly—my expulsion does not.

Cordially,
Oswald Garrison Villard

1. This may be rendered, "Ingratitude is the world's passion."
2. William Allan Neilson was born in Scotland in 1869 and died in Connecticut 13 February 1946. He was educated at Edinburgh and Harvard; taught in Scotland and Canada and then at Bryn Mawr, Columbia, and Harvard; and was president of Smith

The last white president of Fisk University was Thomas E. Jones, who served from 1926 to 1946. At the beginning of Jones's twentieth year of service, his resignation impended and the question of a successor became acute. By this time Atlanta, Howard, Wilberforce, and Lincoln (Pa.) universities all had Black presidents, and that consideration presented the white-dominated board of trustees at Fisk with quite a problem.

Fisk was Du Bois's alma mater; he loved the school and was an active alumnus. His intercession had been largely responsible for the resignations of two previous Fisk presidents—James G. Merrill in 1908 and Fayette A. McKenzie in 1925—and so in this crisis Du Bois again activated himself.

New York City, June 19, 1946

Dear Dr. [Ernest R.] Alexander:[1]

I have talked to [W. L.] Imes and [M. V.] Boutté and some other Fisk graduates and I think perhaps it would be timely for me to say a word publicly concerning the presidency at Fisk; but I should be glad to have your opinion first.

My own feeling is that there is only one candidate for the office who is fitted by training and experience to be president of Fisk University. He happens to be colored but that is irrelevant. He is Charles Wesley, President of Wilberforce.[2]

The power to appoint him lies in the hands of three classes of people: Northern philanthropists, Southern liberals and the alumni of Fisk. The Northern philanthropists have gotten in the habit of kowtowing and being entirely subservient in opinion to Southern liberals. The Southern liberals are not wholly liberal and are sometimes selfishly desirous of the school trade and at other times determined to see that Negroes keep in their places and consequently prefer either a white man as president whom they can handle or a white folk's "nigger." The alumni apparently cannot concentrate on a demand for Wesley.

College from 1917 through 1939. He edited Chaucer, Milton, Shakespeare and was an associate editor of the *Harvard Classics.*

1. Dr. Ernest R. Alexander (1892–1960) graduated from Fisk in 1914 and received his medical degree from the University of Vermont in 1919. He opened an office in Harlem the next year and served in Bellevue and Harlem Hospitals until November 1959, less than a year before his death. In May 1958, he received Fisk's alumni award. There is no written response from Alexander to Du Bois's letter, but since both men lived in New York City it is likely that they met or discussed this question via the telephone.

2. Charles Harris Wesley was born in Kentucky in 1891 and attended Fisk, Harvard, and Wilberforce universities. From 1913 to 1941 he was on the faculty of Howard University; from 1942 to 1962 he was president of Central State College in Wilberforce, Ohio, and most recently he served as executive director of the Association for the Study of Negro Life and History.

If you think that my public suggestion of the above ideas and their implications would do good, I would be glad to make them; and in that case please send me the names and addresses of the committee which is to select the president. I will submit the letter to you and others before I send it.

Let me hear from you at your convenience.

Very sincerely yours,
W. E. B. Du Bois

Some five weeks later—Du Bois meanwhile having conferred with Alexander and perhaps other Fisk alumni—he was ready to publish views on the Fisk situation and turned for appropriate vehicle to the Nation, *for which he had written often and indeed specifically on questions concerning Black higher education.* He wrote to Freda Kirchwey, editor of that magazine.*

New York City, July 26, 1946

My dear Miss Kirchwey:

There is a situation developing at Fisk University which I think calls for some publicity. Fisk has always had white presidents, but a new president is being elected and the best man mentioned for the job is colored, Charles Wesley, a graduate and trustee of Fisk. He is a Doctor of Philosophy from Harvard, former dean at Howard with administrative experience for four years as president of Wilberforce and a writer of distinction. No other candidate approaches him in capability or availability. The alumni demand him almost unanimously. The trustees have not yet elected him apparently for three reasons: first, they hesitate to put a Negro in this job who will administer a college with an endowment of three million dollars; secondly, the alumni object to present financial policies which include annually $12,000 for "publicity" to the New York office and $22,000 for handling the investments; and thirdly, certain Southern leaders of the United Negro Endowment Fund and Southern white trustees of Fisk have said frankly that they have defined as radical any person who supports the FEPC or the CIO. These facts are clearly established.

This brings up a serious problem not only of race discrimination but as to interference of wealth with education. Wesley is not radical but he supported the FEPC and has written a sympathetic book on Negro union labor.[1] I am wondering if you can find space in the *Nation* for a short statement of this

* These articles included "Negroes in College," *Nation* 122 (3 March 1926):228–30, and "The Hampton Strike," *Nation* 125 (2 November 1927):471–72.

1. Charles H. Wesley, *Negro Labor in the United States, 1850–1925* (New York: Vanguard Press, 1927, 1967).

sort which I would like to write. May I hear from you at your convenience?[2]
Very sincerely yours,
W. E. B. Du Bois

Wesley was not appointed president of Fisk; the ensuing letters from Du Bois from later in 1946 may suggest additional reasons why he was not selected.
Charles S. Johnson (1893–1956), who was chosen to succeed Thomas Jones and became Fisk's first Black president, had been in charge of Fisk's sociology department; he was a board member of the Rosenwald Fund (1943–48) and a very close friend of the president of that influential fund, Edwin R. Embree. Johnson was a prolific author and editor and was probably the most widely known Black sociologist in the United States during his lifetime.

New York City, October 1, 1946
Dear Dr. Alexander:
On September 20th I had a long talk with Brownlee of the American Missionary Association about Fisk.[1] He told me very confidentially that Johnson had threatened to resign from Fisk University if Wesley was elected president. Afterwards I sent him a memorandum a copy of which I enclose.
Very sincerely yours,
W. E. B. Du Bois

[Enclosure]
September 23, 1946
Dear Mr. Brownlee:
Thinking over our conversation about Fisk, there are two matters I would like to stress:
1. Do not assume without careful investigation that the amount of Fisk money going to the office of the Vice-President of the Board is small; there is strong testimony that it has reached $12,000 a year. Look into this thoroughly.
2. For a Negro scholar of prominence to resign because he did not want to work under a Negro president would be a difficult matter to live down. Any man who can work under Tom Jones can work under Charles Wesley, UNLESS the matter of color is decisive. And it is precisely that which influential alumni are already charging.
Very sincerely yours,
W. E. B. Du Bois

2. The response was positive and Du Bois published "A Crisis at Fisk," *Nation* 143 (7 September 1946):269–70.
1. Frederick Leslie Brownlee (1883-1962) was born in Ohio and educated at Ohio State University and at Union Theological Seminary in New York City. He served various churches in Ohio and New York and from 1920 to 1950 was general secretary of the American Missionary Association and a trustee of Fisk.

In October 1946, the trustees of Fisk selected Charles S. Johnson to succeed Jones as president. Bitterness persisted, especially among some alumni; a few even suggested an effort to reverse the appointment. In this connection, Du Bois wrote to Ernest Alexander.

New York City, November 9, 1946

Dear Dr. Alexander:

My feeling is that since Mr. Johnson has been elected President of Fisk University the attitude of those who preferred someone else should be that of complete neutrality and silence. We should wait and see. I do not think that we should undertake any campaign of ouster. It is practically impossible today with the university set-up as it is to get rid of a president unless the charges against him are clear and of tremendous importance. No such charge in my opinion can be brought against Mr. Johnson. Moreover there is a possibility that he will make a good president for Fisk; I doubt it, but it may come true. He has the ear of the foundations and he will probably get the money that Fisk so sorely needs. He will probably rebuild the university physically and may be able to get a faculty about him of the sort of teachers that Fisk needs. At any rate, the only thing that we can do now, it seems to me, is to keep still and give him a chance.

Very sincerely yours,
W. E. B. Du Bois

Late in August 1946, Paul Robeson wired Du Bois an invitation to join in an anti-lynching demonstration. Du Bois's response was positive; as will be seen, Walter White interpreted this response as one of the counts against Du Bois.

New York City, August 30, 1946

Dr. W. E. B. Du Bois

The alarming rise of lynchings and continued immunity from prosecution of the lynchers necessitates dramatic, effective action of democratic Americans on a national scale.[1] Will you join Bartley Crum[2] and myself in issuing a call for a

---

1. The *New York Times* of 29 December 1946 (p. 7) reported from Tuskegee Institute that in 1946 there had been six lynchings, as contrasted with one in 1945. The institute added that four "borderline" cases of lynching occurred in 1946 but were not included in the total "because of insufficient evidence." Furthermore, there were in 1946 at least seventeen instances in which lynchings were prevented. All those lynched in 1946 were Black people.

2. Bartley C. Crum (1900–1959) was born in California and practiced law there and in New York City. In 1942 he served as a special counsel to President Roosevelt's Committee on Fair Employment Practices; in 1945 he was a consultant to the United States delegation at the founding of the United Nations; and in 1946 he was a mem-

gathering in Washington on September 22, 23 in commemoration of Lincoln's projection of the Emancipation Proclamation to launch an American crusade to end lynching? This crusade will express the determination of the American people that the lynchers be apprehended and prosecuted and that the Congress of the United States enact a Federal anti-lynch law. Please wire your reply 23 West 26th Street, New York City.

Paul Robeson

September 19, 1946

Memorandum to Dr. Du Bois from Walter White:

I want you to see the enclosed copy of memorandum from Mr. Frank Williams of our staff regarding the experience he had in attempting to follow through NAACP's position on the matter of an unfortunate conflict between two groups with respect to the current wave of lynching and the fight for anti-lynching legislation. I want you also to see copy of personal letter I wrote Paul Robeson explaining why I could not as Secretary of the NAACP nor as an individual participate in this movement.[1]

I want you also to have background of the facts. On August 6th the NAACP invited some fifty or more organizations to send representatives to a meeting held here to discuss joint action against the rising tide of mob violence. It was said by a number of those present that it was one of the most broadly representative groups that had ever been gathered. Out of that meeting came the National Emergency Committee Against Mob Violence, with an Executive Committee consisting of Arthur B. Spingarn, Charles G. Bolte, Edward L. Bernays, Allan Knight Chalmers, Clyde Miller, Mrs. Alfred E. Mudge, Rev. Bernard J. Sheil, Walter White and Max Yergan. This meeting adopted the

---

ber of the Anglo-American Commission on Inquiry on Palestine. Crum was also a member of the National Legal Committee of the NAACP.

1. White refers to Franklin H. Williams, born in 1917 in Flushing, New York, and admitted to the New York bar in 1945. At the time this letter was written, Williams was on the legal staff of the NAACP and was one of its executive officers. He has since held such significant offices as assistant attorney general of California (1959-61), United States Ambassador to Ghana (1965-68), and director of the Urban Center of Columbia University (1968-70). Williams is now president of the Phelps-Stokes Fund. His memorandum to White, dated 17 September 1946, complained of the competing crusade against lynching headed by Robeson and supported by Du Bois and by James Egert Allen, then president of the New York State Conference of NAACP branches. Williams stated that, against his protests, the Metropolitan Area Council of the American Veterans Committee voted to support the Robeson effort; he added that the support of this effort by Du Bois was "both confusing and prejudicial" to efforts of the NAACP. White's letter to Robeson, dated 10 September 1946, was marked "Personal and Confidential"; it told of the formation in August 1946 of the National Emergency Committee Against Mob Violence and gave reasons why White could not support the Robeson effort.

program copy of which is attached.[2] This committee is actively functioning, one of its jobs being the implementation of the number one recommendation, namely a conference with President Truman which was held today at 11:45 A.M.

Some time later on I received a telegram from Paul Robeson asking to join him and forty others to discuss plans for a coalition to oppose mob violence. I wired regrets for the reasons, first that on that date and hour the Political Action Committee voted at our Cincinnati Conference was meeting here in the office and second, because such a coalition had already been formed. When I was invited to participate in the Washington meeting I sent Paul the letter which is attached.

To return to Mr. Williams' predicament, I suggested to him that he inform the Metropolitan Area Council of the AVC [American Veterans Committee] that you had signed the Call for the Crusade Against Lynching wholly and solely in your individual capacity and that this in no wise committed the NAACP. But if you will note from his memorandum, this was without effect. The National AVC had refused to participate stating as did the CIO, the Federal Council of Churches and other groups that they were participating in the organization formed by the NAACP and would not have anything to do with the competing group.

It would be most helpful on issues which are an integral part of the Association's work like the fight against lynching if inquiry could be made by you on such matters inasmuch as the calling of this conference has tremendously complicated and overburdened the office. We have had to answer inquiries from many people who are confused and many of whom believe that the Association is participating in this Washington meeting because of your name on it. This in no wise, however, is meant to influence your judgment. It would just save all of us time and headaches if the facts are obtained before decision is made.

Walter White

23 September 1946

Memorandum to Mr. White:

Your memorandum of September 19 was the first notice I have had of your

---

2. The program contained ten points: the first suggested appointment of a delegation to visit President Truman and Attorney General Tom Clark. Others suggested efforts to involve churches, chambers of commerce, and unions in combat against mob violence and racial prejudice; the reconvening of Congress for passage of anti-lynching legislation; a letter-writing campaign to Congress and to media; and visits to State officials. The *Crisis* of November 1946 (53:339) has a photograph of the delegation meeting with President Truman; on the following page is a story of this meeting, headlined, "Truman Promises to End Mob Violence."

new Anti-Lynching movement. My cooperation was evidently not needed. It was certainly not asked. If I had been notified, I would gladly have cooperated. On the other hand I have been fighting lynching for forty years, and I have a right to let the world know that I am still fighting. I therefore gladly endorsed the Robeson movement which asked my cooperation. This did not and could not have interfered with the NAACP program. The fight against mob law is the monopoly of no one person—no one organization.

W. E. B. Du Bois

October 2, 1946

Memorandum from Mr. White to Dr. Du Bois:

With further reference to your memorandum regarding your participation in the Crusade Against Lynching which was formed in competition to the National Emergency Committee Against Mob Violence formed on August 6th at the call of the NAACP, I wish to call your attention to this further evidence of confusion.

Gloster Current has sent to my desk a letter from the Executive Secretary of our Philadelphia Branch received in answer to special delivery letter Mr. Current had sent to them and other branches explaining why the NAACP was not participating in the Washington meeting.[1]

Mr. Shorter writes, "since the name of one of our National Officers appeared on the Call Release, we did not feel that we could fully comply with the request of your office."

May I add that the tone of your memorandum was distinctly surprising in its tartness. I had sought to make my memorandum to you explaining the complication which had arisen as friendly as possible so that you would understand the facts.[2] You can imagine, therefore, my surprise at the manner in which you received my memorandum.

Walter White

1. Gloster Current, formerly head of the Detroit branch of the NAACP, was appointed director of branches on 1 September 1946. Robeson's "American Crusade to End Lynching" also sent a delegation to visit Truman, on 23 September 1946, after a mass meeting held the previous evening at the Lincoln Memorial. Mayor William O'Dwyer of New York City proclaimed 23 September 1946 as "End Lynching Day" as a result of a request from the city council on behalf of the American Crusade to End Lynching. See New York Times, 22, 23, 24 September 1946.

2. White's flat statement in his previous memorandum that the Robeson effort "was formed in competition" to that of the NAACP would surely have been noted by Du Bois, as would the didactic tone of White's last paragraph. Du Bois would certainly also have observed White's failure to comment on the substance of his complaint: that he, Du Bois, had not even been informed of the 6 August meeting to project an anti-lynching effort.

The "ordinary" burdens of a Black person in the United States regularly confronted Du Bois, and he consistently protested. An example is a letter involving bus service in New York City at a time when employees of public transportation—except those in janitorial jobs—were solely white people.

New York City, September 25, 1946

Fifth Avenue Coach Co.
New York City
Gentlemen:

I write to complain of your service, especially the No. 2 route, which I use once or twice nearly every working day. There are usually too few buses on this route, far fewer than on any other main route. They often refuse to stop for passengers, even when not filled, and their conductors, and more especially their drivers (who do most of the talking to passengers), are insufferably rude. I stood this during the war, but it seems to me that the time has come to protest.

Tuesday, September 24, at about 5 p.m., I tried to board a No. 2 at Fifth Avenue and Fortieth Street. The first one swung out into the middle of the Avenue and refused to stop at my upraised arm, although it was plainly not filled. Its number marking as usual made it impossible to identify it. The next No. 2, plainly marked "168th St.," stopped and I got on and got a seat. Between 125th St. and 132nd Street, I heard the conductor say "155th St. only." But I thought I must have misheard. Before reaching 155th St., we were ordered off the bus. It was raining heavily; there is no car stop there; cabs were utterly out of sight and the street with three lines of traffic is dangerous to cross. I protested to the Conductor and demanded his number. He said 165; but he had no badge in sight and showed none, and I do not know whether or not he was telling the truth. Then the driver interrupted truculently and declared the car had been marked "155th St." which was not true when I boarded. There was nothing for me to do but to get out and walk in the pouring rain more than two long blocks uphill to my apartment at 409 Edgecombe Avenue.

I think this is an outrage; and when such treatment is added to the neglect of this route, the studied discourtesy of the employees, the failure to wear distinguishable badges, and the continued prayer of this company for added privileges in addition to the right to charge an exorbitant fare, I demand that something be done. The people of Harlem may be poor and black, but I trust this is not the reason for this treatment.[1]

Very truly yours,
W.E.B. Du Bois

1. On 30 September 1946, John E. McCarthy, president of the company, replied to Du Bois briefly, apologizing and promising efforts at improvement.

In the fall of 1946, Du Bois's granddaughter, DuBois Williams, entered the Northfield School for Girls in Massachusetts. Soon after getting settled there, she wrote Du Bois a newsy letter, to which the grandfather replied at some length.

New York City, October 8, 1946

Dear DuBois:

I have your nice letter and was of course planning to write you a long note on the whole philosophy of your new school life and so forth.

Your letter brings up certain specific questions and in answer I am sending you a few clippings from newspapers; also I think I will send you a six months subscription to P.M. That is a popular daily newspaper and you may like it if you read and use it. I think that it will be a good reference paper for your use in discussion. I may find some books that will help you, but of course you realize that for current history, newspapers and magazines, especially the weekly magazines, are the only recourse.

I think you are beginning to see what I mean by the higher standards of education in certain schools; they are more aware of what is going on in the world and they keep you on your toes and the competition is keen. I shall be interested to know how you stand up under it.

There is on the other hand, the matter of "race relations"; you are for the first time going to what is called a "white" school and there are two attitudes which children often develop. One is the feeling of withdrawal and isolation, homesickness for your own group and consequent unwillingness even to try to cooperate. There is a equally dangerous opposite attitude, that is the feeling that you have come into contact with unusual and super-human people who can do things better than you and your folks, and are altogether above and beyond you, so that you make every effort to bow down to them. Both of these attitudes are I am sure you see altogether wrong. These people are human beings just as you are. There are among them the good and the bad, the kind, and the cruel and they are part of the world in which you are going to live and work. Person for person they have had in their lives better food, better homes, better clothes, better training than your little colored friends in Baltimore. They have met people with good manners, and good clear English. They are not necessarily better people; they have had better opportunities.

You now have a splendid opportunity to become acquainted with them and be friendly and learn to look upon them as everyday folks and neither fawn upon them nor be unduly uncooperative and unfriendly. Be nice to those who evidently are willing to be nice to you and if there are some who withdraw from you or seem to, be studiously polite but make no undue effort to force yourself into their company.

I sent you your typewriter the other day. I hope you will use it regularly for your reports and letters and things of that kind. It is very necessary that you should learn to use a typewriter well. If there is anything else that I can get for you or any way that I can help, I shall be so glad to try to see if I can.

I have not been to Baltimore since you left but I understand that Grandmother is still improving slowly. The doctor reports that she is doing very well indeed. I shall not be able to get down there for a couple of weeks, but I telephone every once in a while.

Perhaps I forgot to be more specific about my own attitude toward these subjects you mention. The Atom Bomb calls for some understanding of physics and realization of the immense opportunity of atomic power. Of course it ought to be used for peaceful industrial purposes, replacing coal and electricity for the manufacture of power. It is a great calamity that today we think of using the atom as a weapon of war. An international understanding on the subject of the atom involves our willingness to stop making atomic bombs, destroy those which we have except as they are used for industry and share our knowledge of the atom. If we are willing to do this, I am quite sure that Russia can be induced to submit along with other people to inspection of her atomic activities. But of course in cases like that, nations must have faith in each other's honesty and good will. It is impossible for them to insure security simply by treaties.

As to the Peace Conference in Paris, that has very unfortunately gone back to imitation of the old method of power politics; that is, of setting up nations and groups of nations against each other so as to insure their defense. Possibly this was inevitable at first but we must move beyond this or the future is full of danger.

In the United States so far, the United Nations have faced a number of questions and have not made a very good record but we are looking forward to the meeting of the Assembly in the latter part of this month. We have great hopes for the future of the organization. I saw the first Assembly under the League of Nations in Geneva in 1921 and I'm going to meet Trygve Lie in the near future.

I have been making a few speeches; and a few nights ago I spoke at the 115th Street Branch of the Public Library and on the same program with Mrs. Roosevelt whom I met for the first time. I also attended a very splendid dinner at the Waldorf-Astoria celebrating the 100th anniversary of Liberia. Late in the month I am going to Columbia, South Carolina to attend the Negro Youth Conference. I shall see some of the people in Atlanta. Goodby and good-luck and please write me often and tell me all of your difficulties and joys.

Yours with love,
W.E.B. Du Bois

In his letter to his granddaughter, Du Bois referred to his evening at a branch of the New York Public Library. That event evoked a substantive letter from one of the first Black men elected to a municipal court judgeship in New York City. It was marked, "Unofficial."

Du Bois, in his response, enclosed a copy of a long memorandum he had prepared for Walter White; readers will see at once its great consequence as an expression of Du Bois's ideas at the time and also his basic differences with the leadership of the association. Judge Toney was at this time a member of the board of directors of the NAACP.*

New York City, October 10, 1946

My dear Doctor Du Bois,

After your talk the other evening at the 115th Street Branch Library a gentleman sitting near me asked you the question, "What has the American white man to lose by his mistreating of the Negro?" Your answer to him I am sure was as unsatisfactory to you as it was to your questioner. The answer was correct as far as it went, but did not go in my opinion far enough nor enough into the details of the matter, but, of course, this happens to the best of us when a question is put on the spur of the moment. In your writings you have given many better answers and more in detail to that question.

Why I am writing is that I am wondering whether or not a tract upon this subject of what white Americans lose by the mistreatment of Negroes would not be worthwhile. The losses to the American white man because of such treatment, as you have so often pointed out directly and indirectly, are moral, social, economic and cultural. Americans lose the moral strength coming from the sense of having dealt with others with fairness and justice; they lose a worthwhile element in the broadening of their views and the softening and mellowing of human relationships in social intercourse; they lose the impetus and broadening effect coming from a culture having a background and basis different from their own while at the same time it retards the development of that culture; last, but not least, they lose the economic benefits to be had by creating a market desiring and able to buy and use agricultural and industrial products and services.

I am merely making the suggestion as an outline for such a tract, but at the same time I have in mind that you are far more capable of doing this than I am. This comes from me merely as a suggestion.

I am

Yours very truly,
Charles E. Toney

---

* Charles E. Toney (1881–1951) was born in Alabama and received his law degree from Syracuse University. He started his law practice in New York City in 1905 and was elected to a municipal court judgeship in 1930. He held that position until his retirement in 1950.

New York City, November 14, 1946

My dear Mr. Toney:

Answering your letter of October 10, I am sure that a tract on the subject of what white America loses by the mistreatment of Negroes would be worthwhile; but as you see by the enclosed copy of correspondence, my efforts to have the N.A.A.C.P. publish certain information and leaflets have not been successful in the past. I should not like to propose anything further unless the N.A.A.C.P. specifically asks me to do it.

Very sincerely yours,
W.E.B. Du Bois

[Enclosure]
Memorandum to the Secretary for the N.A.A.C.P. Staff Conference
From W. E. B. Du Bois, Director of Special Research

When the flow of progress in a land or age is strong, steady and unchallenged, a suppressed group has one clear objective: the abolition of discrimination, equality of opportunity to share in the national effort and its results. This was true of the American Negro at the end of the nineteenth century and the beginning of the twentieth.

But when, as in the first half of the twentieth century, progress fails and civilization is near collapse, then the suppressed group, especially if it has begun successfully to reduce discrimination and gain some integration into the national culture of America, must adopt something beyond the negative program of resistance to discrimination, and unite with the best elements of the nation in a positive constructive program for rebuilding civilization and reorienting progress.

This revised program in the case of American Negroes must give attention to:
1. Economic illiteracy
2. The colonial peoples, and more especially, Africans
3. Education
4. Health
5. Democracy
6. Politics

Economic Illiteracy The present breakdown of civilization is fundamentally economic: the failure of human labor and sacrifice to bring happiness to the mass of men as rapidly as it increases the efficiency of labor. The leaders of two centuries have called attention to this threat to our industrial and economic organization; but the mass of people, even those of training, have not usually understood the increasingly complicated industrial structure of current society, and consequently have been in no condition radically to improve and rebuild it. Current education has permitted the man in the street to see industry as primarily a method of making individuals rich, and to regard freedom of individual initiative in business enterprise as the foundation for all progress. Again and again great thinkers have warned the world that this anarchy in industry would retain poverty, ignorance, disease and crime beyond possible reduction and culminate eventually in the suicide of war and destruction. This is what we see about us today.

To counteract this, prophets have demanded reform in industry based on curbing by government action the freedom of individual profit-making in the interest of social well-being. Such efforts have varied from palliatives like the New Deal to economic planning like T.V.A., to the O.P.A. and F.E.P.C., to English socialism and Russian Communism. Even Fascism recognized this necessity but placed the power to carry it out in the hands of irresponsible dictators and the object of its benefits was an oligarchy and not the working masses. The whole trend of the forward thinking world, before and since the war, is toward economic planning to abolish poverty, curb monopoly and the rule of wealth, spread education, insure health and practice democracy.

Here then the N.A.A.C.P. must take a stand. To do this intelligently, we must encourage study of economic organization by lectures and forums and lead the masses of Negroes and their children to clear comprehension of the problems of industry; we must not be diverted by witch-hunting for Communists, or by fear of the wealthy, or by the temptation ourselves to exploit labor, white and black, through business, gambling, or by industrial fascism.

Colonies We must look beyond the facade of luxurious cities, behind which modern civilization masquerades, and see and realize the poverty, squalor, slavery, ignorance, disease and despair under which the mass of men labor even today in our own slums, on our farms, and especially among the 200,000,000 colonial and semi-colonial peoples. Above all, we American Negroes should know that the center of the colonial problem is today in Africa; that until Africa is free, the descendants of Africa the world over cannot escape chains. We must believe Africans worthy of freedom, fit for survival and capable of civilization.

The N.A.A.C.P. should therefore put in the forefront of its program the freedom of Africa in work and wage, education and health, the complete abolition of the colonial system. A world which is One industrially and politically cannot be narrowly national in social reform.

Education From its founding in 1910, the N.A.A.C.P. has been curiously reticent on the matter of education. This was because, assuming that education of American Negroes was progressing satisfactorily, we saw at first our main duty in the task of fighting discrimination and segregation in the schools. Meantime education, especially the crucial elementary training in the three R's, has widely broken down in the world and particularly among Negroes in Africa and America. It is safe to say that today the average Negro child in the United States does not have a chance to learn to read, write and count accurately and correctly; of the army recruits, from 18 to 25, one-third of our young American Negroes could not read and write. This is simply appalling. Beyond this, higher education is deprived of adequately trained students and deterred from the facts and reform of industry.

Knowing that Democracy and social reform depend on intelligence, the N.A.A.C.P. should start a crusade for Negro education, and while not for a moment relaxing their fight on race segregation in schools, insist that segregation or no segregation, American Negro youth must be educated.

Health The health of American Negroes, of the Negroes of Africa and of the descendants of Africans throughout the world is seriously impaired and we lack physicians, nurses and hospitals to cope with this situation; we need, too, teaching among the young to curb excessive indulgence in alcohol, loss of sleep and gambling. Here again the N.A.A.C.P. has confined its activities hitherto mostly to fighting discrimination in medical schools, hospitals and public services and has accomplished much in this line. But we cannot be content to stop here. While continuing to contend for admission of Negro students to all medical schools and Negro patients to all hospitals, we ought to make redoubled effort to guard the health and cure the disease of Negroes the world over, by any method practical. Such planned effort should have immediate place on our national program.

Democracy We, with the world, talk democracy and make small effort to practice it. We run our organizations from the top down, and do not believe any other method is practical. We have built in the N.A.A.C.P. a magnificent organization of several hundred thousand persons, but it is not yet a democratic organization, and in our hearts many of us do not believe it can be. We believe in a concentration of power and authority in the hands of a small tight group which issues directives to the mass of members who are expected to be glad to obey.

This is no new theory; it is as old as government. Always the leader wants to direct and command; but the difficulty is that he does not know enough; he cannot be experienced enough; he cannot possibly find time enough to master the details of a large group widely distributed. This has been the history of government, until men realized that the source of wisdom lies down among the masses because there alone is the endless experience which is complete Wisdom.

The problem—the always difficult and sometimes well-nigh insoluble problem —is how to tap this reservoir of wisdom and then find leadership to implement it.

This the N.A.A.C.P. has not adequately tried. It has regarded the demand of regions and branches for increased autonomy as revolt against the New York headquarters while in truth it has been a more or less crude attempt to teach New York the things New York must know in order to cooperate with Texas or California or New Jersey in the Advancement of Colored People.

The N.A.A.C.P. should set out to democratize the organization; to hand down and distribute authority to regions and branches and not to concentrate authority in one office or one officer; and then to assure progress by searching out intelligent, unselfish, resourceful local leaders of high character and honesty, instead of being content with the prominent and rich who are too often willing to let well-enough alone.

This securing of mass leadership of character and authority among young colored people of training and high ability can only be accomplished if we offer them not only adequate salaries, but even more, power, authority and a chance for initiative. This should begin right in the central office; the staff heads should be chosen not only to obey orders but to bear responsibility; the chief executive should be relieved of infinite details by distribution of real authority among his subordinates, reserving only broad matters of policy for himself and avoiding the paralysis of the whole office when he has no time personally to settle details. No one man can possibly attend to all details of an office like this and no assistant can work without power.

From such a top organism, power could flow down to the branches through chosen men armed with responsibility and power until it touches the mass of people themselves. All this is far easier said than done, but it is the essence of democracy and if it fails, Democracy fails.

Very soon a committee should be appointed to consider the reorganization of the New York office, with this in view. Such a committee, composed possibly of both office personnel and experts, should seek to consolidate and streamline the staff, reassign duties and powers, fix authority and responsibility and do away with overlapping. The office needs at least twice the space it now occupies to prevent unsanitary overcrowding and lack of privacy for work and consultation. Possibly the publishing, filing and more purely business functions might be physically separated from executive and research functions, or such a committee might seriously consider the removal of our head offices to the suburbs, to a building especially designed for this work with offices, archives, reference library, printing-plant and bindery, museum and art center, cafeteria, transient lodgings, large and small auditoriums and radio broadcasting facilities.

Politics Finally, in our political program we should adopt two objectives—an immediate and a long term objective.

At present, realizing that party government in this nation has definitely and disastrously broken down, we should in future elections ignore entirely all party labels and vote for candidates solely on their records and categorical promises. Each state, each county, each election precinct, should find out for itself carefully and as completely as possible the record of each candidate and strive to elect or defeat him whether he be Democrat, Republican, Labor Party or Communist. This should be a continuous job and not merely a pre-election activity; and it cannot be done on a national scale; it is a local job.

But this is only preliminary; efficient democracy depends on parties; that is, on groups united on programs for progress. We must in this land make such party government possible. Today it is impossible because of the premium put on disfranchisement by making population instead of actual voters the basis of representation in legislatures and Congress, and by the failure to function of that separation between the Executive and the Legislature, which the Constitution tried to make. We must work for a constitutional amendment, concentrating both power and immediate popular responsibility on a Congress elected by popular vote, with membership based on the voting electors.

Today Congress is owned and directed by the great aggregations of Business— the Steel Trust, the Copper Syndicate, the Aluminum Monopoly, the Textile Industry, the Farming Capitalists and a dozen others, while the Consumers and mass of workers are only partially articulate and can enforce their demands only by votes which are largely ineffective; the great interests can compel action by offering legislators financial security, profitable employment and direct bribes.

The N.A.A.C.P. should lead in such political reform, all the more because no other American group has yet had the foresight or courage to advocate it.

W.E.B. Du Bois
October 10, 1946

*An exchange between Villard and Du Bois about an attempt to help a young scholar named Arthur S. Link affords interesting commentary on Du Bois's relationship with the 1912 campaign of Woodrow Wilson.**

New York City, October 10, 1946

Dear Dr. Du Bois:

I enclose the letter from Prof. Link and the six pages of his manuscript. I am glad that your recollection is fresh and that you can help out, because he obviously wants to tell the truth. Will you kindly send your reply to me at Thomaston, Connecticut?

With thanks for your cooperation,

Cordially yours,
Oswald Garrison Villard

New York City, October 18, 1946

My dear Mr. Villard:

I am returning Mr. Link's manuscript with this comment:[1]

---

* Arthur Stanley Link was born in 1920 in Virginia and educated at the University of North Carolina. He taught briefly at North Carolina State College (1943–44) and in 1945 began his long association (with brief interruptions) with Princeton University. He has published widely but is best known for his volumes interpreting aspects of the life of Woodrow Wilson; he is the editor of the multi-volumed *Papers of Woodrow Wilson*, which began to appear in 1966 and is still ongoing.

1. The manuscript was that published as "The Negro as a Factor in the Campaign of

There were three approaches to Mr. Wilson concerning his attitude toward Negroes when he was elected president; the first was that of [J. Milton] Waldron and [W. Justin] Carter who represented an independent movement. They are the ones that got the statement from Mr. Wilson quoted in the *Crisis* for September, 1912.

The second was the effort of Bishop [Alexander] Walters; he was an enrolled Democrat; and third was the approach of Mr. Villard. Bishop Walters obtained a clear and straight-forward statement from Mr. Wilson much more acceptable to Negroes than that given to Mr. Waldron. This is referred to in my biography *Dusk of Dawn*, pages 234–235. The approach of Mr. Villard was independent of the other two and while he and I talked over the matter the actual letter writing was between him and Mr. Wilson. At no time did I see Mr. Wilson or talk to him.

I hope this will help in some respects. The exact quotations from Mr. Wilson's letter to Bishop Walters and the circumstances of his sending it may be found in Bishop Walters' biography *My Life and Work*.[2] I am copying it in case Mr. Link cannot find the book.

Very sincerely yours,
W. E. B. Du Bois

An effort to identify the writer of the following letter, beyond information given in his letter itself, has been unsuccessful except for a tragic note in the New York *Times of 5 March 1946. The* Times *noted the arrival at San Francisco of several hundred "war brides" from Australia, stating that Mrs. Marjorie B. Bialek died aboard the ship of "natural causes" and that her husband was "former Sgt. Thaddeus L. Bialek of Baltimore."*

Baltimore, Md., October 30, 1946

Dear Dr. Du Bois,

Earlier today, after nearly two weeks of careful digestion, I finished reading your *Color and Democracy*. I must give you some idea of what this book meant to me.

After nearly five years in the army, three of them in the Pacific, including

---

1912" in the *Journal of Negro History* 31 (January 1947):81-99. It had been given as a paper at the Meeting of the Association for the Study of Negro Life and History in Philadelphia, 26 October 1946. The letter from Du Bois to Villard published here—presumably forwarded to Link—arrived too late to influence his paper, but the paper does contain, of course, extensive references to Du Bois's role in the 1912 campaign. In a letter to this editor, dated 13 April 1976, Link states that he never did correspond with Du Bois; he adds that he checked his "files pretty carefully and could not find any Du Bois letters."

2. New York: Fleming H. Revell, 1917.

the first six months of Leyte, more than a year ago I became a civilian again. My selection of courses at [Johns] Hopkins, my whole thinking for years, had been geared to engaging myself in some form of helping of society. Then my years in the service, combined with what I witnessed for a year as a civilian —witnessed and experienced—served somehow to throw me into total confusion. Not to lessen my zeal to help society, but to confound it and to deprive me of goals and purpose. One result of my confusion has been my unemployment of the past two months.

As I read your simple, truthful and purposeful book I felt a gradual return of perspective, a steady return of dynamism to my values, until when I finished it I felt reinspired with purpose and felt whole again. The feeling is good and for that alone I thank you. I hope I can help justify your effort by working toward the world-wide democracy we must have.

Sincerely yours,
Thaddeus L. Bialek

New York City, November 8, 1946

My dear Mr. Bialek:

May I thank you very much for your letter of October 30. I have seldom received a communication which gave me greater satisfaction.

Very sincerely yours,
W. E. B. Du Bois

Late in 1946 Du Bois received a personally inscribed copy of Nehru's biography of Gandhi—a gesture indicative of the esteem in which he was held by the colored world in particular.*

New York City, November 7, 1946

My dear Mr. Nehru:

I cannot tell you how deeply I appreciate the gift of your book on "Gandhi, his life and work." I shall treasure it among my most valued possessions. May I add that you have the sympathy of myself and my people in the great work that you are attempting to do for India.

Very sincerely yours,
W. E. B. Du Bois

* Jawaharlal Nehru (1889–1964), as a leader in the cause of Indian independence, was jailed by Britain from 1930 to 1936 and from 1942 to 1945. In 1946 he was vice-president of the interim Indian government, and in the summer of 1947—after the formation of Pakistan—he became the first prime minister and minister of foreign affairs of independent India.

*One of the best-known Southern-born white journalists and writers of the
1940s wrote an appreciative letter to Du Bois in late 1946.*

New York City, November 19, 1946

Dear Dr. Du Bois,

I have been in New York for a month and have tried from time to time
without success to reach you by telephone. Am editing a special issue of *Survey
Graphic* on segregation.[1] I wanted simply to come by to pay my humble
respects to a great man. I do not believe there are many "scholars" who know
the real dimensions of your life-work and the place you must occupy in American history. But more of us who do know it, who have been profoundly influenced by the truth you kept alive, are going to own tomorrow, because we
must. And the name of W. E. B. Du Bois will never be without the greatest
honor.

Thomas Sancton

New York City, November 25, 1946

My dear Mr Sancton:

I was very glad to hear from you and know of your whereabouts; I had
quite lost track of you.[1] I am in my office almost every afternoon at 20 West
40th Street and would be very glad if you would call. Usually I am there between two and four. Thank you for your kind words.

Very sincerely yours,

W. E. B. Du Bois

Du Bois's writings began to appear in the Communist-edited weekly New
Masses *in 1945.* Late in 1946, its chief editor, Joseph North, asked Du Bois if
he would be interested in contributing a series of pieces to the magazine in
1947. The reply was enlightening.*

New York City, November 21, 1946

My dear Mr. North:

Concerning a possible series of articles which I might furnish the *New*

1. The special issue was dated January 1947 (vol. 36, no. 1). A long list of contributors included Robert E. Cushman, Louis T. Wright, Carey McWilliams, Robert C.
Weaver, Loren Miller, E. Franklin Frazier, Alain Locke, and Henry Lee Moon. The
issue repays study today.

1. Volume two of this work contains an exchange of letters between Sancton and
Du Bois, extending from June through September 1942. (pp. 327–30)

* Du Bois's first article in *New Masses* was published 24 April 1945; entitled "What
He Meant to the Negro," it was an estimate of the life and work of the recently
deceased Franklin Delano Roosevelt. In the issues dated 10 and 27 September 1946, the
magazine reprinted a chapter on Georgia that had appeared in a book first published
in 1924.

Masses in 1947, let me say that for some time I have had in mind a small book which might be called "Prolegomena to a Science of Human Action" or more simply perhaps "Steps Toward a Knowledge of How Men Act." What I wanted in this book was to explore from my own thought and experience, the way in which we progress from Curiosity to Science, from Natural Science to Social Research, from Social Research to Plans for Social Progress, and from Ethics to Art.

I have laid down something like thirteen divisions which might make five or six magazine articles of not too great length.

Of course the real question is how far this kind of thing would appeal to the ordinary reader. I want however to bring it down from dry theory to my actual personal experience—my early thinking of the problem of knowing and being certain; the lack of logic in doubt; my efforts to measure facts, especially social facts; and the whole idea of the working hypothesis and the willingness to change it in face of new facts.

Then I want to express the thesis, which I have always had, of regarding sociology as Science of the limits of chance in human conduct, and the concept of creative force as another expression of the old idea of free will: that is, the assumption that people can have some effect in changing their own destiny and the destiny of the world.

I am not at all sure that I can make this human and readable, but if you think that there will be a possibility of this filling your need, I might try a first cycle of say three articles and see how they will be received by your readers.

I will be glad to hear from you on this subject.[1]

Very sincerely yours,
W. E. B. Du Bois

John Collier, the former United States commissioner of Indian affairs, in his then capacity as president of the Institute of Ethnic Affairs, wrote to Du Bois as a result of a letter from Du Bois in the New York Times.* *No evidence exists of a reply from Du Bois.*

Washington, D.C., November 22, 1946

Dear Dr. Du Bois:

If only every American would read and pay heed to your Letter-to-the-

---

1. Du Bois did contribute to *New Masses* in 1947—the last year of its existence—but not on the subject here outlined. These articles appeared 14 January, 12 February, 4 March, and 10 June 1947.

* Collier (1884-1968) was born in Georgia and educated at Columbia and in France. His life was devoted largely to the cause of the Native American Indian peoples; from 1947 to his death he was professor (and professor emeritus) of anthropology and sociology at the College of the City of New York. Perhaps his best-known book is *The Indians of the Americas* (1947).

Editor appearing in the New York *Times*.[1] The problem of Africa looms high among the problems of all the world's non-self-governing, dependent peoples. Indeed the problems of all are so inter-related they become virtually inseparable. It is with [these] problems that the Institute of Ethnic Affairs has been working. I call your attention to the section in the November News Letter (enclosed) headed "Spotlight on Africa."[2]

Any suggestions as to how we might do more would be welcome.

Sincerely yours,
John Collier

Late in October 1946, Anson Phelps Stokes completed thirty-five years as a director of the Phelps-Stokes Fund; at that time he resigned and turned his duties over to Jackson Davis. To complete his works, he produced a report on the labors of those thirty-five years* and in that connection sent Du Bois, on 5 November 1946, a table of important dates in Afro-American history. On 18 December 1946 Du Bois sent Phelps Stokes a list of some errors, initiating an interesting exchange.

Lenox, Mass., December 20, 1946

Dear Dr. Du Bois:

Thank you immensely for your letter of December 18th and for the six suggestions of minor corrections and additions in my Table of Dates. They are all appreciated. It may interest you to know that I took the 1917 date for the founding of the Pan African Congress from Dr. Woodson's *The Negro in Our History*, page 555, fifth revised edition. It may also interest you to know that *The New Republic* article is referred to by Myrdal. On page 1178 the reference to it [is] thus stated:

1. Du Bois's letter headed "Problems of Africa," was on p. 28 of the 12 November 1946 *New York Times*. Several paragraphs in the original letter were omitted in the newspaper printing, including quotations from appeals of South African Black leaders opposing the incorporation of South-West Africa into the Union of South Africa and others from appeals of leaders in Angola protesting conditions. Also omitted was the following paragraph: "How shall colonies, like Nigeria, the Gold Coast, Angola, Mozambique, Uganda, the Sudan, French West and Equatorial Africa, the Belgian Congo and others, make effective their demand for freedom, education and political power, if they are deprived of the right to free speech and of open impartial investigation?"

2. The section was actually entitled "Spotlight on South Africa." It appears on pages 3–6 of the November 1946 (1, no. 5) issue of the *News Letter* of the institute.

* The report, dated 31 October 1946, was published by the Phelps-Stokes Fund in New York City in 1948 as *Negro Status and Race Relations in the United States, 1911-1946: The Thirty-Five Year Report of the Phelps-Stokes Fund*, by Anson Phelps Stokes et al.

WASHINGTON, Booker T., "My View of Segregation Laws." *The New Republic*, vol. 5, no. 57; December 4, 1915; pp. 113-114.[1]

I am particularly grateful for catching the error with reference to General [Benjamin O.] Davis. I hope that I would have caught it myself in my revision, but I cannot be sure. The putting of his appointment as General in *1914* instead of *1940* was undoubtedly due to a misunderstanding in dictation.

Again many thanks. I am glad that you think the list an interesting one. The corrections will be noted.

While on the subject of dates in the history of the Negro I most earnestly hope that you are making arrangements either for the publication yourself of a full autobiography, or for leaving your papers to some institution or individual with the idea that an autobiography will be finished after your death. I know of course the delightful little pamphlet that you published some years ago on your development in each of seven decades,[2] but what is needed is a full length story, for whether you will acknowledge it or not, the part that you have played in the progress of the Negro in this country and in Africa is a most notable and important one. You have had a unique position. As you know, during your middle period, when your work was so largely that of a controversialist, I did not always see eye to eye with you, but I have never for a moment questioned your ability, your unselfishness, or your ideals, and have generally heartily agreed with your ultimate aims. I see more clearly than ever, as I consider the progress in the past thirty-five years, what a large part you have had to play in it. Surely if you have not time to prepare an autobiography there are some very competent Negro scholars such as Charles H. Thompson, or Alain Locke, or Dr. Logan, or others who could do the work admirably. Would that our mutual friend James Weldon Johnson were here to do it.

I imagine that friends or relatives must have frequently presented this idea to you, but I want at least to be among those who reinforce the suggestion.

Always sincerely yours,
Anson Phelps Stokes

New York City, December 31, 1946

My dear Mr. Stokes:

Thank you for your letter of December 20th. You will be glad to know that Miss Shirley Graham who wrote the book on [George Washington] Carver and has just received the Messner Prize for a biography of Frederick Douglass, has long insisted that one of her projected books will be a biography of myself.

1. Booker T. Washington died 14 November 1915; the article noted here was published posthumously and the citation as given in Myrdal is correct.

2. The reference is to a forty-four-page pamphlet published in 1938 by the Atlanta University Press: *A Pageant in Seven Decades: 1868–1938; An Address Delivered on the Occasion of His Seventieth Birthday at the University Convocation of Atlanta University, Morehouse College, and Spelman College, February 23, 1938.*

In the meantime, Herbert Aptheker, a Columbia doctor in philosophy, is going over my letters and articles with view to publication. Between these two it is possible that something will be done in the matter which you mention. I trust that you and family had a pleasant holiday.

> Very sincerely yours,
> W. E. B. Du Bois

No more is known about the writer of a letter received by Du Bois late in December 1946 than what he tells us—that he was a student as Long Island University and that like so many students then and since he waited until the last moment to work on a paper! Du Bois, as usual when faced with a straightforward and interesting question, answered promptly and pointedly.

> Jamaica, N.Y., December 29, 1946

Dear Dr. Du Bois:

My English course at Long Island University includes a term paper, due date, January 7, 1947.

Owing to the lack of any course in Negro History, I thought it would be enlightening and appropriate to choose a topic of this nature; and in so doing, it seems fitting to write on two of the most outstanding contributors to race education and scientific race knowledge, yourself and the late Dr. Booker T. Washington. I have read several publications by and about both you and Dr. Washington in preparation of this term paper. May I hear from you in regard to the following questions? Any other comments would be appreciated.

Do you still believe that special attention to the "Talented Tenth" (relative to solving the Negro racial problem) is the best method of approach to the task of improving race relations between the whites and blacks in America?[1] What is your opinion regarding the quality of race relationship now prevalent as compared to that when you conceived the idea of the "Talented Tenth"? Do you believe that, had your idea been put into effect in the manner in which you desired, present relations would be much better than they are?

Thank you for your kind attention.

> Very sincerely yours,
> Cecil Peterson

> New York City, January 6, 1947

My dear Mr. Peterson:

Answering your letter of December 29th let me say that if I were writing

---

1. "The Talented Tenth" appears in a book whose editor is not known: *The Negro Problem: A Series of Articles by Representative American Negroes of Today* (New York: James Pott and Co., 1903), pp. 33-75.

today about "Talented Tenth" I would still believe in the main thesis but I should make rather different emphasis. When I wrote in 1903 I assumed that educated persons especially among American Negroes would do two things: first, devote their main energy and talent to the uplift of the mass of the people; and secondly, recognize that their talent was not exceptional but should be continually enforced and increased by the talent among the masses which is so often forgotten and frustrated.

Of course those two assumptions cannot be made at any time or among any people with complete assurance. Talented Negroes like other human beings are going to produce a large number of selfish and self-seeking persons, who will not work for the best interests of the masses of the people. Secondly, there is always the temptation to assume that the few people who have gotten education and opportunity are the only ones who are capable or worthy of reaching the heights. As a matter of fact there is at least ten times as much talent undeveloped as there is in process of development.

Very sincerely yours,
W. E. B. Du Bois

In 1946 Du Bois's major preoccupation, again, was the struggle against colonialism in general and for the liberation of the African continent in particular. His 1946 correspondence on this subject may be divided into three main components: letters to and from E. Sylvia Pankhurst;* efforts to further the work of the Pan-African movement; and efforts within the NAACP to advance the movement against colonialism and against domestic racism.

Ensuing letters are illustrative of the Pankhurst exchange during this year.

Essex, England, March 27, 1946
Dear Mr. Du Bois,

I was sorry not to see you again before you left England. I am enclosing herewith a copy of "New Times and Ethiopia News" just to give you the latest information. I hope that you will see your way to agitate in America against the proposals of Mr. [James F.] Byrnes of placing the Ex-Italian Colonies under

---

* Estelle Sylvia Pankhurst (1882–1960) was one of the most remarkable figures in twentieth-century British history. She was a leader in the Women's Social and Political Union, which agitated very actively for women's equality prior to the First World War; for this activity she was jailed several times and—refusing food—subjected to forced feeding. She was jailed for opposing the First World War and for actively supporting the Bolshevik Revolution. She was a very early opponent of Mussolini's Italy and especially active against the Italian invasion of Ethiopia; this interest formed the major concentration of her last twenty-five years and she edited the *New Times and Ethiopia News* from 1936 to 1956. In her final years she lived in Addis Ababa, where she died in September 1960. She was the author of a score of volumes, including *Ethiopia: A Cultural History* (1955).

Trusteeship. This will really mean a new Colony for someone, probably Britain. Ethiopia is going ahead well, and her progress will be a help to the whole of the coloured races. I do hope for your energetic support.

Yours sincerely,

E. Sylvia Pankhurst

New York City, July 31, 1946

My dear Miss Pankhurst:

I am very sorry I did not have the chance to talk with you frankly while I was in England. I do not think that you or most English liberals have any clear idea of the status and effort of American Negroes. Whenever we try, as of course we must try, to help our fellow Africans in other parts of the world, our work is looked upon as interference and with that attitude goes usually the assumption that we are busybodies who must be ignored.

As a matter of fact, time will prove, if it has not already proven, that the fight which descendants of American slaves have made in the United States is one of the most significant in the world; and that its results are of importance not simply for themselves and for Americans but for all peoples of the world who are today in contact and commerce with the darker races.

We American Negroes have not only the wish but the duty to do all we can in the interpretation of interracial problems for the benefit of the world and particularly for Great Britain, the leading world colonial power.

No one has appreciated more than I the long and courageous effort which you have made for the freedom of Ethiopia; but I strongly believe that you would be helped if your alliance with American Negroes and your understanding of their efforts were more complete. The Ethiopians themselves for a long time have been misled by the idea that any appearance of sympathy between them and American Negroes would be unwise. This of course is simply yielding to the divide and rule philosophy of colonial powers. It is not simply a matter of common blood, which is certainly great between Ethiopia and us, but much more than that, it is a question of cultural status and sharing the same problems of oppression.

There was a time when the Negroes of Haiti kept as far as possible from intercourse with and knowledge of American Negroes; but they found out in the attempt which the United States made to conquer Haiti, that it was the political power of American Negroes which blocked the effort and secured at least the beginning of their release. In the same way, Ethiopia, needing as it does capital and technical knowledge, may easily obtain that, at least in part, from America and at the same time have behind that political power on the part of American Negro which may save this power of capital from turning Ethiopia into a semi-slave state of American imperialism.

What I want is not blind acceptance of any thesis of this sort on your part or that of Ethiopia, but I do want sympathetic conference and understanding and frequent exchange of ideas. Certainly that cannot hurt and that is what is absent today.

The mass of American Negroes is still poor and ignorant but it has a large and growing intelligentsia and leadership. We are represented in Congress, in the State legislature, in the city governments and on the bench both federal, state and city. I deeply desire that in the future there shall be increasing conferences between Americans of Negro descent, Africans, and their white friends, looking to cooperation of every sort in order to free the African peoples.

I had hoped that we might have conferences on this matter and lay some plans for the future, but unfortunately we were both so busy that that did not take place during my last visit to England. I trust that something in this line may be done in the future.

> Very sincerely yours,
> W.E.B. Du Bois

> Essex, England, October 11, 1946

Dear Mr. Du Bois,

I also was sorry not to have a chance to talk with you again.

I have always had sympathy for the American Negro and had some lively experiences when I was in the United States on that account.

I have always desired that the American Negroes should give political support to Ethiopia and I often observed that whilst they were very generous in helping various war funds I could have wished that they might have concentrated on Helping Ethiopia rather than British and other funds which had great support from other sources.

I have tried to make the cause of Ethiopia more known in America, especially to the Negroes, through "New Times and Ethiopia News" and by other efforts, but thus far my success has not been very great.

The Ethiopian Diplomatic Officials in America are, of course, handicapped. It would not be considered correct for them to take part in any political movement in the United States and if they were to appear to do so on behalf of the Negroes, this would be officially resented by the United States Authorities. That is their view and no doubt it is correct.

Unofficial people do not work under the same obstacles. At the present time the policy of the United States at the Peace Conference has been decidedly pro-Italian and if Ethiopia is to win back her lost Colonies, much requires to be done to improve United States policy.

Can the Negroes of America take this up in a wholly disinterested manner without asking for any official support or expressions of approval from the Ethiopian Legation? This is the line we take here; we never ask for any official approval for what we do for Ethiopia. The Legation is perfectly able to tell the Foreign Office, if it chooses, that we are acting independently and cannot be controlled from any Ethiopian source; the same consideration applies here as in the United States.

I am fully sympathetic with your view that capital, whether from America or abroad, may have dangerous results in Ethiopia, both to the Country and to the individual worker. My advice is, as far as possible, to get everything done, as much as possible by the Government or the Cooperatives, which have been started, and not to encourage the private capitalists from abroad into the Country, but lack of capital forces people sometimes to resort to methods which are not the best. Ethiopia has achieved a great deal in the short time since her liberation and is making good progress, but under extreme difficulties.

I feel that for the time being she cannot do much to help others but requires help from every possible source. When she is strong she will be a great support to the African people all over Africa and also to the American Negro.

I fully agree with you that there should be sympathetic conference and understanding and exchange of ideas. I make a few suggestions which I think would help Ethiopia and promote understanding.

1. You should send us lists of addresses where we could send literature about Ethiopia (pamphlets, etc.). Some of these could be given away, but there is a limit to that; it would be good also to have addresses of places where it would be possible to sell literature on Ethiopia, in order that the financial strain could be reduced.

2. Are there any Negro newspapers in the United States who would like to receive a weekly or monthly letter about Ethiopia?

3. Would you join with others in forming in America a Branch of the International Ethiopian Council for Study and Report?

4. Could you get some members of Congress to act as advisers and to ask questions in Congress relative to United States policy on Ethiopia?

The Council you form might consist of Negroes and Non-Negroes—I express no opinion about that; you know conditions in the United States better than I do; or it might be all Negro and there might also be a joint body.

The Council, when formed, might be mainly of individuals, or it might be formed by representatives of Societies or it might be formed both of individuals and of representatives, but if it is to be formed it should be formed at once, or you might form a special Sub-Committee of your own Organization and leave it to others to do anything they thought fit independently.

For Ethiopia the coming year is of vast importance because the question of Eritrea and Somalia will be settled during the coming year.

As you say the Negroes are represented in Congress and in the State Legislatures.

I am enclosing "New Times and Ethiopia" Issues with reports of the Paris Conference which may be fuller than others which you have been able to see. These will acquaint you of what happened in Ethiopia during the Conference.

I am not sure whether you are taking the Paper, but I shall put you on the list if you are not. If you will send a subscription I shall be obliged, as our free list is unduly large and we have a struggle to make ends meet.

5. *Princess Tsahai Memorial Hospital.* This is exceedingly important for Ethiopia, as it will be the first medical and nursing Training School in Ethiopia and is the only existing Hospital with plenty of room for extension and, therefore, the capacity to become a really important Institution.

We have appealed to the British public and received a good deal of support, but last year money came in very slowly owing to British and European claims and to the fact that Britain is now very poor and the sources to which we have to go are bled white. Could our efforts be reinforced in the United States by a Committee there raising funds independently it would indeed be helpful. At present we have not raised enough to pay for the building and equipment and money is urgently required.

It is essential for Ethiopia to get out of the hands of foreign Missionary Societies, British Institutes and foreign Governments and their officials and be able to run her own affairs independently of foreigners. When she can do that help will be received without great difficulty, but she has to achieve an independent status of her own; and for her people to be trained instead of having to rely on foreign Doctors and Technicians is essential.

The difference which an efficient Ethiopia would make to the rest of Africa is beyond computation.

Foreign Military rule over the African people, an example of which we have recently seen in Eritrea, must be terminated, and we have to work both politically and culturally to this end.

I have put forward a few of my views and should be glad to receive your comments.

I am sending under separate cover a few pamphlets which I hope will be of interest.

I am very anxious to get the Memorial Hospital going; after that there are many other developments which we might help to promote if we have a body of people prepared to give their support.

Yours sincerely,
E. Sylvia Pankhurst

In the struggles for the liberation of Africa and against racism in the United States, Du Bois concentrated his efforts in 1946 upon bringing both matters before the United Nations and thereby, hopefully, attracting worldwide attention. Though these efforts went on simultaneously, for clarity the illustrative correspondence concerning each is presented separately. Matters concerning Africa are given first.

New York City, January 28, 1946

My dear Mr. Padmore:

I have been so busy getting into my new office and attending to Mrs. Du Bois in her severe illness that I have not had a chance to write you. Won't you please let me know how things are going? What is the cocoa situation?

Mr. White has not yet offered to call a public meeting with regard to the Pan African Congress and American Negro aid but if he doesn't act pretty soon, I shall go ahead.

How is the office getting on? What publications have been made or planned? Let me hear from you as soon as possible.

My regards to you and all my friends.

Very sincerely yours,
W. E. B. Du Bois

London, England, February 27, 1946

My dear Dr. Du Bois:

I am afraid this letter is very long overdue, but I have been in bed for the best part of two months and after that I had to put the finishing touches to a novel my publishers want to issue in June, so I hope I am forgiven. Don't waste sympathy for my illness, I saw it coming and did not take the proper care; but it's a lesson I shall not forget soon.

I saw George the other day. He told me that Mrs. Du Bois had been ill. I trust she is completely recovered now; and I hope you are keeping in good health as well. I am afraid I cannot tell you much about the Pan-African business as I am just beginning to pick up the threads again. The French have done something about it and I shall get a copy of a paper in which they deal with the Congress and send it over to you in a day or two.

Dorothy [Mrs. Abrahams], who is in fine fettle, asks me to send her love (you have made a complete conquest there!) and asks to remind you to try and find a secondhand copy of *Dark Princess* for her. She's prepared to send any book you like in exchange.

Are any of your publishing friends biting on *Song of the City?* The Czechs and Norwegians are interested in translating it.[1]

Keep well.

Yours sincerely,
Peter Abrahams

1. Peter Abrahams (b. 1919), the exiled South African novelist, served as the press representative for the Manchester Pan-African Congress. In 1942 a collection of his short stories, *Dark Testament*, appeared and in 1945 his first novel, *Song of the City*. In 1954 his autobiography, *Tell Freedom*, was published. Among his best-known works of fiction are *A Wreath for Udomo* (1956) and *This Island, Now* (1966).

New York City, July 15, 1946

My dear Mr. Abrahams:

There is absolutely no excuse for anyone neglecting good friends as I have you and Mrs. Abrahams. But I have been busy and worried since returning. Mrs. Du Bois had a bad fall last fall, and had no sooner partially recovered from that then she had a slight cerebral hemorrhage which has left her left side partially paralyzed.

She has been in the hospital for eight months, but at last, in June, returned to our home in Baltimore where she is resting comfortably and recovering slowly. This came at just the time when we were to celebrate our Golden Wedding. Naturally it put rather a damper upon the celebration; nevertheless it went through and we had very pleasant messages from our friends including you.

In addition to that, as usual, I have been writing a book and have just got it in the publisher's hands.[1] We have had hectic times here in the United States and are far from being out of the woods. Our food situation is not as bad as that in England, but it's bad enough. And the thing that hurts is that it is much worse than it needs to be.

I have not had opportunity to bring your book before any publishers, I am ashamed to say. But when your new one comes out send me a copy and I will put both before the Viking Press and Harcourt Brace. Just now publication here while not impossible is difficult in various ways. The matter may clear up in a few months.

Give my regards to your wife and assure her that admiration is mutual! If I can find a copy of *Dark Princess*, I shall certainly send it to her. With best regards and cordial remembrances,

Very sincerely yours,
W. E. B. Du Bois

New York City, April 1, 1946

My dear Mr. Padmore:

This is in answer to your kind letter of February twenty-seventh. I have just finished the manuscript of a book, "The World and Africa," and this explains my delay. I am off for California but am asking my assistant to send you this letter while I am away.

I am enclosing a manuscript of Pan Africa which you are at liberty to use in your publications and to cut if necessary.[1]

1. He refers to *The World and Africa*.
1. This manuscript was published as "The Pan-African Movement," in George Padmore, ed., *Colonial and Coloured Unity: A Programme of Action: History of the Pan-African Congress* (Manchester: Pan-African Service, Ltd, [1946]), pp. 13-26. This publication also contains (pp. 8-9) the text of the "Memorandum to the U.N.O." which Du Bois drafted and with which much correspondence hereafter published deals. His remarks at the congress, made 19 October 1945, also are given in this source (p. 54).

I would like to approach the General Assembly of the United Nations Organization in September with a plea to allow some of us to sit in as consultants and speak as friends of the colonies of Africa. Could you arrange some sort of statement from the Pan African movement which would justify such a request and send it to me?

I shall write you again as soon as I return from California.

Very sincerely yours,
W. E. B. Du Bois*

* Dictated but not signed.

London, England, April 16, 1946

Dear Dr. Du Bois:

I have to thank you for your letter of the 1st of April, with enclosed manuscript, which we shall gladly use. When writing previously I was not certain whether we had a transcript of your survey of the Negro Problem in America, which you made at the Congress. I find now that we have not, and I should be very grateful if you could let me have a few pages at your earliest convenience, as we are now going ahead with the printing of the Congress report.

The Committee has the matter of credentials for you to the General Assembly of the United Nations in hand, and we shall be sending them to you in due course. Your proposals should be in conformity with the decisions taken at our Congress last October, and you may be assured of our fullest support.

The Federation is shaping well, but our great need is money, as there is absolutely nothing in the till. Anything you can do to help financially will be much appreciated.

I have taken over more or less the international work, as it seems to me that this needs an experienced hand. We are meeting with great response, and I am quite astonished at the amount of enthusiasm and fervour that is manifesting itself among the rank and file of the Colonial movements. There is almost spontaneous movement towards unity in all parts. Lately we have been approached by an organization in Tanganyika, which speaks of East African unity.

I hope to hear from you again soon. Meanwhile, my very best wishes.

Very sincerely yours,
George Padmore

London, England, May 21, 1946

Dear Dr. Du Bois:

This is by way of giving you a brief report of the varied activities on which the Federation has been engaged during the past several weeks, as I know you would like to know what we have been doing and with what results.

We carried on a campaign for the Jamaica strike which occurred earlier this year, and held meetings in several places. Mr. Nethersole of the Trades Union Congress, and Manley's party, was over here, and we took advantage of his presence to have him address meetings on behalf of Jamaica. We were successful in collecting almost £100, and we are receiving letters of grateful appreciation from the militant organisations in Jamaica.

The question of flogging in the Colonies, in particular its reintroduction in Trinidad, about which you will read in the copy of the Colonial Parliamentary Bulletin which I have sent to you separately, has been one of our concerns. We have also taken up the case of the suppression of Zik's (Nnamdi Azikiwe's) press in Nigeria. To keep you informed about this I am sending you, under separate cover, a pamphlet, which will give you the details. The Governor is trying by every possible means to force Zik to abandon his papers, because he supported the Nigerian strike. The Government of Nigeria is anxious to abolish any kind of militant press, and is going all out to this end.

Following the strike in Buganda last year, a number of persons were deported to Seychelles island, and this matter has been agitating a number of liberal-minded persons here. We are taking it up, too. Then there is the question of food for the starving Africans in South Africa.

All these matters mentioned in the two paragraphs above we have been discussing with the Center Against Imperialism, about which I have already written to you, to see whether by joint action, and through the connections they have with Parliamentary members, we cannot get something done. At our last meeting, we had reluctantly to decide about the South African natives that there was little we could do to help them in a material way, as there is little enough food to spare in this country and it is extremely difficult to export anything. We can only leave it to the coloured people of America to continue their support and assistance. They already recognize the seriousness of the problem, and we must hope that they are doing everything possible to help alleviate it. With regard to the other matters mentioned, we are arranging a combined delegation to the Colonial Office, where we shall raise them all, and I will let you know the results of our conversations. I have forgotten to mention that we have been in touch with a number of African organizations in connection with the removal of the Kikuyu from their lands in Kenya. The restrictions being placed on these people are becoming tighter than ever. The problem is most serious, and we must raise world-wide support in behalf of the natives there.

In the Colonies, as soon as we get out our short history of Pan-Africanism, it is our intention to make a world wide drive for affiliation of the various organisations to the Federation. In this I would like to solicit your moral support, which you can demonstrate in this way. We shall send you the addresses of the Colonial organisations to which we shall write, and we would then like you also to write to them, pointing out to them the importance of the Federation and how essential it is for them to join it.

At the moment there is over here, to take part in the Conference of International Farmers and Agriculturalists, Prof. Ranga of India.[1] He is Secretary of the Foreign Department of the Indian Congress and a member of the Central Legislative. He is very anxious to draw together in unity all Asiatics and coloured peoples throughout the world. He is coming over to America and wants to come and see you about building up a world association of Asiatics and coloured peoples. He wants your support in connection with the bringing together of the Federation, the Indian Congress, the Javanese, and other groups. They would like us to send a delegate, and we are proposing that you should go to India to represent us, and if possible, one of us from this side.

I am getting all the documents ready for the September conference of UNO, as well as credentials. We are taking care of this, and by July or August you will have everything. We are drawing up the documents about the various questions and matters which the people want remedied or altered.

The next All West Indian Trade Union and Labour Conference takes place in Jamaica some time at the end of this year, and we should like you, on account of your proximity, to go down there. It will be either in November or December, but we will let you know more about it. Meantime, Dr. [Peter M.] Milliard is preparing to leave for British Guiana Trade and Labour Conference taking place in June. He will try and pass in at New York and see you.

Now there is a personal matter in which I would like your assistance. I believe there has been a recent shake-up at Howard University. I do not know to what extent it will affect the appointments of new people, but I am interested to do something for a very gifted young man, named [William] Nicholson, now wasting his time here to his complete frustration, disappointment and misery. The enclosed recommendations from his various professors speak for themselves and will leave you in no doubt as to Nicholson's capabilities. I should be most grateful if you could use your influence to get him a professorship, even if only a temporary one. It would help him not only financially, but more important, spiritually, and it would make it easier, I have no doubt, for him to get a post at the West Indian University, when that is ultimately established.

Finally, we all here hope that you had a very happy celebration. We were very delighted to hear about it, and all our thoughts were with you.

Most sincerely yours,
George Padmore

New York City, July 12, 1946

My dear Mr. Padmore:

I know that my delay in writing you has been inexcusable but there is some-

1. The reference is to N. G. Ranga (1900–1973), educated at Oxford and active since 1931 in the Indian independence movement. In the 1950s he left the Congress party and founded the Swatantra party; in the late 1960s he was a member of the Indian parliament. He was the author of many books, notably *The Colonial and Coloured Peoples: A Programme for Their Freedom*, published in Bombay in 1946.

thing to say in my behalf. As I told you before, Mrs. Du Bois has been in the hospital all this year, and just about two weeks ago we got her back to her home in Baltimore. She is improving slowly but will be an invalid all her life and it has taken a great deal of my time to arrange for her comfort.

In addition to that I found my publisher was anxious to issue immediately my new book, *The World and Africa*. I had planned it last year, but of course had not begun writing. So just as soon as I got a little time I began at the book and practically gave it all the time I could spare from Mrs. Du Bois, from the beginning of the year through June.

I have now in the hands of the publisher a book called *The World and Africa*, which is an attempt to rewrite world history and integrate the Negro into it; and to put the blame for his being so long excluded upon the African slave-trade to America, and the capitalistic system built upon it. It is, of course, a gigantic task and will bring endless criticism because the theme is large enough to take a whole lifetime instead of a few months.[1] But I am convinced that unless I can get this published now, it will be a long time before anyone else will undertake it.

In addition to these two tasks, I have had numbers of lectures in six or seven states, in which I have discussed the Pan-African Congress and its objects; several articles and of course numberless letters.

The chief difficulty, however, in the United States, is one that I am sure you have already sensed. We have some powerful Negro organizations but there is naturally a great deal of jealousy between them and difficulty in cooperation. The NAACP, outside of the church organizations, is the oldest and has a firm foundation; it has endowed funds and a very considerable annual income.

As you know, I left the NAACP in 1934, because I was not altogether sure of its program and did not want to undertake, at my age, any radical change. I went to Atlanta University and expected to end my days there as a writer and teacher. But it turned out otherwise. My friend, President [John] Hope, who had asked me to return there, died and after ten years I was retired, and again asked to return to NAACP, which I did.

One of my chief objects in that return, and one in which I thought I had the cooperation of the organization, was to revive interest in the Pan-African Congresses. When, however, I made a specific proposal to attend the Congress which was being called in England, I found a great deal of opposition among younger men who had come in the organization. They rather doubted if a "Pan-African" Congress was what we wanted; they thought perhaps a Pan-Colonial Movement would be better, etc. I insisted that our particular mandate

1. Actually, the reviews were numerous and on the whole quite positive. Sales also were good—for a book of this kind—and from 1947 through 1951 about ten thousand copies were bought. See this editor's introduction to the Kraus-Thomson edition of *The World and Africa* (Millwood, New York, 1975).

was Africa and after great difficulty and delay, I finally was able to take the trip to England.

But before coming, I did not have time or authority to enlist the sympathies and cooperation of a number of other organizations who ought to have been invited to join us. There is, for instance, the Council on African Affairs, headed by Paul Robeson and Max Yergan. It is, as a matter of fact, chiefly interested in South Africa where Yergan was a Y.M.C.A. secretary for a number of years. But it has a constituency and is doing good work. It is charged that the Council is financed by the Communists which is probably true. I wanted their cooperation but was not able to ask them officially because of the hesitation of the NAACP. There is the African Academy, run by Nigerian and other West African students; they would cooperate. There are a number of other organizations, especially the large church organizations which always have an interest in Africa, chiefly religious, but nevertheless it is possible to guide them to a social program.

Ever since I returned I have been trying to get the NAACP to sponsor a public meeting by which these cooperating organizations could be brought in to join us in an American Pan-African Movement so as to help the parent body. Although I have appealed to the Board and the Secretary, I have not been able to accomplish anything. I did not want to start out on a movement of this sort on my personal initiative, as it might involve a certain disloyalty to the NAACP which I do not want to appear to promote.

However I am certain of this; first of all, as I wrote you before, we must make a concerted and widely signed appeal to the U.N. assembly on behalf of the colonies of Africa when it meets in September. Fortunately, as matters now stand, it will not be until about the end of September when it meets which will give us part of July, all of August and most of September to prepare. What I have in mind, is to ask first a number of individuals to meet me in New York next month and talk over the plan. The immediate start which I have in mind is a small "Pan-African Exposition"; a series of charts and maps which will show the exact status of the various parts of Africa. This can be carried out on a small scale and from time to time extended and enlarged. I have talked to the American Minister to Liberia who has just resigned after more than a decade of service there, and I have suggested that perhaps such an exposition might be used as part of the Liberian Centennial.[2] I shall see him again in a few days and get his reaction. Sometime during the week of July 14, I am going to get together a small committee and talk about the possibilities of my plan, especially of the possibility of arranging an exhibit for the benefit of the United Nations As-

2. This was Lester A. Walton (1882–1965), with whom Du Bois maintained a close friendship. Several letters exchanged between the two men are given in the second volume of this work, along with a photograph of Walton. He served as United States minister to Liberia from 1935 to 1946. Du Bois's column in the *Chicago Defender* of 1 June 1946 was devoted to Walton.

sembly in September; also a method of approaching the assembly so that the Pan-African Congress could sit as observer or consultant at their meetings. I will let you know the result of the preliminary Conference as soon as possible.

After that I shall hope to call a larger Conference during August or early September. Out of that, it is possible that financial help may come. I don't know how much but it has not been feasible for me to do anything toward that as yet. I attended the meeting at Madison Square Garden to send food to South Africa. I spoke briefly as a representative of the Pan-African Congress.[3]

Meantime I wish you would let me have the information on several matters: first, just what has been done since I left concerning the West African cocoa situation? Secondly, what is the situation with regard to our offices in London, and what persons are working there? How are the publications getting on?

I hope to hear from you soon. My best regards to friends and especially to yourself. I have forwarded copies of Mr. Nicholson's recommendations to the President of Howard with a personal letter. I hope something may come of it.

> Very sincerely yours,
> W. E. B. Du Bois

> Paris, France, August 9, 1946

Dear Doctor:

It was a great relief to me to have your letter, as it clarifies a number of points. We are all profoundly sorry to hear about the seriousness of Mrs. Du Bois's condition. You had mentioned about her illness in a previous letter, but we had thought that she was on the way to recovery. In the circumstances we can very well appreciate your difficulties, and sympathise with you.

We have not been unmindful of your request regarding credentials from the Federation, so that you can make representations on behalf of the African communities concerned in connection with the problem of trusteeship. You will be receiving a formal credential signed on behalf of the Executive Committee, which we would like you to present to Mr. Trygve Lie, the Secretary General, asking that facilities be extended to you as an observer at the Trusteeship Committee (No. 4) meetings. For there is where the big issue will be fought out.

---

3. The meeting occurred on 6 June 1946; according to the report of the *New York Times* published the next day, fifteen thousand people were present. Du Bois was not mentioned in the report, which referred to the sponsor—the Council on African Affairs—as "a Communist-controlled organization supported mainly by Negroes." Until this account in June 1946, the *Times* did not so label the council; an 8 January 1946 *Times* report of a meeting held under the council's auspices in Harlem—attended by forty-five hundred people—simply noted that the council's purpose was to seek aid for starving people in South Africa. The *Times* also reported of the 7 January meeting that Judge Hubert T. Delaney chaired and that Marian Anderson was "one of the speakers."

I am enclosing a copy of the letter, which will be coming to you direct from Manchester.

I am writing this letter from Paris, where I am reporting the Peace Conference. You will no doubt read my despatches in the *Chicago Defender*. I am, however, carrying out the assignment primarily for the *Free Press Journal* of Bombay, who have appointed me their special correspondent to cover the Conference. I shall not take up any time in discussing the trends here. You will no doubt follow my interpretations. Unfortunately, the Colonial issue is excluded from the agenda here though the Abyssinians are trying to get the matter raised when the Italian draft treaty comes up for discussion.

I have with me certain documents concerning the South African question which I shall post directly from Paris. They contain sufficient material to enable you to get a clear appreciation of the position of the African population within the Union of South Africa on the question of the inclusion of South West Africa. You will be pleased to know that the World Federation of Democratic Youth has been holding a conference here during the past week at the Lycée Henri IV, at which they adopted a resolution on the non-inclusion of South West Africa in the Union, and I am enclosing a copy.

Now concerning the work of our Pan-African Federation. Since your departure we have concentrated upon the immediate tasks of popularizing the decisions of our Congress, and this has been quite successful. We have had no difficulties in getting our resolutions printed in the various Colonial newspapers, and we now have in the hands of the printers a small brochure containing the resolutions and your excellent historical review of Pan-Africanism. We hope to have this out at an early date and you shall receive copies for distribution on your side of the Atlantic. We intend to give this brochure as wide as possible a circulation in the Colonies. This should not be difficult since we have contacts not only with individuals but with organizations in all of the Colonies. After this publicity campaign has been crystallised, we intend to consolidate the organisational structure of the Federation by drawing in all Colonial organisations of a progressive character as affiliated bodies.

Objectively the task we set ourselves is fairly easy. Our difficulty is that we have not enough cadres in England who can afford sufficient time to carrying out the work. We are handicapped in just the opposite way from the NAACP. They have a machinery and the means to maintain the machinery; we have neither the machinery [nor the means] to create one. However, we are not allowing this to stand in our way. We shall find ways of overcoming it. Ideologically speaking, Pan-Africanism, it can safely be said, has found wide response throughout the black world. This is indicated by the wholehearted support which our Congress has received. The only criticism which I have noted comes from [George S.] Schuyler, and we all know of Schuyler's cynicism. Therefore, a criticism from that quarter need not be taken seriously.

While we have found no opposition to our ideas, we cannot just sit upon our past achievements; we must push forward. And that is what I have constantly in mind. If you think it advisable I will get the Federation to address a letter to Mr. White, asking the NAACP for a contribution. The auditor has just presented us with the financial statement of the Congress, which shows a small deficit, and if we could get a contribution of, say $500, from the NAACP, it would not only help us to pay off the deficit but enable us to pay for the Congress Report and defray its distribution. It is upon these concrete needs that I would make our appeal to the NAACP. I am confident that in time we shall find a solution to our temporary financial difficulties, for the organisation is very mindful of the need of keeping our overheads down to the minimum. Our present financial position has prevented us from embarking upon the formal establishment of the London headquarters, as we did not want to undertake this responsibility without an assured income. However, the work is being carried on from my London address, and in this I have the close co-operation of Abrahams and Miss Pizer, who is giving her secretarial services voluntarily. Manchester has engaged Mrs. Livings as a full-time worker, so much of the work is distributed between the two centres.

Now, unfortunately, Dr. Milliard, the President of the British section, has a a heart attack and is laid up in hospital. At one time he was in a very dangerous situation. I saw him just before I left for Paris, and I must say that he is now showing signs of improvement and we hope that he will soon be out of danger. His breakdown came suddenly while he was driving his car and was the result of strain and overwork. It will be necessary for him to take a long rest. Just before this unhappy happening we were planning to send him to America to join you at the September conference of UNO; he had already secured his passport and made arrangements for his passage when he had this attack.

Your letter confirms what we knew about the Council of African Affairs. We are very glad to note the assistance they were able to render to the natives of South Africa in collecting food, and in this connection you will be disturbed to know that the South African Government, not satisfied with allowing these people to starve and trying to prevent their receiving outside help, is making capital out of the parcels which American Negroes are sending them. I met a young fellow from South Africa who was a delegate to the Youth Conference and he told me that the Government of South Africa has imposed a tax of 20% on the food which Max Yergan is sending there. As this fact may not be generally known, I think you should use it in your column.

In regard to Yergan, I do not know the man personally, but there are now quite a number of South African Negro doctors here in England, most of whom are in Manchester and Birmingham; and as they are connected with the Federation, I have had the opportunity of getting their opinions on Yergan. To say the least, it is very low. It would appear from what they assert that Yergan identified himself as much as possible with the white church community in

South Africa (the YMCA) and treated the Africans, even the intellectuals at Fort Hare, the students and Professor [D. D.] Jabavu, with the greatest contempt. He was so disliked that it affected his work among the Africans and contributed to his having to leave South Africa. Whatever the truth of these assertions, his name undoubtedly stinks among the South Africans in Britain. No doubt his present efforts constitute an attempt to redress his lost status, for he seemed to have had a warm welcome when he originally went out. No doubt, too, he has contacts with the Communist Party in South Africa and that gives a link with the communists in this African Council, but I am afraid that it will take more than a few food boxes to make this man Max Yergan persona grata with the African intellectuals. However, that should not prevent us from collaborating with them as far as possible.

About your book. I think it very wise of you to make hay while the sun shines. The points of view which we seek to present in a hostile white world have to be put forward at psychological moments, so when one can get a publisher receptive to the idea of presenting our manuscripts, one has to put all other matters aside and seize the opportunity. There has recently been an awakening interest in Britain in the American Negro problems. Gunnar Myrdal's books have been brought out, and the others in the same series, and Horace Cayton's book on Chicago has been well reviewed.[1] I would like you to send me a copy of your manuscript and I will try to see whether [Victor] Gollancz will publish it. He has just brought out Mrs. [Eslanda] Robeson's *African Journey*, and as a Jew and one of the biggest English publishers he is usually receptive to minority points of view.

Regarding the cocoa situation. Mickey has had to return home.[2] His mission was a failure from the point of view that he never got an audience with the Colonial Office. On the other hand, the Colonial Office has promised Parliament to issue a new statement on the cocoa affair. Up to the time Parliament went into recess this was not done, but as soon as the white paper appears I will send you a copy. So matters remain as they were when you were here. Cocoa is being bought by the Government and marketed by them, principally in America.

As to the publications, I am writing a letter to the Socialist Book Centre, the wholesale distributors of the Pan-African Federation publications, asking them to send you a dozen copies of "The Voice of Coloured Labour," which is the

1. The Myrdal books mentioned are the two volumes of *An American Dilemma*, published by Harper and Bros. in 1945; other studies resulting from this Carnegie-sponsored effort included books by Otto Klineberg and Richard Sterner. The Horace Cayton book is *Black Metropolis: A Study of Negro Life in a Northern City*, by St. Clair Drake and Horace R. Cayton, published in 1945 by Harcourt, Brace and Co.

2. "Mickey" refers to Ashie-Nikoi, who represented the Aborigine Rights Protection Society of the Gold Coast at the 1945 Manchester Pan-African Congress.

latest pamphlet we have brought out. I do not remember whether I sent you a copy of it.

The Federation is not in touch with Yergan's group, although we had invited them to the Pan-African Congress as well as the Garvey organisation and the African Academy of Arts and Research. The latter replied to our invitation and expressed their regret that they were unable to send over a delegate as the time was so short. The Yergan group never replied. Since the Congress we have maintained close contact with the Garvey group and the African Academy of Arts and Research.

I am acquainted with several of the young men associated with this organisation. They are chiefly from West Africa and they are in wholehearted agreement with the aims and objects and the resolutions of the Congress. So there should be no difficulty in your collaborating with them.

I think that the best policy to adopt in the situation as it exists in America is not to create a new organisation, but merely to set up a sort of co-ordinating committee, with a council composed of representatives from all of the organisations interested in Africa and peoples of African descent; this would serve as a kind of rallying point whenever action round some concrete problem is desirable. For example, I would make as the immediate campaign the Trusteeship problem in connection with the forthcoming conference. I had an article shortly after the last Trusteeship meeting here which I sent to the *Crisis*.[3] I do not know whether it has appeared, but in that article I attempted to give an interpretation and analysis of the Trusteeship idea and made a comparison with the Old League of Nations mandates. I wanted to have it reprinted as a pamphlet so as to send it out to the Colonies as an eye-opener, but unfortunately I have no money to pay for the printing of it. Lack of money is our greatest handicap, for unlike in America, we have no rich ones among us, and you will no doubt be surprised to know that all of the work that has been done all these years has been done on a purely voluntary basis. We have never had a paid secretary or anything of the kind. To a large extent this is merely in keeping with the British tradition of public service. For few people in England get paid for their public work. It has its virtues—it avoids a lot of corruption; but it also has its drawbacks, for men must eat, and in a community such as ours consisting of the poorer citizens, it imposes an unusually hard strain. As you will see from the financial account when you receive it, all of the money which was contributed towards defraying the Congress expenses was on a voluntary basis.

I have read the document you enclose with your letter.[4] It is a good document and contains a concrete proposal. It has the endorsement of the Pan-African Federation, and I am attaching a list of organisations to whom I would

3. George Padmore, "Trusteeship: The New Imperialism," *Crisis* 53 (October 1946): 302-5.

4. This document was dated 24 July 1946; it is given below, pp. 149-51.

suggest that you send copies of the document for their endorsement. I think, if time is against us, it is safe to assume that the document has the endorsement of these people.

I am in Paris for a little while, but I shall be returning to London at the end of the Conference, and therefore it will be best for you to address all communications to my address there. If I stay here longer, they will be forwarded to me.

Please give our very kindest wishes to Mrs. Du Bois and assure her of our deep sympathy. Please also accept our best regards for yourself.

Very sincerely yours,
George Padmore

Shortly after writing to Padmore on 12 July, Du Bois sent a letter to Mrs. Eleanor Roosevelt, enclosing a draft of his plan to begin pressuring the United Nations to make some arrangements so that the views of African peoples might be heard. There is no evidence of any written response from Mrs. Roosevelt.

New York City, July 17, 1946

My dear Madam:

Enclosed is a copy of a letter which has not yet been sent but which I am proposing to send to various organizations named in the first paragraph.

I am writing to ask if you would glance at this and let me know what your reaction is and give me any advice that you may have.

As a member of the Economic and Social Council of the United Nations, it may be that you would be willing to indicate just what action in the direction of this statement it would be wise for me to follow. I shall appreciate any word that you can send me. You will find my biography in *Who's Who in America*.

Very sincerely yours,
W. E. B. Du Bois

The final draft of the letter Du Bois had in mind when writing to Mrs. Roosevelt was sent out very widely on 24 July 1946. The postscript to the letter indicates just how wide was this mailing. The copy here used is that sent to Oswald Garrison Villard, the original of which is now in the Villard Papers at the Widener Library, Harvard University.

New York City, July 24, 1946

My dear Mr. Villard:

Next September there will assemble in the United States the first session of the Assembly of the United Nations. The peoples of earth will meet to discuss openly and face to face the problems of human progress. All nations will be

directly represented. But Colonial peoples will, for the most part, be represented either by the nations owning and governing them or at best by representatives chosen by these master nations. Particularly in the case of Africa it
is quite possible that not a single person of Negro descent will have any voice
save in the case of Ethiopia and Liberia, which are free nations. There will be
at least 150,000,000 Africans who will be unrepresented and unheard, and will
be denied all opportunity to plead their own cause, complain of injustice or
defend themselves from calumny and attack.

This is not only unfair, it is dangerous for the peace and progress of the
world. Despite all assumptions to the contrary, the Negro peoples are today to
no inconsiderable degree ready to plead their cause before the peoples of the
world. Six times during the twentieth century, African peoples have met in Pan
African Congresses and sued for redress of grievances. It is true that these Congresses were only partially representative of the mass of Africans, and that this
mass is not today, by reason of poverty and ignorance, capable of clear and
coherent expression. Nevertheless black Africa has leaders and thinkers, and
black Africans, despite their handicaps in the modern world, are increasingly
able to discern their needs and ills. They must and will be heard if this world
advances from war and exploitation to peace and progress for all mankind.

Therefore as President of the Pan African Congress which met last October
in its Fifth Congress in the city of Manchester, England, with two hundred
delegates from East, West and South Africa and the West Indies, I am asking
you to join me in seeking a way by which the people of Africa may be represented in the United Nations Assembly, at least as observers, if not participants.
While this concession is of fundamental importance in any real democratic
world, its accomplishment will be beset with difficulties. The empires—Britain,
France, Holland, Belgium, even the United States of America—are going to
contend that representation of colonial peoples is an invasion of national
sovereignty and that these people are not capable of intelligent expression; and
that the empires are governing them for their good and know their condition
best. This argument can only be countered by close and intelligent cooperation
among the African peoples, their descendants and their friends, and by insistence on the obvious fact that the countries profiting from the ownership of
colonies are not the best judges of the interests of colonial peoples; and that
there is no human group incapable of voicing at least in some degree its distress, if the world is willing to hear and makes reasonable effort to know the
truth.

As a movement toward this, the suggested committee would be a logical first
step. Especially could it voice the almost universal feeling of mankind at the
utterly indefensible position of the Union of South Africa in its treatment of
Africans and Indians and its demand for absorption of Southwest Africa.

I suggest, therefore, first, that a petition to the Assembly be prepared, consisting of a careful survey, with charts, maps and plans, social condition of the

African colonies; secondly, that a record be made of the complaints and demands of these colonies as expressed in the last hundred years by spokesmen of these peoples; third, a demand be drafted signed by Africans, descendants of Africans the world over, and all friends of humanity of whatever color and race, to have appointed in some equitable way a small committee, which should have the right to attend all meetings of the Assembly, with the right to discuss all matters pertaining to African colonies.

Assuming, as we surely may, that many of the nations with colonies are seeking the welfare of colonial peoples, nevertheless there is no reason that the elementary basis of democracy—the right of peoples to speak for themselves—should be entirely ignored in international consideration of African questions.

For this purpose I am asking you to write me saying

1. if you are willing to cooperate in this enterprise;

2. if you will send representatives to a meeting in New York in August to explore ways and means of implementing this plan.

Very sincerely yours,

W. E. B. Du Bois

P.S.   The above letter has been sent to the heads of the following organizations: The National Association for the Advancement of Colored People, The Council on African Affairs, The African Academy of Arts and Research, The Federation of Negro Churches, National Council of Negro Women, The Grand United Order of Odd Fellows, the Improved Order of Elks of the World, The Grand Lodges of Masons Prince Hall Jurisdiction, The Nigerian Youth Council, The National Council of British West Africa, The Native Congress of South Africa, The Native Congress of East Africa, The Soudanese Nationalist Organization, The Federated Trades Unions of The West Indies, the Governments of Ethiopia, Haiti, Liberia, and other persons and bodies in freedom and self-rule in Africa.[1]

The response to the 24 July letter was considerable and positive, but those who responded did not indicate personal willingness to carry this effort forward. Three illustrative replies are given here.

Thomaston, Conn., July 29, 1946

Dear Dr. Du Bois:

Replying to yours of the 24th of July, I shall wish to cooperate in your enterprise so far as my limited strength, power and time permit, but I cannot attend

1. The text of this letter was sent out early in August by the Associated Negro Press. It was widely published in the Black press, although not the white; see, for example, the *Atlanta* (Ga.) *World*, 4 August 1946.

a meeting in August in New York. If my name is of any value to you, however, in this cause, use it freely.

With best regards,

Sincerely yours,
Oswald Garrison Villard

Kennebunk Beach, Maine, July 31, 1946

Dear Doctor Du Bois:

I have read with a profound sense of gratitude and admiration your noble letter of the 24th, setting forth your proposal for appeal to the Assembly of the United Nations on behalf of the neglected and even forgotten peoples of Africa. Here is one more example of the statesmanship which has been the glory of your career, and the vision and courage which have never failed you.

I feel deeply honored that you are including me among those whom you are asking for cooperation. I am not only willing but eager to join hands with you and I stand ready to do anything in my power to follow your leadership in this supremely important matter. I regret that I shall be unable to attend the meeting you are calling in August, as I shall be out of the city at that time, but I shall hope to have a full report of what is done.

Very sincerely yours,
John Haynes Holmes[1]

Washington, D.C., August 10, 1946

My dear Dr. Du Bois:

Your communication regarding the United Nations assembly received and its contents carefully noted. I agree with your plan one hundred percent. Be assured of my desire to help although my time at the present is limited. Because of my interest, hope you will keep me informed.

Sincerely yours,
A. C. Powell, Jr.[1]

After the publicity given the 24 July letter had dissipated without any real public follow-up in the United States, Du Bois decided, with Padmore's en-

1. John Haynes Holmes (1879–1964) was born in Philadelphia and educated at Harvard. From 1907 to 1949 he was minister of the Community Church in New York City. He was a founder of the NAACP and of the American Civil Liberties Union. For a summary of Du Bois's very high estimate of the man, see Aptheker, *Annotated Bibliography*, p. 522.

1. Adam Clayton Powell, Jr. (1908–72), was born in New Haven, Connecticut, and educated at Colgate University. He was pastor of the Abyssinian Baptist Church in Harlem, a fighter for civil rights, a member of the New York City Council in 1941, publisher of influential newspapers, and, beginning in 1945, a member of Congress.

*couragement, to move toward the preparation and presentation of a petition to the United Nations from African and African-derived peoples and their friends. Accordingly, he sent a letter early in September to Trygve Lie, the secretary-general of the United Nations. So far as available records show, there was no written response.**

New York City, September 4, 1946

[Mr. Trygve Lie]

Sir:

The Pan African Congress of which I am president is proposing to lay before the Assembly of the United Nations, a plea for the right to send to their meetings a consultant to represent the Negro colonial peoples of Africa. This petition is in the course of preparation and is being signed by African organizations and by descendants of African residents in America and friends of the Negro race. I am writing to ask if such a petition will be received; to whom it should be addressed; and whether any decisions have already been made as to the possibility of appointing such a consultant.

I may say that I am sure you will yourself realize how helpless and voiceless a hundred and fifty million Negroes under colonial control are and that they have made complaints in the past and are complaining now. It is surely desirable that these people have at least the right to listen to the action of the Assembly of the United Nations if not the actual permission to speak in behalf of the Negro peoples of the world. The Pan African Congress is an international organization which has been holding meetings intermittently for fifty years, and to which at various times all the black nations of Africa have sent representatives and addressed statements. The last Congress met in Manchester, England in 1945. I am sir,

Very sincerely yours,

W. E. B. Du Bois, Ph.D. (Harvard), Member of the National Institute of Arts and Letters; Fellow of the American Association for the Advancement of Science, President of the Pan African Congress.

Du Bois sent the text of the petition to the United Nations, dated 18 September 1946, to many organizations and individuals in the United States and through-

* On 9 October 1946, Du Bois wrote to Lie again, stating that he had had word from Gunnar Myrdal in Sweden that Lie was ready to meet with Du Bois for "a few moments" on the substance of the 18 September petition. Again, however, there is no ascertainable written record of a reply. Du Bois does not mention meeting with Lie in any of his letters, nor in any of his newspaper columns, nor in his *Autobiography*.

out the world. Two of the endorsements came from significant individuals and organizations which—for some reason not known to the editor—are not among those listed with the publication of the petition.

Space being a major problem in this work, published material is not normally again reproduced. An exception is made in this case, because of the consequence of the matter and because the pamphlet edited by George Padmore in which the text appeared ("The Pan-African Movement") is rather rare, and the petition is given here in full.

The undermentioned organizations and individuals representing or supporting the rights of African Negroes and descendants of Africans in the West Indies and the United States of America, strongly endorse and respectfully submit the following proposals initiated by the Pan-African Congress.

1. The great need of the world today is intelligent citizenship capable of controlling the actions of men by democratic methods of government.

2. One of the greatest obstacles to this accomplishment is the poverty, ignorance and disease in colonies, especially those in Africa.

3. In spite of all efforts to overcome these conditions by the colonial powers, by philanthropy and missions, and by the efforts of the Negroes themselves, progress is hindered by the difficulties which these Negroes have in making known their needs and wants and the opposition that confronts them. In addition, there is the widespread assumption that Negroes lack the intelligence to express their views and can only be represented by imperial governments or by other spokesmen not of their own choosing.

4. It is just, proper, and necessary that provision be made for the participation of designated representatives of the African colonial peoples in such business of the United Nations as concerns them. The truth of this principle cannot be denied. Provision should be made for such participation to the maximum extent possible under the present charter of the United Nations, so that the grievances and demands of the Africans can be freely expressed.

Already for nearly half a century peoples of African descent have been holding Congresses. Their object has been to increase mutual knowledge of each other and co-operation among the various African peoples and their descendants in America. Such Congresses have been held in London, 1900[1]; Paris, 1919; London, Paris, Brussels, 1921; London, Paris, Lisbon, 1923; New York, 1927; Manchester, England, 1945. Other conferences of African peoples have also been held during recent years. The organization of the Pan-African Congress has not been wholly representative, but it has far-reaching and increasing influence among Negroes and has helped to bring persons of Negro descent in the Americas in sympathy and co-operation with their African brethren.

---

1. The original petition gives this date erroneously as 1910.

American and West Indian citizens of Negro descent regard it as especially appropriate that they should share in the responsibility for the liberation and modern development of Africa. They have already shown the world that they contribute to human progress. Moreover, African Negroes themselves have made far more progress in modern culture than they are usually given credit for and have a growing class of educated persons capable of expressing their desires. Even those who lack modern education have the training of ancient and highly developed cultural patterns which render their opinions and desires of value.

[The published text then gives the following list of organizations and individuals who have supported the petition[2]]:

New York State Conference, NAACP; James Egert Allen, President.

National Council of Negro Women, Inc.; Mary McLeod Bethune, Founder, President.

Delta Sigma Theta Sorority; Mae Wright Downs.

National Sunday School, B.T.U. Congress; Dr. W. H. Jernagin, President.

National Bar Association; Earl B. Dickerson, President.

West Coast Regional Office, NAACP; N. W. Griffin, Regional Secretary.

American Teachers' Association; Walter N. Ridley, President.

National Association of Colored Women, Inc.; Mrs. Christine S. Smith, President.

Non-Partisan Interfaith Citizens Committee; C. B. Powell, A. Clayton Powell, Co-Chairmen.

National Negro Congress; Max Yergan, President.

Council on African Affairs; Max Yergan, Executive Director.

Southern Negro Youth Congress; Esther V. Cooper, Executive Secretary.

Improved Order of Elks of the World; J. Finley Wilson, Grand Exalted Ruler.

Negro Newspaper Publishers Association; Frank L. Stanley, President.

National Baptist Convention, U.S.A.; D. W. Jemison, President.

Phi Beta Sigma Fraternity, Inc.; George A. Parker, National President.

National Medical Association; W. A. Younge, President.

Kappa Alpha Psi Fraternity; Augustus G. Parker, Grand Polemarch.

Second Episcopal District, A.M.E. Zion Church; Bishop W. E. Walling, Presiding.

Alpha Phi Alpha; Bedford Lawson, President.

Pan-African Federation, Manchester, England, affiliated with 12 organizations of Negroes in Europe and Africa; Peter Milliard, M.D., President; T. R. Makonnen, Treasurer.

League of Coloured Peoples, M. Joseph-Mitchell, Secretary.

---

2. Du Bois sent the petition to Walter White, as head of the NAACP; although White did not endorse it, two regional sections of the NAACP did.

National Council of Nigeria and Cameroons, representing 140 organizations, 110 towns in British West Africa; Nnamdi Azikiwe, President.

Non-European Unity Committee, Union of South Africa; Z. R. Mahabane, Chairman.

His Excellency Ras Has Immru of the Imperial Ethiopian Legation [in Washington] has expressed "his sympathy for your efforts in the interest and welfare of the African people and to wish you success."

Nyasaland African Congress; C. Matinga, President-General.

The African Development Association; F. C. Archer, Founder, Secretary-Treasurer.

St. Kitts-Nevis Trade and Labor Union; Jos. N. France, General Secretary.

Trades Union Congress of Jamaica; Ken Hill, Vice-Chairman.

The Barbados Workers' Union; H. W. Springer, General Secretary.

International African Service Bureau; George Padmore, Chairman.

Kenyan African Union; W. W. W. Awori, Secretary.

Kikuyu Central Association of Kenya; Jomo Kenyatta, Secretary.

West African Youth League (Sierra Leone); Wallace Johnson, Secretary.

Caribbean Labor Congress; Richard Hart, Secretary.

Washington, D.C., September 25, 1946

Dear Mr. Du Bois:

In order to help you secure endorsement of the petition which you have prepared for presentation to the Assembly of the United Nations, a copy of which you enclosed in your letter dated September 18th, I enclose a list of the names and addresses of the representatives of State Federations of Labor and City Central Bodies chartered by the American Federation of Labor. You may communicate with the officers of these organizations, calling their attention to your petition and requesting them to support you and endorse the petition which you brought to my attention.

Very truly yours,
Wm. Green[1]
President,
American Federation of Labor

The West African National Secretariat
London, England, November 4, 1946

Dear Doctor Du Bois,

I am writing to acknowledge receipt of your letter of the 18th September and the enclosed petition which the Pan African Congress is presenting the United

---

1. William Green (1870-1952), born in Ohio, held high offices in the United Mine Workers and from 1924 until his death was president of the American Federation of Labor.

Nations Organisation. At a recent meeting of the West African National Secretariat the text of the petition was read, discussed and unanimously approved. The Secretariat fully supports the Pan African Congress in this step which it has taken to bring to the notice of the U.N.O. the important question of the treatment of Africans and peoples of African descent, racial discrimination and colonial matters generally, which are all vital to the making of world peace.

Yours very sincerely,
Kwame Nkrumah[1]
Secretary-General

An exchange between Padmore and Du Bois from the final month of 1946 terminates this presentation of Du Bois's preoccupation with the Pan-African petition to the United Nations.

London, England, December 12, 1946

Dear Doctor:

I have seen a number of Colonial newspapers with a report of the Resolution which you sent to UNO claiming representation there for the colonial peoples. It would seem that this Resolution has received pretty wide publicity. I am including it in the Congress Report, which I have now sent to the printers, and I would like you to send me as soon as possible a list of the organizations who were among the "undersigned."

After all this time I have had myself to get down and take the Congress Report into shape and get it ready for the printers, as no one else seemed to have got on with the job. It seems that the brunt of the work does fall upon me, and I am trying hard to keep up with it. As far as the Report is concerned, there is also the question of finance, and I would like you to advise me as to how to approach Walter White to help us to pay for it when it has been printed. When it is ready, I shall start a campaign among the Colonial organizations for affiliation on the basis of the Report, and get them to send affiliation fees, but I have been holding my hand until the Report is out, as I feel that it is better for us to go to these people with something concrete in our hands.

I am keeping well in touch with all our contacts in Africa and the West Indies, and also with our Asiatic friends. The Indians are anxious to build up an Asiatic-African Unity Front, and we have actually established in London an Asiatic-African Unity Committee, which sponsored a meeting to put the Sudanese case on December 2nd, as you will see from the enclosed handbill and

1. Kwame Nkrumah (1909-72) studied in West Africa, the United States, and England. He was an outstanding leader in the struggle for independence of the Gold Coast—now Ghana—and suffered imprisonment on that account. He was prime minister of Ghana from 1957 to 1960 and president from 1960 until his overthrow in a coup in 1966. He was a prolific author and a devoted follower of Du Bois.

Resolutions. I had a word with Nehru when he was here, just for a moment before a meeting at which he spoke, and he would like the Pan-African Federation to send a representative to the Conference of Asiatics and Africans which they are proposing to hold some time next year. I am wondering whether it is possible for you to go, particularly as you could perhaps get there more easily. I understand, however, that there might be difficulty about your leaving Mrs. Du Bois in her present condition. But let me know what your feelings are about this.

Norman Manley came over to defend a young RAF (Royal Air Force member) from Jamaica who was brought on a charge of murder, and for whose defense the Federation set up a Fund. The man was acquitted without the case even going to the Jury. We used the opportunity, which was very short, to have Manley speak at the Sudan meeting, and it was extremely successful. I am in constant touch with the members of the Umma Party who are here in a delegation concerned with seeing that the British do not sell out their country to Egypt, and I am sending you all the relevant documents under separate covers.[1]

With the entry into Moody's League of Coloured People of a progressively-minded Secretary, Mr. Joseph-Mitchell, we are now collaborating most successfully with that organization, which took the initiative in getting out a Resolution on South-West Africa, which our Federation, as well as other coloured organisations in this country, signed and sent off to UNO. We watched very closely the proceedings on this matter and are quite up to date on it.

I am, if anything, more busy than ever. There is a constant stream of people passing through here, and there is always some question being brought up which takes up time and attention. I am anxious to build up the Federation but I want it to be something solid, and am not anxious to build up a following before we have our programme concrete, as outlined in the Report. I have always in my mind the fate of Garvey's organisation, and the situation it left when it failed. Nevertheless, I am using my influence to assist the growth of movements and a forward-looking vanguard wherever the opportunity seems to be ripe, and at last I see a definite stirring in East Africa which needs nurturing and assisting in the right direction.

I do hope that you are well, and that Mrs. Du Bois is bearing up. Please give her my warm wishes; accept the same for yourself.

Sincerely yours,

George Padmore

P. S.   I am being frequently asked by Asiatics going to the States to place them in touch with you as the person most likely to help them in reaching organisa-

1. In 1946 a crisis developed, with Sudan—guided by major elements in its Umma party—seeking to achieve recognition of its independence from both Britain and Egypt. For a recent account, see Mohamed Omer Beshir, *Revolution and Nationalism in the Sudan* (New York: Harper and Row, 1974), pp. 168–72.

tions, groups and individuals who will help them in getting acquainted with the problems of our people in America. So please do not be surprised if young men turn up from time to time with letters of introduction. I know you will do your best to help them.

New York City, 30 December 1946

My dear Mr. Padmore:

I have your letter of December 12. First of all remember that the N.A.A.C.P. is not yet definitely committed to the African program. Against the desire of the secretary and several powerful members of the board, I was sent to the Fifth Pan African Congress. Since then, although I have made several recommendations, the board has taken no action until the last meeting, December 9. They then agreed to the enclosed resolution, and ordered the appointment of a committee, of which I am to be a member, to make recommendations.[1] This is a start but no more than a start. Any effort now to get Mr. White to recommend an appropriation of money for printing the report of its Fifth Pan African Congress would, I am sure, be quite in vain. I do, however, have distinct hopes of getting the whole organization back of the next Pan-African Congress and back of any colonial organization which may be set up or forecast.

I am enclosing the addresses of the organizations which were willing to back our petition to the United Nations. I did not go further than word the petition, because, after all, its presentation and acceptance would have meant very little. Practically all visitors were admitted to most of the sessions and the mere right of listening was not worth contending for. On the other hand, at present, it is out of question to attempt to secure the right of petition on colonial matters. The nearest we got to that was [Carlos P.] Romulo's resolution which merely asked the various imperial powers to convene colonial assemblies. Starting from that we may be able to do something but it is at present rather doubtful.

I am glad to hear of Manley and the Sudan meeting and am awaiting the material which you are sending. I have come in contact with many of the Asiatics; Madame Pandit and the head of the delegation to the Assembly.[2] I shall write again soon. My best regards to you, Mr. Abrahams and others.

Very sincerely yours,
W. E. B. Du Bois

1. The resolution approved in general terms efforts to end colonialism and appointed a committee to look further into proposals for this purpose. It is noteworthy that Du Bois does not discuss in his *Autobiography* the effort concerning the Pan-African petition to the United Nations.

2. Madame Vijaya Lakshmi Pandit, sister of the late Pandit Nehru, was born in 1900 and by 1931 had been jailed for her efforts in behalf of India's independence. She was jailed again in 1932, 1941, and 1942. She led the Indian delegation to the United Nations from 1946 to 1951 and in 1963, and was president of the United Nations Assembly in 1953 and 1954. She served as India's ambassador to several countries,

The selections that follow are illustrative of internal NAACP *correspondence relating to Du Bois's particular interests and duties in 1946. Here again, his efforts were highlighted by a petition to the United Nations; correspondence concerning this petition extended through 1947.*

In a memorandum dated 18 January 1946, Madison S. Jones, then an administrative assistant to Walter White, asked Du Bois's opinion of a petition being sponsored for presentation to President Truman by the Writers' Board, under the leadership of Rex Stout. This petition called upon the president to help transform the United Nations "into a World Government" in order to prevent future wars.*

New York City, January 18, 1946

Memorandum to Mr. Jones:

I do not believe that any point is so essential to the preservation of world peace as the emancipation of colonial peoples and I do not believe that a world government is in itself necessarily the most effective method to achieve the abolition of the colonial system. I think that the real reason for omitting the colonial question from Mr. Stout's petition was because his committee did not dare face the question of colonies.

Very sincerely yours,
W. E. B. Du Bois

March 23, 1946

Memorandum to Dr. Du Bois from Mr. White:

I would like to have recommendations from you as to what action or recommendations, if any, you think we should make to the UNO Conference opening next week at Hunter College [in New York City] with respect to the colonial human rights or any other issues on which we should act.

March 26, 1946

Memorandum to Mr. White:

There are three things that we ought to put before the UNO Conference:

1. a strong demand for trusteeship not only of mandated colonies but of all colonies; and for quick decisive action toward this end

2. we should ask that the NAACP be given a chance to represent the peoples of Africa before the UNO and to speak for their interests

---

including the USSR and Spain. In his *Chicago Defender* column for 18 January 1947, Du Bois stated that all Negroes should be grateful to Madame Pandit for her leadership in getting the United Nations Assembly to adopt a resolution condemning the racism of the Union of South Africa against Indians.

* The petition was presented to President Truman 10 February 1947. Over one thousand scientists, educators, and public figures signed it, and the *New York Times* reported it quite fully in the issue of 11 February 1946 (p. 2).

3. we ought especially to arraign South Africa for the way in which she has treated the mandates of South Africa; for lack of education or of social uplift; and for deliberate policy to ignore and degrade black people. We should contend that the United Nations ought to recognize that no nation with the background of South Africa has any right to control black people.

W. E. B. Du Bois

March 28, 1946

Memorandum to the Secretary [Walter White]:

Supplementing my memorandum of yesterday [*sic*] concerning the UNO, I am convinced that there is not much we can do with the Security Council except, of course, we ought to have been given a seat in the audience along with other organizations following the pattern laid down at San Francisco.

Our real work should be with the Assembly which meets in September and we should make every effort to be called in consultation not only as representing American Negroes but more especially as representing the peoples of Africa through our work for the Pan African Congresses.

W. E. B. Du Bois

March 28, 1946

Memorandum to Dr. Du Bois from Mr. White:

Thank you for your memorandum of March 26th. May I suggest that with respect to Item 2 that we request that the NAACP be given a chance to speak for Negroes everywhere, including Africa, I doubt that we should use the word "represent" since they would promptly ask us if the colored peoples of Africa, West Indies or any other part of the world had authorized or requested us to do so.

Would you draft a statement, if possible today, so that we can include it in the press release.

March 28, 1946

A Suggested Statement to the UNO

The National Association for the Advancement of Colored People believes that because it represents a large section of American citizens and because of the age and experience of its organization it should have recognition from the UNO as a consulting body on the same basis as the national organizations which have been recently given seats for the public meetings. It believes that the pattern set at [the] San Francisco meeting in the matter of consultants should not be changed.

In addition to this, the National Association for the Advancement of Colored People claims the right to represent before the UNO the colonies of Negro Africa in so far as they cannot be directly represented on their own initiative or through the colonial powers. The National Association for the Advancement

of Colored People as far back as 1918 has promoted a Pan African movement.
In the five Congresses held nearly all the black peoples of Africa have been
represented and have spoken for their rights through this Association. At the
Fifth Pan African Congress held in England in the fall of 1945, an official of this
organization was elected president and demands formulated for the freedom
and social uplift for colonial peoples in Africa. We do not claim through this
act to be the only organization interested in Africa or worthy of hearing, but
we do think that we ought to be the next friend of the African peoples and
to have some recognition in consulting capacity before the Security Council, the
General Assembly and especially before the Economic and Social Council.

W. E. B. Du Bois

Dissatisfaction with the functioning of the NAACP *Board and particularly its
secretary was acute with Du Bois before 1945 ended, and the intensity of his dissatisfaction sharpened until the break in 1947. Illustrative is a memorandum
Du Bois submitted in May 1946 concerning his special responsibilities; he never
received satisfaction on the matter in question.*

May 15, 1946

Memorandum to the Secretary:

Several times since the San Francisco Conference you have asked my opinion
on various subjects concerning colonies and I have given you memoranda
concerning whose use and disposition I have never heard. I think it would be
much wiser for us to lay down a broad plan of dealing with the colonies and
influencing the United Nations. I should be glad to propose such a plan but I
would want to be sure what the plans of the NAACP are and what my place in
them would be. I should want to know what power or responsibility I had in
such a movement.

My own idea which I have touched upon several times to you and the Board
has been that my Department of Special Research should be especially busied
with colonial questions, collecting data, preparing statements, giving lectures,
and proposing plans. Connected with this I have several times proposed certain pamphlets and other publications which are sorely needed at this time. I
should be glad to further elaborate on these plans.

It would be unfair to me and the Association for me to attempt blindfolded
to give advice on so broad and important a matter, without knowledge of the
developments in mind.

I shall be glad to hear from you in regard to this subject at your convenience.

W. E. B. Du Bois

Du Bois sent a momentous memorandum to White in the summer of 1946.

August 1, 1946

Memorandum to the Secretary:

I believe that the National Association for the Advancement of Colored People should direct a petition to the Assembly of the United Nations when it meets in September, touching the situation of American Negroes. The National Negro Congress has made such a petition and it is well done but it is too short and not sufficiently documented.[1]

It would be no duplication of effort if we did an impressive and definitive effort in this respect. The petition ought to begin with a concise statement of grievances, followed by an explanation, carefully arranged by legal experts, of the action which the United Nations, under its charter and decisions already made, might take; then each one of our grievances should be very carefully and factually documented with historical examples. Finally, there should be a bibliography and index.

This petition ought to be at least one hundred and not more than two hundred printed pages, and it should be distributed to every member of the Assembly of the United Nations and to the libraries and distinguished leaders of the various countries of the world.

I should be glad to undertake in this department a document of this sort, if I could have the necessary clerical help and expense account. I can make an estimate of what this expense would be.

The necessity of a document of this sort is emphasized by the fact that other groups of people, notably the Indians of South Africa, the Jews of Palestine, the Indonesians and others are making similar petitions. I have on my desk a letter from Dr. [B. R.] Ambedkar of the Untouchables of India, in which he intimates that they may make an appeal.[2] It would be, I am sure, an omission not easily to be explained if the NAACP did not make a petition and statement of this sort.

W. E. B. Du Bois

1. The delegates to the Tenth Anniversary Meeting of the National Negro Congress held in Detroit in the spring of 1946 voted to present a "Petition to the United Nations on Behalf of Thirteen Million Oppressed Negro Citizens of the United States of America." The present editor wrote the text, and the petition was presented to Trygvie Lie, the United Nations secretary-general, on 6 June 1946; it went from there to the United Nations Economic and Social Council, but opposition from the United States delegates prevented its serious discussion. One hundred thousand copies of this petition were distributed in pamphlet form. The text may be found in H. Aptheker, *Afro-American History: The Modern Era* (Secaucus, N.J.: Citadel Press, 1971), pp. 301–11.

2. There is a recent study, "Dr. Bhimrao Ramji Ambedkar: Rebel against Hindu Tradition," by B. Gokhale, in *Journal of Asian and African Studies* 11 (January-April 1976):13-23.

Walter White's response was immediate.

August 1, 1946
Memorandum to Dr. Du Bois from Mr. White:

I think it is of the highest importance that we should file a petition to the United Nations and it should be given the widest possible publicity and circulation. I would like to know what the expenses would be for clerical help. If you will let me have that, I will take it up immediately. I assume the sum will not be very great.

I would like also to suggest that we get the advice of experts like Dr. Ralph Bunche and Governor [William H.] Hastie on the document as soon as the first draft is prepared.

Du Bois left for his annual Maine vacation in early August; his response to White was therefore dated late in August.

August 26, 1946
Memorandum to Mr. White:

With regard to a petition of American Negroes to the United Nations in accordance with our memoranda of August first:

A. I suggest an editorial board with myself as editor and four contributing editors as follows: Rayford W. Logan, Earl B. Dickerson, Sadie T. Alexander and Henrietta Buckmaster.

B. The four contributing editors would be asked to prepare four parts of the petition substantially as follows:

1. The legal rights of American Negroes under the constitution, the federal and state statutes and court decisions.

2. The denial of these rights from emancipation in 1863 to the beginning of the First World War.

3. The present local and social status of Americans of Negro descent from 1917 to 1946.

4. The charter of the United Nations and its provisions for human rights and the rights of minorities and decisions already taken under this charter.

C. The editor would provide a summary of these four parts and a proposed program of international action.

D. The finished document thus prepared would be submitted to a committee of review who would criticize it and suggest additions and alterations. This committee might include such persons as Arthur Spingarn, Walter White, Louis T. Wright, Thurgood Marshall, William Hastie, Leslie Perry, Ralph Bunche, Morris Ernst.

E. The expense of this effort would be as follows:

1. Honoraria of $100 each to the four contributors $400
2. Stenographer and clerk for one month at $150 each   300
3. postage, books and miscellany   100

                        $800

4. publication of 2,500 copies of 100 printed pages, paper bound.

The publishers of the *Crisis* should be asked to get an estimate of paper and printing for such a booklet.

W. E. B. Du Bois

Du Bois worked on this petition to the United Nations at a pace unusual even for him. Accordingly, he was able to send a memorandum late in November announcing the near completion of the manuscript.

November 21, 1946

Memorandum to Mr. White:

I have consulted the Secretariat of the United Nations concerning our proposed petition on the Human Rights of American Negroes. Mr. Edward Lawson has written me confidentially November 19 a letter from which I quote:[1]

"The Charter gives the Commission on Human Rights no authority to accept petitions. Hence there exists a basic question as to what status should be given communications alleging violations of human rights received by this organ of the United Nations. No decision on this question can be made until the Commission holds its first meeting, which will be after the present session of the Assembly ends.

"The document of which you speak may be forwarded to the Commission or to the Secretary-General of the United Nations, by mail or can be delivered in person. If it comes from a private individual or organization, it would appear to have no legal status unless and until the Commission decides to give it some."

I think that we should proceed with the preparation of the petition, present [it] in manuscript by mail to the Secretariat, have it printed and eventually send a copy to each member of the Assembly. Since the Human Rights Commission will not meet until after the adjournment of the Assembly, we still have time to do this.

The petition has been ready since November 1 with the exception of the chapter by Robert W. Ming, Jr. of Washington, who was strongly recom-

1. Edward Lawson was managing editor of *Opportunity*, the organ of the National Urban League, from 1938 until May 1941, when he became a member of the Office of Production Management. In 1945 he was regional director of FEPC in New York and New England, and the next year he joined the United Nations Secretariat.

mended by Mr. [Charles] Houston. Ming promises to have the chapter ready this week.[2]

W. E. B. Du Bois

Two memoranda Du Bois sent to White late in 1946 detail continuing proposals from the former which failed to evoke satisfactory replies or actions.

November 14, 1946

Memorandum to Mr. White:

The NAACP has taken no stand nor laid down any program with regard to Africa. I have repeatedly urged this since my return from the Pan-African Congress. Individually I have done what I could but I have neither the help, funds, nor authority to accomplish more.[1]

If we are to enter into conference with regard to Trusteeships or other problems we should be prepared with a policy and clear statement of our position. As an organization we have nothing of the sort. I asked two years ago to have authority to collect and publish the various demands of Africans for freedom and autonomy. Permission was never given me. Such a series of documents now would be of invaluable use before the Assembly of the United Nations.

The only authorization I have had was on September 17, to prepare a petition on the rights of the Negro Minority in the United States. This was to

2. Du Bois's correspondence to would-be and actual contributors and others in connection with this petition to the United Nations amounted to hundreds of pages. Delay was a main problem for Du Bois, along with clashes with White, but finally in 1947 there did appear a ninety-four-page booklet: *An Appeal to the World: A Statement on the Denial of Human Rights to Minorities in the Case of Citizens of Negro Descent in the United States of America and an Appeal to the United Nations for Redress,* prepared for the NAACP under the editorial supervision of W. E. Burghardt Du Bois. It is likely that Du Bois—and probably no one else—had a special sense of historical continuity in the title of this petition, for it was identical with the title of the "Appeal to the World" drafted by Du Bois in 1900 for the first Pan-African Conference in London. This booklet contains an introduction by Du Bois and six additional chapters: the legal status of Black people in the United States before 1914, by Earl B. Dickerson; this same matter since the First World War, by Milton R. Konvitz; the present legal and social status of the Negro, by William R. Ming, Jr.; patterns of discrimination in basic human rights, by Leslie S. Perry; and an examination of the United Nations and the rights of minorities by Rayford W. Logan. Subsequent correspondence will further discuss this work (see pp. 178–84 below). See also Du Bois's *Autobiography,* pp. 332-35.

1. One of Du Bois's most important efforts was his initiative in assembling representatives from twenty organizations involved in civil rights to meet at the Schomburg Collection building of the New York Public Library in Harlem on 5 October 1946. Du Bois presided and the substance of the 18 September petition to the United Nations was presented, debated, and adopted. The reportage on this meeting was fairly full in the *New York Times,* 6 October 1946, p. 34.

consist of an introduction, four chapters and a summary. The whole statement is ready, except one chapter from Robert Ming of Washington, which is promised for the 15th. As soon as it arrives the whole report will be sent to the critics already agreed upon for comment. After that it will be ready for presentation and printing.

But this, as of course you understand, has nothing to do with Africa or African problems. I would be glad to submit to the Board at any time a suggested platform on the problems of Africa.

W. E. B. Du Bois

2 December 1946

Memorandum to the Secretary on Africa

Ever since my preliminary report on the work of this department made in 1944, I have stressed in nearly every report to the board certain actions which we ought to take toward Africa. To this the board has paid no attention except in the case of my visiting the Pan African Congress.

In its relations to Africa and the social problems there, this organization is facing a problem similar to that of the whole United States, in the question of the relation of this country to other countries of the world. The unrest and agitation and development in Africa especially during the last twenty-five years is moving toward a crescendo. Never before in the history of the world has there been such evidence of movement on the part of so many people of the African continent. This organization is, of course, at liberty entirely to ignore this by maintaining that our problems have to do with the United States and that there we have more than enough to keep us busy and to use our available funds; and that we should leave the problems of Africa to some other organization.

However, there is no organization taking up this work as it should be performed. The Council on African Affairs is well-equipped to study South Africa and furnishes continuous and interesting information concerning it. The African Academy of Arts and Research and the Nigerian Youth Movement with offices on 42nd Street are doing a similar work for the British West Africa. There is an Ethiopian organization which is the remains of work done many years ago in New York, but the Ethiopians formerly at the head of that have returned to their country; and the present organization is doing very little.

That leaves us practically no active organization or gathering of material in the United States concerning former German Africa, Uganda, Kenya, Nyasaland, Portuguese Africa, Belgian Congo, French Africa, the Anglo-Egyptian Sudan, Morocco, Algiers and Tunis.

In spite what we may wish to do, we are continually asked for information concerning the Negro peoples of Africa, and we are furnishing such information as far as we can get it; and at the same time making no organized effort to collect it.

This matter of overall information concerning Africa is a job that is being left undone now except so far as it is covered by the African studies of the University of Pennsylvania. One of my first proposals to the board of directors of this organization was that they should collect and print the manifestos, petitions and declarations made during the twentieth century by various groups of African peoples. If we had such a collection today it would be invaluable not only for our own knowledge but for giving information to others.

In addition to that there is today need of a careful survey of labor conditions in Africa and of the trade-union movement. This is available in no practical form. There is need for a series of biographical notes on African leaders living now and during the twentieth century, so that when we want to correspond with Africa we would know whom we could write and have some data concerning the person. Especially do we need a pamphlet giving the area, population, physical and geographical characteristics, government and social conditions of the various African countries.

Information such as this will be increasingly demanded by people who look toward the National Association for the Advancement of Colored People for data of this sort. There is no way in which this association can disassociate itself from the interests of the people of Africa.

I therefore suggest again that the association begin to issue a series of pamphlets concerning present conditions in Africa; that they cover the following subjects:

1. Demands for freedom and autonomy on the part of the peoples of Africa during the twentieth century.

2. Labor conditions and trade-union movements during the twentieth century.

3. Biographical notes on African leaders during the twentieth century.

4. Data concerning African organizations during the twentieth century.

I think that beyond this, since the NAACP initiated and founded the Pan African Congresses, they could now afford to take the stand of trying to interest organizations of Negro peoples throughout the world in uniting for the support of the Pan African Congress, for calling future congresses and for carrying on such correspondence between different groups of Africans and persons of African descent throughout the world as would bring them into sympathetic and effective coordination. I have done this to some extent at my personal expense but I cannot continue without help.

W. E. B. Du Bois

Du Bois's main work in 1947 revolved around the petition to the United Nations from the NAACP; *material relative to this effort will be presented as a unit (see pp. 178–84 below). Much else concerned him, however, during the year, and some sense of these other interests can be gained from the letters that follow here immediately.*

The first is from the executive secretary of the Southern Negro Youth Congress, which had been founded in 1937 and had pioneered in the struggle against jim-crowism in the South.* The congress had headquarters in Birmingham, Alabama.

Birmingham, Ala., January 4, 1947

Dear Dr. Du Bois:

I am enclosing a copy of the pamphlet, "Behold the Land," which you were kind enough to permit us to issue.[1] Ten thousand copies have been printed, and fifty more are being sent to you in another mail.

All of us in this office have read with great interest your column in the *Chicago Defender* which offered a Creed for Youth.[2] We are utilizing that article and this pamphlet as the basis for educational discussions in our clubs throughout the South and the response has been encouraging.

Please accept our sincere good wishes for a happy and fruitful 1947.

Cordially yours,
Louis E. Burnham[3]

---

* See Aptheker, *Documentary History*, 3:258-61, for the founding "proclamation" of SNYC, issued in 1937. Accounts of later work of this congress are given in the same volume, pp. 325-32, 354-60.

1. This pamphlet was issued late in 1946 by the Southern Negro Youth Congress in Birmingham, Alabama. Pages 7-15 give the text of Du Bois's speech, which was delivered 20 October 1946 in Columbia, South Carolina, at the closing session of a South-wide conference convened by the congress and attended by almost nine hundred Black and white young people. The *New York Times* of 21 October 1946 carried an account of the event (p. 31).

2. The column appeared on 28 December 1946. He urged youths to fight to eliminate poverty, to get work that would not be demeaning, to get the fullest possible education, to combat disease, and to maintain "in all life equality of sexes."

3. Louis E. Burnham died at the age of forty-four in 1960. In the 1930s and 1940s he was a leading force in the struggle against racism and for union organization in the South. In the 1950s he was an editor of *Freedom*, a paper founded by Paul Robeson

*Lewis Gannett, who conducted a widely read column, "Books and Things,"
that appeared in the* New York Herald-Tribune *and elsewhere, reviewed Du
Bois's* World and Africa *in his 29 January 1947 column.* He admired the book
and suggested that if Governor Herman Talmadge of Georgia would read
it, he would learn surprising things, such as "that some of Egypt's greatest
Pharaohs would have been called 'niggers' in Georgia—among them Akhenaton,
who converted Egypt to monotheism, and the dusky Cleopatra...." This statement brought Gannett some angry letters, including one from Walter Renton
Ingalls, who doubted the authenticity of Du Bois's scholarship and reported
that his own readings had persuaded him that Cleopatra was "a bright blonde."†
Gannett sent this and other such complaints to Du Bois.*

New York City, January 30, 1947

Dear Dr. Du Bois:

You see what you got me into! I've answered them by quoting from p. 140
of your book, from "The Ptolemies were in contact..." to the end of the paragraph. If you want to do anything more about it, God bless you!

Sincerely,

Lewis Gannett

New York City, February 3, 1947

Dear Mr. Gannett:

Thank you for the review and you have all my sympathy for the blows
you are going to get for it. I do not know whether or not Cleopatra was dark
enough to be called "nigger," but if she had been that she would not have
minded it a bit; she would have probably smiled graciously. On the other
hand, Mr. Ingalls would have had a fit. Naturally he thinks that Cleopatra was
"blond." In fact all of the Greeks of generations which we do not know were
"blond," but those of the present generation seem to be largely brunette. The
ancient Greeks had a great deal of commerce with Africa, both physical and
economic.

That purity of blood business is, of course, all nonsense. The marrying of the
Pharaohs with their sisters did not begin with the Ptolemys but was an old

and issued monthly in Harlem; in the late 1950s he was on the editorial staff of the
progressive weekly the *National Guardian.* Burnham was co-editor, with Norval
Welch, of *A Star to Steer By* (1963), by Hugh Mulzac, and author of "Behind The
Lynching of Emmett Louis Till" (1955). See "From the Writings of Louis E. Burn-
ham," *Freedomways* 2 (Winter 1962):10-32. Du Bois spoke at a memorial meeting for
Burnham; his speech was printed in the *National Guardian,* 20 June 1960.

* Lewis Gannett (1891-1966), educated at Harvard, was on the editorial staff of the
Nation from 1919 to 1929 and wrote a daily book-review column published in the
New York Herald-Tribune (and other newspapers) from 1928 through 1956.

† Walter Benton Ingalls (1865-1956) was a construction engineer with offices in New
York City who produced several books on lead and zinc and on mining.

Egyptian custom. Even then black Pharaohs and black Queens appeared by curious accident.

Very sincerely yours,
W. E. B. Du Bois

In the late 1930s and in the 1940s a beginning was made in changing the lily-white character of the faculties of United States institutions serving mainly white students. Volume two of this work published correspondence reflecting the change (pp. 363–64). Another illustration appears in a letter from a student at Oberlin College in Ohio.* The Du Bois papers include a manuscript obviously prepared in response to the Oberlin letter but, for reasons unknown to the editor, never mailed. Together, the documents are of considerable consequence.

Oberlin, Ohio, March 3, 1947

Dr. W. E. B. Du Bois
Dear Sir,

A small group of Oberlin students is seeking to do what it can in concrete campus situations to bring about a greater degree of democracy than has thus far been actualized. We should like to ask of you a brief bit of information which would help us in our attempt to accomplish this aim.

Oberlin does not have any Negro faculty member. This state of affairs should not continue for long. Inasmuch as at least one and probably two new teachers will be selected for the sociology department here for next year, we feel that the time is ripe for a change for one new sociologist, and when Professor Loren Eiseley, chairman of the department of sociology and anthropology at Oberlin, returns next year to his alma mater, the University of Pennsylvania, to be head of the department of anthropology, another replacement will be needed. Since the department has traditionally been a three-man affair, it is fairly certain that two new professors will be employed.

The student group of which I spoke above is the Oberlin committee of the National Student Organization. We would like to present a formal letter to the Student Council for its approval and subsequent submission to the administration of the college, calling attention to the traditional liberal policy of Oberlin with regard to admission of Negro *students*, and urging that there be no discrimination where candidates for teaching positions are concerned. Further-

---

* The writer of the letter—John W. Copeland, now professor of philosophy at Drew University in Madison, New Jersey—stated in a 16 July 1976 letter to this editor (in which permission to publish his own letter was given) that he sent the letter not only to Du Bois but also to "a sociologist then at Wayne State" and to Professor Allison Davis of the University of Chicago. The person at Wayne made no response; Davis supplied "detailed information on several people," but in any case two white professors were hired by Oberlin.

more, that since qualified Negro teachers of the social sciences are teaching in American colleges and universities, some of whom have been employed during the past ten years, namely ———— at U. of ————, ———— at ———— College, ————, etc., it is urged that the administration of the college make known to leading Negro sociologists and anthropologists the openings in the department so that they may become applicants or recommend others for these positions.

Those of us on the committee are not sociology majors and thus are not in possession of the names of such professors as were indicated above. Our purpose in writing to you is to ask if you could suggest several names which we could use in our letter. We have heard that many colleges have hired Negro faculty members in recent years for the first time in their history, and we feel that Oberlin has lagged behind on this matter. Perhaps what we are trying to do is unorthodox; we are open to criticism and suggestion. If you could send us the information noted above, we would be profoundly grateful.

Very sincerely,
John W. Copeland

Du Bois's unmailed reply was headed, "List as of March, 1947."

Negroes teaching in the social science unit of white institutions
University of Chicago: Dr. Abram L. Harris, Allison Davis.
New School for Social Research: Alain Locke, Lawrence D. Reddick.
New York University: Ira DeA. Reid
Hunter College, N.Y.: Warren Brown
Smith College: Adelaide Cromwell Hill
Brooklyn College, N.Y.: Marian Cuthbert, Lloyd Bailor, Mabel Smythe
Queens College, N.Y.: Kenneth Clark
Roosevelt College, Chicago: St. Clair Drake, Alyse Graham
Seton Hall College, South Orange, N.J.: Francis Hammond, Frank Griffin
University of Akron, Ohio: Raymond Brown
College of City of New York: Lawrence D. Reddick
University of Connecticut: Marie Jacobs
Fordham University, N.Y.C.: Olive Streater
University of Minnesota: Forrest O. Wiggins
Olivet College, Michigan: Cornelius Golightly
University of the City of Toledo, Ohio: Constance Heslip
Wayne University, Detroit: Beulah Whitby

NOTE: For a list of Negroes teaching in other fields in white colleges see: *Negro College Quarterly*, Vol. IV, No. 4, December, 1946, beginning on page 184. The periodical may be secured from Dr. V. V. Oak, Editor, Wilberforce University, Wilberforce, Ohio.

The above list does not include Negroes who have held teaching positions during summer sessions in white colleges.

*Carl Van Vechten (1880-1964) was a prolific author, musicologist, and photographer; in photography, he was most famous for his portraits of distinguished Afro-American figures. Du Bois and he were friends and occasionally they exchanged letters. One from Van Vechten in mid-1947 is characteristic.**

New York City, June 1, 1947

Dear Doctor Du Bois:

Last night, the night after you were here, I read *The World and Africa* and the pamphlet, "Behold the Land," with the satisfaction and inspiration that a sympathetic reader derives from idealistic and even poetic writing which is based on fact. Have you by any chance looked into Theodore G. Bilbo's *Take Your Choice: Separation or Mongrelization...?*[1] The senator concedes that you are the most profound and distinguished of the Negro writers: has something there!

My wife, too, speaks of you with great enthusiasm and we hope to see you again soon.[2]

You are, I believe, the only Negro writer to wax dithyrambic about the race, so successfully, indeed, that the reader believes you, and sees with your eyes.

With much admiration,

Carl Van Vechten

A letter not in substance unlike Van Vechten's came to Du Bois from Gunnar Myrdal, at this time executive secretary of the Economic Commission for Europe of the United Nations.

Lake Success, New York, 21 August 1947

Dear Professor Du Bois:

I wonder if you would do me a very great favor. In my study in Geneva I have a corner for photographs of my colleagues and friends and particularly those who have had an influence on my work. I should like, if possible, to have

---

* © Estate of Carl Van Vechten.

1. Theodore G. Bilbo (1877-1947) was a United States senator from Mississippi from 1935 to 1947. He was perhaps the most notorious racist in the Senate during his membership. The Bilbo book mentioned by Van Vechten was published in 1947 in Poplarville, Mississippi, by Dream House Publishing Company. Du Bois is quoted and denounced throughout the book, especially on pp. 62-65, 120-21, 214.

2. Van Vechten's wife was the Russian-born actress Fania Marinoff.

a picture of yourself for my corner. I would appreciate it if you would send the picture to me at the Palais des Nations, Geneva.

With kindest greetings,

Sincerely yours,
Gunnar Myrdal

New York City, August 27, 1947

My dear Mr. Myrdal:

I have your letter of August 21st and am glad to hear from you and know definitely your whereabouts. I am sending you herewith the photograph which you asked. My best wishes to you and Mrs. Myrdal.

Very sincerely yours,
W. E. B. Du Bois

The relationship of Mary White Ovington (1865-1951) and W. E. B. Du Bois was remarkable for its quality and its duration, beginning in 1904 and terminating only with her death. Having received a copy of her autobiography, Du Bois dropped her this note.

New York City, September 23, 1947

My dear Miss Ovington:

I am so glad to have a copy of your book, *The Walls Come Tumbling Down.*[1] It is a very important contribution to the history of race relations in the United States and I am especially grateful for the kind words you have expressed concerning me and my work.

With best regards.

Very sincerely yours,
W. E. B. Du Bois

One of the early acts in what became the full-scale witch-hunt later called McCarthyism was the hounding of progressive-minded directors and writers in Hollywood. The instrument was the House Un-American Activities Committee, at this time headed by J. Parnell Thomas of New Jersey, shortly to be himself convicted of theft. In November 1947, ten leading Hollywood creative figures were cited for contempt of Congress, and the major producers voted to refuse employment to Communists—a term subject to definition by the likes of Thomas.

In this connection, a spokesman for the "Hollywood Ten" wrote Du Bois.

1. Mary White Ovington, *The Walls Came Tumbling Down* (New York: Harcourt, Brace and Co., 1947). Du Bois appears throughout the book from the first to the last chapter, and his central role in the struggle against racism is made clear.

Hollywood, California, December 29, 1947

Dear Dr. Du Bois:

The enclosed statement has been addressed to one hundred leaders of American thought.[1]

We most respectfully request that your response be addressed to us, together with permission to release it to the press, the radio and to secure for it the fullest possible circulation.

Most respectfully yours,
Herbert Biberman[2]
for the "Ten"

New York City, January 12, 1948

Dear Mr. Biberman:

I am in complete sympathy with your "Statement from Hollywood," and share in your apprehension at the result of this despicable witch-hunt on liberty in America.

Very sincerely yours,
W. E. B. Du Bois

By mid-1947, the present editor was actively seeking a publisher for the Du Bois correspondence or parts thereof. Correspondence and meetings were undertaken at that time, continuing intermittently for some twenty-five years, with editors from Little, Brown, Houghton Mifflin, Harper, Harcourt, Brace, Lippincott, the presses of Columbia University and Harvard University, and other houses. All rejected the proposal, some quickly and some belatedly, but all firmly. I usually conveyed my ideas and information to Du Bois either by telephone or in person, but from time to time he wrote me about the effort.

New York City, August 12, 1947

My dear Mr. Aptheker:

I shall be glad to see the documentary records of your effort. I knew you

1. The statement was signed by Alvah Bessie, Herbert Biberman, Lester Cole, Edward Dmytryk, Ring Lardner, Jr., John Howard Lawson, Albert Maltz, Samuel Ornitz, Adrian Scott, and Dalton Trumbo. The central thought of its seven paragraphs was: "A precedent has been established. It would logically follow that any private employer may make conformance with his particular political views a condition of employment. And the mental strait-jacket already casts its lengthening shadow toward the other mediums of communication—the theatre, the schools, book publication and what remains of a free radio and press."

2. Herbert Biberman (1900–1971) was educated at the University of Pennsylvania and Yale University. He was author, director, or producer of many plays and motion pictures, including *Roar China, Meet Nero Wolf*, and *Salt of the Earth*.

were going to have trouble. The difficulty is that most publishers have no idea that Negroes are in the market for books or that the number of people interested in the Negro problem and other matters pertaining to race relations has greatly increased. What you have got to do in approaching your publishers is to let them know that you are quite aware of what their natural reaction is going to be, but that it is time for them to reappraise the situation and make some venture. Of course even with this argument, you are going to have a hard time to find anybody who will finance the book which you have in mind. I think it would not be too difficult for you to get publication if you took on the work and cost of compilation; but of course that is impossible and not fair.

I hope you will keep trying. I shall be glad to see you sometime.

Very sincerely yours,
W. E. B. Du Bois

By the latter part of 1947 I felt some sense of encouragement in certain responses from publishers. This sense was conveyed, with some youthful over-optimism, no doubt, to Du Bois. A brief note resulted.

New York City, December 18, 1947

My dear Mr. Aptheker:

I congratulate you that you have got some response from publishers. Perhaps in the end you will be able to get real cooperation. I certainly hope so.

Very sincerely yours,
W. E. B. Du Bois

Brooklyn, N.Y., January 5, 1948

Dear Dr. Du Bois:

I write, in particular, to inform you of my latest rejection in connection with the contemplated edition of your letters. This one is from Columbia University Press, and here I had gotten to the point of actually discussing the project with the production manager. The letter to me from this personage—one Henry H. Wiggins—is dated December 17, 1947, and reads as follows:

In accordance with our conversation of November 24th, I have discussed this project with other members of the Press staff and have laid it before the Publication Committee.

There is a general agreement that the book which you plan will be interesting and provocative. In view of our heavy commitments and of current high costs, however, the Committee does not feel that it could make any contract [by] which you would be assured of the advance royalty that you would need in order to get the leisure to prepare the manuscript. Indeed, the Committee doubts that we could undertake, even if you did not stand in need of the advance, to commit ourselves at this time to the publication of such a substantial work, given that the manuscript would not be available for nearly two years, and that we have no way of knowing what publication costs will be at that time.

It was good of you to think of us in connection with the project and I am sorry that we cannot be helpful.

In conversation with Mr. Wiggins he made a significant remark. He declared that he hoped I would understand that there might be some members of the Publication Committee of Columbia University who would not be anxious to see the letters of Du Bois published. I replied that this had occurred to me, and I added, somewhat wryly, I fear, that it might also be true that some members of the Committee would not be overjoyed to see as the editor of such letters so notorious a character as Aptheker! His reply was a weak smile of agreement, and the statement that none of this would of course appear in his official communication with me.

So there I am. Other letters are out, and so far as I'm concerned the battle has just begun. I am very much bothered by this consideration, however. The basic point is, of course, to publish your letters and papers because they are indispensable for an understanding of the history of the Negro people for the past half-century. How much deterring effect on the accomplishment of this prime task is my association with it having? This troubles me very much. If you feel for a moment that a somewhat more respectable—and perhaps, more capable—person engaged in this effort might have better luck in accomplishing the main job, please be good enough to indicate that to me.

I send you my warmest greetings for the new year; may it bring consternation to the enemies of the people!

Respectfully yours,
Herbert Aptheker

New York City, January 8, 1948

My dear Mr. Aptheker:

I think that you are by far the best fitted person to edit my letters and I hope you will not consider giving up the job, although, as I said before, it is going to be difficult.

There is at Fisk University a Mr. Cedric Dover, who would be interested in my work, and he has been doing something toward commemorating it through the celebration of my eightieth birthday, which is February 23, 1948. You might communicate with him and tell him what you are doing. Perhaps in some indirect way he could help.[1]

Very sincerely yours,
W. E. B. Du Bois

1. Cedric Dover (1904–61) was born in Calcutta, studied biology there and in Edinburgh, and spent some years in research appointments in Malaya and India. He pub-

*A considerable portion of Du Bois's time in 1947 (and in 1948 as well) was
devoted to the petition to the United Nations. A significant communication on
this matter came to him early in 1947 from the association's national legislative
counsel.*

Washington, D.C., January 7, 1947

My dear Dr. Du Bois:

I had a chance to read the material to be submitted to the United Nations
Assembly as I came down on the train last night, and I can, therefore, let you
have my criticisms forthwith.

Because the body of law being dealt with is, in the main, somewhat limited
it would be exceedingly difficult for three lawyers to write three of the four
chapters without there being some repetition and duplication.[1]

However, I am concerned by what I consider to be an important omission.
We are asking the Assembly to go to the very brink of its authority and it is,
therefore, incumbent upon us to give the fullest possible picture of the disabilities under which the Negro works and lives in the United States. For that
reason I am disturbed by the lack of statistical material in this petition reflecting
the low state of Negro welfare.

I would like to see the following sociological data set forth:

1. Employment
    (a) Stratification in unskilled, personal service and domestic occupations
        (U.S. Census figures)
    (b) *Wage differentials* (Bureau of Labor Statistics, Decisions of War
        Labor Board, Bureau of Education Figures—Teachers Salary Differ-
        entials)
    (c) *Unemployment* (U. S. Census Figures)
2. Education
    (a) *Relative illiteracy or near illiteracy* (U.S. Census and Selective Service
        Figures)

---

lished widely on questions of art and racial relationships; his best-known books are
Half-Caste, with a preface by Lancelot Hogben (London: Secker and Warburg,
1937), *Hell in the Sunshine* (London: Secker and Warburg, 1943), and *American
Negro Art* (Greenwich, Conn.: New York Graphic Society, 1960). After World
War II he served as a visiting professor for some years at Fisk University and at the
New School for Social Research in New York City. Dover was highly interested in the
project of publishing Du Bois's correspondence and was warmly responsive, but in
fact nothing eventuated from that lead.

1. The three lawyers meant were Earl B. Dickerson, former assistant attorney gen-
eral of Illinois and at that time president of the National Bar Association; Milton R.
Konvitz, professor and director of research, School of Industrial and Labor Relations,
Cornell University; and William R. Ming, Jr., formerly connected with the Office
of Price Administration and at that time a professor at the University of Chicago
Legal Institute.

    (b) *Per Capita expenditure Negro and white students* (Bureau of Education)

3. Housing

Statistical material regarding general, urban and rural living conditions, including high rents.

4. Health

    (a) Hospital facilities. "In some areas where the population is heavily Negro, there are as few as 75 beds set aside for over a million Negroes." (*An American Dilemma* page 1224)

    (b) Infant mortality 69 per cent above whites.

    (c) Life expectancy—Negro 53 years, whites 65 years.

Perhaps something like this should be added to Mr. Ming's paper.

You will find in duplicate separate sheets covering my criticisms of the introduction summary and each of the four chapters.

Very sincerely,

Leslie S. Perry[2]

New York City, January 22, 1947

Dear Mr. Perry:

Thank you for the data which you have sent me. I am, on my own initiative, adding a chapter which I am provisionally entitling "Patterns of Social Discrimination Against Negroes" by Leslie S. Perry. Enclosed is an outline of this chapter. This I shall use provisionally but eventually I hope you will prepare a complete statement on these and other discriminations; about 10-20 typed pages. I shall try to get the committee to allow it to be printed.[1] With many thanks.

Very sincerely yours,

W. E. B. Du Bois

By *August 1947 the petition was finished and its text approved by the* NAACP; *mimeographed, it was 155 pages long. Throughout Du Bois's connection with the United Nations, beginning in 1945 in San Francisco, he had found the Indian delegates—and especially its chief delegate, Madame Vijaya Lakshmi Pandit— particularly friendly and sympathetic. Soon after the document was ready, therefore, he communicated with Madame Pandit.*

2. Leslie S. Perry was born in Washington, D.C., in 1906; he was educated at Howard University and practiced law in Washington beginning in 1933. He was national legislative counsel for the NAACP from 1942 to 1950, returning to private law practice in 1950.

1. Perry prepared the suggested statement; it appeared in the petition as the fifth chapter: "Patterns of Discrimination in Fundamental Human Rights," pp. 62-84.

New York City, September 18, 1947

My dear Madam Pandit:

I am sending you by the hand of Mr. Walter White, Secretary of the National Association for the Advancement of Colored People, a copy of the petition and statement which we are trying to get before the Assembly of the United Nations, or the Economic and Social Council. I am also enclosing a letter which I have written to Mr. Trygve Lie. I should be under great obligation if you could do anything to see that we get some chance for a hearing.[1]

Very sincerely yours,
W. E. B. Du Bois

New York City, September 25, 1947

Dear Mr. Du Bois,

Thank you for the copy of the petition and statement which you have sent to Mr. Trygve Lie. I shall certainly do what I can to help you to place this before the Assembly of the United Nations or the Economics and Social Council.[1]

Sincerely yours,
Vijaya Lakshmi Pandit

Other letters from 1947 indicate further developments in connection with the presentation of the petition to the United Nations.

New York City, September 29, 1947

Dear Mr. Du Bois:

The Secretary-General has asked me to thank you for your letter of September 11 regarding the proposed petition to be submitted by the National Association for the Advancement of Colored People to the General Assembly.

1. Walter White sent Du Bois a copy of a letter he had written to Madame Pandit on 18 September 1947, which read:

"Here is a document I think will interest you prepared by the NAACP on the position of the Negro in the United States.

"Dr. Du Bois of our staff has written Mr. Trygve Lie requesting that he set a time when a small delegation headed by Dr. Du Bois and myself will make the formal presentation.

"I thought you would be interested in seeing this document, so I send it to you with our compliments."

1. The Indian delegation did take a positive position on the NAACP petition; after it was presented to a representative of Lie on 23 October 1947, the *Pittsburgh Courier* (25 October 1947) accurately put on its front page the headline, "India Hails NAACP Stand." While there was considerable press coverage of this petition—more will be said of this matter later—the press generally devoted most of its attention to the report of President Truman's Civil Rights Commission of Inquiry, whose *To Secure These Rights* was issued in the fall of 1947.

An earlier answer has been prevented by our desire to look into the question and by the great volume of work which has occupied the Secretary-General in connection with the General Assembly.

Mr. Lie now suggests that you communicate with Mr. John Humphrey, Director of our Division of Human Rights, and consult him as to the method which should be adopted in furthering your plan. Mr. Lie, himself, is not in a position to receive such a delegation as you suggest.

Yours sincerely,
William H. Stoneman[1]

New York City, October 16, 1947

Mr. William H. Stoneman
My dear Sir:

I have your letter of September 29, and have in accordance with it written to Mr. John P. Humphrey. He has replied, that the Economic and Social Council apparently limits the Commission on Human Rights in the reception of petitions to filing them confidentially. I have written him again today, to ask if there is any way to make it possible for us to have our petition officially received by someone representing the United Nations.

I think you will agree with me that this document is not hastily prepared nor carelessly conceived. It is written by scholars who speak with authority, and it is in reasonable language. Its preparation has taken over a year. Already, some twelve delegations to the United Nations have asked to read it, and it is receiving publicity from the press.[1]

Is it not the bounden duty of the Secretariat of the United Nations openly and publicly to let the delegations and the world know that such a document exists: that it has been publicly received, and that all are free to examine it?

The case of American Negroes is not going to be kept from knowledge by denial of the right to petition, no more than in the past slavery could bolster itself by silence. We are going to give world-wide publicity to our complaint; but first, we would like to proceed by regular process and lay this petition before the United Nations publicly and in such a manner as their Secretariat suggests.

Therefore, I am venturing to write you again, and to ask if such a presentation cannot in some way be arranged?

Very sincerely yours,
W. E. B. Du Bois

1. William H. Stoneman was born in Michigan in 1904 and educated at the University of Michigan. He was a well-known news correspondent in Rome, London, Moscow, and Addis Ababa from 1928 to 1946; in the latter year, he became a special adviser to the United Nations secretary-general, in charge of public relations. He held that position until 1949 and then returned to newspaper work. Most recently he has been London correspondent of the *Chicago Daily News*.

1. For example, there was a two-column story by George Streator in the *New York*

New York City, October 14, 1947

Honorable Warren R. Austin[1]
My dear Sir:

On September 29, my assistant, Mr. Hugh H. Smythe, wrote you stating that we had prepared a petition on the denial of human rights to minorities in the case of citizens of Negro descent in the United States, to be presented to the General Assembly of the United Nations. He asked if you would like to receive a copy of this document and after examining it if you would be willing to assist us in bringing it to the attention of the Assembly.

Your answer of October 9 informed us that it would be impossible to get this matter on the agenda of the Assembly this year. We were aware of this, but nevertheless it is important to remember that this statement has already been put before the Human Rights Commission and that in amended form we now wish to make formal presentation to official representatives of the Assembly, even though we cannot actually get it upon the agenda for this year. If we can get it upon the agenda for next year or the year after we will be satisfied. What we want is to have the cooperation and help of the United States Delegation. May I ask again, therefore, if we may send you a copy of the petition for examination and if you will join us and others in giving us the opportunity to make a formal presentation to representatives of the assembly of the United Nations, with the purpose of having this matter put upon the agenda whenever that is possible? I shall be very glad to have an answer at your convenience.

I am, sir

Very sincerely yours,
W. E. B. Du Bois

New York City, October 21, 1947

My dear Dr. Du Bois:

I have received your letter of October 14 with further reference to the petition and statement prepared by your Association on the denial of human rights to minorities in the case of citizens of Negro descent in the United States. You inquire whether you may send us a copy of the petition for examination and whether we would join in giving you the opportunity to make a formal presentation to representatives of the General Assembly of the United Nations.

With reference to your inquiry whether you may send us a copy of the

---

Times on Sunday, 12 October 1947 (p. 52), headlined "Negroes to Bring Cause Before u.n." It quoted at some length from Du Bois's introduction to the petition.
1. Warren Robinson Austin (1877–1963) was born in Vermont and educated at its state university; he practiced law there from 1902 to 1931. In 1931 he was elected a United States senator. He remained in the Senate until 1946, when he was appointed chief of the United States delegation to the United Nations. He retired from that position in 1953.

petition for examination, we would of course be glad to have you send us a copy. As to the question of a formal presentation to representatives of the General Assembly of the United Nations, I indicated in my letter to you of October 9 that because of the deadline for the inclusion of new items on the agenda, it would not be practicable for the United States Delegation to propose the addition at this time of an agenda item concerning a matter of this character. There is therefore nothing that the Delegation can properly do with reference to the presentation of this petition to representatives of the General Assembly. I understand that you have made arrangements to present a copy of the petition to certain officers of the United Nations Secretariat for the attention of the Human Rights Commission.

Upon receipt of a copy of your petition, we will be glad to refer it to the Department of State for appropriate consideration.

Sincerely yours,
Warren R. Austin

New York City, October 28, 1947

The Honorable Warren R. Austin
My dear Sir:

Replying to your letter of October 21, I am taking the opportunity of sending you a copy of our petition to the United Nations. I trust that you will do your best to have this matter put on the agenda of the United Nations Assembly, either this year or next. I think it would be an excellent thing if the United States was able to say to the world: We are perfectly willing to be criticized as to our democracy and to give the public a chance to know what that criticism is.

I am, sir

Very sincerely yours,
W. E. B. Du Bois

October 17, 1947

Memorandum to Mr. White from Dr. Du Bois

Last night, Mr. [John P.] Humphrey of the Commission on Human Rights of the United Nations telephoned me and said that opportunity for us officially to present the petition and statement would be accorded us Thursday, October 23, at twelve o'clock—noon. The event preceding this decision was as follows:

I wrote Mr. Humphrey a letter, which I have already sent to you, and the similar one to Mr. Stoneman, who is the Public Relations man. Before I had a chance to mail Mr. Humphrey's letter, I got a telephone message from him saying that he had written me and that an occasion could be made for the presentation of the petition, that Mr. Russeau (I think that was the name), Assistant to the Secretary-General, would be present, and Mr. Humphrey

himself, and that I might suggest certain dates. He wished me to write and
make the request, as it would not be proper for him to suggest it. Therefore,
I changed my letter slightly, suggesting certain dates, and sent it special
delivery.

As I have said, before the close of the day, he had suggested the 23rd. I trust
that this date suits you. If it does not, will you get in touch with Mr. Humphrey's office and make any further suggestions.

The whole publicity for this affair will, of course, be conducted by your
office. I venture to suggest that we send out immediately something like five
hundred or a thousand invitations, in which the Board of Directors of the NAACP
invites persons to be present on this occasion. I think that we should make
every effort to have a representative gathering of distinguished colored and
white citizens.

In addition to that, this invitation should especially be sent to the heads of all
the fifty-seven United Nations delegations, and, of course, these ought to go out
not later than Monday. Possibly it would be all right to have these invitations
printed on the regular office paper, with the full list of the Board of Directors
and Officers. Of course, invitations should go to all the newspapers, colored
and white, directed especially to the editors.[1]

*Du Bois's patience and energy and his lifelong conviction of the persuasiveness
of reason are reflected in a letter he sent to a West Virginia newspaper which
had editorially attacked the NAACP for its petition to the United Nations.* Du*

1. The December 1947 *Crisis* (54: 362–64, 379–81) carried a condensation of Du
Bois's introduction to the petition and brief summaries of the chapters by Earl Dickerson, Milton Konvitz, William Ming, Jr., Leslie Perry, and Rayford Logan, together
with a picture of Du Bois's actual presentation of the petition to Henri Laugier, Lie's
assistant (not Russeau, as in Du Bois's memorandum). At the 23 October presentation, Walter White made a short introductory statement, concluding by presenting
Du Bois as "one of the most distinguished scholars of the United States." This speech
was followed by a statement from Du Bois, containing perhaps three hundred words
and referring to the petition as "a frank and earnest appeal to all the world for ele-
mental justice against the treatment which the United States has visited upon us for
three centuries...." A factual summary of the petition and its presentation will be
found in two similar articles by Hugh H. Smythe, one in the *Journal of Negro Education* 17 (Winter 1948):88–90, the other in *Phylon* 8 (Fourth Quarter 1947):355–58.

* Full comprehension of Du Bois's letter requires knowledge of the text to which he
responded. An editorial entitled, "Hurting Race Relations," which appeared in the
Morgantown Post, 15 October 1947, stated: "It is difficult to imagine how the cause
of better racial relations in the United States could have been done a greater disservice
than by the action of the National Association for the Advancement of Colored People
in filing a complaint with the United Nations.... It seems to us that, by going to the
United Nations at a time when our international relations are at such a critical stage,
the NAACP has followed a course which, rightly or wrongly, is almost certain to alien-
ate public support and cause a large number of persons to cease their participation in

Bois's letter was not published,† but it still merits publication.

New York City, October 27, 1947

The Editor
The Morgantown *Post*
Morgantown, West Virginia
Sir:
On October 15, you published a leading editorial on the statement which
the NAACP recently placed before the United Nations, and questioned its time-
liness. I write to ask if you are acquainted with the circumstances leading to this
complaint? The Charter of the United Nations, adopted at San Francisco and
ratified by the United States and fifty-six other nations, has the following six
references to the obligation of this new international body to uphold essential human freedoms and rights.

Preamble: The United Nations is "Determined . . . to reaffirm faith in fundamental human rights."

Chapter I, Article I, Paragraph 3: The purposes and principles of the United
Nations are: "To achieve international cooperation . . . in promoting and encouraging respect for human rights and for fundamental freedoms for all without distinction as to race, sex, language, or religion."

Chapter IV, Article 13, Paragraph 1: "The General Assembly shall initiate
studies and make recommendations for the purpose of . . . assisting in the realization of human rights and fundamental freedoms for all without distinction as
to race, sex, language, or religion."

Chapter IX, Article 55, Paragraph 1: ". . . the United Nations shall promote . . . universal respect for, and observance of, human rights and fundamental freedom for all without distinction as to race, sex, language, or religion."

Chapter X, Article 62, Paragraphs 1–2: "The Economic and Social Council . . . may make recommendations for the purpose of promoting respect for,
and observance of, human rights and fundamental freedoms for all."

Chapter XII, Article 76, Paragraphs 1–3: "The basic objectives of the trusteeship system . . . [are] to encourage respect for human rights and fundamental
freedoms for all without distinction as to race, sex, language, or religion. . . ."

---

its program. If the U.N. had some authority in the matter or could do anything to
abate the conditions set forth in the complaint, more justification might be found for
the course which has been followed. But under the circumstances it has been judgement of the poorest sort to seek 'publicity' for NAACP objectives at the cost of embarrassing the country in its foreign relations and furnishing Soviet Russia with new
ammunition to use against us."

† A search of the *Morgantown Post* for November 1947 produced no evidence of the
publication or mention of any letter from the NAACP or Du Bois. The editor appreciates
the assistance on this matter generously given by Robert F. Munn, Director of Libraries
of West Virginia University, in a letter to the editor dated 25 June 1973.

In pursuance to this obligation, the United Nations set up a Human Rights Commission last Spring and next month it will set up a sub-commission on Discrimination. Under those circumstances what was the duty of American Negroes? Should they by silence and inaction let the world assume that they are satisfied with their status in this land, or was it their duty to set down clearly and dispassionately their status and just complaint? The timing of this protest was set by the action of the United Nations who invited the submission of data.

Manifestly, no people who consciously or unconsciously is oppressing another is going to agree upon a proper time when they are willing to listen to protest. For two centuries this country declared that any protest against slavery was untimely and presumptuous; it paid for its unwillingness to listen to reason by blood and destruction. Today fourteen million Americans are deeply resentful and alarmed for themselves and their country at the continuation of color-caste, lynching, and disfranchisement in this land. Is it not their duty to let their attitude be known, when the world asks a report on human rights and discrimination?

It has always been the policy of the NAACP to temper its protests and actions with reason, and because of that it might have been fairer on the part of your writer to have read our petition before criticizing it. But it is a mistake for anyone to assume that this organization awaits popular applause before action. We are not spineless appeasers. When we see wrong or persistence in wrong we protest. We have done this for forty years and we shall continue this program.

Very sincerely yours,
W. E. B. Du Bois

The NAACP petition to the United Nations received extensive nationwide publicity; it was, indeed, commented upon throughout the world. The New York Times of 24 October 1947 headlined the story, "U.N. Get Charges of Wide Bias in U.S.," and gave George Streator half a page to report it. John P. Humphrey, director of the United Nations' Division of Human Rights, was quoted in the story as stating that the division "has no power to take any action in regard to any complaints concerning human rights." He added, however, that a subcommission on the prevention of discrimination was to meet in Geneva on 24 November and that the human rights commission itself was to meet in the same place on 1 December. Therefore, wrote Streator, Humphrey himself "asked the Association to continue its efforts."

Representing the United States on that human rights commission were Mrs. Eleanor Roosevelt (herself a member of the board of directors of the NAACP) and Jonathan Daniels. But the task of taking the fight before that commission in Geneva was entrusted to White and not to Du Bois. When a Soviet proposal to consider the NAACP petition was presented to the commission, it was rejected, on

3 December 1947, by a vote of 11 to 1. In connection with the latter action, Du Bois expressed his views in a letter written in January 1948.

New York City, January 23, 1948

Dear Mr. Mezerik:[1]

Thank you for your letter and for your kindness in permitting me to see the material from Mr. Jonathan Daniels,[2] as well as for passing along the letter from Dr. Jacob Maulen of The Library of the Palace of Peace, The Hague. I am sending you enclosed a copy of a letter which I have sent to Dr. Maulen.

With regard to Mr. Daniels' letter, the fundamental mistake of the Commission on Human Rights, and the Sub-Commission on Discrimination and Protection of Minorities, is to try to attack this problem in a general and overall way. This is simply impossible. It makes very little difference to the man who is having his teeth pushed down his throat that the Commission on Human Rights has declared he was born "free and equal." The Commission ought to begin at the other end of the scale and make a study of a petition, which merits attention. Even in this case a start has to be made somewhere, and it is simply unfortunate submission to the "Red scare" to assume that their motives are "obviously political." They can say the same thing about Mr. Daniels. The NAACP is not "defending Russia" or anybody else; it is trying to get men like Mr. Daniels to stand up and be counted for the decent treatment of Negroes in America. It wishes to have the petition which it has sent in to be put on agenda of the General Assembly of the United Nations.

Mr. Daniels' own proposals are not realistic; he wants our petition considered, apparently along with all the other petitions. This seems to me ridiculous. You have got to start somewhere, and the Russian proposal ought to have had the

1. This was A. G. Mezerik (b. 1901), whose *Revolt of the South and the West* had recently been published by Duell, Sloan and Pearce (1946). He contributed frequently to the *Nation* throughout the 1940s and published a splendid analysis of the NAACP petition to the United Nations in the 13 December 1947 *Nation* (165: 644-46) under the title, "Negroes at U.N.'s Door." Mezerik is currently editor of the International Review Service with offices at the United Nations in New York City.

2. Jonathan Worth Daniels was born in North Carolina in 1902 and studied at the University of North Carolina and at the law school of Columbia University. He was on the staff of the *Raleigh News and Observer* beginning in 1928 and since 1970 has been editor emeritus of that paper. He was on the White House staff from 1943 through 1945; from 1947 to 1953 he was a member of the United Nations Sub-Commission on Discrimination and Protection of Minorities. He has written many books, including *A Southerner Discovers the South* (1938) and *The Randolphs of Virginia* (1972). The letter to Mezerik from Daniels—a copy of which went to Du Bois—was dated Raleigh, North Carolina, 29 December 1947, and took issue with Mezerik's *Nation* article. Du Bois's letter to Mezerik is directly responsive to arguments in the Daniels letter.

wholehearted cooperation of American liberals. To do nothing, because so much is asked, is certainly no way to attack a pressing social problem.

Very sincerely yours,

W. E. B. Du Bois

The NAACP petition to the United Nations was not received at Geneva. Efforts to bring it before the General Assembly of the United Nations in 1948—India, Haiti, Liberia, and the USSR had indicated interest in supporting such an effort —were blocked by opposition from the United States and in particular from Mrs. Roosevelt, the most prominent member of its UN delegation and a member of the national board of the NAACP itself.*

A memorandum from Du Bois to White in the summer of 1948, shortly before Du Bois was dismissed from the NAACP, illuminates this matter.

Memorandum

To: Mr. Walter White
From: Dr. W. E. B. Du Bois
Subject: Meeting with Mrs. Eleanor Roosevelt—NAACP Petition
Date: July 1, 1948

On June 30, I was asked to call on Mrs. Roosevelt at 2 Park Avenue, the offices of the United States Delegation to the United Nations. I talked with her for about one-half hour. She represented Senator Warren Austin, the head of the United States Delegation. What she said was in answer to a letter that I had written to Senator Austin on October 28, 1947. The essence of that letter was as follows:

Replying to your letter of October 21, I am taking the opportunity of sending you a copy of our petition to the United Nations. I trust that you will do your best to have this matter put on the agenda of the United Nations Assembly, either this year or next. I think it would be an excellent thing if the United States was able to say to the world: We are perfectly willing to be criticized as to our democracy and to give the public a chance to know what that critcism is.

Senator Austin wrote: "Upon receipt of a copy of your petition, we will be glad to refer it to the Department of State for appropriate consideration."

Mrs. Roosevelt said that the State Department had communicated its decision,

---

* The presence of Mrs. Roosevelt on the human rights commission and on the national board of the NAACP, together with her resistance to the petition from the NAACP, caused special embarrassment to her and to the NAACP board. The *New Republic*, then edited by Henry Wallace, commented specifically on this matter in an editorial in its 17 November 1947 issue (117:30), referring to Mrs. Roosevelt's "split personality."

and as Mr. Austin was engaged on the Security Council, she was representing him. The Department of State was of the opinion that it would be unwise to put our Petition on the agenda of the next Assembly for discussion, since no good could come from such a discussion. On the other hand, the Declaration of Human Rights, and it was to be hoped also the Convenant, would come up at that session and be discussed and possibly assented to.

I replied that I realized that no international action on our plight was probable nor, indeed, expected; but that I thought that the world ought to know just exactly what the situation was in the United States, so that they would not be depending upon vague references concerning our race problem, but would have factual statements before them; and that if the United States was unwilling itself to put the matter before the Assembly, that one or two other nations had expressed the possibility of their doing this.

Mrs. Roosevelt thought that this would be embarrassing; that it would be seized upon by the Soviet Government and others as an excuse for attacking the United States. Mrs. Roosevelt said that already, several times, she had been compelled to answer attacks upon the United States for its race problem by pointing out the fact that other countries had made similar mistakes. In case, therefore, the matter was discussed in the Assembly, she and her colleagues would be put in the unpleasant position of having to defend the United States. The situation then might be so unpleasant that she would feel it necessary to resign from the United States Delegation to the United Nations.

I expressed the opinion that the placing of facts before an international body need not of necessity be a matter of embarrassment. Naturally, it might be taken up by persons and organizations unfriendly to the United States but that was not a reason for suppressing the truth. That in the early days of the National Association for the Advancement of Colored People, when we proposed to expose the facts concerning lynching and discrimination, there were many good friends of the Negro race who advised against it and said it would bring unfavorable criticism upon us. Nevertheless, we insisted and I think that we did right.

Mrs. Roosevelt asked that if any action was taken toward bringing the matter up for discussion before the Assembly of the United Nations, she be notified as soon as possible, so that she could prepare to act accordingly. I promised that such notification would certainly be given to her.[1]

1. Du Bois sent Mrs. Roosevelt a copy of this memorandum on 1 July 1948, but his papers contain no written response from her. Du Bois devoted several of his *Chicago Defender* columns to detailed discussion of the fate of the United Nations petition in Geneva and to Mrs. Roosevelt's and Mr. Daniels's opposition to its acceptance; see the issues of 27 March, 3 April, 10 April, and 17 April 1948.

1948

*In September 1948 the board of directors of the NAACP dismissed Du Bois, ef-
fective 31 December 1948. Correspondence of 1948 which is directly relevant
to that event will be presented as a group; meanwhile, many other events and
interests were of concern to Du Bois.*

Du Bois sent a letter to the New York Times *early in 1948 which was thought
not "fit to print." He then sent the letter to the New York* Herald-Tribune,
*which published it on 7 March 1948. Its subject matter is as timely now as three
decades ago.*

New York City, January 23, 1948

To the Editor
The New York *Times*
Dear Sir:

Many residents of New York and taxpayers of Negro descent are alarmed
and disappointed at the news recently printed in your columns, that Dr. L. D.
Reddick, Curator of the Schomburg Collection, has resigned and is going South
because of lack of funds and facilities for support of his work.[1]

Most people, unfortunately, know little about this collection. Arthur Schomburg was a bank messenger who had wide knowledge of Negro literature in
English, Spanish, and other languages. He began collecting books, pamphlets,
and other articles on his own account until his collection became one of the
most outstanding in the United States.

The 135th Street Branch of the New York Public Library was beginning to be
a center for Negroes and others interested in reading and research, and for
some time there was friction because it was not the policy of the library authorities to encourage Negro librarians or assistants. After considerable pressure,
however, this ban was lifted, and today there is a Negro librarian in charge of
this and other branches, and assistants in various parts of the city library system.

Meantime, at the 135th Street Branch, Mrs. Catherine Latimer, of Brooklyn,
began to collect Negro literature and was given charge of this work. She
gathered quite a number of books and gradually impressed upon her superiors
that Negro American culture in the United States had a growing, interesting
literature which people ought to know and many wanted to study. Finally, the

1. The account to which Du Bois refers appeared in the *Times* on 15 January 1948,
p. 21.

Schomburg Collection was bought by the City, and after a time Mr. Schomburg, having retired from his work at the bank, was appointed Curator. He was valuable in collecting books, but he was not a trained librarian, and naturally the direction of the Schomburg Collection fell to Mrs. Latimer.

In 1939, L. D. Reddick, a Ph.D. from the University of Chicago, was put in charge of this collection. It began to grow, and especially it became a center where students looked for rare books, and pamphlets, and other materials pertaining to Negroes. The vast manuscript collection of the Myrdal study was entrusted to this collection and there was a considerable collection of objects of art. But the library authorities did not seem to realize the unique place which this collection occupied. When the library was enlarged and rebuilt, the Schomburg Collection was put on the fourth floor, with no elevator, and it was given but meager facilities. It is now difficult for students to use it, and the number of helpers is far too few. Mr. Reddick had many plans which called for additional funds, but, as the library authorities said, it was cramped for funds in all directions, and it still seemed to be under the impression that the Schomburg Collection was nothing more than a branch library for young readers which did not call for any special attention.

Because of this, the Schomburg Collection has lost much material which it would have had. The Arthur Spingarn Collection of Negro literature, one of the finest in the world, was given to Howard University, because Mr. Spingarn was convinced that there it would get the attention which it needed. Many of my own manuscripts and documents have been given to the James Weldon Johnson Collection at Yale University because they were giving especial attention to that sort of thing. There is no certainty that the Schomburg Collection is going to be anything more than the orphan child of the New York Public Library.

Now comes the serious news that the best trained man for this work in the United States is going to leave to go to head up the library of a Southern university [Atlanta University], because he simply despairs of getting the attention, the planning, and the funds which he must have, if the Schomburg Collection is to fulfill its promise. It would be a calamity to have this happen. And it seems to me that someone in the city of New York ought to take it upon his conscience to induce the New York Public Library, and the philanthropically minded citizens, to come to the rescue of this unique adventure in the study of American Negro culture.

Sincerely yours,
W. E. B. Du Bois

A widely read gossip column, called "Grapevine," stated in the 7 February 1948 Chicago Defender that the project for an Encyclopedia of the Negro was allowed to die because of a general feeling that Du Bois was too "advanced"; it was *thought advisable, said this column, to await the good doctor's demise. Alas, "Brother Du Bois gets healthier every year," and so, the report continued, the General Education Board and Dodd, Mead and Company had decided to press forward with the project and has persuaded Dr. F. D. Patterson, president of Tuskegee Institute, to be its editor-in-chief.* The substance for this "gossip" will appear in subsequent letters.*

Washington, D.C., February 16, 1948

My dear Dr. Du Bois:

I am enclosing herewith a copy of a letter which I have just written to Dr. Stokes concerning the reported transfer of the Encyclopedia of the Negro Project from the Phelps-Stokes Fund to the General Education Board, with Dr. F. D. Patterson as general editor.[1]

I would appreciate very much any information which you can give me on this matter. I might say quite frankly that I am in a mood to write an editorial comment on the matter if I can get sufficient and accurate information. If you can aid me, either on the record or off the record, I would appreciate hearing from you.

May I take this opportunity to add my congratulations to the many which I know you have received on the occasion of your eightieth birthday. I regret very much that I will not be able to attend the banquet in your honor because of previous commitments.

Sincerely yours,
Chas. H. Thompson[2]

New York City, February 22, 1948

Dr. Fred McCuistion[1]

My dear Sir:

I have received recently several letters which have so disquieted me, that I

---

* Frederick Douglass Patterson was born in Washington, D.C., in 1901; he was educated at Iowa State College. He headed the veterinary division of Tuskegee Institute from 1928 to 1933, was director of Tuskegee's School of Agriculture from 1933 to 1935, and was president of the institute from 1935 to 1953, thereafter emeritus. From 1953 to 1970 he was president of the Phelps-Stokes Fund.

1. Thompson's letter to Anson Phelps Stokes was also dated 16 February; it asked for information on the reported project for an Encyclopedia of the Negro to be sponsored by the General Education Board. See the index of volume two of this correspondence for numerous references to this project.

2. Charles Henry Thompson was born in Mississippi in 1896 and was educated at Virginia Union and Chicago universities. He served as a professor and a dean at Howard University, but he is best known as founding editor of the *Journal of Negro Education*, beginning in 1932, and he remains editor emeritus of that quarterly.

1. Fred McCuistion was born in Arkansas in 1893 and educated in Hendrix College in Arkansas and Peabody College in Maryland. He was State Director of

am venturing to write the General Education Board. I am addressing the letter to you and asking that if this matter is not in your jurisdiction, you will pass it on to the proper official.

On May 10, 1932, the *Encyclopedia of the Negro* was incorporated in the District of Columbia by Anson Phelps Stokes, Mordecai W. Johnson, W. E. B. Du Bois, James H. Dillard, Waldo G. Leland and others, to edit and publish an Encyclopedia of the Negro. Later I was chosen Senior Editor and Dr. Guy Johnson of the University of North Carolina, as my associate. We tried in various ways to get the project underwritten, but were not successful. However, the Phelps-Stokes Fund, under Dr. Anson Phelps Stokes, furnished a small budget and preliminary work and planning went on from then until 1946, resulting in a preliminary volume of bibliography and history of the project.

Recently letters and notices have gone out stating that the General Education Board has furnished $250,000 for taking over this project and that Dr. F. D. Patterson of Tuskegee has been designated as general editor.

No direct word of this has come to me. There has been, so far as I know, no meeting of the Board of Directors nor of the Editorial Board.

I write, therefore, to you and through you to the General Education Board to ask just what their action has been in this matter. I should like it clearly understood that I have no objection to my replacement as editor. The project is of greater importance than the plans of any one person. But I object to the manner of my displacement, involving as it does unmerited discourtesy. I did not seek the office but was given it to my great surprise at the insistence of Dr. Moton of Tuskegee and the whole Board. I am willing at any time, and still am, to step down if the project can be realized under other leadership.

My stronger objection is the fact that the Board of Directors have apparently been ignored and an editor appointed without their consultation or consent. President Patterson is a worthy person; I have been his friend, a guest in his house, and have defended many of his efforts. But Mr. Patterson was trained as a veterinary surgeon and holds a full-time job as administrator of a great school. He has no knowledge of the social sciences nor history, and is not a writer. I know of no encyclopedia in our day that has been entrusted to an untrained editor. Moreover, an encyclopedia of the Negro race should be edited by a board on which Negroes were represented and had voice in the selection of the staff. It would be intolerable to have the editor of such a project selected by white men or by a white organization exclusively.

Of course I do not know what part, if any, the General Education Board has had in this matter. I, therefore, write for information, before taking any further steps. I am, however, while awaiting your reply, taking the liberty to send

---

Negro Education in Arkansas from 1925 to 1930 and an associate director of the Rosenwald Fund thereafter. In 1939 he was appointed to the General Education Board and at the time Du Bois wrote him was its associate director.

copies of this letter to Dr. Stokes, Dr. Patterson, Dr. [Mordecai] Johnson and a few friends who have already written me and asked for information.

I am, Sir,

> Respectfully yours,
> W. E. B. Du Bois

New York City, February 27, 1948

Dear Mr. Du Bois:

I am enclosing your letter of February 22 in which you report information regarding a General Education Board grant toward the development of an encyclopaedia of the Negro.

I assure you the information is unfounded and that the Board has made no such contribution. We have, however, given preliminary consideration to a proposal from Tuskegee, but the project is inactive at present.

If you have further interest in the project we shall be glad to discuss it with you on your return. In the meantime I have talked with your associate, Mr. Smythe, who will probably give you a report of the situation.

> Sincerely,
> Fred McCuistion

At this same time Du Bois sent a similar letter directly to President Patterson at Tuskegee, which received the ensuing reply. The project went no further.

Tuskegee, Alabama, March 5, 1948

Dear Dr. Du Bois:

I am pleased to send you a copy of the letter which was sent over my signature to a few people regarding an encyclopedia on the Negro, along with the statement suggested by Mr. Edward Dodd, Jr. of Dodd, Mead and Company as to the possible scope and nature of this volume.[1]

1. The enclosure included a copy of a letter sent by Patterson to Charles S. Johnson, president of Fisk University. This letter, dated 14 January 1948, stated that Patterson had been conferring "for nearly two years" with Edward Dodd of Dodd, Mead and Co. and with Claude A. Barnett (an attorney in Chicago and head of the Associated Negro Press) and with "officials of the General Education Board on producing an Encyclopedia of the Negro." The letter stated that he had "permitted the use of my name as Editor in Chief" but that he had intended nothing final in so doing; it asked for an opinion about the effort and asked whether or not Dr. Johnson and Fisk would cooperate in it. The memorandum from Edward Dodd came to some eight hundred words and affirmed "the need for a comprehensive, basic reference book on the Negro" to be called "The Negro: An Encyclopedia," planned to come to about one million words and to sell for perhaps twelve dollars.

The Du Bois papers include a signed carbon copy of a letter to Patterson from Professor Rayford W. Logan, dated Washington, D.C., 16 February 1948, in reply to

Apparently the information which has come to you is greatly misleading as no grant whatever has been made nor is there any assurance that any will be made. I am pleased, however, to be advised of your thinking on the matter. I am sure before anything more of significance is done an opportunity for a thorough discussion with you and others interested will be sought.

Very truly yours,

F. D. Patterson

Dictated by Dr. Patterson but signed in his absence

In writing of the period which Dalton Trumbo called The Time of the Toad *and Lillian Hellman more recently* Scoundrel Time, *the fact of resistance to the intense repression exemplified in the names Trumbo and Hellman is often overlooked or minimized. Du Bois was, of course, a leader in that resistance, and his correspondence reflects both its existence and his leadership. Thus, in 1948, he heard from and responded positively to appeals from both Harlow Shapley and Van Wyck Brooks.* *

New York City, February 17, 1948

Dear Dr. Du Bois:

On January 30th I wrote you urging that you consent to be a member-at-

---

a letter he had received asking for his cooperation. The letter indicated that a copy went to Du Bois and another to Anson Phelps Stokes. Its substantive paragraph reads: "As you probably know, I was associated with Dr. W. E. B. Du Bois during practically the entire period of the Phelps-Stokes Project for an Encyclopedia of the Negro. I have valid reasons for believing that a major reason for the failure of the General Education Board to grant an appropriation of $150,000 was the opposition to Dr. Du Bois because of his alleged radical views. I was further informed, quite reliably, that it was planned to wait until Dr. Du Bois died before further action would be taken on the encyclopedia. Since Dr. Du Bois has not been sufficiently cooperative to pass off the scene, and since there is an obvious need for an encyclopedia of the Negro, it would seem that plans are now being made to publish an encyclopedia with which he will have no connection. Under the circumstances, I am sure that you will understand that it is impossible for me to contribute to the proposed encyclopedia." (In a letter to the editor of 22 July 1976, Professor Logan kindly consented to the publication of this material from his letter to President Patterson.)

* Harlow Shapley (1885–1972), the renowned astronomer, was educated at the University of Missouri and at Princeton; his researches in photometry and cosmogony were especially important. He was author of several books, notably *Of Stars and Men* (1958), *The View from a Distant Star* (1963), and *Beyond the Observatory* (1967). Van Wyck Brooks (1886–1967) was educated at Harvard and taught at Stanford prior to the First World War; he was an editor of the *Freeman* in the 1920s. His main work included critical studies of Melville, James, Howells, Whitman, and others, in separate studies and in the five-volume *Makers and Finders: A History of the Writer in America, 1800–1915* (1936–52). He also translated works by leading contemporary French authors, especially Romain Rolland.

large of the National Council of Arts, Sciences and Professions. Doubtless, under pressure of work the letter has been overlooked, but as it is important to complete our organization, I am writing again to tell you how much we would appreciate your accepting this position.

The following have already consented to serve on the Council: Thomas Mann, Jo Davidson, Max Weber, Lillian Hellman, Paul Robeson, Norman Corwin, Dr. Allan Butler, Dr. Maud Slye, Prof. Curtis MacDougall, Prof. Melville Herskovits, John Cromwell, Dr. Frederick Schuman, Prof. Thomas Emerson, John Howard Lawson, Howard Koch, Philip Evergood, Dr. Theodor Rosebury.

I am sure you will agree with us that the work of this Council is of vital importance to all professional people in maintaining the freedoms so important not only to cultural groups but to all American citizens.

Looking forward to your joining us, I am

Sincerely yours,

Dr. Harlow Shapley

Washington, D.C., February 25, 1948

Dear Dr. Du Bois:

A group of citizens repelled and alarmed by the unconscionable inroads upon our traditional civil liberties that are made daily by the House Committee on un-American Activities, has initiated a Committee of One Thousand whose sole purpose it is to seek the abolition of that committee.[1] Enclosed is a statement of principles.

There is no question that the influence of this committee has spread far beyond Washington. It has inspired state legislatures to draft bills and set up similar committees which tend to create an atmosphere of terror and intimidation throughout this country. We know that many congressmen are opposed to the inquisitorial procedures of the [J. Parnell] Thomas Committee and are awake to the peril of its operations. They know that the committee incites the formation of "little Dies Committees" in the various states; and promotes secondary purges in business, government, and on campuses. But in this presidential-election year these congressmen need the backing of well-known citizens before taking appropriate legislative action.

Those of us who have initiated the Committee of One Thousand have done so with the conviction that such wholly un-American activities must be fought vigorously and effectively.

We would like very much to have you with us as a member of the Committee of One Thousand. Please fill in the enclosed card. There are no membership

1. In addition to Van Wyck Brooks, initiating sponsors included William Rose Benet, Norman Corwin, Olin Downes, Irwin Edman, Albert Einstein, Lillian Hellman, Frederick March, Rexford G. Tugwell, and Rabbi Stephen S. Wise.

dues but any financial contribution you can make would be important in helping us do the job more effectively.

Sincerely yours,
Van Wyck Brooks

The twenty-third of February 1948 was Du Bois's eightieth birthday. The Fisk Club of New York sponsored a dinner marking the occasion at the Roosevelt Hotel in New York; Arthur B. Spingarn served as toastmaster.* Du Bois received numerous congratulatory letters, including one from George Padmore, writing as chief of the African Press Agency. Du Bois's response reflects the almost incredible energy and spirit of this man as he began his ninth decade.

London, England, February 23, 1948
Dear Dr. Du Bois:

I have the honour to convey to you at the request of my colleagues here, on our behalf and on behalf of Africans, African-descended, and British admirers, our heartiest greetings on the occasion of your eightieth birthday. We sincerely trust that you will outlive the allotted biblical span by considerably more than one decade, as we know that you will use all the years that may be given to you in furthering the cause of Pan-Africanism, to which you have devoted so large a part of your life.

Unlike so many who, with shibboleths on their lips and self-interest in their hearts, have been seduced by money and office away from the struggle for the social emancipation and political freedom of our people, you have rejected the path of opportunism and clung steadfastly to your beliefs. Nor have you allowed those beliefs to remain sterile but have kept your mind active and alert to the point of bringing your ideas more into line with the current scene and temper of our people in the United States, in Africa and in the West Indies, in whose hearts you have earned a place as a fighter for freedom and democratic justice.

Holding at heart the belief that freedom and justice are indivisible, you have demonstrated that you are concerned that these prerogatives shall be internationally enjoyed and not confined to any single group, people or race. Your work in the cause of our people, therefore, has not merely a sectarian aim, but the noble objective of international unity in freedom and peace between all peoples.

This objective is indeed worthy of the devoted work you have performed in

---

* There is a photograph showing Du Bois and Spingarn together on this occasion in the April 1948 *Crisis* (55:125); ironically, the same issue carried an editorial, "Keep an Eye on the Communists," which reflected the worst elements in the growing hysteria. A poem in tribute to Du Bois on his eightieth birthday by Bette Darcie Latimer, then a senior at Fisk, appeared in the July 1948 *Crisis* (55:210).

its cause, and we should prove unworthy of our respect for your endeavors if we did not pledge ourselves on this most fitting occasion to pursue to a successful conclusion the fight for the social, political and economic freedom of our people in all parts of the world, and of the oppressed and downtrodden everywhere.

May your work be crowned by this achievement.

George Padmore

St. Louis, Missouri, March 1, 1948

Dear Mr. Padmore:

I am on a lecture trip to the middle West, California, Texas and Georgia. I pause to thank you much for your kind message on my birthday. I appreciated it. I have had an idea. Mull it over without publishing it yet. The Assembly of the U.N. meets in Paris next Fall. How about a real Pan-African Congress: one voting delegate to each million Negroes, with genuine credentials—250 delegates; alternates on strict conditions. That would be 8 delegates from the Caribbean, 15 from the U.S.A., one from Europe. Fraternal, non-voting delegates from Asia.

Demand recognized consultants to the Assembly from Pan-Africa.

Think this over. Best regards.

W. E. B. Du Bois

A delightful congratulatory message came from Channing H. Tobias, then director of the Phelps-Stokes Fund.

New York City, February 24, 1948

Dear Dr. Du Bois:

I am taking advantage of the first time in my office in ten days to express my regret at not being able to attend the dinner in your honor last night and to pass on to you the tribute that I intended to have reach you yesterday. It is this:

The marvel of Du Bois is not that he has reached the ripe age of eighty, but that in spite of years he is today the most vigorously forthright and aggressive advocate of the rights of the darker peoples of the earth. I predict that when he reaches the century mark his head will still be held high, his beard will still be pointed, and he will still be smoking gold-tipped cigarettes![1]

My best wishes to you.

Sincerely yours,
Channing H. Tobias

1. For many years Du Bois smoked gold-tipped Benson and Hedges cigarettes; but with this as with everything in his life (except work!) he exercised moderation: he smoked three cigarettes a day, one after each meal, deliberately and slowly.

*A biographer of the great Africanist Edward Wilmont Blyden also offered
congratulations to Du Bois on his eightieth birthday and added some comments
of consequence.*

Greenwich, Conn., February 23, 1948

My dear Dr. Du Bois:

May I add my congratulations on your eightieth birthday, although rather
belatedly?

I have recently read, with much interest, your book on *The World and
Africa*, and have recommended it to friends.

My special interest is in connection with Liberia, for it was my grandfather,
the Rev. John P. Knox, then a minister on the island of St. Thomas, West Indies,
who was young Edward Blyden's pastor, and who was responsible for his going
to Liberia for his education, when he was refused admittance to an institution
in this country.

A few years ago I tried to find more facts about the life of Dr. Blyden, to
supplement the family story, but not knowing where to look, I was not successful in discovering much more than had come down by word of mouth. But,
just a little over a year ago, Dr. Blyden's grandson and namesake arrived in
this country for post-graduate study, and the leads which he has given me
have revealed a wealth of material on Dr. Blyden's life and accomplishments.

One reference I have found linked your name with his. Do you have any
personal recollection of Dr. Blyden, or anything which can be added to the
material I am now collecting on his life and labors? Edward W. Blyden, III,
hopes to write the story of his grandfather's life, and all the information I am
gathering is to be turned over to him for this purpose.

With best wishes to you in the great work you are doing,

Yours sincerely,

Edith Holden[1]

New York City, March 26, 1948

Miss Edith Holden

My dear Madam:

Thank you very much for your congratulations on my birthday. I never met
Dr. Blyden, but I know of him and have greatly admired his work.[1] If there is

1. Other than the information in this letter, the editor has been able to find little
additional data on Edith Holden. Files at the Schomburg Library in New York City
indicate that she died in 1967. She did produce a massive source book of over one
thousand pages, *Blyden of Liberia: An Account of the Life and Labors of Edward
Wilmot Blyden, LL.D., as Recorded in Letters and in Print* (with a foreword by
Nnamdi Azikiwe), published in 1966 by Vantage Press, New York. The Blyden
grandson mentioned in her letter was a professor at the University of Nigeria when
her book appeared and made the index for the book.

1. There is a letter to Blyden from Du Bois in the first volume of this *Correspond-*

anything I can do to help his grandson in writing his grandfather's life, I shall be glad to do it.

Very sincerely yours,
W. E. B. Du Bois

Some indication of Du Bois's activities as he began his eightieth year is conveyed in a letter he sent his wife in Baltimore.

New York City, March 12, 1948

My dear Nina:

I haven't bothered you with information about my trip as I know Yolande has told you most of it. First of all, in the middle of February I went to Boston and talked at Revere Hall in Mechanics Building for a very busy colored woman who holds an annual art exhibit. There were five or six hundred people there and all listened very carefully. I met, of course, a great many old friends.

Then after a few days I went up to Maine to Colby College at Waterville, a very interesting school which I had never seen before. There were two or three colored students and two teachers who had taught with me at Atlanta. I was very nicely entertained and lectured to students, and held conferences in the parlor and had dinner with students and professors.

Then I came back to New York just in time for my dinner party. I had not been anxious to have this dinner given because it cost so much and put so many of your friends on the spot. You know, of course, that it was $7.50 a plate, which was highway robbery, but I had nothing to do with it. In fact, Mrs. [Lillian A.] Alexander ran it, and naturally she and I had some differences of opinion. For instance, to my surprise she informed me over the phone that Charles Johnson, the new president at Fisk, was going to preside. I said flatly that he was not going to preside at my dinner. She went up in the air and so did I but finally we compromised and Arthur Spingarn presided and Johnson made a speech. It was really an extraordinarily interesting event. Over 300 people were present and lots of your friends: Mrs. Curtis, Mrs. Trotman, Mrs. Bell and the girls, Lottie Cooper, and numbers of others. One white woman friend in Chicago gave me as a present a check for $100.00. The messages were splendid—from the Prime Minister of India, Nehru, and some of the prominent Indians; from Henry Wallace, from Gunnar Myrdal and his wife, etc.

The dinner was over about midnight and next morning at 7:30 I hopped on

ence (p. 146) and several references to his work in the published writings of Du Bois, always showing great admiration; see the index to Aptheker, *Annotated Bibliography.* Hollis R. Lynch gives a different impression of Du Bois's opinion both in his biography of Blyden (Oxford: Oxford University Press, 1967) and in his introduction to *Selected Published Writings of Edward Wilmot Blyden* (New York: Humanities Press, 1971), p. xxxiv.

a plane and was in St. Louis that afternoon. I was so afraid I would be delayed by the bad weather but I made it all right. I stayed with Mabel Byrd Curtis who has two twin sons 12 years of age, most interesting kids. Her sister-in-law is Julia Childs Curtis, you may remember her—she was a student of mine at Atlanta. I spoke there to 800 pupils at Stowe College which is the colored Teachers College. There was a delegation of 65 white high school students to hear me. Two days later I spoke to the Booklovers Club—about 300 persons—in the local church.

Finally I took another plane and came to San Francisco. It was [a] long, rather hard ride with rain and snow almost all of the way until we cleared the last range of mountains. As usual the view of Los Angeles and San Francisco from the air at night was startling in its beauty.

At San Francisco a delegation of white and colored people met me and I went to the Palace Hotel. Since that I have spoken to 600 people in Oakland, to a large banquet of several hundred at the Labor School in San Francisco. Today I speak at Palo Alto where Stanford University is located. Day after tomorrow at Sacramento. On the 12th at the University of California and on the 14th at the Jones Memorial Church in San Francisco. On the 15th I shall go to Los Angeles to stop with Doctors John and Vada Somerville whom you remember. I will write you again from there.

I hope you are comfortable and content. You would have been very pleased to see your daughter and grand-daughter sitting at the head table at the New York dinner.

Yours with love,
Will

While it is disappointing that no reply to a letter from the late Oscar Lewis seems to have survived, Lewis's letter itself is thought-provoking. *

St. Louis, Missouri, April 6, 1948

Dear Dr. Du Bois:

Some time ago Melville Herskovits sent me a newspaper clipping of your column in which you very kindly referred to my article on "Wealth Differences in a Mexican Village."[1] I want you to know that I was very flattered that this article came to your attention and was very pleased that you saw some

---

* Oscar Lewis (1914-70) was educated at the College of the City of New York and at Columbia University. At the time of his letter to Du Bois he was associate professor of anthropology at Washington University in Saint Louis; from 1948 to 1970 he was professor of anthropology at the University of Illinois.

1. In his column in the *Chicago Defender*, 23 August 1947, Du Bois commented favorably on Lewis's book, *Life in a Mexican Village* (Urbana: University of Illinois Press, 1947).

practical value in a fairly technical and academic paper. I confess that it is quite rare for me to feel useful in this sense.

I am writing to you for advice in connection with a research paper that I am now working on. It has been noted by many anthropologists that wherever so-called primitive peoples or folk cultures have come into contact with Western civilization the lives of men and women have been affected in different ways. Thus Margaret [Mead] in one of the few studies available on this subject has shown that in the case of an American Indian tribe which was placed on a reservation following white conquest, the men were much harder hit than the women. When buffalo hunting and warfare—the two major occupations of the men—were gone, the men's lives were stripped of meaning, whereas the women continued with their traditional jobs as child bearers and child rearers and apparently made a better adjustment to the new situation.

I have been thinking of the history of Negro slavery in the New World from this point of view and have wondered whether there is any evidence which would indicate the different ways in which men and women were affected. Of course, I realize that slavery was destructive of the lives of both sexes and of African culture as a whole, but I wonder if a distinction can be made. In rereading the work of Herskovits I get the impression that a good case might be made for the proposition that the lives of the Negro men were much more disrupted than those of the women. Indeed, Herskovits suggests that most of the African cultural survivals in places like Haiti and Trinidad were carried by the women.

Can you recommend any studies or materials which would throw further light on this subject?

Thank you.

Sincerely yours,
Oscar Lewis

Du Bois earnestly supported the third-party presidential candidacy of former Vice-President Henry A. Wallace. Fundamental to that candidacy, and to Du Bois's support, was Wallace's commitment to changing United States foreign policy and terminating the Cold War.

New York City, May 17, 1948

Dear Dr. Du Bois:

I am taking the liberty of sending you a copy of an open letter which I have addressed to Premier Stalin, outlining the basic principles and practical steps which I believe make possible a general settlement of outstanding differences between ourselves and the Russians.

The body of this letter was written before the publication of the recent exchange of notes between Ambassador [Bedell] Smith and Foreign Minister [V. I.] Molotov. That exchange, which seemed to open the door to direct negotiations between the two nations, gave new hope to the peace-loving peoples of the world for an end to the cold war.[1]

It would be tragic if this hope were betrayed and a conference between the United States and the Soviet Union foreclosed by the Administration's flat rejection of the Russian offer to negotiate.

I am therefore addressing you and other men of peace who are leaders of American thought and molders of public opinion to ask that you urge the President, the Secretary of State and the Congress to act in good faith upon Ambassador Smith's statement that "the door is always wide open" to Soviet-American discussions by accepting the Molotov proposal for a conference to settle outstanding differences. Only if that proposal is accepted, and our representatives sit down with the Russians to arrive at a peaceful understanding, can America regain the moral leadership in world affairs that alone can make peace possible.

As I said in my open letter to Premier Stalin; "There is no misunderstanding or difficulty between the u.s.a. and the ussr which can be settled by force or fear and there is no difference which cannot be settled by peaceful, hopeful negotiation." If you believe, with me, in the truth of this statement let me urge you to speak out now for an early, open and fully reported meeting between representatives of the two great powers for the settlement of our differences by negotiations and agreement.

Sincerely yours,
Henry A. Wallace

New York City, May 24, 1948

My dear Mr. Wallace:

May I thank you for a copy of the letter addressed to Premier Stalin. I have read Mr. Stalin's answer. I think that your letter was a splendid achievement and a courageous step toward that peace for which every decent American citizen longs.

Very sincerely yours,
W. E. B. Du Bois

An exchange of substantial interest occurred between Du Bois and a writer in Colorado in the spring of 1948.

1. The text of Wallace's open letter is given in the *New York Times*, 17 May 1948, p. 14. The text of the reply from Premier Stalin, to which Du Bois refers in his answer to Wallace, is in the 18 May 1948 *Times*, p. 4. It is in his welcoming reply that Stalin uses the term "the co-existence of these [two] systems."

Denver, Colorado, May 17, 1948

My dear Dr. Du Bois:

Honesty demands my confession at the very start that the real reason I am writing you is that I need your blessing. My first approach to the so-called 'Negro question' (euphemistic term for the undemocratic treatment by the white of his colored brother) came through your *Black Folk—Then and Now;* since then I have evaluated the writings of others largely through their relation to the ideas you have set forth in *Dusk of Dawn* and other volumes. And it seems both natural and right to me that I should ask your approval of the course I am taking in the book I am now attempting in all humility and with a vivid realization of my own inadequacy, but a book I must nevertheless write because I feel so keenly the tragic injustice of the Negro's situation in an America which preaches democracy and practices its opposite with regard to some 13,000,000 of its people.

My original intention was to campaign for a permanent, well-implemented FEPC above all else, with the idea that wherever compulsion has brought together black and white as fellow-workers, mutual respect has been the outcome, and this, I thought, would be a step towards better racial relations. But this thinking was based largely on the findings of Dr. Robert C. Weaver (in *Negro Labor*), under the extraordinary conditions growing out of a war-begotten tight labor market. You will doubtless remember that the integration and up-grading of Negroes in industries where they had formerly been used only in a menial capacity—in many not at all—was accomplished only after the federal government set its foot down and said Executive Order 8802 must be made to work unless America wanted the obvious alternative of defeat at the hands of totalitarian powers. But under what for the sake of argument we should label 'normal' conditions, could these same gains be accomplished? Again I thought the answer to be 'yes'—provided, that is, the growing strength of the trade unions with liberal constitutions could be counted upon. And now—with the Taft-Hartley Bill an accomplished fact and the Mundt Bill a probability this very week?[1]

---

1. The Labor Management Relations Act was passed in 1947 over a veto from President Truman. It is generally known as the Taft-Hartley Act after Senator Robert A. Taft (R., Ohio) and Representative Fred A. Hartley, Jr. (R., N.J.), who sponsored it. Organized labor strongly opposed the act and was severely hurt by its passage: it outlawed the "closed shop" and made legal "right-to-work" laws, which were immediately instituted in several states, especially Southern ones. A detailed summary is given in *Labor Fact Book* no. 9, ed. Labor Research Association (New York: International Publishers, 1949), pp. 128–32. See also the *New York Times*, 24 June 1947.

The Mundt-Nixon Bill was a product of the House Un-American Activities Committee and was originally proposed in 1948 by two Republican Representatives—Richard M. Nixon of California and Karl E. Mundt of South Dakota, soon thereafter a senator. The same two men introduced the bill—called the Subversive Activities Control Act—again in 1949 and again it was not passed. But in 1950, under the same

Paul Robeson was here on a speaking tour recently and although I did not achieve the discussion I had hoped might be possible, I did fling at him the question: shall I push FEPC above all else in my book on the Negro situation? "No," he said, "to my mind, abolition of the poll tax is more important."

So I came home and began re-orienting myself. If the 10,000,000 votes that could be used in the southern states if there were no poll tax were added to the existing aggregate—even if the 6,000,000-odd poor whites had to be ruled out— Dixie would no longer be the formidable bloc it now is, would it? Do you think the uneducated Negroes in the South would be sufficiently alive to their own interests to vote for liberal candidates, liberal legislation? If out of the kindness of your heart you would tell me how you view this matter, I should be more than grateful.

Forgive my brash scraping of acquaintance—I saw no other way to make the contact I have been wanting to make since I first began to admire both your clear logic and your faultless literary style.

One more thing: as things are now shaping, do you still feel that a carefully and intelligently planned co-operative Negro industrial system in the midst of and in conjunction with a probable forthcoming change in the present economic basis of the nation is the answer? That is, do you still advocate deliberate segregation as a present economic defense and a potential striking force?

Very sincerely yours,
Kathleen R. Bruyn[2]
(Mrs. Marcel Bruyn)

New York City, May 4, 1948

My dear Mrs. Bruyn:

I have your letter of May 17.

Fundamentally and in the long run, it is more important to attack poverty than to attack disfranchisement. I mean by that, that the ignorance which is so often the cause of disfranchisement and always the cause of the mis-use of voting power, is at bottom itself caused by poverty. The same, of course, is true of disease. The fundamental evil then is poverty, lack of work, and low

---

title and with the support of such Democrats as Hubert Humphrey and Herbert Lehman, it was passed; it was generally referred to as the McCarran Act after one of its passionate advocates, Senator Pat McCarran of Nevada.

For an analysis of these laws and the struggle against them see H. Aptheker, *Dare We Be Free? The Meaning of the Attempt to Outlaw the Communist Party* (New York: New Century Publishers, 1961).

2. Kathleen Bruÿn was born in Niagara Falls, New York, in 1903 and privately educated. She worked on a local paper from 1927 to 1933 and then moved to Colorado. Until 1965 she was public relations chief for the Denver Opera House. The University of Colorado Press published her *Uranium Country* in 1955, and in 1971 she published *"Aunt" Clara Brown: The Story of a Black Pioneer* (Denver: Pruett).

wages. However, at any particular time it might be the best policy to fight against restrictions of the ballot when it was not as easy to fight after equitable working arrangements and decent wages.

I think that Consumers Cooperation and other cooperative enterprises among Negroes are of great importance in ameliorating their condition. This, of course, is equally true among whites.

I do not advocate segregation where it can be avoided, without doing harm because of long delay. When, however, you find a situation where Negroes are suffering disabilities because of segregation, I think that a deliberately segregated economy would eventually be the best way toward attacking economic injustice. In other words, I think of segregation as an evil; but there are other evils more fundamental like poverty, ignorance, and disease. While segregation increases these evils in most cases, nevertheless, it would not be sensible to wait for doing away with segregation before attacking these fundamental evils themselves, even if in that attack, you were working within segregated limits.

Very sincerely yours,
W. E. B. Du Bois

Central to Du Bois's post-war interests was the effort to assure that there would be no World War Three. This goal motivated part of his struggles against colonialism, his support of the Wallace campaign, his later leadership in the 1949 Waldorf Conference for Peace, and then his dedication to the Peace Information Center and the Stockholm Peace Pledge. One of the areas in which the National Council of the Arts, Sciences and Professions expended much energy was this effort to prevent a new world war. Jo Davidson, Harlow Shapley, Albert Einstein, Paul Robeson, Thomas Mann, Lillian Hellman, Linus Pauling, and Du Bois were among the world-famous Americans involved in the council and the peace movement. A letter from Du Bois to Shapley in the summer of 1948 refers to this commitment.

New York City, July 2, 1948

Dear Mr. Shapley:

I enjoyed the meeting of June 30 very much and am, personally, in full accord with your objectives.[1] I left my signature on one of the statements. I do not, however, have the right to represent the NAACP officially, and although I

1. On 23 June 1948, Shapley had invited Du Bois to a meeting to be held on 30 June at the Hotel Biltmore. The initiative for this meeting came from Albert Einstein, who had stated in a letter to Shapley; "I feel now sure that the people in power in Washington are pushing systematically toward preventive war"; Einstein therefore urged the launching "of a strong counter-attack" by "leading intellectuals" against this drive. A statement affirming the danger and calling for resistance issued from the 30 June meeting.

am putting the matter before the Secretary and the Board of Directors, I doubt
if they will take any action. Partly, this is because the NAACP has always sought
to restrict itself so far as possible to the matter of race discrimination, particularly in the United States. Usually it has refused to go outside this field.

Personally, I feel that in the present extraordinary crisis, the NAACP ought to
regard the fight against war as one of the first items in its fight against race
prejudice. I have, therefore, written the Secretary and the Board of Directors
asking them if they would be willing to sign this statement. As I have said, I
do not think they will but I have done all that I can.

Very sincerely yours,
W. E. B. Du Bois

*C. B. Baldwin, the campaign manager for the 1948 Wallace effort, tried to in-
tensify and formalize the support Du Bois was giving to Wallace.* This matter
was important to Du Bois's difficulties with the leadership of the NAACP; hence,
his reply to Baldwin is of considerable consequence.*

New York City, July 15, 1948

Dear Mr. Baldwin:

As I have written you before, I am unable to take any active part in partisan
politics during this campaign. This is because of the vote of the Board of Directors of the National Association for the Advancement of Colored People,
passed in 1944. This vote forbids salaried officers of the Association taking active part in political campaigns. Had I known of this action before rejoining the
Association in 1944, I would have insisted on a clearer understanding. I agree
with the aim of the Association to be non-partisan, but I am certain that this
action does not accomplish this, and in fact intense partisan activity on the
part of persons closely connected with the Association is putting us very distinctly in politics.

Nevertheless, my duty is clear to me. I will obey the letter of the Board's
vote, and for that reason, will not attend the Philadelphia meeting or act on
any of its committees.

On the other hand I will retain my right to vote, of which no organization
can legally deprive me, and whenever I consider it necessary I will publicly announce my choice of Henry Wallace for president and the reasons therefore.

* Calvin Benham Baldwin (1902-75) was born in Virginia and educated at Virginia
Polytechnic Institute. He was an assistant to Henry Wallace and to Rexford G. Tugwell in the early New Deal days and from 1940 to 1943 was the administrator of the
Farm Security Administration. In the 1944 election, Baldwin was executive vice-chairman of the CIO Political Action Committee in support of FDR's campaign, but in 1948
he became campaign manager for Wallace and thereafter remained active in the
Progressive party.

In any such announcement, I will be careful to say that this is my personal opinion and in no way expresses or seeks to express the policy of the NAACP or any of its members.

Very sincerely yours,
W. E. B. Du Bois

In 1944 Du Bois projected an effort at cooperation in the social studies among Atlanta University and twenty Negro land-grant colleges;* this effort was disrupted by his dismissal that year from Atlanta University. He labored to save it by trying to get its center moved to Howard University, under E. Franklin Frazier, without any real effectiveness. In the summer of 1948 Du Bois met John W. Davis, the president of West Virginia State College, at a professional meeting, and Davis asked about the cooperative effort. The result was a letter that summarized much of Du Bois's thinking on this subject.

New York City, August 23, 1948

My dear President Davis:

You have done me a great disservice by starting me thinking again, and thereby interfering with the novel which I am writing[1] and with certain vows I have made at the temple of Rest and Peace.

I had about come to the place where I was going to give up further thought about the sociological program. It seemed to me that I could do nothing more without interfering. At the same time it has been very difficult for me to understand why so few others could not see, as we do, the tremendous and epoch-making possibilities of this plan. I laid it down vaguely in 1897, in a speech made at the University of Pennsylvania. I tried to carry it out in the first thirteen years of work at Atlanta University, and then I came to the NAACP with the expressed and distinct idea of continuing my research there.

For 25 years I did nothing because I could get no funds, and was busy with the *Crisis* and other matters. Then returning to Atlanta, I planned it again and ran up against a certain guy named [Rufus] Clement, who succeeded in ruining it. I did think, however, that I had saved the remnants and put it at our largest Negro institution with the best sociologist of our day in charge. As you have said, very little has come of this scheme.

First of all, I think you are one of the few who understand what I have in mind. Here is, for the science of sociology, an extraordinary opportunity for a laboratory experiment; fifteen million human beings with an intriguing his-

---

* Volume two of this *Correspondence* has relevant letters, pp. 393–400.

1. This work reached fruition with the publication of the trilogy *The Black Flame* by Mainstream Publishers in New York City, 1957–61; it was republished, with an introduction by the present editor, by Kraus-Thomson in 1976.

tory, in a situation of world importance just now, who are in such position that they can be studied as a group, more or less isolated from their surroundings, with the aid of trained students of sociology to make the study continuously. If we could even now begin it systematically, within 50 years, certainly within a 100, we would have the most magnificent picture of the development of a group of human beings that the scientific world has ever seen. It might put the science of sociology on its feet.

What can we do? What I had in mind was, in the first place, to get in each state of the Union where there were any large number of colored people, and in the great cities of the North were Negroes have congregated, an organization, either a college or a voluntary group, to make it their business to study continuously, broadly, and as carefully as possible the situation of the Negroes in their territory. They were to use official data, federal, state, county and city; but, also, gradually to collect their own data, so as eventually to cover the whole life of the Negro. To do this, there was needed local scientific scholarship and that would be furnished in the Negro institutions by the professors of sociology.

But, of course, such scholars working alone, might go off at various tangents, and not have the advantage of the latest and most effective technique. For that reason they should be brought into correspondence and touch with each other, so as more and more to work as one coordinated group.

For this reason I wanted to get a sponsoring institution which would furnish funds enough for clerical work, and also be a center where the best sociological thought of the United States and of Europe could be brought to bear for advice and criticism. This was the reason that I called the various conferences at Atlanta University, and hoped that this plan could be continued at Howard.

Manifestly, at Howard neither the president nor Mr. Frazier quite grasp the importance and scope of this study, so that the cooperating institutions are getting uneasy and losing interest, which is quite understandable. What I now propose is to remove the sponsorship, either wholly or in part, from Howard and place it at least temporarily in New York. The advantage of New York is that here one can get in touch with all the great thinkers and workers of the world. Here would be a place where conferences could easily be held and eagerly attended.

The question is, however, what would be the sponsoring body? Naturally, I want it to be, certainly at first, a body with which I am connected, so that in the few remaining years of my work I can give it some attention and guidance. Also, I have with me Dr. Hugh Smythe, a Ph.D. in anthropology, from Northwestern University, who knows something of my plans and had hoped to help at Howard; he probably would have but funds were not available. He is employed now as my research assistant, but is not getting the salary which he ought to have and naturally is seeking wider scope. There are others who might help.

The point then is, to what institution could this be hitched? I think at present of two: first, there is my Department of Special Research in the NAACP. It is possible (although I am not at all certain) that the directors of the NAACP could be induced to let me take up that project as part of my department, provided of course, that it did not entail any considerable increase of expenditure on their part. The NAACP is a great organization and has become a social institution among both colored and white people. It must, however, have broader bases and objectives than it has now; it must become more than an organization of protest and agitation. It must have a constructive program. My plan might meet opposition, and perhaps I could not swing it. I shall be glad to have your opinion.

The second institution which I have in mind is the New School; this is an institution for social research. It has on its faculty a large number of the best scholars of Europe, and I think it would be interested in this project. The only drawback is that it is predominantly a white institution and would get credit for much, if not the larger part, of what we might be able to accomplish. Outside these organizations it might, of course, be possible to interest one of the Funds. The General Education Board would have backed it, if Clement had asked for it. But he preferred the Study of Negro Business. I am writing you just as I happen to be thinking with nothing very clear or definite in my mind. Will you read this over at your leisure and let me have your reactions?

It was very nice to meet you at Wilberforce, and more especially (if you will kindly say this to her!) to meet Mrs. Davis, and also, your daughter.

Very sincerely yours,
W. E. B. Du Bois

Possibly as the result of suggestions made by Du Bois to Sylvia Pankhurst, he received a welcome letter from the Ethiopian minister to Washington.

Washington, D.C., August 30, 1948

My dear Dr. Du Bois:

It has been my earnest desire since my arrival in the United States as Minister Plenipotentiary and Envoy Extraordinary of the Ethiopian Government, to reach as many outstanding leaders of the colored race in America as possible, to acquaint myself with their general condition and to exchange views of mutual interest in cultural, historical and other matters. It is, however, unfortunate that I have been able to contact only [a] few of such representatives so far. I would very much appreciate it therefore, if you will call on me at the Legation, 2134 Kalorama Road, N.W. Washington, D.C., for the purpose of exchanging views as mentioned above.

All expenses incurred by you on this trip will be refunded by me.

I would suggest you call this week, as I have planned to be out of town next week.

Your notifying me of the date of your coming to Washington will be appreciated.

Sincerely yours,
Ras Imru[1]

New York City, September 13, 1948

His Excellency, Ras Imru
Sir:

I have the feeling that our interview, interesting as it was to me, did not quite meet the plans or give the information which you had in mind.

I was interested in the future of your country, whose history I have followed with absorbed interest for the last forty years. I had hoped to discuss with you ways in which two great branches of the black race—the 15 million people of your country and the 13 million Americans of Negro descent, might collaborate in the future for progress, survival and cultural expansion.

On the other hand, your chief interest was inquiry into the discrimination against people of color in the United States and what steps we were taking to eliminate it. You naturally assumed that we as Americans are at least in part responsible for our country's failure to live up to its own laws and declarations and were curious to know my attitude toward discrimination. On the other hand, I assumed that you were more or less familiar with our long struggle for equality in this land and its results.

We were, perhaps, both wrong in part. American Negroes are not responsible for discrimination in this land; they are the victims of it. Only 85 years ago three-fourths of the Negroes were chattel slaves. In less than a century, against the social, political, and economic power of one of the greatest of modern nations, this group of Negroes, back to the wall and opposed by modern civilization have:

1. Fought for their own freedom (Lincoln said that without help of Negro soldiers, the North could not have conquered the South in the Civil War).

2. Helped to reconstruct the nation after the Civil War, by new social legislation including public schools.

3. Reduced our illiteracy so that today over four-fifths of us can read and write.

---

1. Ras Imru was born in 1892. He served as governor of the province of Wallo in Ethiopia from 1922 to 1925 and of Godjam Province from 1933 to 1935; he was jailed during the Italian occupation from 1935 through 1941. He was appointed minister to Washington in 1946. On 15 September 1948, Minister Imru was ejected from the diplomatic section in Constitution Hall, in Washington, while President Truman was addressing the annual meeting of the American Association for the Advancement of Science, a piece of jim-crowism for which the association then apologized. The apology made the front page of the *New York Times*, 16 September 1948.

4. Become an important part of the national economy and also saved money, bought property and founded family life.

5. Continuously during these 85 years fought color and race discrimination.

I am enclosing a short history of our efforts. It is chapter 1 of a petition to the United Nations. I wish you would have this translated into Amharic and then if possible have it printed and distributed among your officials and in your public schools. In this way you would let Ethiopia understand the struggle we have made and are still making for the abolition of the color line in modern civilization.

After you have read this, I wish you would let me confer with you again with the idea of exploring ways of cooperation between Ethiopia and the other dark-skinned groups of the world. I would especially like to suggest the idea of a Pan-African Congress held in your country, with His Imperial Majesty as patron, to confer on present cooperation and future aims.

I am Sir,

Your obedient servant,
W. E. B. Du Bois

Soon after having been the guest of the minister from Ethiopia, Du Bois was asked to be the guest of Robeson. The invitation came on the stationery of the Committee to End the Jim Crow 'Silver-Gold' System in the Panama Canal Zone, of which Charles P. Howard of Iowa was honorary chairman and the three co-chairpeople were Mrs. Charlotta Bass of Los Angeles, Paul Robeson, and Du Bois himself.

New York, N.Y., September 15, 1948
Dear Dr. Du Bois:

Will you come as my personal guest to a luncheon on Saturday afternoon, 12:30 P.M., September 25th, at the Hotel Piccadilly, 227 West 45th Street, New York?

Brother Pascual Ampudia, President of Local 713, United Public Workers, C.I.O., the union of "silver" workers, is arriving from Panama and will be present to give us a first hand report.

We also plan additional activity in our drive to end government sponsored Jim Crow in Panama.

Will you let me know immediately whether you will be able to attend—via the enclosed card?

Sincerely yours,
Paul Robeson

Du Bois attended this luncheon and wrote about the experience in a letter to *the* New York Times. *The* Times, *however, decided that the letter did not merit printing.**

New York City, September 27, 1948

The Editor of the *Times*:

I sat at luncheon Saturday to hear the head of a labor union in the Canal Zone tell of his efforts to improve labor conditions. He was a colored man, earnest and intelligent. He had gone to work at the age of nine to help dig the Panama Canal. He had no formal schooling but spoke English and Spanish quite well.

His wage at first was ten cents an hour. This wage, the workers by organization and agitation had raised to 40 cents an hour. But this was not enough for decent living. They lived in hovels, with poor food and wretched sanitation; their schools were poor and teachers underpaid. All this was taking place under the army rule of the United States Government, who were discriminating against colored workers (called Silver workers) and paying white workers (Gold workers) wages often 100% higher, with good homes, schools and opportunity for promotion. Against this squalor and discrimination this man, with help from union labor in the United States, had organized a union of 10,000 members.

He said, "The whites break up our meetings and throw our leaders in jail." He spoke with deep feeling and restraint for a half hour. He asked our help. Then he sat down. But finally he turned to his neighbor, a white editor, and said: "And they call me Communist? What do they mean by that?"

I did not catch the editor's reply.

W. E. B. Du Bois

A priest of the Primera Iglesia Bautista in Cuba asked Du Bois a plain question; in such cases Du Bois gave plain answers.

Colon, Cuba, October 3rd, 1948

Dear doctor Du Bois,

I am writing this letter to ask a favor of you. I would like to know if you are a believer in God, also what is your opinion about the Lord Jesus.

Sir, with these lines I wish to express my gratitude to you for answering this letter.

Respectfully yours,
E. Pina Moreno

---

* While the *Times* did not print this letter, Du Bois did get it published in the very liberal—and short-lived—*New York Star*, 21 October 1948.

W. E. B. and Nina Gomer Du Bois, 1947

American Labor party candidates, Buffalo, New York, 1950. Left to right: Frank Scheiner, candidate for state attorney general; George B. Murphy, Jr., Du Bois's campaign manager; Du Bois; John T. McManus, candidate for governor.

Du Bois at home, with a portrait of Frederick Douglass, and a photograph of
Du Bois's great-grandson, 1948. Courtesy of the University of Massachusetts
Library.

W. E. B. and Shirley Graham Du Bois with Mao Tse-Tung, Peking, 1959.
Du Bois in a Peking doorway, 1959. Courtesy of the University of
Massachusetts Library.

Du Bois with Nikita Khruschev, Moscow, 1958. Photograph by *Moscow News*. Courtesy of the University of Massachusetts Library.

W. E. B. Du Bois and Shirley Graham Du Bois. Photographs by Carl Van
Vechten. Courtesy of the University of Massachusetts Library.

Du Bois speaking at Holy Trinity Church in Brooklyn, New York, during Negro History Week, February 1953.

Arthur B. Spingarn and Du Bois at a dinner in honor of Du Bois's eightieth birthday, 1948. Photograph by Drucker-Hilbert Co., Inc.

W. E. B. and Shirley Graham Du Bois on Du Bois's eighty-seventh birthday, 23 February 1955. Photograph by Lotte Jacobi.

Herbert Aptheker and Du Bois at the airport before the latter's departure for Ghana, 1961. Courtesy of International Publishers, in *The Autobiography of W. E. B. Du Bois*, 1968.

Du Bois in the garden of Paul Robeson's home in London, 1958. Courtesy of the University of Massachusetts Library.

Du Bois receiving an honorary degree from the University of Ghana on his ninety-fifth birthday, 23 February 1963.

New York City, November 15, 1948

My dear Sir: Mr. E. Pina Moreno

Answering your letter of October 3, may I say: If by being "a believer in God," you mean a belief in a person of vast power who consciously rules the universe for the good of mankind, I answer No; I cannot disprove this assumption, but I certainly see no proof to sustain such a belief, neither in History nor in my personal experience.

If on the other hand you mean by "God" a vague Force which, in some uncomprehensible way, dominates all life and change, then I answer, Yes; I recognize such Force, and if you wish to call it God, I do not object.

Very sincerely yours,
W. E. B. Du Bois

After the election of Harry S. Truman as president, Du Bois sent a letter analyzing the meaning of the event to the editor of the New York Post. *But the* Post *did not print the letter and it is published below for the first time.*

New York City, November 4, 1948

The Editor, N.Y. *Post*
Dear Sir:

The lesson of the election is clear. Since the First World War, the civilized world has been going Left; that is, veering from the 18th century ideal of individual freedom to twentieth Century social control in order to eliminate Poverty, Disease and Ignorance. Alone among the great nations the United States has tried to stand for private enterprise uncontrolled by public welfare. This policy was overthrown by the Great Depression of 1929 to 1933, and the ten year reign of Roosevelt began a "New Deal" for the socialization of America, with curbing of private wealth, social security and long distance economic planning. His program was interrupted and diverted by war, which without questioning the socialization of wealth and social planning turned on the character of the control, whether through dictatorship or by democratic methods. With the indispensable help of Russia, the allies overthrew the dictators. Britain and other lands proceeded toward socialization of wealth and social planning, while in the United States, Big Business, made bigger by huge war profits, determined to turn the clock back and return the nation to the anarchy of industry and the organized fight against socialism, which characterized the Nineteenth Century. President Truman did not realize what the struggle was all about and in face of his vacillation and hesitation, Big Business got almost complete control and prepared to take over with Mr. Dewey.

Meantime Henry Wallace began to fight for a New Deal, for socialism, for understanding with Russia and for world peace. He accepted help and cooperation from all parties, including Communists. Immediately the Big Business interests concentrated their fight against the New Deal by a witch hunt against "Communism." To win their ends, they thrust the nation to the brink of war, intervened on the side of dictators and investors all over the world, and dubbed "Communism" every sane step toward real world progress and democracy. They so overplayed their hand that Henry Wallace began to grow in popularity.

Then Harry Truman got wise. Deserted by his main supporters, bit by bit he accepted the domestic policy of Wallace in price control, labor legislation, agriculture, water conservation and curbing monopoly. Less surely, he began to talk "Peace" and to hesitate on Arabian oil and Chiang Kai-Shek. And finally in the last days of campaigning he even mentioned again civil rights, on which he had been dumb for four months.

What then did the voters have to decide on November 2? Dewey and re-action or Truman on the platform of Henry Wallace. They chose Truman in the hope that he would stand on this platform. But that does not end the matter. It begins it. Will Truman try to carry out the Wallace platform? And will his party let him? The answer is No! Truman had no idea of the world change from uncontrolled private initiative to social control. He has no broad com-prehension of social planning. He does not understand the Russian Revolution nor the Truth that even bombs cannot kill ideas. Personally he likes neither Negroes nor Jews; he hasn't the foggiest idea of the inner struggle of the Bal-kans and Asia. The Democratic party as constituted today would not back Mr. Truman even if he tried to live up to his final campaign promises. The South is reactionary and against democracy. Large elements of the party in the North stand for Big Business, and in foreign affairs the Democrats and Republicans are one.

What to do? The Progressives have done a good job. Without the hard work of Henry Wallace and his followers, the electorate would still be ignorant of fundamental issues and Thomas Dewey and Wall Street would be headed for the Presidential chair. It is no mean feat to induce two million people to en-danger their social security by voting for an unpopular cause, and one they know could not succeed in this election. But now the education of the people of the United States must proceed. The Progressives with tightened organiza-tion and co-ordinated effort must teach the nation:

1. That War is the end of Civilization
2. That Poverty can be conquered
3. That social medicine and research can save and prolong life
4. That Universal Education costs less than Universal military training and does not murder youth.

The meaning of this election is the success of the Wallace campaign and the necessity for its continuance.

Sincerely,
W. E. B. Du Bois

Du Bois sent to Henry Wallace a copy of this letter to the Post. *The reference to Mrs. Blaine in Wallace's response will be explained in subsequent correspondence (pp. 229–36 below).*

New York City, November 29, 1948

Dear Dr. Du Bois:

I have read with deepest interest your letter of November 4. Moreover, I can never forget the marvelous address you made at the Golden Gate meeting in Harlem during the campaign.

Is there any likelihood that you will be in Chicago any time in the near future? If you are going to be there, I want very much to arrange for you to see Mrs. Anita McCormick Blaine. I have spoken to her about you, hoping that you might perhaps have some community of interests.

Sincerely yours,

H. A. Wallace

Du Bois kept files marked "sick" for letters from people more afflicted with racism than most white people in the United States; or at least from those who felt compelled to express their hatred more aggressively and explicitly than others. These letters reflect something of the society in which Du Bois labored and two are printed below; they are published precisely as written. The two were from the same person and both were sent anonymously, as was true of almost all the "sick" letters. These were postmarked Los Angeles, California, 25 and 26 November 1948.

[November 25, 1948]

I just read one of your books. Vastly amusing. You ignore the fact that the great men who signed the Declaration were *all* White—anglo-Saxons—of *English* descent. So were the men who in the Civil War liberated *you*—Grant, Sherman, Lincoln—et al. The English control the greatest Empire in history. Greatest *names* in history—English. Newton, Darwin, Shakespeare and ten thousand others. The poor Irish & German you pretended to despise, could improve their lot & go into society, where *you* would *never* be admitted. The great civilization of the past were all *white*, but they fell when their pure white blood became *polluted* by black blood. It's tragic, Dubious, your being mulatto. Even Jefferson & Lincoln considered Negros inferior. If you believe in re-incarnation, pray that in the next life you may be born a Chinaman. In South Africa, 3 million whites control 40 millions of malodorous half-apes—niggers. Every American's stomach sickens at sight of a coon. But we whites are compassionate. Now down South, the whites are pure Anglo-Saxon. The Southern Europeans—the North were mongrelized by the Tar brush before coming to the U.S.A. No

Dubious, it wont wash, your outpouring of hate. You poor frustrated creature. I am English and *enormously* proud of it. Who would *not* be. *We* are the dominant race—The poor niggers never had any civilization. Just cave men. Dont you wish you could change into a *white* man? But you are doomed to remain a coon—just a cocoanut. A Frisco term. But be happy in the thought that you have *some* white blood—hence your degree of intelligence. I wish you luck, Dubious, you are too far beneath me to rate much attention. It is a pity negros & negresses are so evil smelling. Your tribesmen in the u.s. will *never* get equality; nature withheld it from them. But good luck & good health to you. You are a very amusing WOOLLY.

[November 26, 1948]

I've just seen movie 'Africa Speaks.' Voice of the jungle. Such primitive revolting cannibals. *Your* relatives Dubious. These half apes are funny, too. But mostly obnoxious. Even the yellow races despise them. Negros—lowest & most inferior of all God's creatures. Those poor Irish & Germans you affected to look down upon. How you envied them their pure Caucasian blood & their white skins. And their offspring grew up to order you about. How you seethe with jealousy of the superior white race. The race to which *you* owe something good & decent. In Dixie the whites keep their blood from being polluted by negroid. In Russia there is no dislike of black creatures. Why? Because they are but few. To be close to black's is to despise them. They are loathsome. Now Dubois, you'll *never* get social equality in the u.s.—or anywhere else. Be happy as you are. After all, *God* loves you & He has a special Heaven for his inferior creatures. We whites are *enormously* proud of our heritage. And we Anglo Saxons control the world. Would you be as Doctor Faustus—make the bargain— just to be a *white man* for even one day. How your little negro soul would exhult. The white blood—the modicum of white blood you have was already polluted by your French relatives before they came to America. Yet—favor it. You got your little sense. If you are shut out—excluded—here—why don't you go back to the Congo. You could strut there before the natives. You are an amusing woolly coon Dubious—all Americans—North and South despise you— but they are too polite to say so. Every other race on earth scorns the negro. But good health to you darky. Continue to pour out your hate. You are such an obvious, funny shine

A Black student at the Oberlin Graduate School of Theology in Ohio propounded a series of questions concerning the insurrection led by Nat Turner.

Oberlin, Ohio, December 7, 1948

Dear Dr. Du Bois:

I am currently writing an s.t.m. thesis on the Nat Turner insurrection of

Southampton County, Virginia, in 1831. It is my hope that you will help me with some extremely important and needed materials which, I feel, will make a significant contribution to this thesis.

It is my aim to secure from prominent contemporary thinkers their ideas concerning the Nat Turner insurrection. Would you address your remarks to the following questions:

1. What was the immediate effect of the Nat Turner insurrection on the attitudes and thinking of (a) Negroes and (b) Whites?

2. How important a part does the Nat Turner insurrection play on current (a) Negro and (b) White thought—that is, in religion, journalism, political propaganda, contemporary philosophy of American history, prejudices, etc.?

3. What ideas, if any, are there peculiar to Negro thought of today which stem directly from the insurrection?

4. What do you think of Nat Turner and his idea that "God ordained him for the mission"?

5. What do you think of Brawley's statement: "In the long run, however, he gained, for the insurrections increased the agitation against slavery and thus led on to the Civil War and emancipation"?[1]

The answers to these questions will form the ground work of my evaluation of this movement. Questions 2, 3, 4, and 5 are the most important in our case. Would it be possible for you to answer this inquiry by February 10, according to your convenience? Thank you very much for your help in this matter.

Yours very truly,
P. Rodgers Brown[2]

New York City, December 15, 1948

My dear Mr. Brown:

Answering your letter of December 7, may I respond to your questions as follows:

1. (a) So far as the Negroes heard about these insurrections they were greatly excited and moved.

(b) The whites were widely frightened and as a result passed a great deal of repressive legislation.

1. The source is Benjamin Brawley, *A Social History of the American Negro* (New York: Macmillan, 1921); the quotation—not quite exact—is from p. 148.

2. Peter Rodgers Brown received the degree of Master of Sacred Theology from the Oberlin Graduate School of Theology in 1949; his thesis was entitled, "The Theology of Nat Turner as Reflected in the Insurrection." He had received an A.B. and a B.D. from Shaw University in Raleigh in 1947. Brown was killed in an automobile accident early in January 1950 in Virginia. The assistance of Elaine Druesedow, reference librarian of the Oberlin College Library, was very helpful in supplying data on Brown and his thesis.

2. (a) The insurrection has practically no influence at present because it is forgotten.[1]
3. None that I know of.
4. No comment.
5. I agree with Brawley.

Very sincerely yours,
W. E. B. Du Bois

On 11 December 1948, the New York Times *published a letter from Du Bois complaining of the persistence of racist segregation and discrimination in interstate travel, despite the existence of laws banning this practice in several Northern states. A result was a letter from Carl Murphy, president of Afro-American Newspapers.**

Baltimore, Md., December 14, 1948

Dear Dr. Du Bois:

I read with interest your letter on discrimination in interstate travel which appeared in the New York *Times*.

I want to raise this question. Isn't there something the people of New York themselves can do? Take the Atlantic Coast Line train, the "Champion." Isn't it a fact that colored persons are sold seats in a colored coach only in New York City and New Yorkers must travel from New York through Maryland as jim crow passengers, in states which require no separation of races in interstate travel? Isn't it true also that such discrimination against colored people violates the state anti-discrimination laws in both New York and Pennsylvania?

Very truly yours,
Carl Murphy

1. Du Bois's affirmation that the Turner revolt was "forgotten" was an overstatement, as Brown's own interest indicates; in the preface to his thesis itself, Brown observes: "My interest in the man, Nat Turner, was stimulated ten years ago. I was constantly thrown in contact with persons who used Turner to sanction their many deeds and actions. Parents used him to show their children that only courage would indeed help them." Another inquiry to Du Bois about Nat Turner is given in volume two of this work, p. 143. In 1935–36, the present editor labored on a study of Nat Turner, which was accepted as a master's thesis at Columbia University in February 1937.

* Carl Murphy (1889–1967) was born in Baltimore and educated at Howard, Harvard, and the University of Jena in Germany. He taught briefly at Howard, but his main work was with the *Afro-American* newspaper firm. From 1918 to 1944 he was editor of the paper, and from 1922 to his death he headed the board of directors. He was a trustee of Morgan State College, a member of the national board of the NAACP from 1931 to his death, and Spingarn Medalist in 1955.

New York City, December 17, 1948

My dear Mr. Murphy:

Answering your letter of December 14, may I say that the discrimination which you mention is difficult to get at. What happens is this: If an obviously colored person goes to make a reservation on one of the through reclining coach trains, he may be assigned to coach No. 1. This is not a "Jim Crow" coach, but on leaving Washington, no white person is seated there and all colored persons are segregated there. The same thing happens in Chicago, on through trains South. On the other hand, if the colored person secures an assignment to some other coach, which he can easily arrange, he rides in that coach till he comes to the Mason and Dixon line; even then, on many occasions, he is not disturbed. On other occasions, he is asked to move, but not compelled if he does not want to; and in still other cases he is forcibly removed or even arrested and fined.

In any case in the North, if he is assigned to coach No. 1, and there are seats in other coaches he can make a row and usually get another seat. If not, he can bring suit, but of course it would be difficult to prove that there were vacant seats in other coaches. Any compulsory segregation would violate the state laws of New York, Pennsylvania and I am pretty sure of Illinois.

Very sincerely yours,

W. E. B. Du Bois

When Du Bois was dismissed by the NAACP *in September 1948— a dismissal which was to take effect on the final day in that year—he was in his eightieth year. Except for a small pension from Atlanta University and another promised from the* NAACP, *he was without funds and without any significant source of income. Although several of his books were in print, none of them ever brought him a substantial sum of money, and by 1948 his income from royalties was minimal. Du Bois was, at the same time, the main source of support for his invalid wife in Baltimore, and he was providing funds for the education of their granddaughter.*

It was with this reality in mind that Henry Wallace made mention of wanting Du Bois to meet Anita McCormick Blaine, in the letter dated 29 November 1948 (p. 225 above).* As Du Bois stated in a letter to Wallace of 18 January 1949 (pp. 234-35 below), he called Mrs. Blaine early in December. Sometime after this call and before 15 December 1948 Du Bois sent a memorandum to Mrs. Blaine; it is undated—a most unusual lapse for him.

* Anita McCormick Blaine (1866–1954) was the daughter of Cyrus Hall, the inventor of the reaping machine. She devoted a considerable proportion of her inherited wealth to various philanthropies; she was, for example, the founder of the School of Education of the University of Chicago.

[New York City, December ?, 1948]

My dear Mrs. Blaine:

I think perhaps it would be fairer to you, if I put before you in writing my situation before the interview to which you have kindly assented.

I shall be 81 years of age in February. I am however in good health and may have several years of creative thinking and writing before me, if I have the opportunity to devote myself to it without too much worry.

I was born in western Massachusetts and educated in the public schools, at a Negro college in Tennessee, at Harvard and the University of Berlin. I began work as a teacher at a colored college in Ohio in 1896; I spent a year as assistant instructor at the University of Pennsylvania and then settled down at Atlanta University as teacher and investigator for 13 years. I had already published two books, one of which was the first volume in the Harvard University Historical Series. At Atlanta, I began the first scientific study of the Negro Problem in the United States, and for the next 25 years nearly every book on the Negro published in the country used our work.

But I was disappointed because we could not get funds to finance our studies and because my disagreement with the philosophy of Booker T. Washington cut off contributions to the University. In 1910, therefore, I turned reluctantly from my science to propaganda by joining the new NAACP of which I was an incorporator and founded the *Crisis*. At this time I had added to my first two books, the *Souls of Black Folk*, and 14 social studies on the Negro.

I worked for the NAACP twenty-three years, bringing the *Crisis* at one time up to a circulation of 100,000 copies, entirely self-supporting, including my salary. But the Depression cut down the *Crisis* circulation until it was no longer paying costs. I was at this time over 60, and thought it wise to accept an offer from my close friend, John Hope, to return to Atlanta and round out my days in teaching and writing. I stayed ten years 1934-'44 writing my book on Reconstruction and an autobiography and founding a quarterly magazine, *Phylon*. But poor Hope died of overwork and the new young president retired me preemptorily for age in 1944, when I was 76. I was taken completely by surprise. My family consisted of a wife, with whom I celebrated a golden wedding in 1946; a daughter who has been teaching in a Baltimore high school for 18 years; and a granddaughter just 16 and in high school. My pay had always been low; $1200 a year at Atlanta; first $2500 and finally $5000 in New York; finally, $4,500 in Atlanta again. I had kept my family in comfort, educated my daughter at Fisk and Columbia (A.M. in English) and built an 8 room cottage in Baltimore for the family. I lost all my life insurance in the failure of the Negro company, Standard Life. But the house is without mortgage and I have enough in U.S. bonds to pay my granddaughter's college education. I have no debts. Unfortunately my wife suffered a paralytic stroke two years ago and has been helpless since. Her care is costly, but my daughter shares and keeps the house.

Under these circumstances I was naturally aghast when retired with a small pension ($1800 a year 1944-1950; $1200 thereafter). I was however offered 4 different jobs—three at Southern colleges, and one to return to the NAACP. The three chief officials, with no initiative on my part, urged me to return, promising me $5000 a year, a research assistant and stenographer, offices, etc.; and especially, complete freedom to study and write. I was flattered and accepted.

In the four years I have spent with the NAACP I have written and published two books; edited an appeal to the United Nations; lectured in England, Cuba, Haiti and in 23 of the U.S., beside writing articles in magazines and newspapers and carrying on wide correspondence.

Unfortunately, from the beginning matters did not run smoothly in my new position. Doubtless some of this was my fault; old people are often hard to get on with; but I certainly tried to fit in for this seemed my last chance to work. Nevertheless I never got the office space needed and promised; the Secretary repeatedly tried to block any expression of opinion on public matters on my part, even in my special fields of study; he and the directors forbade any "political activity" in the late campaign; and finally, Mr. White assumed the right to speak for the NAACP in the field of colonial and trusteeship questions. I complained and the complaint, without my knowledge, reached the newspapers. The directors dismissed me as of Dec. 31 for insubordination and publicity.

In some respects my complaint was ill-advised so far as my own fortunes were concerned; I ought to have realized that I had been invited back not to work or think, but to do nothing and let my name be used by the NAACP. If I had done this I would have been secure for life. But I could not. I saw that the NAACP was going wrong in organization, policy and accomplishment. I had to speak out and if the newspapers had not heard my complaint it would have been buried.

So there I am. Except for a small pension of $1200, a home for my sick wife and savings for the grandchild's education, I have nothing. My 15 or more books have been praised and read, but not widely and yield now less than $150 annually. On the other hand, I have had a life of great length and experience. I know something of history and the social sciences; I have a unique library, some 50,000 letters from persons of all sorts and positions and I can write English. I am faced by the necessity of trying some new job and perhaps letting all the knowledge, experience and skill I have accumulated go down in total loss. Of course, at best, I have not long to live and work effectively—perhaps much less than I now think. But I hate to surrender in this day of the world's desperate need. I am now sitting before a manuscript of 150 pages which I had planned to extend to a thousand covering the years of Negro development from 1876 to 1949. I want to finish it.

It was at this crisis of my fortunes that Mr. Wallace and Paul Robeson spoke to me of you; and Mr. Baldwin had me to lunch and said you had some plans in mind for activities after the election into which I might fit. He added that these plans were not yet developed, but advised me to talk with you. I hesitated to ask this—I know how you must be harrassed to help save the world. But I want you to understand the plight I am in and if any of your plans can fit with mine I would be happy.

I shall telephone you about noon Tuesday, December 14, to ask what day you will be willing to talk with me in Chicago. I speak at Yale University Dec. 15 and have an engagement in New York the 17th. I could be in Chicago the 18th, or any day thereafter before Christmas.

Very sincerely,
W. E. B. Du Bois

New York City, December 15, 1948

Dear Mrs. Blaine:

Pursuant to our telephone conversation yesterday, I understand that your thought concerning my work falls into two parts: 1. The question of my immediate needs to insure the continuity of my life work. 2. Exploring, at your leisure and with consultation, plans and means for inaugurating a movement for peace and progress in face of present world conditions, into which my ability and effort might be included.

In accord with the above thought, I am venturing in this letter to outline my immediate needs for continuing my work:

EXPENSES, 1949

Living, including rent, clothes, etc., and support of my sick wife

$5000

Moving my 2500 books, file-cases and papers outfitting a new office (All my present office furniture belongs to the NAACP) $1000

Clerical help $2000

Office rental $2000

INCOME

My pension from Atlanta University, $1200 will cover the expense of moving and setting up a new office.

The Council for African Affairs, of which Mr. Robeson is chairman, has offered to furnish me an office rent free, in return for which I would act as councillor on matters touching Africa and contribute to their publications.

The NAACP in view of my 23 years services will probably offer me a small pension—perhaps $1000 to $1500. If there are no strings attached to make the acceptance impossible, this will cover clerical expense.

If the above assumptions prove true, I would need in addition to the income indicated the sum of $5000. If I had this I would immediately move my offices to 23 West 26th Street, where the Council on African Affairs is now located. I would devote my time chiefly to my projected literary work, but devoting some of my time to the policy and publications of the Council; and also a part to trying to think out and plan in consultation with you, Mr. Wallace, Mr.

Robeson and others just what should and can be done to save our world from further disaster.

I hope I have made myself clear and I know that if you are not able to do what I ask you will say so frankly, knowing that I will understand that ability often falls far short of willingness.

Very sincerely,
W. E. B. Du Bois

New York City, January 7, 1949

Personal

Dear Mrs. Blaine:

I am sorry to have troubled you this morning, but I was afraid my letter of December 15 might have miscarried in the holiday rush of mail.

My present position has changed somewhat since December 15, and is as follows: I have moved my offices to 23 West 26th St., where the Council of African Affairs has furnished me rent-free two rooms for my secretary and myself. They pay the secretary and use her part time. This may entail some extra expense on my part for clerical aid, especially for library research. My library of 2500 books will be installed here, and the council will pay part of the cost of moving and installation.

My other expense for the year will be my sick wife and my own living. For nursing my wife I am paying $2600 a year. My apartment rent is $1000, and I estimate my living, clothes, etc., at $2400. On the income side I have a pension of $1200 from Atlanta University and a grant this year of $2400 from the NAACP which may or may not be renewed. I can earn something by speeches and miscellaneous writing. But travel is high, and writing should not interfere with my main work.

If then I can be certain of $5000 in addition to the help of the Council of African Affairs and my pension, I can concentrate all my efforts (save such advice and writing as I do for the Council) on my main work; this is an attempt to survey and interpret the history of the Negro in America, from 1876, the end of Reconstruction to 1949–"Three score Years and Thirteen." From my own participation, I want to portray from within the feelings, thoughts and stresses of a great modern minority in the mightiest development of European civilization. I believe that I can do this and make a living message for today and the future. But to do this I must have leisure and freedom.

I am not the only person, nor the most important for pressing work of this sort; nor is my age the most promising; but I believe deeply in the urgency of my plan and the weight of my message and my ability to make it.

I am speaking in Detroit, January 12: I can be in Chicago January 10, or on any date from January 13 to 19.

Very sincerely,
W. E. B. Du Bois

RECAPITULATION OF FINANCIAL POSITION OF W. E. B. DU BOIS
AS OF JANUARY 7, 1949

Expense, 1949		Income	
Office rent	$1200	Pension, Atlanta University	$1200
Secretary	1680	Pension NAACP (?)	2400
Research	1000	Miscellaneous writing	
Personal			
		& speaking, net	400(?)
Mrs. Du Bois	3600	Total	$4000
W. E. B. D.	2400	Needed to balance	$5000
rent, N.Y.	1000	TOTAL	$9000
Total	$10,880		
Paid by the Council			
African Affairs	1880		
Deficit	$9000		

Letters from Du Bois to Henry Wallace and to C. B. Baldwin and communications from Mrs. Blaine to Du Bois conclude this correspondence. Mrs. Blaine provided $5000 to help carry Du Bois through from mid-1949 to mid-1950.

New York City, January 18, 1949

My dear Mr. Wallace:

I think I ought to report to you what I have done in the case of Mrs. Blaine. I do not want you to take any further action but since you have been so kind, I want you to know what I have done on my part.

In accordance with your letter, I called Mrs. Blaine by phone early in December and asked if I might have an appointment to see her; she was very pleasant but said that she was quite busy at the time and would I call her again within a few days. Therefore, I wrote to her a rather long letter saying that I thought it would be fairer to put before her the facts in writing and then perhaps have the interview. I told her my age and something of my education and work and the books which I had written. I outlined my service with the Atlanta University and with the NAACP and my return to Atlanta University in 1934 to 1944. I told her about my family, the salaries which I had received, the home which I had bought in Baltimore, my daughter as a teacher and the illness of my wife for two years. I also told her that I have no life insurance and why, but that I had saved up a little to help educate my granddaughter. I then told of my difficulties with the NAACP and my recent dismissal. I said I would phone her on Tuesday, December 14.

On that day again, I had a pleasant talk with her, but she was still too busy to make an appointment to see me; but asked me to write her in detail just what my wants were; I therefore wrote, December 15, 1948 making a detailed schedule of my expenses and asked if it would be possible for her to furnish me $5000 this year and also since I understood that she had planned for inaugurating a movement for peace and progress, I hoped later I might find a chance to cooperate.

I did not hear from this letter and was rather afraid that it might have been lost in the Christmas mail. I therefore phoned again, January 7, asking to talk with Mrs. Blaine's secretary and see if the letter had been received; but Mrs. Blaine answered personally and said that she had received the letter and was going to think it over soon but still could not as yet arrange for an interview. She said that if I had any further facts to lay before her she would be glad to have them. I therefore wrote, January 7, showing some changes in my position but asking again for the same sum, $5000. I told her that I was speaking in Detroit, January 12, and could be in Chicago any time between then and the 19th. I have had no answer from this letter.

I shall not write again or do anything more until I hear from her. I have told these facts to Mr. Robeson and am just outlining them to you; for your information only and not for any further action on your part. I am already deeply under obligation.

Very sincerely yours,
W. E. B. Du Bois

Chicago, Ill., March 27, 1949

[Telegram]
Dr. W. E. B. Du Bois:
I shall hope to have the pleasure of seeing you next week. Will you kindly telegraph me collect what days will suit you best?

Anita Blaine.

New York City, April 6, 1949

My dear Mr. Baldwin:
I had a very satisfactory tea with Mrs. Blaine. She seemed pleased to see me and we talked for over an hour. She finally proposed during the year, April 1, 1949 to April 1, 1950 to provide my salary and to be one of a committee to take up the question of future compensation during my working years. It was a very pleasant visit and I want to thank you deeply for all that you did to bring it about.

I am enclosing, at your request, a memorandum of the cost of the trip, but you are of course under no obligation to meet it.

Very sincerely yours,
W. E. B. Du Bois

Chicago, Ill., April 7, 1949

Dear Dr. Du Bois:

I am sorry there has been so much of an interval between our talking and my following the talk.

I hope there has been no suspense or inconvenience to you on that account.

I was most glad that through the talk it became possible for me to ask for the privilege of being a small part in the arrangements for your work.

It was very good of you to let me come into this region. I am very grateful.

What I understood that you would let me do is to add five thousand dollars to your available funds.

What I imagine you would like to have me do would be to send you a part, say, half of this gift now and send the remainder of it nearer to the end of the year.

If any other way suits you better, please tell me.

With all good wishes

I am sincerely yours,
Anita Blaine

Chicago, Ill., May 18, 1949

Dear Dr. Du Bois:

I learn from a kindly reminder that the check of which I wrote to you has not gone to you.

I am most sorry for this delay and I hope it has not inconvenienced you.

I am enclosing now my check for five thousand (5,000) dollars, to you, to get it immediately into your hand.

I am sincerely yours,
Anita Blaine

Correspondence relevant to Du Bois's dismissal from the NAACP late in 1948 may be illustrated by beginning with a memorandum from Du Bois in January and closing with formal notice of dismissal from Roy Wilkins on the final day in December.

Memorandum
To: The Secretary and Board of Directors
From: W. E. B. Du Bois, Director, Department of Special Research, NAACP
Subject: Memorandum from Madison Jones, Administrative Assistant, of Jan. 27.
Date: January 28, 1948.

Replying to the memorandum of January 27, let me say that I would be willing at any time to move to any suitable offices to relieve the congestion here.

However, since the subject has been brought up, I think that the whole matter of my office accommodations deserves review.

1. When I came to join the NAACP in 1944, it was the understanding that I should have two offices, one for myself and books, and one for my research assistant.

2. When I arrived at 69 Fifth Avenue, it had been found impossible to assign me more than a small space, about 8' x 12'. The Secretary promised that he would soon find me more suitable quarters outside the building.

3. When the Secretary went to the East, I was given the use of his office. I had my books moved into this office, but when the Secretary returned, I had to give up office and books, and confine myself to the smaller office again.

4. I protested and asked for the promised offices outside. Finally, work in the small office became simply impossible. I found office accommodations at 52 West 42nd Street. When I gave notice of this to the Secretary, he objected to my moving and was upheld by the Board. The Administrative Assistant was given my office. I had, therefore, to pay office rent for two months, and the expense of moving in and moving out, a total of about $400.00 which has never been repaid.

5. When the new offices were opened at 20 West 40th Street, I asked for at least one large office which could be divided into two. It was found impossible to arrange this. I, therefore, took the small office which was offered to me and have since tried to accommodate myself to it. My present office is about 12' x 20'. It houses three workers, 2,500 books, 2 desks, a typing table, a dictaphone outfit, [and] 6 four-drawer file cabinets. Much valuable material is still in the basement. Much of my own work is done in my apartment, where I have installed at my own expense a desk, dictaphone, and typewriter.

6. I did not complain further about office space, for I realize that the failure to accommodate me was not necessarily personal, but due to the fact that the total space available for the Association was too small. As I said to the staff conference in October, 1946, "The Association needs at least twice the space it now occupies to prevent unsanitary overcrowding and lack of privacy for work and consultation." A large part of the office space at 69 Fifth Avenue should have been retained, and only important parts of the Association, such as planning and research functions, should have been moved. The small increase in space which will be gained by eliminating my quarters will make very little difference in the long run. By another year the overcrowding will be just as great as it is now.

If now, the Board wishes me to occupy offices outside of this building and in any place where I can be accommodated with reasonable comfort, I shall be very glad to comply. I shall always insist, however, that I was unfairly treated in the refusal of the Board to pay for the office space which I was compelled to have in 1945.

February 25, 1948
Memorandum from Mr. White to the staff:

At the meeting of the Committee on Administration held on February 24, 1948, upon motion, duly seconded, it was *voted* that the following resolution passed by the Board of Directors of the Association at its meeting on March 13, 1944 be sent to each staff member in order to emphasize the Association's position with regard to political activity on the part of individual staff members:

"Employed Executive Officers of the NAACP are prohibited from any partisan activity. They may not sign or issue statements in support of party candidates or party policies and programs. They may not speak at meetings called by partisan political groups.

"The National Office of the NAACP may not officially support any political party or take any action which can be interpreted as support of a political party."

Please acknowledge.

Memorandum

To: The Board of Directors of the National Association for the Advancement of Colored People
From: W. E. B. Du Bois, Director, Department of Special Research
Subject: Policy on Political Activity of Staff Members
Date: March 8, 1948

The Secretary has just sent me a copy of a resolution passed by the Board, March 13, 1944, forbidding employed Executive Officers of the NAACP from partisan activity in political campaigns.

I fully appreciate the necessity in an organization as large as ours, comprising such diverse points of view, of guarding against the possibility of having any officer or official presume to speak officially for the whole organization. I have sought to avoid that in the past and will certainly do so in the future.

But I assume that the Board could not possibly have meant to forbid any individual, in his capacity as a private citizen, from casting his ballot as he pleased or of defending his convictions and candidates publicly. To do this would be seriously to interfere with that political freedom for which this organization has fought for nearly forty years.

I am aware of how critical an election is upon us and how bitter the feelings are that have been aroused. I know for the future of this organization how careful all of us must be to do no harm to its unity and efficiency. But on the other hand, the liberty, honesty, and integrity of the individual must not be forgotten. I have taken part in nine presidential elections. I have never been a member of any party organization,[1] nor taken the stump for any candidate. But I have in each election let it be known by written and spoken word whom I supported and why. I do not believe that the Directors would want me to do any less in this my tenth presidential campaign. I shall certainly exercise the utmost care to make it at all times clearly understood that in political matters I am speaking as a private individual and not presuming to speak for the NAACP; and in any case where there is any doubt as to this being understood, I shall refrain from speech or action.

With these limitations, I shall assume, unless otherwise informed, that my right to my own ideas as a private citizen is not questioned.

W. E. B. Du Bois

March 29, 1948

Dear Dr. Du Bois:

On March 11th I wrote you as follows:

"Your memorandum to the Board of Directors of March 8, 1948 was carefully considered and discussed at the Board meeting of March 8th. At the conclusion of the discussion it was voted that the Board uphold its ruling of 1944 which was quoted in my memorandum sent at the instruction of the Committee on Administration of February 25th, and that no exception be made to that ruling.

"I would like to add that the Board's position is in accordance with the mandate upon it of the 1946 Cincinnati and the 1947 Washington Annual Conference."

As yet I have received no reply to this letter.

In the New York *Times* of March 26th appeared a story headed "Committee to Set Third Party Conclave," telling of the formation of a 700-member organization for Wallace in which is included your name identified as "research director, National Association for the Advancement of the Colored People."

Will you kindly advise me by return airmail for the information of the Board of Directors whether you consented to serve on this committee for Wallace, and if so, whether this consent was given before or after you received my letter of March 11th.

Every sincerely,
Walter White
Secretary

Prairie View, Texas, April 2, 1948

Dear Mr. Spingarn:

Frankly I am bewildered. Consider the following facts:

1. Before I left on this lecture trip, I wrote several columns for the Chicago

1. A slip; for one year—1911–12—Du Bois was a member of the Socialist party.

Defender, one of which was on Wallace and other candidates. This was long
before I had any knowledge of the Board action on political activity. I wrote
my assistant to hold up any matter touching politics until I had looked it over.
But this column had already been mailed.[1]

2. Mr. White has written me, saying my name was signed to a call for the
Third Party convention. I replied that I had signed no such call and indeed had
not seen it. I presume that since I had long ago endorsed Wallace and was a
Vice-President of the PCA, they felt justified in assuming I would sign the call.
But under the Board decision, I would not have signed it had I known it. In
replying to Mr. White, I said that since I received notice of the action of the
Board, I had taken no part in organized political activity.

3. But this does not settle the matter. For instance in this morning's mail
come the following requests:

a. From Madame Sun Yat Sen, to become an honorary member of her China
Welfare Fund.

b. From the American Council for a Democratic Greece, to become a Co-
Chairman, with Louis Adamic and Carey McWilliams, in a proposed National Conference.

Ordinarily, I should not hesitate to assent to both these requests. But both
are in a sense "political." Does it mean that, hereafter, I must not thus express
my ideas? Once in 1909, at a similar request, I served on a committee of 100
which resulted in the NAACP.

c. I have delivered, since February 15, 12 lectures in 5 states. In no case was
the occasion political; but also in every case I discussed subjects which had
political implications; indeed how can anyone speak of current topics and
avoid politics? My interpretation of the Board's ruling was that, the occasion
must not be a political rally for a party candidate; and even on other occasions, the talk must not be aimed at asking support for a particular political
candidate. But am I right in this conclusion?

For instance: again before I had notice of the Board action, I accepted an
invitation to address the Chicago Forum, April 16, on "What the Negro
Wants in 1948." I addressed this forum in 1947, and I accepted this invitation.
But I wrote to Lochard, who runs it, after receiving White's letter, that I understood this was not a political meeting but a forum; and gave the reasons.
Now I am wondering: Shall I be discussing Civil Rights, Poll Tax, Segregation,
etc.? The city will be Wallace-conscious from a recent convention. Even if I
avoid mentioning candidates, suppose a question comes from the floor? Does
this make the meeting "political"? Must I, to follow the Board's ruling, hereafter refuse to address forums?

A forum in Philadelphia, headed by Dr. S. S. Bloom, 606 Medical Arts Build-

1. Du Bois's arguments favoring the candidacy of Henry Wallace appeared in two
columns of the *Chicago Defender*, 21 February and 20 March 1948.

ing (16th and Walnut Streets), has asked me repeatedly to address them. I
have refused to, [claiming] lack of time and strength. Today comes another
invitation: "We need him so badly here that our committee urges me to write
once more. . . . We planned on having Mr. Rainey with him.[2] You know that
the Progressive Party is running Mr. Rainey for Congress and his chances are
good."

I have refused to go, since the meeting is evidently political. And yet in
what position does this leave the NAACP, in the case of a prospective congressman who is a member and officer of the Association?

You will realize the dilemmas in which I find myself; they will increase as
the present crisis continues. What I must ask myself is, how narrowly is this
Board ruling to be interpreted? Is the interpretation outlined above valid, or
if I continue to discuss current topics in non-political meetings, and if I continue to write on current political and social problems, am I going to face
sudden loss of bread and butter?

When you and Louis Wright urged me to return to the NAACP, there was
no warning that my usual freedom of expression was to be curtailed, except of
course general conformity with the NAACP program, and (as I myself insisted)
no attempt on my part to make its policy. Certainly, if I had thought that rejoining the NAACP meant an end to my writing and speaking I would never have
come back. Hitherto, in my books, articles and talks, I have heard no criticism
that I was going contrary to your general policy. This makes it all the more
difficult for me to interpret this latest order, which, broadly interpreted, I
willingly assent to; but narrowly applied, practically closes my mouth and stops
my pen, with about the sharpest threat a man can face at the end of his life.

This letter requires no answer. I realize that you are not in much better
position to answer it than I, myself. I simply want to make myself clear for
the record when clarity is demanded.

Very sincerely,
W. E. B. Du Bois

P. S. Two other cases occur to me: On February 9, I was asked to attend a civil
rights banquet in Washington and received from the American Veterans Committee an award as "AVC Man of the Year for 1948." I accepted. The dinner is
April 12. (Since changed to May 15.) Is this political? Again I have just been
asked by the Southern Negro Youth Congress to be a sponsor for the Conference for 1948. I spoke for their 1946 conference and my speech was published
(10,000 copies). In a certain sense this movement is political. I have not yet
replied.

2. Joseph H. Rainey was a Black man who served as a municipal judge in Philadelphia from 1938 to 1951. He was a candidate for Congress on the Wallace ticket in
1948; he also was chairman of the Philadelphia branch of the NAACP.

New York City, May 28, 1948

Dear Doctor Du Bois:

The Administrative Committee, on May 24, 1948, directed me to write you that, as a paid Executive of the Association, it disapproved your being an initiating sponsor of the March on Washington Movement for Civil Rights on June 2.[1]

The Committee voted that paid Executives did not and should not have the right of independent action, in areas in which the Association works, without clearing such action beforehand with the Association.

Your name has received, in this connection, much publicity and has caused confusion among Association members because they felt that you voiced the opinion of and represented the Association. This was not so.

An Executive of the Association cannot invite the Association to participate in a movement that the Association did not inaugurate. Actually, the Association began and fostered its own civil rights program.

The Committee recommended that this matter be presented to the Board of Directors at their next meeting to the end that the Board will decide as a matter of policy what Executives can do.

A conflict exists here and, fortunately or unfortunately, your name as an Executive of the Association cannot be separated from your activities as an individual, and the Committee feels that you, therefore, should not act in any way that would be harmful to the best interests of the Association.

In this specific instance the call for a March on Washington Movement was considered by the Administrative Committee to be badly timed, contrary to the Association's strategy, and that it will be harmful to the establishment of the aims stated.

With the kindest personal regards, I am

Very sincerely yours,
Louis T. Wright, M.D.[2]

1. Very early in 1948 several nationally known Black leaders had urged rallies, demonstrations, parades, and petitions to end the system of discrimination and segregation and to achieve in 1948 legislation wiping out the poll tax, outlawing lynching, and establishing a federal fair employment practices act with teeth for enforcement. These leaders were Dr. J. Finley Wilson of Washington, D.C., Dr. Benjamin F. Mays of Atlanta, Dr. William H. Jernagin of Washington, Bishop D. Ward Nichols of New York City, John Wesley Dobbs of Atlanta, Dr. William H. Borders, also of Atlanta, and Du Bois. This effort merged with the Progressive party's strong fight against racism, even in the South, and participating in this movement then, as for decades earlier, was the entire political left. The mass character and left-orientation of this struggle was objected to by the Truman administration—and by the leadership of the NAACP.

2. Louis Tompkins Wright (1891-1952) was born in Georgia. He was educated at Clark University in Atlanta and at Harvard, where he gained his M.D. in 1915; he was one of the most distinguished physicians and surgeons of his time. A Spingarn Medalist

*In the midst of these formal and unpleasant memoranda, it is a relief to observe
that Walter White sent Du Bois a one-sentence note, undated, reading: "To:
Dr. Du Bois: Why didn't you tell me you owned half of Harlem?" Clipped to
the note was an item from the New York City newspaper* PM, *3 June 1948,
quoting a Washington* AP *dispatch of 2 June with excerpts from a Voice of
America broadcast, beamed to South America in Spanish, which contained this
dialogue:* Narrator: *"This street is Harlem's Fifth Avenue, where colored mil-
lionaires live."* Voice: *"I thought all colored people were poor!"* Narrator:
"There is a Mr. Du Bois who owns half of Harlem."

*The final straw for Du Bois came when he learned that Walter White was to
join the United States delegation at a meeting of the United Nations in Paris;
when White asked Du Bois to give him a memorandum that might assist him in
Paris, Du Bois decided that the time had come for a showdown.*

Memorandum
To: The Secretary and Board of Directors of the N.A.A.C.P.
From: W. E. B. Du Bois
Subject: The United Nations and the N.A.A.C.P.
Date: September 7, 1948
    The Secretary has asked me to give him a memorandum on matters which
are likely to come up at the Paris meeting of the United Nations this month,
and in which we should be interested. I regret to say that I am unable to comply
with his request, and I wish to state the reasons why.
    According to the understanding by which I joined the National Association
for the Advancement of Colored People in 1944, my fields of research were
left indeterminate and largely in accordance with my desires, subject to the
directives of the Board of Directors. But there was a fairly clear understanding that problems of the Darker Races outside the United States and particularly
in Africa would engage most of my time. For that reason I have attended the
Pan African Congress in England; prepared a petition to the United Nations on
our status; written two books on democracy for colored peoples and the relation
of Africa to the world. Also, at the request of the *Atlantic Monthly* I have prepared a statement on present conditions in Africa, which the editors are now
considering for possible publication.[1]
    With regard to these matters I have reported to the Board of Directors from
time to time. Whether my suggestions have reached the Board, and what action
it has taken, I seldom know, since the Secretary does not send me copies of the
agenda of the Board meetings nor minutes of the actions of the Board.

---

in 1940, he was chairman of the board of the NAACP at the time of this letter. He and
Du Bois were close friends for decades.
    1. It was not published.

Therefore, I have been proceeding practically without directives from the Board and without any clear idea of its attitude with regard to what might be called the Foreign Policy of this Association. In the past, for the most part, this lack was unimportant and our action limited. Today however, the situation has changed drastically, and just as the United States has become international in its action, so the NAACP is called upon to take a stand concerning Africa, Asia, the islands of the Pacific and the Caribbean, not to mention the colonial problems of all colored and oppressed peoples. We ought to have investigation, consultation, and a plan of action. So far as I know we have had nothing of the sort. Certainly I have not been called into consultation, nor have I been commissioned to investigate or propose a policy.

The Secretary announces now that in the name of the NAACP he has accepted, at the hands of the Truman administration, appointment as a Consultant to the United States Delegation to the United Nations, for the Paris meeting of the General Assembly. The United States Delegation to the United Nations has expressed clearly its attitude toward matters in which the NAACP is interested; it has refused to bring the curtailment of our civil rights to the attention of the General Assembly; it has refused willingly to allow any other nation to bring this matter up; if any should, Mrs. Eleanor Roosevelt has declared that she would probably resign from the United States Delegation. In the Trusteeship Council the United States has sided with the imperial powers; it has sided with Italy in taking all but an unimportant part of Eritrea from Ethiopia; it has opposed the best interests of India, the only nation which has defended Africa before the Assembly; it has not defended Indonesia, and is clearly straddling on Israel.

If we accept a consultantship in this delegation without a clear, open, public declaration by the Board of our position on the Truman foreign policy, our very acceptance ties us in with the reactionary, war-mongering colonial imperialism of the present administration. It is certain that no influence applied in Paris is going to have the slightest influence on our delegation. Their minds are made up and their policy set. The only change that can be made is in Washington and in the United States.

I do not know the attitude of the Board of Directors of the NAACP on these matters, nor, so far as I know, does anyone else. But I insist that here if anywhere, in a democratic organization seeking the welfare of the millions of colored people the world over, is the place for careful knowledge of all the facts and thoughtful consideration as to just what our plans and purposes are in this crisis of the world.

If, on the contrary, we are to be loaded on the Truman bandwagon, with no chance for opinion or consultation, we are headed for a tragic mistake.

Our international policy concerning Africa, Asia, Indonesia, and Israel is not only being determined without consultation or investigation, but even discussion of these matters here in public have in my case been met by five threats and warnings from the officials of the NAACP not to engage in "political activity." My request for clarification of what "political activity" consists has never been answered. On the other hand, the political activity of various members of this Association has been widely known.

I thoroughly agree that no official of this organization, salaried or unsalaried, should commit the organization as such to any one political party. But I insist that this rule should apply to all officials and not to a few;[2] and I also insist that it is not only the right but the bounden duty of every official and member of the NAACP as an American citizen to investigate, interrogate, vote and defend his vote in every election, and I deny the right of any official to tie this organization to the foreign policy of the present administration as long as it stands against the public discussion of our civil rights, for the despoiling of Ethiopia, for the delaying of recognition to Israel, and, in general, against the interests of colonial peoples.

For these reasons I am not attending the committee meeting called by the Secretary for today, Tuesday, September 7, 1948. And I am insisting that:

1. Hereafter I receive the agenda for the meetings of the Board of Directors and minutes of their meetings.

2. There be put before the Board of Directors at their next meeting a proposal for steps leading to a declared foreign policy for this Association.

Du Bois sent a copy of the foregoing memorandum to each of the nearly fifty members of the national board of the NAACP and to its office staff; he did not send a copy to the press, but the press obtained it. A story quoting from it at length appeared in the New York Times, *9 September 1948, under the headline, "Racial Unit Scored As Aiding Truman/Dr. Du Bois Charges Dropping of Efforts to Help Peoples of the World."*

The result was a letter sent special delivery from the chairman of the board of the NAACP.

New York City, September 13, 1948

Dear Dr. Du Bois:

I am enclosing a copy of a motion passed today by the Board of Directors

2. Du Bois not only meant that White's acceptance of the position with the United States delegation was a political act; he also had in mind White's speeches attacking the Republicans and, especially, the Progressive party candidates in the 1948 election. This, for example, was a main theme of his speech at the thirty-ninth Annual Conference of the NAACP held in Kansas City, Missouri, which was published in the *Crisis* 53 (August 1948):247.

of the NAACP. I am sure that all the members of the Board regretted the fact that they felt it necessary to take this action.

Sincerely yours,
Louis T. Wright
Chairman of the Board.

[Enclosure]
Motion Passed by NAACP Board of Directors
at the Regular Meeting, September 13, 1948

That in view of Dr. Du Bois' written refusal to cooperate with the NAACP executive staff of which he is a member in preparation for representation at the forthcoming meeting of the General Assembly of the U.N., in view of his distribution of his memorandum of September 7, addressed to this Board, before its consideration by this Board, and in view of Dr. Du Bois' expressed willingness that the memorandum in question be made public before its consideration by this Board, it is the conclusion of this Board that it will not be in the best interest of the Association to continue the employment of Dr. Du Bois as a staff member beyond the term of his present contract; that formal notice of this decision be transmitted to Dr. Du Bois.

As may be expected, Du Bois received many letters when news of his dismissal from the NAACP *became public; the following are representative.*

Brooklyn, N.Y., September 15, 1948
Dear Dr. Du Bois:

I read with profound shock and chagrin, in the New York *Times,* September 14, the decision of the Board of Directors of the NAACP regarding yourself.

I think that your memorandum to the Board of Directors of the NAACP regarding the [position the] Association is taking in these turbulent times strengthens the ever growing movement of progress and of the Negro people here and abroad in particular.

It expresses their best vital interests. They should be made aware of it, and then they will tear away those elements of corruption, who cringe before imperialism, from their struggles and thus strengthen their fight for dignity, freedom and social progress.

Expressing my personal opinion and sincere best wishes, I am

Sincerely yours,
James W. Ford

Norfolk, Virginia, Sept. 24, 1948
My dear Dr. Du Bois:

I want you to know that I am with you wholeheartedly in your position with regard to Mr. Walter White. No one but a person suffering from an inflated

ego and an acute case of selfishness would step in front of you for an international assignment on the Colonial question involving Negroes.

I am amazed at Mr. White's interest in his personal advancement. Not a
single Negro in America has done as much as you have to focus the attention
of the white world on the oppression and exploitation of Negroes in Africa and
other parts of the world. You are the most noted and most widely recognized
Negro statesman in the world on the color problem in the world.

Any Negro of good sense and a balanced judgment of his own worth would
have had sense enough to realize that you more than any other Negro anywhere
in the world deserves the post for consultant on Negro problems in colonial
Africa.

I am a reporter for the *Journal and Guide*. We discussed this matter as we
do many others in the news room at the *Guide*. What is said, of course, was our
personal opinion, but everyone in the news room who entered the discussion
said White is too self-centered and that you should have had the post or assignment which he engineered for himself.

No Negro has done as much for the NAACP as you have, but Mr. White
probably would not agree to this. You are my spiritual father—the man who
with others helped to keep me from giving up in utter despair when I was in
my teens.

I am afraid most Negroes don't realize the value of a man who does the work
you did as founder and editor of *The Crisis*. *The Crisis* under your editorship
saved hundreds and thousands of young Negroes from spiritual death. Their
hope and aspirations were kept alive because you wrote and said the things they
wanted someone to write and say. In my own case I don't know what would
have happened to me "spiritually and morally" but for you and *The Crisis* and
Negro leaders like you. I'll never forget your editorial on John R. Mott in
which you discussed Mott's admonition "Don't Be Bitter."[1]

Walter White is a shoe shine boy in comparison to you. Of course he has
done a good job as NAACP Secretary but he was never and never will be the
scholar or statesman that you are or that my late friend James Weldon Johnson
was.

Most sincerely yours,
Thomas L. Dabney

P. S. You might not remember—I once taught school in Buckingham County,
Va. and started the fight in Virginia in 1931 for higher salaries of Negro
teachers.[2]

1. An editorial strongly suggestive of the one mentioned by Dabney is entitled "The
Gall of Bitterness." It appeared in the *Crisis* 3 (February 1912):153.
2. Du Bois had a very high regard for the pioneer efforts of Dabney in fighting
against discrimination in education. See the present work, 2:273–75.

Evanston, Illinois, Sept. 28, 1948

Dear Dr. Du Bois:

I just want to be added to the list of those who are highly indignant over the action of the NAACP.

My reaction, as a matter of fact, goes beyond indignation. I am frightened at this new indication of how successful the Goebbels-like red smokescreen has been in this nation. When each new incident occurs I ask myself, shuddering, "What next?"

On the personal side I recall pleasantly having met you two or three times about a decade ago when I was state supervisor of the Illinois Writers Project and you consulted with Arna Bontemps and me regarding several research proposals.

Cordially yours,
Curtis D. MacDougall[1]

Boston, Mass., October 5, 1948

Dear Mr. Du Bois:

I have received, presumably from the NAACP, a report dated September 13th of a meeting of the Board of Directors and a statement purporting to come from W. E. B. Du Bois and if it was not written by you I would be interested to know it.

You seem to be unconscious of the fact that when a man accepts employment from any other man or organization or joins any representative body he thereby curtails to a certain extent his freedom as a private citizen with regard to publication of his views, and if he does not possess good judgment as to what this extent of curtailment should properly be, he may cease to be a desirable employee or associate and may lose his employment.

In advocating the views of Henry Wallace I think you have been, according to the statement which is supposed to be yours, an enemy to the best interests of your country and of the people of the world. It seems to me that Russia, a country in which I have traveled many thousands of miles, has been now enslaved by 14 men, commonly called the Politburo and that since the year 1917 the policy announced by Leningrad, that no treaties or agreements would be made with other countries excepting with the purpose of breaking them at any time that it might suit the interests of Russia, has been continuously the Russian policy in all of her foreign relations.

1. Curtis Daniel MacDougall was born in Wisconsin in 1903. After studying at Northwestern and the University of Wisconsin, he worked as a newspaperman in Wisconsin, Illinois, and Missouri; served as state supervisor for the Illinois Writers' Project, 1939-42; and thereafter was a professor of journalism at Northwestern University. He is the author of many books in journalism and of the two-volume study of the Wallace-Progressive movement *Gideon's Army*, published in 1965. He was a candidate for United States senator on the Wallace ticket in Illinois in 1948.

I think Henry Wallace's conduct is actuated chiefly by selfish ambition and anger against Truman. I do not, in general, approve of Truman's conduct of the affairs of the United States and hope that he will be replaced by Thomas E. Dewey this fall, but I do think he and his predecessor deserve greater credit for accomplishing more to enforce the constitutional rights of colored persons in this country than had been accomplished in the previous fifty years, and I surmise that your following and promulgating the doctrines of this man would render you persona non grata to the Board of Directors of the NAACP. I imagine that if your connection with the NAACP was severed that no one therewith connected would attempt to interfere with your constitutional rights of speech and publication, but they also have a constitutional right to promulgate and support the views that they hold, under the limitations of the federal statutes and the common law, and the right to employ or not to employ you. I trust you will find some future employer with whom you will get along in harmony, but if you require that he should coincide with you in all of his views, it is unlikely you will be able to discover such a man, for there is an infinite diversity of views among members of our race.

It is well to remember that there is no policy so righteous and good that it may not be carried to unwise extremes and diminish the usefulness of the person who thus pursues it too far. For instance: there is nothing on which a larger portion of the human race are agreed than the evil of murder, but if a man were to refuse to take quinine, in order to cure himself of malarial fever, by reason of the microbes that had been squirted into his blood by the anophyles mosquito, he would be in a camparatively small minority, and I judge that neither you nor I would consider him a wise man.

Yours truly,

Godfrey L. Cabot[1]

Copy to: Mr. Walter White, Secretary, NAACP

New York City, October 13, 1948

Dear Mr. Cabot:

It seems to me that your letter of October 8 is not quite logical. Apparently you assume that the complaint of the NAACP against me is because I shall vote for Mr. Wallace. That may be true in the case of some members like you. But their declared reason was that I did not "cooperate" with the Secretary in his trip to Paris and revealed my reasons therefore, which became public before the Board had considered them. Before this action the Board had declared that none of the employed personnel should take active part in political campaigns for any candidate, Dewey, Truman, Wallace or Thomas. I was in accord with

---

1. Godfrey Lowell Cabot (1861-1962) was born in Boston and educated at MIT and Harvard. He was a naval aviator, chemical engineer, and manufacturer; he also was, at this time, one of the vice-presidents of the NAACP.

that decision, in so far as "taking part" meant active political canvassing. But I asked the Board if they meant to deny my right to vote or announce my candidate or even tell publicly whom I preferred, so long as I was careful to make it clear that I wasn't speaking officially for the NAACP. The Board never answered this query.

The Secretary, openly, by word written and spoken, announced his choice of Truman and atttacked both Dewey and Wallace. His position as Secretary made his words sound much more official than mine, especially since I, in the few pronouncements which I made, was especially careful to say that these were my personal views.

It has always been the custom in the NAACP (in which I have been an official for 27 years) for officers to announce their political choices publicly. It was so in Wilson's campaign, in the Bull Moose fight, in the election of Harding, Hoover, and Roosevelt. Of course we never presumed to speak officially for the organization, nor did the organization order us to keep silent.

It seems to me, therefore, that your objection to Mr. Wallace is beside the point. I regard Mr. Wallace as a great and good man. You do not. Both of us have a right to our opinion. The real question is: did I mislead the public in appearing to commit the NAACP to Wallace or did the Secretary commit the organization to Truman? If either of us did, we were wrong. My contention is that I distinctly did not and that the Secretary did. The Board has never taken action on this point.

Very sincerely yours,
W. E. B. Du Bois

Lenox, Mass., October 6, 1948

Dear Dr. Du Bois:

I cannot let your separation from the active service of the NAACP pass without a word of appreciation for the magnificent work which you have rendered over the years in this and other capacities. You state the results while modestly restraining from mentioning your own part in the extremely interesting article in the current number of *Phylon* entitled "Race Relations in the United States 1917-1947."[1] But I was sorry for the little slap at Booker Washington which I do not think justified. As I have always seen it, it was not an "either or" with him as far as the different types of education were concerned, but the point of emphasis for his particular activity in his part of the south. I do not think that the Tuskegee ideal and the Atlanta University ideal, for instance, were in any way inconsistent.

You beat me to it in your 30-year study of race relations. Remember that I showed you a couple of years ago my Table of Dates for the 35th Anniversary Report of the Phelps-Stokes Fund, which was to cover the period from 1911

1. The article appeared in *Phylon* 9 (1949):234-47.

through 1945. My material has been in for over a year and a half, but owing to the great rush of office work and our small staff the other portions of the Report have not been completed until very recently. I hope that my Table of Dates in the volume which is to be called "Negro Status and Race Relations 1911-1946" may be of some service.[2]

I of course know nothing at first hand about the difference of opinion between you and the Trustees of the NAACP. I imagine it is something like the case of my old friend, Gifford Pinchot, in connection with the Taft administration and the Ballinger case. Gifford was undoubtedly right in his insistence on the highest standards of conservation and in making sure that there was no letdown. On the other hand, as he himself wrote me—and I have the letter on file— the President was right in asking him to resign as part of an administration which he was criticizing.[3] Perhaps it is a somewhat similar issue, although I don't know.

I am constantly gratified, as I see recognition such as the one by Gunnar Myrdal in his recent article, on "Social Trends in America," pay tribute to your extraordinary services to the cause of Negro advancement.[4] It has been heroic work and although I have not agreed a hundred percent with your points of view I have agreed a hundred percent in admiring your devotion to the cause of Negro and of American democracy, and have almost always agreed with the objectives which you have aimed at.

I notice that the Board in arranging for your retirement has duly expressed its appreciation of your services, and trust that it will arrange for some suitable pension.

Always sincerely yours,
Anson Phelps Stokes

New York City, October 21, 1948

My dear Dr. Stokes:

Thank you very much for your letter of October 6. I do not think that my mention of Mr. Washington in the *Phylon* article was in any sense a "slap." There were three statements of fact: First, what Charles Dudley Warner said;

2. This eighty-nine-page work was published by the Phelps-Stokes Fund late in 1948. The table of "Dates in the History of Negro Progress" begins with the establishment of the fund in 1909 and concludes with Truman's appointment of the President's Committee on Civil Rights in 1946; it appears on pp. 73-88 of the report and remains of value.

3. The quarrel between Gifford Pinchot and Richard Ballinger in 1909-10 resulted in President Taft's dismissal of Pinchot; this incensed Theodore Roosevelt and played a part in the split between Taft and Roosevelt which had momentous results in the 1912 election. See George E. Mowry, *The Era of Theodore Roosevelt: 1900-1912* (New York: Harper and Row, 1958), chap. 13.

4. Gunnar Myrdal, "Social Trends in America and Strategic Approaches to the Negro Problem," *Phylon* 9 (1948):196-214.

secondly, that he was a supporter of Mr. Washington; and thirdly, that these two things made defense of higher education in 1900 difficult. It does not seem to me that there could be any question about these three matters and their relations.

I remember now your showing me your data concerning race relations, but I had forgotten it, when I wrote the *Phylon* article. I shall hope to see them in print in the future.

I do not think that my relations to the NAACP exactly parallel the Pinchot case. It is rather a case of concentration of power in the hands of the Secretary, which makes it impossible for a person with any independence of thought to work with him. Eventually, of course, this power must and will be curbed.

I thank you very much for your kind references to my work. I may say, with regard to your last sentence, that no mention of a pension or other compensation has been made.[1]

I trust that this will find you in good health.

> Very sincerely yours,
> W. E. B. Du Bois

> Tougaloo, Miss., October 7, 1948

My dear Dr. Du Bois:

Your communication relative to the NAACP was read with deep concern. It is my fondest hope that you will not separate yourself from the organization at this nor at any future time. From my point of view, we can ill afford to be without the light of your leadership and experience, along with that of Mr. White, in times like these. To those of us in benighted Mississippi, and elsewhere, I am sure, the thought of your leaving the NAACP is a most regrettable one. May we dare express the hope that the separation from the NAACP will be that last thing ever to come to pass. To do so would bring irreparable loss to us all, measured from any point of view.

May I call your attention to the fact that many of the things for which you and others have fought for many decades are now coming to fruition right here in Mississippi where I was born and reared. For instance, Negroes are voting in the Democratic Primaries here in Jackson and in other spots about the state, in fairly large numbers; a young woman who is a graduate of this college has filed suit for equalization of salaries in the schools of Jackson, and other suits are coming up. You are aware of the fact that it was Negroes of Jackson, of whom I am one, that initiated the fight against Bilbo. Even the others got hold of our thunder—I mean the NAACP started the fight that put an end to Bilbo.

---

1. As noted in Du Bois's 7 January 1949 letter to Mrs. Blaine, the NAACP did give Du Bois $2,400 on his severance from its employment; thereafter, the NAACP paid him a yearly pension of half that sum.

Leaders like you, over a period of years, put the fight in us. Because of the untarnished leadership of men like you, some of us have resolved to stay down here and "fight it out if it takes us all summer." Don't desert us at this stage. To do so, will be tragic.

I have enclosed a clipping from the Jackson *Daily News* of two days ago to contrast this type of leadership with the true and tried from men like Mr. White and yourself. This so called New Jersey "leader" has been writing about our group for some time. We have consistently ignored it until now. He attracted the attention of Governor Fielding Wright, second in command among the Dixicrats, and it is reported that this Negro was in Jackson a few days ago. Now this is the type of trash that sells us down the river.[1] We thank God for the NAACP and for everyone of you men who have held high its principles for forty years. May the fight never falter or fall.

With every good wish for you and your work, I am

Very sincerely yours,
W. A. Bender[2]

New York City, October 21, 1948

Mr. W. A. Bender
My dear Sir:

I appreciate deeply your kind letter of October 7. Whatever my relations may be with the NAACP in the future, I shall certainly not desert the cause.

Very sincerely yours,
W. E. B. Du Bois

Washington, D.C., October 8, 1948

My dear Doctor Du Bois:

Mrs. Myra Colson Callis and I wish you to know that you have our whole-hearted support in the recent controversy which has resulted in your separation from the N.A.A.C.P. for the second time.

It seems so perfectly clear that one cannot carry our State Department on one shoulder and the cause of oppressed peoples on the other. The very philosophy

1. The enclosure was not found. The reference, however, is to one Clarence A. Ward of Plainfield, New Jersey, who seems to have specialized in traveling through the South and "exposing" the criminal and fraudulent activities of the Progressive party. There is a story based on Ward's charges on page one of the *Atlanta* (Ga.) *Constitution*, 6 October 1948, and the same issue carried an editorial based on that story entitled, "The Wallacites for What They Are."

2. Bender was the minister of Tougaloo College and assistant to the college president. He also was president of the Jackson, Mississippi, branch of the NAACP.

beneath The Marshall Plan envisions the exploitation of Africa with the aid of American Tax Dollars.

Sincerely,
Henry Arthur Callis[1]

New York City, October 21, 1948

My dear Dr. Callis:

I appreciate very deeply your kind letter of October 8.
My best regards to you and your wife.

Very sincerely yours,
W. E. B. Du Bois

The official termination of Du Bois's relationship with the NAACP *came in a letter from its assistant secretary, Roy Wilkins. It is unfortunate that Wilkins seems not to have made time to sign this letter personally.*

New York City, December 31, 1948

Dear Dr. Du Bois:

I am enclosing your pay check for December 31, 1948, and in addition, a check to cover vacation time earned to December 31.

I should like to express my regret that circumstances developed which resulted in your leaving the Association as of today.

Very sincerely yours,
Roy Wilkins (per ELJ)

1. Henry Arthur Callis (1887-1974) was born in Rochester, New York, and educated at Cornell University and Rush Medical College in Chicago. Beginning in 1923 he practiced medicine in Washington, D.C.; he was an associate professor of medicine at Howard University from 1930 to 1939. He was a founder of Alpha Phi Alpha, Du Bois's fraternity. Myra Colson Callis was born in 1892 and educated at Fisk and the University of Chicago. She taught chemistry in high schools and at Virginia State College; at the time this letter was written she was a social worker in Washington.

1949

As part of the Cold War and Red-baiting hysteria, early in 1948 the attorney
general of the United States placed the Council on African Affairs upon what
was called the "subversive list"—that is, a list of suspect and treasonous organizations. At the same moment Dr. Max Yergan—who, with Paul Robeson, had
been a main founder of the council in the late 1930s—issued a press statement
attacking "Communists." This action led to a fierce inner struggle and Yergan
was ousted from his position; Paul Robeson remained and with him remained,
as secretary, Dr. W. Alphaeus Hunton, formerly a professor at Howard University.

Du Bois was part of the group seeking to save the council; indeed, early in
1948 he was chairman of the interim executive committee of the council and a
member of the policy committee. When Du Bois left the NAACP at the end of
1948 he was invited by Paul Robeson to join with him. He accepted with the
title of vice-chairman; he received no salary but was furnished an office at the
council headquarters, rent-free, and also the services of a council secretary.
Du Bois remained with the council and actively participated in its work from
then until its dissolution in 1955—a dissolution largely attributable to the constant hounding of the federal government and the hostility of the commercial
media.*

No sooner did Du Bois get settled in his new office than he sent a letter to
the president of Howard University, Dr. Mordecai W. Johnson. The suggested
conference was not held.

New York City, January 26, 1949

Dear President Johnson:

I am writing to ask, if you would not be willing to promote a conference on
Africa? The Council on African Affairs would be glad to cooperate with you.
We would want, as I am sure you would, all phases and attitudes on the subject

---

* The present editor was a member of the Council on African Affairs. Du Bois writes
of his relationship with it in his *In Battle for Peace* (New York: Masses and Mainstream, 1952), pp. 15-19; Hunton also describes it briefly in an appendix to Paul Robeson's *I'll Take My Stand*, originally published in New York City in 1958 by Othello
Associates, pp. 126-28. In the Beacon Press reprint this appendix appears only in the
second printing (1972), pp. 117-19.

represented: the colonial powers such as Great Britain, France, Portugal, Belgium, and Italy: and the African countries like Egypt, Ethiopia, the Union of South Africa and all of the African colonies.

There should be organizations like The Phelps-Stokes Fund and what is left of the Colonization Society; and Big-Business as represented by Stettinius and other investors. I should think we might make a conference of tremendous importance, lasting three or four days and bringing to the world the great and growing importance of Africa.

If Africa is going to be developed as the last stronghold of colonial imperialism, that will drag the world in one direction. On the other hand, if it is going to develop toward independence and self-sustaining cultures, as part of a new democratic world, that is another thing. We ought, of course, to bring in the United Nations and the various organizations for world government and world unity: Russia and her colonial attitude ought to be represented.

I am writing you simply to get your reaction, and would be glad to hear from you in the near future.

My best regards to you and the family.

Very sincerely yours,
W. E. B. Du Bois

Washington, D.C., February 3, 1949

Dear Dr. Du Bois:

Please forgive me for my delayed answer to your letter. I have been under such heavy pressure during the last few days in respect to our budget requests now pending before Congress that I have not been free until now to have the conferences preparatory to answering your letter. Today, however, I have talked with Professor [Alain] Locke, Chairman of the Division of Social Sciences in the University. He agrees with me that a conference with such broad representation as you have outlined in your letter would be of great importance and that Howard University should be willing to promote such a conference.

Professor Locke is to be in New York possibly on the twelfth of February, but certainly on the nineteenth. He will call you by telephone for a preliminary conference on the whole matter if this seems desirable to you.

All good wishes to you and to your loved ones!

Sincerely yours,
Mordecai W. Johnson

Shortly before writing the preceding letter to the president of Howard University, Du Bois wrote to the present editor concerning ideas for the republication of his classic, The Souls of Black Folk. *Du Bois's attempt to interest leading publishers in a new edition of the book was not successful, and so in 1953 the new edition was published by the Blue Heron Press in New York City—a press established by Howard Fast as a vehicle for the publication of his own work, since he was among the* verboten *authors of the McCarthy era.*

New York City, January 7, 1949

Dear Mr. Aptheker:

The plates on the *Souls of Black Folk,* published in 1903 in Chicago, have been offered to me for $100. I am going to buy them January 15. There will then come the question as to what can be done with them.

I wish you would think this over and advise me. I have been thinking that possibly a sort of jubilee edition might be undertaken, perhaps with some addition taken from the *Times* article or the Petition to the United Nations.[1] Howard Fast, I think, has some ideas. Let me hear from you at your leisure.

Very sincerely yours,

W. E. B. Du Bois

A series of telegrams and letters exchanged between the president of Morgan State College in Baltimore and Du Bois gives an inkling of the state of hysteria in this "time of the toad."

Baltimore, Md., March 23, 1949

[Telegram]

Dr. W. E. B. Du Bois:

Would like to have you deliver commencement address Morgan State College June 6th at 6 P.M. on subject of your own choosing. Honorarium $100 plus traveling expenses from New York. Please wire your reaction by Friday, March 25.

Martin D. Jenkins[1]

Du Bois replied, by wire, on 24 March 1949.

1. The *New York Times* published an essay by Du Bois, which it entitled, "The Negro Since 1900: A Progress Report," in its Sunday *Magazine,* 21 November 1948, pp. 24, 54-57. On the *Souls of Black Folk* republication, see the editor's introduction to the Kraus-Thomson edition, published in 1975.

1. Martin David Jenkins was born in Indiana in 1904 and was educated at Howard and Northwestern universities. He was a professor of education at Howard from 1938 to 1948 and from 1948 to 1970 was president of Morgan State College. Most recently he has been director of urban affairs for the American Council on Education in Washington, D.C.

Martin D. Jenkins
President, Morgan State College
 Will speak Monday, June 8, subject: "The Future of the Negro State
College."[1]

W. E. B. Du Bois

Baltimore, Md., April 23, 1949
Dear Dr. Du Bois:
 This belated letter will confirm my telegram of March 23, 1949, in which I
invited you to deliver our Commencement Address. As stated in the telegram,
we will pay you an honorarium of $100 plus first-class railroad fare from New
York City to Baltimore and return. I am glad that you have accepted this invita-
tion and we look forward, with a great deal of pleasure, to your visit with us.
 The Commencement Exercises will be held in the Hughes Stadium of Morgan
State College on Monday, June 6, 1949, at 6:00 P.M., D.S.T. The academic pro-
cession will move at 5:30 P.M., probably from the Morgan Christian Center.
 There will be a luncheon for the Commencement guests at 3:30 P.M. in the
dining hall, which is located in Spencer Hall. You are invited to be present at
this affair.
 Since Baltimore is your home, you may not wish us to provide sleeping accommodations for you. If you wish us to do so, however, please advise me.
 The college will furnish the academic costume, unless you care to provide
your own. I am enclosing a form which I wish you would fill out entirely, if
you desire us to procure a costume for you, or partially, if you wish to furnish
your own academic costume. Of course, we must have the information concerning your name, degrees, and so on. A self-addressed stamped envelope is being
inclosed for your convenience.

Cordially yours,
Martin D. Jenkins

New York City, April 28, 1949
Dear President Jenkins:
 Your letter of April 23, has been received. Dr. Du Bois is abroad in Paris in
attendance at the Peace Congress. He is expected to return early in May.
 I will bring your letter and its enclosure to his attention immediately upon
his return. He will, I am sure, let you know in time about the costume. However, I do not think you need to provide sleeping accommodations for him.

Very sincerely yours,
Lillian Murphy
Secretary to Dr. Du Bois

 1. What Du Bois might have said on this subject at this time one does not know. It
may be relevant to read what he did say on "The Future of the Negro State Univer-

Baltimore, Md., April 29, 1949

[Registered Mail]
Dear Dr. Du Bois:

I am writing to withdraw our invitation to you to deliver the Commencement Address at the Commencement Exercises at Morgan State College on June 6, 1949. This invitation was extended to you as a tribute to your outstanding contributions in the field of scholarship. You were among the first of the great Negro scholars, and you have been for many, many years a symbol and a source of inspiration to the younger Negro scholars who are attempting to follow in your footsteps. Now that you are approaching the end of your career, we thought it desirable, particularly in view of your Baltimore residence, to present you in person to the members of our graduating class.

Your appearance with Mr. Paul Robeson at the recent World Peace Congress held in Paris and, particularly, your failure to condemn his treasonable statement made at that meeting have linked you in the public mind with the Communist movement in this country.[1] I do not deny you the right to your own views. I feel, however, that if you were to speak at Morgan State College, even on a non-political topic as you had planned, it would give the appearance of our being in sympathy with your general views. As a matter of fact, we are far from being sympathetic in this matter. I think that Mr. Robeson's views and approach are to be severely condemned.

I regret very much that it has been necessary for us to take this action.

Sincerely yours,
Martin D. Jenkins

New York City, May 4, 1949

Dear President Jenkins:

Your letter of April 29 to Dr. Du Bois has been received. Dr. Du Bois, as you no doubt know, is still in Paris.

I shall bring your letter to his attention when he returns to his office.

Very sincerely yours,
Lillian Murphy
Secretary to Dr. Du Bois

---

sity" in 1941 and "The Future and Function of the Private Negro College" in 1946; see Du Bois, *The Education of Black People: Ten Critiques*, 1906-1960, ed. H. Aptheker (Amherst, Massachusetts: University of Massachusetts Press, 1973), pp. 129-48.

1. At the World Peace Congress held in Paris in April 1949, Paul Robeson said, among much else: "The Black folk in America will never fight against the Soviet Union." There was a debate on the propriety of this statement between Du Bois and Walter White, published in *Negro Digest* 7, no. 5 (March 1950):8,10-14, with Du Bois supporting and White attacking the Robeson view. The May 1949 *Crisis* bitterly attacked Robeson in an editorial and specifically denounced the Council on African Affairs—"long ago labeled a Communist-front by the Department of Justice" (54:137).

From 25 March through 27 March 1949, under the auspices of the National
Council of the Arts, Sciences and Professions, a Cultural and Scientific Confer-
ence for World Peace was held at the Waldorf-Astoria in New York City. The
program committee, in addition to Du Bois, included Harlow Shapley; Sarah
Gibson Blanding, the president of Vassar College; Herbert John Davis, the
president of Smith College; Olin Downes, the music critic; Lillian Hellman, the
playwright; Louis Untermeyer, the poet; John Martin, the dance critic; and
Philip Morrison, the physicist; as well as O. John Rogge, former United States
assistant attorney general. Foreign guests and speakers included J. D. Bernal of
England, Paul Eluard of France, Carlo Levi of Italy, and A. I. Oparin and D. D.
Shostakovich of the USSR.
Du Bois wrote of this event to his wife in Baltimore.

New York City, March 30, 1949

My dear Nina:

This is a report of this week. I have been almost too busy to think. You know
that there has been meeting, in New York, a Conference on Peace held by the
Council of Arts, Sciences and Professions. I am a member of that Council and
serve on its board of directors. I also helped to plan this program.

Well, in the first place, we invited artists, musicians and scientists from all
over the world and got an astonishing response. Then the Department of State
stepped in and refused at least half of them visas; but they did allow representatives to come from Russia, Czechoslovakia, Yugoslavia and Poland, one from
England and one a West African Negro from North Ireland. He was invited
at my request.

The papers tried to do everything they could to smear the meeting and there
were counter demonstrations and picket lines; but it has been an astonishing
conference.[1] Last night, I opened the meeting at Madison Square Garden.
There were 20,000 people there crowded to the rafters and two or more thousand people could not get in. It was a magnificent demonstration.

I spoke of the general results of the Conference and introduced the presiding
officer, Harlow Shapley of Boston. Shostakovich, the great Russian composer,
played and there were speeches from a half dozen different countries. It was a
marvelous occasion.

Before that in Carnegie Hall we had a meeting, with the whole edifice packed;

1. Henry A. Singer made a careful study of the coverage of this event by the main
newspapers of New York City: "An Analysis of the New York Press Treatment of
the Peace Conference at the Waldorf Astoria," *Journal of Educational Sociology* 23
(January 1950):258–70. The reportage in such periodicals as *Life* and *Time* reached
depths that rivaled the journalism of Streicher in Nazi Germany.

The West African living in Ireland and invited by Du Bois was R. E. G. Armattoe.
Dr. Armattoe was a physician and director of the Lomeshie Research Centre in
Londonderry.

also we had a dinner at the Waldorf Astoria, where all of the guests and some of the sponsors, including myself, sat at three high tables. Various speeches were made. The audience paid $10 a place for their dinner and in addition to that gave $19,000 for the cause! The work is going on. The visitors are going to travel across the whole country appearing in a dozen different cities, including Baltimore, Los Angeles, St. Louis, Cleveland, Chicago and Philadelphia. I have just been to a meeting of the Action Committee.

You will not, of course, see many reports and probably no honest reports of these meetings in the Baltimore papers, but don't mind that. It was an epoch making effort to stop war.

I hope that you are getting on well. Although I have been working hard and am tired, I am not too tired and am going to rest this week; except that tomorrow, I fly to Chicago in order to have an interview with a person who is very much interested in my work.

With love to all.

Yours,
Will

Much of the national leadership of the Communist party of the United States went on trial in 1949, charged, under the 1940 Smith Act, with conspiring to advocate the forcible overthrow of the government. The present editor was one of the witnesses for the defense in that case; I also sought to obtain others whose testimony might be helpful and in this connection I, together with the late Harry Sacher, one of the attorneys for the defense, spoke with Du Bois at some length. In that discussion he expressed great sympathy for the defendants and no doubt of their innocence, but he did have reservations about testifying. A result was a letter written early in 1949.

New York City, April 11, 1949

My dear Dr. Aptheker:

Despite my resolutions, I could not help mulling over the proposal you and the lawyer made me.

As I have assured you before, anything that I can do in reason to help the accused martyrs, I will do. But again in this case, I think the analogy between the American Negro, whose position I know fairly well, and the Marxists is not good.

Undoubtedly, the Negroes, since the fifteenth century in America, have been subject to force and violence and also just as clearly, wherever they had the intelligence and reasonable opportunity, they revolted; until their revolts culminated in the Haitian Revolution, the Underground Railroad and in their assistance in the American Civil War.

Since that time, while there have been proposals here and there of force and violence against the treatment which they are receiving, it has never amounted to much, because by peaceful methods and agitation, they gradually began to win their fight. It would, therefore, be untrue to say that force and violence against the Negro never evoked corresponding conspiracy and effort to gain their rights by force.

Comparing this now with the Marxists, there is the initial and vast difference that working people are always the vast majority; while the Negro slaves were usually a minority, except of course in the West Indies. The working people are not only oppressed but incur force and violence whenever they show disposition to resist their pressure even by democratic methods. While I do not know the action of all of the working groups, certainly it has been my understanding that whenever they thought they could gain their rights Communism advised them to attempt to do so.

Can it be said that joining the Communist Party involves a determination to use force and violence? This I am not in position to say in all cases, but I am afraid that if I went on the stand to testify for the accused—a good attorney might easily elicit from me a confession that force and violence have been used by Communists and certainly may be used just as in the case of Negro slaves.

I do not, of course, believe for a moment that this accused group here ever had any overt plans of the sort for America. At the same time, that is simply my belief. Of the accused persons I have only met two, and only know one well.[1] I have no information at all as to the action of the party. From 1933 to 1944 I was resident out of the city.

I therefore conclude again that I would do the cause no good, in trying to draw an analogy between the American Negro and the working class of modern days.

Very sincerely yours,
W. E. B. Du Bois

In June 1949 Du Bois sent a letter full of news of activity to his dear friend, the author Shirley Graham. She attended the Peace Congress in Paris in April 1949 but did not return to the United States at once. Rather, at the invitation of a Danish publisher, she visited Denmark and participated in the celebration of the eightieth birthday of Martin Anderon Nexö. She returned to the United States late in July 1949.*

1. Du Bois had met Eugene Dennis; he knew Benjamin J. Davis, Jr., quite well and had known his family in Georgia.
* See Shirley Graham's "Comments" in Du Bois's In Battle for Peace, pp. 31–32.

New York City, June 24, 1949

My dear Shirley:

You have tremendous faith in the American Express; I suppose they do deliver at least three-quarters of the letters which they receive. I am not so sure of the other quarter. But this is going to you in care of them at Copenhagen.

We had a tremendous mass meeting at the Rockland Palace which used to be the old Manhattan Casino. It was filled with people and they paid from $1.20 to $2.40 for seats. I was the first speaker after an introduction by Alphaeus [Hunton] and the audience was very receptive; they rose when I began and rose again when I finished. I left immediately because it was a hot afternoon and I did not want to stay in that crowded room too long. The session began with music at three o'clock in the afternoon and did not close until eight. There was a fine succession of speakers: Ben Davis, Marcantonio and of course, Robeson, who received a tremendous ovation. I think the Council took in a goodly sum of money. Persons have spoken to me about the good impression which the meeting made.

I attended the board meeting of the Arts and Sciences with Shapley in the chair and many distinguished persons present. It was a restaurant dinner very excellently served and everybody was cordial. I sat beside Lillian Hellman, and Ella Winter and her husband [Donald Ogden Stewart] were there. The movement seems to be flourishing. They gave their first "Art Center" night at Carnegie Hall with a dramatic presentation of the picture which Fox movies turned down after paying $35,000: "The Journey of Simon McKeever" [based on a novel by Howard Fast] and also another sketch which was very excellent. Outside of these two nights, I have stayed home, going to a couple of movies in the late afternoon; and going out once to treat myself to a dinner at Longchamps.

I have also written a petition on the Rosa Ingram case for a committee of colored women headed by Mary Terrell.[1] I think it is a pretty good document and they thought so too. It is going to be presented to the United Nations. Work is also progressing on the novel and on the whole I am satisfied. I have also written out two tentative chapters of a sociology of the American Negro for Prentice-Hall. I rather doubt if they will accept it but as they asked for it, I thought it was a good thing to try. It will not take much time if I have to do it.

My rugs are up for the Summer and replaced by a few pieces of matting. The whole apartment is going to be painted a grey-green next week. During that

1. On 4 November 1947 in Georgia, Rosa Lee Ingram, a Black widow with twelve children, was set upon by an armed white man, John E. Stratford; he was in the act of beating her when two of her sons, Wallace, aged seventeen, and Sammie, aged fourteen, came to her aid and killed Stratford. Early in February 1948 an all-white jury, after a trial lasting one day, found all three guilty of murder in the first degree and sentenced them to die. Appeals followed appeals and their lives were saved, but all three served eleven years in prison. There is a photograph of Mrs. Ingram and her two sons in the May 1948 Crisis (55:141).

time I am going down to Laster Cottage at Spring Lake, taking my typewriter with me. I can get in, I think, about 4 or 5 days of work there; then I shall return to the apartment. I have bought a floor fan which I think is going to keep me fairly comfortable.

I am so glad of the magnificent trip which you are having. You are going to have a view of Europe which is worth while. Unfortunately I have never been to Scandinavia but I know of what they have accomplished in socialism and what they will yet accomplish if they are let alone; of course I am still hoping that you will get a chance to see the Soviet Union.

Yours with love,
W. E. B. Du Bois

*Du Bois was one of the conveners of a Continental Congress for World Peace held in Mexico City in September 1949. In this capacity he wrote to distinguished people in the United States urging their participation. One of the responses came from Linus Pauling.**

Pasadena, California, July 27, 1949

Dear Dr. Du Bois:

I am very pleased that you are going to serve as one of the United States vice-presidents for the American Continental Congress for World Peace. I regret that, because of the great distance of Pasadena from New York and some local problems that are keeping me tied up this summer, it is not possible for me to come to the meeting of the United States Committee on Monday, nor to attend the Congress itself.

I feel that the fine group of people not only in the United States but elsewhere in the Western Hemisphere who have already responded to the call for the Continental Congress for World Peace assures its success. Please feel free to call on me whenever I can be of help.

With very best wishes to you and your colleagues, I am

Sincerely yours,
Linus Pauling

New York City, August 5, 1949

Dear Mr. Pauling:

Thank you very much for your kind letter of July 27. I sincerely hope that

---

* Linus Carl Pauling was born in Oregon in 1901. He has served as a professor of chemistry at California Institute of Technology, at Stanford, at Oxford, and elsewhere. He was awarded the Nobel Prize in chemistry in 1954 and the Nobel Peace Prize in 1962.

our cooperation may be successful in strengthening the stand for Peace which the world today needs more than anything else.

Very sincerely yours,

W. E. B. Du Bois

The typewriter Du Bois took with him on the brief holiday noted in his June letter to Shirley Graham no doubt clattered away on the manuscript that became the trilogy Black Flame. *In its first volume Du Bois treats the rise of the Populist movement and the role of Thomas Watson and his Black associate, Sebastian Doyle. While collecting information on Doyle he wrote to Channing Tobias—who had known Doyle—and to Doyle's son. The replies are of great interest.*

New York City, July 27, 1949

Dear Dr. Du Bois:

I have yours of July 24th asking for information concerning the life and activities of the late H. Sebastian Doyle. First let me say that I am glad that you are writing to his son, Dr. Bertram Doyle, Municipal College, Louisville, Kentucky, for I am sure that he can supply you with exact data involving dates, birth and death and other facts that I do not have in my possession.

I know that he died in Kerrville, Texas where he spent the last five or six years of his life in a losing fight against tuberculosis. I am quite sure that he received his education at Clark College in Atlanta and Ohio Wesleyan University. He came to Augusta, Georgia to serve as pastor of the Trinity Colored Methodist Episcopal Church. This was when I was in my late teens. As a youngster I was greatly impressed by his learning, his eloquence and his courage. He was a lover of the classics and got a lot of fun out of stumping some of us who were just beginning our studies in Latin and Greek. While his sermons were shot through with emotion, he never stooped to the methods of some trained ministers who purposely played upon the emotions of the people in order to get their support.

In addition to his pastoral and preaching services, he was the one minister in Augusta who had the courage to challenge racial discrimination, even though he knew that his statements might be used against him by the so-called "Uncle Tom" Negro type of leadership so prevalent at the time. Not only had he the courage to challenge jim-crowism, he also had the courage to challenge the effectiveness of the dominant political parties. It was this that led him into the Agrarian movement led by Thomas E. Watson. Although in later years Watson denied it, it was a fact that Doyle was his chief supporter and protagonist. Doyle's name was almost as much of a household word as Watson's among the poor whites as well as the Negroes in Georgia. He stumped the State in the interest of the People's Party ticket with Watson and on one occasion spent the night at Watson's home in Thomson to avoid a threatened attack on his life. Although the third party movement passed off the scene, Doyle never became reconciled to the Republican Party as a medium through which equal rights for the Negro could be secured. Of course there was no such thing as a Negro Democrat at the time because the door of that party was securely closed against the black man. So Doyle was a partyless man from the time of the dissolution of the Populist movement until he died.

I am glad that you are going to mention him in your book and I regret that I do not have more authentic information to give you, but as I said in the beginning, I am sure his son will be able to help you considerably.

With cordial good wishes, I am

Sincerely yours,
Channing H. Tobias

Louisville, Ky., August 23, 1949

My dear Dr. Du Bois:

Here is such information as I have been able to recall concerning my father, Henry Sebastian Doyle, Sr. I do not know what assistance this will be in your investigation, or if there is any other information that I can give.

Cordially yours,
Bertram W. Doyle[1]

[Enclosure]

Biographical Sketch of the Life of Henry Sebastian Doyle, Sr.

Henry Sebastian Doyle, Sr., was born at Eastman, Georgia, January 8, 1867. Died at Kerrville, Texas, October 31, 1913.

He attended Clark University, Atlanta, Georgia; and Ohio Wesleyan University, Delaware, Ohio. It may be that he received his stimulus to enter politics at Ohio Wesleyan, where, as I have heard him relate, he was associated with Joseph B. Foraker, of the Ohio Forakers. (But whether the father or the son, I am not sure and have not taken the time to check except that in the Ohio Wesleyan Yearbook, 1891, a Joseph B. Foraker is listed. I think this was the son rather than the father.)

At Clark University, young Doyle was a classmate of R. S. Lovinggood, later President of Sam Houston College, Austin, Texas and attended Clark at the time when Doctors J. W. E. Bowen, and W. H. Crogman were names with which to conjure.

1. Bertram Wilbur Doyle was born in Alabama in 1897 and educated at Ohio Wesleyan and the University of Chicago. He taught at Paine College and at Fisk University and was ordained in the Christian Methodist Episcopal Church ministry in 1925. He then pastored in Tennessee and South Carolina but returned to teaching in the late 1930s at Atlanta and Hampton. From 1942 to 1950 he was dean at the Municipal College in Louisville, Kentucky. He became a bishop in his church in 1950. His book, *Etiquette of Race Relations*, was published in 1937.

Bishop Wilbur P. Thirkield was then President of Gammon Theological Seminary and became interested in young Doyle, as the legend goes, because of Doyle's marked oratorical talent and ability, as expressed in the literary societies which flourished in those days.

Bishop Thirkield was a graduate of Ohio Wesleyan and assisted Doyle both financially and otherwise in changing to that institution. At a later date Doyle gave Bishop Thirkield's name to his second son, Bertram Wilbur.

After leaving Ohio Wesleyan, young Doyle taught a while at Toccoa, Georgia; very soon entered the ministry and received a pastorate at Waynesboro, Georgia where as I understand he was pastoring at the time of his association with Thomas Watson.

For a long time as a memento of this association, the family has treasured an autographed copy of Senator Watson's *The French Revolution.*
Doyle later pastored at Birmingham, Alabama (where he met his later wife, Anna Magnolia Walker).

Later pastorates were at: Talladega, Alabama; Washington, D. C.; Lowndesborough, Alabama; Augusta, Georgia; Shreveport, Louisiana. During this period he was honored by Morris Brown College with the M.A. degree, and by Paine College with the D.D. degree.

It was at Shreveport, Louisiana that he did his most effective work in erecting the Williams' Temple C.M.E. Church which even in 1949 is one of the most prominent churches of the city.

He was prominent in his church, and was a candidate for the episcopacy in 1908, at Memphis, Tennessee. He lost his health in 1907 and was never able to again fill a full-time pastorate.

He had four sons: Albion Walker, Bertram Wilbur, Levi Carter and Henry Sebastian, Jr. Albion the eldest died in 1921. Levi Carter did not survive infancy. His widow, Anna Magnolia Walker Doyle, passed in 1937. Two sons survive.

I have heard several apocryphal stories of his life in Georgia for all of his associates are not yet dead.

You will find published information in: C. Vann Woodward: *Tom Watson, Agrarian Rebel* (New York: Macmillan, 1938, p. 239–240) along with references to source materials.

For example, I have heard two versions of the murder at Louisville, Georgia, and have heard also of a near murder at Sparta, Georgia, when a man shot at my father and creased his chin with a bullet.

Around Augusta, stories may still be heard of the time when he spoke from a platform, on which every associate was armed; Doyle, himself, had two pistols, one on each side of the speaker's stand.

My father died when I was in High School, and had been away from home for two years. I had not then, as I do now, of course, indicated any interest in his political activities.

*Du Bois was a guest at a peace congress held in Moscow in August 1949. He
was in Europe during most of August and much of September and wrote of
his trip to Anita McCormick Blaine, whose generosity had made it possible for
him to undertake the voyage.*

New York City, September 27, 1949

My dear Mrs. Blaine:

I returned from Europe, Friday, September 16, at noon. I wrote you from
Moscow and I trust you received that letter. I left Moscow after two weeks
stay on Saturday, September 3. I spent three days in Warsaw, Poland and three
in Prague, Czechoslovakia. I never thought it possible that human beings could
do to each other in modern days what the Germans did to Warsaw. Here was
a great modern city which they bombed from the air, raked with artillery on
the ground and finally soldiers with pails of gasoline ran from house to house
setting them on fire. The result was incredible devastation. In some cases there
was nothing but dust left and all over the city there is a panorama of ruined
walls which tell of the unbelievable destruction. Notwithstanding this the city
is rising again and anew and the spirit of the people is extraordinary. Six bridges
across the Vistula River were destroyed and have now been restored and rebuilt in beautiful pattern. Streets are being relaid; in some cases it is possible
to restore them only by the aid of photographs.

Parks are being laid out and flowers planted. There is yet wide evidence of
distress and inconvenience. For instance, I found to my dismay in my very
nice hotel room that the great wide window looking out on the city had no curtains whatsoever; and I had to ask to be transferred to a more simple room on
the fourth floor where curtains where available.

I recognized Prague from what I had seen of it in 1893 as a German student.
It is still a busy and beautiful city and did not suffer war destruction; although
it suffered all other sorts of inconvenience because of occupation by the German troops for a long time.

In both Poland and Czechoslovakia, the officials received me very kindly and
gave me every convenience for seeing the city and for translation of the language. I went to several theaters and finally on the 9th came to Paris where I
had a few days. I wandered for two days in the Louvre; I went to the Bois de
Boulogne; I walked along the banks of the Seine where books and drawings
are for sale and at last came back to this country.

It was a most illuminating and informing trip and I am deeply grateful for
the opportunity of making it.

I trust that this letter will find you in good health. I am still well.

Very sincerely yours,
W. E. B. Du Bois

Complete racial exclusion in the mass media remained quite unbroken until the 1960s. There were, however, many efforts in earlier years which helped in bringing about some change. One of the groups leading such efforts in the 1940s was the Voice of Freedom Committee, headed by Dorothy Parker.* In this connection, she sent a telegram to Du Bois in late 1949.

New York City, October 10, 1949

Dr. Du Bois:

Voice of Freedom Committee conducting campaign to get Negro commentator on a network as public service feature, to dramatize shameful lack of adequate employment for Negroes in the radio industry. Preliminary to actual campaign has been conducting nation-wide poll to ascertain cross section of opinion as to whom the people would like to hear. According to the results of the poll and in the considered judgment of our panel of distinguished judges we are proud to announce that you, Mary McLeod Bethune and Paul Robeson were named as the three around whom we would be most apt to wage successful campaign. Among the judges were two vof monitors, two vof officers and S. W. Garlington, managing editor of *Amsterdam News*, Dr. J. Raymond Walsh, Rev. Jack McMichael of Methodist Federation of Social Services, James E. Allen of naacp and Walter Christmas of Committee for Negro in the Arts. Please let us know as soon as possible if we may have the privilege as we plan to launch our campaign officially at our rally at Town Hall on October 22. We would appreciate it if you could be with us on this occasion as your presence would stimulate the entire movement and help to rally the people around you. The success of our project depends on you.

Dorothy Parker

New York City, October 12, 1949

My dear Miss Parker:

Frankly I do not think that your selections for radio work, with exception of Paul Robeson, are very good. However, I will be glad to help in any way I can.

Very sincerely yours,
W. E. B. Du Bois

One of the eleven leaders of the Communist party indicted in 1948 under the

---

* Dorothy R. Parker (1893-1967) was born in New Jersey. She was on the editorial staffs of *Vogue* and *Vanity Fair* and was one of the best known poets, playwrights, and short-story writers of her time. She won the O. Henry short story award in 1929.

conspiracy section of the Smith Act was Benjamin J. Davis. He was at that
time a member of the city council of New York, having first been elected to
that position, under a proportional representation system, in 1943, when he
received over 44,000 votes. He was re-elected in 1945 with over 63,000 votes.
While on trial—a trial which lasted nine months, into the latter part of 1949—
Davis remained a member of the council, but upon his conviction he was
ejected. While on bail he ran again for the council from a state senate district
representing part of Harlem and also the upper West Side, predominantly
white. Proportional representation was abolished, and a Black man, Earl Brown,
was supported by a coalition of the Republican, Democratic, and Liberal parties to oppose Davis; he was defeated under these circumstances by a vote of
63,000 to 22,000.*

*Du Bois strongly supported the campaign of Davis. He served as chairman
of the Independent Non-Partisan Citizens Committee seeking Davis's re-election; with him on this committee were Olin Downes, Muriel Draper, Hope
Stevens, Richard Boyer, and Ollie Harrington. On the stationery of the committee, Du Bois wrote an open letter to encourage voting registration and support of Davis.*

New York City, October 7, 1949

Dear Friend:

In these days when we have so recently faced the terror of Peekskill,[1] the
right to vote is indeed a mighty weapon in our hands. But we cannot vote
unless we *register*. This is primarily to remind you that registration week is
from October 10th to 15th.

We *must* register to vote, and as citizens of a New York State that has already witnessed, and to a large degree bears the responsibility for Peekskill in
the eyes of the nation and the world, we *must vote wisely*.

---

* Benjamin J. Davis, Jr., was born in Georgia in 1903. He was educated at Morehouse College in Atlanta, Amherst College in Massachusetts, and the Harvard Law
School. He was attorney for Angelo Herndon in Georgia, 1932-33; he joined the
Communist party as a result of his work with Herndon and thereafter was an outstanding leader of that party. He began serving a five-year sentence after conviction
under the Smith Act in 1951 and was jailed again on a "contempt" charge in Pennsylvania after completing the first sentence. After his prison sentences were finished he
returned to leadership in the Communist party, but his health was never good thereafter; he died on 22 August 1964. International Publishers issued posthumously, in 1969,
his *Communist Councilman from Harlem: Autobiographical Notes Written in a Federal Penitentiary*.

1. Nazi-like mobs, incited by the press and supported by the town and state police,
physically attacked crowds gathered to hear an open-air concert featuring Paul Robeson held in Peekskill, New York; many people were injured. Robeson returned to
nearby Cortland; guards surrounded the grounds and the second concert was held
despite fierce provocation and assaults. These events occurred on 27 August and
4 September 1949; altogether about two hundred people were seriously injured.

Councilman Benjamin J. Davis's re-election is of utmost importance in this campaign. He is the only Negro representative in the New York City Council. His record proves that he has been constantly on the side of the people—so much so that the political machines of the three other parties have united to defeat him. Significantly, they did not nominate a Negro for any other office throughout the city in this present election.

Ben Davis must remain in the City Council! This means that we must see to it that everyone of voting age registers next week, October 10th to 15th.

An all-out registration insures victory for our candidate!

Cordially yours,
W. E. B. Du Bois

New York City, November 14, 1949

My dear Mr. Davis:

May I congratulate you upon the good fight which you put up in the last election. I trust you will not lose courage. In the long run, you will be vindicated.

Very sincerely yours,
W. E. B. Du Bois

New York City, November 22, 1949

Dear Dr. Du Bois:

It was a great privilege to receive a letter from you expressing your confidence in the ultimate victory of the cause of democracy, freedom and peace over the forces of imperialism and reaction. My campaign for re-election was only one tiny segment of that fierce battle which is going on all over the world and I considered it a honor to have been a spokesman of the people's cause in that struggle.

I am one of the thousands who have been greatly inspired by the contributions which you have made over a long and fruitful career to the cause of human freedom and dignity, and I am looking forward to your continued contribution which history will place high upon mankind's honor roll.

None of us can even think of losing courage. Even in the last election there were signs in Harlem that the Negro people are beginning to break with the two parties of economic greed and political reaction. As the struggle develops in the immediate future there will be even more decisive breaks, not only among the Negro people, but among the workers and democratic forces, irrespective of races, creeds, colors and political affiliations. You have been working skillfully and uncompromisingly for the victory that is surely going to come. I salute you and send you my warm personal regards.

Sincerely yours,
Benjamin J. Davis Jr.

With evident reference to a meeting of leaders of the Wallace Progressive party, Du Bois shared some musings in a letter to the former vice-president. If there was a written response, it seems not to have survived.

New York City, December 2, 1949

Dear Mr. Wallace:

At the meeting the other night I indulged myself in a line of imagination and analogy which was too long and involved for me to take the time to state it with its implications. But I am venturing to do this by letter, realizing that analogies like this do not go on all fours.

Suppose that instead of being in New York in 1949, we had been meeting on lower Broadway in 1849. Naturally I would not have been present, but, for that matter, I was not much present last night.

We would have represented the Liberty party, formed some years before and representing middle ground between the Abolitionists and the Whigs. The Anti-Slavery societies of that time numbered some 200,000 members, but were of many minds and tendencies. They were all unpopular and suspect; they harbored Atheists, and the Church for that and other reasons disowned them. Some of them attacked Property, not only in men, but in things which men needed, like Land. They had a lunatic fringe who went in for Communism and rights of women. They were favorite objects of repressive legislation and court injunctions and mob law. Garrison had been dragged through the streets; Douglass had his right hand permanently crippled and Lovejoy was killed. Finally the group split. One wing went into politics. They wanted not only to free the slaves and permit no more slave territory, but were suspected of being subservient to a Foreign Power, undemocratic England, with King and lords, who jealous of our prosperity based on the Cotton Kingdom was now abolishing slavery in the West Indies and starting her colonial Imperialism in Asia and Africa. She was also trying to steal Oregon.

The Liberty Party started in 1840. They were not Abolitionists, although they wanted to abolish slavery; but they had no other dangerous 'isms and no fear of England and her designs. They chose the name "Liberty" as a designation which was vague enough to catch all but the Die-hards. They started in the election of 1844, when the South was aiming toward a new slave empire in central and South America and the Caribbean area. The Liberty Party cast 62,000 votes and beat Clay for the presidency; but unfortunately, this helped elect Polk who promptly annexed the vast slave state of Texas and forced us into a war with Mexico. He also looked viciously at England and yelled "Fifty-four forty or Fight!"

Although the Liberty Party kept at it and cast a good vote in 1846, it began to be discouraged. And the main cause of this discouragement was the "smear" of Abolition. So in 1849 (historically, it was 1847, but the analogy is not too far astray) they sat down together and took stock. Their leader was a bit discouraged. He had been subjected to mud-slinging of efficient quality and he was pretty well fed up. His family was even (to coin a word) fedder upper. Especially he resented being called an enemy of property, an instigator of servile revolt or an advocate of votes for women. He hated slavery, yes; but he was not an Abolitionist in the current sense of the term. What shall we do, he asked and suggested that the persons present poll their friends and the public as to what they wanted the Liberty Party to stand for.

The discussion was long, but tended to divide in two directions: How can we avoid being classed with Abolitionists; they are unpopular and no party with that label can win in the United States; they may not be wrong in ideal, but they are impossible in method and their foreign entanglements with British radicals are undoubted. Some argued: ignore the Smear and the differences; so far as both we and they oppose slavery and want Peace, let's work together and perfect organization. Others answered, but the Abolitionists push in, use our offices to attack slave-owners and work like Hell to twist our aims and push theirs. Our best bet is openly to disassociate ourselves from the Abolitionists and join forces with the Free Soil Party now forming. "Free Soil? What's that?" "Free Soil, Free Men, Free Speech?"

"Do you mean land owned in common, no slaves, and the right to discuss and write about property and woman suffrage?"

"No, we mean no extension of slave territory, rights for men already free and reasonable discussion which does not attack legal private property in land or men."

There, or somewhere around there, we adjourned; what happened historically thereafter, is another story.

And here, Mr. Wallace, this admittedly lame analogy ends.

Very sincerely,

W. E. B. Du Bois

P. S. To complete the record, the Liberty Party committed suicide; the Free Soil Party took over, were met by the pro-slavery Compromise of 1850 and died peacefully in the election of 1852. In 1854, their ashes fertilized a Party which moved still further right, recognized slavery but opposed its extension. It won the election of 1860 by a minority vote and went into the Civil War pledged to defend the institution. But in order to win that war they had to abolish slavery.

1950

A graduate student at Harvard put some consequential questions to Du Bois early in 1950, in a letter addressed to the NAACP; *as usual in such cases, the response was candid and precise.*

Cambridge, Mass., February 6, 1950

Dear Dr. Du Bois:

Having read your many books, I know that you have a very active interest in the colonial problem; indeed, you have been one of the outstanding spokesmen in our country on this question. Hence, I am taking the liberty of writing to you for certain information.

At the present time I am a Teaching Fellow in Government at Harvard University where I am working on my doctoral dissertation. The title of the latter is "The United Nations and Non-Self-Governing Territories." My specific interest is in the rise and decline of the ideal that there is a legitimate international interest in colonial territories, and that the latter are more of the nature of the international public domain than the private possession of certain Colonial Powers. I am less interested in the mandates (now trust territories) than I am the bulk of the colonial domain.

As you undoubtedly know, one of the chief arguments the Colonial Powers use against any form of international action regarding colonies (and more especially international administration or international trusteeship) is that such action would be contrary to the wishes and interests of the inhabitants of the territories concerned. This argument has been used against a generalization of the Mandates/Trusteeship Systems as well as against an expansion of the activities of the United Nations under Chapter XI of the Charter. If the contention of the colonial powers is valid, then the ideal of international trusteeship would seem to be a vain endeavor. If their argument is not based on fact, then it should be so determined.

From such research as I have done thus far, I have not been able to obtain sufficient data to document a case in either direction. It has been made clear by white settlers of Kenya and Tanganyika that international trusteeship is not desired by them as inhabitants of those territories. The question, of course, immediately arises, "What are the views of the native inhabitants?" The Nigerian author of the book *Without Bitterness* does not seem too interested in international action. Indeed, he seemed to feel that the study made by the Committee on Africa, the War, and Peace Aims (of which you were a member) was not a true reflection of the native sentiments of West Africa.[1] A graduate student here at Harvard who is a native of Sierra Leone has, during frequent conversations with me, manifested a distrust of any form of international trusteeship. Furthermore, a British West Indian delegate at the United Nations on one occasion challenged Soviet criticism on the grounds that the West Indians would work out their own destiny with Great Britain.[2] In short, on the basis of such attitudes as these it seems that certain members of the native intelligentsia reject any form of international supervision on one of several grounds: (1) that it is ineffective; (2) that international commissions merely become forums for verbalizing the power struggle between nations in which the welfare of native inhabitants is forgotten; (3) that they are willing to remain within the framework of larger confederations and commonwealths if they are given internal autonomy and the rights of self-government, but that they prefer to win that status by their own efforts; or (4) that independence only would meet their true aspirations.

The foregoing arguments are not too unreasonable; but the following questions immediately arise: (1) Do these few sources I have cited represent the views of the majority of educated native Africans regarding the international trusteeship? (2) Even if they are a correct representation, does the attitude of the native intelligentsia necessarily reflect the sentiments of the bulk of the native inhabitants who have not expressed themselves on the subject? (3) Even if the latter is found to be the case, is international trusteeship an institution which can be justified on the basis of a legitimate interest of the non-colonial world, irrespective of whether or not either the colonial power or the native inhabitants desire it?

I realize that it would be highly presumptuous of me to even suggest that you answer any or all of these intriguing questions. I would be most grateful, however, for such comments as you might feel disposed to make regarding them. Furthermore, I would greatly appreciate any information you can give me about where I could obtain a record of the proceedings and resolutions of the

1. The reference is to A. N. Orizu, *Without Bitterness: Western Nations in Post-War Africa* (New York:Creative Age Press, 1944). Du Bois was critical of the work of the Committee on Africa; see volume two of this *Correspondence*, pp. 331-35. Du Bois reviewed the published findings of that committee, with some critical comment, in the Sunday book section of the *New York Herald Tribune*, 10 January 1943.

2. Grantley Adams, of Barbados, upheld British rule and attacked the USSR first at a meeting of the trusteeship committee of the United Nations Assembly held in Paris on 13 October 1948 and again several times thereafter that same month. The *Times* (London) gave these attacks prominent coverage, 14 October, p. 4; 22 October, p. 3; 4 November, p. 3. The *New York Times* also reported Adams's statements quite fully: 14 October, p. 2; 22 October, p. 9; 24 October, p. 26.

Pan-African Congresses you have been so instrumental in arranging which have been held since 1944.

Very truly yours,
James S. Coleman[3]

New York City, February 18, 1950

My dear Mr. Coleman:

I found your letter of February 6 here on my return from a lecture tour in the West. May I state that with the set-up today in the colonies, it is difficult if not impossible to get any real reflection of native opinion. Every effort is taken to see that the natives have little chance to communicate with persons outside the colony. In addition to that if one gets at native opinion, that opinion would necessarily be limited by the horizon about them. You can imagine what an educated native in a British colony must think about the world. He has been indoctrinated with the idea that the British Empire is the only country and that even when its rule is bad, it is better than rule outside the Empire. The natives have very little opportunity to know about the United States or the other countries of Europe and learn almost nothing of Asia.

In consulting the native African students you must remember that they know nothing about Africa, except their own colony, as inter-colonial travel is practically prohibited. The opinion therefore of a native of Sierre Leone, as to the Sudan or the Belgian Congo or even of Liberia, would be of little value.

My effort in pushing the Pan-African Congresses, beginning in 1919, was to try to get the intelligentsia among the blacks of Africa and America in touch with each other, not for any prearranged program, but in the hope that conference would bring understanding and some concerted action. The program, however, was very successfully sabotaged by the colonial powers, acting directly and indirectly through the peoples under their control.

The last congress was held in England in 1945. You might get information concerning that and some documents by writing to:

Mr. George Padmore
22 Cranleigh House
Cranleigh Street
London, N.W. 1 England

Another difficulty in the proposed United Nations trusteeships is the question as to what the United Nations as an organization could and would do. If they are successful in Somaliland and Eritrea, this will be a very strong argument for

3. James S. Coleman was born in Utah in 1919 and educated at Brigham Young University and Harvard University, from which he received a doctorate in 1953. Until 1967 he served as a professor at the University of California in Los Angeles and at Makerere University in Uganda. Since 1967 he has been associated with the Rockefeller Foundation in New York City. He has published studies on Nigeria and other areas in southern Africa; his *Nigeria: Background to Nationalism* (1958) is well known.

widening of such trusteeship; but the outlook just now is to my mind not very favorable.

The British West Indian Delegate to the United Nations, to whom you refer, did not speak for the best opinion in the West Indies and was evidently a stool-pigeon. He incurred a great deal of criticism at home.

Perhaps these statements may be of some help to you.

Very sincerely yours,
W. E. B. Du Bois

Not all presidents of colleges for Black youth dealt with Du Bois as did the president of Morgan State (see above, pp. 257–59). An inquiry came to Du Bois early in 1950 from the president of Texas State University for Negroes.

Houston, Texas, February 16, 1950

Dear Dr. Du Bois:

We are wondering whether or not you would be interested in serving as Visiting Professor at Texas State University during the Summer Session beginning June first through August 31st. Also, we wonder if you would be interested in serving for the ensuing year as Visiting Professor?

At present we are able to offer $500.00 per month for the Summer School Work and $535.00 per month for the regular term of nine months.

You would be expected to teach six credit hours during the Summer Session, or two classes of one hour forty-five minutes for five days per week. During the regular school year you would be expected to teach from nine to twelve clock hours each week.

Please do not consider this an offer for employment but an attempt to find out whether or not you would be available or interested.

Sincerely yours,
R. O'Hara Lanier[1]

P. S. I expect to be in New York—Feb. 24-25—and hope that I can see you. Give me a call if you can, Broadway Central Hotel.

New York City, February 22, 1950

Dear Mr. Lanier:

Unfortunately I shall be out of town at the time of your visit. I shall not return until the 27th.

1. Raphael O'Hara Lanier (1900-1962) was born in North Carolina and educated at Lincoln (Pa.), Stanford, and Harvard universities. He was on the faculties at Tuskegee and Hampton and from 1946 to 1948 was United States minister to Liberia. In 1948 he became president of Texas State University for Negroes in Houston; he held this position until his death.

I have not had time to consider your suggestion fully, but I am jotting down my first reactions:

I would not be interested in an ordinary teaching job for the summer; but if it could be made part of a social project, I might be attracted.

For instance: the social development of the Negro in Texas, past and present, would be an interesting study; there is much material already collected, needing examination and interpretation. If I could have a dozen to twenty-five good students, with clerical help, offices and books, we might in a summer start something, which in continuing work over the years, could become an out. tanding scientific contribution. It might be interspaced with general lectures for the school body and perhaps school cooperation in the overall study.

This is just a suggestion. Beyond this is the question of the availability and cost of comfortable existence in Houston during the summer. I would be glad to hear from you on the matter at your leisure.

Very sincerely,
W. E. B. Du Bois

Houston, Texas, March 9, 1950

Dear Dr. Du Bois:

Thank you for your letter of February 22nd.

I am very sorry indeed that I did not get a chance to see you in New York.

I regret that we do not have any way of providing for the type of research which you suggest. Our program is purely a teaching program at the present time.

When we come to the point that we can provide a plan for research such as you mention I shall be very happy to write you.

With kindest regards from Mrs. Lanier, Mrs. Nance and myself, I am

Sincerely yours,
R. O'Hara Lanier

Birthday greetings to Du Bois as he reached his eighty-second year were numerous. One from Thomas L. Dabney of Virginia contained striking biographical information.

Norfolk, Virgina, February 23, 1950

My dear Dr. Du Bois:

Please accept this belated greeting on your 82nd birthday. You deserve to be congratulated on writing of two more volumes on your birthday.[1] I wish to add my congratulations and best wishes on this occasion.

1. Presumably, Dabney refers to Du Bois's *Color and Democracy:Colonies and Peace* and *The World and Africa*.

I heard you speak on "War and Prejudice" at Virginia Union University in Richmond in 1916 when you were the house guest of Dr. and Mrs. J. B. Simpson, and the next day the Rev. E. D. Caffeem and I secured an automobile and carried you to several historical places in Richmond. When we went to the Mechanics Bank at 3rd and Clay, John Mitchell Jr. joined us and we went to other places including St. John's Church on Churchill where Patrick Henry made his "Give me liberty or death speech."

While we were at St. John's Church the attendant recited Patrick Henry's speech for us and you went into the pew where Henry stood and stood there for a while in silence.

I also heard you at the commencement for the Norfolk Division of Virginia State College at First Baptist Church, Bute Street, in June, 1947.

I have excerpts of your testimony on August 8, 1949, before the House Committee on Foreign Affairs in which you rightly pointed out that "Russia and Communism are not your enemies."[2] James N. Rhea, an intelligent *Journal and Guide* reporter, and I have often talked about your intelligent and statesmanlike position on international affairs.

Rhea and I often discuss your point of view on racial and international questions and we feel indebted to you for your broad position and intelligent attitude on world problems.

I wish to congratulate you on your record. I have always thought a lot of you for your intellectualism and liberalism. God bless you.

Very sincerely yours,
Thomas L. Dabney

When I was a poor struggling student at Virginia Union University, I sold the *Crisis* and supported the NAACP without which I would have died in despair. I owed my spiritual existence to *The Crisis* under your editorship and the NAACP under the guidance of the late James Weldon Johnson.

New York City, March 17, 1950

Dear Mr. Dabney:

Thank you very much for your birthday greetings. I remember that visit to Virginia Union University and my correspondence with you later.

Very sincerely yours,
W. E. B. Du Bois

Two results of the meeting proposed in a telegram that reached Du Bois just

2. Du Bois's testimony is printed in U.S., Congress, House, Committee on Foreign Affairs, *Hearings on Mutual Defense Assistance Act of 1949*, 81st Cong., 1st sess., 1949, pp. 261-70. Part of his testimony was published in the *National Guardian*, 22 August 1949.

*after his birthday were the Peace Information Center and Du Bois's leadership
in the campaign to ban use of atomic bombs—the well-known Stockholm Peace
Pledge. This activity nearly brought Du Bois to the penitentiary, and the sender
of the telegram was the government's witness against him! Du Bois discusses
this meeting and the work of the center in his* In Battle for Peace, *pp. 34-42.*

New York City, February 24, 1950

W. E. B. Du Bois, Council on African Affairs:

Strongly urge your participation meeting my house 400 East 52 street at 8
O'clock Wednesday evening March 1. Purpose is to discuss certain vital problems relating to current activities for promotion of world peace.

O. John Rogge[1]

In 1949 Dennis Dobson in London published George Padmore's Africa:
Britain's Third Empire. *Padmore sent a copy to Du Bois and asked if it might
be possible to find a publisher for the book in the United States; he wondered,
too, if President Charles S. Johnson of Fisk might help in such an effort.*

New York City, March 17, 1950

My dear Mr. Padmore:

Thank you so much for your latest book which has just come. I am going to
read it, and I appreciate the dedication.[1]

I am writing a book on Russia, covering my three trips in 1926, 1936 and
1949. I am not sure of a publisher, but hope for one.[2]

I am wondering if you have any ideas of a Pan-African Congress in Africa?
I suppose that there will be difficulty in getting permission from anybody. I
met Azikiwe when he was here the last time and was impressed.

I shall be very glad to write a preface for your book in its American edition.
I do not know whether a publisher can be found; this country has gone stark
crazy and our Civil Rights are only glimmering.

1. Oetje John Rogge was born in Illinois in 1903 and was educated at the University
of Illinois and the Harvard Law School. He practiced law in Chicago from 1925 to
1937 and served as a counsel for the Reconstruction Finance Corporation and the
Securities and Exchange Commission in the late 1930s. From 1943 to 1946 he was
special assistant to the United States attorney general. In 1949 he published *Our Van-
ishing Civil Liberties* and ten years later, *Why Men Confess.* He is now in private
practice in New York City.

1. The book was dedicated to Du Bois, " 'Father' of Pan-Africanism, Scholar and
Uncompromising Fighter for Human Rights," and to J. E. Casely-Hayford, barrister
and founder-president of the National Congress of British West Africa. The book's
preface is dated May Day 1948.

2. The manuscript was sent to several publishers; all rejected it and it remains
unpublished.

I do not have much hope that Johnson of Fisk would extend any help, although it would not hurt to write him. He is, if not reactionary, certainly very cautious.

With best regards,
W. E. B. Du Bois

Note has been made earlier of the furor created by Paul Robeson's speech in Paris in 1949 at a World Peace meeting. Du Bois was present and agreed with Robeson's position. The March 1950 issue of the Negro Digest *published a debate on the challenge in Robeson's speech—that Black people in the United States would not and should not support Washington should there be a war between the* ussr *and the* usa—*with Walter White attacking and Du Bois supporting Robeson.*

A physician in Pittsburgh, who signed his letter, "Chairman of Americanization Committee, Pennsylvania Society, sar,"* *took issue with Du Bois.*

Pittsburgh, Pa., March 23, 1950

Dear Mr. Du Bois:

I was interesting in reading your presentation in the *Negro Digest* for the month of March, entitled "Paul Robeson—Right."

It seems to me that your viewpoint regarding Russia, her present government and conditions needs re-orientation. Certainly if you face the facts as presented by ample demonstration coming from closer observers, who are in the know, you would realize that the greatest slave system in the world is in force in their labor camps. You would realize that Russia's big objective is world domination and our destruction. Her whole ideology is entirely foreign to the principles of our government. We have only to follow the course of events in the neighboring countries to her, to realize what portends for the rest of the world.

I think your premises as to our motives in this country and the motives in Russia are entirely erroneous. I think Paul Robeson needs to know these things, quite as much as you do. A man with your background and standing ought to be leading your race in the principles of American democracy and liberty, rather than the contrary.

Very truly yours,
H. R. Decker, M. D.[1]

* In 1908 Du Bois was asked to join the Sons of the American Revolution (sar); he applied but was rejected when his Black ancestry was discovered. In 1928 the dar condemned Du Bois as subversive; Du Bois thanked the dar for this honor in the *Crisis* 35 (May 1928):169. See this work 2:212–13.

1. Harry Ryerson Decker was born in 1883 and graduated from Columbia University's College of Physicians and Surgeons in 1907. At the time he wrote to Du Bois,

New York City, March 30, 1950

Dr. H. Ryerson Decker

Dear Sir:

I have visited the Union of Soviet Socialist Republics three times in the last 25 years. I have seen both European and Asiatic Russia and many of the chief cities. I am familiar with much of the literature on Russia both by Russians and others.

My conclusion is that Russian labor is not enslaved; that Russia does not seek world domination; that her ideology differs from ours but is a great effort for human good which we are already in many ways following; that her neighboring countries are better off than ever before.

I believe that my knowledge of the motives and actions of this country are quite as good as yours and that whatever leadership of the Negro race in America I have been able to furnish has increased democracy in this land.

Very sincerely yours,

W. E. B. Du Bois

On 3 April 1950 Dr. Carter G. Woodson, the pioneer in Afro-American historiography, died. This was the occasion for a substantial exchange between Du Bois and Rayford W. Logan, then chairman of the history department at Howard University.

New York City, April 26, 1950

Dear Dr. Logan:

I see by the Pittsburgh *Courier*, that you are still in circulation.[1] There has been such sonorous silence down Howard-way lately, that I thought most of you were dead.

I am writing to ask you something about Woodson. His death is a great loss. I am writing an article about him in *Masses & Mainstream*.[2]

Will you tell me this: how did he play? Was he interested in baseball or football? Did he play cards of any kind, whist or poker? Did he like children and

---

Ryerson was assistant professor of surgery at the Medical School of the University of Pittsburgh.

1. Logan had written articles for the *Pittsburgh Courier* on 22 and 29 April 1950, suggesting the names and careers of outstanding Black figures who would grace the Truman administration in both domestic and foreign endeavors.

2. Du Bois's essay, "A Portrait of Carter G. Woodson," appeared in *Masses & Mainstream* 3 (June 1950):19-25. He also wrote about Woodson briefly but with great admiration in his column in the *Chicago Globe*, 29 April 1950 (the *Globe*, established by Du Bois's friend Metz T. Lochard, carried a column by Du Bois from April through December 1950).

have any contact with them? I imagine that his brother, to whom *The Negro in our History* is dedicated, helped him with his education: were they close to each other and did the brother have any children whom Woodson helped or who helped Woodson? Did he have any close and confidential friends?

How is the *Journal* left and is it going to be carried on? Do you suppose there would be any way of our getting his encyclopedia and our Encyclopedia of the Negro together now for completion? I presume not, but I would be glad to have any information that you can give me; I will not of course reveal its source.

I am in good health and hope that you are. My best regards to you and your wife.

Very sincerely yours,
W. E. B. Du Bois

Washington, D.C., April 29, 1950

Dear Dr. Du Bois:

I was delighted to receive your letter of April 26. We might just as well all be dead here at Howard.

Woodson's death is indeed a great loss as are those of Drew and Houston.[1] Rarely have we been hit so hard in such a short space of time.

Dr. Woodson at one time played tennis and was very much interested in it. I do not recall that he was interested in baseball or football. I have never known him to play cards of any kind. He appears to have had a real liking for children. The children in the block felt a real affection for him, an affection which they would not have had if he did not feel close to them. It is my recollection that Dr. Woodson's brother did help him with his education, but I cannot recall the exact details. A grandson of his sister's is a sophomore at West Virginia State College. I am sorry that I do not know his name but I am certain that President John W. Davis can supply it. I doubt very much that Dr. Woodson had any close or confidential friends. I imagine that I was as close to him as anyone until I began working with the *Encyclopedia of the Negro*.

My article in *Phylon*, 4th Quarter, 1945, will give some details which may be of interest to you.[2] I remember especially the story about a lady with whom he was apparently at one time engaged. He approached a lady in a hotel at

---

1. Charles Richard Drew, distinguished surgeon and pioneer in blood banking, was awarded the Spingarn Medal in 1944; he headed the surgery department of Howard's medical school. He died in an auto accident in North Carolina, 1 April 1950. Charles Hamilton Houston was one of the leading attorneys of his time and received the Spingarn Medal in 1950; he died in Washington in his fifty-fourth year on 22 April 1950.

2. Logan's article appeared in the Profile series in *Phylon* 6 (Fourth Quarter 1945): 315–21.

Asbury Park, as I recall, and said to her: "Don't I know you?" She said: "You ought to. You were engaged to marry me at one time." This is the only time that I ever heard him refer to any interest in the ladies.

In reply to your telegram, my own categorical answer would be that he neither drank nor smoked. I was as certain of that as I could be of anything. One of my colleagues told me confidentially that some bottles of Canadian Club were found in his room after his death. I am sure these were used for medicinal purposes.

I should like to add my own observation that Dr. Woodson was a bundle of contradictions. He was vindictive and mean and a Silas Marner. On the other hand, he was kind and generous and would go out of his way to support causes other than his own.

Ruth's biscuits are not better than they ever have been, but we will always be delighted to have you visit with us whenever you want to.

Sincerely yours,
Rayford W. Logan

Having completed her preparatory work, Du Bois's granddaughter, DuBois Williams, was to enter Fisk University in the fall of 1950. Du Bois arranged a trip for the young woman to western and eastern Europe for the summer months and sent to her, at Baltimore, a long letter offering suggestions and guidance.

New York City, July 17, 1950

Dear DuBois:

You are going to have one of the greatest opportunities that any young person could have today. I have gone to trouble and expense, which I can hardly afford, because I believe this trip is necessary for your education and life. I am therefore putting down in the shape of a steamship letter as we used to call it, which you can read and re-read on the voyage, certain matters for you to think about. I shall also give you other literature and books.

You, of course, realize that the world today is sharply divided into two main parts, the Soviet Union on the one hand, and the United States on the other. There are also other important divisions especially between the wealthy independent and investing countries and the poor colonial and semi-colonial regions, but the American-Russian division is of first importance. You are going to see something of the great centers of western European civilization and then you are going, as we say, behind the "Iron Curtain." This phrase was first used by Winston Churchill in a speech which he made several years ago in Missouri, and it typified the separation that has grown up between Russia on the one hand and western Europe and the United States.

I want to say a word briefly about this difference. It is of course a long story and eventually you will have to study and read about it carefully for yourself. But there are certain general outlines which perhaps I can set down before you.

The root of the difficulty and characteristic of human life is the scarcity of certain materials which human beings need for living; scarcity of food, clothing, shelter, etc. This scarcity makes it necessary for people to work, and in primitive times, a tribe or clan working together with accumulated knowledge and experience supplied for each other the materials necessary. What they had to fear was the weather and accidents and the attacks of other tribes who might try to take their accumulated materials from them, being themselves in want. Gradually, however, by combining units there grew up large nations able to defend themselves against their enemies.

Gradually within such nations there arose great disparity in social condition and wealth, due to difference in strength, to craft and crime, and especially to family inheritance of wealth and privilege. In time there arose social classes of rich idle nobles, and hard working artisans and slaves. And then much more gradually there came widely organized work and the use of capital. Capital consists of the materials and food gathered but not consumed immediately; but either saved or some of it used in order to make other things; for instance, a part of the wheat saved in order to grow more wheat; or iron used not for weapons but for tools in order to make other weapons or to build houses. This wealth in the form to be used to make more wealth was called capital, and gradually, especially in the 18th century instead of being paid directly by the products of their toil, [workers] entered into contracts with the owners of capital and received wages which were paid usually before the products which they produced were ready for actual use. Thus the wage contract arose and two social classes of employers and laborers was instituted.

Very soon it was evident that while wealth was accumulating by this organization of work and invention of machines, the workers tended to be very poor, living from hand to mouth; while the owners of capital became rich, often having more than they really needed. This situation was discussed by thinkers and statesmen for a long time.

The French Revolution was a revolt of capitalists and artisans against the privileges and monopoly of the hereditary nobility and resulted in putting owners of capital or as the French called them the Bourgeoisie in control of the state.

In the 18th and early 19th century with new ability free to work and save, new inventions and machines, and new discovery of lands, wealth grew immensely, but poverty also increased through oppression of the workers and there arose what we call the doctrine of socialism: namely, the idea that the government should direct the production of goods and control the wage contract and the distribution of consumers' goods. Almost all of the great philosophers in the world in the 18th and 19th centuries agreed that there must be some such government control.

Then in the 19th century came an emphasis upon socialism which we call communism, which was a method of attaining complete socialism by having the mass of the workers seize all capital and the control of the state, and then conduct the state permanently for the benefit of the working class. This of course was bitterly opposed. The wealthier and educated classes said that, first of all, ordinary workers, being ignorant and inexperienced, could not conduct industry successfully and even if they tried to there would not be enough goods to go around. There must be poverty in order to support a ruling and directing aristocracy of industry. This remained for many years an academic question with only spasmodic attempts to realize the plan until the time of the First World War.

The First World War was precipitated by what we call Colonial Imperialism: that is, the owners of wealth not only invested capital in their own lands but with expanding trade seized other countries and held them as colonies in order to use their labor and material for enriching the leading countries in the civilized world. Thus in the 19th century we had rich and civilized British, French and Spanish empires, who were not only very efficient in producing goods and had large amounts of capital to distribute but also owned the larger part of the world inhabited by the darker peoples as colonies. The greater part of these colonies were owned by England and France; Spain and Portugal had a considerable amount. Germany and Italy had few colonies but strongly desired more, while the United States, also with only a few colonies, profited greatly by trade with the empires and their colonies. In the early 20th century, Germany developed as a great manufacturing country and began to demand a larger share of colonial trade. She was eventually joined by Italy and Austria and opposed by Britain, France and at last by the United States in a world war. The First World War was really fought over ownership of colonies and proved so destructive that it pretty nearly destroyed the whole world organization of industry and distribution of wealth.

As a result there was revolt in many countries. In Russia this revolt took the form of an attempt to establish a communistic state; that is, a state which would control not only public work but also what we call private industry; and in which the workers must be in complete control. The ownership of capital would not be allowed in the hands of private persons. Most of the Western world was outraged at this attempt. They knew that the Russian people had suffered greatly in the past and during the war. Some of their soldiers were sent against the Germans without fire-arms and without shoes in the snows of this bitterly cold land. For many years the plight of the Russian peasant received the sympathy of the civilized world. It was different now when these workers, with their ignorance and inexperience, tried to take charge of all industry. Fourteen different nations, including the United States, assumed that this effort was bound to fail disastrously and they made war upon Russia, invaded it, furnished much money and materials to overcome the new revolutionary government. The war on Russia lasted from 1918 to 1924, but finally the Soviet government was successful and established a strong government. This government was not a democracy in our sense of the term, because the mass of the people at first could neither read nor write. There was less freedom in choice of work and the leaders like Lenin were in control of the state and guiding it toward socialism.

The progress of Russia since that time has been remarkable, although of course there have been vast internal difficulties and various disturbances fomented from the outside. But on the whole Russia has succeeded in establishing a strong state and in taking complete charge of industry, abolishing extreme poverty, giving the people wages sufficient for decent life and a splendid system of education and health control, with drama, music and art.

On the other hand, the people of the United States believed this method of government was wrong and bound to fail in the long run. Persons who had lost invested capital in Russia bitterly resented this regime. England adopted a limited socialism and France a social state still more limited and with a powerful capitalist class. But Germany and Italy, impoverished by war and threatened with communism, adopted Fascism; i.e. leadership of a small group with total power supported by the capitalists and run for their benefit, but allaying the complaints of the workers by full employment, better wages and many social gifts like housing and social medicine. This seemed to western Europe and America a dangerous substitute for democracy. But they accepted Hitler and Mussolini until they united to overthrow the democracies and rule the world.

The Second World War was an attempt to restore the former industrial organization of the world so as to keep the Fascists from overwhelming the democracies. At first the United States and Great Britain avoided any alliance with Russia, and the Soviets were left standing alone between the two great forces until Germany offered alliance, which Russia accepted; but almost immediately Germany got the idea that they would seize Russia in order to have her resources and manpower to fight the United States, France and Great Britain. The result was that finally, through the efforts of Franklin Roosevelt, Russia became allied with the western democracies and it was Russian help that enabled these democracies to conquer in the Second World War. Russia's sacrifices were tremendous—fifteen million of her people died.

At the end of the Second World War there was close alliance between the United States, Great Britain and Russia. This soon stopped, because the people of the United States and most of the people of Great Britain began to realize that the Russian method of controlling industry was different from theirs and we believe that the "American Way of Life," as we called it, was the better. Moreover, many countries bordering on Russia, like Poland, Czechoslovakia, Bulgaria and Rumania turned communist. We charged that the Soviet Union forced this change and would force others. The Soviets replied that the change came at the demand of the workers and peasants and was opposed by landholders and employers and that all the Soviet Union did was to protect her borders from aggression and prevent further attack on Communism from the West.

Now in a reasonable world, the way to settle this matter would have been to let each country go its own way and prove by its success which was best or in what respect each method of conducting industry excelled the other so that modifications could be made. There were some evidences of this; in the United States there was a great increase of social control, under the New Deal, as for instance in the building of the great dams and power control in the Tennessee Valley, social security for unemployment and old age, etc. In the Soviet Union there were some modifications in the control of industry; some small industries and individual workers were allowed.

But unfortunately after two world wars, the world in general was not reasonable and the result is that there has been growing, since the end of the Second World War, increasingly bitter enmity and rivalry especially between the United States and Russia. The United States continues to charge that Russia was forcibly imposing her method of industry on border states like Czechoslovakia, which you are going to visit. And that the Russians were threatening countries like Turkey and Greece.

On the other hand, the Russians say that the United States tried desperately and with the expenditure of over six billion dollars to fasten a Fascist regime on the Chinese under Chiang Kai Shek, when the Chinese revolted and drove him out. We refused to recognize the Communistic regime in China. The result has been that the attempt to unite the world in something like a world government has been but partially successful. This was attempted after the First World War, by the League of Nations, but the League of Nations failed when Italy attacked and conquered Ethiopia. The United Nations was formed in 1945, and you remember that I was one of the Consultants and attended the meeting in San Francisco. The United Nations is now in danger of disruption because of the refusal to seat the Chinese Communists and the consequent refusal of Russia to take part, and now at last by the Korean War. Here then we are at the beginning of the third world war, with the terrible weapon of the atom bomb.

The whole situation is very confusing; for instance, the Catholic Church has said bitter things about the Soviet Union and the Communists; on the other hand, many catholics do not believe that the church has any right to enter politics and industry but is a religious organization; and there are Catholic Priests who defend Communism and its control of industry. Nevertheless the organized church as a whole is against communism and because of this has been curtailed in its activities in Russia, Czechoslovakia and elsewhere. The churches have not been closed and the priests officiate but they are not allowed to interfere in political matters.

All these things you will have to read more widely than can be imparted in a comparatively short letter like this; but I do want you to understand the controversy into which you are entering, and from which you can learn so much. You are going behind "the Iron Curtain"; do not boast of America. Learn about Russia and Czechoslovakia; do not get angry, listen; be perfectly frank about the fact that Negroes for instance, and other minorities, are not free citizens of the United States; that democracy applies to them only in part; on the other hand, you will of course learn that the situation in the communist countries is not perfect and could not be supposed to be so. These countries are run by human beings just as our country is.

The great thing is to learn what the facts are; remember what Goethe, one of the great thinkers of the world, said: "Light, more Light!"

You are having a great opportunity to see the world in which you are to live. I hope you will take every advantage of this trip. Finally certain minor matters; be careful of your money; protect your travelers' checks; cash only one or two at a time. You are going to be among poor people; do not spend money conspicuously; do not buy anything you do not really need; make a list of your travelers' checks and keep that list separate from the checks themselves; if you lose your checks, write immediately to the bank, and let them know what checks have been lost. They will in all probability reimburse you.

Keep a daily record of what you do, and hear and think. Do not forget this, it will be invaluable in the future. Collect photographs in order to remind you of the trip. Make friends and keep names and addresses. Take part in all activities that you can, see all you can and ask questions so that you will understand. Write to us regularly, to your mother if you wish and she can forward the letters to me or vice versa; but keep in close touch with us, and in case of emergency send a cablegram. "Du Bois, 23 West 26, New York."

With love,
W. E. B. Du Bois

On 1 July 1950 Nina Gomer Du Bois passed away, after suffering for five years as an invalid after a stroke. A letter beginning with condolences on this event came from Padmore in England.

London, England, August 21, 1950

Dear Dr. Du Bois:

It is with deep regret that I read of the death of Mrs. Du Bois in a recent issue of the Pittsburgh *Courier*.[1] Please accept my heartfelt sympathy in the loss you have sustained. We are following your activities, and rejoice in the knowledge that, in spite of advancing age, you are still with us to inspire and lead the

1. Nina Gomer, a graduate of Wilberforce University, married Du Bois in 1896. Her death was reported on the first page of the *Pittsburgh Courier*, 8 July 1950. Du Bois published a very moving tribute to his wife in the *Chicago Globe*, 15 July 1950.

struggle for African liberation. Your many young friends and admirers here and in Africa sincerely hope that your life will be spared to see the final success of your unselfish labours on behalf of our people in Africa and abroad.

Peter Abrahams has just returned from France and hopes to settle down to a new book soon. I am also working on a new one. My last had a tremendous success, but I am trying to find an American publisher. Can you recommend one? If so, I would like you to write a short introduction to it.

Clements Kadalie of South Africa has done an excellent book on his life and the history of the I.C.U. (Industrial and Commercial Union) but cannot get a publisher for it in S. Africa.[2] I am trying to find one here. What are the chances in the U.S.A.? A word from you will be appreciated. With all our best wishes,

Yours very sincerely,
George Padmore

New York City, September 18, 1950
My dear Padmore:
Thank you for your sympathy and kind words.

I have just come back from a month in Czechoslovakia and France. I wanted to come to London but was too busy to take time off. It is almost impossible to get any radical books published now in the United States. I have a volume on "America and Russia," which Harcourt Brace has just turned down. Sometime when this hysteria has passed, we will get back to normal attitudes in this country.

I am interested too in Kadalie's work; I have long followed his career.

Very sincerely yours,
W. E. B. Du Bois

A fascinating letter dealing with the Catholic church and Black people reached Du Bois in September 1950. The letter is published verbatim.

St. Louis, Missouri, September 11, 1950
Dear Dr. Du Bois:
This I know is unusual, but I am so interested and anxious. I wish to write a small novel entitled—*Betrayal of The Cloth*. In this book I want to trace Chris-

2. Clements Kadalie (1896–1951) was born in Nyasaland and migrated to Cape Town in South Africa. In 1919 he led a strike of dockworkers from which emerged the Industrial and Commercial Union under his leadership. He was harassed by officials and repeatedly arrested. After World War II he lived in exile in England and died in East London. His book, *My Life and the I.C.U.: The Autobiography of a Black Trade Unionist in South Africa*, edited by Stanley Trapido, was published posthumously by Cass in London in 1960 and reprinted by Humanities Press (New York City) in 1970.

tianity from the days of the Catacombs to the present day. To show how in America, which is spoken of as a christian country, the churches have practiced and upheld white supremacy.

Most of my book will be on the Catholic Church—which I am an active member, many Negroes have lost the faith—among such were my grandparents left because they could not see Christ in the Catholic Church, which rejected them from schools, hospitals, Home for Aged and all their institutions and lastly the church's last pew was labeled *Colored Only* and ushers held back all Negroes until every white man, woman and child had left the Communion rail.

My college training was at Xavier Univ. New Orleans, Louisiana (One remains in grace with Sisters as long as their thinking is followed—never differ this goes double for instructors and there is white and colored salaries) My husband also a catholic has two degrees from Loyola of Chicago. This summer we did much research reading at St. Louis Univ. Library on Negro during slavery also after and the inactive part the church played in defending rights of Negro on christian principles. And even today she toys with white supremacy; look at these few cases:

St. Louis is a catholic city—the *good* white catholics choose to give a small hospital rather than to admit any in the many here in the city, of course, there are some rare cases where colored catholics knew some white protestants of good means who would ask the nuns to admit their Negro in their private rooms—this granted but to be kept a secret. Few years ago a small colored boy was injured on the school campus, priest in charge rushed him over to nearest hospital—the Sister in charge refused to treat him, the priest demanded to see the Sr. Superior stating this is a catholic boy injured on catholic school campus calmly she looked at the bloody boy in pain and said she was indeed sorry but he was colored and we only treat white by this time the priest was justly angry and got pretty nasty and she finally consented she would only for the sake of the priest, but the child would need farther treatments and please do not return him.

About couple of years ago the Registrar catholic weekly carried a picture of Negro nurse accepted in a white religious order (nuns in charge of largest catholic hospital—St. Louis Univ.) today they number some ten or twelve but they are segregated given their own sleeping and eating quarters. Recently one almost about to take her perpetual vows announced she could not be in the order and suffer such humiliation it was accepted and the white nuns had the nerve to feel she was ungrateful. And this I believe to be the pattern followed.

Our present Archbishop Joseph E. Ritter is trying to eliminate many of his predecessor lily-white rules—first he ordered all catholics to go to the nearest church, then all catholic schools must accept all catholic students.[1] This was

1. Joseph Elmer Ritter was bishop of Indianapolis from 1934 until appointed archbishop of Saint Louis in 1946; he was designated cardinal in 1961. He died in 1967.

met by a group secretly supported by many priests to an appeal to the Holy Father. They ordered him to change his plans or be transferred, this they were unable to do but the religious, priests and nuns have shown their resentment by humiliating the students on every occasion.

I am a step-mother of five and my children are in mixed schools, they get along nicely with the students, the insults come from nuns and the priest in charge which leaves the children defenseless. My eldest step-son was a altar boy in other parish so upon telling his schoolmates they told him to hurry and list his name so he could be in on the many parties and treats given by the pastor—before coming to this parish the boy had decided to be a priest, quite sincere since he would from his odd jobs donate to the Missionaries. A nun had charge of assigning boys so after checking him over placed his name on list, and for the week he was on time and had to serve alone when his white partner fail to show up twice. When the pastor learned of this the nun had to be transferred immediately and my son was told he could not serve again. I immediately went to see the pastor—he was rude and charged the Archbishop for all this mess. This was last October, to this present day not another colored boy has served as altar boy. Today my son is a crushed and confused catholic boy, yet daily we are asked to pray to crush communism but if this was done what would become of all the colored races whose only hope depends on it since christianity (as lived) Has failed.

Seeing the children so ill affected I have tried with literature to show how much they have to be proud of and to be a member of this great race. Your book—*Souls of The Black*—have indeed help them. This year they are prepared. We are now reading your book *Black Reconstruction in America*. That is why I know you and only you can master that which I wish to say so badly.

Dr. Du Bois, would you have the time to make rough outlines into smooth reading, I know you are a busy man—but the nation and the world need this shocking bitter truth.

Very gratefully yours,
(Mrs) Monica Morrison

New York City, September 18, 1950

My dear Mrs. Morrison:

I am very much interested in your letter of September 11, but of course no author could accept the cooperation of another author in a work which he wanted to be really his own.

Your story is interesting and the best thing to do is to write it out frankly and fearlessly. I recommend that you correspond with the editors of *America*, which is the liberal Catholic monthly. I am sending them a copy of your letter.

Very sincerely yours,
W. E. B. Du Bois

Du Bois's Indian friend Cedric Dover wrote of a projected volume—never published—consisting of autobiographical essays by Claude McKay and himself.*

London, England, November 3, 1950

My dear Dr. Du Bois:

I understand that Mr. Carl Cowl is sending (or has sent) you *East Indian, West Indian* by Claude McKay and myself.[1] He hopes, as I do, that you will be able to find the time to read it and write an evaluatory Foreword for it. In more callow days I once asked Bernard Shaw to write a Foreword to a book of mine. He replied: "If it is a bad book it would neither help you nor do me credit if I introduced it; if it is a good book it needs no introduction." I feel that *East Indian, West Indian* is "a good book" and I thought it needed no introduction, but I have come to realise how very appropriate a Foreword from yourself would be. For you are the Father of the movement towards colored unity and, outside America, I have been perhaps your most vocal disciple. Moreover, in its authorship alone (I believe it is the first by an Indian and a Negro) the book is a practical expression of coloured unity, while its intention is to show, through reminiscences of childhood in Calcutta and Jamaica, some of the shaping influences that create this sense of unity.[2] The resemblances are, I think, quite striking—all the more so because there was no collaboration between Claude and myself and there could hardly be two writers more separated by temperament and political convictions.

The criticisms I have had are as follows:

1. Claude McKay's part is very slight. So it is, but he is dead and nothing more can be done about it. I feel, too, that the account of his childhood is the best and most surprising thing that Claude ever did, for it is benign, charming, completely without venom and full of meaning under its apparent simplicity— and I am very keen that it should be published and preserved.

2. It is not "dramatic." But it is not meant to be—and the universal complaint against Richard Wright's *Black Boy* is that it is over-dramatised.

3. *West Indian* should be deleted, and I should continue the book as my own story. Apart from the obvious point of honour involved, this criticism shows gross misunderstanding of my purpose, which is essentially to provide a socio-

---

* On Dover, see above, p. 177, n.1.

1. Carl Cowl, a literary agent, wrote Du Bois from New York City, 24 October 1950, discussing the joint McKay-Dover work and urging that he undertake a foreword. Du Bois responded positively, though belatedly, on 7 December 1950.

2. Claude McKay's "Boyhood in Jamaica," excerpted by Cedric Dover from McKay's "My Green Hills of Jamaica," was published in *Phylon* 13 (Second Quarter 1953): 141–46. The Schomburg Collection has a typescript. Wayne F. Cooper, editor of *The Passion of Claude McKay: Selected Poetry and Prose* (New York: Schocken Books, 1973) remarks that McKay and Dover had had plans to publish in one volume a joint autobiography (p. 348, n. 5).

logical study, autobiographically treated and with some regard for style, of childhood in two supposedly very different parts of the coloured world. This has never been done and I believe it is important.

4. The last section—"The Vast Similitude"—is not relevant and should be deleted. This criticism has been made by some who are evidently afraid of its content. Progressives, on the other hand, have said that it is the best thing I have written and that I must resist suggestions to delete it. Technically, it is an appendix, additional to the "story," but it is not an afterthought. Its intention is to give the feel of the sense of coloured unity, in a contemporary setting and personally approached, and in so doing to lend additional understanding to those who read the two accounts of coloured childhoods. Without it these accounts would be interpreted too much as merely personal reminiscences, whereas their purpose is as contributions to a deeper understanding of the coloured world.

I have thought about this book for many years and there is not much I can do to improve it, except to ask you to give it the distinction of a Foreword by yourself which will discuss it, criticise it, sharpen its implications and perhaps summarise again the germinal ideas which you have pioneered for so long. How much, and for how long, you have been the Master and myself the pupil is clear even from this book, though I have reserved for a later autobiography a portrait of yourself and a discussion of your great role in the emancipation of the coloured world.

With every good wish,

Yours very sincerely,
Cedric Dover

P. S. I have written about some other matters separately.

London, England, November 4, 1950

My dear Dr. Du Bois:

I wrote you yesterday through my agent Carl Cowl, but omitted one point that might not have appealed to him and to Hope McKay.[1] It is that Claude McKay has been much used by Catholics and anti-progressives, but this last book makes no mention of Catholics (though referring a good deal and very sympathetically to rationalism), while its few references to communism are friendly and understanding. In fact, his only criticisms are of America. Therefore, this book brings him back into our fold—and this, too, is important.

I have sent you separately twelve variously inscribed copies of *Brown Phoenix*.[2] It seems to me that they might be sold, *after* the usual collection, for at least one dollar each at your smaller meetings as my small contribution to

---

1. The reference is to Mrs. Hope McKay Virtue, Claude McKay's daughter.
2. Cedric Dover, *Brown Phoenix* (London: College Press, 1950) was a forty-page book of poems.

the Council's funds. And I shall happily send further copies for the same purpose if these are sold. I will also set aside a proportion of my royalties (if any!)
on *East Indian, West Indian* for the Council, whose work seems to me to be of
exceptional importance.

You might also be interested to know that I have decided to use my collection of books and materials on "race and colour"—which is perhaps the most
extensive in Britain—as the basis of a collection (which I am now working on
and elaborating) for some academic institution in London that will give it
special accommodation. I want, with your permission, to call it the W. E. B.
Du Bois Collection—and I hope that you will remember it from time to time
when you come across duplicates or other unwanted material.

I have an enormous amount of work to come in the fairly near future:
(1) a book in the press on Eurasian poetry socially considered; (2) a large
sociological study now in draft of Negro poetry; (3) a book of ideas, persons
and places to be called *I Keep and Pass;* and (4) the integration of a great mass
of material, much of it from sources never considered by the race experts, into
a book which will revalue and extend the whole problem of race and research
on race. This I am doing now—and when these tasks are done I shall feel that
I have carried out the first phase of my intention to survey and penetrate within
my coloured world. I wish I had worked harder and more purposively, but
at least I hope you will not be ashamed that *The Souls of Black Folk* and *The
Negro* started a Eurasian boy in his early teens along a path he has never lost
sight of for over thirty years. I remember, too, how generously you helped
with my magazine *The New Outlook* in 1925—and that my first non-scientific
note in America was published in that year in *The Crisis* under the names of
Mercia Heynes Wood and myself—a coloured solidarity note as I recall.[3]

Has *Color and Democracy* been published by Padma Publications (Bombay)
yet?

There have been times recently when I could easily have felt ashamed of
being a coloured man, if it were not for the inspiration of countries like China
and individuals like yourself. I never thought I should see Nehru being so
pathetically diplomatic, or that even the new *Crisis* and N.A.A.C.P. would be so
craven as to pass and publish its lickspittling resolution on Korea.[4]

With every good wish,

Yours very sincerely,
Cedric

3. Efforts to identify the article mentioned here have not been successful.
4. The October 1950 *Crisis* notes that "In its first meeting since the beginning of
hostilities in Korea, the board of directors of the Association voted 'support of the
efforts of the United States and the United Nations to halt Communist aggression
in Korea" (57:586). The board went on to "condemn unreservedly this breach of
peace by the armed forces of the government of North Korea abetted by the Soviet
Union." This NAACP meeting was held 14 September 1950.

New York City, February 14, 1951

Dear Cedric Dover:

I am just returning the "East Indian West Indian" ms. to Carl Cowl with the enclosed inadequate foreword.[1] I am ashamed to have been so long getting at this but America has literally gone mad since your leaving and I have been dragged into all sorts of activities—like running for United States Senator—which took me hopelessly from my literary work.

I did not continue my course at the New School; I gave them opportunity to decline my services by insisting on $40 a lecture; they offered only fees. I have been pushing Peace campaigns to the extent of being in danger of federal prosecution.

I have not been able to do anything with the copies of "Brown Phoenix"; the Council on African Affairs is very wobbly, with no funds and in debt. Paul is stopped from his income and career by persecution and I'm not sure how long the organization can survive. But perhaps they may recover later. They fill as you say a vital field in America. They are promoting my 83rd birthday dinner and a "Du Bois Foundation Fund" of $10,000. I doubt its success, but it is a kindly gesture.

I would be delighted to have your book collection named after me. Keep up your literary work. I too am still at it and have recently been trying short stories as an experiment in escapist literature. Your program looks interesting. I find your "East Indian, West Indian" most interesting and hope it will get in print. "Color and Democracy" has not to my knowledge yet appeared in India.

My best regards and good wishes; and by the by, I am marrying Shirley Graham this month and we plan a month in the Bahamas and Cuba.

With best regards,
W. E. B. Du Bois

In two letters to his granddaughter at Fisk, Du Bois described his efforts in the 1950 elections.

New York City, October 27, 1950

My dear DuBois:

I have been meaning before this to write you something about the campaign for Senator. You see the Democratic and Republican parties both stand for the

---

1. In a telephone conversation with the editor on 22 July 1976, Mr. Cowl stated that he recalled reading this foreword, that he did not possess the copy, and that he believed the widow of Claude McKay had the manuscript. The editor has not seen a copy.

same thing practically, that is for war, universal military service and opposition to the Soviet Republic and to Communism and Socialism.

I was asked to run on the American Labor Ticket of which [Vito]Marcantonio is the candidate for re-election as congressman from New York. He has done splendid work in Congress. I will help him as much as possible and [it was] thought that my name on the ticket would be of service. Ordinarily there would be no chance of election, but I do have an opportunity to say to the public what I think about the present situation.

I shall have made by the time I finish, November 6, ten speeches and seven radio broadcasts. I regret having to be a candidate for public office, but in these days of hysteria and cowardice it is necessary for somebody to stand up for the obvious truth. I have travelled in the northern part of the state, Buffalo, Rochester, Syracuse and Albany, and in the different boroughs of New York. I have had one television broadcast and six other broadcasts.

I have subscribed for you for the magazine, *Masses & Mainstream*. It is well written and I think you will enjoy it. I am wondering if you have received the typewriter and how the language question of German has gotten on? Also have you enquired about your scholarships and when they are payable? I hope you are having a pleasant time. My best regards to Bonita [a school chum].

Yours with love,
W. E. B. Du Bois

New York City, December 4, 1950

Dear DuBois:

The campaign is over. There were five million votes cast in the New York election. I received:

New York City

Bronx	37,094
Kings	52,453
Queens	18,480
Richmond	1,637
Manhattan	85,935
Up-State	29,000
	224,599

This was more than I had any idea of getting, because election means money these days—large funds contributed by big business organizations and rich men who expect and get political and other concessions in return. Governor Dewey for instance paid $35,000 for one whole day on the radio. While the two old parties spend millions, we had only thousands—and few of those—but it was a good and honorable fight for a great cause.

I made ten speeches: at Golden Gate Casino in Harlem, to several thousand; at Hotel Theresa [in Harlem] for the newspapers; in the Bronx, Queens, and

Brooklyn for several hundred; and to 17,000 people at Madison Square Garden. With the other candidates, I took a trip up-state: to Buffalo, Rochester, Syracuse and Albany. The audiences there were small, for the people were scared of losing their jobs; but they were very eager and enthusiastic. Beside these talks I made seven broadcasts on the radio, one of which was televised, one statewide and the rest local from New York. The last broadcast was spectacular and combined a hook-up with a great rally for Marcantonio at "Lucky Corner" at 116th Street and Lexington Avenue and a series of broadcasts from all the candidates from the studio.

Election day after voting, I disappeared: three days at Shirley's in Long Island, three days at a fine estate of the Sterns' in Connecticut (he married a daughter of Julius Rosenwald and after her death the daughter of the last American Ambassador to old Germany).[1] Then I spent a week in Washington and finally had Thanksgiving dinner with mother in Baltimore. The home is beautiful and mother seems more cheerful. Being now quite rested from the campaign, I returned to my desk and went to work editing my speeches for publication.[2] Soon I shall return to my fiction. I did not try to go to the last Peace Congress in England and Warsaw, although invited and put on the International Committee.

By this time you realize how different the atmosphere is at Fisk than in Czechoslovakia. The better class of Negroes are petty bourgeois and narrowly American in ideals. I hope you will not succumb to their chauvinism, but will calmly maintain your broader outlook, without unnecessary antagonism. Read carefully the classics of communism and also read the *Guardian*.

Greet the Professor from Penn. State for me.[3] I hope you keep in touch with him. He's modern and courageous.

Have you heard from Marek?[4] There may be some censorship on his mail. If you have not heard, send me a sealed letter by mail and I will forward it through a friend.

What I propose is this: do not spend beyond our means; do not waste too much on socials and games. Study and study hard. Read and read widely. Be careful of your eyes and get much sleep. Plan to spend Xmas with Mother and

1. Shirley Graham's home was then in Saint Albans, Long Island. By "the Sterns" Du Bois refers to Alfred Stern and his wife, Martha Dodd Stern—the daughter, as Du Bois writes, of the historian and ambassador to Germany, William E. Dodd.

2. No collection of Du Bois's election speeches was published. Through the Peace Information Center there did appear late in 1950 a four-page pamphlet, *I Speak for Peace*, which was the text of the statement Du Bois made at a press conference held in Harlem, 24 September 1950, announcing his candidacy.

3. He refers to Dr. Lee Lorch, the mathematician, who had difficulty retaining academic positions during the Cold War era; his employment at Fisk lasted but a short time. Future correspondence will elaborate on this matter (see below, pp. 363-65).

4. This was the Czech historian and journalist Franz Marek.

get acquainted with her. She is really lonesome. Do not plan any Xmas trips here or elsewhere. Spend the vacation reading. Try for a job this Summer. Then try to talk your Mother into a trip to Europe together during the Summer of 1952. This can be worked out I am sure. I cannot promise much aid, but Mother's insurance policies and your economy, with the $500 a year I have saved for your education, ought to pay for such a trip; of course a scholarship would cinch it! Think and plan and work.

With much love and all my hope,

W. E. B. Du Bois

Du Bois's verve and energy and his habit of projecting major projects are shown in a letter written to Rayford W. Logan soon after it was announced that Logan had been appointed director of the Association for the Study of Negro Life and History and editor of its journal, to succeed the recently deceased Carter G. Woodson.

New York City, November 3, 1950

Dear Dr. Logan:

I hear you have been elected editor of the Negro History Publications. Congratulations!

Here is a project; think it over. I propose that we undertake a new broad definitive study of Reconstruction with the cooperation of the best students and teachers of history, throughout the South and of course with the cooperation of those in the North. I would suggest that I be a sort of editor in a more or less honorary position and simply because of my work in Reconstruction; that you be the executive editor and that is the real director; and that we secure in each of the Southern states the best teachers of history and that they go to work to exhaust documents and facts covering the American Negro in their states from 1866 to 1876; putting great stress on biographical facts, documents and economic conditions. If there are two or three good men in the state, as there would be for instance in Georgia, each could take some particular part of the state or divide it by subject.

In this way I think that the Negro scholarship might have a final word to say on Reconstruction. A general board would review and rationalize the local histories and make a general study of books and documents and give interpretations. This whole scheme would call for comparatively little finances at first; each one of the history teachers could ask at first simply for time from his regular teaching to do this research; and then perhaps after a year or so, something for expenses; if we can, later raise by a general fund something more for reimbursement.

The central editorial board in the same way could work on its own time and let individuals pay their own expense until some funds could be raised. Parts when finished could be published in the *Journal of Negro History* and papers could be read before the American Historical Association. It seems to me that in this way we might start a really great project. Think it over. I expect to be in Washington sometime about November 20. I would be glad to call and talk with you.

My best regards to yourself and Mrs. Logan.

Very sincerely yours,
W. E. B. Du Bois

Washington, D.C., November 10, 1950

My dear Dr. Du Bois:

Thank you very much for your letter of November 3 and especially for your kind congratulations.

Your project for a new broad definitive study of Reconstruction definitely appeals to me. Here, however, is the present difficulty. Most of the books published by Dr. Woodson were brought out by the Associated Publishers. Until his estate has been settled, it will, of course, be impossible for the Associated Publishers to bring out any new books. Under the terms of Dr. Woodson's will, the Associated Publishers will become the property of the Association. If at that time I am still Director of the Association, I shall be glad to consider the project in detail with you.[1]

As always, I shall be delighted to see you whenever you come to Washington. According to my personal plans, I shall be in town about November 20 and if you will make your wishes known, I will do my best to see that they are fulfilled.

Sincerely yours,
Rayford W. Logan

Elechukwu N. Njaka (1921-75) was born in Nigeria; he did his undergraduate work at Xavier University in New Orleans and graduate work at the University of California in Los Angeles. From 1958 to 1968 he was a high school principal in Nigeria, from 1968 to 1971 chairman of the political science department at Tuskegee, and from 1971 to his death head of the African American Department at the University of Maryland in Baltimore.

1. Nothing came of Du Bois's proposal. Logan resigned as director of the association and editor of the *Journal of Negro History* when he went to France in October 1951 on a Fulbright Research Fellowship. (This information was kindly supplied to the editor by Professor Logan in a letter dated 2 August 1976.)

* Information about Njaka's death was provided the editor through the courtesy of Bernetta L. Hux, secretary of the African American Studies program at the University of Maryland in Baltimore.

While a student at Xavier he sent Du Bois a letter, complimenting him on his anti-imperialist efforts, but mainly arguing against Du Bois's use of the word "Negro"; Njaka preferred the term "Ethiopian." Du Bois's response reflected his consistent position on this matter.

New York City, November 27, 1950

Mr. Elechukwu Njaka

Dear Sir:

I thank you for your letter of November 18. You must remember that a name is not a matter of individual choice or even of historical accuracy, it is a matter of general understanding and agreement and the result of long and intricate growth of culture patterns. When, therefore, we say the "black race" or the "Negro people," everybody on earth understands exactly what we mean.

It is not a question of historical accuracy or scientific definition, but a clear and indisputable fact. It can be changed only by a long and intricate process involving complete change of culture patterns, and since in this case the change would have no real meaning, why worry about it?

If black people were called epilogimistes instead of Negroes they would still be the same people with the same problems, with the same past and future.

Very sincerely yours,

W. E. B. Du Bois

The dean of the School of Library Service at Atlanta University put interesting questions to Du Bois late in 1950 and received a significant reply.

Atlanta, Ga., December 6, 1950

Dear Dr. Du Bois:

One of our students in the Atlanta University School of Library Service is writing, for a master's thesis, an historical sketch of the development of public library service to Negroes in Atlanta, Georgia.[1] We have learned that on the day of the opening of the Carnegie Library in Atlanta for whites you, representing a committee of Negro citizens, called upon the president of the new public library board to protest because no provision was made for Negro citizens to use the library and to ask that public library facilities be made available for Negroes and that there be appointed a Negro member of the public library board.

I am writing to ask if you have or can refer us to any records kept of the

1. The student was Barbara Adkins Ridley; her thesis, entitled, "A History of Public Library Service to Negroes in Atlanta, Georgia," was accepted for her master's degree in 1951. This information was kindly supplied the editor by Virginia Lacy Jones, now dean of the School of Library Service of Atlanta University, in a letter dated 27 July 1976.

work of the committee that you represented on this occasion. Could you give us the names of the members of the Committee? If you could lend us any materials from your files pertaining to this struggle of Atlanta Negroes to secure public library service, we would be most appreciative. We would be happy to pay the postage on such material and return it to you promptly. Whatever information you can give us on this development will be most useful. We plan to do a series of such historical sketches for several southern cities.

My husband joins me in kindest personal regards and best wishes.[2]

Sincerely yours,
Virginia Lacy Jones[3]

New York City, December 19, 1950

My dear Mrs. Jones:

Answering your letter of December 6, I have been hoping to find time to go through my files and get hold of some of the original documents on the library matter; but the task is too much and I shall have to simply say: that the year after the Carnegie Library was opened in Atlanta, a committee of Negroes was formed of which I was one. I am not quite sure of the other members; I think John Hope and probably Dr. Porter were but that I cannot now remember.[1]

We made an appointment with the trustees and met them once. There were four or five of us and five or six of the trustees. I was the main speaker. I hesitated at first as to whether I should make a straight out demand for full rights or compromise by asking for a branch library. I decided to make the full demand.

I demanded of the committee the same rights to use the library as were accorded white citizens. I pointed out that the discrimination was unfair; that although my own books were in the library, I could not take them out; and that this sort of discrimination was not democracy. Some of the trustees were quite angry at the demand and showed it in their faces and by what they said. The result of the visit was that we not only got no rights in the Central Library but for 10 years no branch library was established.

If your student should ever be in New York and want to examine my files for the original documents, I should be glad to give him such facilities as I can.

I trust this will be of some use to your student.

Very sincerely yours,
W. E. B. Du Bois

2. This was Edward Allen Jones.

3. Virginia Lacy Jones was born in Cincinnati in 1912 and educated at Hampton Institute and the universities of Illinois and Chicago. She has been connected with the library service of Atlanta University since 1939 and has been dean of the School of Library Service since 1945.

1. Du Bois published a contemporary account of this incident, "The Opening of the Library," *Independent* 54 (3 April 1902):809–10.

On 12 July 1950, Dean Acheson, secretary of state, issued a statement attacking the World Peace Center, the Stockholm Peace Pledge and those Americans who were circulating it. The opening paragraph of his statement read: "I am sure that the American people will not be fooled by the so-called 'world peace appeal' or 'Stockholm resolution' now being circulated in this country for signatures. It should be recognized for what it is—a propaganda trick in the spurious 'peace offensive' of the Soviet Union." This charge received first page headlines in the press of the United States—and in much of the rest of the world; see, for example, the New York Times *of 13 July 1950, where the text of Acheson's brief statement was published (p. 7).*

This background explains a letter Du Bois sent Acheson on the fourteenth of July. Part of Du Bois's letter was published in the New York Times, *17 July 1950 (p. 5), with the headline: "Dr. Du Bois Calls on Acheson to Promise U.S. Will 'Never Be First to Use Bomb.'" At least one newspaper published Du Bois's open letter in full: the* Syracuse (N.Y.) Post-Standard, *26 July 1950, under the headline, "We've Got to Live with Russia."*

New York City, July 14, 1950

Dear Mr. Acheson:

Your public statement of July 12, on the campaign to outlaw atomic warfare which we have been helping, appears to us of so great significance as to call for a reply and rectification of certain assertions.

At a moment in history when a world fearful of war hangs on every American pronouncement, the Secretary of State, simultaneously with the Committee on Un-American Activities of the House of Representatives, joins in condemning any effort to outlaw atomic warfare. There is in your statement no intimation of a desire for peace, of a realization of the horror of another World War or of sympathy with the crippled, impoverished and dead who pay for fighting.

Surely throughout the world hundreds of millions of people may be pardoned for interpreting your statements as foreshadowing American use of the atom bomb in Korea. Nowhere in your statements can be found evidence of a spirit which would seek to mitigate the present dangers of war by mediation.

The main burden of your opposition to this appeal and our efforts toward peace lies in the charge that proposals to outlaw atomic warfare, as the Geneva Convention outlaws gas, and the World Peace Appeal, stem from communist sources, are the "propaganda tricks in the spurious peace offensive of the Soviet Union," and persons signing this Appeal are either Communists or gullible fools.

The best answer to these assertions is to list a few of the great minds and figures of our times who, with more than 200,000,000 ordinary men and women who want peace, have signed their names to the World Peace Appeal. George Bernard Shaw, Arnold Zweig, former President Cardenas of Mexico, former Premier Vittorio Orlando of Italy (who was one of the Big Four at Versailles), Osvaldo Aranha, Brazilian statesman and former president of the UN General

Assembly, M. Mongibeaux, Chief Justice of the French Supreme Court, M. Mornet, Attorney General of France, Dr. Sholem Treistman, Chief Rabbi of Poland, Edouard Herriot, President of the French Senate and former Premier, Mme. Sun Yat Sen, Jose Bergamin, renowned Catholic philosopher, Cardinal Sapieha, Roman Catholic Primate of Poland—these are but a few of the great names in other countries.

Nobel Peace Prize winner, Emily Greene Balch, in signing declared: "A statement like the World Peace Appeal is essentially important at this time because it cuts across all ideological and political lines and merits the support of all those who want peace, regardless of any other differences among them."

Thomas Mann, one of the great figures of the world, writes: "The atom bomb is a great threat to humanity. I have signed the Stockholm Appeal. I support any movement which has peace as its aim."

In our own country, among one million American men and women who are sick at the threat of war and have therefore signed the World Peace Appeal are scientists like Dr. Anton J. Carlson of the University of Chicago, cancer specialist, Dr. Philip R. White of Philadelphia, the Rt. Rev. Arthur W. Moulton, Protestant Episcopal Bishop (retired) of Utah, Bishop Sherman L. Greene, A.M.E. Church of Birmingham, Justice James Kolthoff of the University of Minnesota, publisher Aubrey Williams.

The appeal has been endorsed by the Egyptian Council of State, by the Roman Catholic Episcopate of Poland, by eight Catholic Bishops of Italy, by the Prime Minister and Cabinet of Finland, and by the Parliament of the Soviet Union.

You must also address yourself to those other groups and individuals who, concerned with the possibility of atomic destruction, have likewise called for outlawing atomic weapons though they may not have specifically endorsed the World Peace Appeal. May we draw your attention to the appeal issued on April 5 of this year by the International Committee of the Red Cross, an appeal to the governments of sixty-two countries urging them to "begin work on outlawing atomic weapons." The International Red Cross statement pointed out, "Against the atom bomb no protection is possible" and urged an international convention similar to that outlawing poison gases signed in June 1925.

The Cardinals and Bishops of the Roman Catholic Church of France, the Methodists, Presbyterians and Quakers and other religious groups in the United States, that world figure Dr. Albert Einstein—all have called for the banning of atomic warfare in as simple and direct a manner as called for by the World Peace Appeal.

The main burden of your opposition to this Appeal and to our efforts lies in the charge that we are part of a "spurious peace offensive" of the Soviet Union. Is it our strategy that when the Soviet Union asks for peace, we insist on war? Must any proposals for averting atomic catastrophe be sanctified by Soviet opposition? Have we come to the tragic pass where, by declaration of our own Secretary of State, there is no possibility of mediating our differences with the Soviet Union? Does it not occur to you, sir, that there are honest Americans who, regardless of their differences on other questions, hate and fear war and are determined to do something to avert it?

An answer to your argument has already been given. We borrow the words of Israel Galili, former commander-in-chief of the Haganah in Israel, who declared upon signing the Appeal: "When the Soviet Union supported the struggle for the creation of the state of Israel, no one said that help to Israel should be opposed because the Soviet Union was supporting Israel, and Britain was attempting to destroy it. So, too, no one has the right today to smear the campaign for peace because the Soviet Union and the communist movement support it."

We have got to live in the world with Russia and China. If we worked together with the Soviet Union against the menace of Hitler, can we not work with them again at a time when only faith can save us from utter atomic disaster? Certainly hundreds of millions of colonial peoples in Asia, Africa, Latin America and elsewhere, conscious of our support of Chiang Kai-Shek, Bao-Dai and the colonial system, and mindful of the oppressive discrimination against the Negro people in the United States would feel that our intentions also must be accepted on faith.

Today in this country it is becoming standard reaction to call anything "communist," and therefore subversive and unpatriotic, which anybody for any reason dislikes. We feel strongly that this tactic has already gone too far; that it is not sufficient today to trace a proposal to a communist source in order to dismiss it with contempt.

We are a group of Americans, who upon reading this Peace Appeal, regarded it as a true, fair statement of what we ourselves and many countless other Americans believed. Regardless of our other beliefs and affiliations, we united in this organization for the one and only purpose of informing the American people on the issues of peace. In furtherance of this, we have made available the World Peace Appeal and offered it to all those who wish to work for peace.

More than one million Americans have signed the World Peace Appeal to date and in the next few weeks several millions more will sign because the American people in overwhelming majority want peace.

Today we received a letter from a small town in Oregon: "Enclosed find five signatures to the World Peace Appeal and a small contribution to help carry on the good work. We have one son in the Army, Korea bound, and one in the naval blockade of Korea." Letters like this reassure us that we are serving the best interests of the American people in trying to prevent further slaughter of their sons.

While there is yet time, Mr. Acheson, let the world know that in the future,

the Government of the United States will never be the first to use the atom
bomb, whether in Korea or in any other part of the earth.[1]

Respectfully yours,
W. E. B. Du Bois, Chairman
Peace Information Center

*One month after Acheson's public attack upon the Peace Information Center,
a registered letter was sent to the center from the Department of Justice. Before presenting this letter, it may be helpful to offer a brief chronological account of the confrontation between the United States government and Du Bois
and his associates of the Peace Information Center.*

*The center, headed by Du Bois, functioned from 3 April 1950 to 12 October
1950. From August 1950 to November 1950, Du Bois campaigned on the American Labor Party ticket for the office of United States senator from New York.
On 9 February 1951 he and others at the center were indicted as unregistered
foreign agents; Du Bois was arraigned in Washington on 16 February 1951, one
week before his eighty-third birthday. The trial date was set for 2 April 1951
but, after protest from the defense, was changed to 14 May 1951. The need of
both prosecution and defense for testimony from witnesses in Europe led to
a further postponement to 3 October 1951, and then again to 2 November. The
trial actually began in Washington on 8 November 1951. On 11 November,
Armistice Day, there was a three-day recess; trial re-opened on 15 November
and the prosecution completed its case on 19 November. On 20 November
1951 came the directed verdict of acquittal.*

United States Department of Justice
Washington, D.C., August 11, 1950

Peace Information Center
Gentlemen:

The Peace Information Center is engaged in activities within the United
States which require its registration with this Department under the terms of
the Foreign Agents Registration Act of 1938, as amended. There is enclosed
for your information in this respect a pamphlet which contains a reprint of the
Act, together with the rules and regulations prescribed thereunder by the
Attorney General.

Your attention is specifically invited to Section 1 (c) of the Act which states
in substance that any person who acts within the United States, whether or
not pursuant to contractual relationship, as a publicity agent for a foreign

1. There was no reply to this letter. The next month, however, the legal machinery
was put into action which would eventuate in the indictment and trial of Du Bois
and four associates from the Peace Information Center.

principal falls within the purview of the registration requirements of the Act. The term "person" includes any Combination of individuals and the term "foreign principal" includes any organization organized under the laws of or having its principal place of business in a foreign country.

Section 2 (a) of the Act states in substance that no person shall act as an agent of a foreign principal within the United States unless there has been filed with the Attorney General a true and complete registration statement.

Registration is accomplished by the filing of a registration statement, supported by the appropriate number of exhibits, each in duplicate, and by the filing of supplemental statements at six month intervals for as long as the agency relationship continues to exist. An Exhibit A should be filed for every officer and director of the organization as well as any person who renders any assistance to the registrant in a capacity other than stenographic or clerical.

Enclosed herewith for the use of the Peace Information Center in filing its registration statement are three copies of Forms FA-2, three Exhibit C forms and twenty-four Exhibit A forms. No special forms are provided for Exhibit B. Additional copies of the forms supplied may be had upon request.

In view of the length of time that has elapsed since the Peace Information Center has been acting as an agent of a foreign principal without having filed its registration statement as required by law, it is expected that the registration statement will be submitted forthwith.

> Sincerely yours,
> William E. Foley, Chief
> Foreign Agents Registration Section

[Sent from New York City; undated]

J. Howard McGrath
Attorney General of the United States
United States Department of Justice
Re: Peace Information Center
Dear Sir:

On August 11, 1950, the Peace Information Center, of which I am the Chairman, received a request from the Foreign Agents Registration Section of your Department to register pursuant to the applicable act, as "publicity agent" for a "foreign principal." At that time I was out of the country, unable to take personal charge of this matter. Since a request to the Chief of the Section, William E. Foley, to defer discussions until my return was not honored, I authorized the organization to take such steps as it deemed necessary to meet your Department's request.

Gloria Agrin, Esq. was retained as attorney for the Peace Information Center, and, I am informed, she conferred and corresponded with Mr. Foley, concerning the view of the organization of the inapplicability of the Foreign Agents Registration Act to it.

On September 19, 1950 Miss Agrin received a letter from Mr. Foley, indicating that his Section was not satisfied that this was so. Since I believed the Justice Department's persistent adherence to its original demand to be an absurdity, unfounded in fact, and unwarranted in law, and because I am, perhaps, the person best informed concerning the organization, I requested Miss Agrin to arrange an appointment for me with Mr. Foley. I have since been informed that this request was denied.

I cannot but feel that, in a matter of such serious concern, Mr. Foley's denial to me of an opportunity to be heard must necessarily reflect adversely upon the Department of Justice. I should think that the possible consequences of an unjustified enforcement of the Act would impel the Justice Department to bend every effort to make certain of its conclusions. The Department's arbitrary and capricious refusal to confer with me compels me to infer that either the Department is unaware of the import of the statute which it seems to enforce, or that it is unwise enough to deal cavalierly with the rights of American citizens.

Whatever be the motivation, I consider the end product indefensible and outrageous. It is for that reason that I am writing to you, as the head of the Justice Department. I believe it to be of the utmost importance that an appointment be arranged for me.

Although, as you know, I am a candidate for the United States Senate from the State of New York, and, therefore, am laboring under a heavy schedule, I shall seek to accommodate myself to any date you may set, if it is at all possible.

I await your early reply.

Very truly yours,
Dr. W. E. B. Du Bois

[Sent from New York City; undated]

William E. Foley, Chief
Foreign Agents Registration Section
Department of Justice
Re: Peace Information Center
Dear Sir:

It has come to my attention that the Washington, D. C. Grand Jury is in the process of investigating the possible violation of the Foreign Agents Registration Act, from which I have drawn what I believe to be a reasonable inference, that the investigation may have some relation to the Peace Information Center.

This is surprising to me, in light of the fact that the Peace Information Center and your department were engaged in discussion concerning the position of your department that this organization was obliged to register pursuant to the terms of this law. In fact, our last communication with you was a letter, which I wrote to Attorney General J. Howard McGrath, early in October, urgently requesting that he grant me the opportunity to discuss the matter with the Department, and to which I have not been favored with the courtesy of a reply.

At no time has the Peace Information Center intended to act in violation of the law; its conflict with the department related to the propriety of the application of the law to it.

Furthermore, it seems to me that the entire matter is now moot and academic, since the governing body of the Peace Information Center, on October 12, 1950, voted to disband the organization, which since then has been in the process of winding up its affairs and has undertaken and conducted no new business. Even this last process, I believe, is all but completed.

My own resignation as chairman was handed in this Fall to be accepted at pleasure, but not later than January 1, 1951.

In any case, however, I again urge the importance of a discussion with you in which I may have the opportunity to participate. Any confusions to the position either of the Department of Justice or the Peace Information Center may, in this way, be clarified, and both the Government and the organization save the unpleasantness and expense of unnecessary legal contests.

Very truly yours,
Dr. W. E. B. Du Bois

Washington, D. C., February 2, 1951
Re: Peace Information Center
Dear Dr. Du Bois:

Receipt is acknowledged of your undated letter, postmarked at New York on January 26, 1951, concerning the Peace Information Center.

You have been fully advised through exchange of correspondence and through conferences with the Center's attorney regarding the obligations of the Peace Information Center under the terms of the Foreign Agents Registration Act of 1938, as amended. In this connection, your attention is invited to Section 8 (3) of the Act which states in substance that failure to file the required registration statement shall be considered a continuing offense for as long as such failure exists.

Your attention is also invited to Section 7 of the Act which places each officer and director of an agent of a foreign principal which is not an individual under the obligation to cause such agent to execute and file the required registration statement.

Dissolution of an organization relieves neither the organization itself nor its officers from complying with the provisions of the Act.

Sincerely yours,
William E. Foley, Chief
Foreign Agents Registration Section

On 9 February 1951 the grand jury in Washington indicted Du Bois and four
other members of the Peace Information Center for violation of the Foreign
Agents Registration Act. The four indicted with Du Bois were Sylvia Soloff,
who had served as the center's secretary and whose indictment was voided;
Abbott Simon, an attorney; Elizabeth Moos, a teacher and educator; and Kyrle
Elkin, a businessman and Harvard graduate. They were arraigned on 16 Feb-
ruary 1951; Du Bois was fingerprinted, searched for weapons, and manacled to
Elkin until protests from his lawyers led to the removal of the handcuffs.

At the time of his arraignment, Du Bois read a statement that has not hitherto
been published:

It is a curious thing that today I am called upon to defend myself against
criminal charges for openly advocating the one thing all people want—Peace.
For 83 years I have worked and studied hoping that in some way I might help
my people and my fellowmen to a better way of life, free of poverty and
injustice.

My interest in world affairs is long standing. For two years, from 1892 to
1894, I studied at the University of Berlin and travelled in Germany, Austria,
Hungary, Italy and France. I attended the World Races Congress in 1911 in
London. I organized the Pan-African Congresses in Paris, London, Brussels
and Lisbon in 1919, 1921 and 1923. I was in consultation in 1919 and 1921 with
the founders of the League of Nations. I attended the first meeting of the
League Assembly in Geneva and met with the Directors of the Commission
on Mandates and the International Labor Organization. In 1924 I had the
honor of serving as Special Minister from the United States to Liberia. In
1936, as a Fellow of the Carl Schurz Foundation, I spent five months in
Germany and then went on to China, Japan, Manchuria and Russia. I was
appointed special consultant and attended the founding conference in San
Francisco of the United Nations. Later, in 1945, I attended the Pan-African
Congress in London [actually Manchester]. I cite these facts simply to indicate that my personal concern and activities for peace these last few years are
fully consonant with my entire life interest in the cause of promoting peace
through understanding among the peoples of the world.

With me today are three of my co-workers in the Peace Information Center, persons of integrity and principle who share with me the deep moral
conviction that differences between nations must not be allowed to bring
about the destruction of the human race.

It is a sad commentary that we must enter a courtroom today to plead
Not Guilty to something that cannot be a crime—advocating peace and
friendship between the American people and the peoples of the world. These
indictments are a shameful proclamation to the world that our Government
considers peace alien, and its advocacy criminal. In a world which has barely
emerged from the horrors of the Second World War and which trembles

*on the brink of an atomic catastrophe, can it be criminal to hope and work
for peace?*

*We feel now as we have always felt that our activities for peace, and in
particular, the outlawing of atomic warfare cannot conceivably fall within
the purview of a statute such as the Foreign Agents Registration Act. As
Chairman of the Peace Information Center during its existence, I can categor-
ically state that we were an entirely American organization whose sole objective as Americans was to secure peace and prevent a third world war.*

*It is revealing that the Justice Department can find no statute which pro-
vides protection for the Negro people from such outrages as the execution of
the Martinsville Seven,* yet it displays great ingenuity in distorting legislation
to make it apply to advocates of peace.*

*A great demand for peace is being voiced throughout the country. Men
and women everywhere are questioning our tragic military adventure in
Korea and the prospect of war with China. There is deep apprehension at
the thought that an atomic war may be unleashed. In the light of this, the
shabby trick of branding those who seek peace as "aliens" and "criminals"
will not stem this tide. I am confident that every American who desires
peace, Negro and white, Catholic, Jew and Protestant, the three million
signers of the World Peace Appeal and the tens of millions more will join us
in our fight to vindicate our right to speak for peace.*

*Committees, organizations, and individuals labored to inform the world of the
indictment and forthcoming trial of Du Bois and his co-defendants. Letters of
protest poured into Washington and many letters of support came to Du Bois.
Among them was one from George Padmore in his capacity as a member of
the executive committee of the Pan-African Federation.*

London, England, March 21, 1951

Dear and esteemed Dr. Du Bois:

The news has just reached us that you have been indicted by the so-called
Un-American Activities Committee [sic], for your heroic fight for Peace.
We consider this attempt to blackmail you into silence an outrage against the
fundamental principles of democracy and an insult to Africans and peoples of
African descent throughout the world. For in you, sir, we see the finest representative of our people's hopes, dream and aspiration. You have done more
than any other man during the first half of the twentieth century to blaze the
way and chart the course for Negro rights in America and African and Colonial
freedom. We, therefore, beg you to accept our heartfelt sympathy and assure

---

* Seven young Black men from the town of Martinsville, Virginia, were executed
in Richmond on 2 and 5 February 1951 for alleged rape of a white woman, who,
according to law enforcement agencies in Virginia, had disappeared since the original
conviction.

you of our unqualified solidarity and support. Please let us know what concrete steps we can take to help you in your defence. Meanwhile, we are giving the matter the widest publicity in the African and West Indian Press. We have already distributed a release based on the facts of the indictment taken from recent issues of coloured American newspapers reaching us. We have also read of your marriage to the former Miss Shirley Graham.[1] Please permit us to take this opportunity of sharing with you this good news and to wish you both many, many years of happiness. We sincerely hope that your honour and character will be vindicated against this outrageous charge, which we consider one of the greatest travesties of American justice! We are sorry to say it, but your country is fast losing its claims to be a civilized nation. When it is not lynching the bodies of Negroes, it tortures the minds of its finest citizens. Come what may, we want to assure you, Dr. Du Bois, that you will always remain deep in our hearts and minds, the greatest champion of our oppressed race—unselfish, uncompromising and incorruptible!

You will no doubt be pleased to hear that as a result of our sweeping victory in the recent Gold Coast election, Kwame Nkrumah, the Leader of the Convention People's Party, who made the report on West Africa at our Fifth Congress in Manchester, has agreed to take the initiative of convening a sixth Congress on African soil later this year. We sincerely hope that you will be able to be with us and to share in our victory inspired by your vision and work. Again our best wishes to yourself and Mrs. Du Bois. Do arrange for someone to keep in touch with us on the progress of your case. With God's blessing on you and our assurances of warmest respect and admiration.

Yours sincerely,
George Padmore

New York City, April 11, 1951

My dear Mr. Padmore:

I thank you very much for your letter of March 28, which came to hand through Dr. Hunton. The indictment is of course a serious matter. Under ordinary circumstances it could be easily beaten in court, but in this era of hysteria and persecution which has developed in the United States, it is quite possible that we might be sent to jail, or fined or both.

The most important thing is to let the peoples of the world, white, black and yellow, know just what is happening in our case and in that matter you can help very substantially. The accusation is not that we have done anything treasonable, or anything that we did not have the right to do; it does not accuse

1. Du Bois and Shirley Graham were married, at the bride's home, on 27 February 1951. Shirley Graham describes the wedding in her "Comments" in Du Bois's *In Battle for Peace*, pp. 65–68, and in her own *His Day Is Marching On: A Memoir of W. E. B. Du Bois* (Philadelphia: J. B. Lippincott, 1971), pp. 140–48.

the five defendants of being representatives of a foreign government, but as
the curious statute says "representatives of a foreign principal," which means
that if this conviction stands, anybody who repeats in the United States anything that anyone in Europe or Russia says can be accused of being an agent.
Of course there must be some proof that the relation of agent and principal had
actually been set up, but in our present attitude, of course that may be assumed
simply because we, for instance, circulated the Stockholm Peace Pledge and
gave the same advice to Americans that the Partisans for Peace were giving to
the world. So it is a very dangerous situation, and it ought to be clear to the
peoples of the world what is happening and just how far freedom of speech
and of thought is being curtailed in the United States.

I shall be glad, very glad from time to time to keep you in touch with what
is happening and to send you any documents or other matters which will be
of interest.

I am glad to hear of the election of Nkrumah, and of the proposed sixth
Pan-African Congress in Africa. I should certainly try to be there if in any
way it is possible.

My very best regards to you. I assume you have heard of my marriage to
Shirley Graham, and she joins me in best wishes.

Very sincerely yours,
W. E. B. Du Bois

*The chief counsel for Du Bois was Vito Marcantonio, the former congressman
from New York. Gloria Agrin and Stanley Faulkner of New York City were
part of the counsel. In addition, the Washington law firm of Cobb, Howard
and Hayes, and George Parker, another Black attorney in the capital, were
part of the defense team.*

*After the arraignment but prior to the trial, Du Bois learned that a govern-
ment official had approached Marcantonio to suggest that if Du Bois pleaded
"nolo contendere" he would be let off with a suspended sentence. This act explains a letter Du Bois sent to James A. Cobb—which letter he showed, before
mailing it, to each of his other attorneys in New York City.**

New York City, April 10, 1951
Dear Judge Cobb:
Shirley and I have just returned from four weeks complete rest in the Ba-

* James A. Cobb (1876-1958) was born in Louisiana, graduated from Fisk, and received his law degree from Howard in 1900. In 1926 President Coolidge appointed
him to the municipal court bench in Washington; he served in that capacity until
1935 and thereafter returned to private practice.

A copy of this letter and information surrounding it came to me through the kindness of Stanley Faulkner, Esq., in a letter dated 25 March 1974.

hamas and Cuba and feel renewed in strength. I want to thank you for your deep interest in my case and the help which made the trip possible.

Also in view of some rumors I've heard of the willingness of the Government to compromise or at least not press the suit, I want to make clear to you my own attitude after careful thought and deliberation; I regard this case as a great opportunity to vindicate the right of free speech and advocacy of peace. On this line I want the case fought and under no circumstances will I curry favor or ask leniency if that involved declaring that I have ever acted as an agent for any foreign person, organization or government. I would prefer to rot to death in jail than utter that lie. I have refused too many offers to sell out in America to be bribed in my old age.

I know you will respect my decision and I put it down in plain words in order to be sure it is understood. I was always cranky as you know and this grows with the years. At the same time I am not really hankering for jail and want your best efforts to keep me out.

Very sincerely,
W. E. B. Du Bois

*Soon after his arraignment, Du Bois tried to interest the American Civil Liberties Union in aiding the defense. The note of final failure in this effort came from Arthur Garfield Hays.**

New York City, April 26, 1951

My dear Dr. Du Bois:

I have taken up the matter of the indictment with the Civil Liberties Union and with several men on the Board who were active in the discussions in March as to whether or not the Union should go into your case.

At the time the matter came up I was not present at the meeting of the directors of the Union, and I had supposed the matter was rather cursorily handled. I find, however, that it was given very serious consideration. The general opinion seemed to be that we should take no position in connection with the indictment since we have not opposed the constitutionality of the law, and there is no indication that the trial would be in any way unfair. Other views were that we should not take a position since we have never opposed the law and any indictments under it, and since we did not oppose the indictment where unpopular Nazi groups were involved we should not oppose it now merely because friends of ours are involved.

* Arthur Garfield Hays (1881–1954), a graduate of the Columbia Law School, was a leading civil liberties attorney and national director of the American Civil Liberties Union for many years. He was involved in the Sacco-Vanzetti case and appeared for the defendants in the Reichstag fire trials in 1933; he was the author of several books, including *Let Freedom Ring* (1928) and *Trial by Prejudice* (1933).

Having talked to some of the key men among the directors, and those who would be most favorable toward our going into the matter, and not having met their support, I feel there is no possibility of the American Civil Liberties Union's taking up this matter until after trial. I am sorry because personally I should like to have helped in this case.

I am returning your correspondence herewith.

Sincerely yours,
Arthur Garfield Hays

While some life-long associates, especially many in the leadership of the NAACP, *offered no support, and certain personal friends also turned their backs upon him, a matter of great satisfaction to Du Bois was a Resolution of Faith that came to him from the alumni association of his beloved Fisk.*

RESOLUTION

WHEREAS, William Edward Burghardt Du Bois, distinguished graduate of Fisk University, has made an outstanding contribution to scholarship, literature, and social action, and

WHEREAS, he has gained the respect, admiration, and gratitude of his fellow alumni and has received the highest award from his Alma Mater, and

WHEREAS, the government of the United States has indicted him and is now about to bring him to trial, and

WHEREAS, the General Alumni Association of Fisk University in its annual meeting assembled May 26, 1951, are desirous of expressing at this time their continued respect, gratitude, and admiration of him therefore be it

RESOLVED, that we reaffirm our faith and confidence in him and in his integrity and loyalty to the principles and ideas of his Alma Mater and again express our sincere appreciation for his courageous leadership in the struggle for the full emancipation of his people and the realization of total democracy for all men.

GENERAL ALUMNI ASSOCIATION OF FISK
UNIVERSITY
L. Howard Bennett
President

George Padmore was an important source of international support for Du Bois at this difficult time.

London, England, May 29, 1951

Dear Doctor:

I was pleased to note the hopeful tone of your letter and sincerely wish you and your co-defendants all success. I can assure you that we shall continue to give the widest publicity to your case in the African and Colonial Press. Already our efforts are meeting with great success. We have circularised all our contacts and requested them to express their solidarity with you in whatever ways they consider most effective. Enclosed are a few clippings from West Africa. You will no doubt remember Ja-Ja Wachuku who was a delegate to the Fifth Pan-African Congress. He has recently started a Pan-African Party in Nigeria to spread the ideas of which you are the worthy father. I am planning to leave for the Gold Coast and Nigeria this month to help the comrades there in preparing for another meeting of the Congress. I might travel out together with Nkrumah who is visiting the u.s. to receive an honorary doctorate from Lincoln University [Pa.] on June 5. He will no doubt see you if he visits New York. Drop him a line in care of Lincoln as it is important for you both to meet before he leaves America. I shall keep you informed of developments on my return to London. Apart from the publicity which I have been able to get into the overseas press, Cedric Dover and Peter Abrahams have released statements through my press agency which will also help the campaign as they are both well known in the Colonies. Dorothy had a pleasant holiday in the West Indies and succeeded in getting some of the local political and trade union leaders to take an interest in your case. They plan to send protest resolutions to the State Department through the local u.s. Consuls. Be assured that we shall leave no stone unturned to voice our indignation and condemnation of the reactionary policies of the American authorities, who the Colonial peoples everywhere consider the main bulwark of Colonialism in Asia, Africa and the West Indies today. What a tragedy for a nation which had its birth in the struggle against British Colonialism! But we are also conscious that there is still an anti-imperialist sentiment among progressive Americans, even if their voices are not always heard abroad. With best wishes to yourself and Mrs. Du Bois.

Yours in solidarity and friendship,
George Padmore

New York City, July 10, 1951

My dear Mr. Padmore:

I am sorry that I was away when your last letter came and am especially disappointed not to see Mr. Nkrumah.

Shirley and I took a trip to the Middle West and the West Coast and made a series of speeches on my case and the Peace Movement. We were greatly encouraged and I made a speech to the Peace Congress in Chicago to 5000 delegates and at least 10,000 spectators.[1]

I especially however wanted to see Nkrumah. I have a rather fantastic idea

1. Du Bois's speech was delivered in Chicago on 30 June 1951; it was published in the *National Guardian*, 11 July 1951.

which may lead to something: and that is I want to write out a Declaration of Independence for Africa, including all the peoples of Africa and making a forecast of their desires and demands, with as strong a stand toward socialism as is possible; so that in the future the young men of Africa may realize that the methods of the capitalistic world are dying out. I want to make this and a statement which shall be used in the Call for a Sixth Pan-African Congress. It may be quite possible that I shall not attend because of death, or being in jail or inability to get a passport; but at any rate I think this will be a gesture. I shall wait until you return from Africa before I send it to you, and would like to have some news of the conditions you found there.

My best regards to you and Dorothy, from Shirley and myself.

Very sincerely yours,
W. E. B. Du Bois

A stirring message of support for Du Bois came to the National Council of the Arts, Sciences and Professions—one of the groups alerting the world to his trial and mobilizing support for him—from the senior bishop of the African Methodist Episcopal Church.

Wilberforce, Ohio, October 26, 1951
National Council of the Arts Sciences and Professions
Dear Sir:

In addition to your communications I also have a circular from the National Committee to Defend Dr. W. E. B. Du Bois, whose address I have in a letter from 16 West 29th Street, Room 1224, New York 1, New York. I have the time to come to Washington to the hearing on November first, but I do not have the physical strength. Du Bois is eighty-three, I am almost ninety-one years of age, but I want both you and him to know that with all my puny strength and influence I am with you one hundred percent.

I have known Dr. Du Bois more than fifty years, ever since he graduated from Harvard University. I have worked with him in organizations and committees fighting for justice, freedom and equality for almost two generations.

Even if I could, I would not bother President Truman about this case. I think I know him well enough to know he will have nothing to do with this monstrous attempt at intimidation and suppression of an outstanding American citizen. I have the same confidence in United States Attorney General [J. Howard] McGrath. By the accident of birth Dr. Du Bois is classed with Americans of African descent, but he is much more than that. He is bound by no creed of race, or color. His writings are voluminous and easily accessible. He is one of the best known Negroes in America or for that matter in the world.

This blow at him looks like a strike at the intelligentsia of Negro Americans and the millions who trust and follow their leadership. It may be in the case at

hand that Dr. Du Bois like millions of us stopped here and there to listen to the
song of some siren, who sought to lure him. But I am sure that his loyalty to our
government has never leaned in the direction of Russian Communism.

For over fifty years, Dr. W. E. B. Du Bois has stood for the things for which
George Washington fought, that Thomas Jefferson wrote in the Declaration of
Independence, and the guarantees contained in the Constitution of the United
States. Millions of Americans of African descent though inarticulate aspire to
achieve the things advocated by Dr. Du Bois. Namely, full and complete integration into every phase of American life on the basis of absolute equality.
Negroes are fighting and dying in Korea today, they are working in the mines,
on the farms, and in the great industrial plants without a murmur or complaint
to sustain and support our government.

If this case comes to trial, will they try to end this man's brilliant career by
placing on him a martyr's crown? In case they do it, it would be the most
powerful blow for Negro Freedom and Equality that has happened since
Abraham Lincoln issued his proclamation emancipating the slaves. We are not
turning back a single inch. Americans of African descent are on the March for
Freedom against Segregation, Proscription, Denial, and every influence that
would prevent them from obtaining their goal of complete freedom and equality as American Citizens.

I know that the forms of law must be observed, but when it is administered
in the spirit of hysteria or to frighten and discourage we shall not retreat a
single inch. Millions of us here have courage without fear. And shall firmly
stand to support the foundation upon which this nation was established, and
upon which it stands today. It remains the brightest hope for all Americans
regardless of race, creed, or color. If we could ascend from the depths of slavery
from which we came to the place we occupy today, we can also achieve the
goals of brotherhood and peace for which we strive.

Faithfully yours,
Reverdy C. Ransom[1]

*On 20 November 1951, immediately after the presentation of the prosecution's
case, Judge Matthew F. McGuire directed the acquittal of all the defendants.
Letters of congratulation and rejoicing were numerous. One, addressed to the
National Committee to Defend Dr. Du Bois, in New York City, came from a*

1. Reverdy Cassius Ransom (1861–1959) was born in Ohio and educated at Oberlin
College and Wilberforce University. He was ordained a minister in the AME church
in 1885; he edited the AME *Church Review* from 1912 to 1924 and in the latter year was
elected a bishop. He was president of the board of trustees of Wilberforce University
from 1932 to 1948. From 1948 until his death he served as director of the church's
Bureau of Research and History, located at Wilberforce. His autobiography, *The
Pilgrimage of Harriet Ransom's Son*, was published in 1949.

woman who was serving as secretary of the chapter of the American Peace Crusade movement in a town in Idaho.

Coeur d'Alene, Idaho, November 21, 1951

Dear Committee:

On the eve of America's Thanksgiving Day it occurs to us that we can be thankful to those lovers of justice and freedom who still have the courage to fight for peace and liberty.

We consider the acquittal of the four officers of the Peace Information Center as a remarkable victory for the growing sentiment for peace.

Enclosed is an announcement from our local daily press which devoted many columns over a period of several weeks to a red-baiting barrage upon the indictment of these valiant fighters for peace. You will notice the contradiction between the title and the body of the news item, characteristic of our commercial press in America.[1]

Also enclosed is $5.00.

Sincerely yours,
Opal Brooten

*Three other letters inspired by Du Bois's acquittal are noteworthy. One was from Hubert T. Delany, a Black justice of the Domestic Relations Court in New York City; the second (here translated from the French in which it was written) was from Frédéric Joliot-Curie in Paris; and the third was from Du Bois to Albert Einstein.**

1. The enclosed clipping, about half an inch long, is headlined, "Indicted." The news item in its entirety then reads: "Washington, Nov. 20—(AP) The Peace information center and five [sic] of its officers were acquitted today of charges of violating the foreign agents registration act."

The 1 December 1951 *Nation* commented editorially on Du Bois's acquittal that the failure of the government to present any credible or even relevant evidence led one "to conclude therefore that the original indictment was intended to intimidate the defendants and thereby to discourage the circulation of the Stockholm petition." The concluding sentence will strike home to the post-Watergate generation: "Not only was the indictment an incredible propaganda blunder, but it is further evidence that a thorough house-cleaning in the Department of Justice is long overdue" (173:462–63).

* Hubert T. Delany (b. 1901) was born in North Carolina and educated at the City College of New York and the law school of New York University. He was assistant United States attorney for the Southern District of New York from 1927 to 1933 and tax commissioner of New York City, under Mayor LaGuardia, from 1934 to 1942; he became a justice of the Domestic Relations Court in New York City in 1942.

Frédéric Joliot-Curie (1900-1958), the renowned physicist, was France's high commissioner for atomic energy from 1946 to 1950 and—when this letter to Du Bois was written—president of the World Peace Council.

New York City, November 27, 1951

Personal

My dear Dr. Du Bois:

I send you this note to express my gratification that the indictment against you was dismissed.

It has seemed to me from the very beginning that your indictment was, to say the least, unusual in that the effect of your indictment tended to silence all champions of minority rights in this country. I am sorry to say that if this was the motive of the government, it was in far too many respects successful, because our so-called leaders today have folded their tents, closed their mouths and have become apologists for all of the injustices our government permits against the Negro people of America.

You probably do not know it, but I was subpoenaed to testify as a witness at your trial. I, of course, cannot be sure of the reason that I was subpoenaed, but I assume I was subpoenaed as a character witness. I also assume that whoever subpoenaed me knew that regardless of the issues involved, I would tell the truth. While I am glad that you did not have to go through the ordeal of having your case presented to the jury, I would have considered it an honor to have given testimony to the excellent reputation you have always borne in the community in which you live and far beyond that.

As I look over the record I know of no single individual in this country who has fought longer, harder, more consistently and more militantly for the rights of Negroes than you. If I could not make that statement today, I could not face myself, and that is why I am glad to make it not only to you, but would have not cringed if I had been asked a question that would have permitted that answer on the stand.

With kind personal regards to you, I am

Sincerely yours,
Hubert T. Delany

Paris, France, November 28, 1951

Professor Du Bois

Dear Friend:

For several months we have all followed the news of your case with great interest.

Today I wish to express our great joy at the news of your acquittal.

You give new proof to the fact that perseverance and courage in the struggle for a just cause constitute a powerful force, a force which is invincible when it is supported by millions and millions of honest people.

Dear friend, please accept our fondest wishes,

Frédéric Joliot-Curie

New York City, November 29, 1951

Personal

My dear Dr. Einstein:

I write to express my deep appreciation of your generous offer to do anything that you could in the case brought against me by the Department of Justice.

I was delighted that in the end it was not necessary to call upon you and interfere with your great work and needed leisure, but my thanks for your generous attitude is not less on that account.

Mrs. Du Bois joins me in deep appreciation.

Very sincerely yours,

W. E. B. Du Bois

Du Bois appreciated the support of those who remained convinced of his integrity despite the effort of the United States government to send him to prison. But he was deeply hurt (and rather shocked) at the number of people who did not support him or, in some cases, actually turned against him.. The latter included his brothers from the Boule in New York City of the Sigma Pi Phi fraternity. Hence the exchange that follows.

New York City, November 27, 1951

To Arthur Elmes
Grand Sire Archon
Sigma Pi Phi Fraternity
Sir:

I hereby present my resignation from the Sigma Pi Phi Fraternity and specifically from Zeta Boule, New York City, to become effective immediately. My dues for 1951 have been paid.

I remain respectfully yours,

W. E. B. Du Bois

New York City, December 29, 1951

Dear Archon Du Bois:

With genuine regret, we heard your letter of resignation from Zeta Boule read at our meeting on December 14th. We freely acknowledge our neglect, common discourtesy and lack of Boule spirit with regard to your 83rd Birthday Dinner and at the enforced defense of your good name and reputation in the recent action by the Justice Department of the U.S.

It was the unanimous decision of Zeta that the resignation be NOT ACCEPTED. A Committee of three was appointed to inform you of the deep concern of Zeta. The committee earnestly requests a conference with you. In this connection, with your permission Zeta wishes to call the attention of the officers of the Grand Boule to its discourtesy experienced by you in cities of other Boules. We understand the single exception in demonstrating Boule spirit was that of Epsilon, of Washington, D. C.

Trusting you will grant this conference,[1] we remain,

Fraternally yours,
The Committee
John S. Brown, Chr.

The leadership of the NAACP *adopted a hostile attitude toward Du Bois during his indictment and trial. Though the board did pass a resolution which offered no judgment "on the merits of the recent indictment of Dr. Du Bois," it did affirm that he was "one of the great champions of civil rights" and that the indictment lent "color to the charge that efforts are being made to silence spokesmen for full equality of Negroes." No further action was taken, however, and the board did not publicize even this resolution. In fact, some among the* NAACP *leaders affirmed belief in Du Bois's "guilt." This background explains, in part, a letter Du Bois sent to Judge Delany late in December 1951.*

New York City, December 21, 1951

My dear Judge Delany:

Will you let me again trespass upon your time? I want to bring to your attention the attitudes of the N.A.A.C.P. toward me. I know that you are acquainted with most of it, but I should like to put into your hands a memorandum that I have sent to Mr. Marcantonio, which I am enclosing.

Especially do I want to emphasize the recent attitude of Walter White, Gloster Current, Alfred Baker Lewis, and others. After the Department of Justice had ordered the Peace Information Bureau to register, and we were in controversy with it about it, my pension, or whatever it is that they call it, was without notice cut in half, so that for the year 1951 I have been receiving from them $1200 instead of $2400. There is nothing to prevent them from reducing this to nothing for the year of 1952.

I have heretofore refrained from any attack upon the N.A.A.C.P., since it is, in part, my child. But since this indictment the executive officers of the N.A.A.C.P. have tried to put me in jail.

Arthur Spingarn said frankly to Shirley Graham that of course the Soviet Union was furnishing funds for the Peace Information Center, although he admitted that "possibly" I might not be aware of it.

1. The editor does not know the result of this request; nothing in the Du Bois papers indicates that he changed his decision to resign. Du Bois refers to this fraternity's failure to support him in his *Autobiography* (p. 371).

The executive officers of the N.A.A.C.P. have warned and frightened their branches from helping in my defense, and on the very day of the verdict, Walter White was telling persons at a meeting in Milwaukee that my guilt was proven by irrefutable evidence in the hands of the Department of Justice.

You know, of course, his testimony at the meeting of the Board, when the question of advice to branches came up. He assured them, from a direct interview in Washington, of the evidence of my guilt.[1]

Now, I am tired of this sort of thing, and if any further talk is made, or refusal to pay me a decent pension, I am going to take Walter White, and, if necessary, the N.A.A.C.P. into court. I want you to know this, and think it over. If you have any advice I shall be glad to receive it.

A Merry Christmas and a Happy New Year.

Very sincerely yours,
W. E. B. Du Bois

1. See Du Bois's *Autobiography*, p. 372, and also *In Battle for Peace*, pp. 147–48, 153–54. Sidney Berger of Milwaukee—a son of the former congressman Victor Berger —stated that Walter White affirmed Du Bois's guilt. The same charge appears in other correspondence in the Du Bois papers, especially that with an insurance man in Milwaukee, a friend of Du Bois's named Lawrence Hautz. Du Bois's pension of $1,200 a year continued from the NAACP until his death.

1951

Friends planned a public celebration and dinner for Du Bois's eighty-third birthday, 23 February 1951. A dinner committee was established with Professor E. Franklin Fraizer as chairman,* Dr. Walter Beekman—Du Bois's dentist for several decades—as treasurer, and Mrs. Alice Burghardt Crawford—a cousin of Du Bois's, who lived in Brooklyn, New York—as secretary. Reservations were made at the Essex House, near Central Park in New York City, and invitations went out.

Meanwhile, as already noted, Du Bois was indicted on 9 February and arraigned on 16 February. On 19 February, four days before the date for the dinner, the Essex House cancelled the reservations with a telegram. The dinner was held at a restaurant in Harlem, jammed to the walls with guests; it was chaired by Frazier and addressed by Bedford Lawson, head of Du Bois's graduate fraternity, Alpha Phi Alpha, and by Paul Robeson. The previously designated speakers—President Mordecai Johnson of Howard, President Charlotte Hawkins Brown of Palmer Memorial Institute in North Carolina, and Rabbi Abba Hillel Silver of Cleveland—all withdrew.†

* Edward Franklin Frazier (1894-1962) was head of the department of sociology at Howard University for many years and was one of the most distinguished sociologists in the United States. Among his noteworthy books were *The Negro Family in Chicago* (1932), *The Black Bourgeoisie* (1957), *The Negro in the United States* (1949, 1957), and *Race and Culture Contacts in the Modern World* (1957). Du Bois had the highest regard for Frazier; correspondence between the two appears several times in the first two volumes of this work. See also the index to Aptheker, *Annotated Bibliography.*

† Charlotte Hawkins Brown (1882-1961) was born in North Carolina and educated in the public schools of Cambridge, Massachusetts, and at Simmons College in Boston. She was founder-principal of Palmer Memorial Institute, serving from 1901 until 1952. Abba Hillel Silver (1893-1963) was born in Lithuania and brought to the United States as a child. He graduated from the University of Cincinnati in 1915 and was ordained a rabbi from Hebrew Union College the same year. From 1917 to his death he was rabbi of The Temple in Cleveland, Ohio. Silver had been a president of the Zionist Organization of America and was president (1945-47) of the Central Conference of American Rabbis. Several of his books found a wide readership, especially, *Religion in a Changing World* (1930) and *Vision and Victory* (1949).

For fuller details on the dinner, see *In Battle for Peace*, pp. 62-68.

Sedalia, North Carolina, February 5, 1951
Gentlemen [of the Dinner Committee]:
   I shall do my best to be present with a ten minute address for the Du Bois testimony for Friday, February 23, 1951.
   Please send an invitation at my request to Dr. and Mrs. A. M. Rivera, 54 Hawthorne Ave., Yonkers, New York.

Gratefully yours,
Charlotte H. Brown

Sedalia, N. C., February 21, 1951
[Telegram]
Mrs. Alice Crawford: Secretary Du Bois Testimonial Committee.
   Immediately following your telephone message important New York Trustee threatens resignation if I appear on Du Bois program. Cannot risk School interest so near the end of my fiftieth year. Great fear of Communist influence. Sorry.

Charlotte Hawkins Brown

Cleveland, Ohio, February 5, 1951
Dear Mrs. Crawford:
   Will you please reserve a room for Rabbi Silver at the Essex House for February 23rd in connection with the testimonial dinner for Dr. Du Bois. Dr. Silver will arrive early in the afternoon and will leave the following morning.

Sincerely yours,
Elizabeth Rice
secretary to
Abba Hillel Silver

Cleveland, Ohio, February 15, 1951
[Telegram]
Dr. E. Franklin Frazier: Du Bois Testimonial Committee
   In view of the unexpected and embarrassing developments I regret that it will not be possible for me to address the Du Bois Testimonial Dinner on February 23. Should you decide to postpone the meeting until the situation is clarified I shall be very pleased to address it then. Kindest regards.

Abba Hillel Silver

It is a pleasure to observe that, on the other hand, the distinguished poet and *author Eve Merriam sent Du Bois a poem, dated 12 February 1951, and signed it "with love and longevity."**

FOR W. E. B. DU BOIS

In California there are giant redwoods,
A car can pass through the colossal trunk;
In Mexico, tourists attend the fabulous tule tree,
Fifty hands cannot span its girth.

Here, in our midst, stands the surest of all,
Tall and unfabled;
Great branches echoing over oceans to Johannesburg, Malaya,
Roots struck deep into Louisiana bayou,
Forcing through the rock of city slum.

Mightier, unwavering as it grows,
Tears and tempests only nourish.
Nothing can stunt this growth.
Behold, below, the pygmy mounting atomic stockpile,
Remains a pygmy.

While higher, and rising higher
Our freedom tree;
Has no winter,
No leafless bough,
No April daring now sighing down to a dusty November wind.
Constant creator,
Green archway to the future
Beckoning—

Surrounded with our love and labor,
Nothing can cut it down;
Not the lyncher's knife nor the bayonet greased by gold.
Scatter its fruit wide,
Raised above heaven,
Bearing the seed beyond the stars,
Level with humanity itself,

* Eve Merriam was born in 1916 in Philadelphia. In 1946 she won the Yale Younger Poet's Award and in 1949 the Collier's Star Fiction award. Her *Inner City Mother Goose* (1969) and *Double Bed* (1972) have been widely read, as has *Growing Up Female in America* (1971), which she edited. She is also a leading writer of children's books.

With our hands in working brotherhood:
Oh blessed be
This flowering tree of life,
Our topmost tower
Of peace!

*Du Bois very much valued courtesy; he also practiced it, and his letter to
Frazier, who had chaired the testimonial dinner, is illustrative.*

New York City, April 11, 1951

My dear Dr. Frazier:

I have waited already too long to say the word of thanks due you for your
courageous stand in my defense. Shirley and I, after the dinner, hastened off to
the West Indies and took four weeks of complete rest. I am very glad we did.
We have lost some time, but nevertheless we have renewed strength and clear-
ness of thought.

Ordinarily the stand such as you took was what could be expected of any
American and particularly of any educated Negro. It happened however that
the number of people with guts and ordinary clarity of thought was astonish-
ingly small among both black and white. That made your stand all the more
fine and creditable.

I thank you for it very deeply. You may suffer some, but I do not think that
in the long run you will find anything but praise and approbation among people
who think and know. I shall want to see you as soon as possible and have a
long talk.

We are still in of course for the rather nasty fight in the matter of this indictment, but we are going to fight to the end. It's a big opportunity and I am
willing to go to jail in order to make the courts face the issue and make the
United States and especially Negro Americans know what they are up against.

With the deepest appreciation of your work.

Yours very sincerely,

W. E. B. Du Bois

*Milton Morris James of Philadelphia, an art historian, was interested in writing
an account of his friend, the Black painter Laura Wheeler Waring (1887-1948).
Mrs. Waring had frequently spoken of Du Bois and his influence upon her;
hence James wrote Du Bois in January and again in April 1951 requesting information. Du Bois's response not only offered some of the requested information but presented a fine vignette of himself.*

New York City, April 10, 1951

My dear Mr. James:

There is not much that I can do to help you in the case of Laura Wheeler Waring. If I had time to go through my letter files, perhaps I could find some letters, but I am so harassed with business just now that I cannot do this.

I knew Laura Wheeler for twenty-five years or more. I did not see her often or long, but always once or twice a year as I came through Philadelphia, we met and had talks and compared notes. I was particularly interested in her art work.

Then when she went to Cheyney, I saw a little more of her because I was there quite often as a guest of Principal [Leslie P.] Hill and his wife. I remember particularly an incident which happened there: they were having an afternoon reception for the students and faculty and Laura and I were sitting there when the orchestra struck up an unusually pleasant tune. I asked her to dance. She looked at me a little startled at first and then rose and we began to waltz. There was, if I remember correctly, at first a little flurry and then others began to dance and even Principal Hill joined us. I afterward learned to my astonishment that this was the first time there had been any public dancing in Cheyney. After that the custom of dancing kept up.

I knew Mr. Waring through his sister, Nora, who is a good friend of mine and I was pleased when the union between Laura Wheeler and Mr. Waring took place.

Laura wanted to paint my picture, but I was so busy at Atlanta that I could not sit, but sent her a number of photographs, and from them she painted a portrait. She also copied the portrait of Frederick Douglass which I have and the copy was very successful. Then as time went on, I lost contact with her and did not see her more than once in two or three years. The news of her death took me by surprise. I am sorry that I did not see more of her during her last years.

I think that her painting was conscientious and good and that it will live in the history of art. As I have said, this is very little to contribute to your work, but I will try to look through my files in the next few months and see if I cannot come across letters and documents which will help further.[1]

Very sincerely yours,
W. E. B. Du Bois

From the days when Du Bois's mother sang him to sleep with an African lullaby,

1. Milton M. James wrote about Laura Wheeler Waring in the *Negro History Bulletin* 19 (March 1956):126–28 and 22 (October 1958):16. Her work is represented in the collections of the National Archives and the National Portrait Gallery. Mrs. Waring was head of the art department of Cheyney State Teachers College in Pennsylvania at the time of her death.

throughout the rest of his life, Africa was seldom out of his mind. At the end of
October 1951 he wrote to Padmore.

New York City, October 27, 1951

My dear Padmore:

I am glad to learn through Miss Citron that you are back from West Africa.[1]
I am hoping to hear from you soon.

I am sure that Africa today, more and more, is wheeling into the center of
world thought and activity and that we ought to be correspondingly aware. I
did not know of Nkrumah's visit to the United States until too late. Even if I
had known, I doubt if I could have gotten in touch with him. Through British
connivance, the State Department held him almost incommunicado while he
was in this country. Many of his friends could not get in touch with him. I had
planned to have a confidential talk with him concerning a sixth Pan-African
Congress in West Africa and concerning a Declaration of African Independence. Finally, I heard from you and learned that you were on the way to West
Africa. There again I wish I had a chance to send messages by your hand. You
will, of course, have a great deal of information and many proposals which I am
waiting to hear with interest.

I have heard expressed from Africa and other sources some rather serious
doubts of Nkrumah's integrity. One correspondent writes: "The government
here led by Kwame Nkrumah is no longer a resistance movement nor a revolutionary people's movement since the leaders have been captured thru luxury
and flattery. It never really was much despite a lot of foreign propaganda, most
of the Cabinet leaders being vile self-seekers who want to get rich quick. This is
a great disappointment for us as a people but there is hope that the masses will
soon see thru all this."[2]

I am enclosing a proposed Declaration of Independence for your criticism.

One thing that we need here and must have is authentic information direct
from Africa. There is no doubt but what African mail to America is tampered
with. Letters do not reach their destination. We can keep up with occurrences
in British West Africa, and with some difficulty, in French West Africa. We
can get no information from the Sudan or Uganda or Portuguese Africa, very
little from Kenya and Tanganyika, something but not much from Nyasaland,

1. He refers to Alice Citron, executive secretary of the Du Bois Defense Committee.
In 1950 she was summarily dismissed from her position as a public school teacher—she
had taught in Harlem for eighteen years—because she refused to respond to red-baiting
inquiries. Du Bois writes of her effective work on the defense committee in his *In
Battle for Peace*, p. 94.

2. Du Bois is quoting from a letter, marked "confidential," sent to him from Kumasi,
the Gold Coast, on 27 August 1951; the writer of the letter was Dr. R. G. Armattoe—
the physician invited by Du Bois from his (then) Irish research station to attend the
1949 Waldorf Peace Conference.

the Rhodesias and the protectorates, nothing from the Belgian Congo. A good deal of information comes from the Union of South Africa but nothing from Southwest Africa. We ought to get all of these areas together with the United States and the Caribbean into a mutual exchange of information and thought. I hope we can do so.

Best regards from myself and wife to you and Mrs. Padmore.

Sincerely yours,
W. E. B. Du Bois

1952

Early in 1952 Du Bois put a question to Arthur Shutzer, the executive secretary of the American Labor party in New York, which evoked a reply he had not expected.

New York City, January 24, 1952

Dear Mr. Shutzer:

Do you remember the number or proportion of votes cast for me in Harlem in the senatorial campaign of 1950?

My impression is that my candidacy did not make much impression on the Negro vote; that the machines of the Republican and Democratic parties held their following pretty well.

If you can give me some figures on this matter, I shall be obliged.

Very sincerely yours,
W. E. B. Du Bois

New York City, January 28, 1952

Dear Dr. Du Bois:

In reply to your letter dated January 24, 1952, I am pleased to set forth below the official tabulation of votes cast in Harlem in the senatorial campaign of 1950:

DR. W. E. B. DU BOIS (ALP)	7,344
JOE R. HANLEY (Republican)	10,262
HERBERT H. LEHMAN (Democratic)	35,232
HERBERT H. LEHMAN (Liberal)	4,750

The vote for you was approximately 12.6% of the total vote cast in Harlem for the office of U.S. Senator.

The official tabulation of votes cast in Harlem in the *gubernatorial* campaign of 1950 is as follows:

JOHN T. MCMANUS (ALP)	5,393
THOMAS E. DEWEY (Republican)	19,241
WALTER A. LYNCH (Democratic)	31,885
WALTER A. LYNCH (Liberal)	3,704

The vote for Mr. McManus was approximately 8.9% of the total vote cast in Harlem for the office of Governor.

I shall be pleased to furnish any additional information you may desire.

Sincerely yours,

Arthur Schutzer

On 31 January 1952, Du Bois was asked by the World Council of Peace, in a letter signed by two of its officers—the Frenchman Jean Lafitte and the American Reverend John W. Darr, Jr.—to represent it at a planned meeting scheduled for Rio de Janeiro in Brazil later that year. As a result, Du Bois applied to the State Department for permission for Mrs. Du Bois and himself to travel to Brazil. From Ruth B. Shipley came the official response—dated on Lincoln's birthday, not then a holiday in Washington.

Washington, D.C., February 12, 1952

My dear Mr. Du Bois:

The Department has received your recent application for a passport for travel to Brazil accompanied by your wife, Mrs. Lois Shirley Graham Du Bois.

The Department has given careful consideration to your request. However, since it appears that your proposed travel would be contrary to the best interests of the United States, a passport is not being issued to you.

The sum of $9.00, which accompanied your application, will be returned to you at a later date. The passport which was issued to Mrs. Du Bois on April 5, 1949, is being retained in the Department's files.

Sincerely yours,

R. B. Shipley

Chief, Passport Division

Du Bois favored independent political activity throughout his life. After World War II he believed that such activity would have to be conducted outside and in opposition to the two major parties: Hence his support of Henry Wallace in 1948 and his own candidacy, on the American Labor party ticket, for United States Senator in 1950.* Du Bois sent a letter reflecting this position to the distinguished Chicago attorney Earl B. Dickerson. Dickerson, then visiting in Los Angeles, was an officer in the Liberty Life Insurance Company, whose president was Truman K. Gibson.

* For Du Bois's account of this aspect of his life, see his essay, "From McKinley to [Henry] Wallace: My Fifty Years as a Political Independent," *Masses & Mainstream* 1, no. 6 (August 1948):3-13.

New York City, February 12, 1952

Dear Mr. Dickerson:

I had just written you a letter to Chicago, when Beanie [C. B.] Baldwin tells me that you may be in Los Angeles. I cannot send you a copy of the Chicago letter because I wrote it in a hurry myself, and made no copy, but this is the gist of what I said:

You know, of course, that at the meeting of the Executive Committee of the Progressive Party last Sunday, the candidates chosen for the next campaign were Hallinan and Dickerson. No publicity would be given to this until we get your consent. I am writing to urge that you give this consent.

I know that it is asking a good deal to demand that a person like you stick your neck out in these difficult times, but I have a feeling that you will not lose by this. A vast change is coming in the United States, not necessarily next fall, but within five or ten years, and the people who have dared to stand up and be counted, and especially those who enter the front ranks, are going to get deserved popularity.

Moreover, in this case I do not believe you could lose anything. Your place is established. It is not yet a crime to run for office even in the Progressive Party. The campaign will give you wide publicity. Of course, there is the difficulty of Hallinan's possible sentence to jail, but even this may be avoided, or if not, have a good effect on the campaign.

Of course, there is one matter of which only you can judge, and that is the effect of this campaign upon your private fortunes. I am, however, disposed to think that in the case of the Liberty Life Insurance Company, men like Gibson may have sense enough to see that it would be good business to be on the side of the workers and the progressives, rather than stick to reaction and Big Business.

At any rate, I am writing to urge you to take this designation. Of course I could not take it myself, even if physically I could stand the campaign at 84, which is doubtful. Politically it would only bring ridicule upon the party to nominate so old a man. Many would be sure that the party was not sincere.

Moreover, if you are not designated, perhaps with mistaken zeal some man would be nominated because of his color who has not the qualifications or the character. This is a real danger.

Please think this over and wire me an address where you can be reached by telephone.[1]

Very sincerely yours,
W. E. B. Du Bois

1. Dickerson did not accept the nomination. There is no written reply to this letter in the Du Bois papers; Dickerson probably communicated with Du Bois via telephone or in person. Vincent Hallinan, the well-known San Francisco attorney, was the candidate for president on this ticket; for vice-president, the Progressive party in 1952 nominated—for the first time in history— a Black woman, Mrs. Charlotta Bass, an

When the Canadian Peace Congress held a national conference for peace in Toronto, 10-11 May 1952, its secretary, Mary Jennison, invited Du Bois to speak.

New York City, April 30, 1952

Dear Miss Jennison:

The [American] Peace Crusade is going ahead with arrangements for myself and Mrs. Du Bois to go to the Canadian Peace Congress.

I am writing, however, to warn you that the United States Government may try to prevent our going.

We are planning to go by plane, and it would be well for you to make arrangements beforehand to see that there are no obstacles to our coming so far as the Canadian Government is concerned.

You will be notified later as to the time we start and the airline.

Very sincerely yours,
W. E. B. Du Bois

Canadian officials—probably at the suggestion of Washington—met Dr. and Mrs. Du Bois at the Toronto airport and prohibited their entry into Canada; they were required to take the next available plane back to New York City. Thoughtfully, Du Bois had sent along a tape of his remarks for just this contingency, and the tape was played at the meeting.

Burlington, Ont., Canada, May 12, 1952

Dear Dr. Du Bois,

I am one of the nearly eight thousand people who attended the Peace meeting at which you were to speak yesterday.

Please be assured there was an outpouring of indignation and sadness with regard to the appalling treatment meted out to you and your wife at Malton airport on Friday.

I am ashamed and alarmed for Canada!

The ovation given at every mention of your name, and especially when your recording was played, I hope will be some small consolation to you—it was inspiring and heart warming.

---

editor and publisher of the *California Eagle* in Los Angeles and a well-known civil-rights leader. Hallinan was jailed early in the campaign on an income-tax charge.

Remarks by Hallinan and Bass and the text of a speech by Paul Robeson at the national convention of the Progressive party, held in Chicago, 4 July 1952, are given in *Masses & Mainstream* 5, no. 8 (August 1952):9–14. Du Bois delivered the keynote speech at this Chicago meeting; major portions of his address were published in the *National Guardian*, 10 July 1952. A Du Bois essay, "The Negro Voter and the 1952 Elections," appeared in the 11 September 1952 *National Guardian*.

We saw through tears . . .

Through the hopeless fog and despair of the day, men like you and Dr. Endicott shine like beacon lights.[1]

Long may you continue to light the way! You are truly man's best hope.

God Bless you!

With warm regard

Sincerely,

(Mrs.) Ivy Stoetzer

Early in June 1952 the National Institute of Arts and Letters, of which Du Bois was the first and only Black member, issued a statement assuring all proper authorities that it was not a Communist organization. Other groups—the American Historical Association, for instance—were doing the same thing; city educational systems, including New York's, were banning the Nation; *library systems were forbidding the circulation of* Robin Hood; *and when people were asked, in the mid-West, to sign a petition whose words consisted of the Declaration of Independence, many refused on the grounds that it was Communist propaganda. Such was the moment for an exchange between Du Bois and the president of the institute.*

New York City, June 23, 1952

My dear Mr. Moore:[1]

I have pondered over your letter of June 4, 1952, and am constrained to write to you simply to relieve my feelings, and not in expectation of any action or reply on your part.

The second paragraph of your letter says:

"I can assure you that any suggestion that the Institute or Academy has been infiltrated or controlled by Communists or engaged in subversive or other like activities is without any foundation."

The third paragraph adds:

"I firmly believe that any fair investigation will disclose that there never has been the slightest evidence of any communist or other insidious influences operating in our organization at any time in its long history."

Nevertheless you also declare that "we as creative artists can state with pride that the Institute and the Academy stand for unswerving devotion to American

1. The reference is to James G. Endicott, chairman of the Canadian Peace Congress.

1. Douglas Stuart Moore (1893–1969) was the president of the institute from 1946 to 1953. A composer and college professor, Moore was born in Long Island, New York, and educated at Yale. He was a member of Columbia University's department of music for many years and in 1951 received the Pulitzer Prize in music. His books, *Listening to Music* (1932) and *From Madrigal to Modern Music* (1942), remain in print.

traditions of freedom and democracy," and that our purposes are "the furtherance of the interests of literature and the fine arts."

It seems to me that you are calling a belief in Communism an insidious influence, and are asserting that all believers in Communism are "engaged in
subversive or other like activities."

Would it not have been a much fairer statement in accord with traditions of
freedom and democracy to have said that the Institute and the Academy are
not trying to control the thought or opinions of their members; that the very
tradition of freedom and democracy allows and should allow a person perfect
freedom of thought? If in any way his consequent action becomes illegal, he is
subject to punishment by law, and that is no concern of these institutions.
Neither do these institutions assume the right to call any honest opinion insidious, no matter how much its various members disagree with it.

In other words, I am neither defending nor attacking Communism, but I do
think that for an organization like the National Institute to hand the red-baiters
of this era an opportunity to see that these organizations for freedom of opinion
are willing to curtail such freedom when it comes to a great line of thinking
like Socialism and Communism, is unworthy of our objects and ideals.

Very sincerely yours,
W. E. B. Du Bois

New York City, July 2, 1952
Dear Dr. Du Bois:

My reference in the letter of June 4, 1952 to the absence of Communist infil-
tration or influence in the Institute refers to the generally accepted fact that the
Communist Party in the United States has attempted to influence for its own
political purposes various art organizations, and that to the best of my knowledge we have been free from this pressure. We are a non-political organization
and as president I shall do everything in my power to see that we remain so.

The Institute, however, cannot accept responsibility for the beliefs of its
members nor is there any suggestion in my letter that membership in the
Institute imposes any restriction upon freedom of thought. For a society of
creative artists such censorship would be intolerable.

We are an association of American artists and we glory in the tradition of
American freedom and decency. To accept dictation as to what we are to think
and believe is to borrow from the Communist party a principle which violates
the very essence of our national tradition.

Yours sincerely,
Douglas Moore

*A young professor asked a series of probing questions about a formerly signifi-
cant Southern political official; Du Bois's reply was concise and informative.*

Greensboro, N.C., August 22, 1952

Dear Dr. Du Bois:

For the past several years I have been engaged in writing a biography of Hoke Smith, a political leader from Georgia with whose work you are well acquainted. References to Smith in some of your writings lead me to believe that you may have additional information about and impressions of this leader that would be of help to me in the preparation of my biography. I would be most grateful if you would write me as fully and specifically as you are able on this matter. I would especially appreciate your answers to the following questions.

1. Do you feel that Smith deliberately and insincerely took up the cry for disfranchisement in Georgia in 1905-1906, in order to obtain Watson's support and to win votes? (I myself have been unable to find any evidence that Smith was a fanatic on the subject of disfranchisement before the campaign of 1905-1906.)

2. Was Smith more than an ordinary demagogue? Please elaborate as fully on this point as you can.

3. Irrespective of his position on racial questions, what would you say his main contributions were as a political leader? His major shortcomings?

4. Did you ever have occasion to meet Smith or to work with him on any matter? What sort of impression did he make on you? What personal qualities of the man impressed you most strongly?

5. With whom, if anybody, would you compare him as far as the political leaders of his day were concerned? As far as current leaders are concerned?

6. Would you say that Smith was progressive in any way? Did his position on questions of race make it impossible for him to be liberal on all other matters?

I shall appreciate very much your help.

Very sincerely,
Dewey W. Grantham, Jr.[1]

New York City, September 3, 1952

Dear Mr. Grantham:

I am afraid I cannot give you very much information concerning Hoke Smith. I never met him personally and cannot remember ever having seen him,

1. Dewey Wesley Grantham, Jr., was born in Georgia in 1921 and educated at the universities of Georgia and North Carolina. He taught history briefly at North Texas State College in Denton and from 1950 until 1952 was an assistant professor at the Woman's College of the University of North Carolina. In 1952 he went on to Vanderbilt University in Nashville, where he is now professor. The book he was working on when he wrote Du Bois was published as *Hoke Smith and the Politics of the New South* (Baton Rouge: Louisiana State University Press, 1958). In 1973 Grantham edited *The Political Status of the Negro in the Age of FDR* (University of Chicago Press) from the many unpublished manuscripts prepared for Gunnar Myrdal in 1940 by a team headed by Ralph J. Bunche.

but I lived in Atlanta from 1896 to 1910 and observed his political campaign.

I believe that in that campaign Smith started out to attack the corporations, especially the railroads. The corporations at that time were lawless and deserved severe criticism, but they practically owned Atlanta. There used to be a current saying that the railroads told the city that they were there before the city was, and if the city did not like their actions it could leave it.

Smith's attacks were stinging, and I have no doubt but what he was offered great inducements, certainly for his political future and perhaps inducements of other sorts, to change the direction of his attacks, and that he found that the easiest way to do that was to direct his attack upon the Negro. This brought the support of Watson and his followers, warded off the wrath of the corporations, and made him Governor of Georgia.

But on the other hand, his attack upon the Negro was all the more terrible because it was based on no real conviction, and utterly unlimited by any fear of retaliation. I have never heard a more vicious attack. He held meetings, from which Negroes were excluded, in which he told school directors that in selecting teachers they should select deliberately the poorest trained and most ignorant Negro candidate, rather than the best.

He allowed his own newspaper to lie about Negro crime until he had stirred the lower elements of Atlanta into a frenzy which resulted in the Atlanta riot [of 1906]. I have a feeling that his unrestrained bitterness caused him some qualms after the riot.

Smith was certainly not an ordinary demagogue; he was extraordinary. He had brains, experience, and wide acquaintance, but was absolutely without conscience when it came to his political career. As Georgia was then organized, a politician followed a regular course; member of legislature, member of Congress, Senator, governor. Once out of line in this political career and he was apt to be dead forever. Smith had stepped out of line when he supported the gold standard against Bryan. He paid for reinstatement with the murder of Negroes in the Atlanta riot.

I am afraid that this is as much as I can furnish you.

Very sincerely yours,
W. E. B. Du Bois

Despite repression, Du Bois's writings found fertile ground, and with gratifying regularity he received letters of appreciation. While the National Institute of Arts and Letters was taking the stance just illustrated, a young woman in the Bronx was writing Du Bois.

Bronx, New York, September 15, 1952

Dear Dr. Du Bois,

"Blessed are the peacemakers for they shall be called Communists," you wrote.[1] Well, I write and I hope it comes true, "Blessed are the peacemakers for they shall be justified by History."

I just finished reading your book *In Battle For Peace*, and I remembered with great shame, that a few years ago I refused to sign the peace petition. Ignorance and indifference is the only excuse I can think of. (Also, criminal miseducation as I was attending high school and in four years I had never heard of you.) I, and many others like myself, did not know that you were in danger of being put into jail because of your "radical" ideas. Now that I am aware of the progressive forces (and the P. Party) and I look back and see how long it took me to wake up, I am appalled by the almost impossible task of bringing these ideas to the common, ignorant, indifferent people like myself.

May I thank you for the pleasure I have had in reading your great works of literature?

Thank you

Marilyn O'Toole

New York City, September 23, 1952

Dear Miss O'Toole:

Thank you very much for your kind letter of September 15th.

Very sincerely yours,

W. E. B. Du Bois

In 1952 Arna Bontemps, then chief librarian at Fisk University, inquired of Du Bois about the possibility of his depositing his library and papers at Fisk at some appropriate time. Du Bois replied to this inquiry and—since Bontemps was working on a manuscript treating the lives of Frederick Douglass, Booker T. Washington, and Du Bois—added a note of interest on that matter, too. See below, p. 423 and note, for Du Bois's ultimate arrangements with Fisk.

New York City, November 3, 1952

Dear Mr. Bontemps:

I thought I had already written you about my library, but presume I must have forgotten it.

For a long time my wife, Shirley Graham, has regarded it as her chief object in the world to preserve and arrange my library, and to write a definitive biography on the basis of my books, papers and letters. For this reason we bought a house [in Brooklyn, N. Y.] which is considerably larger than our needs, which has a dry stone basement and other rooms, and there pretty soon my library will be transferred for her use and to an extent the use of the public.

Also, Dr. Herbert Aptheker has already begun a study of my letters and

1. The quotation is from *In Battle for Peace*, p. 160.

papers and probably would have gone through with it if he could have secured the finance from publishers or foundations, but that he has not yet been able to do.

So that you see the future of my library has been provided for at least in theory, and there would be no chance, unless my plans were changed, to deposit it at Fisk University. I appreciate your interest in my collection, and if at any time there are parts of collections that could well go to Fisk, I would certainly be glad to send them.

Also, there is one other matter that Shirley keeps asking me to emphasize, and that is that my career did not end with Booker T. Washington, and if, therefore, you are still working on those comparative biographies I hope you will not either over-stress that earlier part of my career or forget that latter part. There seem to be a considerable number of persons who think that I died when Washington did, which is an exaggeration.

Very sincerely yours,
W. E. B. Du Bois

A young graduate student at Yale, having read Du Bois's In Battle for Peace, *propounded a significant question and thus induced a consequential response.*

New Haven, Connecticut,
December 31, 1952

Dear Sir:

I have read your book, *In Battle for Peace,* with great interest. With your ordeal in the courts I deeply sympathize. I am at the same time ashamed, as an American, to share responsibility for this matter.

At the same time I am incredulous of and concerned about many of the statements in your book. You say on page 28 that the main cause of the unrest and threat of war is American imperialism. I am aware of the fact that America has used its money abroad to gather support for its policies but I do not appreciate the link between this and such facts of disorder as Korea.

Perhaps the major difference between your point of view and mine lies in my belief in many of the analyses of the world situation published by our government and by American newspapers. You imply in your book that American big business controls our government and our press, not to mention other sorts of opinion sources, such as schools, which you imply are also thus controlled. I find it hard to believe that such control is so absolute.

One very disturbing aspect of your book was the several references to the control of American education and research by big business. On page 174 you say, "The realm of scientific enquiry is increasingly limited, with economics tabu, sociology limited, and history strictly conventional." You also mention art. As a budding social scientist and teacher I am not aware of this.

Could you possibly lead me to material documenting your contentions about this control of big business over government, the press and education? Also about the implied conspiracy of big business to colonialize the world at the risk of embroiling this country in a third world war?

Sincerely,

Dean Pruitt[1]

Brooklyn, N.Y., January 6, 1953

Dear Mr. Pruitt:

Your letter of December 31 has been forwarded to me.[1] I feel very strongly that American imperialism financed by Big Business is the cause of our being today the chief world advocate of war. This imperialism started, of course, with the annexation of Hawaii, the Spanish War, and Central and South American investments. It reached its height, however, between the first and second World Wars when many of our industrial leaders who had been prominent in the European cartels were convinced that America was going to succeed the declining British Empire as the leader in colonial imperialism.

This was implemented by our attempt to control China. We were desperately disappointed when China, despite our expenditure of millions of dollars, escaped our control; we are still trying to punish the persons whom we think were to blame for the rise of the New Chinese Republic.

We were strong supporters of South Korea in its determination to extend its rule over North Korea, consolidate our investments there, and expand to Manchuria and China. Indeed, the book by I. F. Stone proves that it was the proposed adventure of Syngman Rhee which caused the present Korean War.[2] Add to this, the book by Carl Marzani, *We Can Be Friends*, for proof.[3]

In addition to this, our investments in Africa are the main support of the present capitalistic control of that country. The money which we have furnished the [D. F.] Malan government of the Union of South Africa is larger in amount than that of the British Empire. Our largest industries have been investing great sums and building large plants in South Africa since the Second World War. We are among the chief supporters of exploitation in the Belgian Congo, and our help to Europe was not so much relief as funds which enabled European

---

1. Dean G. Pruitt was born in Philadelphia in 1930 and educated at Oberlin and Yale. He has been on the faculties at the University of Delaware and the State University of New York at Buffalo; since 1969 he has been director of the graduate program in social psychology at the latter institution. With R. C. Snyder, he edited *Theory and Research on the Causes of War* (1969).

1. Pruitt had sent his letter to Du Bois in care of Masses and Mainstream, publishers of *In Battle for Peace*.

2. *The Hidden History of the Korean War* (New York: Monthly Review Press, 1952).

3. (New York: Topical Books Publishers, 1952). Du Bois wrote the foreword.

capitalists to maintain their power against labor organizations, to make profitable new investments for themselves, and later to arm themselves for a Third World War.

Finally, the control of our government by American Big Business reveals itself in Mr. Eisenhower's appointment of cabinet officials who represent Big Business almost exclusively. Government subsidies of universities today make them subservient to government policies, while government policies follow Big Business. No university president would dare to attack current business methods as they did during the administration of Theodore Roosevelt. On all the trustee boards of the universities and institutions of research and philanthropy Big Business is prominently represented, if not in complete control.

The fact that the Morgan banking interests own the *Saturday Review of Literature* must surely indicate to you the interest of Big Business in literature;[4] while distribution of news by papers, periodicals, radio and television is owned by Big Business and directed in the interests of its propaganda.

This line of reasoning is not an attack upon American initiative, technology or business organization. It is simply making it clear where the power lies today, how it is being used, and what we must do if we are going to escape making the main objects of our nation private profit rather than the uplift and progress of our social institutions.

I think that this is as much as I have time to give you as a general indication of my line of thought. You will, I am sure, have no difficulty in documenting this argument further.

> Very sincerely yours,
> W. E. B. Du Bois

---

4. In 1953 the president of Saturday Review, Inc., was Harrison V. Smith, executive vice-president of the Morgan Guaranty Trust Company. The chairman of the board of *Saturday Review* was Everette Lee De Golyer, then a leading oil geologist and producer, who held executive positions on Amerada Petroleum Corporation and Amerada Refining Corporation; the banker for the Amerada corporations was Dillon Read and Co.

An important letter dealing with Du Bois's classic, The Souls of Black Folk, *came to me early in 1953.*

Seattle, Washington, February 27, 1953

Dear Mr. Aptheker:

Shirley and I have had fifteen days of perfect sunshine in California; I have spoken eight times and Shirley eleven, to very sympathetic audiences, on "Africa" and on "Peace." We are now ending with talks in Seattle and Portland. We reach New York, March 5.

In Los Angeles, a friend gave me a copy of *Souls of Black Folk*. I have had a chance to read it in part for the first time in years. I find in chapters VII, VIII and IX, five incidental references to Jews. I recall that years ago, Jacob Schiff wrote me criticising these references and that I denied any thought of race or religious prejudice and promised to go over the passages in future editions. The editions however succeeded each other without any consultation with me, and evidently the matter slipped my mind.

As I re-read these words today, I see that harm might come if they were allowed to stand as they are. First of all, I am not at all sure that the foreign exploiters to whom I referred in my study of the Black Belt, were in fact Jews. I took the word of my informants, and I am now wondering if in fact Russian Jews in any number were in Georgia at that time. But even if they were, what I was condemning was the exploitation and not the race nor religion. And I did not, when writing, realize that by stressing the name of the group instead of what some members of the [group] may have done, I was unjustly maligning a people in exactly the same way my folk were then and are now falsely accused.

In view of this and because of the even greater danger of injustice now than then, I want in the event of re-publication [to] change these passages. How this can best be done I am not sure; but I am going to think it over and when I return, I hope you will have some suggestions. The passages which I have noted are on pp. 126, 127, 132, 133 and 170. I think there was one other, but I have not yet found it. Please think this over and give me your advice.[1]

Our love to you, your wife and daughter from both of us,

Sincerely yours,

W. E. B. Du Bois

1. This letter was part of Du Bois's preparatory work for the fiftieth anniversary edi-

One of the leading Communists victimized by the McCarthy witch-hunting
was V. J. Jerome, a member of the party's national committee; editor of Political
Affairs, *its theoretical organ; and a poet, playwright and novelist. Jerome was*
jailed shortly after Du Bois wrote the ensuing letter to Dashiell Hammett, and
served two years. He died in 1965. Dashiell Hammett, the distinguished author,
was chairman of a committee to defend V. J. Jerome and in that capacity had
written to Du Bois reminding him of a dinner in Jerome's honor to be given in
New York City on 20 March 1953.

New York City, March 9, 1953

Dear Mr. Hammett:

I have your reminder of the Jerome dinner.

I have just returned from a trip of about 7000 miles to the Pacific coast where
I delivered ten lectures on Peace and Revolt in Africa.

I do not think that I should undertake any further public speaking in the
near future, but I have the highest regard for Mr. Jerome and am enclosing a
statement which you may use at the dinner if you think proper.[1]

Very sincerely yours,

W. E. B. Du Bois

[Enclosure]

Of all sins against the Holy Ghost, the stopping of Thought, the silencing of
the Thinker is the worst. The Thinker may be wrong and often is; Thought
may mislead and has often done so. But with all, in the end, Thought rights
itself, and for human kind there is no other way but logical thinking to approach the stars; than this there is no surer salvation.

But too, and here rests the hope of mankind, the Thinker may be right; and
on the Truth and Beauty which he has during eternal years revealed, has been
built the civilization of Man. At long last Thought must be right or there is
neither Right nor Hope for Mankind.

---

tion of *The Souls of Black Folk*, published in October 1953 by the Blue Heron Press
of New York City, owned by Howard Fast. In response to Du Bois's suggestion, I
spoke with him and suggested that the offending passages be changed and that in a
foreword Du Bois state what he was doing and why. After writing this letter to me
and conferring on the question, Du Bois at first decided to let the work stand precisely as published in 1903, with a paragraph containing remarks similar to those in
the letter to me. Sometime during the summer of 1953, however, he changed his mind
and made alterations at seven places for the 1953 edition. In his foreword to this edition he stated that a few changes had been made but did not otherwise identify them
or comment upon them. In his correspondence there were no letters to or from Jacob
Schiff; I think that the exchange with Schiff probably took place in person and not in
letters. For details and further information, see my introduction to the Kraus-Thomson edition of *The Souls of Black Folk*.

1. Du Bois's statement was read at the dinner.

The vicious and utterly unjustifiable persecution of our greatest Marxist philosopher, V. J. Jerome, is more than unjust, it is obscene; it is sacrilegious. It seeks to put back the clock of Progress by crucifying an artist and writer and by punishing his wife and sons in futile effort to keep Truth hidden, and by forbidding a nation to think. This attempt must fail or we, our country and our time fail too.

W. E. B. Du Bois

Du Bois was one of the large number of people forbidden the use of their United States passports on political grounds during the McCarthy era. He had repeated exchanges with Mrs. Ruth B. Shipley, the chief of the passport division of the State Department. Illustrative is an exchange from March 1953; the Shipley letter from which Du Bois quotes is given above, p. 332.

Brooklyn, N.Y., March 28, 1953

Mrs. Ruth B. Shipley
Dear Madame:

When I last applied for a passport in February 1952, I was informed that "your proposed travel would be contrary to the best interests of the United States" and a passport was denied me and my wife.

I write to ask if the State Department is still of the same mind and if, consequently, it would be useless for me to make another application.

You will permit me to remind you that I have held United States' passports since 1892 and my wife since 1927. During that time neither of us has in any way violated the laws of this nation or been convicted of any crime. I have always here and abroad within the limits of the law expressed my opinions and naturally I expect to continue to do so.

I and my wife wish to make two trips:

1. To visit Budapest, April 10, 1953 to attend the meeting of the World Peace Council of which I am a member. The Council proposes at this meeting to present prizes to persons who have worked for peace in the leading nations of the world. I have been nominated as one of these recipients. 2. We wish in October, 1953, to attend the Inter-continental Conference of the Bahai Faith to be held in New Delhi, India.

I would like therefore to know whether or not the State Department has altered its decision of last February, with regard to my right to travel.

I am, Madame,

Very sincerely yours,
W. E. B. Du Bois

Washington, D. C., April 6, 1953

My dear Mr. Du Bois:

The Department has received your letter of March 28, 1953 in which you state that you and your wife desire to travel to Hungary during this month and to India in October, 1953.

You are informed that since May 1, 1952 travel to Hungary has been forbidden to American citizens.

With respect to your proposed travel to India, you may wish to raise that question at a later date. However, if you and Mrs. Du Bois are communists, the Department under the new regulations, copy of which is enclosed, would be obliged to refuse to provide you with a passport. However, the Department would consider the matter when you care to present it. At that time you and your wife should each submit to the Department a sworn statement as to whether you are now or ever have been communists.

Sincerely yours,
R. B. Shipley

Enclosure: Supplement to Passport Regulations.[1]

Letters from Du Bois to either his granddaughter, DuBois Williams, or his daughter, Mrs. Yolande Williams, a high-school teacher in Baltimore, are prime sources for detailed information on his myriad activities. An example is one written from his Brooklyn home in April 1953.

Brooklyn, N.Y., April 20, 1953

Dear Yolande:

I am so sorry that I have neglected writing you for so long. I did not realize, although naturally I have plenty of excuses.

We arrived from the West March 5th. Since then I have had six meetings of my seminar on Africa at the Jefferson School; prepared my income tax returns; spoke at Brighton Beach, at the Stalin Memorial Meeting and at the Warsaw Ghetto meeting; attended the annual meeting of the American-Soviet Friendship Council and a meeting in honor of Paul Robeson by the *New World Review*; appeared on television with Marcantonio and went to a party after-

---

1. The enclosure was a three-page mimeographed document, consisting of title 22, chapter 1, part 51, subpart B, paragraphs 51.135, a, b, c, and 51.136. Taken together, these sections stated that "persons supporting [the] communist movement" were to be denied passports and forbidden the use of passports; there was no definition of "communist movement," and passport authorities could determine that given persons were acting in support of this undefined entity by concluding that "there is reason to believe, on the balance of all the evidence, that they are going abroad to engage in activities which will advance the Communist movement. ..."

ward; written several articles for the *National Guardian* and one for the *Monthly Review* and for *Freedom;* wrote a book review for *Science and Society*.[1]

We have attended the theater twice, the circus once, and several good movies. I was in bed with a bad cold for a couple of days, and have begun again writing on that eternal novel.

In addition to this there has been a little correspondence and a few thousand phone calls. So you see I have an excuse although it is inadequate.

I did write DuBois once and also wrote Dr. Higgins about your health, which worries me a bit. You must plan to get out of Baltimore this summer for a rest. I hope to help you do it when and if the Peace Council prize money comes to hand.[2] I am expecting it some time in May.

We are going to the Bahamas for three weeks, leaving the 26th unless, of course, the United States government should step in, although I do not expect any such trouble.

I hope you will look after yourself, and above all things do not worry. My mother, your grandmother, used to always worry, and our aunts and uncles said that she worried about things that never happened. I perhaps go too far the other way and do not worry when I ought to.

I hope DuBois is getting on reasonably and that the house is still comfortable. At the present writing you are not going to need your air conditioning for some months.

Yours with love,
W. E. B. Du Bois

*Under the provisions of the Internal Security Act of 1950—the so-called McCarran Act—a Subversive Activities Control Board (*SACB*) was established with power to order groups or organizations to register as "Communist" or "Communist-action" or "Communist-controlled." Organizations—which is to say their officers—so registering would then not be subject to penalties under the McCarran Act, but the Smith Act made membership in such organizations a crime subject to ten years' imprisonment!*

*Late in April 1953 Herbert Brownell, the United States attorney general, asked the *SACB* to force the registration of twelve organizations as "Communist-front" groups; this list included the Council on African Affairs, of which Paul*

1. Du Bois led a seminar treating different nations in Africa at the Jefferson School of Social Science in New York City. Articles by Du Bois appeared in the *National Guardian* on 16 March, 23 March, and 6 April 1953; in the *Monthly Review* in April 1953; and in *Freedom* in June 1953. His review of E. S. Sachs, *The Choice Before Us* (New York: Philosophical Library, 1952), appeared in *Science & Society* 17 (Summer 1953):269–70.

2. In January 1953 the World Peace Council awarded its annual prize to Du Bois; the presentation was made in October 1953.

Robeson was chairman, Du Bois vice-chairman, Rosalie L. Pinckney treasurer, and W. Alphaeus Hunton secretary. This was page one news in papers throughout the nation, and the charge and publicity—given the atmosphere in the country at the time—meant the demise of the accused groups. The council managed to exist until 1955, but its battle against registration and the intensely hostile propaganda to which it was subjected did force its closing. Even before Brownell's action, indeed, Hunton (and others) had gone to jail for "contempt of Congress" in refusing to turn over to McCarthy's committee the names of people who had at any time supported or contributed to the Civil Rights Congress Bail Fund.*

Du Bois devoted much time and energy to the battle against this persecution. Indicative is a letter asking for help which he drafted after the Brownell move, and mailed to many people in the United Nations.

New York City, June 18, 1953

Dear_____:

You are, no doubt, aware of the fact that the Council on African Affairs has been forced to take legal steps to defend its right to exist and continue to work for African liberation, as a result of Attorney General Brownell's petition to the Subversive Activities Control Board to order the Council to register as a "Communist-front organization" under the terms of the Internal Security (McCarran) Act of 1950. Through its attorney, Mr. James T. Wright of Washington, our organization has moved for dismissal of the Attorney General's petition and for protection of our constitutional rights in other respects. Oral argument on these motions is now pending.

This action of the Government is one more step in the process of making Americanism synonymous with McCarthyism, of interpreting patriotism to mean conformity to the most reactionary political and social creed, and of meting out punishment to those who dissent from that creed.

For refusing to act as an informer, the Council's secretary, Dr. Hunton, was forced to serve five months in jail. For advocating and working for peace, I was also threatened with jail. And both Paul Robeson and I, and no one knows how many hundreds of others, are denied the right to travel abroad—Mr. Robeson, so the Government argued, because of his "frank admission that he

---

* No history of the council has yet been published. There is some material in the second chapter of Du Bois's *In Battle for Peace* and in his *Autobiography*, pp. 344-47. An article by Doxey A. Wilkerson in *Freedomways* (Third Quarter 1970), in a group of writings by and about W. Alphaeus Hunton, discusses Hunton's work at the council in some detail; and Hunton's "Note on the Council of African Affairs" appears as an appendix on pp. 126-28 of Paul Robeson's *Here I Stand* (New York: Othello Associates, 1958; reprinted ed., Boston:Beacon Press, 1972). Lloyd L. Brown, who is preparing the authorized biography of Paul Robeson, has been helpful in providing information on this point.

has been for years extremely active politically in behalf of the independence of the colonial peoples of Africa . . . [and] the diplomatic embarrassment that could arise from the presence of such a political meddler. . . ." Now, invoking the notorious McCarran Act, the Government aims to inflict still more drastic punishment on the officers of the Council.

Please do not misunderstand me. I make no personal plea to you on my own behalf. Neither do my colleagues in the leadership of the Council on theirs. I write to you because I feel you share my conviction, first, that it is important and essential to defend the right of our organization to continue its work; and, second, that if the Government is successful in its attack upon us and the other organizations whose cases are now before the SACB, the way will have been opened for *legally* imposing fascist thought-control upon *all* organizations and *all* the people of our country.

The Council during the past several months has been collecting funds to aid the people's resistance struggle against Malanism in South Africa. You are probably among those who have enabled us to send more than $2,500 for the support of that cause. It now becomes necessary for us to ask your help in the Council's defense, on this particular front of the people's battle against McCarthyism in the U.S.A.

We are confronted with the necessity of raising at once a minimum of $2000 for immediate legal and other expenses incidental to the conduct of our case before the SACB. We have not the time nor the means for mounting a general public campaign to raise this sum, although we do, of course, intend doing all we can to spread the proper understanding of our case and enlist broad support. We are seeking to raise the $2000 quickly by using this means of asking a few friends to contribute as substantially as possible.

Paul Robeson is now in California on concert tour; that is why his signature does not appear below with mine. But I know that he joins with me in the earnest hope that you will respond generously to this appeal, either individually or in association with other friends, despite whatever heavy obligations you may already have.

Faithfully yours,
W. E. B. Du Bois

P. S. All contribution in response to this letter will be entered in a special Defense Fund account and will be used exclusively for the purposes indicated. Checks may be made payable to me or to Rosalie L. Pinckney, treasurer.

The left-wing weekly paper Tribune *of Sydney, Australia, held its second annual festival in October 1953. In preparation for it, the editors asked Du Bois to send a message appropriate to the paper's interest in furthering the cause of socialism and peace. Du Bois responded and, as was customary with him, used the opportunity to pen very much more than mere formal greetings or good wishes.*

New York City, July 13, 1953

The Editor of the "Tribune"
Dear Sir:

In answering to your kind letter of May 17, 1953, I thank you for your information concerning your second annual festival to be held at the end of October. I should like to greet this meeting with these words:

The day is coming, and it is not far distant, when ordinary intelligent people are going to look upon the world as it revealed itself in the middle of the 20th century, and to ask what possibly could have driven civilized people into the hysteria and near-insanity which characterizes us now. It will be then impossible to explain how people who call themselves Christians or Jews or Mohammedans or followers of the great Buddha, could have persuaded themselves that civilization was going to be preserved and increased and broadened by world war. And yet today an extraordinary number of human beings are depending upon force, and force to the utmost, in order to accomplish what they seem to think will be a new and better world.

In that coming day we shall all know that such an idea was crazy; that neither armies nor navies, atom bombs or unlimited funds are going to remake the human soul; that what we have got to have in this world is a change of heart and of object. We have got to respect our fellow beings no matter what their color or race is, or their history or their present situation. We have got to see that the poverty of the mass of men disappears, that ignorance is eliminated and that disease yields to scientific knowledge. Then, starting upon that foundation, we have got to do justice to human beings without regard to the lines of separation that appear, and we have got, so far as is humanly possible, to give thought and desire the widest freedom compatible with the freedom and progress of all.

I hope that this thought will be emphasized and spread in your coming meeting.

I am,

Very sincerely yours,
W. E. B. Du Bois

Du Bois believed in planning and rational living for individuals and societies. He applied his standards to his own life, including his health. He ate carefully, slowly, and never to excess; he smoked no more than three cigarettes a day; he took care to sleep eight hours out of twenty-four; he exercised; he took vacations; and he regularly visited dentist and physician. Indicative of this aspect of his life is a letter to the Life Extension Institute, to which Dr. Harry J. Johnson

*responded by complimenting Du Bois on his approach to problems of health
and suggesting he consult a particular physician whom Johnson named—a piece
of advice Du Bois did not follow.*

New York City, July 16, 1953

Director, Life Extension Examiners
My dear Sir:

I have your card asking me to arrange for my annual health examination. I
have not answered it yet for this reason:

I have been, as you may know, a visitor to your Life Extension Institute and
Life Extension Examiners for over 30 years; but recently it seems to me that
you are not organized to be of service to me. Your attention and facilities are
chiefly directed to young persons who are sick, and to middle-aged persons
who are in danger from some of our chief diseases of the lungs, heart, and
cancer and so forth.

Now I am not sick, but in my 86th year I need careful and regular advice
concerning senescence. This you did not seem prepared to give. When I visit
your office I am always asked what I am chiefly complaining about, and my
answer is, naturally, that I am not complaining about anything. I am as well as
a person of my age could hope to be. But it does seem to me that in a day when
the number of persons of advanced age is increasing, that you ought to give at
least some attention to their well being. On the contrary, if I say to your examiners that my muscular coordination is not as good as it used to be, or that I
feel some dizziness, they either are not interested or say that this, of course, is
to be expected in old age—which I know perfectly well. But what should be
done to retard the increase of these symptoms they do not say and apparently
they do not know.

Now there is in the world increasing knowledge and experiment concerning
old age. If you are aware of this you ought to be able to give me advice, and if
you are not you ought to gather such knowledge or tell me where I could get
advice of this sort. In that case I should be glad to hear from you and to make
further appointments. Otherwise it would be a loss of time on my part and on
yours for me to visit you.

Very sincerely yours,
W. E. B. Du Bois

*Because Du Bois was forbidden to travel abroad, the award made to him by the
World Peace Council in January 1953 was finally presented to him in October
1953, in a ceremony presided over by his Harvard classmate Robert Morss
Lovett. On this occasion Du Bois read a statement, dated 14 October 1953.*

Mr. Lovett and Friends:

The meeting in Paris in the Spring of 1949, of the Partisans of Peace, now known as the World Peace Council, was the most impressive gathering of human beings which I have ever seen. The high ideal of Peace, after two devastating world wars and in the shadow of a third, was voiced in the swarming hundreds of thousands who thronged the Buffalo Stadium and echoed from far Prague, where Asia met to greet us. Later meetings all over Europe and in Asia and Africa, culminating in the unforgettable Stockholm Appeal against the horror of the Atom Bomb, have made this organization one of the greatest among men, holding high the ideal of release from the worst threat of our day to Civilization.

I am embarrassed when this body of great, learned and self-sacrificing persons regards my few and ineffective efforts for Peace worthy of notice. I know that through me the World Peace Council wishes to express the conviction that the United States of America today more than any other nation is to blame for the terrible danger of continued murder and destruction, and wishes therefore to recognize any word no matter how unheard and unheeded, which has been raised here for Peace. For this reason alone I receive in all humility these tokens of regard for what I have tried to do. Before this brutal Juggernaut of Wealth and Force my words have been fruitless and futile; but at least they have been spoken.

W. E. B. Du Bois

Paul Robeson sent Du Bois a telegram, in care of Dr. Lovett, on this occasion.

Ours is a mighty tradition—one to be forever treasured, ever to be fought for, never to be surrendered. Today evil men supported by those of wealth and power dare to vainly hope that the people of our nation will at last be terrorized and bludgeoned into submission. As at other times in our glorious history, men and women of valor, of endless courage, of deepest wisdom arise to defend us and ours. We are privileged to stand side by side with such a human being, endowed with all the foregoing and more—a matchless poet, a proud son of the Negro people from whom he has sprung—indeed, of all the American people and of all the progressive world. We through him are deeply honored and most important are moved to a higher awareness of our sacred responsibilities in the struggle for peace. All my best, dear Dr. Du Bois, to you and Mrs. Shirley Graham Du Bois on this historic occasion. With you we hold our heads high certain of final victory for a peaceful and abundant world.

Sincerely,
Paul Robeson

Du Bois knew how to enjoy life. As often as duties and opportunities made possible, he attended theaters, concert halls, and circuses. Mrs. Du Bois and he knew Dorothy Parker, joint author of a play which he thought excellent but which had a short run on Broadway. Soon after it closed he wrote to her.

New York City, November 30, 1953

My dear Dorothy Parker:

Shirley and I saw "Ladies of the Corridor" Saturday afternoon.

We thoroughly enjoyed it. It is a sad commentary upon the New York critics of the theater (or upon those who own them) that this magnificent satire did not run at least a year.[1]

Our best regards.

Very sincerely yours,
W. E. B. Du Bois

1. *The Ladies of the Corridor*, by Dorothy Parker and Arnaud d'Usseau, was produced by Walter Fried and ran at the Longacre Theatre on Broadway from 21 October to 28 November 1953. Viking Press in New York City published it in 1954.

1954

Again, a student's question raising significant issues drew a prompt and careful response from Du Bois.

Princeton, New Jersey, February 11, 1954

Dear Dr. Du Bois:

As an undergraduate in the Woodrow Wilson School of Public and International Affairs, I am at present pursuing a study of the complexities and implications of the plural community in the Union of South Africa. In the course of my research I have of course read *Dark Water*, in which you made the following oft-quoted statement:

"... this shameful war ... *is nothing to compare
with that fight for freedom which black and
yellow men must and will make unless their
oppression and humiliation at the hands of the
white world cease* ..." p. 49.

In addition, I have noted your remark of June 2, 1949:

"... the Dark World is moving towards its destiny
much faster than we in this country [now] realize."
p. 10, *N. Y. Times*.[1]

In the context of the above quotations, I wonder if you would assist the thinking of a student who at the moment is plagued by fear of an academic, non-realistic approach to perhaps the most significant problem of our time, *i.e.*, the plural or multi-racial community. Admittedly, throughout all of Africa, the Middle East, and Asia, nationalism, in various forms, is the dominant political and social force. Particularly in the Union of South Africa is this phenomenon in evidence. In South Africa there seems to exist a repressive pseudo-biological nationalism and a gradually emerging counterpoise nationalism. Essentially then, it seems that history is step by step confirming your hypothesis of 1920 cited above. However, Dr. Du Bois, in view of the vast disparity in technological and industrial capacity, and in view of the various international and regional agreements, and finally in light of the frequent, patent dissension within the ranks of "... the Dark World," how realistic is it for one, in this case a perplexed student, to surmise as to the possibility, in the world of today, of a form

1. Du Bois made this remark 1 June 1949 in an interview after his return from the peace congress held in Paris. The bracketed word is in the original source.

of *pan-pigmentism* suddenly bursting forth and precipitating a world conflict? Perhaps this group identification would never adopt violent methods? Perhaps it is a matter of a century or centuries hence? Perhaps the situation in the Union of South Africa will ignite and spread? This student is perplexed. Will you assist him, Dr. Du Bois? He would be indebted to you.

Sincerely yours,
Robert C. Bennett[2]

New York City, February 16, 1954

Dear Mr. Bennett:

I have your letter of February 11th.

In the 19th century I thought, with most people, that progress could only be assured by war. I was convinced that if the black people or the yellow people of the world ever gained their right to freedom it would be through conquest or armed defense against the white European world.

Since then and after the experience of two, virtually three world wars, I have given up that idea. Force is not going to insure progress and no people is going to gain freedom and justice through war. I do not therefore expect, as I intimated in *Darkwater*, a great war of races as prelude to Negro freedom.

On the other hand, unless the determined aggression of the white race is curbed in some way, freedom for the colored races is not now in sight. Probably that curb, however, is coming through the very mistakes of white civilization. The present determination, for instance, of the United States, Britain and France to control Asia, Africa and South America will probably break down of its own weight and out of that, with reasonable commonsense based on science, we will be able to plan a better and more united world.

In short, then, I do not believe that a Pan African movement in Africa based on colored nationalism is going to be the final answer to the present African problems. I do believe, however, that it is going to be the beginning and probably will involve a great deal of bloodshed and misery before this racial effort resolves itself into a new world cultural striving which will bring the African nationalists and the progressive people of the whole world into union and understanding.

Very sincerely yours,
W. E. B. Du Bois

2. Mr. Bennett, in granting permission for the publication of his letter, states that he went on to serve as an officer in the United States Navy, earned a postgraduate degree, and has "undertaken a career in international finance which I now pursue" (letter to the editor from Scarsdale, New York, 14 September 1976). The registrar at Princeton University was helpful in locating Mr. Bennett.

An exchange of letters with Sylvia Pankhurst, editor of the New Times & Ethiopia News, *early in 1954, raised several questions of lasting concern.*

New York City, February 16, 1954

My dear Miss Pankhurst:

I learned from the *New Times & Ethiopia News* that His Majesty, the Emperor of Ethiopia, is going to visit the United States in May.

I am aware and I know you are, that every effort will be made by the United States Government to see that His Majesty does not come into close contact with American Negroes or have any opportunity to consult with them. This had been the case in many instances. When, for instance, the Ethiopian delegation of prominent citizens visited the United States in the '20's they were so guarded and hemmed in that few of us got a chance to see them.

This is of course unfair. There are in the United States fifteen million persons of Negro descent, and some of us have long been interested in Africa, and Ethiopia as its greatest Negro representative. The Pan African Congresses which I inaugurated and which are to a large extent responsible for the present aspirations of Africans toward nationhood, included Ethiopia from the first. One of the delegates to the meeting in 1919 was the former physician of the Emperor Menelik.

In the present instance when the Emperor visits this country, there ought to be opportunity and occasion for some of us at least to meet him and make known to him our situation and objects.

There are two Negro Congressmen, there are a score or more members of the Legislature. There are several high-placed judges. The chances are that they will be entirely ignored unless the Emperor should express some wish to meet Negro Americans. In that case, there are two Negro Americans mentioned in the British *Who's Who,* perhaps half a dozen in the International *Who's Who,* and a dozen or more in *Who's Who in America.* They ought to be among those invited to meet the Emperor. And on the other hand we ought to guard against the natural pushing forward of persons who want to approach him for personal, unimportant reasons.

I venture to put this before you and ask you to bring this matter to the attention of His Majesty. I realize that it is a delicate matter and that perhaps nothing can be done or could be attempted. But I would not feel that I had done my duty unless I brought the question up.

The present attitude in America is to make it impossible for American Negroes to express themselves concerning their situation unless they confine their remarks or writings to fulsome praise of the United States.

I hope I may hear from you on this matter.

Very sincerely yours,
W. E. B. Du Bois

Essex, England, February 26, 1954

Dear Mr. Du Bois:

I will write to the Emperor mentioning to him the matter you refer to, but perhaps I might mention to you that Ethiopia does not recognise the term "negro" as applied to the whole African people, and regards it as rather an Americanised version of the matter. The term African is greatly preferred and Ethiopia is very keen on her own name, Ethiopia, which dates back to before the Christian era, and is prized on that account and on account of Biblical references. In ancient times it was applied to all people of dark colour, both Africans and even Indians by the Greeks and probably by others. This is of course only a small matter in a sense, though not to Ethiopians who are much impressed by the Biblican references to Ethiopia and certain claims based on them. I think myself that Mr. [Edward] Lawson is not wrong in referring to the negroes of America as Afro-Americans, for I believe the term Negro can only apply to one part of Africa and the Africans in America have come from many parts.

It is just like the terms Copts and Coptic, which is applied generally by foreigners to the Ethiopian Orthodox Church, but to do so is not at all correct; the Ethiopian Church is now independent, and in any case, Alexandrine would have been a more correct term because the Copts are definitely a certain people who inhabit Egypt, and the term Coptic has nothing whatever to do with Ethiopia.

Africa has its many peoples, just as Europe and Asia have, and I would not suggest that any have the preference, but at the same time I think it wise to inform you that Ethiopia does not welcome the name Negro, not because she wishes to cast any slur on the Negro of America or of Africa, but because it does not seem to appear to be correct as applied to Ethiopia and appears to be a foreign term given by the Americans and probably the British before them to all Africans whom they took to America.

It is just like Eritrea. The name was invented by the Italians, and though it persists at present it will probably die out and the old name Hamasein will be substituted. The people of what we used to call Persia now call their country Iran and this sort of change is bound to be made when peoples become free of the countries which, for a time in their history, dominated them. European domination of all these peoples will, in time to come, be realised to have been but a brief incident in their long, long history.

Having concluded these remarks, I promise you that I will put the matter to his Imperial Majesty, and I am sure he will do what he can to meet the desire of the Afro-Americans, or Negroes, if you prefer to call them so.

You will remember that Ras Imru was very helpful in expressing his disapproval of the colour bar, and so far as the hospitality accorded to the Emperor will allow him to be free to dispose of his time, I am sure he will do his best in the same direction. Of course it may not be quite so easy as would be the case were he going to America just as a tourist and not as the guest of the President, but if he has any freedom of movement at all and if he is there long enough to make arrangements for himself, I am sure he will act on the lines you desire.

Yours sincerely,

E. Sylvia Pankhurst

On 10 March Du Bois sent a letter, telling of the disastrous impact of McCarthyism upon intellectual, cultural, and political freedom in the United States, to leading personages of his acquaintance in many parts of the world. Sylvia Pankhurst was among those replying.

Essex, England, March 15, 1954

Dear Mr. Du Bois:

I have just received your letter dated March 10th. I share your anxiety, and in the course of a few days will decide what to do and to whom to write.

I would add, however, that in view of the present situation in Kenya I feel that we British are not really in a very good position at the moment for criticizing other people's governments, as we have such a mess-up in a territory for which we are responsible!!! See *Kenya; the History of Two Nations* shortly to be published.[1]

I was very much struck by the fact that the great Einstein, having escaped persecution in Germany, is now being attacked by McCarthy for his opposition to Franco who was financed by the odious Mussolini in his rise to power.

With all good wishes.

Yours sincerely,

E. Sylvia Pankhurst

New York City, March 31, 1954

My dear Miss Pankhurst:

I thank you for your letters of February 26th and March 15th. I have been out of my office for three weeks on vacation in the Caribbean.

The adoption of the name "Negro" as a group designation by American Negroes was a result of long controversy and misunderstanding. We know that it is not, of course, the logical name for the darker Africans or even for Americans of African descent, but in order to clarify our statements and be able to discuss these groups without misunderstanding it was necessary to agree upon some name for the people who now number over fifteen million in this country.

In the earliest days they called themselves Africans, but of course their children and grandchildren were not Africans. They used the word "colored" but that referred mainly to mixed bloods and was not applicable to those of unmixed descent. Hyphenated words like "Afro-American" are awkward.

1. Richard K. P. Pankhurst, *Kenya: The History of Two Nations*, with a foreword by Frida Laski (London, Independent Publishing Co., 1954).

Then there was another reason for adopting the word "Negro." Analogous to the use of the word "Quaker" in England, "Negro" and "nigger" were used in America as terms of contempt. The word "Negro" was not capitalized. We therefore determined to make it respectable, and today all official publications and nearly all authors capitalize the word, and when it is used in America the meaning is perfectly clear.

On the other hand it is quite understandable that the word which came into use in America and in connection with slavery would not be suitable for Africans of today and we naturally have no desire to insist upon or expect its use. The one point that we want to emphasize is that the darker peoples of Africa and the Americas who are descended from African slaves belong to a group which is not only unified by descent but by its relation to the white European world; that on that account it has common problems and should try to come into close touch, understanding and cooperation.

Names, of course, are important but seldom logical or historically accurate. Their use is a matter of convenience and precision, and only by recognizing this can we make ourselves clear in argument and exposition.

I am very grateful for your willingness to bring the existence of our fifteen million people to the attention of the Emperor of Abyssinia and also for your offer to do something to help the American people in their present oppression by the Smith Act.

Very sincerely yours,
W. E. B. Du Bois

As part of his work on what became the trilogy The Black Flame, *Du Bois from time to time wrote to individuals who, he thought, might be helpful on some particular point. Correspondence with John Adams Kingsbury brought forth data on Harry L. Hopkins, who had been very influential throughout the administrations of Franklin Delano Roosevelt.* *

New York City, May 6, 1954

My dear Doctor Kingsbury:

I learned that between 1917 and 1921 Harry Hopkins was an official in the Red Cross. He went to New Orleans to direct the Gulf Division, and later became Director of all Red Cross activities in the southeastern states, with headquarters in Atlanta.

* John A. Kingsbury (1876-1956) was born in Kansas and educated at the University of Washington and Columbia and Syracuse universities, from the latter of which he earned a Doctor of Laws. His contribution, however, was in social work, starting with the State Charities Association of New York (1907-11). He was commissioner of public charities in New York City from 1914 to 1918 and during the war was assistant director of general relief in France. During the New Deal he was connected with the Works Progress Administration (WPA).

In this work he must have learned about the Negro problem. Do you have any recollection as to what his reactions were? Did he have any hand in relief from Mississippi floods?

Please do not undertake any research, but if you remember anything pertinent kindly let me know at your leisure.

With best wishes to you and Mrs. Kingsbury.

Very sincerely yours,
W. E. B. Du Bois

Shady, N.Y., May 7, 1954

Dear Dr. Du Bois:

I was in France and Yugoslavia during the time Hopkins was with the American Red Cross, and quite out of touch with him. Soon after my return from World War I, and post-war service in Europe, I rescued Hopkins from the Red Cross!

I persuaded him to return to New York and take charge of Public Health Work under the Milbank Fund. Of course I talked with him about his work in the south, and I am sure he did learn a great deal about the Negro problem. I don't, however, have any specific recollection of his reactions, but I am sure they were what one would expect of a liberal social minded man. If he has been unsympathetic to racial equality, I certainly would remember that.

I have no doubt that he had a hand in the relief from Mississippi floods, and I can tell you who can give you specific information. I refer to Aubrey Williams, Editor of *Southern Farmer*, Montgomery, Ala., whom you surely know. His attitude on the Negro problem is well known. He has recently "stood on the press"—to use a phrase of President Taft!

I regret that, without research, I cannot be more helpful.

Mrs. Kingsbury joins me in kind regards to you and Mrs. Du Bois.

Sincerely yours,
John A. Kingsbury

In her twenty-fourth year the vibrant and brilliant Lorraine Hansberry served as director of special events at Camp Unity, conducted and attended by left-wing people and located in upstate New York. Her initiative provided one of Du Bois's very happy weekends in the generally distressing 1950s.*

* Lorraine Hansberry was born in Chicago in May 1930 and died in New York City in January 1965. She studied at the University of Wisconsin and at the Jefferson School of Social Science in New York City. Her play *A Raisin in the Sun* was first produced on Broadway in 1959; it has since been made into a motion picture and the plot line for the musical play *Raisin*. In 1964 her *Sign in Sidney Brustein's Window* appeared on Broadway, and that same year her book *The Movement: Documentary of a Struggle for Equality* (a text) was published. Other books include *To Be Young,*

Wingdale, N.Y., June 15, 1954

Dear Dr. Du Bois:

With regard to the coming Independence Day weekend, Camp Unity plans
to present a series of memorable and stirring programs in honor of this great
national holiday. To complement the character of the occasion we would be
particularly proud if you would consent to be our guest lawn program speaker,
Sunday, morning, July 4th.

In the event you find it possible to consider this tardy invitation, I think you
would like to know the following specifics: Topically we have conceived of
the program as one which will deal with the most meaningful features of "Our
American Heritage"—before and since 1776. Your contribution would mean a
45 to 60 minute address in the context of a program which in its entirety (address, readings and music) will not exceed one hour and a half. The camp of
course will attend to your travel expenses and to the speakers fee which I
hope you will be good enough to specify in a return communication.

You and Mrs. Du Bois are cordially invited to spend the entire holiday,
Friday evening through Monday, as guests of the camp.

Again, please accept our deep apologies for the tardiness of this request.
Unfortunately matters beyond our control have delayed the planning of many
of the season's activities. May I add that I shall personally look forward to seeing you and Mrs. Du Bois again and truly hope your plans will permit you to
be with us.

With very best wishes, I am

Sincerely yours,
Lorraine Hansberry

New York City, June 22, 1954

Dear Miss Hansberry:

In answer to your letter of June 15th, may I say that I could speak for you
Sunday morning, July 4th. I cannot guarantee that my talk will be "stirring"
but I will do my best, and speak for about thirty minutes, with questions afterwards if wanted.

My fee would be $50 in addition to expenses of travel and lodging for me
and Mrs. Du Bois for the weekend. I am not sure that Mrs. Du Bois will be able
to leave her work so as to come, but it is possible.

Very sincerely yours,
W. E. B. Du Bois

Gifted and Black (1969, 1970) and *Les Blancs: The Collected Last Plays of Lorraine
Hansberry* (1972).

Wingdale, N.Y., June 25, 1954

Dear Dr. Du Bois:

In answer to your letter of June 22nd, we are extremely happy that you have consented to be our guest Lawn Program speaker for July 4th.

Your traveling expenses and fee will be entirely attended to. Accommodations have been reserved for you and Mrs. Du Bois. I do hope she will find it possible to come.

I should like to know, by telephone or note, when you will arrive, and if by train, the hour of arrival. If you come by train you will be met and escorted to camp.

Regarding your references to whether or not your talk will be "stirring," I am altogether certain that your message will more than honor the occasion and that your distinguished presence will in itself be one of the most stirring events in the camp's experience.

The management and staff of Camp Unity look forward to greeting you and Mrs. Du Bois this weekend.

Sincerely yours,
Lorraine Hansberry

New York City, July 7, 1954

Dear Miss Hansberry:

May I tell you how much I enjoyed my stay at Camp Unity.

Please give my best wishes to all of your staff, and especially to your husband who was so very thoughtful in taking care of us.[1]

Shirley and I join in best love.

Very sincerely yours,
W. E. B. Du Bois

Alain Leroy Locke died on 9 July 1954; he had been chairman of Howard's philosophy department for many years and was a leading art, music, and literary critic who—along with Du Bois—fathered the literary renaissance of the 1920s. Du Bois spoke at memorial services for him;* chairing the occasion was Arthur Huff Fauset.†

1. Lorraine Hansberry and Robert Nemiroff were married in June 1953.
* Du Bois's remarks were published in *Phylon* 15 (Third Quarter 1954):251–52.
† Arthur Huff Fauset was born in New Jersey in 1899 and educated at the University of Pennsylvania; he served as a teacher and principal in Philadelphia public schools from 1918 to 1946. Best known among his books are a biography of Sojourner Truth published in 1938 by the University of North Carolina Press and his *Black Gods of the Metropolis,* University of Pennsylvania Press, 1942.

New York City, July 17, 1954

Dear Dr. Du Bois:

You were very kind to come to the services for Alain Locke and bring along with you that fine spirited message so reminiscent of the man who has stirred and directed the mind of youth in particular in our country for so many years.

I know that Alain Locke would have rejoiced. Over and over in these latter years he spoke to me of you in terms of warm appreciation, of support and also endearment. You were one of the few and perhaps the only representative from those who remain of the titans of a former generation who in his estimation had retained that constancy and devotion to inner belief which alone merits the profound respect of intelligent and sincere admirers.

You did all of us a great service with those remarks. If I may speak personally, not only did they cause rejoicing because Alain Locke had carried the torch in his own earnest manner, but as well because we, the people of your race and all the peoples of America and the world have you still with us and your clear voice, still vibrant and assured and wise, guiding us who need guiding as perhaps never so much in the past have we needed it.

God Bless you, Dr. Du Bois.

With warmest regards to you and to Mrs. Du Bois,

Most sincerely yours,
Arthur Huff Fauset

One of the teachers who was most frequently harassed during the Cold War period was the mathematician Lee Lorch. An exchange between him and Du Bois concerns Lorch's problems at Fisk.*

Nashville, Tenn., September 20, 1954

Dear Dr. Du Bois:

As the enclosed materials indicate, IT has happened. Just as the fight for desegregation is moving into high gear on the heels of the Supreme Court decision of last May, some one has decided that I am too great a nuisance to have in this region.

* Lee Lorch was born in New York City in 1915; he was educated at Cornell and the University of Cincinnati. He was on the faculty at City College of New York from 1946 to 1949 and at Pennsylvania State College from 1949 to 1950. From 1950 until his dismissal in 1955 he was a professor and chairman of the mathematics department at Fisk. Thereafter he taught at Philander Smith College in Arkansas until 1958 and finally felt it necessary to leave the United States. Since 1968 he has been a professor at York University in Ontario, Canada. Lorch and his wife Grace, who died in 1974, were active in anti-racist struggles in New York City, in Tennessee (where they were the first white parents to enter their child in an all-Black school after the 1954 Supreme Court decision), and in Little Rock, Arkansas.

I read in yesterday's paper, since Dr. [Charles S.] Johnson does not inform me of these things, that the question of my dismissal from Fisk will be laid before the regular meeting of the Board of Trustees scheduled for October 28th and that, if possible, a special meeting of that Board will be called sooner to consider this question.[1] Good support for my position is developing in the community, among the faculty [and] students. But the morning newspaper, the *Nashville Tennessean,* has been baiting Dr. Johnson with considerable success. Panic seems to have descended upon him and he has done many foolish things. For example, he has issued statements in advance of events and thereby given this newspaper its stories. The afternoon paper, the *Nashville Banner,* a generally reactionary paper by the way, has taken this whole matter very calmly. Interestingly enough, I have received no threatening phone calls (in contrast to what happened after we first raised the question of entering Alice in Pearl Elementary School, previously a Negro School) and there have been no letters to the editor screaming for my blood.

I should be appreciative of any advice and help that you may see fit to render. Petitions are being circulated locally which will be directed to the Board of Trustees and letters from mathematicians at various Institutions who are opposed to witch-hunting can also be expected. Rev. T. B. Brumfield, Professor emeritus of Biblical Literature, has been educating the local alumni to the significance of this issue. He has some considerable hopes of gaining some support from this quarter.

My wife and daughter join me in the very warmest greetings to you and Shirley. We hope that both of you are enjoying the best of health and spirit.

Sincerely,

Lee Lorch

New York City, September 24, 1954

My dear Dr. Lorch:

I am sure you know how deeply I sympathize with you in the attack now being made on you. If there is anything that you think I can do please let me know immediately.

I hesitate to take any action on my own initiative for fear it may do you more harm than good. I am on speaking terms with President Johnson but I opposed his election in the first place and have had little contact with him since, and he has never called on me.

Most of the alumni whom I knew well are dead, and I am not certain as to whether or not any of those living would listen to anything I would say.

1. On 23 November 1954 the board of trustees of Fisk decided not to renew Lorch's contract when it expired in June 1955. On 19 November Lorch had appeared before the House Un-American Activities Committee and had denied that he was a Communist party member, but would not answer any other question. He was cited for contempt by the committee, but the Congress as a whole took no action on the citation.

Despite all this let me know if you think of any action I could take or any letters I could write.

Shirley joins me in very deep sympathy and regards for you, your wife and little girl.

Very sincerely yours,
W. E. B. Du Bois

[Enclosure]

To Whom It May Concern

The dismissal of Dr. Lee Lorch from his professorship at Fisk University would be a calamity. It would be an unwarranted attack upon a man of high character and of learning, and a denial of freedom of thought and expression in a nation founded to protect liberty.

It would be a deliberate attack upon a man who has tried to implement the unanimous decision of the Supreme Court despite the reactionary and fascist forces of the white South.

If the American Negro and particularly the graduates of Fisk University do not stand up and oppose this unwarranted punishment of a man who deserves reward rather than attack, they will do irreparable harm to a great university and to a struggling race.

W. E. B. Du Bois

When the board of trustees at Fisk decided not to renew Lorch's contract, Du Bois wrote to him again.

New York City, December 1, 1954

Dear Mr. Lorch:

I have heard with shame and sorrow of the decision of the Board of Trustees of Fisk University.

I presume we will have to gird ourselves for a bitter attack on progressives in America during these coming years when the United States is compelled to give up the crazy dream of conquering Communism by war. We are going to attempt to conquer ourselves by unprecedented injustice and suppression.

I wish there was something I could do in your behalf. If you think of anything let me know.

Mrs. Du Bois and I join in sympathy and love to you, Mrs. Lorch, and the little girl.

Very sincerely yours,
W. E. B. Du Bois

The author of a pioneering effort in the history of women in the United States had a brief exchange with Du Bois five years prior to the book's appearance.

New York, N.Y., September 20, 1954

Dear Dr. Du Bois:

I am presently working on a history of the women's equal rights movement in this country, and several persons have urged what my own instinct already had suggested—that I seek your advice regarding sources of information on the activities of Negro women in particular.

I live not far from your office, and would deeply appreciate the opportunity to call on you there at your convenience. I am mindful that there are many demands made on your time and energies, and would be as expeditious as possible!

Sincerely yours,
Eleanor Flexner[1]

New York City, September 24, 1954

My dear Miss Flexner:

If you will phone me: MU-3 3855, Ex. 10, and make an appointment, I can see you some afternoon next week.[1]

Very sincerely yours,
W. E. B. Du Bois

An outstanding sculptor in the United States in the twentieth century was the Black woman Meta Vaux Warrick Fuller.* When Du Bois was in Paris in 1900 he met Miss Warrick, then a student in that city, and his admiration for her work remained constant. Late in 1954 the two exchanged letters.

1. Eleanor Flexner was born in New York City in 1908 and was educated at Swarthmore and Oxford; in 1939 her *American Playwrights: 1918–1938* was published (Simon and Schuster). In 1959 Harvard University Press published her *Century of Struggle: The Woman's Rights Movement in the United States.* Its revised, 1975, edition contains much additional material on Black women.

1. In a letter to the editor of 3 September 1976, Eleanor Flexner stated that she did visit Du Bois and asked "whether he thought it was a viable scheme to treat of Black women's history as part of the mainstream of American women's struggles, and to the best of my recollection he answered 'Yes'—period." In his writing, as in his lecturing and conversing, Du Bois rarely used two words if one would do.

* Meta Vaux Warrick Fuller was born in Pennsylvania in 1877 and died in Massachusetts in 1967. She exhibited in Paris in 1898 and her last exhibit was held at the City College of New York the year of her death; her work is part of the permanent collection of museums and libraries throughout the United States. There is an excellent account of her life and work by Sylvia Dannett in *Profiles of Negro Womanhood*, volume 2 of the *Negro Heritage Library* (Yonkers, New York: Education Heritage, 1966), pp. 31-46. Du Bois called attention to her work in the January 1918 *Crisis* (15:133), and a drawing of her appears in that issue on p. 129. Much information on Mrs. Fuller is given in T. D. Cederholm's *Afro-American Artists: A Bio-bibliographical Directory* (1973).

New York City, September 16, 1954

My dear Meta:

The other day my barber, Mr. Meek, told me that he had been in your home in South Framingham and had seen a bust of me. He also said that you were in a sanatorium, but I am writing and hoping that this letter may get to you.[1]

It has been a long time since I have heard of you although I read of the death of Dr. Fuller a year or so ago.[2]

I remember very well our meeting in Paris, and the times when I visited your home in Framingham. I hope that you are able still to enjoy life, as I am.

Specifically I am writing to ask what disposition you plan to make of my bust. Is it for sale? I should so like to have some work of yours.

My wife, Shirley Graham, joins me in love and best wishes.

Very sincerely yours,
W. E. B. Du Bois

Waltham, Mass., September 26, 1954

My dear Dr. Du Bois:

It was a great pleasure to have your letter handed to me a day or so ago and I feel eager to reply.

First of all, I do not recall the visit of Mr. Meek but that is not strange for he was probably visiting my son Solomon. Be that as it may, he did *not* see a bust of you, much as I wish that I had one. All that I have are some photographs which Dr. Fuller made of you—rather successful ones but nothing in sculpture. The only portrait head is one I made of Dr. F. years ago when he was in good health but it could never have been mistaken for one of you.

Sue Bailey Thurman visited me a couple of weeks ago, and expressed a determination to have me do a portrait of Howard Thurman but that is as far as that has gone. She has a way of bringing about what she wants and if she is successful on that issue, well, we may yet be able to produce one of you.

I have a few pieces that you might be interested in seeing but at present my work is scattered about some at home and some in storage with the tenant to whom I sold the studio when I gave up the work.

My very best wishes to you and to Mrs. Du Bois and hope that I may hear again ere long.

Very sincerely yours,
Meta Warrick Fuller

1. He addressed the letter to Mrs. Fuller at South Framingham; she was, however, convalescing from tuberculosis at the Middlesex County Sanatorium in Waltham, Mass.

2. Meta Warrick married Dr. Solomon C. Fuller in 1909; he died 16 January 1953. Fuller, a 1909 graduate of the Boston University School of Medicine, was a neurologist at the Massachusetts State Hospital and, later, a faculty member at the Harvard Med-

Waltham, Mass., Oct. 5, 1954

Dear Dr. Du Bois:

Since my last letter to you it has occurred to me that you might like to have the photographs of "The Slave Ship." In as much as your "Suppression of the Slave Trade," which you wrote long ago, was the inspiration for this subject, it seems fitting that you should possess the four views which I had made some time ago. Of course it is only a sketch about five or six inches high but I originally intended to enlarge it to at least three feet and possibly even more—much more for purpose of exhibition—but this is the best I can do for the present. It is very indistinct, I know, but you know how sketches are, mere problems in composition.

At any rate you may be able to understand it as no one else can and imagine it in grander proportions and proper finish.

Please accept it for what it is and if and when I am discharged from Middlesex "San" "The Slave Ship" will be one of the first subjects I shall attempt to finish.

With best regards to you and to Mrs. Du Bois.

Sincerely yours,
Meta Warrick Fuller

New York City, October 28, 1954

My dear Meta:

I thank you so much for your kind letter of October 5th and the photographs enclosed.

My friend must have mistaken some other bust in your home for me. I could not imagine how you could have done the bust, except possibly from photographs.

I have copies of the photographs which Dr. Fuller took.

I hope this will find you in better health and I should be glad to hear from you at any time.

Yours with love,
W. E. B. DuBois

In October 1954 Du Bois received a letter from a Missouri college student.

Nevada, Missouri, October 31, 1954

Dear Mr. Du Bois:

You are probably quite curious to know who would write to you from a small college in Missouri, of which you have probably never heard, and also why.

---

ical School; he was a pioneer in investigating mental disorders. Du Bois commented upon Fuller's work in the *Crisis* 6 (May 1913):17 and 9 (November 1914):44.

I guess that I myself don't quite know, except that I have recently read two of your books, *Black Men: Then and Now,*[1] and *The World and Africa,* and was deeply impressed by both.

Before I go further into this, I would like to tell you a little about myself. I am a second-year student here at Cottey, a junior college, and was born 18 years ago in Fairmont, West Virginia. This summer I went to summer school at Northwestern University, where I plan to go next year. There I met one of the most wonderful people I have ever met in my life. It isn't usual, I guess, at my age to meet such a person and to fall in love, but I think in my case it was. You see this man is from Mozambique, and is a member of the Tsonga peoples.

For me this experience has opened the door to knowing and understanding half the people of the world, which, even though in my home I had never felt prejudice toward, were still apart from me. I gained an insatiety to read and learn about Africa, its land, its history and its peoples. And this is where your books come in.

Like most people of European descent I had the rather vague notion that Africa was all a land of wilderness, the people were and always had been savages, etc. However, I had always kept an open mind, but I never had filled in the gaps of "Why," "When," and "Where," about Africa.

Your books have indeed helped me to fill in these gaps and to crystalize my viewpoint on Africa. I now realize that there is wilderness in Africa, as there is even in our own country, and if the people are savages, it is due mostly to the effects of slavery and colonization.

I feel a burning shame for all the treacherous exploits of my "fellow" Europeans in their dastardly draining of resources—human and natural—from Africa. "It is sad," my Chinese roommate this year said, "when an inferior culture overruns a superior one."

Your books have made me feel even more strongly about the need for an understanding of Africa in this country, and they have also strengthened my desire to go to Africa, not to share the so-called "white-man's burden," but to try to amend some of the wrongs which my forefathers did.

Now I would like to tell you about my friend. You may have heard of him already. He was the first person ever to come to the u.s. from Mozambique. He went to school at a white university in Johannesburg till Dr. Malan made him leave. Then he went for a year to the University of Lisbon and spent a summer at the Sorbonne in Paris. He came to this country the summer of 1951 and went to Oberlin College in Ohio for two years. Last year and at the present he is at Northwestern working on his doctorate in social psychology.

He has given hundreds of speeches since he came to this country and was a Youth Consultant at the recent World Council of Churches. He is co-author

1. The correct title is *Black Folk Then and Now.*

of "Chitlangou, Son of a Chief," which has been translated into five languages. He himself, Eduardo C. Mondlane, speaks seven.[2]

I know that if you are ever in the vicinity of Chicago, he would enjoy very much talking to you.

Again I want to say "Thank you" for two of the most inspiring books I have ever read. I have been recommending them to all my friends here and I hope they will get as much food for thought out of them as I did.

I hope some day I may have the pleasure of meeting you, Sir, and I would like to say that if you ever pass through Nevada, Missouri this year I would be honored to talk to you.

With hope for the future of Africa, I am

Sincerely yours,
Miss Maribel Meisel[3]

New York City, December 10, 1954

Dear Miss Meisel:

I have your letter of October 31 and am glad that two of my books have meant something to you. There are two more republished in which you may be interested, and [you] probably will find them in libraries. They are *Souls of Black Folk* and *Suppression of the African Slave Trade*.

I am glad to know of Mr. Mondlane, and if he comes to New York I shall be very glad to have him call. The chances of my getting west in the near future are very slim.

With best regards,
W. E. B. Du Bois

An exchange with his friend of many years, Anson Phelps Stokes, reveals something of Du Bois's temperament and humor.

2. Eduardo Chivambo Mondlane was born in 1924. After obtaining his doctorate at Northwestern University, he was employed in research work at the United Nations and in 1961 joined the faculty of Syracuse University. The next year he returned to Mozambique and helped found FRELIMO (Frente de Libertacao de Mozambique); he was elected its president and led the armed struggle against Portuguese colonialism. Mondlane was assassinated in Dar es Salaam in February 1969. In that year Penguin Books published his *Struggle for Mozambique*.

3. Maribel Meisel (b. 1936) was graduated from Cottey College in 1955 and has since received degrees in music from Oberlin, the American Conservatory of Music (Chicago), and West Virginia University. She began in the late 1960s to lecture and publish extensively in musicology. Her assistance and permission to publish her letter are gratefully acknowledged; Adele Ausink of Cottey College also was very helpful in this connection.

Lenox, Massachusetts, November 12, 1954

Dear Dr. Du Bois:

I was pleased to see a few days ago your tribute to our mutual friend the late Alain Locke. It was well deserved. It reminded me of you and of the days when we worked together on the *Negro Encyclopedia*, the Committee on the Negro in Defense Industries, and other projects. I remember those days mostly twenty or so years ago with great pleasure. I know little of what you have been doing lately, but I am sure your interest in the improvement of the Negro's condition and his attaining first-class citizenship in every respect is still a dominant one with you.

I could not help think when I read the fine and unanimous decision of the Supreme Court on Segregation that you had done much to lay the foundations for this progressive and appropriate Court action.

I have not always agreed with you, but I have always known how loyal you were to the best interests of your group and what you believe to be the best interests of the country.

I have passed my 80th birthday, and I know you are a few years ahead of me.

With every good wish, I am

Sincerely yours,
Anson Phelps Stokes

New York City, November 16, 1954

Dear Dr. Stokes:

I was very glad to receive your letter this morning. I have thought about you often and been wondering whether you were still in circulation. It is rather queer to have you younger men talk of your age. I shall be 87 in February.

I was looking over the preliminary volume of the *Negro Encyclopedia* the other day and regretting again that we could not have gone ahead with that. It would have been valuable today.

My wife died in 1950 and the next year I married Shirley Graham, a writer, who had long had a youthful ambition to help me die. We moved from Harlem to Brooklyn Heights, a half block from the water, where we have the right to pay interest and taxes on a rather pleasant home with a beautiful, lofty living room and a fireplace that works, and at the back a little garden where the crimson sage is still blooming. If you ever come to New York we would be very glad to have you call.

I have been quite busy since I saw you. First, keeping out of jail, the story of which I am sending you in case you haven't read it. The United States Government and the publishing business have tried to keep this book from being known so far as possible. Still, many people have read it and it is being translated into Czech.

I have done some other writing and am just finishing an historical novel covering the history of the American Negro from 1876 to this year. It is long and heavy and there is much doubt if any American publishers will take it. Nevertheless I have written it and it is being copied, and that's that.

I have lectured a good deal in the east, middle west and west, at Princeton, Chicago University and other schools. I am lecturing once a week now at the Jefferson School of Marxism,[1] on "Reconstruction."

My best regards to you and your wife. I have read of the promotion of your son.[2]

Very sincerely yours,
W. E. B. Du Bois

Du Bois's daughter, not having heard from him for a prolonged period, called from Baltimore on the evening of 14 November 1954. A result was a long and newsy letter.

New York City, November 15, 1954

Dear Yolande:

I was terribly upset last night to know that you were worried about me or any fancied neglect. You must realize that as people get older time goes faster and they do not know how much rushed by. I had thought about you almost every day and had meant to call. I did not at all realize that it had been three months since I had written.

I am quite well, although of course getting steadily older so that I feel effort more and more, and we have had a great deal to do and to think about. First of all, as I told you, I am writing this novel which is going to be 1500 pages, in 42 chapters, and I have been giving every working hour to that, including dreams at night! Then I have done some articles, and planned another book which a publisher asked for but which there is slight chance of his taking.

Then, as you know, Marcantonio died.[1] Without his experience and unselfish devotion I might be in jail now and I felt I had to do everything I could.

Shirley, too, has had her troubles. You know her heart was set on publication of this novel about Aaron Burr on which she has been working six years or more. Finally, after 17 rejections, a publisher took it and gave her a contract and made a down payment. The editor was very enthusiastic. And then, at the

1. The school certainly was Marxist in its orientation, but its name was Jefferson School of Social Science.
2. The Reverend Dr. Anson Phelps Stokes, Jr., rector of Saint Bartholomew's Church in New York City, was elected Bishop-Coadjutor of the Massachusetts Episcopal Diocese in June 1954; he accepted this position in July.
1. Vito Marcantonio died in August 1954; Du Bois offered the eulogy at his funeral. Much of his statement was published in the *National Guardian*, 23 August 1954; and in *Freedom*, August 1954, Du Bois published a tribute to Marcantonio; "Politician in the Finest Sense."

last moment, the publishing house broke the contract. Of course in such a case there is no use going to law. If compelled, he would publish it and ruin it forever. So that made Shirley feel pretty low and she has had a hard time pulling up. However, the manuscript is now in England with some chance of its being published there.[2] In the meantime she has written a new teen-age book on Booker Washington.[3]

You can see with a few other things like this that we have been pretty busy, although I have kept to my schedule of getting to bed at 11 o'clock and up at 8 or later. This has kept me in good health.

I hope that you are taking care of yourself. I know you must have had some experience with the Integration muddle, and I shall want to hear about it. Shirley and I would like so much to have you come up Thanksgiving. Do you think you could make it?

I shall write to you again long before I have an answer to this.

Yours with love,
W. E. B. Du Bois

Almost always, the exchanges between George Padmore and Du Bois were meaty. One occurred late in 1954.

London, England, December 3, 1954

Dear and esteemed Dr,

Although you have not heard from me for quite a while, be assured that you are constantly in our thoughts. Hardly a day goes by unless your name comes up in some conversation with our young African friends who are frequent visitors to our apartment. You will be pleased to hear that in order to let the younger generation know of your contributions to Africa's freedom, I have been commissioned to do a book on the Pan-African Congress which I hope to have published by the middle of 1955. Dr. Nkrumah is keen on it as he plans to convene a sixth Pan-African Congress on the Gold Coast as soon as independence is formally declared. We cannot do it before as we don't want to create undue alarm before we have full power in our hands. All goes well there despite last minute attempts by the imperialists to incite tribalism to disrupt the united national front. The recent victory of Dr. Azikiwe's N.C.N.C. in Nigeria is a blow against tribalism[1] and if he plays his hands correctly we hope to consolidate a united Nigerian front. It is a skilful game of manoeuvering and we cannot afford at this stage of the struggle to give the imperialists any excuse to

2. This novel on Burr still has not been published; the manuscript is with Abbott Simon.

3. *Booker T. Washington, Educator of Hand, Head and Heart* (New York: Julius Messner, 1955).

1. The reference is to the National Council of Nigeria and the Cameroons.

intervene as in British Guiana. They are ready to pounce the first opportunity we give them. We are fully aware of what is going on between them and the Yanks. The editor of *United Asia* magazine has requested Mr. Douglas Rodgers, the secretary of the Movement for Colonial Freedom, and myself to prepare a special number of the journal on Africa in time for the coming Asian-African conference to take place in Indonesia next year. Cedric [Dover] should have assisted, but he is away in China at the moment and time is short. Could you send us an article on Pan-Africanism, as "father" of this idea?[2] We will greatly appreciate it. Rogers will be writing to you as he is in charge of official correspondence on the subject and will also send you copies of a series of information pamphlets we are bringing out for the benefit of educating the British public on the various colonies. Our victory in Uganda is now assured. It will move forward as an African State and detached from any association with Kenya, where the struggle goes on. If our people hold out for another year, the whites will have to quit. It is a bloody battle but unavoidable. So was Haiti. Believe me, dear Dr, no force on earth can now hold back the forward march of Africa. Without the outside support of the Tories here and the u.s. the writing would be clear for all to see that Africa will soon take her place among the free nations. It is a great pity that the Afroamerican newspapers are not giving the struggle the publicity it deserves. Even the *Courier* and *Defender* that at one time carried my despatches are no longer interested. I presume they feel that they have nothing in Africa. How unlike the Jews in their support of Israel. Dorothy joins in sending love to you and Shirley. Hope your health is good.

Ever yours

George Padmore

Will order a copy of your *Suppression of the Slave Trade* from Social Science Press.[3] Did you read Richard Wright's book on G. C.?[4] Very good! Will you be able to visit G. C.? Nkrumah would like you and S[hirley] to do so. Let me know. D[orothy] was there this summer.

New York City, December 10, 1954

My dear Padmore:

I am sending you in a separate package two of the latest reprints of my books: *Souls of Black Folk* and *Suppression of the African Slave Trade*. My secretary suspects that we have already sent you the *Souls of Black Folk* but I am not sure. If we have, hand this copy to some of the heathen.

I am very glad to hear about Africa. I understand the policy of you and Dr.

2. The article appeared as "Pan-Africanism: A Mission in My Life," in *United Asia* 7 (March 1955):23–28.
3. The Social Science Press in Brooklyn, a venture of Eugene D. Genovese, reprinted Du Bois's *Suppression of the African Slave Trade* in 1954.
4. The reference is to Richard Wright, *Black Power: A Record of Reactions in a Land of Pathos* (New York: Harper Bros., 1954).

Nkrumah, although I am a little afraid of it. The power of British and especially American capital when it once gets a foothold is tremendous. But of course I realize that once political power is in your hands you can curb capital, providing your own bourgeoise permits it. I am watching the struggle with great interest.

Naturally I did not like Richard Wright's book. Some of his descriptions were splendid but his logic is lousy. He starts out to save Africa from Communism and then makes an attack on British capitalism which is devastating. How he reconciles these two attitudes I cannot see.[1]

I sincerely hope that a Sixth Pan-African Congress can be held soon. Of course, in all probability I will be unable to get a passport to attend, although I will try. Also, I will send you within a week or so a short statement concerning the Pan-African Movement which you can use as you wish.

Johnathan Cape is considering a novel by Shirley which has been turned down by all the leading American publishers with the note that it is a "fine novel, but—."

I have just finished an historical novel which will run to 2000 pages covering the history of the American Negro from 1876 to the present time. It may never get publication but I shall do my best.

Sincerely,
W. E. B. Du Bois

Du Bois had affection and admiration for Leslie Pinckney Hill, a fellow alumnus of Harvard and, like Du Bois, one of the very few Black class orators at that institution (Du Bois in 1890 and Hill in 1903).* A moving exchange occurred

1. In a later letter to Padmore, dated 27 January 1955, Du Bois returned to Richard Wright and his book *Black Power*. He wrote: "The publishers sent me Wright's book and I read it. But I have not reviewed it. I don't like Wright. The Communists of America started him on his career. It is quite possible that some of them presumed on this help and tried to push him around. They, like most human beings, are often narrow and ignorant. But because of that to slur Communism as such, to slander Russia and above all, to spit on American Negroes is too much for an honest artist. Wright has great talent and his descriptions of West Africa are literature; but to write a book to attack Communism in Africa when there has been no Communism in Africa, and when the degradation of Africa is due to that Capitalism which Wright is defending—this is sheer contradiction."

* Leslie Pinckney Hill (1880-1960) was born in Virginia and, as noted above, educated at Harvard. He named one of his daughters Natalie Du Bois. He taught at Tuskegee and at Manassas, Virginia, Industrial School from 1904 to 1913, and from 1913 to 1951 was head of what was called first Institute for Colored Youth, then Cheyney Training School for Teachers, and finally State Teachers College in Pennsylvania. He was administrator of the Mercy-Douglass Hospital in Philadelphia from 1953 to 1956. Hill was the author of a lyrical work, *Wings of Oppression* (1927), and of a drama, *Toussaint L'Ouverture* (1929), but he did not write the other dramas he

*between the two men at the close of 1954, when both were in the last decade
of their lives.*

New York City, December 6, 1954

My dear Hill:

I spent the weekend at Cheyney. I was with some friends in a small new
cottage, and did not invade the campus. But of course I heard the usual stack of
rumors. One was that your wife, Jane, had been very ill but was now recovered.

I do hope that the illness was not too severe and that the recovery is still real
and permanent. Please give her my love.

Also, I understand that you are thin and working like the devil. This is a
great mistake. As a matter of fact, you are a poet and not an executive but you
were kicked into executive work and did a fine job at Cheyney. But after you
were released from that imprisonment I had hoped you would go to writing,
and I would have told you so had I not been so busy at the time keeping out of
jail.

I myself have for the last two years given my time entirely to literature. I am
writing a chef-d'oeuvre masterpiece, which is a novel of the development of the
Negro from 1876 where my book *Reconstruction* broke off, to the present. I
have had a gorgeous time working on it, putting in four or five hours a day. It
is nearly finished.

I wish you would think this over and see if you can't plan to give up your
executive work and go to writing entirely. Of course, I know you won't but I
am getting this off my chest.

Shirley and I have a very fine house in Brooklyn Heights, quiet and comfortable. It cost about twice as much as we could afford to pay but our choice was
between something like that or life in the country, which after repeated investigation I have learned is impossible.

Fortunately I am still in good health and spirits despite what the world seems
to be doing to itself.

Our best regards to you and again to your wife. I shall be glad to hear from
you.

Very sincerely yours,
W. E. B. Du Bois

Philadelphia, Pa., December 17, 1954

Dear Doctor:

Your letter has been a refreshing experience. It warrants my taking issue with
many of our mutual friends who think more of your remarkable head than of
your great heart. I want you to know, in this hour of great anxiety about Mrs.

---

mentioned in the letter to Du Bois. Hill also contributed to Rayford Logan's *What
the Negro Wants* (1944).

Hill's serious condition, that I value deeply your generous concern about me. You express what a number of my influential friends have urged—that I get off somewhere and write.

That wonderful experience to which I have looked forward now frankly for a number of years has not yet come to pass. I have long since planned to complete a trilogy of dramas beginning with *Toussaint L'Ouverture*, which has gone out to evoke some remarkably encouraging criticism, with *Christoph* and *Desselines* following. I have a store of reading back in my head somewhere and still intend to accomplish this threefold task.

The work of our enormous undertaking here at the hospital is demanding and engrossing, and leaves little or no time for anything else. Of course I have no thought of continuing here indefinitely, but want to see the establishment carried over to the new basis with my part done. I intend then to buckle down to some hard study and to the writing to which I have been called in important directions. It would be a delightful privilege to develop an imaginary conversation between you and Sir Winston, if he can be induced ever to retire. I imagine a world of fun in that composition. And so on with much else.

I rejoice that you have been working on your chef-d'oeuvre, and promise you to be one of the first subscribers when it appears. The fact that you have had a "gorgeous time working on it" means that we shall have the joy of your heart in evidence as you terminate this major undertaking. I rejoice also that you are in good health and spirit for your work, in spite of the world and all its besetments.

I keep well, but I am tired and need a rest, which may be forthcoming before too long.

Mrs. Hill, who is still in a critical condition after six weeks of hospitalization, for the most part in an oxygen tent, but now at home with nursing care day and night, enjoyed your letter with me and sends along with mine to you and your spouse every good wish and prayer not only for Christmas, but for years more of productive work.

Your letter makes me think of the inward turmoil of Matthew Arnold, who had to spend days and years in the writing of dry educational reports when he ought to have been up on his wings with an essay or poem.

Again with every good wish to you and Shirley Graham Du Bois, I am

Cordially yours,

Leslie Pinckney Hill

While Du Bois had read Marx quite fully by the 1930s and gave a course on Karl Marx and the Negro in the 1933 summer session at Atlanta University, he studied Lenin's writings a good deal later. Indicative is an exchange with this editor from late in 1954.

New York City, December 21, 1954

My dear Aptheker:

I have just been reading again Lenin's "Imperialism." I wonder if you will be so good as to tell me where I could find the best logical follow-up of this argument? It leaves me a little dissatisfied, or perhaps I would better say, a little at sea in my own thinking.

We still remember with great pleasure our evening with you and hope you will explain to Bettina that I was not privy to the plot that spirited her away.[1]

Very sincerely yours,
W. E. B. Du Bois

Brooklyn, N.Y., December 24, 1954

Dear Dr. Du Bois:

There is, of course, a very considerable literature illuminating the concepts Lenin put forth in his *Imperialism*. Indeed, in the sense that Leninism is Marxism of the epoch of imperialism, practically everything written by Marxists, since the 1890s, falls into this category in one way or another. There are, however, certain works which deal more directly with certain fundamental aspects of imperialism, in an effort to apply or develop Lenin's theory.

Among these are:

New Data for Lenin's "Imperialism," by Eugene Varga and L. Mendelsohn
Marxism and the National Question, by J. Stalin
The Crisis of Britain and the British Empire, by R. Palme Dutt
The Problem of India, by R. Palme Dutt
American Imperialism, by V. Perlo
Atomic Imperialism, by J. S. Allen

By the way, while these books are not published by New Century Publishers, they can supply them.[1] I hope this is of some service.

We are very happy that you had a pleasant evening with us; certainly Fay and I enjoyed it very much. Our warmest wishes to Mrs. Du Bois and to you for a splendid New Year.

Cordially,
Herbert Aptheker

1. He refers to our daughter, then ten years old. She was always loath to retire for the evening, and especially so when the Du Boises were visiting.

1. I was then engaged in editorial work for *Masses & Mainstream* and *Political Affairs;* both magazines were distributed at that time by New Century Publishers.

1955

In its broadest sense, education was Du Bois's central preoccupation throughout his life. One aspect of his views on education is revealed clearly in the course of arrangements for a lecture which he gave at a private, experimental high school in New York City; this was the Elizabeth Irwin School, whose director was Dr. Randolph B. Smith. Du Bois comments in the first paragraph of the following letter that he had become "upset"; the circumstances responsible are not known.

New York City, January 27, 1955

Dear Dr. Smith:

I was, I confess, a little upset by all the circumstances surrounding your invitation to speak for your school, but I realize my obligation to those of your students who did want me, and I am prepared to speak Monday, February 14th, under the following conditions:

My subject will be *freedom of opinion*, and I shall seek to stress the essential thing about education as the right to reach one's own opinions, and the ability to reach opinions after thought and research.

I shall seek to illustrate this as the foundation of real democracy, and show how force has never been able to act as a substitute. I shall refer to the religious wars and the inquisition in Europe; to the question of slavery in the United States, and the present problem of Communism in the modern world. I shall emphasize the fact that I am not interested at the moment in what conclusions on any subject persons come to, but my supreme interest is that they should have the right freely to come to their conclusions; and that their conclusions should be based on their own effort to know the truth.[1]

Secondly, I have found it necessary always to charge a fee for my lectures, which in this case would be $50.

If the above conditions are satisfactory to you, will you kindly let me know.

Very sincerely yours,
W. E. B. Du Bois

Du Bois and E. Sylvia Pankhurst exchanged letters again early in 1955.

1. See Du Bois's essay, "The Freedom to Learn," in a publication of Lincoln University (Mo.), *Midwest Journal* 2 (Winter 1949):9–11.

Essex, England, April 7, 1955

Dear Dr. Du Bois:

Mr. Ngumbu Njururi is a Kikuyu. He was studying here for law, but the income he received from his father has completely stopped, and he can get no contact with his family. He knows that his mother and grandmother were killed or died when in the hands of the Kenya Police, and his sister was imprisoned for a time but has been released.

He has a letter from the Foreign Office to state that owing to the fact that the people of his area would not give information about the Mau Mau, there was collective punishment, and his father's plantations were destroyed.

He has been offered a scholarship at one American University, which would involve paying his fare and finding $200 for his board and lodging, above what the University would allow him on the scholarship.

He has also been offered a scholarship at Fisk, but this would mean $500 above what the University would allow.

I wonder whether there is any hope in America through any other Institution? Can you advise?

Yours sincerely,
E. Sylvia Pankhurst

New York City, May 4, 1955

My dear Miss Pankhurst:

I have your letter of April 7th concerning Mr. Ngumbu Njururi. I would advise him writing to President Horace Bond, Lincoln University, Pennsylvania. This is the institution where Nkrumah and Azikiwe studied and they have a considerable number of African[1] students.

Personally I would have no connections or influence which would help him secure scholarships at any universities. I am at present, as I have told you, what is called in America "a controversial person" because I insist that a man can be a Socialist or a Communist or anything else that he so desires and that punishment and discrimination because of belief is barbarism.

I am not enthusiastic about the kind of teaching that Africans are going to get in American universities but I realize that it is probably their best chance for getting any teaching at all.

Very sincerely yours,
W. E. B. Du Bois

Benjamin J. Davis, Jr., the Black attorney in the Angelo Herndon case and the former Communist councilman in New York City, wrote Du Bois from his

---

1. The original reads "Negro"—an obvious slip.

prison cell in the Allegheny County, Pennsylvania, jail. The letter is undated
but was written probably late in March or early in April 1955.

Pittsburgh, Pa.

Dear Dr. Du Bois:

Your interest in my case, your personal statements, during my 4 years of
imprisonment, have been a source of inspiration and great pride to me. I thank
you very deeply, and none the less because they were made out of your devotion
to the cause of peace and social progress. This is the first opportunity I've had
during the last 4 years to make this personal acknowledgment and to express
my appreciation.

When I entered prison in '51 you were then facing a virtual death sentence
yourself. The victory in your case was celebrated by us, in our own way, in
prison; for we regarded it as a victory of the peace voices and Negro people
and as a tribute to your magnificent contributions.

In August, 1953 when I was preparing to testify in Pitts. in behalf of 5 Smith
Act defendants, I was permitted a number of books, under close custody, at
Terre Haute. One of them which I most enjoyed was yours on your 83rd
birthday—the story of your frameup. It was indeed a fine experience to read
it—worth all the incredible red tape to get it, and though it had to be read
under the eyes of a special guard.

I should have been released with my five white co-defendants on March 1.
But none know better than you the fury of a white supremacy gov't against a
Negro who dares to file suit in person against the racist segregation maintained
in the federal prison system. But I hope to greet you soon in person.[1]

Regards to Shirley.

Sincerely,
Benjamin J. Davis

New York City, April 18, 1955

Dear Ben Davis:

Your letter from Pittsburgh reached me just as I returned from three weeks
rest in Haiti. I was more than glad to have this word from you and to know
that your spirits are still high.

I have suffered with you in your incarceration, and have been, of course,
very helpless to do anything except now and then to speak a word.

---

1. On 1 March 1955 six leaders of the Communist party were released from federal
penitentiaries, having completed forty-four months of five year sentences. In addition to Davis, they were John B. Williamson, Jacob A. Stachel, John Gates, Eugene
Dennis, and Carl Winter. Davis had also been sentenced to sixty days in jail for contempt of court—that is, refusing to be an informer—in the trial of other Communists in
Pittsburgh. Davis was released from the Allegheny County jail on 16 April 1955; his
release was reported in the next day's *Times* in a three-inch story on p. 84.

I confess the situation in this country has gone beyond anything that I ever dreamed, but it is bound to change in time, and signs of change are already here. For instance, I expected to be turned back from my trip to Haiti but was not. I was received with courtesy and kindness although of course there was little official recognition.

I am now returned to my work and hope to get my long novel in process of negotiation for publication soon.

My best regards from myself and wife, Shirley Graham, and every good wish for your success. We will be on hand to welcome you when you are again free.

Very sincerely yours,
W. E. B. Du Bois

P. S. You were freed before this got typed. Hallelujah!

In the days of difficulties when Du Bois was facing trial in Washington, D.C., he and Mrs. Du Bois were the guests of Eugene and Edmonia Davidson; they were old friends, and Mr. Davidson's parents had also been friends of Du Bois's. An exchange between Du Bois and Mr. Davidson reflects this experience and illuminates the atmosphere of the period.

New York City, April 18, 1955

My dear Eugene:

Someone came up from Washington to our house the other day and was talking about you, and to my great surprise intimated that you felt that we had not treated you just fairly in the book about the trial because we had not mentioned by name and in other ways the fine hospitality which you proffered us.

Perhaps this is merely gossip and exaggeration. But for fear that there may be something in it, let me say that I was very careful *not* to mention your name and not to say too much where I had stayed because I was afraid that it might hurt you in your business. The attitude of Ophelia and some of my other Washington friends made me realize what a dangerous acquaintance I was, and therefore I was careful not to mention either your name or that of your wife and simply incidentally and in passing to say that we were taken in while others were afraid.

If I had known or suspected that you were willing for me to go into greater detail, I should have been only too glad to do so.

As I say, perhaps all this is merely unwarranted gossip, and yet I could not let the possibility go by without saying at least a word to you concerning it.

Shirley joins me in best regards to you and your wife. We have both just returned from a three weeks' trip to Haiti which was a beautiful experience.

Very sincerely yours,
W. E. B. Du Bois

Washington, D.C., April 27, 1955

My dear Dr. Du Bois:

I hasten to answer your recent letter relative to your last visit to our home. I regret exceedingly that you apparently have not realized that our mutual friend, George [Murphy, Jr.], is puckish even to the extent sometimes seeming sadistic. His mischievous purpose could only have been to watch your brilliant mind react to such an alleged situation. His suggestions to you as related in your letter, concerning our feelings, are inaccurate and reflect on both our innate courage and sense of publicity values.

The facts are as follows:

1. Our invitation to you to visit with us during a very trying period in your life was sincere and absolutely without ulterior motives. The invitation was motivated solely by a deep sense of friendship which began many years ago when over a period of years you made the home of my mother and father your Washington home. That such a friendship should be broken merely because of a possible difference in ideologies to me was inconceivable.

2. We were fully aware of the hysteria which besets the country at this time and of unwarranted implications of association. This did not prevent us from welcoming you and your wife as our personal guests, nor did it prevent me from being an interested spectator at the trial.

3. Neither Edmonia nor I are seekers of publicity. We resent, even, newspaper publicity on our guests from foreign embassies. It would be absurd for us to have desired mention in your book of your visit to our home by identification of your hosts. Frankly, I think it wise that you did not do so, merely because there are so many bigots who could and would misinterpret our basic reason.

4. Our only reaction to this portion of your splendid book was that instead of relating that courageous friends had made you and Shirley welcome in spite of the atmosphere, you used the words "boarding and lodging" which negated the friendship motive and by connotation suggested that you paid for our hospitality. Moreover, we both felt that without mentioning names, history should record that the man who had contributed so much to the race struggle did have such friends in his darkest hour.

Edmonia sends her best regards to you and Shirley and joins with me in inviting you to be our guests whenever you can come to Washington.

Sincerely yours,
Eugene

The subject of family relationship appeared in the course of correspondence with Arna Bontemps. Bontemps, in a letter from Nashville, Tennessee, dated 26 April 1955, enclosed a copy of a lecture he had recently presented in Chattanooga to the first fully integrated meeting of Tennessee librarians. Bontemps

*based the lecture on materials from a book on which he was then working—
biographical studies of leading figures in Black history. As will be seen, Du
Bois's reply was somewhat sharp. Bontemps's response assured that he had not
meant to convey what Du Bois resented but did think it of some importance
that the upbringing of Frederick Douglass, Booker T. Washington, and Du
Bois was entirely the work of a mother and not a father.*

New York City, April 29, 1955

My dear Mr. Bontemps:

There is one thing that I greatly dislike in your lecture to the Tennessee
Library Association. On page 12 you say:

"As individuals the three men had some interesting similarities. None of
them knew their fathers, or at least not well."

The intimation is that all three of us were illegitimate. I do not want any
such vague statement to stand.

My mother and father were married and lived together, and while he left to
secure work elsewhere, you have no right to intimate that this was a broken
family. I was not old enough when he left to remember him distinctly, but I
did know him.

Very sincerely yours,
W. E. B. Du Bois

*No one had so long and deep an influence upon Black intellectuals, writers, and
poets as did Du Bois. A letter of mid-1955 from a Black poet is to the point.*

Washington, D.C., May 12, 1955

Dear Dr. Du Bois:

I am anxious to know just what your personal reaction is to the import of
this poem.

I have gathered numerous *sayings*, thoughts, etc., during the past years, some
of which remind me of you in their interpretation of you. Shall send them
when I can. I am absolutely buried in papers, notes, etc., that have accumulated
through the years. Naturally, there is no one to help me systematize these
findings so it must wait.

I have collected, written and etc., about twenty-two books, only a few of
which, four I guess, are published. Have tried every fellowship and writer's aid
operating but have been turned down each time (they say age) some of them
even four times.

As you may know the young writers of Washington used my home as a sort
of literary center for a long time. It therefore is a fact that I know the truth
concerning their beginnings as no one else could since they were at my home
each Saturday night and some of them, daily. I feel sad to think that the truths

I know may never reach the ears of the future. It may be that you could see the aperture, the rift in the sky, the star shining in the darkness, that I cannot discern.

I know how busy you are, I know how far from receiving the crowns and plaudits you have so fully and richly deserved and how on the other hand, you have been misrepresented, persecuted, reviled and above all maybe, mostly envied, and yet, with your superlative intellect you can see beyond, above, through and around the present mountains obstructing the view of ordinary persons. Therefore, somehow I write this to you when I only meant primarily, to ask you the first question of this letter.

This may be fruitless, it may be useless, it may be presumptuous, it may be an imposition and yet, so I have written and will send it on nevertheless..

Give my love to your dear wife, please.

Sincerely and with deep regard,
Georgia Douglas Johnson[1]

[Enclosure]
The Man to Be

I ride a-tilt because
Life charges through my veins—
Mixed forces guide the reins
And I must on.

Astride the universe
I go, nor pause, nor rest,
With sharp swords at my breast
To lean upon.

These fierce contending bloods
Churn in the depths of me,
Merged in a mighty sea,
They urge me on.

1. Georgia Douglas Johnson (1886-1966) was born in Georgia and educated at Atlanta University and the Oberlin Conservatory of Music. She was very active in civil-rights movements and in efforts to abolish capital punishment. Her first book of poetry, *The Heart of a Woman*, appeared in 1919. Du Bois wrote the foreword for her second book, *Bronze* (Boston: B. J. Brimmer, 1922), commenting, "As a revelation of the soul struggle of the women of a race it is invaluable." When Du Bois edited the *Crisis*, he published her poetry fairly often; see, for example, the issues of November 1924 and August 1925. In the February 1924 *Crisis*, when writing of "The Younger Literary Movement," Du Bois called special attention to the promise of five newer poets: Langston Hughes, Countee Cullen, Gwendolyn Bennett, Claude McKay, and, Georgia Douglas Johnson. A biography of Mrs. Johnson is needed.

O white men, black and red,
Look through God's lens and see
This fused intensity—
The man to be,
Your son!
   Georgia Douglas Johnson

New York City, May 31, 1955

Dear Georgia Johnson:
   I have your letter of May 12th.
   I always find your poems good, clear and inspiring, and only wish that I
had some way to get them in print, but the opportunity for public expression
today is for everyone very, very difficult.
   Shirley and I attended the annual ceremonial of the National Institute of
Arts and Letters. It was disappointing. The chief speaker, Eelco N. Van Klef-
fens, whose subject was "The Spoken Word," said absolutely nothing.
   I therefore can give you no advice except to keep on writing, and that, of
course, you will do because you have to.
   Shirley joins me in best regards.

Yours with love,
W. E. B. Du Bois

*In a letter that does not seem to have survived, Du Bois asked the distinguished
artist, Rockwell Kent to serve as a United States member of the World Peace
Council.*

Ausable Forks, New York, May 20, 1955

Dear Dr. Du Bois:
   Before I could answer your letter of the 16th, I received a phone call from
Albert Kahn, and I asked him to convey to you what I am here writing: That
I will accept the nomination to be a member of the Peace Council. My only regret will be that I live too far from New York to be of much service.
   I received an interesting light on how reviews are managed: George Biddle,
at his request, was assigned to review my book for the *Herald Tribune*. His
review was received, pigeon-holed, and, though paid for, eventually rejected.
It was found to be an enthusiastic review and was held by Irita Van Doren
to be not sufficiently "objective" about a "controversial figure." I am wondering
if Philbrick will be assigned to do it.
   With best wishes,

Faithfully yours,
Rockwell Kent[1]

1. Rockwell Kent (1882–1971) was a well-known author and, especially, painter,

Two names forbidden in the respectable communication media during the worst years of the Cold War were Paul Robeson and Du Bois. Correspondence with Dodd, Mead publishers is illustrative on Robeson.

New York City, September 17, 1955

Dear Dr. Du Bois:

Langston Hughes suggested that we send you an advance copy of his new book, *Famous Negro Music Makers,* which we are publishing on September 26th, and the book was mailed to you late last week. We hope you will schedule it for early reading, and shall, of course, appreciate your sending us your comments on it.

Sincerely yours,
Dodd, Mead & Company, Inc.
Mary McPartland
Publicity Department

New York City, September 27, 1955

Edward H. Dodd, Jr.,
President, Dodd, Mead & Co.
Dear Sir:

A week ago, your publicity agent, Miss Mary McPartland, sent me a copy of Langston Hughes' *Famous Negro Music Makers* and asked my comment. I wrote her today saying that I could not conceive of a reputable publishing house issuing this book and omitting Paul Robeson. No Negro in the world has done so much to make Negro music known over the globe as Robeson. I said that if in this omission you followed the advice of Hughes I am bitterly disappointed in him as an honest man and that I had known him for 35 years. I published some of his first work. I added that if this omission was forced on him by the policies of your firm, I regarded your action as beneath contempt.

A friend of mine who also knows you was in my office when this matter came

---

wood engraver, and lithographer; his works are represented in the Metropolitan Museum of New York, the Art Institute of Chicago, the Hermitage in Leningrad, and elsewhere. Several of his profusely illustrated books had wide sales, especially *N. by E.* (1930) and *Greenland Journey* (1963). The book to which he refers in this letter was his autobiography, *It's Me, O Lord,* published by Dodd, Mead in New York City in 1955. The author Albert E. Kahn was a founder in 1949 of the World Peace Council and has recently published studies of Galina Ulanova and of Pablo Casals. The Philbrick reference signifies Herbert Philbrick, one of the better-known professional anti-Communists, whose "I Led Three Lives" was being viewed regularly by millions in the United States via television. George Biddle was the internationally known painter and sculptor.

up and he was sure you could not be privy to this situation. He asked me to write you and I am so doing.

Very sincerely
W. E. B. Du Bois

New York City, October 4, 1955
Dear Mr. Du Bois:

We have looked carefully into the factors which caused the choice of the characters for Langston Hughes's book and I can assure you that no pressure was put on Mr. Hughes in this office. He was told by experts of his acquaintance and probably also told by our library advisers that the inclusion of Paul Robeson would probably eliminate the book from acceptance by a good many school libraries, state adoption lists, etc. Evidently he decided that it would be unwise in a book of this sort to damage the circulation to the degree which he thought would eventuate. This book, as you know, is a juvenile and he wanted it to be noncontroversial.

Yours very truly,
Edward H. Dodd, Jr.[1]

One of the more bizarre episodes during "scoundrel time" revolved around a Czech translation of Du Bois's In Battle for Peace. The story began in 1954 and extended through 1955.

In August 1954 the firm of Melantrich of Prague signed a contract to publish three thousand copies of the Du Bois book in the Czech language. Copies were ready in December 1954, and that month six complimentary copies were mailed to Du Bois from Czechoslovakia. In January 1955 Du Bois thanked the Prague publishers for a royalty payment (of $126.12) and stated that he hoped soon to see the book. Some months later, Du Bois received a letter from an official of the Czechoslovak Theatrical and Literary Agency.

Prague, Czechoslovakia, October 21, 1955
Dear Dr. Du Bois:

We are sorry to tell you that according to a communication from the Post Office dep[artment's] Bureau of Transportation in Washington the parcel containing your complimentary copies of the Czech edition of your book In Battle for Peace with Messrs. Melantrich of Prague has been confiscated.

We cannot understand why the u.s. Post Office has confiscated copies of

1. Edward Howard Dodd, Jr. was born in New York City in 1905 and educated at Yale. Since 1929 he has been associated with Dodd, Mead and Co., and at the time of this correspondence he was its president. He is the author of The First Hundred Years: A History of Dodd, Mead & Co., published in 1939.

the Czech edition of a book which has been freely published in your country. Perhaps you will yourself approach the Post Office and explain to them that in this case there is no reason for detaining the books sent to you.

Sincerely yours,
Dr. Vojtech Strnad

Du Bois at once sent a letter to the postmaster general, who at that time was Arthur E. Summerfield.

New York City, November 4, 1955
The Postmaster General
Sir:

Last month Messrs. Melantrich, publishers of Prague, Czechoslovakia, sent me six copies of a translation of my book, *In Battle for Peace,* which they have just published.

This book was published in English in 1952 and duly copyrighted in the United States, by Masses and Mainstream, 832 Broadway, New York.

The Czech translation of this book was confiscated by your Bureau of Transportation and refused delivery to me.

I write to protest this high-handed action which is plainly illegal and insulting. I demand the immediate delivery of these books.

W. E. B. Du Bois

Washington, D.C., November 22, 1955
Dear Dr. Du Bois:

Reference is made to your letter of November 4, 1955, addressed to the Postmaster General, concerning your book *In Battle for Peace* and your failure to obtain delivery of six copies of a translation of the book which were sent to you from the publishers in Prague, Czechoslovakia.

I note that your book was originally published and copyrighted in the United States, and your statement, "The Czech translation of this book was confiscated by your Bureau of Transportation and refused delivery to me."

This matter will be given attention and you will be further advised relative thereto.[1]

Sincerely yours,
Abe McGregor Goff
The Solicitor
By: William C. O'Brien
Assistant Solicitor
Fraud and Mailability Division.

1. It is perhaps needless to remark that Du Bois never heard again from the post

A classical illustration of bureaucratic arrogance in this period is provided by exchanges between Du Bois and the passport division of the State Department through the latter half of 1955.

Washington, D.C., July 1, 1955

Dear Mr. Du Bois:

The Department has received your application for a passport to enable you to proceed to Poland to attend the fifth International Youth Congress at Warsaw, Poland.

I regret to inform you after careful consideration of your application for passport facilities, the Department of State is obliged to disapprove your request tentatively on the ground that the granting of such passport facilities is precluded under the provisions of Section 51.135 of Title 22 of the Code of Federal Regulations. A copy of the pertinent Regulations is enclosed for your information.

In cases coming within the purview of the Regulations above referred to, it is the practice of the Department to inform the applicant of the reasons for the disapproval of his request for passport facilities insofar as the security regulations will permit. In your case the Department has concluded that your case falls within the scope of Sections (a) and (c) of the aforementioned Regulations since it is alleged that you are a Communist and as the Congress which you wish to attend is Communist inspired.

Under Section 51.137 of the Regulations you may present your case and all relevant information to the Passport Office. If you desire to take advantage of this provision you may appear before a hearing officer of the Passport Office and you may be represented by counsel. In such cases, you will be required to submit a sworn statement as to whether you are now or ever have been a Communist.

If you do not desire a hearing, the Department will give consideration to any written statement under oath which you may desire to submit concerning the matter, provided that you include therein a statement as to whether you are now or ever have been a Communist.

You are assured that any information or evidence which you may supply will receive most careful consideration and that every effort will be made to act upon your application promptly and justly. The Department desires to emphasize that the passport records are confidential Government records and any information which you may submit or which may be received from other sources in connection with your application will not be made known to the public or to any unauthorized person unless you release it. The Department

---

office department about this matter. Just where the package of six Czech books now reposes is not known.

reserves the right to disclose factual information to supplement or correct any statement which a passport applicant may release for publication concerning the reasons why he was denied a passport or the Department's action in his case.

If a reply to this letter is not received within thirty days, it will be assumed that you do not wish to have your case reconsidered at this time.

Sincerely yours,
For the Secretary of State
Frances G. Knight, Director
Passport Office

Brooklyn, New York, July 13, 1955
Re: F130—Du Bois, William Edward Burghardt
Mrs. Frances G. Knight, Director
Passport Office
Dear Madame:

I have your letter of July 1, 1955 refusing at present to issue me and my wife passports for travel abroad and in particular for attending as guest of honor the World Festival of Youth to be held at Warsaw, July 31 to August 14, 1955. I enclose a copy of this invitation.

I regard the reasons which you give as both illegal and personally insulting. For sixty years I have held passports from the United States, beginning with Passport No. 42015, issued June 24, 1892 by the Acting Secretary of State, William F. Wharton. With these passports I have made thirteen trips to Europe and visits to Asia, Africa and the West Indies. During this time I have never been accused of crime and have received recognition of many kinds including the rank of United States Special Minister Plenipotentiary and Envoy Extraordinary to the Republic of Liberia.

My continued and continuing advocacy of world peace once brought the demand that I register as a Foreign Agent. I refused, was indicted and acquitted by a Federal Court.

The regulations of your department which you adduce are not statute law, but represent the effort of the State Department to arrogate to itself the judicial right to inquire into and judge my political beliefs and opinions. This is an unconstitutional assumption of power. As a free American citizen, I maintain that it is none of your business what I believe or think so long as I transgress no law. Nor will I be intimidated by secret "allegations" of unnamed informers which have no status in law.

I therefore absolutely refuse to sign or submit to you or anyone else any affidavit concerning my beliefs nor have you any right to decide what lawful assemblies I shall attend or whose voices I shall listen to.

I therefore repeat my demand for a passport, in accord with the Constitution of the United States, the laws of the land and the decision of the courts. Further refusal will confirm my conclusion that you are resting your hope for continued illegal procedures on the cost of litigation which you assume only the rich can afford.

Yours very truly,
W. E. B. Du Bois

Washington, D.C. [undated]

Dear Mr. Du Bois:

The receipt is acknowledged of your letter of July 13, 1955 in regard to your passport case. The matter is being given careful consideration and you will be advised as soon as a decision is reached.

Sincerely yours,
Frances G. Knight
Director, Passport Office

New York City, September 8, 1955

Miss Frances G. Knight
Dear Madame:

Referring to your letter without date, F-130, Du Bois, William Edward Burghardt, may I say that in my application for a passport, June 7, 1955, I asked to attend the World Festival of Youth in Warsaw, July 31 to August 14, 1955; and also to visit Czechoslovakia and other countries for reasons of health and recreation.

You have delayed decision on my passport until the World Festival with 30,000 youth from 114 nations is over. This was I assume deliberate on your part. Nevertheless, I write to say that my application for a passport still stands and I wish to repeat my application to visit Poland, the Soviet Union, Czechoslovakia, Germany, France and England for health and recreation. My wife wishes to accompany me. In accord with your letter of mid-July without date, may I ask for a decision in my case as soon as possible.

Very sincerely,
W. E. B. Du Bois

Washington, D.C., October 6, 1955

Dear Mr. Du Bois:

With reference to your letter of September 22, 1955 regarding your pending passport application you are informed that your file has been sent to another office of the Department for evaluation. Upon the completion of the evaluation you will be advised of the Department's decision.

Sincerely,
Frances G. Knight
Director, Passport Office

New York City, November 4, 1955

Miss Frances G. Knight

Dear Madame:

Almost exactly a month ago (October 6, 1955—F130—Du Bois, William E. B.) you informed me that my application and that of my wife, Shirley Graham Du Bois, made June 7, 1955 was in process of evaluation "by another office of the Department." I have heard nothing since. May I inquire when to expect a decision or if I must take steps in another direction.

Very sincerely,

W. E. B. Du Bois

Washington, D.C., November 25, 1955

Dear Mr. Du Bois:

With reference to your letter of November 4, 1955 regarding your pending passport application you are informed that this office has not yet received the evaluation of your case referred to in my previous letter to you. I am unable to advise you when a decision will be reached.[1]

Sincerely,

Frances G. Knight

Director, Passport Office

1. No decision was ever reached. The State Department continued to deny passports on the basis of alleged political opinion until the 1964 Supreme Court case of *Aptheker* v. *Rusk*.

1956

Late in 1955 my History and Reality *was published in New York City by Cameron Associates. I sent a copy, with my compliments, to Du Bois. Early the next year he sent me a long letter, induced by his reading of that book.*

New York City, January 10, 1956

Dear Aptheker:

Last night I finished reading your "History and Reality." I want to thank you most sincerely for this scholarly and inspiring work. For one who like myself has spent so much of his life immersed in a small part of the vast field of the social problems, and depending on the press for a general knowledge of the world, it is easy, especially today, to get an unreal story of what is happening outside his specialty. I needed, for instance, your splendid review of American relations with China, of which I knew much but not enough for a connected story; I needed to have the story of Franco put together, and American lies about the Soviets set in order. I have known Walter Lippmann for 44 years and yet have never followed carefully his philosophy. I know nothing of [David] Riesman. I met [Alger] Hiss in San Francisco and read Jowitt;[1] but I enjoyed your interpretation of his frame-up. Curiously enough I had never heard more than a fragment of the truth of the official murders on Guam. It is a bit frightening for one who considers himself as fairly intelligent to realize how much of the present he does not know and does not know that he does not know.

Your first chapter, however, is to me of the first importance. I have read it twice. Perhaps you do not remember that it was in search of answers to the fundamental problems which you discuss that I went to Harvard. I had taken a course in "Philosophy" at Fisk in my senior year, in the spring of 1888. It was ruined for me by the interpolation of religious dogma and inexcusable contradictions of logic in the reasoning of a good man, President [Erastus] Cravath, innocent father of one of the greatest of Big Business attorneys [Paul Cravath]. I determined to go to the best university in the land and if possible in the world, to discover Truth, which I spelled with a capital.

For two years I studied under William James while he was developing Prag-

---

1. The reference is to *The Strange Case of Alger Hiss* by the Earl Jowitt (Garden City, New York: Doubleday, 1953). The author had been Lord Chancellor of Great Britain.

matism; under [George] Santayana and his attractive mysticism and under [Josiah] Royce and his Hegelian idealism. I then found and adopted a philosophy which has served me since; thereafter I turned to the study of History and what has become Sociology.

I think in general I agree with your conclusions and criticism; but I would express my philosophy more simply. Several times in the past I have started to formulate it, but met such puzzled looks that it remains only partially set down in scraps of manuscript. I gave up the search of "Absolute" Truth; not from doubt of the existence of reality, but because I believe that our limited knowledge and clumsy methods of research made it impossible now completely to apprehend Truth. I nevertheless firmly believed that gradually the human mind and absolute and provable truth would approach each other and like the "Asymtotes of the Hyberbola" (I learned the phrase in high school and was ever after fascinated by it) would approach each other nearer and nearer and yet never in all eternity meet. I therefore turned to Assumption—scientific Hypothesis. I assumed the existence of Truth, since to assume anything else or not to assume was unthinkable. I assumed that Truth was only partially known but that it was ultimately largely knowable, although perhaps in part forever Unknowable. Science adopted the hypothesis of a Knower and something Known. The Jamesian Pragmatism as I understood it from his lips was not based on the "usefulness" of a hypothesis, as you put it, but on its workable logic if its truth was assumed. Also of necessity I assumed Cause and Change. With these admittedly unprovable assumptions, I proposed to make a scientific study of human action, based on the hypotheses of the reality of such actions, of their causal connections and of their continued occurrence and change because of Law and Chance. I called Sociology the measurement of the element of Chance in Human Action.

At this time I knew little of Marxism and I had studied but beginnings of natural science—a bit of Astronomy, a course in Chemical Analysis, Geology under [Nathaniel] Shaler, and Experimental Psychology under [William] James. Nor have I followed recently the development of those who, refusing assumption or hypothesis, have landed in mysticism and complete doubt. I read with interest your account of the thinking of [Benedetto] Croce, [Charles A.] Beard, and others.

For myself I set out in 1896 on the task of studying human action in exhaustive detail by taking up the Negro Problem. I set forth my thesis at a convocation of the University of Pennsylvania in 1897 and then for fifteen years at Atlanta University. I began to count and classify the facts concerning the American Negro and the way to his betterment through human action. I assumed that human beings could alter and re-direct the course of events so as to better human conditions. I knew that this power was limited by environment, inheritance and natural law, and that from the point of view of science these occurrences must be a matter of Chance and not of Law. I did not rule out the possibility of some God also influencing and directing human action and natural law. However I saw no evidence of such divine guidance. I did see evidence of the decisive action of human beings.

Here most persons who understood what I was saying left me quite alone and reverted to firm belief in unalterable Law, thus to my mind changing Man to an automaton and making Ethics unmeaning and Reform a contradiction in terms. After reading your first Chapter, I was not certain of your attitude or how far dialectical materialism agreed with my formulation. A second reading reassured me somewhat. So I am setting my thought down for your consideration.

Again I thank you deeply for your book.

Very sincerely,
W. E. B. Du Bois

Du Bois was not vindictive; he did not nurse grudges. This characteristic was part of his attractiveness—and may well have helped account for his longevity. A graduate student's request drew from Du Bois a reply reflecting this element in his personality.

Madison, Wisconsin, January 27, 1956

Dear Dr. Du Bois:

While it has been quite a few years ago, you might recall that I was one of several youngsters who grew up on the Morehouse-Atlanta University campuses between the mid-1920's and the early 1940's. My father, a teacher of English, was a colleague of yours in Atlanta.[1]

I am now studying toward the Ph.D. degree in political science at the University of Wisconsin, after teaching for a total of eight years in colleges in Texas, Virginia and Alabama. As a dissertation topic I have chosen to do a study in leadership with the late Walter White as its subject. This is not to be a biography, but an analysis and interpretation of Mr. White's career as a leader— his philosophy, techniques, situational environment and significance as related to theories and practices of interest group leadership.

Because of your experience and interest in social science research and your intimate knowledge of Mr. White and the N.A.A.C.P. I should like to have your comments and suggestions as to methodology, sources of materials and persons I should see and talk to. I have already asked for permission to review the Association's records and Mr. White's private papers. I plan to canvass them for data which will be pertinent to my project. I am also drawing up a list of persons to interview and preparing to arrange to carry through on that.

1. Nathaniel Patrick Tillman was associated with Atlanta University for many years and was a professor of English and a dean during the decade 1934 to 1944, when Du Bois was there.

I shall be very grateful for whatever assistance and advice you can give me, and will be looking forward to seeing you personally, if convenient, when I come to New York later in the year.

Very truly yours,
Nathaniel P. Tillman, Jr.[2]

New York City, March 1, 1956

My dear Mr. Tillman:

Answering your letter of January 27, may I say that I think you will have no difficulty in getting an abundance of material concerning the late Walter White. The archives of the N.A.A.C.P. are full of material. His widow would co-operate and you might get much from his former wife, Gladys White, and from their two children.

Personally, I would not like to undertake to help you in any but a very general way. Mr. White and I disagreed fundamentally on so many matters that my interpretation might be quite unfair.

Very sincerely yours,
W. E. B. Du Bois

Among the most stimulating letters Du Bois received were those from rank-and-file readers who followed his writings and who numbered in the thousands for over sixty years. One such letter came from Florida early in 1956.

St. Petersburg, Fla., Feb. 1, 1956

Dr. W. E. B. Du Bois
Dear Friend:

I have followed your writing in the *National Guardian* with great interest and learning. Your work in the intellectual field stands up with the giants. Perhaps my few years of activity in this struggle does not qualify me to take issue with the old reliables. Nevertheless, I feel that I should register my optimism by taking issue with you on one insignificant point in your Jan. 30 article, "A Bitter Battle Is Shaping Up." In the 5th paragraph from the bottom you said, "The battle for political and civil rights; for labor uplift and monopoly control in the South in this century and the next, will be one of the bitterest the world has seen." Your statement "—in this century and the next—" seems to imply that the battle will rage for another century.

2. Nathaniel P. Tillman, Jr., was born in Atlanta in 1924 and educated at Morehouse and the University of Wisconsin. Prior to 1956 he had taught at Saint Philips Junior College in Texas, Hampton Institute in Virginia, and Miles College in Alabama. He subsequently was on the faculty at Howard and at Delaware State College, and since 1971 he has been president of Olive-Harvey College in Chicago. Tillman's work on White never reached publication.

I fail to see how serfdom in the South can prevail while the balance of the world is throwing it off. Take the intensified industrialization of the South, with its rapid transformation of the small and middle farmers into the pauperized proletariat. Recently, the head of the University of Florida was singing the swan song. Among other things he said, "The small farmer is retarding the South." If the small farmers could be let down slowly into the jobless working class it might not disturb them so quick, but today the liquidation of his position is so rapid it amounts to the shock treatment. Heretofore the small farmer had some choice about when to go. Not so today, he is drove like the hurricane drives sand.

What is to be done with this great increase in production from farm and factory? It is assumed by some that it can be traded on the world market value for value, if need be. I think this is an illusion. For how can the people buy what was traded for if we cannot buy what was traded? No sir Doctor, there is but one way out of a hole and that is UP and we must rise soon.

Very truly yours,
Emmett Carter

New York City, March 1, 1956

My dear Mr. Carter:

Answering your letter of February 1, may I say that it is impossible to know how long such a social and economic problem as the South now faces will require for its solution. A century seems long to the living, but it is quite short and reasonable in the history of the world. I should be very glad if the South straightened itself out in much less time than a century, but I doubt it. As you say, "There is but one way out of a hole, and that is up." But when you add, "We must rise soon," I would advise putting the period after "rise."

Very sincerely yours,
W. E. B. Du Bois

Allan Nevins proposed to Du Bois that he record highlights of his life;* while more will be noted about this project in subsequent correspondence (see pp. 440–42 below), Nevin's approach dates from early 1956.

* Allan Nevins (1890–1971) was born in Illinois and educated at the University of Illinois. He taught English there briefly in 1912–13 and thereafter, until 1931, was an editorial writer for several New York City newspapers. From 1931 to 1958 he taught history at Columbia University and went on from there to be associated with the Huntington Library in California. Nevins was the author of many significant biographies and histories. The "American Academy" in the letter is the American Academy for Arts and Letters, of which Nevins was president from 1966 to 1968.

There was no copy of Du Bois's response to Nevins in his papers; the original is among the papers of the Oral History Research Office at Columbia University, and the editor appreciates the courtesies extended him by Louis M. Starr, its director.

New York City, March 8, 1956
Dear Doctor Du Bois:
Ever since we last met at the American Academy, I have been thinking what a fine thing it would be if you could be persuaded to give us, in a series of tape-recorded interviews, something out of the rich storehouse of your experience for the benefit of posterity.

As you may know, the Oral History Office is a project of mine established for that very purpose: to secure the reminiscences of persons who have made important contributions to American life in our time. Our young men have interviewed Supreme Court Justices, Senators, former cabinet members, publishers, authors, and a host of others. The tapes are transcribed into manuscripts which are then deposited in Special Collections in this library, subject to whatever restrictions the donor wishes to impose. Some, for example, cannot be opened until after the death of the subject; others are restricted for fifty years, and of course some are open to any qualified scholar. The subject receives his own copy.

The idea is to provide a vast reservoir of unique, uninhibited recollection from which the future historian may draw. I can think of no one who could make a more valuable contribution in a field which has engaged the hearts of all men of good will than yourself, and though you have written much, I know that the full story would be abundantly worth the telling. No one can write "the full story" of his life for publication, as we all know; but this method affords the opportunity to do it for those who survive you, and for all time.

Sincerely,
Allan Nevins

New York City, March 23, 1956
Dear Mr. Nevins:
I shall be glad to record for your Oral Research Office some of my reminiscences, when I return from California in the Spring.

Very sincerely,
W. E. B. Du Bois

Sometime in March, the Du Boises sent a letter to Dr. Martin Luther King, Jr., in Montgomery, Alabama. No copy has been found as of this date, but there is a reply from King.

Montgomery Improvement Association
Montgomery, Ala., March 19, 1956
Dear Friends:
This is just a note to express my deepest gratitude to you for your kind

letter. Such letters from friends sympathetic with our momentous struggle for justice give us renewed vigor and courage to carry on.

With every good wish, I am

Cordially yours,
M. L. King, Jr.
President

[Enclosure]

Rev. Martin Luther King, Jr.,
Dexter Avenue Baptist Church
Montgomery, Ala.

Fear not o little flock the foe
That madly seeks thine overthrow
Dread not his rage and power
What though thy courage often faints
Its seeming power o'er God's saints
Lasts but a little hour

It is unfortunate that a conversation between Du Bois and Benjamin J. Davis that took place in May 1956 was not recorded—so far as the editor knows! But a letter from Davis does indicate the questions which these two men discussed.

New York City, May 14, 1956

Dear Dr. Du Bois:

Pursuant to our telephone conversation a couple of days ago, I intend to call [on] you one day this week, perhaps Friday, May 18.

Among various things we might discuss, I want to raise the central matters on my mind so that you might consider them before we get together.

First, what do you think of our Party's theoretical position on the Negro question in the South—involving the question of self-determination for the Black Belt—in the light of the direction of the Negro people's movement in the South today, particularly in Montgomery?

Secondly, what do you see as a realizable perspective for the solution of the Negro question in the South today, in terms of guarantees of the Negro's full political, economic and social equality?

Thirdly, what do you consider the key issue—that is, popular issue—for advancing the whole struggle for democracy and Negro advancement in the South today?

Fourthly, how do you view the struggle for Negro rights in the North—that is, principally in the large urban Negro centers like Harlem, Chicago's South Side, etc.?

Our Party, as you doubtless know, is undergoing a thorough review and reexamination on all questions. But, of course, my conversations with you are entirely personal and unofficial.

I don't need to summon you to complete frankness in discussing the questions with me, because frankness is one of your prime virtues.

The fact is that my own participation in our Party's review will not be adequate until I have gotten the opinions of many who, from their own points of view, have given the Negro question long and wise consideration.

I hope to see you Friday afternoon at your office. Warm regards to Shirley.

Sincerely,
Benjamin J. Davis[1]

A lovely letter that must have brought much pleasure to Du Bois came to him from Langston Hughes—that poet whose greatness first found print in Du Bois's Crisis *a generation earlier.*

New York City, May 22, 1956

Dear Dr. Du Bois:

I have just read again your *The Souls of Black Folk*[1]—for perhaps the tenth time—the first time having been some forty years ago when I was a child in Kansas. Its beauty and passion and power are as moving and as meaningful as ever.

1. Reflecting Davis's thinking in this period is his article "The Challenge of the New Era," *Political Affairs* 35 (December 1956):14–27; esp. pp. 21–24, where he deals with questions of the struggles of Black people.

1. Hughes probably read the Jubilee edition of *The Souls of Black Folk*, published on the fiftieth anniversary of its first appearance in 1903.

The reference Hughes makes to Du Bois's impact upon him renders pertinent another letter of 1956, one written 29 October from Big Sur, California, by the author Henry Miller (b. 1891) to Carey McWilliams, editor of the *Nation*. That magazine published an essay by Du Bois, "I Won't Vote," on 20 October 1956, and Miller wrote McWilliams: "That was a splendid article by W. E. Burghardt du Bois! I didn't know he was still alive. When I was a very young man I attended his lectures, read his books. I owe a great deal to him—he was one of the truly deep influences in my life." McWilliams sent this penned letter to Du Bois; a notation, probably in McWilliams's hand, reads: "Address [of Du Bois] sent 11/2/56," but there appears to be no direct correspondence between Miller and Du Bois. Miller devotes several pages in his *Plexus* (New York: Grove Press, 1965) to an account of Du Bois's impact upon him; he mentions particularly attending one of Du Bois's lectures (pp. 559–66). Miller states here that his own writing was first published by Du Bois (p. 560), but I have not been able to find any evidence and he does not make the same statement in his letter to McWilliams. See also Harold T. McCarthy, "Henry Miller's Democratic Vistas," *American Quarterly* 38 (May 1971) :221–35 esp. p. 225.

My very best regards to Shirley and continued good wishes to you both.
Sincerely,
Langston Hughes

Shattering developments in the Soviet Union and eastern Europe, in particular, produced widespread crisis among left movements everywhere and not least in the United States. While many people reacted with despair or apathy or great change, Du Bois's left commitment and partisanship toward socialism remained firm and even intensified.

Reflecting some of his thinking in 1956 on aspects of this development was a letter written to Anna Melissa Graves, a participant in anti-imperialist and anti-racist movements. Du Bois had known her at least from the early 1930s and had great respect for her.*

This letter was addressed to Miss Graves in care of a friend, Dora Jaufroid, who lived in Covington, Louisiana.

New York City, July 8, 1956

My dear Miss Graves:

I think your letter to Anna Louise Strong was very, very fine. I and Shirley have read it with great interest, and I thank you for sending it. I have had it copied and I wonder if you would mind if I sent it to the editor of the *Guardian* and perhaps to the *Worker*.¹ It may be late for news value, and there has been so much debate that the editors may think enough has been said, but nevertheless I would like them to read it.

Personally I agree with you almost completely. As I wrote to an editor not long ago, I still regard Stalin as one of the great men of the twentieth century. He was not perfect; he was probably too cruel; but he did three things: he established the first socialist state in the modern world; he broke the power of the kulaks; and he conquered Hitler. If in his later years he became an irresponsible tyrant, that was very bad and I am sorry for it. But he was not the first tyrant in the world and will not be the last. Moreover, I am not at all satisfied with Khrushchev's testimony. It seems to me irresponsible and muddled. He lumps together Stalin's fight against Trotsky and the various victims of the purge. From the testimony which I read at the time, I believe that justice was done to these men on the whole. In the critical struggle then going on, some innocent men might have suffered, but as to the general fairness of these trials, even reliable American observers like Raymond Robbins testified.

---

* Correspondence with Miss Graves from 1934 appears in volume two of this work (p. 27). Du Bois thought highly of her book, *Benevenuto Cellini Had No Prejudice against Bronze* (Baltimore: Waverly Press, 1943), recommending it in his column in the *Amsterdam News*, 31 July 1943.

1. A search through both newspapers failed to reveal the publication of this letter.

As to the war against Hitler, it is pure poppycock to assert that Stalin was not fully aware of the menace of Germany, and that any preparation on his part could have stopped the Wehrmacht any sooner than it did. That the victory over Hitler was due entirely to Stalin I of course doubt, and he, or, what is more likely, his friends, later boasted of the victory too much and gave him too much credit. Nevertheless, it remains true that under Stalin's rule Hitler was stopped and turned back, and for this the whole world is Stalin's debtor.

As to what happened in later years, and what the role of Beria was, I do not know and have no present way of finding out. It may have been quite as bad as Khrushchev is reported to have testified, but the facts are not before me.

On the other hand, I am not in the least cast down. The Soviet state is great and progressing, and the beginnings of natural democratic argument and disagreement are encouraging. Not even the upheaval in Poland disturbs me. I saw Poland in 1893 and in 1950. Its progress, contentment, and peace is unquestionable. Of course the old landlord and military clan bribed by the United States is going to make trouble for a long time to come.

I trust this will find you and Miss Jaufroid in good health. The quotation: "It is the stars," and so forth, is taken from a poem by my fellow student William Vaughan Moody.[2] I am not sure about the name of the poem but I think it is "The Fire-bringers."

With love from Shirley and myself, I remain,

Very sincerely yours,
W. E. B. Du Bois

Neither the project conceived by Du Bois nor that projected by Woodson for an Encyclopedia Africana has yet reached fruition. Correspondence relative to both projects was exchanged late in 1956 between Du Bois and Dr. Charles H. Wesley, when the latter was president of Central State College in Wilberforce, Ohio.

Wilberforce, Ohio, October 17, 1956

Dear Dr. Du Bois:

The Association for the Study of Negro Life and History has been planning for a number of years to publish an *Encyclopedia Africana*. Dr. Carter G. Woodson in 1921, when the Associated Publishers, Incorporated was organized, began the development of this idea. A considerable body of data has been collected and is stored in the offices in Washington, D. C. It has been projected to

2. William Vaughan Moody (1869–1910) graduated from Harvard in 1893. The line in question comes from Moody's play *The Fire-Bringer* (1904), in Act II where Pyrrha cries out: "It is the stars! It is the ancient stars! It is the young and everlasting stars!" Du Bois frequently quoted these lines in speeches and essays.

treat in a general way Negroes and Negroid peoples throughout the world. A goodly body of material has been assembled in the rough and some of the editing has been done for the first two volumes. I recall your project under the caption of the *Encyclopedia of the Negro* and that it was incorporated. Neither Dr. Woodson nor I was acquainted with the details of your plan, although I attended one meeting at Howard University at the invitation of President Johnson. I am writing to inquire concerning the status of this plan and what your reaction would be to the proposal of the Association concerning an *Encyclopedia Africana*. Funds are always an obstacle in these types of projects. However, our Association has been discussing this subject at a number of its Annual Meetings and particularly since the passing of Dr. Woodson and our opportunity to examine some of his assembled materials.

The Association will meet at Texas Southern University, Houston, Texas, October 26–28, at its Forty-First Annual Meeting. In order to determine future planning and future approaches to some agency for financing, and to develop plans for editing, it seems desirable that we should have some word from you concerning your project which seems also to have advanced beyond the assembly of materials.

With cordial personal regards, I am

Sincerely yours,
Charles H. Wesley

New York City, October 22, 1956

My dear Mr. Wesley:

Answering your letter of October 17, may I say that as early as 1910, I proposed an Encyclopedia Africana and secured on its editorial board a number of scholars including the greatest of Egyptologists, Flinders Petrie.[1] This of course was but a dream and never got beyond mere paper planning, although in 1911 I discussed the matter with several scholars in England.

I did not return to the subject until Anson Phelps Stokes planned the Encyclopedia of the Negro. A conference on the matter was held in Washington November 7, 1931. Twenty persons were present, but I was not invited. However, at this meeting it was unanimously recommended that Carter Woodson, Alain Locke, and myself be added to the board.

In January, 1932, the *Journal of Negro History* made public for the first time Mr. Woodson's plan of an Encyclopedia Africana. The Board immediately, on motion of President Hope, seconded by me, voted to send a statement to Dr. Woodson, commending the work of his Association and the *Journal;* assuring him that no member of the Board had heard of his proposed Encyclopedia, and welcoming him to join our conference. Dr. Woodson, however, re-

1. Actually Du Bois began work on the encyclopedia no later than 1909; see the present work, 1:145-47.

fused to cooperate.[2] We proceeded with our effort to lay down a broad basis for the proposed Encyclopedia. We corresponded with the chief scholars of America and Europe, and received commendation from Charles Beard, Franz Boas, John R. Commons, Edith Abbott, Felix Frankfurter, Carl Van Doren, H. L. Mencken, Carleton Beals, Roscoe Pound, John W. Vandercook, Robert E. Park, Professor [W. L.] Westermann, Raymond Moley, Broadus Mitchell, Sidney Hook, Francis P. Graham, Harold Laski, and scores of others.

I prepared several general statements and in consultation with the editors of the Encyclopedia of the Social Sciences worked out a careful budget. We applied to the General Education Board for a grant and were much encouraged, but finally the grant was refused. We then decided to go on with the planning of this work and finally published a small preparatory volume in 1946, of which there were two editions.

I have in my office a large amount of correspondence and data which you are quite at liberty to use. Also, Dr. Anson Phelps Stokes, whose address is Lenox, Mass., has a great amount of material which I am sure he would place at your disposal. Much of it is probably filed in the office of the Phelps Stokes Fund. I am enclosing some material from my files which I wish you would be careful to return.

Very sincerely yours,
W. E. B. Du Bois

P. S. Let me impress upon you: there is no such thing as a cheap encyclopedia. If you propose to publish a work of scholarship which will stand up beside the *Catholic Encyclopedia*, the *Jewish Encyclopedia*, and the *Encyclopedia of the Social Sciences*, it cannot be done for a cent less than $250,000. If, of course, you have in mind something like the Tuskegee Yearbook, then don't for god's sake call it an encyclopedia.

A letter which reflects Du Bois's habits of planning far ahead and of concentrating on major issues—and not personalities— was sent to the board of directors of the NAACP *late in 1956.*

New York City, November 5, 1956

Gentlemen:

I am venturing to write to remind you that the year 1957 will usher in a series of centenaries which deeply affect the history of the Negroes and of this country. May I point out a few:

1957: One hundredth anniversary of the Dred Scott decision.

1959: One hundredth anniversary of the death of John Brown.

2. For relevant correspondence, see the present work, 1:447–49.

1961 to 1965: One hundredth anniversary of the participation of American Negroes in the Civil War.

1963: One hundredth anniversary of the Emancipation Proclamation.

1968: One hundredth anniversary of the death of Thaddeus Stevens, of the enfranchisement of the freedmen, and of the Freedmen's Bureau.

1972: One hundredth anniversary of the birth of Paul Laurence Dunbar.

1976: One hundredth anniversary of the Bargain of 1876.

There are many other significant anniversaries which recall Negro history and the cultural tie of the black man with American history. If we neglect to mark this history, it may be distorted or forgotten. Already repeated effort is being made to prove that slavery was not the cause of the Civil War; to minimize the part of Negroes in the slavery controversy and the war; to slander friends of the Negro; and to represent his enfranchisement as a serious mistake.

It would be wrong to make these celebrations occasions for controversy or exacerbation of race hate. Rather they should be occasions for calm and scientific inquiry into the past, participated in by persons of authority, white and black, Northern and Southern. We must only be sure that every point of view has adequate and worthy representation.

I suggest that these celebrations be varied in character and place and in sponsorship; we have only to be sure that no important event or person is forgotten in these centenaries of the first participation in the civilization of the United States of the Negro masses as free citizens. Colleges might celebrate jointly or singly the birthdays of distinguished men; newspapers might issue special editions to recall great events; organizations might hold special meetings or alert their branches and fraternities might offer prizes for essays or even books on certain subjects.

I trust you will agree that this is a vital matter and will take such action as seems to you appropriate.

Very sincerely yours,
W. E. B. Du Bois

A letter such as that printed below compensated, we may be certain, for much of the pain felt by one treated as a pariah by the high and the mighty.

New York City, May 1, 1957

Dear Dr. Du Bois:

You told me this morning that I should call you next Thursday, May 9th, to make an appointment to see you. In our brief telephone conversation this morning you also asked me why I wanted to see you? I replied that I just wanted to speak to you. I believe, however, that I should explain why I "just wanted to speak to you." The reason is rather simple: I want to see and speak to the person who started to fight for me before I was even born. You can even say that I want to make a pilgrimage to see, who is to my mind, one of the most important men in the world today. That is all I want.

I do not want a job, nor money, nor a help in publishing anything. You can even say that after the "blood and toil," I am reaping the reward. I received a fellowship to study in French West Africa, and now I am the second Negro to be appointed to the faculty of Columbia University. I am sure that all this is possible only because people like you have struggled for our rights.

My seeing you can spare me a great deal of embarrassment when, on any future trip to Africa, I am asked by a barely literate African whether I know one Dr. Du Bois. If you think that it is not necessary that I come to see you please have your secretary call me at TR 5-2272 and let me know.

Sincerely yours,
Elliott P. Skinner, Ph. D.[1]

Correspondence initiated by Dr. Carlton B. Goodlett evoked from Du Bois significant opinions about medicine and the nature of its practice.

1. Elliott Percival Skinner was born in Trinidad-Tobago in 1924. He was educated at New York University and Columbia University and served on the faculty of both institutions; since 1969 he has held the chair of Franz Boas Professor of Anthropology at Columbia, and since 1972 he has been chairman of anthropology at Columbia. His books include *The Mossi of the Upper Volta* (1964) and *African Urban Life: The Transformation of Ouagadougou* (1974).

In kindly giving permission for the publication of his letter to Du Bois, Professor Skinner wrote the editor (in a letter dated 14 September 1976, also quoted with per-

San Francisco, Calif., June 26, 1957

Dear Dr. Du Bois:

I am writing you about a project that has interested me for some months. Moreover I realize that your vast knowledge of the current political, social and economical developments in Africa qualified you to give advice to "a Dreamer" in these matters. Briefly stated our interests are as follows: Several men who are trained in medicine are interested in organizing a Medical Team for service in West Africa, preferably Ghana. This medical group would consist of specialists in several areas of medicine: Public Health, Internal Medicine, Gynecology and Obstetrics, General Surgery, Pediatrics, Radiology, Pathology and Parasitology. Our objectives would be twofold: first, to establish a medical clinic for treatment and demonstration purposes; and secondly to assist in the medical profession in Ghana in establishing a Medical College for West Africa. With Nigeria approaching independence, I feel that the need for medical training facilities in West Africa will be imperative. Do you think that such a project has some merit? If the answer is favorable, would you be kind enough to aid me in bringing this matter to the attention of Dr. Kwame Nkrumah? In the initial planning of this project, I am associated with two brilliant young medical scientists:

Nathanial Burbridge, M.D. and Ph.D., Assistant Professor of Pharmacology, Univ. of California Medical College. Dr. Burbridge spent three years in the Medical College, Univ. of Indonesia, where he established the Department of Pharmacology.

Wendel Lipscomb, M.D. and M.S. (Public Health), present Director of Research in the Alcoholic Rehabilitation Program, Department of Health of the State of California.

A statement of my training might be in order: Ph.D. (Psychology) and M.D. Formerly on the teaching staffs of West Virginia State College, Fisk University, Tennessee State A & I College, Fort Valley State College, Meharry Medical College, and Stanford University Medical School.

If we are successful in interesting Dr. Nkrumah in this project one of us would make a trip to Ghana for the purpose of studying and developing a detailed prospectus for the implementation of such a project.

---

mission) that he received a phone call in response to his letter, inviting him to the Du Bois home. He recalls that Du Bois "was extremely gracious" and that "he quizzed me at length about my trip to Africa, about work among the Mossi, and about my appointment at Columbia. Apparently he had read about the Mossi of Upper Volta while researching the African background for his study of the Negro. He recalled that he had met Franz Boas of Columbia's Anthropology Department in Atlanta several years before, but did not go into details. Du Bois was interested in my West Indian background and education. . . . I was also intrigued by his advice to me to learn Chinese."

I trust you will be able to fit the consideration of our problem into your very busy schedule.

Yours very truly,
Carlton B. Goodlett, M.D.[1]

Brooklyn, N.Y., July 6, 1957

Dear Dr. Goodlett:

I have your letter of June 26, concerning a Medical Team for service in West Africa. Of the need of medical service in Africa, there is no question. There are however grave questions as to the way in which such an institution as you outline should be established, and as to its objects and methods. I do not know Dr. Nkrumah's thought on this matter but I shall send him a copy of your letter and of this reply.

Americans regard the practice of medicine as a way of making a good income, with their fees protected by their very efficient trade union the American Medical Association. They are especially set on practicing where they choose and not necessarily where they are most needed; and choosing their patients and fixing their fees according to the amount they can get, with of course some professional limitations.

On the other hand, Great Britain, the Soviet Union, many Scandinavian states and eastern European states have an entirely different plan. There physicians are state officials and paid limited fees by the state. Hospitals and sanatariums are under state control. In the Soviet Union the physician is educated at state expense and must locate and practice where the state orders him to. In other words in the modern state, increasingly medicine is not a private profession for private gain, but a state institution for public welfare.

Just what the attitude of the new state of Ghana is going to be with regard to medicine and hospitals I do not know. I would assume however that it will approach British state controlled medicine and it may go even further toward the Soviet ideal. The reaction of your group toward this will depend much on your attitude toward African health; whether you are interested in medicine as science and philanthropy; or in medicine as well-paying business.

As I have said, I shall send a copy of your letter and my reply to the Prime Minister without comment. He of course will reply as he sees fit.

Very sincerely yours,
W. E. B. Du Bois

1. In addition to his medical practice, Goodlett is the publisher of the weekly *Sun-Reporter* in San Francisco and has been a leader in the international peace movement for many years. In a letter to the editor of 19 September 1976 giving permission for the publication of his letter to Du Bois, Dr. Goodlett wrote, "We followed up the recommendations of Dr. Du Bois with several letters to the President [that is, Nkrumah]." Such efforts continued until the early 1960s and were joined by other groups, including Jefferson Medical College of Philadelphia and the Kaiser Group Medical Plan.

Another young man at the threshold of what is already a distinguished career was invited to the Du Bois home; there is no doubt that inspiration resulted for both hosts and guest.

Chicago, Ill., August 6, 1957

Dear Dr. Du Bois:

I should like to extend my gratitude for having been so warmly received by you and Mrs. Du Bois.

The conversation with you, getting to know Mrs. Du Bois, the exceedingly impressive portraits of Frederick Douglass and Harriet Tubman—these together with everything associated with my visit will remain forever among my most treasured experiences.

You remain now as always my greatest single inspiration, for you represent not only the New Negro in his finest form but, more importantly, through your breadth of knowledge and universality of humanity, you point the way to the man of tomorrow, to a man free from the pettiness and eternal stupidity of a society predicated upon selfishness. For this I, and the youth of the world, can never thank you enough.

I do hope that you and Mrs. Du Bois are in good health. Please extend my warmest regards to her.

Thanks again for having received me at your home.

I remain

Faithfully yours
Sterling Stuckey[1]

A veteran of Black liberation efforts whom Du Bois had known since the years just after World War 1, William A. Domingo, sent Du Bois a pamphlet arguing against West Indian Federation. The resulting exchange touches on the views of both men.

Brooklyn, N.Y., June 11, 1957

Dear Mr. Domingo:

I hope you will pardon me for neglecting so long to answer your letter of last November. I believe in West Indian Federation, although there are some ob-

1. Stuckey is now a professor of history at Northwestern University. In a letter to the editor dated 5 October 1976, permitting publication, Professor Stuckey remarked that the invitation was arranged through the good offices of Du Bois's daughter. The meeting occurred on 17 July 1957; Dr. Stuckey remarks: "He was surprisingly warm, which helped as I was nervous."

jections like those which you mentioned in your pamphlet.[1] I did not want to review it unfavorably and therefore I kept silence. I was, however, glad to know that you are still active and thinking vigorously as in the old days.

Very sincerely,

W. E. B. Du Bois

New York City, August 11, 1957

Dear Dr. Du Bois:

I should have written before to thank you for your letter of two months ago, but a variety of circumstances interfered.

It was very kind of you not to review my pamphlet adversely; but I can assure you I would not have been hurt personally. I believe in the widest latitude of views on controversial questions. British Honduras, with whose leaders I corresponded and to whom I sent copies of my pamphlet, expressed full agreement with me. This was reflected in the overwhelming vote against Federation registered in that country a few months ago.

British Guiana goes to the polls this week and the result should be interesting. I sent copies of my pamphlet to the two outstanding leaders, [Linden F.] Burnham and [Cheddi] Jagan, who are both, if newspaper reports can be trusted, opposed to federation.

Long ago I should have sent you the enclosed clippings from the Jamaica *Gleaner* [not found]. They speak for themselves. West Indians know little of your work for Africa and credit Garvey with a great deal. Jamaicans have even erected a statue to him.

I answered Mrs. Garvey's letter by quoting from Nkrumah's autobiography, *Ghana*. I cited Aggrey's rejection of Garvey and Nkrumah's repudiation of the fantastic and impractical ideas of Garvey regarding the freedom of Africa from Western imperialism. Indeed, Garvey frequently proclaimed that he was a "capitalist" and Rogers quotes him as claiming to be the "first Fascist."[1]

1. The reference is to a nineteen-page pamphlet by William A. Domingo, *British West Indian Federation: A Critique* (Kingston, Jamaica: Gleaner Co., 1956). In 1958, Domingo himself published in New York City a twenty-five-page pamphlet, *Federation: Jamaica's Folly*. Domingo (1889-1968) is briefly identified in volume one of this work (pp. 263-64), where an exchange from 1923—also dealing largely with Garvey— is printed.

1. The reference is to *Ghana:The Autobiography of Kwame Nkrumah*, first published in London in 1957 by Thomas Nelson and Sons and reissued in 1971 in New York City by International Publishers. Nkrumah noted Kwegyir Aggrey's attack on Garveyism on p. 14 of this book but stated at that point that he did not fully agree with Aggrey either. On p. 45 he wrote that his reading of Garvey's *Philosophy and Opinions* (1923) in the United States in the 1940s "did more than any other [book] to fire my enthusiasm." But he did differ substantively with Garvey and so stated on p. 184 of this book. The quotation from Garvey attributed to J. A. Rogers is accurate and will be found in *The Negro in New York: An Informal Social History* ed. Roi Ottley and W. J. Weatherby (New York: New York Public Library, 1967), p. 237.

The whole concept of Garvey as revealed in his organization with its "Lords" and "Dukes" and his designation of his successor in a sealed envelope is reminiscent of Hitler.

In a cautious way I have tried to debunk the Garvey myth in Jamaica, but, as the Greeks used to say, "Against stupidity (in this case ignorance, w.a.d.) even the gods fight in vain."

Yours sincerely,
W. A. Domingo

Du Bois sent a remarkable letter, reflecting his deeply held convictions at this time, to the Literary Gazette *in the Soviet Union in time for that country's celebration of the fortieth anniversary of the Bolshevik Revolution.**

Brooklyn, N.Y., September 26, 1957

To the Foreign Editor of the
Literary Gazette
Sir:

On the Fortieth Anniversary of the Russian Revolution, I beg the privilege of saluting the Union of Soviet Socialist Republics, its leaders and its workers; its writers, artists, and musicians; and particularly its school children, students, and teachers.

I first read of Russia when I was in High School in 1885. I read of the splendor and extravagance of Czars and nobles, and of the misery of the workers, and the fierce repression of all who sought freedom. Particularly did I suffer with the peasants who had been freed from serfdom at almost the same time that my people had been emancipated from slavery, and like the moujiks, still lingered in ignorance and poverty.

When in 1917 I heard of the Russian Revolution, I was overjoyed, as I think were most Americans; but we were just entering the First World War and authentic news was hard to get. By that time I had studied at Harvard and in Germany and had earned my Bachelor's and Master's degrees and taken my doctorate in history. I had taught American Negro students and tried to start a scientific study of race relations. The American people would not support this work, and in 1910, I turned to propaganda to teach the nation the meaning of Negro education and Negro rights for human progress. I founded and for 23 years edited a monthly magazine which spoke out boldly for the uplift of all men, but particularly for the oppressed black folk in the United States.

When the Revolution came in Russia, I could give it but scant attention: my

* This letter was published in the *Literary Gazette* in Moscow (in Russian translation, of course), no. 133, October 1957. I am indebted to Harry Freeman of the TASS agency in New York for obtaining this information.

eyes were blinded and my ears deafened by the mob murder and lynching of my people; by gross discrimination in civil and political rights; and with persistent insistence by American science that Negroes were sub-human. When the Armistice came, I rushed to Paris to hold a Pan-African Congress so as to bring to the attention of the peace-makers the plight of Africans and their children overseas. In this effort and during visits to London and Geneva, I became aware of the Labor Movement and of the development of Marxian socialism and I sensed the real meaning of the Russian Revolution.

However, neither then nor after my return to America did I learn much about what was really taking place in Russia. The war of the West against Russia was now beginning and newspapers, periodicals, and books contradicted each other endlessly. It was impossible for me to extricate truth from slander, especially as I was driven to distraction with the post-war development of the Negro Problem in America. Save for vague references to the Russian Revolution, I was silent on its real implications because I simply did not know the facts. Then in 1926, one morning, three Russians entered my office: a man and wife of evident experience and breeding; a tall blond giant of vigor and enthusiasm. They had come to secure my influence in helping the Soviet Union gain the diplomatic recognition of the American government. I smiled at their ignorance and explained: I had little influence; I was a second-class American citizen. Most Negroes could not vote; they were discriminated against in civil rights and privileges. They wanted to take me to dinner, but no respectable restaurant in New York would admit me. I was a pariah, subject to insult and possible violence in this Land of the Free.

But, they insisted, you write and speak to eleven million of your own people and many whites listen. I had to explain further that I knew little about Russia and about what had happened and was happening there. I had no access to the facts, and without facts I could not write. "Then," they said, "why do you not visit Russia and see for yourself?"

I went to the Soviet Union in 1926 and stayed two months. I visited Leningrad, Moscow, Nizhni Novgorod, Kiev, and Odessa. I visited schools, factories, churches, and homes; I talked with workers, officials, and peasants; I saw poverty, hunger, ignorance, and toil; and I saw a new people, re-born and filled with determination and hope; and with sympathy for me and my people. I learned what slander was when I read in the New York *Times*, dated the very day I landed in peaceful Kronstadt, that this dead town was then in revolution, and was "flowing with blood."[1]

Since that day I have visited the Soviet Union twice: in 1936 I went to Mos-

1. Du Bois was in the USSR in the summer of 1926. From 8 August through 20 August 1926 the *New York Times* ran stories, usually on its first page, reporting "revolts at Kronstadt, Leningrad and other cities" (to quote the issue dated 8 August). These reports came from Bucharest, Warsaw, and Berlin, and from time to time the *Times* reported their denial.

cow and for a week rode the Trans-Siberian Railway from Moscow to Otpur; we rode slowly and talked with fellow travellers and with Russians along the way. In 1949, 25 Americans were invited to attend an All-Russian Peace Congress. I alone accepted. I met leaders and workers from all over the Soviet Union and from many parts of the world.

For this visit and for attending the previous Peace Congress in Paris and distributing in the United States the Stockholm Appeal against atomic weapons, the Government of the United States indicted me for not admitting that I was "agent of a Foreign Power." They fingerprinted me, manacled me, and tried desperately to sentence me to jail for five years and fine me $5,000. It cost $30,000 in funds given by my friends, supported by the protest of workers and writers all over the world, to secure finally my acquittal from the absurd charge.

From this experience, I stand with bared head before the miracle of the Union of Soviet Socialist Republics; before a great nation which in forty years, in little more than a generation, has raised itself from superstition, disease, and poverty to health and industry; from almost 90 percent of illiteracy to an intelligent people with probably the best system of education in the world; from a degraded peasant agriculture to an economy of farm and factory which is becoming the most efficient in the world, freed from the blight of religious dogma and priest-ridden tyranny.

I know that this miracle has been accomplished in the face of the armed attack from nearly every civilized nation in the world including my own; that it has been carried on doggedly in the midst of economic boycott and a vicious slander and barrage of lies which reached a depth of infamy which this world has seldom if ever seen before. And even after thirty years of this unparalleled assault, it was this same Soviet Union which gave millions of her sons and daughters and a large part of her blood-bought industry to rescue the world which has traduced her, from the Hell of Hitler.

I do not wonder that this marvelous accomplishment cost the Russian people blood and tears from internal strife and dissension as well as from foreign aggression; that Russia reeled and starved and quarreled under this superhuman effort. The Russians were not and are not angels; they are just ordinary human beings, for centuries degraded and exploited by the very nations who now seek their destruction. Who flattered and fawned on Czars and Grand Dukes more than the United States and Britain? Who spent more eagerly the results of the starvation of Russian serfs and workers than France and the United States? And when this awful debt was paid, the blood spilt was less than that which flowed in the French Revolution; or that in which India was drowned for two centuries; or that which gushed from black slaves for three hundred years to build America, the land of the Free and the Home of the Brave.

I am astonished at the wealth of ability and strength and moral courage which the Soviet Union has given the world in the Twentieth Century. No other nation has produced any group of men who compare with Lenin, Stalin, Gorki, Litvinov, Vishinsky, Shostakovich, Prokofiev, Oistrakh, Lysenko, Stanislavsky, Kapitza, Oparin, Shokolov. I am quite prepared to believe that Stalin was at times a cruel taskmaster; I do not doubt that suspicion and unjust punishment have been rife in the Soviet Union when tolerance and justice would have served better. But this was to be expected in a nation with so tragic a history as Russia, which in our own day has been treated with such utter contempt as the people of Russia, and had to drag self-respect out of their own entrails. Americans should be the last to demand consistency of others. We declared "all men" equal when half a million were in slavery. George Washington held and traded in slaves; Abraham Lincoln offered to let the South continue to enslave Negroes if it would not secede from Northern business. On occasion, human nature is horrible and human beings beastly, but the world progresses; men reel and stagger forward; and never before in the history of man, have they made so gallant and successful a struggle as in the Soviet Union since the Revolution of 1917.

Again, Comrades, I salute you, and thank you for being the first nation of the modern world to recognize the colored inhabitants of Africa and Asia, America and the islands of the sea, as the equals of the white nations of the earth.

I am Sir, very respectfully yours,

W. E. B. Du Bois

Du Bois sent a letter to one of the United Nations committees late in 1957; it was not acted upon by the organization.

Brooklyn, N.Y., October 10, 1957

To the Membership of the Third Committee[1]
United Nations General Assembly
New York City
Sirs:

I am one of the sixteen million Americans who are deprived of their rights as full citizens and whose fathers for one hundred eighty-one years and more have been so deprived. We have been slaves, serfs and members of a lower caste, for a long time with "no rights which the white man has been bound to respect." Even today we are still discriminated against in work and wages, in homes and schools, in civil and political affairs, in courts and jails, in social and philanthropic effort and in public treatment and esteem.

The progress of Negroes in the United States since 1776 has been great. It

---

1. The Third Committee was the Committee on Social, Humanitarian, and Cultural matters; each of the member nations was represented on this committee.

has come about, however, largely by our own efforts, not simply by the efforts of whites. We led the movement for escape of fugitive slaves and were an effective part of the legal abolition of slavery; our soldiers turned the scales of civil war and made the emancipation of slaves the result of the war and not mere union of states. Negroes fought and died for the right to vote and for civil rights; Negroes gave free public education to the former slave states and were the shock troops who prevented reactionary Southern provincialism from preventing the formation of a unified federal democracy.

We acknowledge with deep gratitude the unselfish effort of many white Americans who have over the years helped us in our struggle upward, but we insist that it was mainly our own efforts that freed us, so far as we are free. Today we are not yet free citizens and will not be free without the force of world's public opinion being brought to bear. We do not ask intervention into the internal affairs of the United States by force or violence, but we do ask the right to be heard, the right to state our own case. We ask that the United Nations and its committees refuse to permit our enemies alone to speak for us.

May we remind the United Nations that there are more Negroes in the United States than persons in half the nations which today compose this great organization. We rejoice that these smaller nations have and use the right to speak and vote in this federation of the world. We especially beg their support in giving us the right to express our grievances and not to have opinions thrust down our throats and broadcast to the world by persons ignorant or inimical to our interests. The other day George Meany undertook to tell you of the success which the United States has made in the social progress of Negroes.[2] Yet no institution has fought harder or longer to degrade and retard Negroes than the American Federation of Labor—which Meany heads. Many of his unions still exclude Negroes. Other white Americans who know nothing and care less about Negroes have been selected to tell the United Nations about the "Negro Problem," while not a single Black man has been given opportunity to speak.

Since the United States has sent no Negro to your Committee to speak from his own knowledge about his own people, is it too much to ask that the United Nations itself invite some Negro to address them on this problem which is not local nor merely internal but affects the majority of the peoples of the earth?

2. George Meany, a member of the Third Committee for the United States, spoke before it on 30 September 1957; the text of his speech is printed in U.S., Department of State, *Bulletin* 37 (28 October 1957):688-93. Mrs. Oswald B. Lord at that time was the remaining member of the committee representing the United States. The quotation from Meany given further on in the letter appears toward the close of Meany's speech, on p. 692. It is relevant that the NAACP Legal Defense and Educational Fund honored Meany "as an American who has contributed in great measure to the betterment of race relations in this country." The honor was given on 16 May 1957; the Catholic magazine *America* reported the matter rather fully in its issue of 8 June 1957 (97:294).

It is false to assert that the Negro problem in the United States is being progressively and satisfactorily settled. The nation has continually advanced and retreated, progressed and fallen back toward barbarism in its treatment of Negroes. Only the unremitting struggle of Negroes themselves has saved it repeatedly from utter collapse. Such a crisis fronts the nation and the world today. In 1787 this nation was on the edge of abolishing slavery but was induced to postpone action for a couple of decades. During these years slavery made the South rich and it fought a civil war to preserve slavery. By 1876 the Negro was free and a voter, but the nation was induced to disfranchise him and beat him down into an underprivileged caste. For thirty years Negroes writhed against this condition until gradually they began to regain the right to vote and to have their children educated; then their schools were made inferior and most of the Negroes in former slave states were still kept from voting. At last came court decisions insisting that segregation by race was unconstitutional. Immediately five states where six million Negro children live declared they would not obey the law and today they are not obeying it and are openly threatening armed resistance. Other states are giving only token and often false obedience to the law. Is this the time for Negroes to suck their thumbs and permit Meany to describe their plight as "one phase of a great advance"? On the contrary, it is threatening evidence of a great retreat and as such the United Nations should at least know the facts.

This is not the first time that American Negroes have appealed to the United Nations for a hearing. Exactly ten years ago, at the direction of the National Association for the Advancement of Colored People, of which I was then an officer, I prepared an "Appeal to the World: A Statement on the Denial of Human Rights to Minorities in the Case of Citizens of Negro Descent in the United States of America and an Appeal to the United Nations for Redress." We presented this to the Human Rights Commission which at first refused to receive it; then the Commission received it but refused to discuss it; then discussed it briefly, but refused to present it to the Assembly.

Today I no longer represent the NAACP or any other organization. As a simple citizen who has devoted the larger part of a century to the situation of Negroes in the United States I ask the right to discuss this matter before the Human Rights Commission or before the Assembly itself. So far the United States has not designated any one of its Negro citizens to talk, but chooses white citizens who have in the past stood for the oppression and degradation of the Negro race.

Respectfully submitted,
W. E. B. Du Bois

An attorney in Buffalo in 1957 posed a question which remains a matter of wide debate.

Buffalo, N.Y., November 8, 1957

Dear Dr. Du Bois:

Some time ago I became interested in the Planned Parenthood Program promoted by the Planned Parenthood Federation of America, Inc. Manifestly, the plan consists of four principal parts: (1) conception control, (2) treating for infertility, (3) education for marriage and parenthood, and (4) research in human reproduction.

As a young parent and a Negro lawyer who deals daily with the problems that torment poverty-stricken, over-populated families, I felt and still feel that this four-part program is a fine scientific effort which makes possible a more stable and happier family life for those availing themselves of its fruits. Accordingly I undertook to contribute what little talent I had to help the program achieve its goal, especially in the local Negro community.

Speaking frankly, in the main, the Negro community was found to be responsive to parts two, three and four of the plan as indicated above. However, in regard to part one (conception control) I found many Negroes, particularly community leaders, who harbored suspicions. Many felt that—from a broader, racial group point of view—a rapidly growing Negro population is an advantageous phenomenon which, if continued, will result in the American Negroes having sufficient political might to demand economic, political and social equality.

Whether this contention is well or ill founded is not the question. The real question is, I feel, that these anxieties are real and the contention itself is formidable. Because these anxieties are so real I have decided to solicit some ideas on the matter from minds more profound than mine. Being a great admirer (and an unmatriculated student) of yours I further decided that you would be among the first to whom I would direct the following question for thought and, I hope, a reply:

"Should the American Negro oppose birth control upon the ground that a larger Negro population will mean greater political power which can be employed to achieve equality more effectively?"

If your busy schedule permits please give me the benefit of your thinking on the matter; and if you desire that your position be kept confidential, I will of course honor such a request.

I am anxiously awaiting your reply.

Very truly yours,
Will Gibson

p. s. I have just finished reading *The Ordeal of Mansart* and I am looking forward to "Book Two." Like your other works devoted to the Negro, *The Black Flame* trilogy will serve as another fork in the spade to unearth the many centuries of lies and half-truths told about Negroes generally, and the American Negro in particular.

Brooklyn, N.Y., November 27, 1957

My dear Mr. Gibson:

Answering your letter of November 8, may I say that for many years I co-operated with the birth control movement under Margaret Sanger. In answer to your question, I should say strongly that American Negroes should not oppose birth control upon the ground that a larger Negro population would mean greater political power, which can be employed to achieve equality more effectively. What any population needs is quality, not quantity, and among Negroes as among others, the increase in population comes usually from that part of it which is least able to support, educate and guide its children. We need, as Negroes especially, conception control and education for marriage and parenthood.[1]

I thank you for your kind words.

Very sincerely yours,
W. E. B. Du Bois

1. On Du Bois and Margaret Sanger, and his attitude toward birth control, see the exchange in volume one of this work, pp. 301-2, and references cited therein. Du Bois published a brief essay on the question raised by Gibson in *Birth Control Review* 16 (June 1932):166-67, entitled, "Black Folk and Birth Control." For a recent study of this matter as a whole, see Robert G. Weisbord, *Genocide? Birth Control and the Black American* (Westport, Ct.: Greenwood Press, 1975).

1958

*A letter from Anna M. Graves to which Du Bois responded early in 1958 seems
not to have survived; the answer, however, is clear and consequential.*

Brooklyn, N.Y., January 6, 1958

My dear Anna Melissa:

I do not agree with your estimate of the United Nations, as compared with
the League of Nations. True it is that the United Nations is not wholly successful, is in many respects unsatisfactory and discouraging. But the League of
Nations was from the first doomed to failure by the stubborn refusal of the
richest and most powerful industrial nation of the world to join; by withdrawal of Japan in protest to color prejudice; and by the fact that the presence
of China under the regime of 1918 with Western control was worse than the
absence of China today under Communism and with every prospect of early
admittance despite the efforts of the United States.

The United Nations had to be located in the United States. Only here could
it get world publicity and American publicity, and carry on its battles in the
face of and before the eyes of its most vicious enemy, which is the United
States. In London and Paris the United Nations would have been the catspaw
of colonial imperialism, at first hand as attacks on Egypt and Algeria proved.

In Brussels or Geneva the United Nations would have been under the same
powers at second-hand and without publicity. In New York imperialism and
capitalism are in control but they are naked and unashamed. There is no camou-
flage of titled and aristocratic concealment. It shows lying, stealing and murder,
open and not denied. Either we conquer it or the world falls.

Nor is the failure of the family to teach unselfishness, the failure of the city
to teach sacrifice, and the failure of the state to teach socialism, any argument
for immediate effort to establish the world state. Of course we want the world
state, we must have it, and sometime we'll get it, but not until the nations have
established socialism, not until the cities have practiced sacrifice, and not until
the families have become unselfish units.

How in God's name can we have a world state if the nations composing it
are determined to fight each other, if our cities continue to stew in crime, and
if the institution of the family continues to disintegrate?

One tremendous advantage which the United Nations has over the League
of Nations is that in 1918 it could be argued that socialism was a dream which
never had been realized in modern times. Today, on the contrary, one Socialist

state is in many respects the most powerful member of the United Nations and
cannot be ignored. A second Socialist State is only temporarily excluded and
socialism is growing in other parts of the world at an irresistible rate. With such
Socialist states and the education which they promote, the peace which is their
goal and the morality toward which economic justice opens the way, a world
state would gradually be realized.

Very sincerely yours,
W. E. B. Du Bois

*The Reverend Clennon King, then a professor of history and head of his de-
partment at Alcorn College—now known as Alcorn State University, in Mississippi—wrote Du Bois on 10 January 1958, asking him to clarify both his views
on so-called self-segregation and also his attitudes toward Booker T. Washington and Marcus Garvey—attitudes which seemed to King to fail to appreciate
the two sufficiently.*

Brooklyn, N.Y., January 29, 1958

Mr. Clennon King[1]
Dear Sir:

   Answering your letter of January 10, may I say that in my book *Dusk of
Dawn* I was trying to answer the question as to how the American Negro
would survive if color caste continued for two or three generations as I thought
it would. I advocated a Negro group socialism to furnish work, encourage
surroundings, and advance literature and art among Negroes. I did not advocate
increase of segregation, but use of such segregation as was inevitable to preserve
American Negroes for future integration into American and world culture.
This attitude had nothing to do with my resigning from the NAACP in 1934. This

---

   1. Clennon King gained national attention in 1957 and 1958. According to *Time
Magazine*, 18 March 1957 (69:49), the Reverend Mr. King was born in 1921; he was a
graduate of Tuskegee and took graduate work at Western Reserve in Cleveland. In
1957, while teaching history at Alcorn, he wrote several letters to the *Jackson State
Times* denouncing the NAACP for arousing the antagonism of white people. Students at
Alcorn then demonstrated against him and demanded his dismissal. In March 1957
President J. R. Otis announced King's dismissal (*New York Times*, 8 March 1957,
p. 23), but this dismissal did not take effect until June 1958 (*New York Times*, 3 May
1958, p. 2). Then, in June 1958, King was arrested for trying to enroll in the all-white
University of Mississippi (*New York Times*, 6 June 1958, p. 25) but was allowed to
leave for his home town (Albany, Georgia); in August 1958 he was serving as a pastor
in Gulfport, Mississippi, and demanding that President Eisenhower assist him in enroll-
ing his daughter in a white school (*New York Times*, 31 August 1958, p. 26). Whether
Du Bois knew of the 1957 excitement when he wrote King early in 1958 is not known.
This is the same Reverend C. L. King who in 1976 and early 1977 caused embarrassment at the church in which President-elect Carter worshiped, through attempts to
change its lily-white character.

resignation was caused by the fact that *The Crisis* ceased to pay its expenses. If it continued, it would necessarily have to depend upon subvention from the NAACP. Such help was offered but necessarily, if received, the independence of the editor would be curtailed.

This philosophy of group socialism was not out of keeping with my earlier or later ideas, and was guided by Marxian philosophy.

Negroes did not fail to appreciate Booker Washington. They followed him too blindly. They also appreciated Garvey and gave him thousands of dollars to waste on projects which were economically unsound. From time to time I gave Washington and Garvey words of appreciation for what they did that was beneficial and words of criticism for their failures.

Very sincerely yours,

W. E. B. Du Bois

The letter that follows may have been written in response to a verbal suggestion. The "Friends" in the salutation were Dr. Corliss Lamont and Kyrle Elkin, a Harvard graduate, a businessman, and the treasurer of the Peace Information Center who was among those indicted with Du Bois as unregistered foreign agents. The present editor remembers discussions with Elkin about his idea of a Du Bois scholarship at Harvard.

Brooklyn, N.Y., February 4, 1958

Dear Friends:

I have thought over carefully the proposal of you and Corliss Lamont concerning the endowment of a Du Bois scholarship at Harvard for colored students. I have concluded that this attempt would not be wise unless the University itself initiated the proposal. Except with a few of my professors, I have never been popular at Harvard. I have conducted classes and given lectures at Yale, Vassar and Princeton at the invitation of the University authorities, but never has Harvard invited me on any occasion except in the case of student organizations. My *Suppression of the Slave Trade to America* became the initial volume of the Harvard Historical series over sixty years [ago]. The University has never in any way mentioned this rather unusual happening. Last year a Harvard man wrote the President on his own initiative on some recognition of my work. No action followed. I have heard from Negro graduates of Harvard some disparaging remarks made by professors about the undesirability of encouraging any other Negro students of my "bitter" type.

I have gotten the impression that Harvard was not particularly proud of me; if this is true I am sure that an offer of an endowed scholarship named after me would not be welcome.

Also such a scholarship for Negroes would sound a little like racial segregation. Such segregation is common and must be as long as public opinion is what it is; yet under the circumstances I would prefer that Harvard on its own accord and from its own funds should establish such a scholarship.

On the other hand, Fisk University at Nashville, Tenn., is in dire need of funds. I got my first A.B. there seventy years ago and have since been cited and given an honorary degree. I have reason [to believe] that Fisk is not ashamed to list me as a graduate. She admits now both [white and] colored students, but it was founded for Negroes and for many years they will form the main student body. I should think that Fisk might welcome an endowment scholarship, or a collection of literature or art named after me and commemorating my work.[1]

Finally, as I said to you: of more importance to me than my memory is the certainty of having my works so perpetuated in print that their message will not be lost, even if the name is forgotten.

Let me thank you very much for the thought which you and Mr. Lamont have given this matter.

Sincerely yours,
W. E. B. Du Bois

The first wife of Marcus Garvey, Amy Ashwood-Garvey, had a substantive exchange with Du Bois early in 1958.

Ghana, West Africa, February 6, 1958

Dear Doctor:

I hope this letter will be to you a pleasant surprise. I can imagine you casting your mind back to the time we met in England at the Pan African Conference [in 1945] and you surprised me with a letterhead of the U.N.I.A. of 1914 in Jamaica, with my name thereon, and I suppose the question in your mind is: Why this letter out of the blue?

I am on the threshold of the publication of the biography of the late Marcus Garvey, and at first I thought of asking you to do me the honour of writing its preface.

Having regard, however, to the time and concentration it would demand and not being unaware how busy a person you are, I decided to change the preface idea and ask you instead to allow me to include an answer from you in a questionnaire-review. I am sure you will not grudge giving to Marcus just five lines now that he is dead.

1. Fisk University purchased from Du Bois in 1961 a considerable portion of his library and some of his papers. In 1959 Fisk erected on its campus a Du Bois Dormitory. Du Bois received an honorary Litt.D. from Fisk in 1938, and in 1958, the seventieth anniversary of his graduation, he was cited by the university as one of its most illustrious sons. The *Fisk News*, an alumni magazine, graced its cover for Spring 1963 with a striking photograph of the aged Du Bois and published an appreciation of him by Lewis W. Jones (pp. 7-8).

The question is:

In the evolution of Pan Africanism, looking in retrospect, what contribution, in your opinion, has the Garveyan ideology made to it?

I would also like to include the following extract from your book *The Negro* and I would have you know of my intention:

"There came simultaneously another movement stemming from the West Indies. This was a peoples' movement, rather than a movement of the intellectuals. It was led by Marcus Garvey and it represented a poorly conceived but intensely earnest determination to unite the Negroes of the world, especially in commercial enterprise.

"It used all of the nationalist and racial paraphernalia of popular agitation, and its strength lay in its backing by the masses of West Indians and by increasing numbers of American Negroes.

"Its weakness lay in its demogogic leadership, poor finance, intemperate propaganda and the natural apprehension it aroused among the colonial powers."[1]

The proceeds of the book is devoted to a trust for educational purposes among Negroes beginning with an educational institution here in Ghana. I have already secured land sufficient for the project, survey and building plans are completed for an early start.[2]

Wishing you more years of useful service in the field,

Sincerely yours,
Amy A. Garvey

Brooklyn, New York, February 19, 1958

My dear Mrs. Garvey:

I have your letter of February 6 and had some time ago a similar communication from a Mrs. Osborne.

Anyone has a right to quote from my published works as long as I and the publisher are given due credit.

I do not wish, however, to add any present remarks concerning Mr. Garvey. First, I am not in a position to estimate the effect of Mr. Garvey's work on present-day Africa; and secondly, I do not feel that I am under any obligation to add to what I have already written concerning Marcus Garvey. I have never at any time attacked Mr. Garvey and have always treated him and his work

1. The quotation is accurate but the source is not *The Negro* (1915); it is, rather, Du Bois's *World and Africa* (New York: Viking Press, 1947), p. 236.

2. There is a helpful account of Amy Ashwood-Garvey and Amy Jacques Garvey, the two wives of Marcus Garvey, by Lerone Bennett, Jr., in *Ebony*, March 1960, pp. 53-61; photographs of both women appear there. Amy Ashwood Garvey visited New York City in 1968 and was interviewed by C. Gerald Fraser for the *New York Times*, 17 August 1968 (p. 29). In both *Ebony* and the *Times*, mention is made of the manuscript dealing with Marcus Garvey's life, but it never was published. Amy Ashwood-Garvey died 3 May 1969, in Jamaica, West Indies; Amy Jacques Garvey died 22 July 1973, also in Jamaica.

with courteous consideration even when I attacked what seemed to me its shortcomings.[1] On the other hand, Garvey repeatedly slurred and insulted me, and accused me of action against him which was absolutely false.

To this day his followers in many cases have repeated these accusations, and accused me of being responsible for his incarceration in the United States and his final expulsion. This, as you yourself know, is absolutely untrue. No word or move of mine was responsible for the treatment which he received.

Under these circumstances, I think you can see why I am unwilling to add anything to what I have already said.

Very sincerely yours,
W. E. B. Du Bois

Ghana, West Africa, March 1, 1958

Dear Dr. Du Bois:

It was pleasant receiving your letter.

I quite understand your lack of enthusiasm to respond to my invitation, and thanks for your permission to quote from your book.

I, who like you, have known the pain of Garvey's tongue and pen, will not add to your past unhappiness. Rather, in my book, I have tried to do what I could to defend your absence of guilt and conduct that made Marcus' attacks on you absolutely unjustifiable.

I repeat the hope that we will meet somewhere once again, and please accept in the meantime, my best wishes for your health and prolonged usefulness to the Negro cause. In ending I would pass on the following lines of consolation and which will appear also in my book:

Life is too short for any bitter feeling;
Time is the best avenger, if we wait.
The years speed by, and on their wings bear healing,
We have no room for anything like hate.

Yours sincerely,
Amy A. Garvey

On 23 February 1958 Du Bois celebrated his ninetieth birthday. Public affairs marking the event were held in New York City on 2 March and in Chicago on 21 May.* Messages came from the presidents of many Black colleges and from

1. Du Bois did exercise restraint in the face of repeated personal and very bitter attacks upon him from Marcus Garvey; he did, however, once publish a sharp attack on Garvey himself, as well as on his program, in a two-page piece headed, "A Lunatic or a Traitor," in Du Bois's "Opinion" section of the *Crisis*, May 1924 (28:9-10). At that point Garvey had become "an open ally of the Ku Klux Klan." See also Du Bois's essay, "Back to Africa," in *Century Magazine* 105 (February 1923):539-48.

* Du Bois briefly describes the events marking his ninetieth birthday in his *Autobiography*, pp. 396-99.

*individuals as varied as Corliss Lamont, the humanist philosopher and outstand-
ing advocate of Soviet-American friendship, and Richard J. Daley, the late
mayor of Chicago. Very active in promoting the affair in New York City was
Carl Marzani, an author with left sympathies who had been among the earliest
political prisoners of the Cold War and was at this time a director of the Liberty
Book Club; in Chicago, the leadership was taken by Truman K. Gibson, an
outstanding Black businessman who headed the Supreme Liberty Life Insurance
Company. Several of the letters published below were addressed to Gibson,
others to Du Bois directly.*

New York City, February 19, 1958

Dear Dr. Du Bois:

I am very sorry indeed that I shall be unable to come to your 90th birthday
party on March 2. However, I shall be in Chicago for the entire weekend attending a meeting of the American Humanist Association and making a couple of
speeches. My heartiest congratulations and good wishes on this important and
splendid anniversary!

In writing Carl Marzani about the matter, I said this: "I can think of no
American who has made a more outstanding record than Dr. Du Bois to the
great democratic and humane causes of our time. He has shown a simply
remarkable combination of ability in scholarship, writing, lecturing and courageous political leadership. And he will always remain an example of what the
good life can be. It is wonderful that at the age of 90 he is still fighting as ably as
ever. I only wish that all progressives could live as long and as fruitfully."

Seriously, I think you ought to tell us younger persons how to live in health
and happiness beyond the century mark. It is at last time for you to reveal
that secret!

Cordially yours,
Corliss Lamont

[Telegram, Chicago, 5 May 1958]

[Truman K. Gibson]

The tribute to Dr. William Edward Burghar[d]t Du Bois to be tendered by
you and your associates on May 21 is commendable in every way—a timely
testimonial to the distinguished work of a renowned leader whose life span has
encompassed much of the most significant and stirring history of our nation. I
deeply appreciate your gracious invitation to be present and regret that previous
commitments make it impossible for me to be in attendance. Kindly extend to
the guest of honor my greetings, best wishes and birthday congratulations.

Richard J. Daley
Mayor

Atlanta, Ga., May 16, 1958

Dear Dr. Du Bois:

I salute you on your ninetieth birthday. Few men in America have fought as valiantly as you have for justice and fair play for all peoples irrespective of class, race or culture. You have used your great talent to assist men and women to free themselves of prejudice; and you have done it in a manner which thinking men everywhere had to respect and admire.

I am happy to send you and Mrs. Du Bois greetings on this your ninetieth birthday.

With kindest regards and best wishes, I am

Yours truly,
Benjamin E. Mays
President
[Morehouse College]

Tuskegee, Alabama, May 16, 1958

Dear Dr. Du Bois:

On behalf of Tuskegee Institute, I extend congratulations and best wishes on your ninetieth birthday. We are pleased to join a host of Americans in paying tribute to your fruitful career.

Sincerely yours,
L. H. Foster
President
[Tuskegee Institute]

Atlanta, Ga., May 16, 1958

Dear Dr. Du Bois:

I wish to take this, your ninetieth birthday, as an opportunity to salute you for your many and varied contributions to American life.

As a member of the Atlanta University System, I am acquainted with the excellent job you did as professor and as head of the department of sociology at Atlanta University. I have read many of your writings, which show clear thinking and cast a strong light on many of the problems faced by the Negro.

Your name will long be revered in the fields of education, literature, and public service. You have lived a rich, full life, and in so doing, you have done much to make life rich and full for others.

With every good wish, I am

Sincerely yours,
Albert E. Manley
President
[Spelman College, Atlanta University]

Nashville, Tenn., May 20, 1958

My dear Dr. Du Bois:

It is with very real pleasure that the staff, students and administration of your Alma Mater, Fisk University, join with the group of Citizens of the City of Chicago in commemorating your recent ninetieth birthday.

During the past sixty-five years, few men have done as much as you have to lift the social, economic and civil horizons of the Negro, and the recognition being accorded you at this time is, in some measure, an expression of gratitude to a great man from an appreciative racial group.

May God's richest blessings of good health and strength be with you many years to come.

Respectfully yours,
S. J. Wright
President
[Fisk University]

Atlanta, Ga., May 21, 1958

Dear Dr. Du Bois:

It is a pleasure to add my congratulations and best wishes to the thousands which you must be receiving today commemorating your ninetieth birthday.

Very few men have had the privilege of looking in retrospect upon a life as crowded with high adventure and meaningful endeavor and achievement as yours. Like an acorn which has burgeoned into a great oak with wide-spread branches, the work which you began in Atlanta many years ago now stretches across the world.

As we look back over the past five decades, we realize that the fight of the American Negro for civil rights, which culminated in the Supreme Court Decision of May 1954, had its beginning when *The Crisis* was founded. We realize, further, that you had much to do with the recognition of common cause and brotherhood which now binds the darker races of the world.

"This Is Your Life," Dr. Du Bois. We wish for you more useful and happy years.

Respectfully yours,
John H. Lewis
President
[Morris Brown College,
  Atlanta University]

Chicago, Ill., May 21, 1958

Dear Dr. Du Bois:

The Chicago Branch of the National Association for the Advancement of

Colored People considers it a distinct privilege to join with the citizens and leadership of the city of Chicago in honoring you here tonight.

It is the view of the Chicago Branch, which considers that you are the parent of our great organization, that the colored people of our country and our city, as well as all others of our nation have benefited by your influence.

Our city and our nation are improved as places in which men may live in improved dignity because of your contribution.

Best wishes.

> Very truly yours,
> National Association for the Advance-
> ment of Colored People
> Theodore A. Jones, President
> Chicago Branch

Merle Curti (b. 1897), the distinguished historian now professor emeritus at the University of Wisconsin, exchanged letters with Du Bois in 1958.*

Madison, Wis., May 26, 1958

Dear Dr. Du Bois:

I am working on an historical study of American philanthropy and in connection with it have read a master's essay by Mr. Esmo Woods on the development of your own education and historical ideas.[1] Mr. Woods suggests, and seems to have some evidence, that your plan for interesting Jacob Schiff in supporting a publishing venture did not materialize—possibly because Booker T. Washington did not favor it. I am wondering whether this is your impression? Also, I should be very grateful to you indeed for any suggestions you may have regarding the role of philanthropists in Negro education and welfare. The record seems to indicate that for the most part philanthropists preferred to give to the vocationally oriented schools. I am wondering whether within your own experience you found some who took a broader point of view and who in any important way supported your work at Philadelphia, at Atlanta, and elsewhere?

Naturally, I will give full credit to any suggestions or help you may give me. With good wishes.

> Sincerely yours,
> Merle Curti

* For other correspondence between Curti and Du Bois, see volume two of this *Correspondence*, pp. 266–67.

1. I have not been able to locate this thesis; there is no record of it at the University of Wisconsin.

Professor Curti published *American Philanthropy Abroad: A History* (New Brunswick, N.J.: Rutgers University Press) in 1963. Du Bois is not discussed in the book, though its pages on philanthropy in Africa (320–22) would have benefited by a consideration of his opinions.

Brooklyn, N.Y., June 4, 1958

Dear Professor Curti:

I have been out of town and so am late answering your letter of May 26th.

I have had but small experience in approaching rich men for contributions. Perhaps my most successful case was with Jacob Schiff. Just how this came about, I am not sure, but I did make his acquaintance and for several years secured an annual contribution for the N.A.A.C.P. I approached him and others for help in starting a monthly magazine on the Negro problem. At his invitation, I called on him and he was interested. I think, although I do not know, that he finally declined to help because of the influence of Booker T. Washington and his friends.

During my whole career, I have tried not to be put in a position where collecting money from philanthropists would be any considerable part of my work. For that reason I have always declined to be candidate for the presidency of any college or organization, where I had to raise funds. This kind of work interferes, to my mind, with study and investigation, and inevitably puts the scholar under obligation to the rich men and to business interests. Most philanthropists, I presume, start their giving because of finding themselves with more money than they need, and realizing that persons and causes may be helped. Then comes the very difficult problem of knowing what causes are worthy; and there follows the second problem of giving where the use of the money may hurt institutions in which the philanthropist is interested, especially business. This, I have seen clearly in the help of Negro education in the South.

During the Civil War and up until the '80's, this philanthropy sprang primarily from sympathy with freedmen. Then it became an effort to build up a school system for ignorant people. This was halted by the fear of many people, especially in the South, that Negroes might be educated too fast and in wrong directions, and in antagonism to the White South. After that, philanthropy in the South was directed by special business interests to what was called "industrial education," designed to train servants and cheap labor.

In the same way, today, philanthropy is being guided by Big Business to ward off Socialism and Communism, to control labor unions, and to curb all sorts of "radical" thought.

Perhaps these random statements may be of some service to you.

Very sincerely yours,
W. E. B. Du Bois

Madison, Wis., June 8, 1958

Dear Dr. Du Bois,

Warm thanks for your letter of June 4 about the relation of philanthropy to Negro education, and to other matters. There is certainly a good deal of documentary evidence to support your position.

I hope you are writing a long and full autobiography, and that you may have many good years ahead.

Sincerely,
Merle Curti

A 1958 exchange between Du Bois and Corliss Lamont illuminates Du Bois's political thinking, especially that of the period from the end of the Second World War to his own death.

Brooklyn, N.Y., June 27, 1958

Dear Mr. Lamont:

I understand that you are considering the call to run for senator on the proposed Third Party ticket this Fall. I hope you will consent. It will of course be a task calling for time, work and money; and in all ordinary ways it will be thankless. But unless soon the people of the United States can count upon citizens willing to sacrifice for the great ends of this nation's existence, the end of our attempt at Democracy is in sight. The tragedy of our day is not Crime, but silence and inaction when the call of Duty is clear. Today as seldom before we need a Third Party to enable honest citizens to vote against War and Greed and for the Welfare State; and not be compelled as we have been now for three elections to have no choice save to vote for one party under two names. I sincerely hope you will make the sacrifice.

Very sincerely yours,
W. E. B. Du Bois

New York City, July 16, 1958

Dear Dr. Du Bois,

I greatly appreciated your letter of June 27 about the matter of my running for Senator on the proposed Third Party ticket next fall. At the end of May I had told the group that was organizing the Conference that I could not see my way clear to taking on the responsibility of being a candidate for any office in 1958. They urged me to keep my mind open on the problem, and this I did.

Your note was one of the serious factors that I considered as I kept reconsidering the whole proposition. I talked the problem over with my friends and of course with my family. But I finally came to the conclusion a week or so ago that I simply could not alter my original decision.

Primarily this is because I have so many other commitments for the fall, including my teaching at Columbia. In 1952, when I ran for the Senate on the A.L.P. ticket, I was able to postpone my Columbia course to the spring. This time, however, the proposal came too late for me to do this. In addition to the teaching, I have numerous writing jobs and my regular work for civil liberties and international peace. I cannot do everything, and my weakness has been to spread myself too thin. I feel, then, that I can make my best contribution by continuing the work upon which I am already engaged.

The United Socialist Party is still planning to run a ticket; and I shall of course support it to the best of my ability.

With kindest regards to you and your wife,

Cordially yours,

Corliss Lamont

P. S. Also I hope to use my passport soon before it is taken away.[1]

From the summer of 1958 until the spring of 1959, Dr. and Mrs. Du Bois traveled abroad; they visited Western and Eastern Europe, the Soviet Union, and the People's Republic of China. Mrs. Du Bois, for reasons indicated below, also visited Africa. Few letters from Du Bois written during this period survive, but two examples are given here. The first was addressed to George B. Murphy, Jr., at his home in Baltimore; Murphy was a devoted friend of the Du Boises for many years and was (and is) an executive of the Afro-American *newspaper enterprise. The second was addressed to Abbott Simon, a New York attorney who had been a leader in the Peace Information Center and one of the co-defendants with Du Bois in the trial of 1950-51.*

Moscow, USSR, December 26, 1958

Dear George [B. Murphy, Jr.]:

We have been in Europe, Asia and Africa and if we have neglected our best friends it is not because we have been idle. I have been abroad 13 times but this is my longest and most significant journey. Both I and Shirley are well and in overflowing spirits.

We spent a month in London where I was on television and gave three lectures. Then we were a week in Holland with television and lectures. In Paris at election time we kept still but were entertained and I sat on the rostrum at the Joliot-Curie Memorial meeting, sitting at the right of the Chairman, [Maurice] Thorez. Then we were almost dragged to Tashkent in middle Asia to a most interesting Afro-Asian Writers' conference. I spoke and was enter-

1. The original of Du Bois's letter to Lamont is in Dr. Lamont's possession. He kindly sent a copy to the editor when giving permission for the publication of his own letters. In addition, on 21 April 1976, Dr. Lamont sent me the following note:

"After my letter of July 16, 1958, President Eisenhower sent several thousand Marines into Lebanon on the mythical grounds that a Communist revolution was in progress there.

"I was so appalled at this interventionist action that I consented, after all, to run for United States Senator from New York on the Independent Socialist Party ticket. I received less than 40,000 votes."

tained. Then two weeks as guests of the Czechoslovakian government with an honorary degree;[1] then to east Germany with another degree and finally to Moscow.

We were on the Red Square for the annual display and Khruschev saluted me; in the reception in Kremlin we had a short talk. By this time however nature had caught up with me; I had a few days in bed in London but after returning from the long round told the Soviets that I needed rest in a sanitarium. I came here November 9 and leave the day before the New Year. They have gone over me and through me with all possible instruments: cardiograms, blood-pressure, blood tests, urine examination, massage, baths, gymnastics and walks. While I was here [came] the invitation to Ghana. I wanted to go and had a duty; but I had been here but three weeks and the council of physicians said "No." So Shirley, who was here with me and in perfect condition, put my speech in her pocket[2] and off she flew to Belgrade, Athens, Cairo, the pyramids and sphinx; the Nile, Khartoum and Kano and Accra. She was gone three weeks. Here I had all the service and care I could use: nurses put me in the hot bath and tucked me in bed and Moscow sent an interpreter who was at call day and night.

Xmas eve they put a lighted tree in our room and Xmas night six guests came out from Moscow; Shirley directed the cooking of the turkey and we had champagne.[3] Then Shirley and I went to the piano in the parlor and sang spirituals.

Next week we go to work in Moscow. We are both having books published here and one case I want to take up with you; I am going to try to get *John Brown* published here and in China in '59, in both English and in the vernacular. East Germany and Czechoslovakia will probably join. Maybe England, though that is not certain. Now then, can anything be done in Negro America? Are the Elks still hopeless? Could we get "One Hundred Sponsors" among Negroes?[4] It will be possible to get copies here in English for almost nothing, provided we can arrange with customs. Think this over.

This is a beautiful place—50 miles southeast of Moscow with tall pines and birches and snow. This morning we took a walk by the frozen lake at 30 below zero (centigrade) and wrapped in boots and furs. Every night we look at movies from upholstered fauteuils. I often think of you and am still grateful

1. Du Bois's *Autobiography* includes two photographs taken during his 1958 visit to Czechoslovakia; one shows the bestowal of an honorary doctorate in historical sciences from Charles University in Prague.
2. The Du Bois speech delivered by Mrs. Du Bois in Accra is published in his *Autobiography*, pp. 402-4.
3. That Christmas of 1958 and Mrs. Du Bois's culinary activity are described by her in *His Day Is Marching On*, pp. 266-68.
4. In 1962 a new, revised edition of Du Bois's *John Brown*, first issued in 1909, was published by International Publishers in New York.

for all you have done. We expect to reach New York by next May. Best regards to the wife and boy. With love,

W. E. B. Du Bois[5]

Leningrad, USSR, January 27, 1959

My dear Abbott [Simon] plus Priscilla [Mrs Simon], [and] the young man and young lady [their children] who favor you with their presence, Greeting from me and Shirley:

We're having an extraordinary time which defies present description but will serve for endless conversation in the future. We've been in England, Holland, France, Czechoslovakia, Germany and the Soviet Union. We have several more nations in mind. In fact, I went so fast that I landed in a nice Soviet sanitarium while Shirley went to Ghana and read my speech. Incidentally she took in Egypt with Sphinx, and pyramid, the Nile and Khartoum. We visited the conference at Tashkent (find it?) and have been several weeks in the Soviet Union. We interviewed Khrushchev last week and had New Year's dinner at the Kremlin where Paul Robeson sang! Now we're here, then back to Moscow and then another great nation.[1] It's too good to be true. Shirley's out to a museum but joins in love,

With me,
W. E. B. Du Bois

p. s. Hope to see you in May!

D.

---

5. This letter carries a postscript from Mrs. Du Bois, noting that Du Bois "was a very sick man when he came to the sanitarium November 9th" but adding, "W. E. B. is fine now. He's dropped twenty years. . . ."

1. He refers to the People's Republic of China; at the time, it was illegal for a United States citizen to visit that country. There are two photographs in the *Autobiography* illustrating the 1959 visit, as well as the text of a radio address Du Bois gave in Peking on his ninety-first birthday, 23 February 1959 (pp. 405–8). For biographical information from 1958 to his death in 1963, see especially Shirley Graham Du Bois's *His Day Is Marching On*, pp. 275-369.

Du Bois letters from the 1960s—he died in August 1963—are relatively few. Ex-
tant letters include personal communications; a momentous letter, written
1 October 1961 to Gus Hall, general secretary of the Communist Party of the
United States, applying for membership; several letters concerning his memoirs
for the Oral History Project of Columbia University; a fairly substantial num-
ber of letters dealing with the Encyclopedia Africana project; and, finally,
letters dealing with his work on his last book, a Du Bois reader selected and
edited by himself and published, under the title An ABC of Color, *one month*
before his death.

Three personal letters from this period, written to Paul Robeson, to me, and
to Bettina Aptheker, are included here.

Du Bois wrote to Paul Robeson in London, whence Robeson had gone when
McCarthyism and its aftermath made it impossible for him to function as an
*artist in the United States.**

Brooklyn, N.Y., January 5, 1961

Dear Paul:

I don't often proffer advice, but here is an exception. I have heard of your hesitation as to your next step. My advice is go to China and make a tour of from three to six months. Consult the Chinese Chargé d'Affairs in London about arrangements. Write the American Ambassador and say that you have promised not to visit any country with which the United States has no diplomatic relations; but upon reflection you cannot keep this promise which you now think was extracted unfairly. On return from China arrange for a three month trip to Africa. By that time Kennedy will be president. Apply to him for a renewal of your passport. If he refuses, take out citizenship in a European or African country.

Our love to you and Essie.

Sincerely,
W. E. B. Du Bois

* The original of this letter is in the Paul Robeson Archives, Berlin, German Democratic Republic. A copy was kindly sent to the editor by Mr. Lloyd L. Brown of New York City, the biographer of Paul Robeson.

At the very end of December 1961, I received this letter.

Accra, Ghana, December 12, 1961

Dear Herbert:

My world is still quite unreal. This is December. Yet last night looking out my window balcony I could see the Gulf of Guinea and hear its low roar; above on my right was the new moon and a little star; above on my left, the crimson beacon atop the old Christianburg castle, where perhaps my great-great grandfather lay once in chains. The city twinkles left and right and the air is warm and still. I am comfortable and reasonably well—no pains, nor definite ills and yet consciously old and increasingly forgetful especially of little matters. I am lonesome for my few friends and news is so scarce and scrappy that I can't imagine what is going on especially in America. Here all are more than kind and thoughtful—a car and driver whenever I will—servants—but all is strange and unknown and the heat tho not excessive yet must be yielded to and I must get used to doing nothing. No real work on the Encyclopedia can begin before the new year and then will be hazy for a long time.

I read with glee [of] your trip to Detroit.[1] I really wonder how much America will submit to. I listen for each day's news with bated breath. And today News is a fantastic mixture of truth and lies. Here I see Revolution face to face and know not how to interpret it. I am not at all sure of the use of living just to see when there is little opportunity to act effectively.

Apropos of nothing, do you know my volume on Georgia in Gruening's *United States*.[2] It is one of my best jobs. Well, I'll stop. I have Bettina's newsy letter. I'll answer some time. Love to her and Fay and to you from us both.[3]

W. E. B. Du Bois

Bettina Aptheker knew Du Bois from her early childhood and visited the Du Boises fairly often when they (and she) lived in Brooklyn, New York. They exchanged letters, also, quite often. The last such exchange began with a letter from the new college student in the latter part of 1962.

Berkeley, Cal., September 15, 1962

Dear Dr. Du Bois,

Please forgive my very long delay between letters. Less than a week after

1. In November 1961 I lectured at Wayne State University in Detroit, Michigan; that university—like most others at the time—had banned Communist speakers, but this ban was then broken. I had written to Du Bois about the Wayne State experience.

2. Du Bois refers to his essay, "Georgia: Invisible Empire State," in *These United States*, ed. Ernest Gruening, 2 vols. (New York: Boni and Liveright, 1924), 2:322-45.

3. The references are to Fay P. Aptheker, my wife, and our daughter, Bettina, then seventeen years old.

graduation [from high school] I began working at the Jefferson Book Shop in New York. It was a splendid job, although I worked 6 days a week. There was, however, a great opportunity to meet many wonderful people.

On August 12, my parents drove me out here to Berkeley. We had a magnificent trip across the nation visiting many of the National Parks—Yellowstone, Grand Tetons, Bryce, Zion and Yosemite, and the Grand Canyon. Each sight was very distinctive, but as far as I was concerned the Grand Canyon put the icing on the cake. I have never seen anything quite so massive and awesome!

Berkeley is a beautiful city—all residential with the Campus in the center. Have you ever seen the UC Campus? It's really a garden, with a creek running through its middle, and fountains everywhere. The library is one of the finest I've seen anywhere, including the New York Public Library.

The courses I'm taking are somewhat limited for the first year or two because of the large number of requirements necessary for a B.A. This semester I'll be studying Philosophy (Locke, Plato and perhaps Sartre), English (standard course but Prof. is excellent—his name is [Thomas] Parkinson. Several years ago a maniac decided he was going to murder all the so-called "Communists" at U.C. He came into Parkinson's room, shot and killed one of his students, and seriously wounded him), Anthropology (Physical Anthro. dealing with evolution) and Spanish (literature course—reading and discussing books in Spanish). This will give me a total of 15 units which is two above what is required per semester. Classes start on Monday.

Vincent Hallinan (ran for President in '52) is now living near Berkeley, practicing law. Two of his sons are at UC. The sons have a home in Berkeley and that is where I am living, at least for this semester. There is one other student who is rooming with us. It's a fine set-up, and only three blocks from campus.

There is, of course, tremendous political activity at UC. The Civil Rights movement is quite strong as well as the peace movement, and there is a strong Civil Liberties group which is becoming a united front kind of thing, gaining more and more political power. We are now in the midst of an important campaign to put Brown in office as governor and defeat Nixon. I'm afraid it's going to be a very close election.[1]

How is work on the Encyclopedia progressing? Have you regained your health, and how are you in general?

Please give my warmest regards to Shirley.

I remain, as always,

> Very truly yours,
> Bettina

1. In the November 1962 election, the Democrat Edmund G. Brown received slightly over 3,000,000 votes and Richard M. Nixon received almost 2,750,000.

Accra, Ghana, November 27, 1962

Dear Bettina,

I am at last back in Accra and getting settled.[1] I am in better health and Shirley is very well indeed.

I have before me your letter of September 15, telling me about your magnificent trip across the nation, visiting many of the National Parks, especially Grand Canyon (I remember riding down on the back of a mule). I am glad to hear about the Hallinans; they are good friends of ours and very interesting people.

We are working slowly on the *Encyclopedia Africana*. It is still in the preparatory stage and it will be many years before we can get it into print.

We are very well, and with love,

Sincerely yours,
W. E. B. Du Bois

Du Bois's acquaintance with Marxism and socialism went back to his German university days in the 1890s. By 1904 he indicated that much in his understanding of socialism seemed to make sense, and by 1907 his speeches reflected quite clearly the influence of Marxian analysis. In 1911 he joined the Socialist party and, while he resigned from it the next year, he ever thereafter thought of himself as a partisan of socialism, though his definition of a socialist society was to alter with the years.

In the 1930s, although often in sharp disagreement with the Communist party and it with him, he undertook a systematic study of Marx and even taught a course in the summer of 1933 at Atlanta University on "Karl Marx and the Negro." His writings, especially Black Reconstruction *(1935) and later books, reflect this growing attraction to Marxism. In the 1940s, particularly after World War II and with the coming of the Cold War, Du Bois moved significantly to the left; internal and international developments in that decade and the 1950s confirmed him in the wisdom and propriety of that orientation.*

When in 1961 the United States Supreme Court upheld the constitutionality of elements of the Subversive Control Act—the so-called McCarran Act—Du Bois was horrified and angered. The implementation of the act made it likely, moreover, that his own passport would be sequestered and that travel outside the United States would be prohibited. Such a state of affairs would jeopardize his cherished plan to go to Ghana at the invitation of President Nkrumah to begin serious work on producing an Encyclopedia Africana. It was in the context of all these events and forces that Du Bois decided to join the Communist

1. In the summer of 1962 Du Bois went to England for medical treatment. After a major operation, he recuperated in Switzerland, went on to China and then to the USSR and returned to Ghana in November.

*party of the United States and to hasten his departure from the United States
for his work in Ghana. The application was made 1 October 1961, and a few
days later, on 5 October, Dr. and Mrs. Du Bois left the United States for Ghana.**

Brooklyn, N.Y., October 1, 1961

To Gus Hall:

On this first day of October, 1961, I am applying for admission to membership in the Communist Party of the United States. I have been long and slow
in coming to this conclusion, but at last my mind is settled.

In college I heard the name of Karl Marx, but read none of his works, nor
heard them explained. At the University of Berlin, I heard much of those
thinkers who had definitely answered the theories of Marx, but again we did
not study what Marx himself had said. Nevertheless, I attended meetings of the
Socialist Party and considered myself a socialist.

On my return to America, I taught and studied for sixteen years, I explained
the theory of socialism and studied the organized social life of American
Negroes; but still I neither read nor heard much of Marxism. Then I came to
New York as an official of the new NAACP and editor of the Crisis Magazine.
The NAACP was capitalist oriented and expected support from rich philanthropists. But it had a strong socialist element in its leadership in persons like Mary
Ovington, William English Walling and Charles Edward Russell. Following
their advice, I joined the Socialist Party in 1911. I knew then nothing of practical Socialist politics and in the campaign of 1912, I found myself unwilling to
vote the Socialist ticket, but advised Negroes to vote for Wilson. This was
contrary to Socialist Party rules and consequently I resigned from the Socialist
Party.

For the next twenty years I tried to develop a political way of life for myself
and my people. I attacked the Democrats and Republicans for monopoly and
disfranchisement of Negroes; I attacked the Socialists for trying to segregate
Southern Negro members; I praised the racial attitudes of the Communists, but
opposed their tactics in the case of the Scottsboro boys and their advocacy of
a Negro state. At the same time I began to study Karl Marx and the Communists; I hailed the Russian Revolution of 1917, but was puzzled at the contradictory news from Russia.

Finally in 1926, I began a new effort: I visited Communist lands. I went to
the Soviet Union in 1926, 1936, 1949 and 1959; I saw the nation develop. I
visited East Germany, Czechoslovakia and Poland. I spent ten weeks in China,
traveling all over the land. Then, this summer, I rested a month in Rumania. I

* For a description of the Du Boises' life just prior to 5 October 1961, see *His Day
Is Marching On*, pp. 321–29. I drove Dr. and Mrs. Du Bois to the airport for their
flight from New York City; they reached Ghana (after a stopover in London) on 7
October 1961.

was early convinced that socialism was an excellent way of life, but I thought it might be reached by various methods. For Russia I was convinced she had chosen the only way open to her at the time. I saw Scandinavia choosing a different method, halfway between socialism and capitalism. In the United States I saw Consumers Cooperation as a path from capitalism to socialism, while England, France and Germany developed in the same direction in their own way. After the depression and the Second World War, I was disillusioned. The Progressive movement in the United States failed. The Cold War started. Capitalism called communism a crime.

Today I have reached a firm conclusion:

Capitalism cannot reform itself; it is doomed to self-destruction. No universal selfishness can bring social good to all.

Communism—the effort to give all men what they need and to ask of each the best they can contribute—this is the only way of human life. It is a difficult and hard end to reach, it has and will make mistakes, but today it marches triumphantly on in education and science, in home and food, with increased freedom of thought and deliverance from dogma. In the end communism will triumph. I want to help bring that day.

The path of the American Communist Party is clear: It will provide the United States with a real Third Party and thus restore democracy to this land. It will call for:

1. Public ownership of natural resources and of all capital
2. Public control of transportation and communications
3. Abolition of poverty and limitation of personal income
4. No exploitation of labor
5. Social medicine, with hospitalization and care of the old
6. Free education for all
7. Training for jobs and jobs for all
8. Discipline for growth and reform
9. Freedom under law
10. No dogmatic religion

These aims are not crimes. They are practiced increasingly over the world. No nation can call itself free which does not allow its citizens to work for these ends.

W. E. B. Du Bois[1]

As March 1956 correspondence between Du Bois and Allan Nevins showed

1. The text of this letter and a photographic reproduction of the original appeared in the *Worker*, Sunday, 26 November 1961; the same paper carried Gus Hall's reply welcoming Du Bois into the party in the name of its national board. Both letters were published in *Political Affairs* 42 (October 1963): 31-34, and Du Bois's letter is also reprinted in *His Day Is Marcing On*, pp. 325-27.

*(see pp. 398–99 above), Du Bois agreed to participate in Columbia University's
oral history project. The story of this undertaking is completed in letters
between Du Bois and the project's director, Dr. Louis M. Starr, in the 1960s.*

New York City, June 15, 1960

Dear Mr. Du Bois:

I had a pleasant phone conversation with Mrs. Du Bois today, confirming
what Mr. Ingersoll, alas, had told me: that you have concluded to end the
highly interesting series of interviews you have had with him.

I could well understand why you should feel compelled to do so. I do wish
to say, however, that we are deeply grateful to you for the cooperation you
have given us and that we would be more than pleased to resume the interviews
in the fall or later, in the event that you should for any reason change your
mind.

As you will note from the catalogue we sent you last February, some of our
more distinguished contributors have carried on at considerable length in order
to give a full recital of their lives. We would be honored to add your name to
this category.

Thanking you again, I am,

Cordially yours,
Louis M. Starr

New York City, March 6, 1961

Dear Doctor Du Bois:

I am pleased to enclose a copy of the transcript of your interviews with Mr.
Ingersoll last year. This is a fascinating memoir, and one which we are anxious
to submit to the Special Collections department of this library.

I beseech you, in editing this manuscript, to do so lightly, with accuracy
alone in mind. We like to retain the spontaneity of the original interviews. The
reader is enjoined to bear in mind, in a notice inserted in the front matter of
each memoir, that he is reading the spoken, rather than the written, word.

As Mr. Ingersoll may have explained to you, you are free to choose four
alternatives for the use of your memoir: the manuscript may be made available
to qualified scholars; it may be closed except with your written permission; it
may be left open with written permission required to quote or to cite; and it
may be closed until a specified date. Will you let us know your wishes when
you return the edited manuscript? We will transfer your corrections to the
copies for submission and return an edited copy to you for your own use.

We are very grateful to you for your cooperation, and trust we may have
this fine manuscript back from you very shortly so that we may submit it to
Special Collections.

Cordially yours,
Louis M. Starr

Brooklyn, N.Y., September 5, 1961

Dear Mr. Starr:

I have before me your letter of March 6th which I have not answered because of long absence from my desk in Rumania and elsewhere.

I have the manuscript of my oral biography. I have not been able to finish correcting it but I very much want to make certain minor corrections since otherwise it would not be satisfactory. However, I cannot do this immediately as I am leaving the country again, but sometime in the next few months, I will send you a corrected copy bearing in mind your advice to retain the spontaneity of the original interviews. This corrected manuscript can then be made available to qualified scholars in time.

Very sincerely yours,
W. E. B. Du Bois

Apparently unaware that Du Bois had left the United States in October 1961, Starr wrote him at his former Brooklyn address on 14 February 1962, hoping that he would soon receive the corrected manuscript; there followed this final letter on the subject.

New York City, March 13, 1962

Dear Doctor Du Bois:

It has been some time since we have heard from you regarding your oral history memoir which we sent you for checking so that we could submit it to the Oral History Collection in this library. Editing, as you know, should be done with accuracy alone in mind.

One of the more stubborn problems we face is the fact that a considerable number of our memoirists simply do not get around to editing and returning their transcripts. Faced with prospect of an ever-increasing pile of memoirs in this suspended state, we have been obliged to adopt the procedure of submitting the material as it stands after due notice has been given. Accordingly, we propose to submit your memoir in April, unless we hear from you to the contrary before then.

Cordially yours,
Louis M. Starr[1]

In mid-February 1960, shortly before his ninety-second birthday, Du Bois and

1. The letters dealing with the Oral History Project were kindly supplied by Louis M. Starr, director, who also gave permission for the publication of his own letters. Although Du Bois's memoir was finally entered without correction, it will be remembered that Du Bois, in his letter of 5 September 1961, did feel that "minor corrections" were necessary and that without them the memoir "would not be satisfactory."

his wife left for a month's vacation in the Virgin Islands. Upon their return to Brooklyn, they received notice from Ghana that they would be receiving official invitations to attend the inauguration of Kwame Nkrumah as the first president of Ghana, to take place in July 1960. The Du Boises's passports had been sequestered upon their return from China (such visits then being illegal), but an attorney's request at the State Department resulted in their being issued new passports. Soon a letter arrived from Nkrumah.

Accra, Ghana, June 18, 1960

Dear Dr. Du Bois:

I have heard with particular pleasure the news that you have accepted our invitation to attend the celebrations connected with the establishment of the Republic of Ghana.

I shall have many things to talk over with you and I should like you to know that whilst you are in Ghana, you and your wife will be my personal private guests.

I sincerely hope that you are enjoying very good health and that you are looking forward to this visit to Ghana with as much pleasurable anticipation as I and your many friends are.

Yours very sincerely,
Kwame Nkrumah

Du Bois was in Ghana for six weeks during the summer of 1960; in an informal meeting with Nkrumah, the president suggested that he would be pleased if Du Bois would consent to head a project, to be located in Accra, for the production of an Encyclopedia Africana. Despite Du Bois's protests about his health and strength, Nkrumah persisted in the invitation, and Du Bois—who had projected such an encyclopedia over fifty years earlier—agreed. His work on this encyclopedia was the major undertaking of the last three years of his life, and the correspondence concerning it is voluminous; illustrative are the letters that follow.

After leaving Africa, the Du Boises spent four weeks in Western Europe and returned to New York in mid-September 1960.

Brooklyn, N.Y., October 10, 1960

Personal

My dear Mr. Nkrumah:

I have already written you once concerning preliminary work on the "Encyclopedia Africana." In this letter, I am summing up what I have done to date in the hope that the Encyclopedia can be brought up and discussed in the reorganization of the University of Ghana.

I should also preface this letter by thanking you again for your hospitality while I was in Ghana and my appreciation of your work before the United Nations.

Enclosed is the general statement which I have sent out already to the following persons and which I am continuing to transmit to other scholars.

Mr. Cedric Belfrage	Mr. Thomas L. Hodgkin
Professor John D. Bernal	Mr. Kuo Mo Jo
Mr. Fenner Brockway, M. P.	Mr. L. S. B. Leakey
Miss Gertrude Caton-Thompson	Mr. William Arthur Lewis
Mr. Basil Davidson	Mr. Richard Pankhurst
Mr. Daryll Forde	Lord Bertrand A. W. Russell
Lord Hailey	Dr. Eric Williams
Dr. Melville Herskovits	

I shall send you as soon as possible a copy of such replies as I receive.

In the meantime, I think it would be wise if the new University of Ghana should do two things: first, assign to some faculty or establish a particular faculty to take charge of the "Encyclopedia Africana" and arrange for its editorial control and publication. The bulk of the members of the Editorial Board should be African scholars, but there should also be included European scholars who are devoid of prejudice and who are willing to work with Africans. Second, there should be set up as soon as possible a Ghana University Press that would be like the Oxford University Press is to Oxford University and the Cambridge University Press to Cambridge University which could take care of publications. A printing establishment should be set up which could issue the Encyclopedia and eventually other works which Ghana would like to publish.

Your government should make known to the Supervisory Board its willingness to finance and support the "Encyclopedia Africana" and the University Press, and let them know to what extent this Board could go. Meantime, if you wish, I will continue the work I have begun, corresponding with as many persons as I can and gathering their replies and making such personal contacts as is possible. This will involve some expense from my office and for this I will make a calculation and enclose it in this letter.

I trust this will find you in good health and I beg to send this greeting from myself and wife to you and your wife and the children.

Very sincerely yours,
W. E. B. Du Bois

The ensuing letters are indicative of the replies received by Du Bois to his letters to various scholars outlining the scope and scientific character of the encyclopedia he projected.

London, England, October 19, 1960

Dear Dr. Du Bois,

Thank you for your letter. I am very sorry to hear that you had a mild stroke whilst in England, and I do hope that you have completely recovered now. It was wonderful to find you in Lagos for the Nigerian Independence Celebrations. I am amazed by your physical and mental energy at your age. It is marvellous.

I am much attracted by your idea of an Encyclopedia Africana. I shall, of course, be ready to help in any way I can. I should have thought the best initial action would be to write to every kind of organization associated with Africa, as well as to the Cultural Ministries in African states or to the national movements where independence has not yet been gained, and ask them to suggest African contributors and give particulars of their educational and scientific qualifications. In this way you ought to be able to get a considerable list of possible contributors, whom you might sift and co-ordinate. In America you have the Committee of African Affairs. In this country you have the Movement for Colonial Freedom, 374 Grays Inn Road, London W.C.1—The Fabian Commonwealth Bureau, 11 Dartmouth Street, London S.W.1.—The Committee of African Organisations, 200 Gower Street, London, N.W.1., and Africa Bureau, Denison House, Vauxhall Bridge Rd., London, S.W.1. All these organisations could help in this way. In addition to the above, I suggest that you should get someone to go to the best library in America and make a survey of books about Africa. You would then get good names for different subjects.

I am not writing to you about the technical process of deciding on the contents. You have all the ability to work this out yourself.

With affectionate greetings as ever,

Fenner[1]

Nairobi, Kenya, 27 October 1960

Dear Dr. Du Bois,

I acknowledge receipt of your letter of the 18th October, with enclosure.

In principle, I certainly think that an Encyclopaedia Africana, as set out by you, would be most worthwhile and I should be happy to cooperate in the preparation of certain aspects of the Encyclopaedia in due course.

My only fear is whether you might not find that some African contributors may get carried away by much of what is now false history; it would need the utmost care to ensure that the work comes up to international standards of accuracy.

1. Archibald Fenner Brockway (b. 1888) was a leader of the Labour party and from 1950 to 1964 a member of Parliament. During World War 1 he was jailed for opposition to the war, and he was long associated with British movements for Indian independence. He was created baron in 1964. Author of many books, he has most recently published *The Colonial Revolution* (1973).

However, I do not regard this as an insuperable difficulty, although it is one of which you must be fully warned.

> Yours sincerely,
> L. S. B. Leakey[1]

Washington, D.C., December 5, 1960

Dear Dr. Du Bois:

I have read carefully the copy of the plan for an "Encyclopedia Africana" and have given it much thought. Although at the present time I can not give you a list of persons who might contribute to what I have suggested as an alternate proposal, I am sending on my reflections about the plan.

1. The idea of an African Encyclopedia is especially important at this period in the history of Africa when there is need to make explicit the historic tradition of peoples who are emerging from a pre-literate past and are seeking to "affirm the African personality" in the modern world.

2. However, it is my opinion that an attempt to bring out an Encyclopedia which would represent what the world has meant and means to Africa and by implication what Africans would make of themselves is premature in view of the human resources available for such an undertaking.

3. In the place of an Encyclopedia an attempt should be made to bring out a large volume to which Africans or people of African descent could make fundamental contributions on the history, culture, and philosophy of African people.

I trust that your recovery is continuing. With warmest regards to you and Shirley,

> Sincerely,
> Frazier

Brooklyn, N.Y., January 4, 1961
[mailed from Paris, France]

My dear Dr. Nkrumah:

I have already written you three times: once concerning preliminary work; then on October 10 giving you a list of fifteen scholars to whom I had written and then on November 6 with a list of fifty-one persons to whom I had written and copies of five replies.

In the present letter I am enclosing replies of nineteen more persons making a total of twenty-four replies received from ten countries.

I have received no acknowledgement of these letters; however, I know how

---

1. Louis Seymour Bazett Leakey (1903-72) was a foremost archeologist and paleontologist; he was curator of the Coryndon Memorial Museum in Nairobi from 1945 to 1961. His *Stone-Age Africa* was first published in 1931; *Progress and Evolution of Man in Africa* was issued by Oxford in 1961. He was chief editor of the three-volume work *Fossil Vertebrates of Africa*.

busy you have been during this time and how worried over the situation in the Congo. I have now a further list of twenty-four persons to whom I shall write in the near future. Also since I have seen you I made a trip to witness the inauguration of Dr. Azikiwe as Governor-General of Nigeria and while there I took the opportunity of laying the plan of the "Encyclopedia Africana" before him and asking his cooperation. He seemed much interested.

I also visited Dr. Kenneth Dike, principal of University College at Ibadan, and talked and dined with him and five young candidates for the Doctorate in History. They were all very enthusiastic and promised cooperation.

On this trip we had to land in Accra on account of the weather before reaching Lagos and I telegraphed your office and left a message with your secretary.

In my last letter I made an estimate of the expense involved in this work as about $64 a week. This expense has been exceeded because of the high postage and the cost of help. The revised cost is:

Office Help	$60.00
Paper & Supplies	10.00
Postage	12.00
TOTAL	$82.00

I have worked from September 13 to January 4, a total of 16 weeks or $1312. This of course includes no compensation for my own time and work.

If you approve of what I have done and wish me to proceed then you should write those African states whose cooperation you wish and inform them of what I am doing. I will prepare a digest of all replies received and write to perhaps a dozen other authorities. After you get that digest, these persons should be written to and arrangements made for an advisory committee, a center of editorial work and a start toward selecting an editorial staff.

I shall await word from you before I take any further action.

Very sincerely yours,
W. E. B. Du Bois

Accra, Ghana, January 23, 1961

My dear Dr. Du Bois,

Thank you for your letter of the 4th January which you had posted from France, and also for your previous one.

This letter is merely an acknowledgement of your letters. I shall write to you again as soon as I have had an opportunity of going further into this matter.

The trouble now is that I am finding increasing calls upon me which make it necessary for me to journey either out of Accra or out of the country. It is rare that I get two consecutive weeks at my desk in Accra!

My greetings and very warm wishes to Shirley and to yourself. I hope that you are both keeping well.

Yours very sincerely,
Kwame Nkrumah

Accra, Ghana, February 15, 1961

[Cable]

Dr. Du Bois

Your proposals in respect of the Encyclopedia African have been accepted and endorsed by the Ghana Academy of Learning. Substantial financial support has been voted. A detailed letter is on its way to you about it. You can be assured that my interest in the Encyclopedia remains unabated and everything will be done by me to promote it. Best wishes.

Kwame Nkrumah

Brooklyn, N.Y., March 7, 1961

Mr. A. A. Kwapong, Acting Secretary

Ghana Academy of Learning

My dear Mr. Kwapong:

I have received your kind letter of February 10 (No. 041), and, also, communications from President Nkrumah. I am making a provisional reply now, and before the end of the month, I shall make some more definite proposals.

First, may I thank you for your interest in this matter and your kind words concerning what I have done.

What I have in mind now is a planning office of which I shall act as director. In charge of this I shall have to have a trained assistant who can carry on correspondence even when I am out of town. That correspondence will cover first, letters to persons all over the world who have been interested in African history, ethnology and sociology, and who have contributed in their writings and explorations to those subjects. My correspondence has already covered Britain fairly well, although there are other persons to whom I shall write. I am trying to get a more complete coverage of French scholars and writers, and especially, of Portuguese and Spanish writers. My idea, eventually, is to get the consent of most of these scholars to act as an advisory committee without power or responsibility, but with expressed willingness to cooperate by advice in any matters which the editorial board may bring up. I am especially eager to get in close touch with Egyptian and other Arabic scholars. And I think I shall be able to do this.

What we have got to do as soon as possible is to get a list of African scholars and persons of African descent who have written on African history, sociology, ethnology, etc., and who are making studies or planning to make studies in these fields. I shall correspond with such persons as I find names for from here, and I suggest that you do the same from Accra. In such correspondence we would make no promises but simply seek information.

You will, of course, begin in Accra to collect an African library and to ask persons who have written or are writing to contribute to it; and, of course, in time, to offer to buy such matters.

The matter of the actual choosing of an editorial board should go slowly, and I should imagine that no final setting up of the board could take place before 1962. At any rate, I am sure that you will agree with me that it is much easier to appoint a man to a board than to get rid of him later.

You mentioned the name of Dr. Horace Mann Bond. He is a scholar of ability whom I've known for many years, and I also knew his father. He is capable of assisting us but I have hesitated in getting in touch with him for one reason, and that is, he is in the pay of the United States State Department and of the Rockefeller interests. They are supporting an organization called the American Society of African Culture, which purports to study African history and culture, has an office at 15 East 40th Street, New York, and officials, and gives public exhibitions and dinners. This is perfectly within their right, but the objects of the United States State Department are not the objects of a scientific work like the Encyclopedia Africana. I will, however, see that Dr. Bond gets any material going out from this office.

I shall probably be able to give most of my time to this work during the year 1961, and, if I continue in my present health, for some time beyond that, provided my services are needed. This will entail, as I have said before, office expenses and some remuneration for my services. These matters we can take up in future letters. As I have said, I shall write you again before April 1st.

I am Sir,

Very sincerely yours,
W. E. B. Du Bois

P. S. I have received a remittance from the Bank of Accra for which I am thankful.

Brooklyn, N.Y., April 7, 1961

My dear Mr. Kwapong:

I have your letter of February 10 and your remittance of 600 pounds which netted me $1,678.50. From September through December, 1960, this office was open 14 weeks. During January, February and March, 1961, it was open 10 weeks. I propose that through April, May and June it will be open 12 weeks. In July I shall be in Rumania, but in the fall I plan to consult with students of history and social science in Czechoslovakia and, possibly, in the Soviet Union and in London and Paris. I will let you know my plans in this regard later. I am enclosing certain letters received since I wrote you: one from the Presence Africaine, Paris, one from the University of Capetown, one from African Studies Association, one from Fabian Commonwealth Bureau, and one from the University College of Rhodesia and Nyasaland.

I have in mind a program something like this: April, May and June, 1961, continued correspondence with interested persons, especially with colleges and universities in Africa, with European institutions of higher learning which have

African students, and with American universities which have African students. I also have in mind tentative letters to heads of African states, apprising them of our general plans and preparing them for communications on a higher level.

I am quite aware that this office must be careful not to assume too much authority. But, on the other hand, I wish those with whom I correspond to realize that this is not merely a personal proposal, but that back of it is the State of Ghana and the Ghana Academy of Learning. I shall try not to speak for these sponsoring bodies, but at the same time to let it be known that I am speaking with some authority. It is for this reason I have had printed the stationery on which this letter is written.[1]

I am writing the University College to know how far they have gone in their organization. I should imagine that it would be a year or two before definitive steps toward organizing a directing board or thinking of actually appointing an editorial board. By 1964, or 5, the editorial board could be definitely at work, and then we could definitely plan to issue the first volume of the Encyclopedia not later than 1970.

There is also the question of a publication office. I shall be glad to know if this will be under University auspices or under the Academy of Learning.

I shall await with interest any comments or suggestions that you may have.

Very sincerely yours,
W. E. B. Du Bois

Brooklyn, N.Y., April 26, 1961

My dear Mr. Kwapong:

Enclosed please find copies of 14 letters from Africa, China, United States and Germany, in answer to my letter on our plan for an Encyclopedia Africana. I have written additional letters to other American colleges and especially, Negro American colleges, and also to India and Egypt. I plan further letters to Spain and Portugal as soon as I receive addresses. I still await information from the University of Ghana concerning any action which it may have taken with regard to a Faculty devoted to the Encyclopedia Africana.

This office has been at work for 28 weeks and plans 8 more weeks until the 1st of July, a total cost, for September to July 1, 36 weeks, of $2,952. I have received from you $1,678.50, leaving a balance of $1,273.50 due on or before July 1st.

I think it is fair to say that our project has been received favorably almost everywhere in the world, although there are still important places which we hope to hear from. I shall be glad to hear from you at your convenience.

Very sincerely yours,
W. E. B. Du Bois

1. Printed on the stationery, with Du Bois's address, was: *Encyclopedia Africana* W. E. B. Du Bois, Ph.D., LL.D, Hist.Sci.D. Director Preliminary Planning.

Brooklyn, N.Y., May 23, 1961

Ghana Academy of Science and Learning

Gentlemen:

I have received from Mr. A. A. Kwapong, your Secretary, his letter of May 6, 1961, informing me that you wish that I should become the first Director of the Secretariat which will carry out the planning of an Encyclopedia Africana.

May I say that I am greatly honored and thankful for this wish on your part. There are, of course, certain obvious objections. I am, as you must know, in my 94th year and in the course of nature cannot hope to do effective work much longer. My acceptance, therefore, of this appointment must be with the knowledge that you have this clearly in mind. On the other hand, it is possible that I can do something to get this great and necessary work started.

I propose, therefore, the following procedure. I have been invited by the Peoples' Republic of Rumania to visit that country in June and to put myself under the care and treatment of its sanitarium for several weeks. After that, if I am in proper condition, I shall be glad to consult with scholars in various parts of the world on the best procedure in forwarding the Encyclopedia. I have been invited by the World Council of Peace, with headquarters in Vienna, to head a delegation to various African countries in December of this year. This would give me opportunity not only to work for the abolition of war in Africa but also to talk with the heads of various African peoples concerning the Encyclopedia. During this visit I could meet with members of the Academy and report further of my work.

If all goes well and I am still able to pursue this enterprise, I should hope to be in Accra for such active work as is possible and necessary some time during the year 1962.

In the meantime, may I suggest that by way of helping the project the government of Ghana and the Academy of Science and Learning should do three things: first, let the various African states know that an Encyclopedia Africana is being planned and under whose auspices; secondly, that they should also give this information to all higher schools of learning in Africa and ask their cooperation; thirdly, that they should secure the names of African scholars in history, ethnology, archeology and other cognate subjects, and find out what work has been done and is being done in these subjects. These matters have been partly covered by my correspondence, but it would strengthen the impression if they got further correspondence from an authoritative African source.

Again thank you for your consideration and action.

I am, Gentlemen,

Very sincerely yours,
W. E. B. Du Bois

Du Bois's connection with an encyclopedia project in the 1930s had produced

rejection and hostility from Dr. Carter G. Woodson, as correspondence in
volume two of this work showed (pp. 448-49). Du Bois's efforts to interest the
Association for the Study of Negro Life and History in the early 1960s were
also not met with favor. Illustrative is correspondence with Charles H. Wesley,
then president of Central State College in Ohio and a member of the executive
council of the ASNLH. *Du Bois and Wesley held each other in high esteem.*

Wilberforce, Ohio, May 24, 1961

Dear Dr. Du Bois:

I have received your letter and the plan of the proposed Encyclopedia Africana. We are having a meeting of the Executive Council of the Association for
the Study of Negro Life and History on June 24 in Washington, D.C., and I
will bring this to the attention of the board at that time and will write you
shortly thereafter.

We are interested, and Dr. Woodson had planned for an Encyclopedia Africana, using this title, when you were planning the Encyclopedia of the Negro.
My own personal opinion is that there might be developed a co-editorship in
Africa and the United States so that our two groups would be equally represented, and, as small as it [the United States group] may be, some of us believe that we could make a contribution to its planning, development and
realization.

Sincerely yours,
Charles H. Wesley

Brooklyn, N.Y., June 13, 1961

My dear Dr. Wesley:

I have your letter of May 24 and will be glad to hear from you further. Since
writing you I have been made chairman of the Secretariat which will appoint
the editors and publish the Encyclopedia Africana. I may say that this work
must be done in Africa and mainly by African scholars. There can be no question of division of control or authority. However, of course we will be glad to
have the cooperation of all interested persons, especially our American Negro
students in the History of the Negro in America.

Very sincerely yours,
W. E. B. Du Bois

Wilberforce, Ohio, September 20, 1961

Dear Dr. Du Bois:

In response to your inquiry concerning the *Encyclopedia Africana* proposed
by the Association for the Study of Negro Life and History, I am advising that
at the annual meeting in October, 1960 at Huston-Tillotson College, Austin,
Texas, the Association representatives decided to continue their plan for an *En-*

cyclopedia Africana under the auspices of our Association. The Executive Council in its 1961 session also approved this plan and appointed a committee to work upon the project.

The above gives you the information which you requested. Some of the committee expressed surprise that the title of your book had been changed from the *Encyclopedia of the Negro* to the *Encyclopedia Africana*. The latter was the title selected by Dr. Carter G. Woodson in 1920 and collection of material was undertaken under this title. We are of the opinion that such an encyclopedia can be published to best advantage here in the United States, and this is our program at present.

Sincerely yours,
Charles H. Wesley[1]

Brooklyn, N.Y., August 25, 1961

Ghana Academy of Science and Learning
Gentlemen:

On May 23rd I wrote you with regard to your kind letter informing me that you wished I should become the first Director of the Secretariat to carry out the project of the Encyclopedia Africana.

I spoke then of my age and my plan to visit Rumania and put myself under the care and treatment of the Sanitarium for several weeks. I have just returned from Rumania after two months stay. I feel improved in health and think that I will be able to give one or two years service to the planning of the Encyclopedia. Also the situation in the United States is such that I have changed my plans in other matters.

I propose to go to Ghana in October and to spend several weeks in consultation with you and the authorities of the University concerning the Encyclopedia. I shall also take up with you, at the time, the question of participation in the peace mission with various African States and other matters. I trust that this plan will be satisfactory to you.

I am Gentlemen,

Very sincerely yours,
W. E. B. Du Bois

Brooklyn, N.Y., August 28, 1961

My dear Dr. Nkrumah:

I am enclosing a letter which I have sent to the Ghana Academy [published immediately above]. Shirley wrote you August 24th that we would be arriv-

---

1. In a letter to this editor of 26 July 1976, Dr. Wesley, in addition to giving permission for the publication of his letters, added: "By the way, no progress was made on the Encyclopedia, as we had to turn to sources for funds and undertook the International Library of Negro Life and History which was a more immediate and available project."

ing in Ghana about the middle of October. I hope her outline of plans is satisfactory to you. She will soon be applying for our visas from your Consulate in Washington. I have returned from Rumania feeling considerably improved and remember with great joy our meeting there.

Very sincerely yours,
W. E. B. Du Bois

On 11 September 1961, E. A. Boateng, who had replaced Dr. Kwapong as acting secretary of the Ghana Academy of Learning, wrote to Du Bois in response to a recent letter and stated that because President Nkrumah was out of the country the arrival of the Du Boises in Ghana in October would not be convenient; they were asked, therefore, "kindly to delay making any firm arrangements for your visit until you have heard from us."

This background explains the text of a letter written to Du Bois in mid-September 1961.

Accra, Ghana, September 16, 1961
Dear Dr. Du Bois:

Following my letter of the 11th September, 1961, the President's office has just passed on to me a copy of a letter from Mrs. Du Bois informing the President of the arrangements you are making to ship your things in the latter part of September and to fly to Accra about the 10th October, 1961.

As I explained in my letter of the 11th September, which no doubt reached you some time after your wife's letter to the President, it is not very easy for us at this time to make adequate arrangements for your arrival in this country in connection with the Encyclopaedia Africana. The President has been away from the country for several weeks and is only now arriving back. Moreover, the country is now busy making preparations for the Royal Visit which is to take place in November. As a result of this the preparatory work which needs to be done in connection with your visit has been greatly delayed.

In the circumstances, the Council of the Academy feels that it would be very much better from our point of view if your arrival could be delayed for a few weeks. I intend to see the President as soon as possible after his arrival to discuss the matter with him and I will let you know the final position shortly afterwards.

I need hardly say how anxious the members of the Council are to see you back in Ghana and we hope that it will be possible to make firm arrangement for your arrival in the near future.

Yours sincerely,
E. A. Boateng

Brooklyn, N.Y., September 21, 1961

Dear Mr. Boateng:

Answering your letter of the 16th of September, 1961, may I beg you not to be too disturbed. My coming early will involve no activity nor expense on the part of the Academy.

We arrive on the morning of October 11th at 6:50 A.M. on Ghana Airways from London. We leave this early because there is grave possibility that if we wait until a later date, we would not be allowed to leave at all. This is by no means certain but it is quite possible. Our coming, however, should not disturb the Academy in the least. We do not want any welcoming arrangements or any expenditure or fuss.

Please secure for us, in my name, accommodations at the Ambassador Hotel or at any other suitable place in or out of Accra where we can await the pleasure and leisure of the President. We want a suite of rooms with living room, bedroom and bath and no other attention whatsoever. Do not bother the President about this matter until he has settled other pressing matters and especially arranged for the royal visit. After all this is over and the President has a chance to breathe, the Academy can take up the matter of arranging for my Secretariat. I am writing these details directly to the President.

Very sincerely yours,
W. E. B. Du Bois

A communication from Ghana's permanent representative to the United Nations—dated simply with the month—settled this matter of the departure date.

New York City, September, 1961

Dear Dr. Du Bois,

I have been instructed by the Osagyefo, Dr. Kwame Nkrumah, to convey to you the following message.

"Much regret impression created by Boateng for which he had no authority whatever. Please come as soon as ever you are ready. Let nothing stop you. I await your arrival."

I would appreciate hearing from you indicating when it would be convenient for you to undertake the trip to Ghana.

Yours sincerely,
Alex Quaison-Sackey

Accra, Ghana, November 30, 1961

Dear Dr. Nkrumah,

I want to say a word of congratulation to you on the work you have done in the last two months. I was distressed to intrude on you at this time of stress and I explained why we came so early. I sincerely trust that we have interfered with your tremendous schedule of work as little as possible.

Meantime, I have witnessed the Queen's visit, I have seen you installed as the first Chancellor of the University of Ghana and I have heard your installation as First Chancellor of the Kwame Nkrumah University of Science and Technology. These were three great accomplishments. In the first, you induced England to recognize Black Ghana as an equal, and yet did it in courtesy and beauty and with a public cooperation seldom seen, and this despite bitter provocation. In the two installations, you set the highest standard of African training with world-wide recognition and took the great step forward toward uniting the old classical learning and modern technology into one broad plan of education for human uplift.

Few men have had the opportunity in one life to bring so much to two such great causes. I tender you my warmest congratulations and my wife joins me.

Very sincerely yours,
W. E. B. Du Bois

The Du Boises were placed in comfortable quarters at the Windsor Lodge in Accra upon their arrival; meanwhile, a home was being prepared for them a mile or two outside the city itself, with a lovely garden and little summer cottage. It was here that the Du Boises lived until his death.

Accra, Ghana, December 4, 1961
Dear Dr. Du Bois,

Thank you very much indeed for your kind letter of the 30th November.

Believe me, I am delighted that you arranged to come to Ghana when you did. You must not think that your arrival in any way inconvenienced me. My only regret is that owing to my heavy schedule since you arrived, I have been prevented from seeing as much of you as I would have liked.

I hope that your house will be ready soon. Tell Shirley that she must keep an eye on it and arrange for things to be done the way she wants them.

I hope to see you before very long.

Yours very sincerely,
Kwame Nkrumah

An urgent requirement for Du Bois in undertaking direction of the encyclopedia project was a fully capable assistant—one he knew and trusted. Such a person was then in Guinea as a teacher; this was Dr. Alphaeus Hunton, Jr., whose distinguished parents Du Bois had known and whom Du Bois had known since Hunton was a boy. As readers will remember, Hunton was secretary of the Council on African Affairs when Du Bois and Paul Robeson were co-chairmen.

Early in 1962 Du Bois wrote to Sekou Touré, president of the Republic of Guinea.

Accra, Ghana, January 16, 1962

Dear Mr. Touré:

On April 17th, 1961, I brought to your attention my plan for an Encyclopedia Africana. You were kind enough to indicate your interest in the venture and your willingness to cooperate. You kindly suggested, however, May 12, 1961, that much work in African geography, history and art should precede this effort. There is, however, no conflict between our ideas; an encyclopedia must not wait until complete knowledge has been accumulated, but rather must summarize from time to time what has already been accumulated. On the other hand, as you suggest, a certain amount of historical, geographical and cultural research must of course precede an encyclopedia. Hence our plan will proceed with deliberation. It will take time. If it is ten years before we bring out the first volume we shall be satisfied. Meantime, local bodies and individuals must be working on the various preliminary subjects.

For this reason I have in the last year been in correspondence with most of the scholars who have devoted themselves to African history and sociology in Britain, America, Europe east and west, and many parts of Africa; there are still scholars in France, Spain and Portugal to be gotten in touch with. Nevertheless, already I have received nearly two hundred letters from the leading scholars of the world on the subject. They have on the whole been exceedingly encouraging. Most of my correspondents have expressed concurrence with the idea and willingness to cooperate. A few have pointed out the present scarcity of African scholars, and several have doubts as to the possibility of their scientific objectivity. I shall as soon as possible publish a digest of this very interesting correspondence.

But first I must get an office started and a staff at work. I have closed my office of preliminary planning in New York. An Encyclopedia Africana must be planned and written in Africa. We want to make this enterprise, as it develops, an increasingly all-African undertaking, with many states sharing in its work and expense. But for the sake of efficiency it must be centered more or less in one place and carried on by a united body of workers. I have therefore come to Accra and, under the sponsorship of the Ghana Academy of Sciences, have begun to organize an office. A preliminary appropriation has been promised to set up a secretariat under my direction.

I need first an assistant whom I know and trust and who knows me. Here of necessity I turn to you and beg your aid. I have known Dr. Alphaeus Hunton all his life, and I knew well his father and mother. He is teaching English at your Lycée Classique in Donka and is under contract to the State of Guinea. I am asking you to release him from his contract to you and let him come here as my secretary to work on the Encyclopedia Africana. He is trained in research and has published one of the best recent books on African conditions.[1] Valuable as he is as a teacher, I believe he would be of far greater value to Africa and the future of Africa if for the next five years he worked with me on this project.

I know this is asking a great deal of you. I do it not for selfish reasons but because of my conviction of what Africa needs today. Teachers of English are needed, but students of African history and culture are needed more. I would like Dr. Hunton to join me in March, if possible, but any convenient time later would have to suffice. My work must wait largely on his coming before it can really go forward. Will you give my request your careful thought and let me hear from you as soon as convenient.[2]

I am, Sir, your obedient servant,

W. E. B. Du Bois

Copy to Dr. Hunton

In May 1962 Du Bois was formally appointed director of the Encyclopedia Africana Secretariat. Toward the latter part of that month, he and Hunton presented a preliminary report of the work and needs of the secretariat.

Accra, Ghana, June 9, 1962

My dear Dr. Du Bois,

Many thanks for your letter of 25th May enclosing a copy of the report on the work of the Secretariat for an Encyclopedia Africana. It shows that Dr. Hunton has started his work in earnest and that the field to be covered is vast and impressive, but this naturally demands that great energy should be put into its achievement, and I can expect all of you associated with it to give of your best.

The details of estimates and personnel, which you refer to in paragraph 2 of your letter, are matters to be examined carefully by the Committee charged with responsibility for such work. If there are any problems arising out of this examination, I hope that they will be brought to my notice at the earliest opportunity. I think it would be a good thing if the African Affairs Secretariat were brought into close association with the work you are doing on this Ency-

1. W. Alphaeus Hunton, *Decision in Africa: Sources of Current Conflict* (New York: International Publishers, 1957), with a foreword by Du Bois. A revised edition was issued by the same publishers in 1960.

2. The request was granted and Hunton and his wife, Dorothy, came to Ghana in March 1962; they remained until those responsible for the 1965 coup forced them to leave.

clopedia, and I shall instruct Mr. Dei-Anang to get into touch with you about this in due course.

I was also glad to see how hale and hearty you looked at the very enjoyable dinner we had a few days ago. I trust that you will continue to maintain this high standard of health. I am arranging to pay you and Shirley a visit.

> Yours very sincerely,
> Kwame Nkrumah

While Du Bois and Hunton made a valiant beginning, the inexorable passage of years was now taking its final toll, even upon Du Bois.

> Accra, Ghana, July 8, 1962

Dear Mr. President:

I regret to inform you that my doctors have ordered special hospitalization for me and I am leaving for London today. I must therefore request sick leave from my duties with the Secretariat for an Encyclopedia Africana until such time as I can return to Ghana with restored health. I leave Dr. Hunton in charge of the work of the Secretariat and will keep in touch with him.

I am, Sir,

> Sincerely yours,
> W. E. B. Du Bois

> Vevey, Switzerland, September 14, 1962

My dear Alphaeus,

I want to tell you how deeply I appreciate all you have been doing for me and for the work in which we are both interested. Your last report, received this morning, is splendid. My only criticism is that no where do you mention your own name as my assistant. I hope you will do this in the future.

We plan to be in Ghana in October* and I [hope?] then to be of some more assistance in the work. It has unfortunately been necessary for me to stay away a long time in order to receive the medical and surgical care which only seemed available in London. I have now had two serious operations which have been very successful and my present condition is reported by the physicians as unexpectedly good. At the same time recovery is slow and tedious and it has taken me a long time to be myself again.

I hope when I return I can be of some little use in the great work we have started. My grateful thanks to you and love to Dorothy and respects to the entire office force.

> Sincerely yours,
> W. E. B. Du Bois

[Du Bois's note]
* Shall be here until Sept. 23

Accra, Ghana, December 19, 1962

Dear Dr. Porter:[1]

I wish to express to you my personal thanks and that of the Secretariat for your kindness and cooperation in serving as Chairman of the Opening Plenary Session of our Conference at the University of Ghana yesterday. I should thank you, also, for your remarks in introducing me.

We earnestly hope that from this first meeting of scholars on the subject of the proposed Encyclopedia Africana will come the development of real and effective cooperation in the gigantic task which lies ahead of us.

Very truly yours,
W. E. B. Du Bois

Apparently, the final letter Du Bois wrote as director of the Encyclopedia Africana Secretariat was one he addressed to President Nkrumah.[*]

Accra, Ghana, December 21, 1962

Dear Osagyefo, the President:

I have the honour in presenting to you a copy of the report on the one-day Conference of Africanists organised by our Secretariat on December 18, 1962. The Secretariat deeply appreciates your support and that of the Ghana Academy of Sciences in furthering our work.

May I take this opportunity, Mr. President, on behalf of our Secretariat to wish you and your family a very good Christmas and a long and happy life in the next coming years.

I am,

Your obedient servant,
W. E. B. Du Bois

1. Du Bois is addressing Arthur Thomas Porter (b. 1924), who was educated at Cambridge University in England and at Boston University in Massachusetts. For a period in the 1950s he was on the faculty at the University of Edinburgh; when Du Bois wrote him he was at the University College in Freetown, Sierra Leone. Since 1974 he has been vice-chancellor, University of Sierra Leone.

* What seems to be the last-dated letter that Du Bois received in his official capacity was written to him by Amba Prasad of the history department of the University of Delhi in India. Dated 8 March 1963 it thanked Du Bois for keeping him informed of the encyclopedia's progress and told something of Prasad's own work. On the margin, in ink, Du Bois wrote: "Please answer and thank—WEBD."

The 1965 coup stopped work on the encyclopedia project, and to date (1977), Du Bois's dream remains unaccomplished.

The last book produced by Du Bois was his ABC of Color, *published in the summer of 1963 by Seven Seas Books, Berlin, German Democratic Republic.*

The founder and director of that publishing house was the late Gertrude Gelbin, who was born in the United States but chose, with her husband, the well-known author Stefan Heym, to live in the GDR. *In 1959 Du Bois was in the German Democratic Republic and Gertrude Gelbin and her husband visited him. On the way, Heym suggested to his wife that a Du Bois reader, selected by Du Bois himself, would be a fine book for the Seven Seas list. Wrote Mrs. Gelbin: "Dr. Du Bois reacted immediately to the idea of a Du Bois Reader. Shirley was worried that it would mean too much work for him; but Dr. Du Bois was sure it would not and he promised to put together such a book when they returned to the United States."* Letters complete the story.*

Brooklyn, N.Y., January 13, 1960

My dear Gertrude Heym:

I am engaged in selecting extracts from the *Crisis* which might be used as a *Du Bois Reader*. If you still want to consider it, I shall be able to mail the manuscript early in February.

Did you have in mind 100, 200, or 300 pages?

Our best regards to you and your husband.

Very sincerely yours,
W. E. B. Du Bois

Brooklyn, N.Y., June 17, 1960

My dear Gertrude:

I have just sent out to be photostated 300 pages of *The Crisis* which I have selected from editorials and articles written in that magazine. Meantime, I am taking a trip to Africa and Czechoslovakia which may last two or three months. As soon as I return I will arrange the photostats and write an introduction and interconnecting matter. The completed manuscript should reach you early in the fall. This is a little later than I had intended, but you know what to expect of authors.

Shirley joins me in best regards to you and your husband.

Very sincerely yours,
W. E. B. Du Bois

Brooklyn, N.Y., February 4, 1961

Dear Gertrude Gelbin:

Enclosed is the "Du Bois Reader" in a manuscript of 200 pages. It is probably too long. But I have cut and cut until I can do no more. My view is limited to

---

* Gertrude Gelbin wrote to me from Berlin about the book and its creation in a letter of 6 December 1963.

what I think people will want to read. You have a broader view of what audiences demand. Therefore cut out what you think best to omit.

With love from us both to both of you

W. E. B. Du Bois

The mails being what they were in the years of the Cold War, the Du Bois manuscript did not reach Berlin for several months.

Brooklyn, N.Y., March 29, 1961

My dear Gertrude:

I am still hoping that the manuscript of the *Du Bois Reader* will reach you. I shall set a tracer after it here. However, in case it does not, I will bring another copy when we come to Europe. This will not be until some time in July, but, whenever it is, we will plan to see you at least for a moment.

Our best regards to your husband and friends.

Very sincerely yours,

W. E. B. Du Bois

Brooklyn, N.Y., June 13, 1961

My dear Gertrude:

I am leaving for Rumania June 15 but I am not bringing another copy of the *Du Bois Reader* as I hoped to do. It has been impossible to finish it in time and also I still hope that the first copy can be found. I am in correspondence with the Chief Inspector of the Post Office Department. I shall probably be back here in August and if the copy sent has not been found by that time, I will start again on finishing this second copy and get it to you somehow by hand.

My best regards to you and your husband from me and Shirley.

Very sincerely yours,

W. E. B. Du Bois

Brooklyn, N.Y., August 30, 1961

My dear Gertrude:

Yesterday I received a cable from Mrs. [Kay] Pankey [Gertrude Gelbin's assistant editor] saying "original manuscript received today." That settles our long waiting.

However, it brings up another problem. The original manuscript covered my writing from 1896 to 1940. After plowing through all that I had written, I concluded that the reader should cover this period and that perhaps in the future, the second reader, from 1940 to 1960, should be issued. However, when the manuscript was apparently lost I started another manuscript, from 1896 to 1958. This one I have just finished and it will be mailed you from London early in October. I prefer it to the original which you have just received; but on the other hand, you may compare the two and make any suggestion that may seem best to you from the publisher's point of view.

I have just returned from six weeks in Rumania and feel considerably improved. If our plans work out, I should hope to see you early next year. I hope this will find you and your husband in good health. Shirley and I are getting along very well.

Yours with love,
W. E. B. Du Bois

London, England, September 13, 1961

Dear Gertrude:

Here is the second manuscript of the proposed Du Bois Reader. I have written you about it and you have that letter. At any rate I am mailing this in London as I pass through to Ghana.

It is the second selection of my writing covering 1896 to 1958. It thus overlaps the first manuscript but is, I think, better. Use your judgment as to which you will use or combine them. I prefer this second.

You can reach me in Ghana for the next three months at this address:

c/o Ghana Academy of Science and Learning

P. O. Box 179

Accra, Ghana

West Africa

Next Spring, we may be in East Germany.

With love,
W. E. B. Du Bois

Accra, Ghana, May 21, 1962

My dear Gertrude:

I hope you have received the contract which was mailed some days ago. I shall await with interest the appearance of the book. I am in fair health, and Shirley also is doing well.

My love to you and your husband.

With best regards,
W. E. B. Du Bois

What appears to have been Du Bois's last letter concerned this book—prepared twice by a man well into his nineties!

Accra, Ghana, July 10, 1963

Thank you, dear Gertrude!

Today we received *An ABC of Color*. I am deeply grateful. I do not feel that I shall be here much longer and I am happy to see this small collection of my writings in such good hands.

Shirley thinks I should immediately order a hundred copies. So, will you please send me at once one hundred copies of *An ABC of Color* which we will distribute in Ghana.

Best wishes to Seven Seas. My love to you.

Sincerely,
W. E. B. Du Bois

INDEX